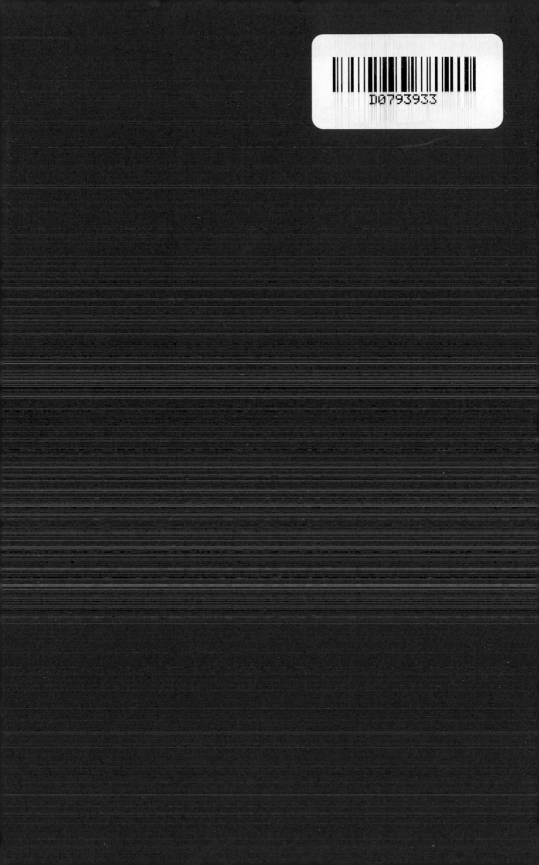

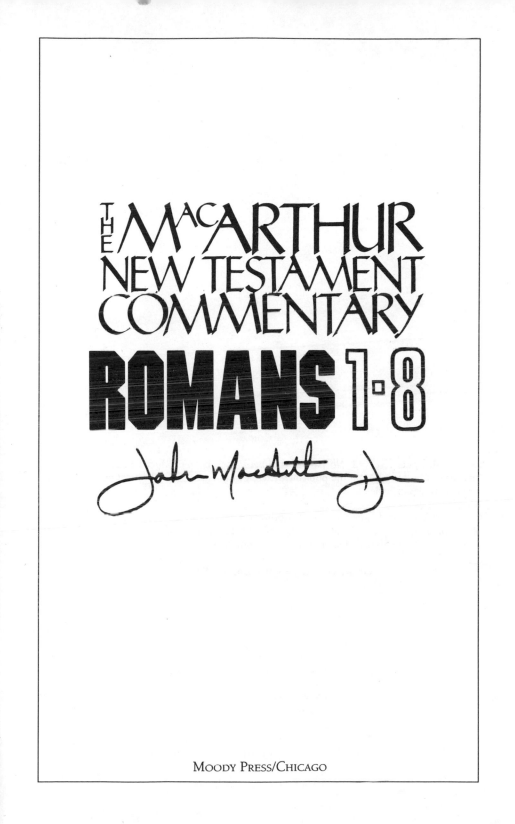

THE MACARTHUR
NEW TESTAMENT
COMMENTARY

ROMANS 1·8

MOODY PRESS/CHICAGO

Unless noted otherwise, all Scripture quotations in this book are from *The New American Standard Bible,* © 1960, 1962, 1963, 1968, 1971, 1972, 1973, 1975, and 1977 by The Lockman Foundation, and are used by permission.

Library of Congress Cataloging in Publication Data

MacArthur, John F.
   Romans

   (The MacArthur New Testament commentary)
    I. Bible. N.T. Romans—Commentaries.
I. Title. II. Series: MacArthur, John F. MacArthur
New Testament commentary.
1900   000.0000   00-0000
ISBN 0-8024-0767-6

15 16 17 18 19 20

Printed in the United States of America

In memory of Thaddeus Woziwodzki.
Though our friendship was brief,
the impact of his love for Christ, the Word, and me,
enriched me permanently.

Other Titles in the
MacAurthur New Testament Commentary Series

MOODY
PUBLISHERS
THE NAME YOU CAN TRUST.

1-800-678-6928 www.MoodyPublishers.org

Contents

Preface

It continues to be a rewarding divine communion for me to preach expositionally through the New Testament. My goal is always to have deep fellowship with the Lord in the understanding of His Word, and out of that experience to explain to His people what a passage means. In the words of Nehemiah 8:8, I strive "to give the sense" of it so they may truly hear God speak and, in so doing, may respond to Him.

Obviously, God's people need to understand Him, which demands knowing His Word of truth (2 Tim. 2:15) and allowing that Word to dwell in us richly (Col. 3:16). The dominant thrust of my ministry, therefore, is to help make God's living Word alive to His people. It is a refreshing adventure.

This New Testament commentary series reflects this objective of explaining and applying Scripture. Some commentaries are primarily linguistic, others are mostly theological, and some are mainly homiletical. This one is basically explanatory, or expository. It is not linguistically technical, but deals with linguistics when this seems helpful to proper interpretation. It is not theologically expansive, but focuses on the major doctrines in each text and on how they relate to the whole of Scripture. It is not primarily homiletical, though each unit of thought is generally treated as one chapter, with a clear outline and logical flow of thought. Most truths are illustrated and applied with other Scripture. After establishing the context of a passage, I have tried to follow closely the writer's development and reasoning.

My prayer is that each reader will fully understand what the Holy Spirit is saying through this part of His Word, so that His revelation may lodge in the minds of believers and bring greater obedience and faithfulness—to the glory of our great God.

Introduction

Most, if not all, of the great revivals and reformations in the history of the church have been directly related to the book of Romans. In September A.D. 386, a native of North Africa who had been a professor for several years in Milan, Italy, sat weeping in the garden of his friend Alyplus, contemplating the wickedness of his life. While sitting there, he heard a child singing, *"Tolle, lege. Tolle, lege,"* which in Latin means "Take up and read. Take up and read." An open scroll of the book of Romans lay beside him, and he picked it up. The first passage that caught his eye read, "Not in carousing and drunkenness, not in sexual promiscuity and sensuality, not in strife and jealousy. But put on the Lord Jesus Christ, and make no provision for the flesh in regard to its lusts" (13:13-14). The man later wrote of that occasion: "No further would I read, nor did I need; for instantly, as the sentence ended,—by a light, as it were, or security infused into my heart,—all the gloom of doubt vanished away" (*Confessions* Book 8, Chapter 12). The man was Aurelius Augustine, who, upon reading that short passage from Romans, received Jesus Christ as Lord and Savior and went on to become one of the church's outstanding theologians and leaders.

Just over a thousand years later, Martin Luther, a monk in the

Roman Catholic order named after Augustine, was teaching the book of Romans to his students at the University of Wittenberg, Germany. As he carefully studied the text, he became more and more convicted by Paul's central theme of justification by faith alone. He wrote,

> I greatly longed to understand Paul's Epistle to the Romans, and nothing stood in the way but that one expression, "the righteousness of God," because I took it to mean that righteousness whereby God is righteous and deals righteously in punishing the unrighteous. . . . Night and day I pondered until . . . I grasped the truth that the righteousness of God is that righteousness whereby, through grace and sheer mercy, he justifies us by faith. Thereupon I felt myself to be reborn and to have gone through open doors into paradise. The whole of Scripture took on a new meaning, and whereas before "the righteousness of God" had filled me with hate, now it became to me inexpressibly sweet in greater love. This passage of Paul became to me a gateway to heaven. (Cf. Barend Klaas Kuiper, *Martin Luther: The Formative Years* [Grand Rapids: Eerdmans, 1933], pp. 198-208.)

Several centuries later, an ordained minister in the Church of England by the name of John Wesley was similarly confused about the meaning of the gospel and was searching for a genuine experience of salvation. For the Wednesday evening of May 24, 1738, he wrote in his journal,

> I went very unwillingly to a society in Aldersgate Street, where one was reading Luther's Preface to the Epistle to the Romans. About a quarter before nine, while he was describing the change which God works in the heart through faith in Christ, I felt my heart strangely warmed. I felt I did trust in Christ, Christ alone, for my salvation; and an assurance was given me that He had taken away my sins, even mine, and saved me from the law of sin and death.

In assessing the importance of the book of Romans, John Calvin said, "When any one gains a knowledge of this Epistle, he has an entrance opened to him to all the most hidden treasures of Scripture" (*Commentaries on the Epistle of Paul to the Romans* [Grand Rapids: Baker, 1979], p. 1). Martin Luther said that Romans is "the chief part of the New Testament and the very purest gospel" (*Commentary on the Epistle to the Romans* [Grand Rapids: Kregel, 1954], p. xiii). Frederick Godet, the noted Swiss Bible commentator, called Romans "the cathedral of Christian faith" (*Commentary on St. Paul's Epistle to the Romans* [New York: Funk & Wagnalls, 1883], p. 1).

The famous sixteenth-century Bible translator William Tyndale wrote the following words in his preface to the book of Romans:

Forasmuch as this epistle is the principal and most excellent part of the New Testament, and most pure *evangelion,* that is to say, glad tidings, and that we call gospel, and also a light and a way unto the whole scripture; I think it meet that every christian man not only know it, by rote and without the book, but also exercise himself therein evermore continually, as with the daily bread of the soul. No man verily can read it too oft, or study it too well; for the more it is studied, the easier it is; the more it is chewed, the pleasanter it is; and the more groundly it is searched, the preciouser things are found in it, so great treasure of spiritual things lieth hid therein. (*Doctrinal Treatises and Introductions to Different Portions of the Holy Scriptures by William Tyndale,* Henry Walter, ed. [Cambridge: University Press, 1848], p. 484)

The popular Bible expositor Donald Grey Barnhouse, who broadcast eleven years of weekly messages on the book of Romans, wrote regarding this beloved epistle,

A scientist may say that mother's milk is the most perfect food known to man, and may give you an analysis showing all its chemical components, a list of the vitamins it contains and an estimate of the calories in a given quantity. A baby will take that milk without the remotest knowledge of its content, and will grow day by day, smiling and thriving in its ignorance. So it is with the profound truths of the word of God. (*Man's Ruin: Romans 1:1-32* [Grand Rapids: Eerdmans, 1952], p. 3)

It has been said that Romans will delight the greatest logician and captivate the mind of the consummate genius, yet it will bring tears to the humblest soul and refreshment to the simplest mind. It will knock you down and then lift you up. It will strip you naked and then clothe you with eternal elegance. The book of Romans took a Bedford tinker like John Bunyan and turned him into the spiritual giant and literary master who wrote *The Pilgrim's Progress* and *The Holy War.*

This epistle quotes the Old Testament some 57 times, more than any other New Testament book. It repeatedly used key words—*God* 154 times, *law* 77 times, *Christ* 66 times, *sin* 45 times, *Lord* 44 times, and *faith* 40 times.

Romans answers many questions concerning man and God. Some of the more significant questions it answers are: What is the good news of God? Is Jesus really God? What is God like? How can God send people to hell? Why do men reject God and His Son, Jesus Christ? Why are there false religions and idols? What is man's biggest sin? Why are there sex perversions, hatred, crime, dishonesty, and all the other evils in the world, and why are they so pervasive and rampant? What is the standard by which God condemns people? How can a person who has never heard the gospel be held spiritually responsible? Do Jews have a greater responsibility to believe than Gentiles? Who is a true Jew? Is there any spiritual advantage to being Jewish? How good is man in himself? How evil is man in himself? Can any person keep God's laws perfectly? How can a person know he is a sinner? How can a sinner be forgiven and justified by God? How is a Christian related to Abraham? What is the importance of Christ's death? What is the importance of His resurrection? What is the importance of His present life in heaven? For whom did Christ die? Where can men find real peace and hope? How are all men related spiritually to Adam, and how are believers related spiritually to Jesus Christ? What is grace and what does it do? How are God's grace and God's law related? How does a person die spiritually and become reborn? What is the Christian's relation to sin? How important is obedience in the Christian life? Why is living a faithful Christian life such a struggle? How many natures does a Christian have?

Still more questions are: What does the Holy Spirit do for a believer? How intimate is a Christian's relationship to God? Why is there suffering? Will the world ever be different? What are election and predestination? How can Christians pray properly? How secure is a believer's salvation? What is God's present plan for Israel? What is His future plan for Israel? Why and for what have the Gentiles been chosen by God? What is the Christian's responsibility to Jews and to Israel? What is true spiritual commitment? What is the Christian's relationship to the world in general, to the unsaved, to other Christians, and to human government? What is genuine love and how does it work? How do Christians deal with issues that are neither right nor wrong in themselves? What is true freedom? How important is unity in the church?

It is no wonder that Frederick Godet, quoted above, once exclaimed, "O Saint Paul! Had thy one work been to compose the epistle to the Romans, that alone should have rendered thee dear to every sound reason."

Romans speaks to us today just as powerfully as it spoke to men of the first century. It speaks morally, about adultery, fornication, homosexuality, hating, murder, lying, and civil disobedience. It speaks intellectually, telling us that the natural man is confused because he has a reprobate mind. It speaks socially, telling us how we are to relate to one another. It speaks psychologically, telling us where true freedom comes to deliver men from the burden of guilt. It speaks nationally, telling us our responsibility to human government. It speaks internationally, telling us the ultimate destiny of the earth and especially the future of Israel. It speaks spiritually, answering man's despair by offering hope for the future. It speaks theologically, teaching us the relationship between the flesh and the spirit, between law and grace, between works and faith. But most of all, it profoundly brings God Himself to us.

An anonymous poet wrote these moving words that capture much of the heart of the book of Romans:

> O long and dark the stairs I trod
> With trembling feet to find my God
> Gaining a foothold bit by bit,
> Then slipping back and losing it.
> Never progressing; striving still
> With weakening grasp and faltering will,
> Bleeding to climb to God, while he
> Serenely smiled, unnoting me.
> Then came a certain time when I
> Loosened my hold and fell thereby;
> Down to the lowest step my fall,
> As if I had not climbed at all.
> Now when I lay despairing there,
> Listen . . . a footfall on the stair,
> On that same stair where I afraid,
> Faltered and fell and lay dismayed.
> And lo, when hope had ceased to be,
> My God came down the stairs to me.

THE AUTHOR

It is impossible to clearly understand the book of Romans without knowing something about its amazing author.

Paul was originally named Saul, after the first king of Israel, and, like his namesake, was of the tribe of Benjamin (Phil. 3:5). He was born in Tarsus (Acts 9:11), a prosperous city just off the northeastern Mediterranean coast in the province of Cilicia, located in what is modern Turkey. Tarsus was a center of Greek learning and culture, the home of one of the three most outstanding universities in the Roman Empire. Saul may have received training there as well as in Jerusalem under the rabbi Gamaliel (Acts 22:3), who was the grandson of Hillel, perhaps the most famous rabbi of all time. Because he was said to personify the law, Gamaliel was often referred to as "the beauty of the law." Saul was therefore learned both in Greek literature and philosophy and in rabbinical law.

Following the Mosaic law, Saul was circumcised on the eighth day (Phil. 3:5). He probably was sent to Jerusalem soon after his thirteenth birthday, the age when Jewish boys became recognized as men. Under Gamaliel, Saul would have memorized and learned to interpret Scripture according to rabbinical tradition, notably that of the Talmud. It was probably during his stay in Jerusalem that he became a Pharisee. Because his father was a Roman citizen, Saul was born into that citizenship (Acts

22:28), a prized and highly beneficial asset. He therefore had the highest possible credentials both of Greco-Roman and Jewish society.

In keeping with Jewish custom, Saul also learned the trade of his father, which was tentmaking (Acts 18:3). In light of the fact that this apostle never encountered Jesus during His earthly ministry, it is likely that he returned to Tarsus after his education in Jerusalem. Because of his outstanding training, he was doubtlessly a leader in one of the leading synagogues of Tarsus, supporting himself by tentmaking. By his own account, he was a zealous legalist, a "Hebrew of Hebrews," totally committed to the law in every detail (Phil. 3:5-6).

It was probably while he was back in Tarsus that he began hearing about the new "sect" that was filling Jerusalem, not only with its teaching but also with its converts. Like most of the Jewish leaders in Palestine, Saul was deeply offended by Jesus' claim to messiahship and dedicated himself to stamping out the presumed heresy. He was still a young man when he came back to Jerusalem, but due to his zeal and natural ability he soon became a leader in persecuting the church. Instead of its softening his heart to the gospel, the stoning of Stephen at first hardened Saul's heart still further, and he "began ravaging the church, entering house after house; and dragging off men and women, he would put them in prison" (Acts 8:3).

Luke reports that Saul was "breathing threats and murder against the disciples of the Lord" (9:1). He became like a war horse with the smell of battle in his nostrils, snorting out unrelenting fury against everyone and everything Christian. Toward the Christians, he became like the wicked Haman—"the enemy of the Jews" who determined to exterminate every Jew in the vast Persian empire of King Ahasuerus (Esther 3:8-10).

Not content with persecuting believers in Jerusalem and Judea, Saul "went to the high priest, and asked for letters from him to the synagogues at Damascus, so that if he found any belonging to the Way, both men and women, he might bring them bound to Jerusalem" (Acts 9:1-2). Saul was consumed by a passion to imprison and execute Christians, and before going to Damascus, he had hounded Christians in many other "foreign cities" outside Israel (see Acts 26:11).

At that time, Damascus was a city of perhaps 150,000 people, including many thousands of Jews. It is therefore possible that the "synagogues at Damascus" to which Saul referred could have numbered a dozen or more. Damascus was the capital of Syria and was 160 miles northeast of Jerusalem, requiring at least six days of travel time from one city to the other.

But on his way there, just as "he was approaching Damascus, . . . suddenly a light from heaven flashed around him; and he fell to the ground, and heard a voice saying to him, 'Saul, Saul, why are you persecuting Me?'" (9:3-4). In his defense before King Agrippa many years later, Paul reported that Jesus then added, "It is hard for you to kick against the goads" (Acts 26:14). A goad was a long, pointed stick used to herd stubborn livestock such as oxen. To keep the animal moving, he was poked in the flank or just above the heel. In Greek culture the phrase "hard to kick against the goad" was a common expression used to indicate opposition to deity, an expression Saul had doubtlessly heard many times while in Tarsus. With that phrase, Jesus was pointing out to Saul that his persecution of Christians was tantamount to opposing God, the very opposite of what he thought he was doing.

In abject fear Saul replied to the heavenly voice, "'Who art Thou, Lord?' And He said, 'I am Jesus whom you are persecuting'" (Acts 9:5). At that moment Saul must have been both terrified and shattered—terrified that he was in the very presence of God and shattered by the discovery that he had been assailing God rather than serving Him. He was devastated to realize that the blood he had been shedding was the blood of God's people. The Jesus whom his fellow Israelites had ridiculed, beaten, and put to death; the Jesus upon whom Stephen had called as Saul stood by consenting to his death; the Jesus whose followers Saul himself had been imprisoning and executing—that Jesus was indeed God, just as He had claimed! Now Paul stood exposed and helpless before Him, blinded by the dazzling brightness of His revealed majesty.

For several years Saul had been totally engrossed in the annihilation of the church, and had he fulfilled his plan, the church would have died in infancy, drowned in its own blood. If the Lord had not immediately added, "But rise, and enter the city, and it shall be told you what you must do" (9:6), Saul could very well have expired simply from fear over the enormity of his sin. Many years later he looked back on that experience and declared,

> I thank Christ Jesus our Lord, who has strengthened me, because He considered me faithful, putting me into service; even though I was formerly a blasphemer and a persecutor and a violent aggressor. And yet I was shown mercy, because I acted ignorantly in unbelief; and the grace of our Lord was more than abundant, with the faith and love which are found in Christ Jesus. It is a trustworthy statement, deserving full acceptance, that Christ Jesus came into the world to save sinners, among whom I am the foremost of all. (1 Tim. 1:12-15)

On that road near Damascus, Saul was marvelously and eternally transformed. Although temporarily blinded and all but speechless, during that experience he submitted his life to Christ.

It is likely that Saul was so vehemently bent on destroying Jesus' followers that no Christian would have been able to present the gospel to him successfully. Only God, by miraculous intervention, could get his attention. He had to be utterly shattered before he would listen to God's truth. He was so feared by the church that even the apostles would not talk to him when he first asked to visit them. They found it impossible to believe that Saul of Tarsus could be a disciple of Christ (Acts 9:26).

Consistent with his natural zealousness, as soon as Saul regained his sight, was baptized, and had some nourishment after three days without food or drink (see 9:9), "immediately he began to proclaim Jesus in the synagogues" of Damascus (v. 20)—the very synagogues to which he had been given letters from the high priest permitting him to arrest any Christians he found among them! It is hardly surprising that "those hearing him continued to be amazed, and were saying, 'Is this not he who in Jerusalem destroyed those who called on this name, and who had come here for the purpose of bringing them bound before the chief priests?'" (v. 21).

By remarkable divine illumination, Saul was immediately able after his conversion not simply to testify to what had happened to him but to defend the gospel so powerfully that he confounded every unbelieving Jew who argued with him, "proving that this Jesus is the Christ" (v. 22).

He was so successful in proclaiming the gospel that soon his former accomplices, along with other unbelieving Jews in Damascus, planned to kill him. In their determination to exterminate this traitor to their cause, they enlisted the political and military support of "the ethnarch under Aretas the king" (2 Cor. 11:32). "But their plot became known to Saul. And they were also watching the gates day and night so that they might put him to death; but his disciples took him by night, and let him down through an opening in the wall, lowering him in a large basket" (Acts 9:24-25).

As Paul himself explains in his letter to the Galatians, it was at this point that he went to Arabia, spending three years there (see Gal. 1:17-18). It was probably there that the apostle learned much and received direct revelation from the Lord. As he had testified earlier in Galatians, the gospel he preached was "not according to man. For I neither received it from man, nor was I taught it, but I received it through a revelation of Jesus Christ" (1:11-12).

After that "divine seminary" training in Nabatean Arabia, Saul went back to Damascus for a brief time (Gal. 1:17). It is possible that it was on this second visit that the ethnarch under King Aretas became involved, perhaps because Saul had raised the royal ire by preaching the gospel while in Arabia, which was under the monarch's control. If so, Saul escaped from Damascus a second time, this time by being lowered through the wall in a basket (see 2 Cor. 11:33).

Only after that three-year period did Saul go to Jerusalem and meet the other apostles. Through the trusting and gracious intercession of Barnabas (Acts 9:27), the apostles finally acknowledged Saul as a true believer and accepted him into fellowship.

The exact chronology of this period in Saul's life cannot be determined, but he spent fifteen days in Jerusalem with Peter (Gal. 1:18), at which time he may or may not have communicated with the other apostles. He soon began preaching and teaching there and was so forceful in "arguing with the Hellenistic Jews" that "they were attempting to put him to death. But when the brethren learned of it, they brought him down to Caesarea and sent him away to Tarsus," his home town (Acts 9:29-30). He probably founded churches in Tarsus and in other places in Cilicia, and we know that the Lord later used him to strengthen the churches of that area (Acts 15:41).

After Barnabas was sent by the Jerusalem church to organize the church at Antioch of Syria, he ministered there for a period of time and then decided to enlist the help of Saul. After searching out Saul in Tarsus, Barnabas "brought him to Antioch. And it came about that for an entire year they met with the church, and taught considerable numbers." It was during this time in Antioch, under the joint ministry of Saul and Barnabas, that "the disciples were first called Christians" (Acts 11:22-26).

When the world-wide famine predicted by Agabus occurred, the church at Antioch received contributions from its members for relief of believers in Judea, who were in special need. The offering was sent "in charge of Barnabas and Saul to the elders" at Jerusalem (Acts 11:28-30).

As the church in Antioch grew, other prophets and teachers were raised up, and eventually the Holy Spirit instructed those leaders: "'Set apart for Me Barnabas and Saul for the work to which I have called them.' Then, when they had fasted, prayed, and laid their hands on them, they sent them away" (Acts 13:1-3). It was at that time that Paul, still called Saul, began his unique ministry as the apostle to the Gentiles.

THE PLACE AND TIME OF WRITING

Paul made three extensive missionary journeys, reported in Acts 13:4–21:17, and then a final journey to Rome to be heard before Caesar (27:1–28:16). On the third journey he went a third time to Corinth, a thriving but wicked port city in the province of Achaia, in what is now southern Greece. It was probably during that stay in Corinth to collect another offering for needy believers in Palestine (Rom. 15:26) that Paul wrote the letter to the church at Rome.

A careful examination by other commentators has arranged the chronological data furnished in the Book of Acts and the epistle itself to set the time in the early spring of A.D. 58, just before Paul left for Jerusalem (Rom. 15:25) to arrive before Pentecost (Acts 20:16).

THE PURPOSE OF WRITING

Paul mentions several purposes for writing the book of Romans. First of all, he had wanted to visit the church at Rome on numerous occasions but thus far had been prevented (Rom. 1:13). He wanted to go there, he explained, "in order that I may impart some spiritual gift to you, that you may be established" (v. 11). Contrary to the teaching of the Roman Catholic Church, the church at Rome was not established by Peter or any other apostle. Paul makes clear at the end of the letter that he was determined not to "build upon another man's foundation" (15:20), that is, not to instruct and lead a congregation that had been founded by another apostle or other Christian leader.

It is likely the church at Rome had been founded by a group of Jewish Christians who came there from Judea. It is possible that there had been Christians in Rome for many years, converts from among the "visitors from Rome, both Jews and proselytes" at Pentecost (Acts 2:10) who witnessed the descent of the Holy Spirit, heard the apostles speak in their own native tongues, and then listened to Peter's powerful sermon. If so, they would have been among the three thousand souls who believed and were baptized that day (v. 41).

In any case, although they were a dedicated and faithful group and lived in the strategic heart of the Roman Empire, believers in the city of Rome had not had the benefit of apostolic preaching or teaching. It was that deficiency that Paul wanted to remedy by visiting with them for a period of instruction and encouragement.

Paul also wanted to do evangelistic work there, suggested by his saying that he eagerly desired "to preach the gospel to you also who are in Rome" (Rom. 1:15).

In addition to those reasons, Paul wanted to visit the church at Rome for his own sake, that "I may be encouraged together with you while among you, each of us by the other's faith, both yours and mine" (1:12). He wanted to go there not only for Christ's sake but also for the sake of the church, for the sake of the lost, and for his own sake.

He longed to get to know the believers in Rome and to have them get to know him. First of all, he wanted them to know him so they could pray for him. Although most of them were strangers, he implored near the end of his letter, "Now I urge you, brethren, by our Lord Jesus Christ and by the love of the Spirit, to strive together with me in your prayers to God for me, . . . so that I may come to you in joy by the will of God and find refreshing rest in your company" (15:30, 32).

He perhaps also wanted them to get to know him so that, after his stay in Rome, they would be willing to help provide the needed resources for his journey on to Spain, where he hoped to minister at a later time (15:28).

Paul's letter to the church at Rome was, among other things, an introduction of himself as an apostle. He clearly set forth the gospel he preached and taught, so that believers in Rome would have complete confidence in his authority. He penned a monumental treatise to establish them in the truth and to show that he was indeed a true apostle of Jesus Christ.

When he finally came to Rome it was at the expense of the Roman government, due to his insistence that, as a Roman citizen, he be tried before Caesar concerning the charges brought against him by the chief priests and other Jewish leaders in Jerusalem (Acts 25:2, 11). His ministry in Rome was therefore as a prisoner, and it was during that imprisonment that he wrote the epistle to the Philippians, in which he sent greetings from "Caesar's household" (Phil. 4:22). It was also likely from Rome that Paul wrote Ephesians (Eph. 3:1; 6:20), Colossians (Col. 4:10), and Philemon (Philem. 1).

The spectacular triumph of the gospel during and through Paul's ministry is impossible to assess, but that incredible man was energized and used by the Spirit of God to accomplish things far beyond what we can imagine. Historians have estimated that by the close of the apostolic period there were a half million Christians! Heaven only knows how many of those were brought to the Lord directly or indirectly by the efforts of Paul. Through the intervening centuries the Lord has continued to use the Spirit-inspired writings of that apostle to win the lost and to edify, strengthen, encourage, and correct countless millions of believers. He had been set apart by God even from his mother's womb, in order that he "might preach [Christ] among the Gentiles" (Gal. 1:15-16).

PAUL'S CHARACTER

Physically, Paul was not attractive (see, e.g., 2 Cor. 10:10; Gal. 4:14). He has been described as being small of stature and having scars over his face and body from his many beatings and stonings. Whatever his physical appearance may have been, in spiritual stature and magnificence Paul is surely unsurpassed among the servants of God.

Paul had personal characteristics that made him useable by God. Obviously he possessed a biblical mind. He was absolutely saturated with the Word of God, which in his day was what we now call the Old Testament. His great intellect was continually immersed in the Hebrew Scriptures, being constantly instructed by God's previous revelation of Himself and His will.

In the book of Romans, for example, Paul speaks with great competence about Abraham. He understood the relationship between grace and law and between flesh and spirit. In teaching about those truths, he draws upon the writings of Moses, Hosea, Isaiah, David, and others. Of the books of the law, he demonstrates special familiarity with Genesis, Exodus, Leviticus, and Deuteronomy. He quotes Jeremiah and Malachi, and alludes to Daniel. He quotes from Joel 2 and Nahum 1 and refers to 1 Samuel, 1 Kings, and Ezekiel 37. His thoughts and teaching continually intersect with the Old Testament, perhaps dominantly with Isaiah, whose prophecies he clearly had mastered.

Quoting Isaiah 28:16, he declares, "Just as it is written, 'Behold, I lay in Zion a stone of stumbling and a rock of offense, and he who believes in Him will not be disappointed'" (Rom. 9:33; cf. 10:11). A few verses later he quotes Isaiah 52:7, saying, "Just as it is written, 'How beautiful are the feet of those who bring glad tidings of good things!'" (10:15). In chapter 11 he asks rhetorically about 1 Kings 19:10, "Do you not know what the Scripture says in the passage about Elijah?" (v. 2). Twice more in that chapter he appeals to unspecified Scripture passages to reinforce what he says, introducing each citation with, "Just as it is written" (vv. 8, 26; cf. Deut. 29:4; Ps. 69:22-23; Isa. 27:9; 59:20-21). Throughout the letter he continues to appeal to scriptural authority (e.g., 12:19; 14:11; 15:3).

The biblical thinking of Paul was combined with a determined and resolute sense of mission which would not be sidetracked or distracted. If beaten, he continued to minister, and if imprisoned, he would start an evangelistic meeting (Acts 16:22-25). If stoned and left for dead because of his preaching, God would raise him up and he would go on his way (14:19-20). When a weary listener fell from a window and died while Paul was preaching late at night, the apostle went out and raised him from the dead and then continued his message (20:9-12).

Paul traversed the greater part of the Roman Empire of his day, from Jerusalem to Rome and from Caesarea to Macedonian Philippi. He was a foundation builder, tirelessly declaring the gospel with conviction for perhaps twenty years. While comforting and warning the elders from Ephesus who came out to Miletus to meet him, Paul said, "The Holy Spirit solemnly testifies to me in every city, saying that bonds and afflictions await me. But I do not consider my life of any account as dear to myself, in order that I may finish my course, and the ministry which I received from the Lord Jesus to testify solemnly of the gospel of the grace of God" (Acts 20:23-24).

Writing to the church at Corinth, he said, "I am under compulsion; for woe is me if I do not preach the gospel" (1 Cor. 9:16). In a later letter to that same church he wrote,

I [am] in far more labors, in far more imprisonments, beaten times without number, often in danger of death. Five times I received from the Jews thirty-nine lashes. Three times I was beaten with rods, once I was stoned, three times I was shipwrecked, a night and a day I have spent in the deep. I have been on frequent journeys, in dangers from rivers, dangers from robbers, dangers from my countrymen, dangers from the Gentiles, dangers in the city, dangers in the wilderness, dangers on the sea, dangers among false brethren; I have been in labor and hardship, through many sleepless nights, in hunger and thirst, often without food, in cold and exposure. Apart from such external things, there is the daily pressure upon me of concern for all the churches. (2 Cor. 11:23-28)

The apostle had experienced all of those things and many more before he wrote the book of Romans. He admonished his young protégé, Timothy, to "be sober in all things, endure hardship, do the work of an evangelist, fulfill your ministry." He then went on to say of himself, "For I am already being poured out as a drink offering, and the time of my departure has come. I have fought the good fight, I have finished the course, I have kept the faith" (2 Tim. 4:5-7).

Though committed to truth and mission, he also had an immense, burning sense of God's love that permeated everything he did, said, and wrote. The great apostle cannot be understood apart from his deep love for God, his love for believing brethren, and his love for unbelieving mankind, especially his fellow Jews. He had such an abiding love for Israel and longed so deeply for their salvation that he could say with perfect sincerity, "I could wish that I myself were accursed, separated from Christ for the sake of my brethren, my kinsmen according to the flesh" (Rom. 9:3).

Paul's love for his spiritual brothers and sisters in the church is evident throughout his letter to Rome. Chapter 16 is almost a continuous list of greetings to various believers who were especially dear to the apostle, including those who had ministered to him and those to whom he had ministered.

He spoke from profound personal experience as well as from divine revelation when he said, "The love of God has been poured out within our hearts through the Holy Spirit who was given to us" (Rom. 5:5). In the same way he declared, "Who shall separate us from the love of Christ? Shall tribulation, or distress, or persecution, or famine, or nakedness, or peril, or sword? . . . In all these things we overwhelmingly conquer through Him who loved us" (Rom. 8:35, 37). As mentioned earlier, near the close of the letter he exhorts his readers: "I urge you, brethren, by our Lord Jesus Christ and by the love of the Spirit, to strive together with me in your prayers to God for me" (15:30).

As it should be with every believer, Paul was totally under the control of Christ's love (see 2 Cor. 5:14). As he more and more understood and experienced God's love, he more and more loved God in return.

Above everything else, however, Paul lived and worked to glorify God. Of the Lord he wrote, "For from Him and through Him and to Him are all things. To Him be the glory forever. Amen" (Rom. 11:36; cf. also 1 Cor. 10:31). He admonished his readers to have that same desire and purpose: "With one voice glorify the God and Father of our Lord Jesus Christ" (15:6). As the specially-chosen apostle to the Gentiles, his great yearning was for them "to glorify God for His mercy" (15:9). The closing words, in effect, dedicate the epistle "to the only wise God, through Jesus Christ," to whom will "be the glory forever" (16:27).

As Donald Grey Barnhouse observed, "Paul could never forget the pit from which he had been digged" (*Man's Ruin: Romans 1:1-32* [Grand Rapids: Eerdmans, 1952], p. 8). He always maintained a realistic and humble perspective on his work and on himself.

Paul was so totally devoted to Jesus Christ that he could admonish his readers with confidence, yet with perfect humility: "Be imitators of me, just as I also am of Christ" (1 Cor. 11:1; cf. 4:16) and "Brethren, join in following my example" (Phil. 3:17; cf. Acts 20:18-24; 2 Thess. 3:7-9).

Every preacher who has proclaimed the gospel since Paul's day has depended on that apostle's teaching for his material. The thirteen New Testament books written by him are the legacy of that great man through the inspiration of the Holy Spirit.

The Good News of God—part 1

Paul, a bond-servant of Christ Jesus, called as an apostle, set apart for the gospel of God, (1:1)

A quick look at any newspaper or passing glance at a weekly news magazine reminds us that in our world most news is bad and seems to be getting worse. What is happening on a national and worldwide scale is simply the magnification of what is happening on an individual level. As personal problems, animosities, and fears increase, so do their counterparts in society at large.

Human beings are in the hold of a terrifying power that grips them at the very core of their being. Left unchecked, it pushes them to self-destruction in one form or another. That power is sin, which is always bad news.

Sin is bad news in every dimension. Among its consequences are four inevitable byproducts that guarantee misery and sorrow for a world taken captive. First, sin has selfishness at its heart. The basic element of fallen human nature is exaltation of self, the ego. When Satan fell, he was asserting his own will above God's, five times declaring, "I will . . ." (Isa. 14:13-14). Man fell by the same self-will, when Adam and Eve asserted their own understanding about right and wrong above God's clear instruction (Gen. 2:16-17; 3:1-7).

By nature man is self-centered and inclined to have his own way. He will push his selfishness as far as circumstances and the tolerance of society will allow. When self-will is unbridled, man consumes everything and everyone around him in an insatiable quest to please himself. When friends, fellow workers, or a spouse cease to provide what is wanted, they are discarded like an old pair of shoes. Much of modern western society has been so imbued with the propriety of self-esteem and self-will that virtually every desire has come to be considered a right.

The ultimate goal in many lives today is little more than perpetual self-satisfaction. Every object, every idea, every circumstance, and every person is viewed in light of what it can contribute to one's own purposes and welfare. Lust for wealth, possessions, fame, dominance, popularity, and physical fulfillment drives people to pervert everything they possess and everyone they know. Employment has become nothing more than a necessary evil to finance one's indulgences. As is often noted, there is constant danger of loving things and using people rather than loving people and using things. When that temptation is succumbed to, stable and faithful personal relationships become impossible. A person engulfed in self-will and self-fulfillment becomes less and less capable of loving, because as his desire to possess grows, his desire to give withers. And when he forfeits selflessness for selfishness, he forfeits the source of true joy.

Selfish greed progressively alienates a person from everyone else, including those who are closest and dearest. The end result is loneliness and despair. Everything that is craved soon yields to the law of diminishing returns, and the more one has of it the less it satisfies.

Second, sin produces guilt, another form of bad news. No matter how convincingly one tries to justify selfishness, its inevitable abuse of things and other people cannot escape generating guilt.

Like physical pain, guilt is a God-given warning that something is wrong and needs correcting. When guilt is ignored or suppressed, it continues to grow and intensify, and with it come anxiety, fear, sleeplessness, and countless other spiritual and physical afflictions. Many people try to overcome those afflictions by masking them with possessions, money, alcohol, drugs, sex, travel, and psychoanalysis. They try to assuage their guilt by blaming society, parents, a deprived childhood, environment, restrictive moral codes, and even God Himself. But the irresponsible notion of blaming other persons and things only aggravates the guilt and escalates the accompanying afflictions.

Third, sin produces meaninglessness, still another form of bad news and one that is endemic to modern times. Trapped in his own selfishness, the self-indulgent person has no sense of purpose or meaning.

Life becomes an endless cycle of trying to fill a void that cannot be filled. The result is futility and despair. To questions such as, "Why am I here? What is the meaning of life? What is truth?" he finds no answers in the world but the lies of Satan, who is the author of lies and prince of the present world system (cf. John 8:44; 2 Cor. 4:4). In the words of Edna St. Vincent Millay in her poem "Lament," he can only say, "Life must go on; I forget just why." Or, like the central character in one of Jean-Paul Sartre's novels, he may say nihilistically, "I decided to kill myself to remove at least one superfluous life."

A fourth element in sin's chain of bad news is hopelessness, which is the companion of meaninglessness. The consumptively selfish person forfeits hope, both for this life and for the next. Although he may deny it, he senses that even death is not the end, and for the hopeless sinner death becomes therefore the ultimate bad news.

Millions of babies are born every day into a world filled with bad news. And because of the boundless selfishness that permeates modern society, millions of other babies are not allowed to enter the world at all. That tragedy alone has made the bad news of the modern world immeasurably worse.

The tidbits of seemingly good news are often merely a brief respite from the bad, and sometimes even what appears to be good news merely masks an evil. Someone once commented cynically that peace treaties merely provide time for everyone to reload!

But the essence of Paul's letter to the Romans is that there is good news that is truly good. The apostle was, in fact, "a minister of Christ Jesus to the Gentiles, ministering as a priest of the gospel of God" (Rom. 15:16). He brought the good news that in Christ sin can be forgiven, selfishness can be overcome, guilt can be removed, anxiety can be alleviated, and life can indeed have hope and eternal glory.

In his Romans letter Paul speaks of the good news in many ways, each way emphasizing a uniquely beautiful facet of one spiritual gem. He calls it the blessed good news, the good news of salvation, the good news of Jesus Christ, the good news of God's Son, and the good news of the grace of God. The letter begins (1:1) and ends (16:25-26) with the good news.

The entire thrust of the sixteen chapters of Romans is distilled into the first seven verses. The apostle apparently was so overjoyed by his message of good news that he could not wait to introduce his readers to the gist of what he had to say. He burst into it immediately.

In Romans 1:1-7 Paul unfolds seven aspects of the good news of Jesus Christ. He first identifies himself as the preacher of the good news (v. 1), which will be discussed in this present chapter. He then tells of the promise (v. 2), the Person (vv. 3-4), the provision (v. 5a), the proclamation (v. 5b), the purpose (v. 5c), and the privileges of the good news (vv. 6-7).

THE PREACHER OF THE GOOD NEWS

Paul, a bond-servant of Christ Jesus, called as an apostle, set apart for the gospel of God, (1:1)

God called a unique man to be the major spokesman for His glorious good news. **Paul** was God's keynote speaker, as it were, for heralding the gospel. A singularly gifted man, he was given divine "insight into the mystery of Christ" (Eph. 3:4), "the mystery which has been hidden from the past ages and generations; but has now been manifested to His saints" (Col. 1:26). That remarkable Jew with Greek education and Roman citizenship, with incredible leadership ability, high motivation, and articulate expression, was specially and directly called, converted, and gifted by God.

Paul crisscrossed much of the Roman Empire as God's ambassador of the good news of Christ. He performed many healing miracles, yet was not relieved of his own thorn in the flesh. He raised Eutychus from the dead but was at least once left for dead himself. He preached freedom in Christ but was imprisoned by men during many years of his ministry.

In the first verse Paul discloses three important things about himself in regard to his ministry: his position as a servant of Christ, his authority as an apostle of Christ, and his power in being set apart for the gospel of Christ.

PAUL'S POSITION AS A SERVANT OF CHRIST

a bond-servant of Christ Jesus, (1:1a)

Doulos (**bond-servant**) carries the basic idea of subservience and has a wide range of connotations. It was sometimes used of a person who voluntarily served others, but most commonly it referred to those who were in unwilling and permanent bondage, from which often there was no release but death.

The Hebrew equivalent (*'ebed*) is used hundreds of times in the Old Testament and carries the same wide range of connotations. The Mosaic law provided for an indentured servant to voluntarily become a permanent bond-slave of a master he loved and respected. "If a slave plainly says, 'I love my master, my wife and my children; I will not go out as a free man,' then his master shall bring him to God, then he shall bring him to the door or the doorpost. And his master shall pierce his ear with an awl; and he shall serve him permanently" (Ex. 21:5-6).

That practice reflects the essence of Paul's use of the term *doulos* in Romans 1:1. The apostle had given himself wholeheartedly in love to the divine Master who saved him from sin and death.

In New Testament times there were millions of slaves in the Roman Empire, the vast majority of whom were forced into slavery and kept there by law. Some of the more educated and skilled slaves held significant positions in a household or business and were treated with considerable respect. But most slaves were treated much like any other personal property of the owner and were considered little better than work animals. They had virtually no rights under the law and could even be killed with impunity by their masters.

Some commentators argue that because of the great difference between Jewish slavery as practiced in Old Testament times and the slavery of first-century Rome, Paul had only the Jewish concept in mind when speaking of his relationship to Christ. Many of the great figures in the Old Testament were referred to as servants. God spoke of Abraham as His servant (Gen. 26:24; Num. 12:7). Joshua is called "the servant of the Lord" (Josh. 24:29), as are David (2 Sam. 7:5) and Isaiah (Isa. 20:3). Even the Messiah is called God's Servant (Isa. 53:11). In all of those instances, and in many more in the Old Testament, the term *servant* carries the idea of humble nobility and honor. But as already noted, the Hebrew word (*'ebed*) behind *servant* was also used of bond-slaves.

In light of Paul's genuine humility and his considering himself the foremost of sinners (1 Tim. 1:15), it is certain that he was not arrogating to himself the revered and noble title of servant of the Lord as used in the citations above. He considered Himself Christ's **bond-servant** in the most unassuming sense.

There is, of course, an honor and dignity attached to all of God's true servants, even the most seemingly insignificant, and Paul was very much aware of the undeserved but real dignity God bestows on those who belong to Him. Yet he was constantly aware also that the dignity and honor God gives His children are purely from grace, that *in themselves* Christians are still sinful, depraved, and undeserving. He wrote to the Corinthian church, "What then is Apollos? And what is Paul? Servants through whom you believed, even as the Lord gave opportunity to each one" (1 Cor. 3:5). Here Paul uses the term *diakonos* to describe his position as servant, a term commonly used of table waiters. But as in his use of *doulos,* the emphasis here is on subservience and insignificance, not honor. Later in the same letter he asks his readers to regard him as a galley slave (4:1). The term used here is *hupēretēs* ("servants") which literally means "underrowers," referring to the lowest level of rowers in the large galley of a Roman ship. This was perhaps the hardest, most dangerous, and most demeaning work a slave could do. Such slaves were considered the lowest of the low.

Because he was called and appointed by Christ Himself, Paul would never belittle his position as an apostle or even as a child of God. He plainly taught that godly leaders in the church, especially those who are diligent in preaching and teaching, are "worthy of double honor" by fellow believers (1 Tim. 5:17). But he continually emphasized that such positions of honor are provisions of God's grace.

PAUL'S AUTHORITY AS AN APOSTLE

called as an apostle, (1:b)

Paul next establishes the authority of his ministry, based on his being **called as an apostle.** Perhaps a better rendering would be "a called apostle," which more clearly points up the fact that his position **as an apostle** was not of his own doing. He did not volunteer for that office, nor was he elected by fellow believers. He was divinely **called** by the Lord Jesus Christ Himself.

While Paul, then called Saul, was still blinded from his miraculous encounter with Jesus on the Damascus Road, the Lord said to Ananias about Paul: "He is a chosen instrument of Mine, to bear My name before the Gentiles and kings and the sons of Israel" (Acts 9:15). In relaying the message to Paul, Ananias said, "The God of our fathers has appointed you to know His will, and to see the Righteous One, and to hear an utterance from His mouth. For you will be a witness for Him to all men of what you have seen and heard" (Acts 22:14-15). Paul later gave the additional revelation that Christ already had given that message directly to him, saying,

> Arise, and stand on your feet; for this purpose I have appeared to you, to appoint you a minister and a witness not only to the things which you have seen, but also to the things in which I will appear to you; delivering you from the Jewish people and from the Gentiles, to whom I am sending you, to open their eyes so that they may turn from darkness to light and from the dominion of Satan to God in order that they may receive forgiveness of sins and an inheritance among those who have been sanctified by faith in Me. (Acts 26:16-18)

Paul told the Corinthian believers, "I am under compulsion; for woe is me if I do not preach the gospel" (1 Cor. 9:16). God had given him a task he had never dreamed of and had never asked for, and he knew he would be in serious trouble if he was not obedient to his divine commission.

Paul was "an apostle (not sent from men, nor through the agency of man, but through Jesus Christ, and God the Father, who raised Him from the dead)" (Gal. 1:1). He went on to declare, "Am I now seeking the favor of men, or of God? Or am I striving to please men? If I were still trying to please men, I would not be a bond-servant of Christ" (v. 10).

Apostle translates *apostolos,* which has the basic meaning of a person who is sent. It referred to someone who was officially commissioned to a position or task, such as an envoy or ambassador. Cargo ships were sometimes called apostolic, because they were dispatched with a specific shipment for a specific destination.

The term **apostle** appears some seventy-nine times in the New Testament and is used in a few instances in a general, nontechnical sense (see Rom. 16:7; Acts 14:14) In its broadest sense, *apostle* can refer to all believers, because every believer is sent into the world as a witness for Christ. But the term is primarily used as a specific and unique title for the thirteen men (the Twelve, with Matthias replacing Judas, and Paul) whom Christ personally chose and commissioned to authoritatively proclaim the gospel and lead the early church.

The thirteen apostles not only were all called directly by Jesus but all were witnesses of His resurrection, Paul having encountered Him on the Damascus Road after His ascension. Those thirteen apostles were given direct revelation of God's Word to proclaim authoritatively, the gift of healing, and the power to cast out demons (Matt. 10:1). By these signs their teaching authority was verified (cf. 2 Cor. 12:12). Their teachings became the foundation of the church (Eph. 2:20), and their authority extended beyond local bodies of believers to the entire believing world.

Although the apostles were "the sent-ones" in a unique way, every person who speaks for God must be called and sent by Him. There are many people preaching, teaching, and presuming to prophesy in Christ's name whom Christ has clearly not sent. They obviously have no anointing of God because their teachings and living do not square with God's Word.

False prophets have always plagued God's people. They corrupted ancient Israel, they have corrupted the church through all the centuries of its existence, and they continue to corrupt the church today. Through Jeremiah the Lord said of such impostors, "I did not send these prophets, but they ran. I did not speak to them, but they prophesied" (Jer. 23:21).

Some religious leaders not only give no evidence of being called by God to preach and teach in His name but even give little evidence of salvation. In his book *The Reformed Pastor,* seventeenth-century Puritan pastor Richard Baxter devotes a hundred pages to warning preachers of the gospel to be sure first of all that they are truly redeemed and second that they have been called by God to His ministry.

PAUL'S POWER IN BEING SET APART FOR THE GOSPEL

set apart for the gospel of God, (1c)

Because Paul was called and sent by God as an apostle, his whole life was **set apart** in the Lord's service. Even a person who has been called by God to a special type or place of service cannot be effective if he is not also separated unto God for **the gospel of God.**

Throughout the Old Testament, God provided for the setting apart of His chosen people. To the entire nation He declared, "You are to be holy to Me, for I the Lord am holy; and I have set you apart from the peoples to be Mine" (Lev. 20:26). Just before He delivered His people from Pharaoh's Army the Lord commanded: "You shall devote to the Lord the first offspring of every womb, and the first offspring of every beast that you own; the males belong to the Lord" (Ex. 13:12). God also demanded the firstfruits of their crops (Num. 15:20). The Levites were set apart as the priestly tribe (Num. 8:11-14).

In the Septuagint (Greek) version of the above passages from Exodus, Numbers, and Leviticus, the words translated "present," "lift up," and "set apart" are all forms of *aphorizō,* the term Paul used for his being **set apart.** It is used of setting apart to God the firstborn, of offering to God first fruits, of consecrating to God the Levites, and of separating Israel to God from other peoples. There was to be no intermingling of the chosen people with the Gentile nations or of the sacred with the profane and ordinary.

The Aramaic term *Pharisee* may share a common root with *aphorizō* and carries the same idea of separation. The Pharisees, however, were not set apart by God or according to God's standards but had rather set themselves apart according to the standards of their own traditions (cf. Matt. 23:1, 2).

Although Paul himself had once been the most ardent of the self-appointed Pharisees, he was now set apart divinely, not humanly. God revealed to him that he had been set apart by God's grace even from his mother's womb (Gal. 1:15). When he and Barnabas were set apart and commissioned for missionary work by the church in Antioch, it was on the direct instruction of the Holy Spirit (Acts 13:2).

Paul's clear understanding of this separateness comes through in his writing to Timothy. Timothy was a genuine servant of God, and he had been personally discipled by Paul and succeeded him as pastor of the church at Ephesus. But at some point in his ministry he may have come dangerously close to being ineffective, perhaps because of fear of opposition or because of temporary weakness. Paul therefore exhorted his beloved friend, "I remind you to kindle afresh the gift of God which is in you through the laying on of my hands. For God has not given us a spirit of timidity, but of power and love and discipline" (2 Tim. 1:6-7). He may also have been tempted to be ashamed of the gospel and of Paul, as suggested in Paul's saying to him, "Be diligent to present yourself approved to God as a workman who does not need to be ashamed, handling accurately the word of truth" (2 Tim. 2:15).

Perhaps because Timothy became distracted from his primary work of preaching and teaching the Word and had become involved in fruitless disputes with unbelievers or immature believers, Paul admonished him further, saying, "Avoid worldly and empty chatter, for it will lead to further ungodliness" (2:16). It is even possible that Timothy was in danger of falling into some form of immoral behavior, prompting Paul to warn: "Flee from youthful lusts, and pursue righteousness, faith, love and peace, with those who call on the Lord from a pure heart" (2:22).

Despite Timothy's high calling and remarkable training, Paul feared that his young disciple was capable of slipping back into some worldly ways. Like many Christians, he discovered that life can appear to be easier and less troublesome when compromises are made. Paul had to remind him that he was set apart by God for God's work and for no one else and for nothing else.

The term *euangelion* (**gospel**) is used some sixty times in this epistle. William Tyndale defined it as "glad tidings" (*Doctrinal Treatises and Introductions to Different Portions of the Holy Scriptures by William Tyndale*, Henry Walter, ed. [Cambridge: University Press, 1848], p. 484). It is the good news that God will deliver us from our selfish sin, free us from our burden of guilt, and give meaning to life and make it abundant.

The most important thing about **the gospel** is that it is **of God.** Paul makes that clear in the first sentence of his epistle in order that his readers have no confusion regarding the specific good news about which he was speaking. *Euangelion* was a common term used in the cult of emperor worship that was common in Paul's day. Many of the caesars claimed deity for themselves and demanded worship from every person in the empire, free or slave, rich or poor, renowned or unknown. Favorable events relating to the emperor were proclaimed to the citizens as "good news." The town herald would stand in the village square and shout, "Good news! The emperor's wife has given birth to a son," or, "Good news! The emperor's heir has come of age," or, "Good news! The new emperor has acceded to the throne."

Especially because he was writing to believers in the Roman capital, Paul wanted to be certain that his readers understood that the good news he proclaimed was of an entirely different order than the trivial and vain proclamations concerning the emperors. The fact that it was **of God** meant that God was the source of it. It was not man's good news, but God's good news for man.

One cannot help wondering why God would condescend to bring good news to a world that rejects and scorns Him. No one deserves to hear it, much less to be saved by it.

The noted expository preacher Donald Grey Barnhouse told the fascinating legend of a young Frenchman who was dearly loved by his mother but in early manhood fell into immorality. He was greatly enamored of an unprincipled woman who managed to gain his total devotion. When the mother tried to draw her son away from the wicked and debased association, the other woman became enraged. She railed at the young man, accusing him of not truly loving her and insisting that he demonstrate his commitment to her by getting rid of his mother. The man resisted until a night when, in a drunken stupor, he was persuaded to carry out the heinous demand. According to the story, the man rushed from the room to his mother's house nearby, brutally killed her, and even cut out her heart to take to his vile companion as proof of his wickedness. But as he rushed on in his insane folly, he stumbled and fell, upon which the bleeding heart is said to have cried out, "My son, are you hurt?" Dr. Barnhouse commented, "That is the way God loves" (*Man's Ruin: Romans 1:1-32* [Grand Rapids: Eerdmans, 1952], pp. 21-22).

Paul himself was living proof of God's great love and mercy. Though he had opposed Christ and persecuted the church, God had made him the Church's chief spokesman. He could imagine no greater role than being set apart to God for the proclamation of His gospel, the good news of salvation in Christ. Perhaps that is one reason he was so effective. Who knew better than Paul just how good the good news really was?

The Good News of God—part 2

which He promised beforehand through His prophets in the holy Scriptures, concerning His Son, who was born of a descendant of David according to the flesh, who was declared the Son of God with power by the resurrection from the dead, according to the spirit of holiness, Jesus Christ our Lord, (1:2-4)

After introducing himself as the preacher of the good news of God (v. 1), Paul then tells of the promise (v. 2) and the Person (vv. 3-4) of the good news.

THE PROMISE OF THE GOOD NEWS

which He promised beforehand through His prophets in the holy Scriptures, (1:2)

The gospel, which originated with God, was not a divine afterthought, nor was it first taught in the New Testament. It does not reflect a late change in God's plan or a revision of His strategy. It was

promised by God **beforehand through His prophets in the holy Scriptures,** that is, in what we now call the Old Testament.

Perhaps especially for the sake of his Jewish critics, Paul emphasizes in the very beginning of the epistle that the good news did not originate with him or even with Jesus' earthly ministry. He was frequently accused of preaching and teaching against Moses and of proclaiming a revolutionary message unheard of in ancient Judaism (cf. Acts 21:20ff). But here he makes clear that the good news he teaches is really old news of the Hebrew **Scriptures** now fulfilled and completed in Jesus Christ.

Paul's use of **prophets** refers to the Old Testament writers in general, all of whom were spokesmen for God, which is the basic meaning of **prophets.** Moses, for instance, was the great lawgiver, yet he also considered himself a prophet (Deut. 18:15). Paul's reference to **the holy Scriptures** was probably to contrast the divinely-inspired Old Testament from the many rabbinical writings which in his day were studied and followed more zealously than was Scripture. In other words, although the rabbinical writings said little or nothing about the gospel of God, **the holy Scriptures** had a great deal to say about it. They did not originate with men or reflect the thinking of men, but were the divinely-revealed Word of the living God.

Most Jews of that day were so accustomed to looking to rabbinical tradition for religious guidance that **the holy Scriptures** were looked on more as a sacred relic than as the source of truth. Even after His three years of intense teaching, Jesus had to chide some of His own disciples for failing to understand and believe what the **Scriptures** taught about Him. Before He revealed His identity to the two disciples on the road to Emmaus, He said to them, "O foolish men and slow of heart to believe in all that the prophets have spoken!" (Luke 24:25). And as He proceeded to teach them about His death and resurrection, He expounded Scripture (v. 27, cf. v. 32).

It was a defective traditional Judaism that was revolutionary, man-originated, man-centered, and that was *not* grounded in **the holy Scriptures.** And it was the proponents of that man-made perversion of Judaism who most strongly opposed Jesus. He denounced the religious devotion of the scribes and Pharisees as being hypocrisy rather than piety and their theology as being the false tradition of men rather than the revealed truth of God.

The phrases "You have heard that it was said" and "You have heard that the ancients were told" that Jesus frequently used in the Sermon on the Mount (Matt. 5:21, 27, 33, 38, 43) did not refer to the Old Testament but to rabbinical traditions that contradicted and invalidated the Old Testament (Matt. 15:6).

It is estimated that the Old Testament contains at least 332 prophecies about Christ, most of which were fulfilled at His first coming.

The Old Testament is filled with truths that predict and lay the groundwork for the New.

Jesus taught nothing that was either disconnected from or contrary to the Old Testament. "Do not think that I came to abolish the Law or the Prophets," He declared; "I did not come to abolish, but to fulfill. For truly I say to you, until heaven and earth pass away, not the smallest letter or stroke shall pass away from the Law, until all is accomplished" (Matt. 5:17-18).

Throughout the history of the church Jews have resisted the gospel by arguing that to embrace it would be to deny their heritage. On the human level that is true, because since long before Jesus' day, popular Judaism has been based more on human tradition that on divine revelation. To become a Christian certainly demands denial of a heritage such as that. But for a Jew to embrace the gospel is for him to truly inherit what his scriptural heritage has always promised. The Jew's greatest heritage is the promise of God's Messiah, and Jesus is that Messiah, the fulfillment of that promise. Every Jewish prophet, directly or indirectly, prophesied of the ultimate Prophet, Jesus Christ. Every Jewish sacrificial lamb spoke of the ultimate, eternal Lamb of God who would be sacrificed for the sins of the world.

Confronting that same issue, the writer of Hebrews opens his letter by declaring, "God, after He spoke long ago to the fathers in the prophets in many portions and in many ways, in these last days has spoken to us in His Son" (Heb. 1:1-2). Peter also accentuated that same truth in his first letter:

> As to this salvation, the prophets who prophesied of the grace that would come to you made careful search and inquiry, seeking to know what person or time the Spirit of Christ within them was indicating as He predicted the sufferings of Christ and the glories to follow. It was revealed to them that they were not serving themselves, but you, in these things which now have been announced to you through those who preached the gospel to you by the Holy Spirit sent from heaven—things into which angels long to look. (1 Pet. 1:10-12)

The prophets spoke generally of the anticipated new covenant (cf. Jer. 31:31-34; Ezek. 36:25-27) as well as specifically of the Messiah who would bring that covenant (cf. Isa. 7:18; 9:6, 7; 53:1-12).

THE PERSON OF THE GOOD NEWS

concerning His Son, who was born of a descendant of David according to the flesh, who was declared the Son of God with

power by the resurrection from the dead, according to the spirit of holiness, Jesus Christ our Lord, (1:3-4)

Both of those verses emphasize the divine sonship of Christ. There is a great mystery in the concept of Jesus as God's **Son.** Although He is Himself God and Lord, He is yet the Son of God. Because Scripture plainly teaches both of those truths, the issue has to do not with whether He is **the Son of God** but in what sense He is God's **Son.**

Clearly, in His humanness Jesus was **born of a descendant of David according to the flesh.** Both Mary (Luke 3: 23, 31), Jesus' natural mother, and Joseph (Matt. 1:6, 16; Luke 1:27), Jesus' legal father, were descendants of David.

In order to fulfill prophecy (see, e.g., 2 Sam. 7:12-13; Ps. 89:3-4, 19, 24; Isa. 11:1-5; Jer. 23:5-6), the Messiah had to be **a descendant of David.** Jesus fulfilled those messianic predictions just as He fulfilled all others. As the descendant of David, Jesus inherited the right to restore and to rule David's kingdom, the promised kingdom that would be without end (Isa 9:7).

The second Person of the Trinity was born into a human family and shared human life with all other humanity, identifying Himself with fallen mankind, yet living without sin (Phil. 2:4-8). He thereby became the perfect high priest, wholly God yet also wholly man, in order that He could "sympathize with our weaknesses, . . . one who has been tempted in all things as we are, yet without sin" (Heb. 4:15). That is the gospel, the great good news, that in Jesus Christ God became a Man who could die for all men, a substitute sacrifice for the sins of the whole world (Rom. 5:18-19).

Even secular history is replete with reports of Jesus' life and work. Writing about A.D. 114, the ancient Roman historian Tacitus reported that Jesus was founder of the Christian religion and that He was put to death by Pontius Pilate during the reign of Emperor Tiberius (*Annals* 15.44). Pliny the Younger wrote a letter to Emperor Trajan on the subject of Jesus Christ and His followers (*Letters* 10.96-97). Jesus is even mentioned in the Jewish Babylonian Talmud (*Sanhedrin* 43a, *Abodah Zerah* 16b-17a).

Writing in A.D. 90, before the apostle John wrote the book of Revelation, the familiar Jewish historian Josephus wrote a brief biographical sketch of Jesus of Nazareth. In it he said,

> Now there was about this time Jesus, a wise man, if it be lawful to call Him a man: for He was a doer of wonderful works, a teacher of such men as receive the truth with pleasure. He drew over to Him both many of the Jews and many of the Gentiles. He was Christ. And when Pilate, at the

suggestion of the principal men among us, had condemned Him to the cross, those that loved Him at the first did not forsake Him; for He appeared to them alive again the third day as the divine prophets had foretold these and ten thousand other wonderful things concerning Him. And the tribe of Christians so named from Him are not extinct at this day. (*Antiquities,* vol. 2, book 18, chap. 4)

An even more reliable witness was the apostle John, who wrote under the inspiration of the Holy Spirit, "By this you know the Spirit of God: every spirit that confesses that Jesus Christ has come in the flesh is from God; and every spirit that does not confess Jesus is not from God; and this is the spirit of the antichrist, of which you have heard that it is coming, and now it is already in the world" (1 John 4:2-3).

John was not speaking of merely recognizing the fact of Jesus' humanity. Countless unbelievers throughout history have been quite willing to concede that a man named Jesus lived in the first century and that He lived an exemplary life and generated a large following. The deist Thomas Jefferson believed in Jesus' existence as a man and in His importance to human history, but he did not believe in Jesus' divinity. He produced an edition of the Bible that eliminated all references to the supernatural. Consequently, the accounts of Jesus in Jefferson's "gospels" pertained to purely physical facts and events.

That is hardly the kind of recognition God's Word demands. The apostle was referring to believing and accepting the truth that Jesus was the Christ, the promised divine Messiah, and that He came from God and lived as a God-man among men.

It was at the time that He became a human being, Paul says, that Jesus **was declared the Son of God.** Though the plan was eternal, the title **Son** is reserved as an incarnational term, applied to Jesus in its fullness only after He put on the robe of humanity. He was the **Son of God** in the sense of oneness of essence and in the role of dutiful, loving submission to the Father in His self-emptying incarnation. There is, of course, no question that He is eternally God and eternally the second Person of the Godhead, but Paul says He **was declared** God's **Son** when He was supernaturally conceived in Mary and was **born of a descendant of David according to the flesh.** We could say, then, that Christ was the **Son of God** from eternity in expectation and was declared God's **Son** in fulfillment at the incarnation and forever.

Horizō (**declared**) carries the basic idea of marking off boundaries. From that term come our English *horizon,* which refers to the demarcation line between the earth and the sky. In an infinitely greater way, the divine sonship of Jesus Christ was marked off with absolute clarity in His incarnation.

Quoting Psalm 2:7, the writer of Hebrews explains that in that text God was declaring to Christ, the Messiah, "Thou art My Son, today I have begotten Thee." In the subsequent quotation from 2 Samuel 7:14, the Father goes on to say of Christ, "I will be a Father to Him, and He shall be a Son to Me" (Heb. 1:5). Both verbs in the last quotation are future tense, indicating that, sometime *after* the psalmist's time, Christ one day would assume a title and role He had not had before.

Psalm 2:7 is also quoted by the apostle Paul in Acts 13:33. This passage points to the resurrection as the declaration of that Sonship. This is not a contradiction. From God's viewpoint He was begotten as Son when He came into the world. The reality of that oneness with God and the perfection of His service to God was publicly declared to the world by the fact that God raised Him from the dead! (For a more detailed discussion, see the author's commentary on *Hebrews*, pp. 24-29.)

Christ was given and took upon Himself the fullness of the title of **Son of God** when he divested Himself of the independent use of His divine prerogatives and the full expression of His majesty, graciously humbling Himself and becoming fully subservient to the will and plan of the Father. In his letter to the church at Philippi, Paul explains that, "Christ Jesus, . . . although He existed in the form of God, did not regard equality with God a thing to be grasped, but emptied Himself, taking the form of a bond-servant, . . . being made in the likeness of men. And being found in appearance as a man, He humbled Himself by becoming obedient to the point of death, even death on a cross" (Phil. 2:5-8).

In His high priestly prayer Jesus said to the Father, "Glorify Thy Son, that the Son may glorify Thee," and a few moments later implored, "Glorify Thou Me together with Thyself, Father, with the glory which I had with thee before the world was" (John 17:1, 5). Christ has existed from all eternity. "He was in the beginning with God. All things came into being by Him, and apart from Him nothing came into being that has come into being" (John 1:2-3). But in accord with the divine plan of redemption, which He Himself planned with the Father and the Holy Spirit, Christ "became flesh, and dwelt among us" (v. 14a). He still possessed some of His divine glory, the "glory as of the only begotten from the Father" (v. 14b), but the glory He retained was a glory veiled in human flesh that could not be observed with human eyes.

As Paul goes on to explain, the most conclusive and irrefutable evidence of Jesus' divine sonship was given **with power by the resurrection from the dead** (cf. Acts 13:29-33). By that supreme demonstration of His ability to conquer death, a power belonging only to God Himself (the Giver of life), He established beyond all doubt that He was indeed God, the Son.

According to the spirit of holiness is another way of saying "according to the nature and work of the Holy Spirit." It was the Holy Spirit working in Christ who accomplished Jesus' resurrection and every other miracle performed by Him or associated with Him. In the incarnation, Jesus Christ was conceived by the power of the Holy Spirit, and in the resurrection He was raised from the dead by the power of the Holy Spirit, **the spirit of holiness.**

Immediately after Jesus' baptism by John the Baptist, "the heavens were opened, and he [John the Baptist] saw the Spirit of God descending as a dove, and coming upon Him, and behold, a voice out of the heavens, saying, 'This is My beloved son, in whom I am well-pleased'" (Matt. 3:16-17). All members of the Trinity were eternally equal in every way, but as mentioned above, in the incarnation the Second Person of the Trinity willingly divested Himself of the expression of the fullness of divine glory and the prerogatives of deity. During His humanity on earth He willingly submitted to the will of the Father (cf. John 5:30) and to the power of the Spirit. The descent of the Holy Spirit upon Him at His baptism was Jesus' initiation into ministry, a ministry totally controlled and empowered by the Spirit, so much so that Jesus characterized willful rejection of Him as blasphemy against the Holy Spirit (Matt. 12:24-32).

Here, then, is the Person of the good news. He is fully man (**a descendant of David**) and fully God (**declared to be the Son of God**). Throughout His ministry, both Jesus' humanness and His divinity were portrayed. When asked to pay taxes, Jesus complied. He explained to Peter that, as God's Son and the rightful ruler of the universe, including the Roman Empire, He was rightfully exempt from taxation. "But lest we give them [the tax collectors] offense," He went on to say, "go to the sea, and throw in a hook, and take the first fish that comes up; and when you open its mouth, you will find a coin. Take that and give it to them for you and Me" (Matt. 17:27). In His humanness He willingly paid taxes, but in His divinity He provided the payment supernaturally.

One evening after a long day of teaching Jesus got into a boat with the disciples and they set out for the other side of the Sea of Galilee. Jesus soon fell asleep, and when a storm arose and threatened to capsize the boat, the frightened disciples awakened Jesus, crying, "'Teacher, do you not care that we are perishing?' And being aroused, He rebuked the wind and said to the sea, 'Hush, be still.' And the wind died down and it became perfectly calm" (Mark 4:38-39). In His humanness Jesus was exhausted just as every person becomes exhausted after a hard day's work. Yet in His divinity He was able to instantly calm a violent storm.

As He hung on the cross, Jesus was bleeding and in severe agony because of His humanness. Yet at the same time, in His divinity He was able to grant eternal life to the repentant thief who hung nearby (Luke 23:42-43).

The Son of God and Son of Man who was raised from the dead by the power of the Holy Spirit was **Jesus Christ our Lord,** Paul declares. **Jesus** means Savior, **Christ** means Anointed One, and the **Lord** means sovereign ruler. He is **Jesus** because He saves His people from their sin. He is **Christ** because He has been anointed by God as King and Priest. He is **Lord** because He is God and is the sovereign ruler of the universe.

The Good News of God—part 3

through whom we have received grace and apostleship to bring about the obedience of faith among all the Gentiles, for His name's sake, among whom you also are the called of Jesus Christ; to all who are beloved of God in Rome, called as saints: Grace to you and peace from God our Father and the Lord Jesus Christ. (1:5-7)

The story is told of a very wealthy man who had many valuable art treasures. His only son was quite ordinary but was dearly loved. When the son died unexpectedly as a young man, the father was so deeply grieved that he died a few months later. The father's will stipulated that, at his death, all his art works were to be publicly auctioned and that a painting of his son was to be auctioned first. On the day of the auction the specified painting was displayed and the bidding was opened. Because neither the boy nor the artist were well known, a long time passed without a bid being offered. Finally, a long-time servant of the father and friend of the boy timidly bid seventy-five cents, all the money he had. When there were no other bids, the painting was given to the servant. At that point the sale was stopped and an official read the remainder of the will, which specified that whoever cared enough for his son to buy the painting of him would receive all the rest of the estate.

That touching story illustrates God's provision for fallen mankind. Anyone who loves and receives His Son, Jesus Christ, will inherit the heavenly Father's estate, as it were. The good news of God is that everyone who receives His Son by faith is blessed "with every spiritual blessing in the heavenly places in Christ" (Eph. 1:3). That is why Paul could exult, "You know the grace of our Lord Jesus Christ, that though He was rich, yet for your sake He became poor, that you through His poverty might become rich" (2 Cor. 8:9). Quoting Isaiah, the apostle declared that the Christian's riches include "things which eye has not seen and ear has not heard, and which have not entered the heart of man, all that God has prepared for those who love Him" (1 Cor. 2:9; cf. Isa. 64:4; 65:17).

In Christ, the believer has riches beyond any imagination. The Christian has life that will never end (John 3:16), a spring of spiritual water that will never dry up (John 4:14), a gift that will never be lost (John 6:37, 39), a love from which he can never be separated (Rom. 8:39), a calling that will never be revoked (Rom. 11:29), a foundation that will never be destroyed (2 Tim. 2:19), and an inheritance that will never diminish (1 Pet. 1:4-5).

In Romans 1:5-7 Paul continues to summarize that good news, describing its provision (v. 5a), its proclamation and purpose (vv. 5b-6), and its privileges (v. 7).

THE PROVISION OF THE GOOD NEWS

through whom we have received grace and apostleship (1:5a)

Paul here mentions two important provisions of the good news of God: conversion, which is by God's **grace**, and vocation, which in Paul's case was **apostleship.**

It is possible that Paul was speaking of the specific grace of apostleship, but it seems more probable that he was referring to, or at least including, the grace by which every believer comes into a saving relationship with Jesus Christ.

Grace is unmerited, unearned favor, in which a believer himself does not and cannot contribute anything of worth. "For by grace you have been saved through faith," Paul explains in his Ephesian letter; "and that not of yourselves, it is the gift of God; not as a result of works, that no one should boast" (Eph. 2:8-9). **Grace** is God's loving mercy, through which He grants salvation as a gift to those who trust in His Son. When any person places his trust in Jesus Christ as Lord and Savior, God sovereignly breathes into that person His own divine life. Christians are alive spiritually because they have been born from above, created anew with the very life of God Himself.

A believer has no cause for self-congratulation, because he contributes nothing at all to his salvation. Human achievement has no place in the divine working of God's saving **grace.** We are "justified as a gift by His grace through the redemption which is in Christ Jesus" (Rom. 3:24), a redemption in which man's work and man's boasting are totally excluded (vv. 27-28).

Salvation does not come by baptism, by confirmation, by communion, by church membership, by church attendance, by keeping the Ten Commandments, by trying to live up to the Sermon on the Mount, by serving other people, or even by serving God. It does not come by being morally upright, respectable, and self-giving. Nor does it come by simply believing that there is a God or that Jesus Christ is His Son. Even the demons recognize such truths (see Mark 5:7; James 2:19). It comes only when a person repenting of sin receives by faith the gracious provision of forgiveness offered by God through the atoning work of His Son, the Lord Jesus Christ.

The great preacher Donald Grey Barnhouse observed, "Love that gives upward is worship, love that goes outward is affection; love that stoops is grace" (*Expositions of Bible Doctrines Taking the Epistle to the Romans as a Point of Departure,* vol. 1 [Grand Rapids: Eerdmans, 1952], p. 72). In an unimaginable divine condescension, God looked down on sinful, fallen mankind and graciously offered His Son for its redemption (John 3:16-17).

The dying words of one ancient saint were, "Grace is the only thing that can make us like God. I might be dragged through heaven, earth, and hell and I would still be the same sinful, polluted wretch unless God Himself should cleanse me by His grace."

Another provision of the good news of God is His calling believers into His service, which is a form of **apostleship.** Paul opens the epistle by speaking of himself, and he resumes his personal comments in verses 8-15. In verses 2-4 he speaks about Jesus Christ. But from the end of verse 4 through verse 7 he is speaking about believers in general and about those in Rome in particular. Paul had already mentioned his own calling and office as an apostle (v. 1), and it therefore seems reasonable to launch from this reference to his **apostleship** to discuss God's divine calling and sending of *all* believers.

The Greek term *apostolos,* which normally is simply transliterated as *apostle,* has the basic meaning of "one who is sent" (cf. the discussion in chapter 1). God sovereignly chose thirteen men in the early church to the *office* of apostle, giving them unique divine authority to proclaim and miraculously authenticate the gospel. The writer of Hebrews even refers to Jesus Christ as an apostle (Heb. 3:1).

But every person who belongs to God through faith in Christ is an apostle in a more general sense of being sent by Him into the world as His messenger and witness. In an unofficial sense, anyone who is sent on a spiritual mission, anyone who represents the Savior and brings His good news of salvation, is an apostle.

Two otherwise unknown leaders in the early church, Andronicus and Junias, were referred to by Paul as being "outstanding among the apostles, who also were in Christ before me" (Rom. 16:7). Luke refers to Barnabas as an apostle (Acts 14:14). The term *apostolos* is also applied to Epaphroditus ("messenger," Phil. 2:25) as well as to some unnamed workers in, or known by, the church in Corinth ("messengers," 2 Cor. 8:23). But those men, godly as they were, did not have the *office* of apostleship as did Paul and the Twelve. Andronicus, Junias, Barnabas, and Epaphroditus were apostles only in the sense that every believer is an apostle, a called and sent ambassador of Jesus Christ.

Sometimes an athletically inept student will be put on a team out of sympathy or to fill a roster, but the coach will rarely, if ever, put him in a game. God does not work that way. Every person who comes to Him through His Son is put on the team and sent in to play the game, as it were. Everyone who is saved by God's sovereign grace is also sovereignly called to apostleship. The Lord never provides conversion without commission. When by grace we "have been saved through faith," Paul explains, it is not ourselves but "is the gift of God; not as a result of works, that no one should boast." But as he goes on to explain, when God saves us we thereby become "His workmanship, created in Christ Jesus for good works, which God prepared beforehand, that we should walk in them" (Eph. 2:8-10). Later in that same epistle Paul entreats believers "to walk in a manner worthy of the calling with which you have been called" (4:1).

A victor at an ancient Greek olympic game is said to have been asked, "Spartan, what will you gain by this victory?" He replied, "I, sir, shall have the honor to fight on the front line for my king." That spirit should typify everyone for whom Jesus Christ is Lord and Savior.

After one of D. L. Moody's sermons, a highly educated man came to him and said, "Excuse me, but you made eleven mistakes in your grammar tonight." In a gracious rebuke Moody replied, "I probably did. My early education was very faulty. But I am using all the grammar that I know in the Master's service. How about you?" On another occasion a man came up to Mr. Moody and said, "I don't like your invitation. I don't think it's the right way to do it." "I appreciate that," Moody responded. "I've always been uncomfortable with it, too. I wish I knew a better way. What is your method of inviting people to Christ?" "I don't have one," the man replied. "Then I like mine better," the evangelist said. Whatever our limitations may be, when God calls us by His grace, He also calls us to His service.

In reflecting on his ordination into the Presbyterian ministry, Barnhouse wrote:

> The moderator of the Presbytery asked me questions, and I answered them. They told me to kneel down. Men came toward me, and one man was asked to make the prayer. I felt his hand come on my head, and then the hands of others, touching my head, and pressing down on his and the other hands. The ring of men closed in, and one man began to pray. It was a nice little prayer and had one pat little phrase in it, "Father, guard him with Thy love, guide him with Thine eye, and gird him with Thy power." I kept thinking about those three verbs, guard, guide, gird. It seemed as foolish as performing a marriage ceremony upon two people who had been living together for a quarter of a century and who had had a family of children together. I knew that I had been ordained long since, and that the Hands that had been upon my head were Hands that had been pierced, and nailed to a cross. Years later the man that made the prayer that day signed a paper saying that he was opposed to the doctrine of the virgin birth, the doctrine of the deity of Jesus Christ, the doctrine of the substitutionary atonement, the doctrine of the miracles of Christ, and the doctrine of the inspiration of the Scriptures, as tests for ordination or a man's good standing in the ministry. When I read his name on the list, I put my hand on the top of my head and smiled to myself, wondering how many dozen times I had had my hair cut since his unholy hands had touched me. And I had the profound consolation of knowing that the hand of the Lord Jesus Christ, wounded and torn because of my sins, had touched me and given me an apostleship which was from God and which was more important than any that men could approve by their little ceremonies. (*Man's Ruin: Romans 1:1-32* [Grand Rapids: Eerdmans, 1952], pp. 76-77. Used by permission.)

Dr. Barnhouse's account reminds me of my own ordination. Before being approved, I was interviewed by a number of men who asked me all kinds of questions concerning such things as my call, my knowledge of Scripture, and my personal beliefs and moral standards. At the ordination service those men gathered around me and placed their hands on my head. Each man then prayed and later signed his name to the ordination certificate. The first name on the certificate was written considerably larger than the others. But not long afterward, that man who signed first and largest abandoned the ministry. He became involved in gross immorality, denied the virtue of the faith, and became a professor of humanistic psychology at a prominent secular university. Like Dr. Barnhouse, I give thanks to God that my ministry did not come from men but from Christ Himself.

THE PROCLAMATION AND PURPOSE OF THE GOOD NEWS

to bring about the obedience of faith among all the Gentiles, for His name's sake, among whom you also are the called of Jesus Christ; (1:5*b*-6)

THE PROCLAMATION

to bring about the obedience of faith among all the Gentiles, (1:5*b*)

Like Paul, every believer is called not only to salvation and to service but to witness for Christ in order **to bring about the obedience of faith** in others. Paul uses the phrase "obedience of faith" again at the end of the letter, saying that "the mystery which has been kept secret for long ages past, but now is manifested, and by the Scriptures of the prophets, according to the commandment of the eternal God, has been made known to all the nations, leading to obedience of faith" (Rom. 16:25-26).

A person who claims faith in Jesus Christ but whose pattern of life is utter disobedience to God's Word has never been redeemed and is living a lie. Faith that does not manifest itself in obedient living is spurious and worthless (James 2:14-26). We are not saved in the least part *by* works, no matter how seemingly good; but as already noted, we are saved *to* good works. That is the very purpose of salvation as far as our earthly life is concerned (Eph. 2:10). The message of the gospel is to call people to **the obedience of faith**, which is here used as a synonym for salvation.

Although Paul does not use the definite article before **faith** in this passage, the idea is that of *the* **faith**, referring to the whole teaching of Scripture, especially the New Testament. It is what Jude refers to as "the faith which was once for all delivered to the saints" (v. 3). That faith is the Word of God, which is the only divinely-constituted authority of Christianity. Affirmation of that faith leads to the practical, lived-out faithfulness without which a professed faith is nothing more than dead and useless (James 2:17, 20). Genuine faith is obedient faith. To call men to **the obedience of faith** is to fulfill the Great Commission, to bring men to Jesus Christ and to the observance of everything He commands in His Word (Matt. 28:20).

It is not that faith plus obedience equals salvation but that obedient faith equals salvation. True faith is verified in obedience. Obedient faith proves itself true, whereas disobedient faith proves itself false. It is for having true faith, that is, obedient faith, that Paul goes on to commend the Roman believers. "I thank my God through Jesus Christ for you all," he says, "because your faith is being proclaimed throughout the whole world" (Rom. 1:8). He gives a similar commendation at the end of the letter. To his beloved brothers and sisters in Christ, most of whom he had never met, he says, "The report of your obedience has reached to all; therefore I am rejoicing over you" (16:19). In the first instance Paul specifically commends their faith, and in the second he specifically commends their obedience. Together, faith and obedience manifest the inseparable two sides of the coin of salvation, which Paul here calls **the obedience of faith.**

God has many titles and names in Scripture, but in both testaments He is most frequently referred to as Lord, which speaks of His sovereign right to order and to rule all things and all people, and most especially His own people. To belong to God in a relationship of **obedience** is to recognize that salvation includes being in submission to His lordship. Scripture recognizes no other saving relationship to Him.

Some years ago, as I was riding with a professor at a well-known evangelical seminary, we happened to pass an unusually large liquor store. When I made a comment about it, my companion said it was one of a large chain of liquor stores in the city owned by a man that went to his church and was a regular attender of an adult Sunday school class. "As a matter of fact, he is in my discipleship group," my friend said; "I meet with him every week." "Doesn't the kind of business he is in bother you?" I asked. "Oh, yes," he said. "We talk about that frequently, but he feels that people who drink are going to buy their liquor somewhere and that it might as well be in his stores." Taken aback, I asked, "Is the rest of his life in order?" He replied, "Well, he left his wife and is living with a young woman." "And he still comes to church and discipleship class every week?" I asked in amazement. The professor sighed and said, "Yes, and you know, sometimes it's hard for me to understand how a Christian can live like that." I said, "Have you ever considered that he may not be a Christian at all?"

A theology that refuses to recognize the lordship of Jesus Christ for *every* believer is a theology that contradicts the very essence of biblical Christianity. "If you confess with your mouth Jesus as Lord," Paul declares, "and believe in your heart that God raised Him from the dead, you shall be saved; for with the heart man believes, resulting in righteousness, and with the mouth he confesses, resulting in salvation" (Rom. 10:9-10). With equal clarity and unambiguity, Peter declared at Pentecost, "Let all the house of Israel know for certain that God has made Him both Lord and Christ—this Jesus whom you crucified" (Acts 2:36). The heart of Jesus' teaching in the Sermon on the Mount is that faith without obedience is not saving faith, but is certain evidence that a person is following the wide and delusive road of the world that leads to destruction, rather than the narrow road of God that leads to eternal life (Matt. 7:13-14).

On the other hand, merely *calling* Jesus Lord, even while doing seemingly important work in His name, is worthless unless those works are done from faith, are done in accord with His Word, and are directed and empowered by His Holy Spirit. With sobering intensity, Jesus plainly declared that truth when He said, "Many will say to Me on that day, 'Lord, Lord, did we not prophesy in Your name, and in Your name cast out demons, and in Your name perform many miracles?' And then I will declare to them, 'I never knew you; depart from Me, you who practice lawlessness.'" As He goes on to explain, the person who claims Him but lives in continual disobedience of His Word is building a religious house on sand, which will eventually wash away and leave him without God and without hope (Matt. 7:22-27). Without sanctification—that is, a life of holiness—"no one will see the Lord" (Heb. 12:14).

Paul's unique calling was to **the Gentiles** (Acts 9:15; 22:21; Rom. 11:13; Gal. 1:16). It is likely that he preached the gospel during his three years in Arabia (Gal. 1:17), but he began his *recorded ministry* by preaching to Jews. Even when ministering in the basically Gentile regions of Asia Minor and Macedonia, he frequently began his work among Jews (see, e.g., Acts 13:14; 14:1;16:13; 17:1; 18:2). As with Paul, the calling of every believer is to proclaim Jesus Christ to all men, Jew and Gentile, in the hope of bringing them to the obedience of faith.

THE PURPOSE

for His name's sake, among whom you also are the called of Jesus Christ. (1:5c-6)

Although God gave His own Son to save the world (John 3:16) and does not wish for any person to perish (2 Pet. 3:9), it must be recognized that the primary purpose of the gospel is not for man's sake but God's, **for His name's sake.** Man's salvation is simply a by-product of God's grace; its main focus is to display God's glory.

The preacher (v. 1), the promise (v. 2), the Person (vv. 3-4), the provision (v. 5a), the proclamation (vv. 5b-6), and the privileges (v. 7) of the good news of God are all given for the express purpose of glorifying God. All of redemptive history focuses on the glory of God, and throughout eternity the accomplishments of His redemption will continue to be a memorial to His majesty, grace, and love.

Because of His gracious love for fallen and helpless mankind, salvation is of importance to God for man's sake, but because of His own perfection it is infinitely more important to Him for His own sake. God is ultimately and totally committed to the exaltation of His own glory. That truth has always been anathema to the natural man, and in our day of rampant selfism even within the church, it is also a stumbling block to many Christians. But man's depraved perspective and standards notwithstanding, the main issue of salvation is God's glory, because He is perfectly worthy and it is that perfect worthiness to which sin is such an affront.

Paul declares that one day, "at the name of Jesus every knee [will] bow, of those who are in heaven, and on earth, and under the earth, and that every tongue [will] confess that Jesus Christ is Lord, to the glory of God the Father' (Phil. 2:10–11). Even the divine truths and blessings that are given for His children's own sake are first of all given "that the grace which is spreading to more and more people may cause the giving of thanks to abound to the glory of God" (2 Cor. 4:15).

When a person believes in Christ, he is saved: but more important than that, God is glorified, because the gift of salvation is entirely by His sovereign will and power. For the same reason, God is glorified when His people love His Son, when they acknowledge His assessment of their sin and their need for cleansing, when their plans become His plans, and when their thoughts become His thoughts. Believers live and exist for the glory of God.

The believers in Rome to whom Paul was writing were **among** those who had been brought to "the obedience of faith" (v. 5) and therefore were **also the called of Jesus Christ.** And, as has already been emphasized, **the called of Jesus Christ,** those who are true believers, are **called** not only to salvation but to obedience. And to be obedient to Christ includes bringing others to Him in faith and obedience.

THE PRIVILEGES OF THE GOOD NEWS

to all who are beloved of God in Rome, called as saints: Grace to you and peace from God our Father and the Lord Jesus Christ. (1:7)

Among the countless, gracious privileges of the good news of God are those of our being His beloved, our being His called ones, and our being His saints.

Paul here address **all** his fellow believers **in Rome** as the **beloved of God.** One of the most repeated and emphasized truths of Scripture is that of God's gracious love for those who belong to Him. David prayed, "Remember, O Lord, thy compassion and Thy lovingkindnesses, for they have been from of old" (Ps. 25:6; cf. 26:3) and, "How precious is Thy lovingkindness, O God!" (Ps. 36:7). Isaiah exulted, "I shall make mention of the lovingkindness of the Lord, the praises of the Lord, according to all that the Lord has granted us, and the great goodness toward the house of Israel, which He has granted them according to His compassion, and according to the multitude of His lovingkindnesses" (Isa. 63:7). Through Jeremiah, the Lord told His people, "I have loved you with an everlasting love; therefore I have drawn you with lovingkindness" (Jer. 31:3).

Paul declares that God is "rich in mercy, because of His great love with which He loved us, even when we were dead in our transgressions" (Eph. 2:4-5). John writes, "See how great a love the Father has bestowed upon us, that we should be called children of God; and such we are" (1 John 3:1).

Every believer has been made acceptable to God through Christ, "to the praise of the glory of His grace, which He freely bestowed on us in the Beloved" (Eph. 1:6). Every believer is a child of God and is loved for the sake of God's beloved Son, Jesus Christ. Paul says that "the love of God has been poured out within our hearts through the Holy Spirit who was given to us" (Rom. 5:5). Later in the epistle he assures us that nothing can "separate us from the love of Christ," not even "tribulation, or distress, or persecution, or famine, or nakedness, or peril, or sword" (8:35).

Second, those who have come to Christ by the obedience of faith are also the **called** of God. Paul is not referring to God's general call for mankind to believe. Through Isaiah He made the appeals "Turn to Me, and be saved, all the ends of the earth" (45:22) and "Seek the Lord while He may be found; call upon Him while He is near" (55:6). Through Ezekiel He warned, "Turn back, turn back from your evil ways!" (Ezek. 33:11). During His earthly ministry, Jesus said to the sinful multitudes, "Come to Me, all who are weary and heavy-laden, and I will give you rest" (Matt. 11:28) and, "If any man is thirsty, let him come to Me and drink" (John 7:37). From heaven, through the apostle John, Jesus said, "The Spirit and the bride say, 'Come.' And let the one who hears say, 'Come.' And let the one who is thirsty come; let the one who wishes take the water of life without cost" (Rev. 22:17).

But in Romans 1:7 Paul is not speaking of that general calling but of the specific way in which those who have responded to that invitation have been sovereignly and effectually **called** by God to Himself in salvation. **Called** is here a synonym for the terms "elect" and "predestined." As the apostle explains in chapter 8, those "whom He predestined, these He also called; and whom He called, these He also justified; and whom He justified, these He also glorified" (v. 30). From our limited human viewpoint, it may seem that we first came to God through an act of our will, but we know from His Word that we could not have sought Him by faith unless He had already chosen us by the gracious act of His sovereign will.

The references to being **called** to salvation are always, in the epistles of the New Testament, efficacious calls that save, never general invitations. Thus calling is the effecting of the plan of election. The doctrine of election is clearly taught throughout the New Testament (cf. Matt. 20:15-16; John 15:16; 17:9; Acts 13:48; Romans 9:14-15; 11:5; 1 Cor. 1:9; Eph. 2:8-10; Col. 1:3-5; 1 Thess. 1:4-5; 2 Thess. 2:13; 2 Tim. 1:9; 2:10; 1 Pet. 1:1-2; Rev. 13:8; 17:8, 14).

Third, believers are God's **saints.** In the NASB text, **as** is printed in italics, indicating that the word is not in the original Greek but is supplied. It seems that a better rendering would be to place a comma in place of the **as**, taking "beloved, "called," and **saints** as related but distinct blessings of the believer.

Saints is from *hagios,* which has the basic meaning of being set apart. In the Old Testament many things and people were divinely set apart by God for His own purposes. The Tabernacle and Temple and all their furnishings—supremely the Ark of the Covenant and the holy of holies—were set apart to Him. The tribe of Levi was set apart for His priesthood, and the entire nation of Israel was set apart as His people. The tithes and offerings of the people of Israel consisted of money and other gifts specifically set apart for God (cf. chap. 1).

Frequently in the Old Testament, however, *holy* refers to a person's being set apart by God from the world and to Himself, and thereby being made like Him in holiness. To be set apart in that sense is to be made holy and righteous. Whether under the Old or the New Covenant, **saints** are "the holy ones" of God.

Under the New Covenant, however, such holy things as the Temple, priesthood, Ark, and tithes no longer exist. God's only truly holy things on earth today are His people, those whom He has sovereignly and graciously set apart for Himself through Jesus Christ. The new temple of God and the new priesthood of God are His church (1 Cor. 3:16-17; 1 Pet. 2:5, 9).

In a beautiful benediction to his introductory remarks, Paul says, **grace to you and peace from God our Father and the Lord Jesus Christ.** The only people who can receive the marvelous blessings of **grace** and **peace** are those who are the beloved, the called, and the holy ones of God. Only they can truly call **God** their **Father,** because only they have been adopted into His divine family through His true Son, **the Lord Jesus Christ.**

True Spiritual Leadership

First, I thank my God through Jesus Christ for you all, because your faith is being proclaimed throughout the whole world. For God, whom I serve in my spirit in the preaching of the gospel of His Son, is my witness as to how unceasingly I make mention of you, always in my prayers making request if perhaps now at last by the will of God I may succeed in coming to you. For I long to see you in order that I may impart some spiritual gift to you, that you may be established; that is, that I may be encouraged together with you while among you, each of us by the other's faith, both yours and mine. And I do not want you to be unaware, brethren, that often I have planned to come to you (and have been prevented thus far) in order that I might obtain some fruit among you also, even as among the rest of the Gentiles. I am under obligation both to Greeks and to barbarians, both to the wise and to the foolish. Thus, for my part, I am eager to preach the gospel to you also who are in Rome. (1:8-15)

In seminary I learned a great deal from the books I read, the lectures I heard, and the papers I wrote. But I learned most from the attitudes and actions of the godly men under whom I studied. While around them, I discovered their true priorities, their true convictions, their true devotion to our Lord.

In the opening verses of his letter to the Romans, Paul also set himself forth for his readers to see before he attempted to teach them some deeper truths of the gospel. He opened his heart and said, in effect, "Before I show you my theology, I am going to show you myself."

People serve the Lord from many motives. Some serve out of legalistic effort, as a means of earning salvation and God's favor. Some serve the Lord for fear that, if they do not, they will incur His disfavor and perhaps even lose their salvation. Some, like Diotrophes (3 John 9), serve because of the prestige and esteem that leadership often brings. Some serve in order to gain preeminent ecclesiastical positions and the power to lord it over those under their care. Some serve for appearance's sake, in order to be considered righteous by fellow church members and by the world. Some serve because of peer pressure to conform to certain human standards of religious and moral behavior. Children are often forced into religious activities by their parents, and they sometimes continue those activities into adult life only because of parental intimidation or perhaps from mere habit. Some people are even zealous in Christian work because of the financial gain it can produce.

But those motives for service are merely external, and no matter how orthodox or helpful to other people the service might be, unless it is done out of a sincere desire to please and glorify God, it is not spiritual nor acceptable to Him (cf. 1 Cor. 10:31). It is, of course, possible for a person to begin Christian service out of genuine devotion to God and later fall into an occasion or even a habit of performing it mechanically, merely from a sense of necessity. Pastors, Sunday School teachers, youth leaders, missionaries and all other Christian workers can carelessly leave their first love and fall into a rut of superficial activity that is performed in the Lord's name but is not done in His power or for His glory.

Even when the Lord is served from a right motive and in His power, there always lingers near a ready temptation to resentment and self-pity when one's work is not appreciated by fellow Christians and perhaps goes completely unnoticed.

The apostle Paul was doubtlessly assailed by many temptations from Satan to give up his ministry when he was opposed, or to give up on a difficult, fleshly, self-centered, and worldly church such as the one at Corinth. But Paul was greatly used of the Lord because, by God's grace and provision, he always kept his motives pure. Because his single purpose was to please God, the displeasure or disregard of other people, even of those he was serving, could not deter his work or lead him into bitterness and self-pity.

In his opening words to the believers at Rome, Paul tells of his sincere spiritual motives in wanting to minister to them. With warmth, affection, and sensitivity that permeate the entire letter, he assures them of his genuine devotion to God and his genuine love for them. Although Paul had not personally founded or even visited the church at Rome, he carried the heartfelt passion of Christ for their spiritual welfare and an eager desire to develop their spiritual and personal friendship. The letter to Rome reveals that Paul not only had the zeal of a prophet, the mind of a teacher, and the determination of an apostle, but also the heart of a shepherd.

When they first received Paul's letter, the believers in Rome probably wondered why this great apostle whom most of them did not know would bother to write them such a long and profound letter. They also may have wondered why, if he cared so much for them, he had not yet paid them a visit. In verses 8-15 of chapter 1, Paul gives the answers to both of those questions. He wrote them because he cared deeply about their spiritual maturity, and he had not yet visited them because he had thus far been prevented. In these few verses the apostle lays bare his heart concerning them.

The key that unlocks the intent in this passage is the phrase "God, whom I serve in my spirit" (v. 9a). Paul had been raised and educated in Judaism. He had himself been a Pharisee and was well acquainted with the other Jewish religious set, the Sadducees, the scribes, the priests, and the elders. He knew that, with few exceptions, those leaders served God in the flesh and were motivated by self-interest. Their worship and service were mechanical, routine, external, and superficial. Paul also was well acquainted with the Gentile world and knew that pagan religious worship and service were likewise external, superficial, and completely motivated by self-interest.

Referring to such religion, Jesus told the Samaritan woman at Jacob's well, "An hour is coming, and now is, when the true worshipers shall worship the Father in spirit and truth; for such people the Father seeks to be His worshipers. God is spirit, and those who worship Him must worship in spirit and truth" (John 4:23-24). Worship that is true and acceptable to God does not involve a particular location, ritual, or any man-made activities or forms.

During the years before his salvation, Paul himself had worshiped and served God in an external, self-interested way (Phil. 3:4-7). But now that he belonged to Christ and had Christ's own Spirit indwelling him, he worshiped and served Him in spirit and in truth, with his whole being. Paul was now motivated by a genuine, inner desire to serve God for God's sake rather than his own, in God's revealed way rather than his own, and in God's power rather than his own. He was no longer motivated by self-interest or by peer pressure and no longer focused on Jewish religious tradition or even on self-effort to keep God's law. He was not interested in trying to please other men, even himself, but only God (1 Cor. 4:1-5).

The focus of his life and his ministry was to glorify God by proclaiming the saving grace of the gospel. He lived in conformity to the divine standard he proclaimed to the Ephesians, serving God "not by way of eyeservice, as men-pleasers, but as slaves of Christ, doing the will of God from the heart" (Eph. 6:6). As he reminded the elders from that church, "I have coveted no one's silver or gold or clothes. You yourselves know that these hands ministered to my own needs and to the men who were with me" (Acts 20:33-34).

Paul did not serve because it was "fun" and self-pleasing. "For even Christ did not please Himself," he points out later in the epistle; "but as it is written, 'The reproaches of those who reproached Thee fell upon Me'" (Rom. 15:3; cf. Ps. 69:9). Nor did Paul serve in order to gain glory and honor from men. "For if I preach the gospel, I have nothing to boast of, for I am under compulsion; for woe is me if I do not preach the gospel" (1 Cor. 9:16). In a later letter to the church at Corinth he declared, "We do not preach ourselves but Christ Jesus as Lord, and ourselves as your bondservants for Jesus' sake" (2 Cor. 4:5; cf. 1 Cor. 9:19).

In verses 8-15, Paul's words suggest nine marks of true spiritual service: a thankful spirit (v. 8), a concerned spirit (v. 9-10a), a willing and submissive spirit (v. 10b), a loving spirit (v. 11), a humble spirit (v. 12), a fruitful spirit (v. 13), an obedient spirit (v. 14), an eager spirit (v. 15). A tenth, a bold spirit, is mentioned in v. 16a.

A Thankful Spirit

First, I thank my God through Jesus Christ for you all, because your faith is being proclaimed throughout the whole world. (1:8)

The first mark of true spiritual service, which Paul had in abundance, is thankfulness. He was grateful for what God had done for and through him, but he was equally grateful for what God had done in and through other believers. He perhaps did not thank the Roman believers themselves, lest it be considered flattery. He said, rather, **I thank my God through Jesus Christ for you.**

Paul's thankfulness was intimate, first of all because of his spiritual closeness to God. **I thank my God,** he declared. No pagan would have made such a statement, nor would have most Jews referred to God with a personal pronoun. For Paul, God was not a theological abstraction but a beloved Savior and close friend. As he testifies in the following verse, he served **God** in his spirit, from the depth of his heart and mind.

Paul gave thanks **through Jesus Christ,** the one eternal Mediator between God and man. "No one comes to the Father, but through Me," Jesus said (John 14:6), and believers in Him have the privilege of calling

Almighty God, **my God.** "There is one God, and one mediator also between God and men, the man Christ Jesus" (1 Tim. 2:5). It is because we have been given access to the Father **through Jesus Christ** that we always can "draw near with confidence to the throne of grace, that we may receive mercy and may find grace to help in time of need" (Heb. 4:16), and can say, "Abba, Father" (Rom. 8:15).

Paul's thankfulness was also intimate because of his spiritual intimacy with fellow believers, even to such as those in Rome, most of whom he did not personally know. **I thank my God . . . for you all,** that is, for **all** the believers in the church at Rome. His gratitude was impartial and all-encompassing, making no distinctions.

In every epistle but one, Paul expresses gratitude for those to whom he writes. The exception was the letter to the church in Galatia, which had defected from the true gospel of grace to a works system of righteousness and was worshiping and serving in the flesh because of the influence of the Judaizers. It was not that the other churches were perfect, which is apparent since Paul wrote most of his letters to correct wrong doctrine or unholy living. But even where the need for instruction and correction was great, he found something in those churches for which he could be thankful.

Paul wrote the letter to the Romans from Corinth, and at the time the Jews there were plotting to kill him (Acts 20:3). He was on his way to Jerusalem, where he knew imprisonment and possibly death awaited him. Yet he was still filled with thanksgiving.

Some years later, as he was prisoner in his own house in Rome while awaiting an audience before Caesar, Paul was still thankful. While there, he wrote four epistles (Ephesians, Philippians, Colossians, and Philemon), commonly called the prison epistles. In each of those letters he gives thanks for the believers to whom he writes (Eph. 1:16; Phil. 1:3; Col. 1:3; Philem. 4). During his second Roman imprisonment, he may have spent time in the wretched Mamertine prison. If so, we can be sure he was thankful even there, although the city sewage system ran through the prison. I was told on a visit there that when the cells were filled to capacity, the sewage gates were opened and all the inmates would drown in the filthy water, making way for a new batch of prisoners. But Paul's thankfulness did not rise and fall based on his earthly circumstances but on the richness of his fellowship with his Lord.

The specific reason for Paul's thankfulness for the Roman Christians was their deep **faith,** which was **being proclaimed throughout the whole world.** From secular history we learn that in A.D. 49 Emperor Claudius expelled Jews from Rome, thinking they were all followers of someone named Chrestus (a variant spelling of Christ). Apparently the testimony of Jewish Christians had so incited the nonbelieving Jews that the turmoil threatened the peace of the whole city. The believers had, then, a powerful testimony not only in the city, but **throughout the whole world.** What a commendation!

By **faith** Paul was not referring to the initial trust in Christ that brings salvation but to the persevering trust that brings spiritual strength and growth. Faith like that also may bring persecution. Believers in Rome lived in the lion's den, as it were, yet they lived out their **faith** with integrity and credibility. Some churches are famous because of their pastor, their architecture, their stained glass windows, or their size or wealth. The church in Rome was famous because of its **faith.** It was a fellowship of genuinely redeemed saints through whom the Lord Jesus Christ manifested His life and power, so that their character was known everywhere.

A thankful heart for those to whom one ministers is essential to true spiritual service. The Christian who is trying to serve God's people, however needy they may be, without gratitude in his heart for what the Lord has done for them will find his service lacking joy. Paul could usually find a cause for thanks so that he could honor the Lord for what had been done already and hope for what God would use him to do.

Superficial believers are seldom satisfied and therefore seldom thankful. Because they focus on their own appetites for things of the world, they are more often resentful than thankful. A thankless heart is a selfish, self-centered, legalistic heart. Paul had a thankful heart because he continually focused on what God was doing in his own life, in the lives of other faithful believers, and in the advancement of His kingdom throughout the world.

A CONCERNED SPIRIT

For God, whom I serve in my spirit in the preaching of the gospel of His Son, is my witness as to how unceasingly I make mention of you, always in my prayers (1:9-10a)

The second mark of true spiritual service that exudes here, and that Paul exemplified in his life, is that of a concerned spirit. Although he was grateful for what had been and was being done in the Lord's work, he was also deeply concerned about balancing those off with what yet needed to be done.

It is here that Paul presents the key phrase of verses 8-15, **God, whom I serve in my spirit.** *Latreuō* (to **serve**) is always used in the New Testament of religious service, and is therefore sometimes translated "worship." Except for two references to the service of pagan idols, the term is used in reference to the worship and service of the true God. The greatest worship a believer can offer to God is devoted, pure, heart-felt ministry.

Godly service calls for total, unreserved commitment. Paul served God with everything he had, beginning with his **spirit**, that is, flowing out of a deep desire in his soul. In chapter 12 of this letter, he appeals to all believers, "by the mercies of God, to present your bodies a living and holy sacrifice, acceptable to God, which is your spiritual service of worship" (v. 1). Such spiritual devotion is accomplished by refusing to "be conformed to this world" and by being "transformed by the renewing of your mind, that you may prove what the will of God is, that which is good and acceptable and perfect" (v. 2).

Paul used a similar statement about true worship in writing to the church at Philippi: "We are the true circumcision, who worship in the Spirit of God and glory in Christ Jesus and put no confidence in the flesh" (Phil. 3:3). When his shipmates had given up all hope of surviving the fierce storm on the Mediterranean Sea as they sailed to Rome, the apostle assured them, "I urge you to keep up your courage, for there shall be no loss of life among you, but only of the ship. For this very night an angel of the God to whom I belong and whom I serve stood before me, saying, 'Do not be afraid, Paul; you must stand before Caesar; and behold, God has granted you all those who are sailing with you.' Therefore, keep up your courage, men, for I believe God, that it will turn out exactly as I have been told" (Acts 27:22-25).

Paul could declare to Timothy, "I thank God, whom I serve with a clear conscience" (2 Tim. 1:3). Because he served God from a sincere heart, he also served with a clear conscience. Paul's worship and service were inextricably related. His worship was an act of service, and his service was an act of worship.

Because his young friend had appeared to stumble spiritually, Paul admonished Timothy: "Be diligent to present yourself approved to God as a workman who does not need to be ashamed, handling accurately the word of truth" (2 Tim. 2:15). A few verses later he also warned: "Flee from youthful lusts, and pursue righteousness, faith, love and peace, with those who call on the Lord from a pure heart" (v. 22).

Paul's primary service to God was **the preaching of the gospel of His Son,** the ministry to which the Lord had called him and to which he gave every breath of his life. But as he goes on to explain, that service to God included deep, personal concern for *everyone* who believed the **gospel,** whether they heard it from him or from someone else. He was not concerned for the saints in Rome because they were "his converts," which they were not, but because he and they were brothers who had the same spiritual Father through trusting in the same divine **Son** as their Savior.

As he mentions several times in the opening of the epistle (1:10-11, 15), and reiterates near the closing (15:14, 22), he was writing to the Roman church somewhat as an outsider and stranger, humanly speaking. That fact makes his intense concern for the believers there even more remarkable and touching.

Perhaps because most of them did not know him personally, Paul here calls the Lord as **witness** to his sincere love and concern for his spiritual brothers and sisters at Rome. He knew that God, who knows the real motive and sincerity of every heart (cf. 1 Cor. 4:5), would testify **as to how unceasingly** he made **mention of** them **always in** his **prayers.** He was not redundant by using both **unceasingly** and **always** but simply gave a negative and positive expression of his concern.

Although he rejoiced in and gave thanks for their great faithfulness, he knew that apart from God's continuing provision even strong faith falters. Those saints were therefore **always in** his **prayers**, never taken off his prayer list. Although for different reasons, the faithful saint needs the prayer support of fellow believers as much as the saint who is unfaithful.

Paul assured the saints of Thessalonica that "we pray for you always that our God may count you worthy of your calling, and fulfill every desire for goodness and the work of faith with power; in order that the name of our Lord Jesus may be glorified in you, and you in Him, according to the grace of our God and the Lord Jesus Christ" (2 Thess. 1:11-12). In his earlier letter the apostle admonished them to have devotion to unceasing prayer (1 Thess. 5:17). He likewise counseled the Ephesian believers to "pray at all times in the Spirit, and with this in view, be on the alert with all perseverance and petition for all the saints" (Eph. 6:18).

Near the end of his Romans letter Paul pleads: "I urge you, brethren, by our Lord Jesus Christ and by the love of the Spirit, to strive together with me in your prayers to God for me" (Rom. 15:30). He did not ask prayer for himself for selfish reasons but for the sake of the ministry, that he might "be delivered from those who [were] disobedient in Judea, and that [his] service for Jerusalem [might] prove acceptable to the saints; so that [he might] come to [Rome] in joy by the will of God" (vv. 31-32).

Although Paul does not state the particular petitions he made on behalf of the Roman Christians, we can safely assume they were similar to those he mentions in other letters. "I bow my knees before the Father, from whom every family in heaven and on earth derives its name," he wrote the Ephesians, "that He would grant you, according to the riches of His glory, to be strengthened with power through His Spirit in the inner man; so that Christ may dwell in your hearts through faith; and that you, being rooted and grounded in love, may be able to comprehend with all the saints what is the breadth and length and height and depth, and to know the love of Christ which surpasses knowledge, that you may be filled up to all the fulness of God" (Eph. 3:14-19).

That is praying in depth! Paul prayed that those saints would be strengthened by the Holy Spirit, that Christ would be at home in their hearts, that they would be filled with God's own love, and that they would be made perfect in His truth and likeness.

Paul prayed that believers in Philippi would abound in love "still more and more in real knowledge and all discernment, so that [they would] approve the things that are excellent, in order to be sincere and blameless until the day of Christ," demonstrating that they were "filled with the fruit of righteousness which comes through Jesus Christ, to the glory and praise of God" (Phil. 1:9-11).

He assured the Colossian church: "We have not ceased to pray for you and to ask that you may be filled with the knowledge of His will in all spiritual wisdom and understanding, so that you may walk in a manner worthy of the Lord, to please Him in all respects, bearing fruit in every good work and increasing in the knowledge of God; strengthened with all power, according to His glorious might, for the attaining of all steadfastness and patience" (Col. 1:9-11).

The content of all Paul's prayers was spiritual. He prayed for individual believers, but he also offered many prayers for groups of believers. He prayed that their hearts would be knit with the heart of God, that their knowledge of His Word would be made complete, and that their obedience to His will would be made perfect. The depth and intensity of prayer measures the depth and intensity of concern.

A WILLING AND SUBMISSIVE SPIRIT

making request, if perhaps now at last by the will of God I may succeed in coming to you. (1:10b)

Paul not only prayed for the spiritual well-being of the Roman church but was eager to be used by God as an instrument to help answer that prayer according to His divine will. The church has always been full of people who are quick to criticize, but seems short of those who are willing to be used by God to solve the problems they are concerned about.

Many Christians are much more willing to give money to an outreach ministry than they are to witness themselves. In his book *The Gospel Blimp* (Elgin, Ill: David C. Cook, 1983), Joe Bayly tells the imagined story of a man who hired a blimp to bombard his neighborhood with gospel tracts. The point of the book, and the popular movie made from it, was that some believers will go to great extremes to avoid personally confronting others with the gospel.

A man once came up to me after a worship service and suggested that the church provide $25,000 to create a sophisticated telephone answering service that would give a gospel message to callers. Like the man in *The Gospel Blimp* story, this man wanted to use his scheme primarily to reach an unbelieving neighbor. I therefore suggested, "Why don't you just go over and tell him the gospel yourself?"

It is much easier, and therefore more attractive to the flesh, to pray for others to be used by the Lord than to pray that He use us. But like Isaiah, when Paul heard the Lord's call for service or saw a spiritual need, he said, "Here am I. Send me" (Isa. 6:8). There is, of course, an important place for praying for others in the Lord's service. But the true measure of our concern for His work is our willingness for Him to use us.

Paul had been **making request** to God for a long time that he could visit the church in Rome in order to minister to them and be ministered to by them (vv. 11-12). Apparently he hoped to make the journey soon, saying, **perhaps now at last by the will of God I may succeed in coming to you.**

Paul's eagerness to serve God was always directed **by the will of God.** He did not serve in the direction of his own desires and insight but according to the **will** of the One he served. When the prophet Agabus dramatically predicted the danger that awaited Paul in Jerusalem, the apostle's friends begged him not to go. But "Paul answered, 'What are you doing, weeping and breaking my heart? For I am ready not only to be bound, but even to die at Jerusalem for the name of the Lord Jesus.' Upon hearing those words, Luke and the others also submitted to God's sovereignty, saying, 'The will of the Lord be done!'" (Acts 21:11-14).

Some people ask, "If God is going to sovereignly accomplish what He plans to do anyway, what is the purpose of praying?" Dr. Donald Grey Barnhouse designed an analogy to illustrate the relationship of a believer's prayers to God's sovereignty.

> We will suppose the case of a man who loves violin music. He has the means to buy for himself a very fine violin, and he also purchases the very best radio obtainable. He builds up a library of the great musical scores, so that he is able to take any piece that is announced on the radio, put it on his music stand, and play along with the orchestra. The announcer says that Mr. Ormandy and the Philadelphia Orchestra are going to play Beethoven's seventh symphony. The man in his home puts that symphony on his stand and tunes his violin with what he hears coming from the orchestra. The music that comes from the radio we might call foreordained. Ormandy is going to follow the score just as Beethoven wrote it. The man in his living

room starts to scratch away at the first violin part. He misses beats, he loses his place and finds it again, he breaks a string, and stops to fix it. The music goes on and on. He finds his place again and plays on after his fashion to the end of the symphony. The announcer names the next work that is to be played and the fiddler puts that number on his rack. Day after week after month after year, he finds pleasure in scraping his fiddle along with the violins of the great orchestras. Their music is determined in advance. What he must do is to learn to play in their tempo, in their key, and to follow the score as it has been written in advance. If he decides that he wants to play Yankee Doodle when the orchestra is in the midst of a Brahm's number, there's going to be dissonance and discord in the man's house but not in the Academy of Music. After some years of this the man may be a rather creditable violin player and may have learned to submit himself utterly to the scores that are written and follow the program as played. Harmony and joy come from the submission and cooperation.

So it is with the plan of God. It is rolling toward us, unfolding day by day, as He has planned it before the foundation of the world. There are those who fight against it and who must ultimately be cast into outer darkness because He will not have in His heaven whose who proudly resist Him. This cannot be tolerated any more than the authorities would permit a man to bring his own violin into the Academy of Music and start to play Shostakovich when the program called for Bach. The score of God's plan is set forth in the Bible. In the measure that I learn it, submit myself to it, and seek to live in accordance with all that is therein set forth, I shall find myself in joy and in harmony with God and His plans. If I set myself to fight against it, or disagree with that which comes forth, there can be no peace in my heart and life. If in my heart I seek to play a tune that is not the melody the Lord has for me, there can be nothing but dissonance. Prayer is learning to play the tune that the eternal plan of God calls for and to do that which is in harmony with the will of the Eternal Composer and the Author of all that is true harmony in life and living. (*Man's Ruin: Romans 1:1-32* [Grand Rapids: Eerdmans, 1952], pp. 122-23. Used by permission.)

The popular practice of demanding things from God and expecting Him to meet those demands is perverted and heretical, an attempt to sway God's perfect and holy will to one's own imperfect and sinful will. Paul sought the advancement of God's kingdom and glory through God's own will, not his own.

Self-styled messiahs are always megalomaniacs. They have grandiose schemes for winning the world for Christ. They always think big, and their plans seldom show evidence of being limited by God's plans, which, from a human perspective, sometimes seem small and insignificant. Jesus' ministry did not focus on converting the great leaders of His day or evangelizing the great cities. He chose twelve ordinary men to train as His apostles, and most of His teaching took place in insignificant, often isolated, parts of Palestine. He did not raise large sums of money or attempt to use the influence of great men to His advantage. His sole purpose was to do His Father's will in His Father's way and in His Father's time. That is the highest goal for us, as well.

A LOVING SPIRIT

For I long to see you in order that I may impart some spiritual gift to you, that you may be established; (1:11)

Another mark of spiritual service is a loving spirit. Paul wanted to visit the Roman believers in order to serve them lovingly in God's name. He did not want to go as a tourist to see the famous Appian Way or the Forum or the Coliseum or the chariot races. He wanted to go to Rome to give of himself, not to entertain or indulge himself.

The Christian who looks on his service to the Lord as a means of receiving appreciation and personal satisfaction is inevitably subject to disappointment and self-pity. But the one who focuses on giving never has such problems. Paul's ministry goal was to "present every man complete in Christ. And for this purpose also I labor," he said, "striving according to His power, which mightily works within me" (Col. 1:28-29).

The apostle's loving spirit is reflected beautifully in his first letter to Thessalonica. "We proved to be gentle among you," he wrote, "as a nursing mother tenderly cares for her own children. Having thus a fond affection for you, we were well-pleased to impart to you not only the gospel of God but also our own lives, because you had become very dear to us. For you recall, brethren, our labor and hardship, how working night and day so as not to be a burden to any of you, we proclaimed to you the gospel of God" (1 Thess. 2:7-9).

The foremost characteristic of genuine love is selfless giving, and it was out of such love that Paul assured the church in Corinth, "I will most gladly spend and be expended for your souls" (2 Cor. 12:15). Willingness to spend was willingness to use all his resources and energy in their behalf, and willingness to be spent was willingness to die for them if necessary.

Paul was burdened for the physical welfare of the Roman believers, but his overriding concern was for their spiritual well-being, and therefore his principal purpose for longing **to see** them was **that** he might **impart** to them **some spiritual gift.**

The **gift** Paul wanted to **impart** was **spiritual** not only in the sense of being in the spiritual realm but in the sense that it had its source in the Holy Spirit. Because he was writing to believers, Paul was not speaking about the free gift of salvation through Christ about which he speaks in 5:15-16. Nor could he have been speaking about the gifts he discusses in chapter 12, because those gifts are bestowed directly by the Spirit Himself, not through a human instrument. He must therefore have been using the term **spiritual gift** in its broadest sense, referring to any kind of divinely-empowered **spiritual** benefit he could bring to the Roman Christians by preaching, teaching, exhorting, comforting, praying, guiding, and disciplining.

Whatever particular blessings the apostle had in mind, they were not of the superficial, self-centered sort that many church members crave today. He was not interested in tickling their ears or satisfying their religious curiosity.

Paul wanted to impart the spiritual blessings in order for the Roman believers to **be established.** He wanted those spiritual brothers and sisters "to grow up in all aspects into Him, who is the head, even Christ" (Eph. 4:15).

A young woman once told me that she had been teaching a Sunday school class of young girls for some while and thought that she loved them dearly. But one Saturday afternoon at her college football game the Lord convicted her about the superficiality of her love for them. Because of her busy Saturdays, she seldom spent more than a few minutes preparing her lesson for the next day. From that day on she determined to make whatever sacrifice and give whatever time necessary to give those girls something of eternal significance. That was the kind of committed, self-sacrificing love Paul had for the church at Rome.

A Humble Spirit

that is, that I may be encouraged together with you while among you, each of us by the other's faith, both yours and mine. (1:12)

Lest his readers think that he had in mind a one-way blessing, Paul assures them that a visit would be to his benefit as well as theirs. Although he was a highly-gifted and greatly-used apostle, having received revealed truth directly from God, Paul never thought that he was above being spiritually edified by other believers.

The truly thankful, concerned, willing, submissive, and loving spirit is also a humble spirit. The person with such a spirit never has a feeling of spiritual superiority and never lords it over those he serves in Christ's name.

Commenting on this passage in Romans, John Calvin said of Paul, "Note how modestly he expresses what he feels by not refusing to seek strengthening from inexperienced beginners. He means what he says, too, for there is none so void of gifts in the Church of Christ who cannot in some measure contribute to our spiritual progress. Ill will and pride, however, prevent our deriving such benefit from one another" (John Calvin, *The Epistle of Paul the Apostle to the Romans and to the Thessalonians* [Grand Rapids: Eerdmans, 1960], p. 24).

Peter warned elders not to lord it over those given to their care but rather to be examples to them. In doing so, "when the Chief Shepherd appears, [they would] receive the unfading crown of glory" (1 Pet. 5:3-4). He then went on to advise both older and younger men to clothe themselves "with humility toward one another, for God is opposed to the proud, but gives grace to the humble" (v. 5).

Paul, the greatest theologian who ever lived, was also one of the most humble men of all. He was blessed beyond measure, yet he had no spiritual pride or intellectual arrogance. Because he had not attained spiritual perfection but genuinely pursued it (cf. Phil. 3:12-14), he was eager to be spiritually helped by all the believers in the Roman church, young as well as old, mature as well as immature.

It is unfortunate not only that many learned and gifted leaders in the church think they are above learning from or being helped by younger and less-experienced believers but also unfortunate that less-experienced believers often feel they have nothing to offer their leaders.

When he was about to board a ship to India to begin missionary service there, some of William Carey's friends asked if he really wanted to go through with his plans. Expressing his great desire for their support in prayer, he is said to have replied, "I will go down [into the pit itself] if you will hold the rope" (S. Pearce Carey, *William Carey* [London: The Carey Press, 1934], pp. 117-18).

A FRUITFUL SPIRIT

And I do not want you to be unaware, brethren, that often I have planned to come to you (and have been prevented thus far) in order that I might obtain some fruit among you also, even as among the rest of the Gentiles. (1:13)

Paul frequently used a phrase such as **I do not want you to be unaware** as a means of calling attention to something of great importance he was about to say. He used it to introduce his teaching about such things as the mystery of God's calling Gentiles to salvation (Rom. 11:25), spiritual gifts (1 Cor. 12:1), and the second coming (1 Thess. 4:13). Here he uses it to introduce his determined plan to visit the saints at Rome. **Often I have planned to come to you (and have been prevented thus far),** he assures his readers. As far as his own plans were concerned, he would have come to them long beforehand had he not **been prevented** from doing so.

His intent was not to make a social call but to **obtain some fruit among** the believers in Rome, **even as among the rest of the Gentiles** to whom he ministered.

Paul's ministry was an unending quest for spiritual **fruit**. His preaching, teaching, and writing were not ends in themselves. The purpose of all true ministry for God is to bear fruit in His name and with His power and for His glory. "You did not choose Me, but I chose you," Jesus declared to His disciples, "and appointed you, that you should go and bear fruit, and that your fruit should remain" (John 15:16).

In regard to spiritual life, the Bible uses the term **fruit** in three ways. In one way, it is used as a metaphor for the attitudes that characterize the Spirit-led believer. This nine-fold "fruit of the Spirit," Paul tells us, "is love, joy, peace, patience, kindness, goodness, faithfulness, gentleness, self-control" (Gal. 5:22-23).

In a second way, spiritual **fruit** refers to action. "Now having been freed from sin and enslaved to God," the apostle declares, "you derive your benefit [lit., 'fruit'], resulting in sanctification" (Rom. 6:22), that is, holy living. The active fruit of a Christian's lips is praise (Heb. 13:15), and the active fruit of his hands is giving (Phil. 4:16-17; "profit" is literally "fruit").

In a third way, spiritual **fruit** involves addition, the increase of converts to Christ and the increase of their spiritual growth in Him. Paul spoke of Epaenetus as being "the first convert [lit., firstfruit] to Christ from Asia" (Rom. 16:5).

Among the Romans, the **fruit** Paul longed for was of the third kind, addition. It included both new converts and maturing converts. They were spiritual **fruit** in the broadest sense of being the product of the gospel's power in men's lives, both to save and to sanctify. The apostle wanted to be used to help the Roman church grow through new converts and grow in sanctification, which includes growth in service to Christ. When, some years later, he wrote to the Philippian church from Rome, he was able to give greetings even from believers within "Caesar's household" (Phil. 4:22), believers he may have been instrumental in bringing to Christ.

As already noted, in the name of the Lord's work some people strive for prestige or acceptance or money or crowds or influence. But a Christian who serves from the heart and whose spiritual service is genuine strives only to be used of the Lord to bear fruit for Him. The Christian who settles for less is one who serves only externally.

Nothing is more encouraging to pastors, Sunday School teachers, youth leaders, and other Christian workers than to see spiritual results in the lives of those to whom they minister. Nothing is more deeply rewarding than the lasting joy of leading others to Christ or helping them grow in the Lord.

An Obedient Spirit

I am under obligation both to Greeks and to barbarians, both to the wise and to the foolish. (1:14)

Paul continues to talk about his attitudes and reasons for ministry, explaining that he did not preach and teach the gospel because of personal reasons or because the calling seemed attractive, but because he was **under obligation.** "I am under compulsion," he said to the Corinthians; "for woe is me if I do not preach the gospel. For if I do this voluntarily, I have a reward; but if against my will, I have a stewardship entrusted to me" (1 Cor. 9:16-17).

When the Lord called him to salvation and to apostleship, Paul was doing anything but promoting the gospel but was rather bent on destroying it at all costs. He seems to be saying to the Romans, in effect, "Don't thank me for wanting to minister to you. Although I love you and sincerely want to visit you, I was sovereignly appointed to this ministry long before I had a personal desire for it" (cf. 1 Cor. 9:16ff.).

Every sincere pastor and Christian worker knows there are times when ministry is its own reward, when study, preparation, teaching, and shepherding are exhilarating in themselves. There are other times, however, when the work does not seem very attractive, and yet you still study, prepare, teach, and shepherd because you are under obligation to God and to those you are serving. Christ is our Lord and we are His servants; and it is a poor servant who serves only when he feels like it.

Paul was **under obligation** in at least two ways. First, he was under obligation to God on behalf of the Gentiles. Because God had appointed him as a unique apostle to the Gentiles (Rom. 1:5; Acts 9:15), he was under divine obligation to minister the gospel to them.

Second, he had an **obligation,** or debt, to the Roman believers directly, because of their spiritual need. That is the kind of obligation a person has to someone whose house is on fire or who is drowning. When someone is in great danger and we are able to help, we are automatically and immediately under obligation to do what we can to save him. Because unbelieving Gentiles, like unbelieving Jews, face spiritual death, Paul was obligated to help rescue them through the gospel.

To Greeks and barbarians and **to the wise and to the foolish** seem to be parallel phrases, **Greeks** representing **the wise** and **barbarians** representing **the foolish.** The **Greeks** of that day included people from many lands who were educated in Greek learning and trained in Greek culture. They were highly sophisticated and were often looked upon as being on a higher level than others. They certainly looked on themselves in that way. The Greek language was thought to be the language of the gods, and Greek philosophy was thought to be little less than divine.

The term **barbarians,** on the other hand, was frequently used to designate those who were not hellenized, that is, not steeped in Greek learning and culture. The word is onomatopoeic, having been derived from the repetition of the sound "bar." To a cultured Greek, other languages sounded like so much gibberish and were mimicked by saying "bar, bar, bar, bar." In its narrowest sense, **barbarians** referred to the uncultured, uncouth, and uneducated masses, but in its wider sense it was used of anyone who was non-Greek.

Paul was therefore expressing his responsibility to the educated and the uneducated, the sophisticated and the simple, the privileged and the underprivileged. Like the Lord he served (1 Pet. 1:17), Paul was no respecter of persons. The gospel is the great equalizer, because every human being is equally lost without it and equally saved by it.

The first person to whom Jesus revealed Himself as Messiah was an adulterous woman who had a number of husbands and was living with a man who was not her husband. Not only that, but she was a Samaritan, a member of a race greatly despised by Jews. Yet Jesus drew her to Himself in loving compassion, and she was used to bring many of her fellow Samaritans to faith in the Messiah (see John 4:7-42).

AN EAGER SPIRIT

Thus, for my part, I am eager to preach the gospel to you also who are in Rome. (1:15)

Paul's external obligation to minister did not preclude his internal desire to fulfill that obligation. He not only was willing but **eager to preach the gospel to** believers **in Rome.**

He was as determined to **preach . . . in Rome** as he was to go to Jerusalem, although he knew great danger awaited him there. "And now, behold, bound in spirit, I am on my way to Jerusalem, not knowing what will happen to me there, except that the Holy Spirit solemnly testifies to me in every city, saying that bonds and afflictions await me" (Acts 20:22-23). In his spirit he was compelled to go because that was God's will for him. Therefore he said, "I do not consider my life of any account as dear to myself, in order that I may finish my course, and the ministry which I received from the Lord Jesus, to testify solemnly of the gospel of the grace of God" (v. 24). Paul knew that "to live is Christ, and to die is gain" (Phil. 1:21), that "to be absent from the body [is] to be at home with the Lord" (2 Cor. 5:8).

Paul had the same concern for the Roman believers as for those in Colossae, to whom he wrote, "I rejoice in my sufferings for your sake, and in my flesh I do my share on behalf of His body (which is the church) in filling up that which is lacking in Christ's afflictions" (Col. 1:24).

Life had but one value for Paul: to do God's work. He was consumed by an eager desire to serve God, which included serving others in His name. That absolute commitment was shared by Epaphroditus, who "came close to death for the work of Christ" (Phil. 2:30). Such godly servants are like racehorses in the gate or sprinters at the starting blocks. They cannot wait to get on with the race of serving Christ.

A final characteristic of spiritual service, a bold spirit, is seen in the following verse, which will be studied in more detail in the next chapter. Paul declared, "I am not ashamed of the gospel" (Rom. 1:16). He knew that Rome was a volatile place and that Christians there had already experienced persecution. He knew that the capital city of the empire was steeped in immorality and paganism, including emperor worship. He knew that most Romans would despise him and that many probably would do him harm. Yet he was boldly eager to go there, for his Lord's sake and for the sake of the Lord's people.

The Gospel of Christ

For I am not ashamed of the gospel, for it is the power of God for salvation to everyone who believes, to the Jew first and also to the Greek. For in it the righteousness of God is revealed from faith to faith; as it is written, "But the righteous man shall live by faith." (1:16-17)

After having gained the attention of his readers by explaining the purpose of his writing and then introducing himself (1:1-15), Paul now states the thesis of the epistle. These two verses express the theme of the book of Romans, and they contain the most life-transforming truth God has put into men's hands. To understand and positively respond to this truth is to have one's time and eternity completely altered. These words summarize the gospel of Jesus Christ, which Paul then proceeds to unfold and explain throughout the remainder of the epistle. For that reason, our comments here will be somewhat brief and a more detailed discussion of these themes will come later in the study.

As noted at the close of the last chapter, the introductory phrase **for I am not ashamed of the gospel** adds a final mark of spiritual service to those presented in verses 8-15, the mark of unashamed boldness.

Paul was imprisoned in Philippi, chased out of Thessalonica, smuggled out of Damascus and Berea, laughed at in Athens, considered a fool in Corinth, and declared a blasphemer and lawbreaker in Jerusalem. He was stoned and left for dead at Lystra. Some pagans of Paul's day branded Christianity as atheism because it believed in only one God and as being cannibalistic because of a misunderstanding of the Lord's Supper.

But the Jewish religious leaders of Jerusalem did not intimidate Paul, nor did the learned and influential pagans at Ephesus, Athens, and Corinth. The apostle was eager now to preach and teach the gospel in Rome, the capital of the pagan empire that ruled virtually all the known world. He was never deterred by opposition, never disheartened by criticism, and never **ashamed,** for any reason, **of the gospel** of Jesus Christ. Although that **gospel** was then, and still is today, a stumbling block to Jews and foolishness to Gentiles, it is the only way God has provided for the salvation of men, and Paul was both overjoyed and emboldened by the privilege of proclaiming its truth and power wherever he went.

Although every true believer knows it is a serious sin to be ashamed of his Savior and Lord, he also knows the difficulty of avoiding that sin. When we have opportunity to speak for Christ, we often do not. We know the gospel is unattractive, intimidating, and repulsive to the natural, unsaved person and to the ungodly spiritual system that now dominates the world. The gospel exposes man's sin, wickedness, depravity, and lostness, and it declares pride to be despicable and works righteousness to be worthless in God's sight. To the sinful heart of unbelievers, the gospel does not appear to be good news but bad (cf. my comments in chapter 1), and when they first hear it they often react with disdain against the one presenting it or throw out arguments and theories against it. For that reason, fear of men and of not being able to handle their arguments is doubtlessly the single greatest snare in witnessing.

It is said that if a circle of white chalk is traced on the floor around a goose that it will not leave the circle for fear of crossing the white mark. In a similar way, the chalk marks of criticism, ridicule, tradition, and rejection prevent many believers from leaving the security of Christian fellowship to witness to the unsaved.

The so-called health and wealth gospel that has swept through much of the church today is not offensive to the world because it offers what the world wants. But that spurious gospel does not offer **the gospel** of Jesus Christ. Like the false teaching of the Judaizers, it is "a different gospel," that is, not the gospel at all but an ungodly distortion (Gal. 1:6-7). Jesus strongly condemned the motives of worldly success and comfort, and those who appeal to such motives play right into the hands of Satan.

A scribe once approached Jesus and said, "Teacher, I will follow You wherever You go." Knowing the man was unwilling to give up his comforts in order to be a disciple, the Lord answered, "The foxes have holes, and the birds of the air have nests; but the Son of Man has nowhere to lay His head" (Matt. 8:19-20). Shortly after that, "another of the disciples said to Him, 'Lord, permit me first to go and bury my father.'" The phrase "bury my father" did not refer to a funeral service but was a colloquialism for awaiting the father's death in order to receive the inheritance. Jesus therefore told the man, "Follow Me; and allow the dead to bury their own dead" (vv. 21-22).

Geoffrey Wilson wrote, "The unpopularity of a crucified Christ has prompted many to present a message which is more palatable to the unbeliever, but the removal of the offense of the cross always renders the message ineffective. An inoffensive gospel is also an inoperative gospel. Thus Christianity is wounded most in the house of its friends" (*Romans: A Digest of Reformed Comment* [Carlisle, Pa.: Banner of Truth, 1976], p. 24).

Some years ago I spoke at a youth rally, after which the wife of the rally director approached me. Expressing an unbiblical mentality that is common in the church today, she said, "Your message offended me, because you preached as if all of these young people were sinners." I replied, "I'm glad it came across that way, because that is exactly the message I wanted to communicate."

Paul's supreme passion was to see men saved. He cared nothing for personal comfort, popularity, or reputation. He offered no compromise of the gospel, because he knew it is the only power available that can change lives for eternity.

In verses 16-17, Paul uses four key words that are crucial to understanding the gospel of Jesus Christ: power, salvation, faith, and righteousness.

POWER

for it is the power of God (1:16b)

First of all, Paul declares, the gospel **is the power of God.** *Dunamis* (**power**) is the Greek term from which our word *dynamite* is derived. The gospel carries with it the omnipotence of God, whose **power** alone is sufficient to save men from sin and give them eternal life.

People have an innate desire to be changed. They want to look better, feel better, have more money, more power, more influence. The premise of all advertising is that people want to change in some way or another, and the job of the advertiser is to convince them that his product or service will add a desired dimension to their lives. Many people want to be changed inwardly, in a way that will make them feel less guilty and more content, and a host of programs, philosophies, and religions promise to meet those desires. Many man-made schemes succeed in making people feel better about themselves, but the ideas promoted have no power to remove the sin that brings the feelings of guilt and discontent. Nor can those ideas make men right with God. In fact, the more successful such approaches are from their own standpoint, the more they drive people away from God and insulate them from His salvation.

Through Jeremiah, the Lord said, "Can the Ethiopian change his skin or the leopard his spots? Then you also can do good who are accustomed to do evil" (Jer. 13:23). It is not within man's power to change his own nature. In rebuking the Sadducees who tried to entrap Him, Jesus said, "You are mistaken, not understanding the Scriptures, or the power of God" (Matt. 22:29). Only the power of God is able to overcome man's sinful nature and impart spiritual life.

The Bible makes it clear that men cannot be spiritually changed or saved by good works, by the church, by ritual, or by any other human means. Men cannot be saved even by keeping God's own law, which was given to show men their helplessness to meet His standards in their own power. The law was not given to save men but to reveal their sin and thus to drive men to God's saving grace.

Later in Romans, Paul declares man's impotence and God's power, saying, "While we were still helpless, at the right time Christ died for the ungodly" (Rom. 5:6), and, "What the law could not do, weak as it was through the flesh, God did: sending His own Son in the likeness of sinful flesh and as an offering for sin" (8:3). Affirming the same basic truth in different words, Peter wrote believers in Asia Minor: "You have been born again not of seed which is perishable but imperishable, that is, through the living and abiding word of God" (1 Pet. 1:23).

Paul reminded the church at Corinth that "the word of the cross is to those who are perishing foolishness, but to us who are being saved it is the power of God" (1 Cor. 1:18), and "we preach Christ crucified, to Jews a stumbling block, and to Gentiles foolishness, but to those who are the called, both Jews and Greeks, Christ the power of God and the wisdom of God. Because the foolishness of God is wiser than men, and the weakness of God is stronger than men" (vv. 23-25). What to the world seems to be utter absurdity is in fact the power by which God transforms men from the realm of darkness to the realm of light, and delivers them from the power of death and gives them the right to be called the children of God (John 1:12).

Ancient pagans mocked Christianity not only because the idea of substitutionary atonement seemed ridiculous in itself but also because their mythical gods were apathetic, detached, and remote—totally indifferent to the welfare of men. The idea of a caring, redeeming, self-sacrificing God was beyond their comprehension. While excavating ancient ruins in Rome, archaeologists discovered a derisive painting depicting a slave bowing down before a cross with a jackass hanging on it. The caption reads, "Alexamenos worships his god."

In the late second century this attitude still existed. A man named Celsus wrote a letter bitterly attacking Christianity. "Let no cultured person draw near, none wise, none sensible," he said, "for all that kind of thing we count evil; but if any man is ignorant, if any is wanting in sense and culture, if any is a fool, let him come boldly [to Christianity]" (William Barclay, *The Letters to the Corinthians* [Philadelphia: Westminster, 1975], p. 21; cf. Origen's *Against Celsus*). "Of the Christians," he further wrote, "we see them in their own houses, wool dressers, cobblers and fullers, the most uneducated and vulgar persons" (p. 21). He compared Christians to a swarm of bats, to ants crawling out of their nests, to frogs holding a symposium around a swamp, and to worms cowering in the muck!

Not wanting to build on human wisdom or appeal to human understanding, Paul told the Corinthians that "when I came to you, brethren, I did not come with superiority of speech or of wisdom, proclaiming to you the testimony of God. For I determined to know nothing among you except Jesus Christ, and Him crucified" (1 Cor. 2:1-2). Later in the letter Paul said, "The kingdom of God does not consist in words, but in power" (4:20), the redeeming power of God.

Every believer, no matter how gifted and mature, has human limitations and weaknesses. Our minds, bodies, and perceptions are imperfect. Yet, incredibly, God uses us as channels of His redeeming and sustaining power when we serve Him obediently.

Scripture certainly testifies to God's glorious power (Ex. 15:6), His irresistible power (Deut. 32:39), His unsearchable power (Job 5:9), His mighty power (Job 9:4), His great power (Ps. 79:11), His incomparable power (Ps. 89:8), His strong power (Ps. 89:13), His everlasting power (Isa. 26:4), His effectual power (Isa. 43:13), and His sovereign power (Rom. 9:21). Jeremiah declared of God, "It is He who made the earth by His power, who established the world by His wisdom" (Jer. 10:12), and through that prophet the Lord said of Himself, "I have made the earth, the men and the beasts which are on the face of the earth by My great power and by My outstretched arm" (Jer. 27:5). The psalmist admonished, "Let all the earth fear the Lord; let all the inhabitants of the world stand in awe of Him. For He spoke, and it was done; He commanded, and it stood fast" (Ps. 33:8-9). His is the power that can save.

SALVATION

for salvation (1:16c)

Surely the greatest manifestation of God's power is that of bringing men to **salvation**, of transforming their nature and giving them eternal life through His Son. We learn from the psalmist that, despite their rebelliousness, God saved His chosen people "for the sake of His name, that He might make His power known" (Ps. 106:8). As God incarnate, Jesus Christ manifested His divine power in healing diseases, restoring crippled limbs, stilling the storm, and even raising those who were dead.

Paul uses the noun *sōtēria* (**salvation**) some nineteen times, five of them in Romans, and he uses the corresponding verb twenty-nine times, eight of them in Romans. The basic idea behind the term is that of deliverance, or rescue, and the point here is that the power of God in **salvation** rescues people from the ultimate penalty of sin, which is spiritual death extended into tormented eternal separation from Him.

Some people object to terms such as *salvation* and *being saved,* claiming that the ideas they convey are out of date and meaningless to contemporary men. But **salvation** is God's term, and there is no better one to describe what He offers fallen mankind through the sacrifice of His Son. Through Christ, and Christ alone, men can be saved from sin, from Satan, from judgment, from wrath, and from spiritual death.

Regardless of the words they may use to describe their quest, men are continually looking for salvation of one kind or another. Some look for economic salvation, others for political or social salvation. As already noted, many people look for inner salvation from the guilt, frustrations, and unhappiness that make their lives miserable.

Even before Paul's day, Greek philosophy had turned inward and begun to focus on changing man's inner life through moral reform and self-discipline. William Barclay tells us that the Greek Stoic philosopher Epictetus called his lecture room "the hospital for sick souls." Another famous Greek philosopher named Epicurus called his teaching "the medicine of salvation." Seneca, a Roman statesman and philosopher and contemporary of Paul, taught that all men were looking *ad salutem* ("toward salvation"). He taught that men are overwhelmingly conscious of their weakness and insufficiency in necessary things and that we therefore need "a hand let down to lift us up" (*The Letter to the Romans* [Philadelphia: Westminster, 1975], p. 19).

Salvation through Christ is God's powerful hand, as it were, that He has let down to lift men up. His **salvation** brings deliverance from the spiritual infection of "this perverse generation" (Acts 2:40), from lostness (Matt. 18:11), from sin (Matt. 1:21), and from the wrath of God

(Rom. 5:9). It brings deliverance to men from their gross and willful spiritual ignorance (Hos. 4:6; 2 Thess. 1:8), from their evil self-indulgence (Luke 14:26), and from the darkness of false religion (Col. 1:13; 1 Pet. 2:9), but only for those who believe.

FAITH

to everyone who believes, to the Jew first and also to the Greek. (1:16d)

The fourth key word regarding the gospel is that of faith. The sovereign power of God working through the gospel brings salvation **to everyone who believes.**

Pisteuō (**believes**) carries the basic idea of trusting in, relying on, having faith in. When used in the New Testament of salvation, it is usually in the present, continuous form, which could be translated "is believing." Daily living is filled with acts of faith. We turn on the faucet to get a drink of water, trusting it is safe to drink. We drive across a bridge, trusting it will not collapse under us. Despite occasional disasters, we trust airplanes to fly us safely to our destination. People could not survive without having implicit trust in a great many things. Virtually all of life requires a natural faith. But Paul has in mind here a supernatural faith, produced by God—a "faith that is not of yourselves but the gift of God" (Eph. 2:8).

Eternal life is both gained and lived by faith from God in Jesus Christ. "For by grace you have been saved through faith," Paul tells us (Eph. 2:8). God does not first ask men to behave but to believe. Man's efforts at right behavior always fall short of God's perfect standard, and therefore no man can save himself by his own good works. Good works are the product of salvation (Eph. 2:10), but they are not the means of it.

Salvation is not merely professing to be a Christian, nor is it baptism, moral reform, going to church, receiving sacraments, or living a life of self-discipline and sacrifice. Salvation is believing in Jesus Christ as Lord and Savior. Salvation comes through giving up on one's own goodness, works, knowledge, and wisdom and trusting in the finished, perfect work of Christ.

Salvation has no national, racial, or ethnic barrier but is given to every person who believes, **to the Jew first and also to the Greek.** It was to **the Jew first** chronologically because Jews are God's specially chosen people, through whom He ordained salvation to come (John 4:22). The Messiah came first to the lost sheep of the house of Israel (Matt. 15:24).

The great Scottish evangelist Robert Haldane wrote,

From the days of Abraham, their great progenitor, the Jews had been highly distinguished from all the rest of the world by their many and great privileges. It was their high distinction that of them Christ came, "who is over all, God blessed for ever." They were thus, as His kinsmen, the royal family of the human race, in this respect higher than all others, and they inherited Emmanuel's land. While, therefore, the evangelical covenant, and consequently justification and salvation, equally regarded all believers, the Jews held the first rank as the ancient people of God, while the other nations were strangers from the covenants of promise. The preaching of the Gospel was to be addressed to them first, and, at the beginning, to them alone, Matt. 10:6; for, during the abode of Jesus Christ upon earth, He was the minister only of the circumcision, Rom. 15:8. "I am not sent," He says, "but to the lost sheep of the house of Israel"; and He commanded that repentance and remission of sins should be preached in His name among all nations, "beginning at Jerusalem." . . . Thus, while Jews and Gentiles were united in the participation of the Gospel, the Jews were not deprived of their rank, since they were the first called.

The preaching of the Gospel to the Jews *first* served various important ends. It fulfilled Old Testament prophecies, as Isa. 2:3. It manifested the compassion of the Lord Jesus for those who shed His blood, to whom, after His resurrection, He commanded His Gospel to be first proclaimed. It showed that it was to be preached to the chief of sinners, and proved the sovereign efficacy of His Atonement in expatiating [sic] the guilt even of His murderers. It was fit, too, that the Gospel should be begun to be preached where the great transactions took place on which it was founded and established; and this furnished an example of the way in which it is the will of the Lord that His Gospel should be propagated by His disciples, beginning in their own houses and their own country. (*An Exposition of the Epistle to the Romans* [MacDill AFB, Fla.: MacDonald Publishing Co., 1958], p. 48)

All who believe may be saved. Only those who truly believe will be.

RIGHTEOUSNESS

For in it the righteousness of God is revealed from faith to faith; as it is written, "But the righteous man shall live by faith." (1:17)

The fourth key word Paul uses here regarding the gospel is **righteousness,** a term he uses over thirty-five times in the book of Romans alone. Faith activates the divine power that brings salvation, and in that sovereign act **the righteousness of God is revealed.** A better rendering is *from* **God,** indicating that He imparts His own **righteousness** to those who believe. It is thereby not only **revealed** but *reckoned* to those who believe in Christ (Rom. 4:5).

Paul confessed to the Philippians, "I count all things to be loss in view of the surpassing value of knowing Christ Jesus my Lord, for whom I have suffered the loss of all things, and count them but rubbish in order that I may gain Christ, and may be found in Him, not having a righteousness of my own derived from the Law, but that which is through faith in Christ, the righteousness which comes from God on the basis of faith" (Phil. 3:8-9). "But now apart from the Law the righteousness of God has been manifested, being witnessed by the Law and the Prophets, even the righteousness of God through faith in Jesus Christ for all those who believe; for there is no distinction; for all have sinned and fall short of the glory of God, being justified as a gift by His grace through the redemption which is in Christ Jesus" (Rom. 3:21-24).

The German pietist Count Zinzendorf wrote, in a profound hymn,

> Jesus, Thy blood and righteousness
> My beauty are, my glorious dress;
> 'Midst flaming worlds, in these arrayed,
> With joy shall I lift up my head.
>
> Bold shall I stand in Thy great day,
> For who aught to my charge shall lay?
> Fully absolved through these I am,
> From sin and fear, from guilt and shame.

From faith to faith seems to parallel "everyone who believes" in the previous verse. If so, the idea is "from faith to faith to faith to faith," as if Paul were singling out the faith of each individual believer.

Salvation by His grace working through man's faith was always God's plan, as Paul here implies in quoting from Habakkuk 2:4, **as it is written, "But the righteous man shall live by faith."** Abraham, the father of the faithful, believed, and it was reckoned to him as righteousness (Rom. 4:3), just as every person's genuine faith, before and after Abraham, has been reckoned to him as righteousness (see Heb. 11:4-40).

There is emphasis here on the continuity of faith. It is not a one-time act, but a way of life. The true believer made righteous will live in faith all his life. Theologians have called this "the perseverance of the saints" (cf. Col. 1:22-23; Heb. 3:12-14).

The Wrath of God

For the wrath of God is revealed from heaven against all ungodliness and unrighteousness of men, who suppress the truth in ungodliness, (1:18)

As Paul begins to unfold the details of the gospel of God in which His righteousness is revealed (see vv. 16-17), he presents an extended discussion of the condemnation of man that extends through chapter 3 and verse 20. He starts with an unequivocal affirmation of God's righteous **wrath**.

The idea of a wrathful God goes against the wishful thinking of fallen human nature and is even a stumbling block to many Christians. Much contemporary evangelism talks only about abundant life in Christ, the joy and blessings of salvation, and the peace with God that faith in Christ brings. All of those benefits do result from true faith, but they are not the whole picture of God's plan of salvation. The corollary truth of God's judgment against sin and those who participate in it must also be heard.

For Paul, fear of eternal condemnation was the first motivation he offered for coming to Christ, the first pressure he applied to evil men. He was determined that they understand the reality of being under God's wrath before he offered them the way of escape from it. That approach makes both logical and theological sense. A person cannot appreciate the wonder of God's grace until he knows about the perfect demands of God's law, and he cannot appreciate the fullness of God's love for him until he knows something about the fierceness of God's anger against his sinful failure to perfectly obey that law. He cannot appreciate God's forgiveness until he knows about the eternal consequences of the sins that require a penalty and need forgiving.

Orgē (**wrath**) refers to a settled, determined indignation, not to the momentary, emotional, and often uncontrolled anger (*thumos*) to which human beings are prone.

God's attributes are balanced in divine perfection. If He had no righteous anger and wrath, He would not be God, just as surely as He would not be God without His gracious love. He perfectly hates just as He perfectly loves, perfectly loving righteousness and perfectly hating evil (Ps. 45:7; Heb. 1:9). One of the great tragedies of modern Christianity, including much of evangelicalism, is the failure to preach and teach the wrath of God and the condemnation it brings upon all with unforgiven sin. The truncated, sentimental gospel that is frequently presented today falls far short of the gospel that Jesus and the apostle Paul proclaimed.

In glancing through a psalter from the late nineteenth century, I discovered that many of the psalms in that hymnal emphasize the wrath of God, just as much of the book of Psalms itself emphasizes His wrath. It is tragic that few hymns or other Christian songs today reflect that important biblical focus.

Scripture, New Testament as well as Old, consistently emphasizes God's righteous **wrath**. Against those who scoff at Him, God "will speak to them in His anger and terrify them in His fury." The psalmist goes on to admonish, "Do homage to the Son, lest He become angry, and you perish in the way, for His wrath may soon be kindled" (Ps. 2:5, 12). Asaph wrote, "At Thy rebuke, O God of Jacob, both rider and horse were cast into a dead sleep. Thou, even Thou, art to be feared; and who may stand in Thy presence when once Thou art angry?" (Ps. 76:6-7). Another psalmist reminded unfaithful Israel of what God had done to the defiant Egyptians who refused to let His people leave: "He sent upon them His burning anger, fury, and indignation, and trouble, a band of destroying angels. He leveled a path for His anger; He did not spare their soul from death, but gave their life over to the plague, and smote all the first-born in Egypt" (Ps. 78:49-51). Speaking in behalf of Israel, Moses lamented, "For we have been consumed by Thine anger, and by thy wrath we have been dismayed. Thou hast placed our iniquities before Thee, our secret sins in the light of Thy presence. For all our days have declined in Thy fury" (Ps. 90:7-9).

The prophets spoke much of God's **wrath**. Isaiah declared, "By the fury of the Lord of hosts the land is burned up, and the people are like fuel for the fire" (Isa. 9:19). Jeremiah proclaimed, "Thus says the Lord God, 'Behold, My anger and My wrath will be poured out on this place, on man and on beast and on the trees of the field and on the fruit of the ground; and it will burn and not be quenched'" (Jer. 7:20). Through Ezekiel, God warned His people that "their silver and their gold [would] not be able to deliver them in the day of the wrath of the Lord. They cannot satisfy their appetite, nor can they fill their stomachs, for their iniquity has become an occasion of stumbling" (Ezek. 7:19).

In many well-known ways God expressed His **wrath** against sinful mankind in past ages. In the days of Noah, He destroyed all mankind in the Flood, except for eight people (Gen. 6-7). Several generations after Noah, He confounded men's language and scattered them around the earth for trying to build an idolatrous tower to heaven (Gen. 11:1-9). In the days of Abraham, He destroyed Sodom and Gomorrah, with only Lot and his family escaping (Gen. 18–19). He destroyed Pharaoh and his army in the sea as they vainly pursued the Israelites to bring them back to Egypt (Ex. 14). He poured out His wrath against pagan kings such as Sennacherib (2 Kings 18–19), Nebuchadnezzar (Dan. 4), and Belshazzar (Dan. 5). He even poured out His wrath against some of His own people — against King Nadab for doing "evil in the sight of the Lord, and [walking] in the way of his father and in his sin which he made Israel sin" (1 Kings 15:25-26) and against Aaron and Miriam, Moses' brother and sister, for questioning Moses' revelations from Him (Num. 12:1-10).

God's wrath is just as clearly exhibited in the New Testament, both in reference to what He has already done and to what He will yet do at the end of the age. The gospel of John, which speaks so eloquently of God's love and graciousness, also speaks powerfully of His anger and wrath. The comforting words "For God so loved the world, that He gave His only begotten Son, that whoever believes in Him should not perish, but have eternal life," are followed closely by the warning "He who does not obey the Son shall not see life, but the wrath of God abides on him" (John 3:16, 36).

Later in his epistle to the Romans, Paul focuses again on God's wrath, declaring, "God, although willing to demonstrate His wrath and to make His power known, endured with much patience vessels of wrath prepared for destruction" (9:22). The apostle warned the Corinthians that anyone who did not love the Lord Jesus was to be eternally cursed (1 Cor. 16:22). He said to the Ephesians, "Let no one deceive you with empty words, for because of these things the wrath of God comes upon the sons of disobedience" (Eph. 5:6). He warned the Colossians that because of "immorality, impurity, passion, evil desire, and greed, which amounts to idolatry, . . . the wrath of God will come" (Col. 3:5-6). He assured the persecuted Thessalonian believers that God would one day give them relief and that "when the Lord Jesus shall be revealed from heaven with His mighty angels in flaming fire, [He will deal] out retribution to those who do not know God and to those who do not obey the gospel of our Lord Jesus" (2 Thess. 1:7-8).

A disease has to be recognized and identified before seeking a cure means anything. In the same way and for the same reason, Scripture reveals the bad news before the good news. God's righteous judgment against sin is proclaimed before His gracious forgiveness of sin is offered. A person has no reason to seek salvation from sin if he does not know he is condemned by it. He has no reason to want spiritual life unless he realizes he is spiritually dead.

With the one exception of Jesus Christ, every human being since the Fall has been born condemned, because when Adam and Eve fell, the divine sentence against all sinners was passed. Paul therefore declared to the Romans that "all have sinned and fall short of the glory of God" (Rom. 3:23). He reminded the Ephesians: "You were dead in your trespasses and sins, in which you formerly walked according to the course of this world, according to the prince of the power of the air, of the spirit that is now working in the sons of disobedience. Among them we too all formerly lived in the lusts of our flesh, indulging the desires of the flesh and of the mind, and were by nature children of wrath, even as the rest" (Eph. 2:1-3).

In the brief scope of one verse (Rom. 1:18), Paul presents six features that characterize God's wrath: its quality, its time, its source, its extent and nature, and its cause.

THE QUALITY OF GOD'S WRATH

of God (1:18*a*)

First, the quality of this wrath is seen in the fact that it is divine, it is **of God.** It is therefore unlike anything we know of in the present world. God's wrath is not like human anger, which is always tainted by sin. God's wrath is always and completely righteous. He never loses His temper. The Puritan writer Thomas Watson said, "Is God so infinitely holy? Then see how unlike to God sin is. . . . No wonder, therefore, that God hates sin, being so unlike to him, nay, so contrary to him; it strikes at his holiness."

Unable to reconcile the idea of God's wrath with his own ideas of goodness and righteousness, one liberal theologian made this claim: "We cannot think with full consistency of God in terms of the highest human ideals of personality and yet attribute to Him the rational passion of anger." But it is foolish, not to mention unbiblical, to measure God by human standards and to discount the idea of His wrath simply because human anger is always flawed by sin.

God's anger is not capricious, irrational rage but is the only response that a holy God could have toward evil. God could not be holy and not be angry at evil. Holiness cannot tolerate unholiness. "Thine eyes are too pure to approve evil, and Thou canst not look on wickedness with favor," Habakkuk says of the Lord (Hab. 1:13). And as Paul declares, neither can love tolerate unholiness, refusing to "rejoice in unrighteousness" (1 Cor. 13:6).

Jesus twice cleansed the Temple because He was incensed at the money changers and sacrifice sellers who made His "Father's house a house of merchandise" and "a robber's den" (John 2:14-16; Matt. 21:12-13). He was furious that His Father's house was flagrantly dishonored. Speaking in place of the sinful inhabitants of Jerusalem, Jeremiah acknowledged the rightness of God's punishment of them, saying, "The Lord is righteous; for I have rebelled against His command; hear now, all peoples, and behold my pain; my virgins and my young men have gone into captivity" (Lam. 1:18). In confessing before Joshua that he had kept for himself some booty from Jericho that was to be reserved for the house of the Lord, Achan acknowledged that the punishment he was about to receive was just and righteous (Josh. 7:20-25).

Even in the warped and perverted societies of men, indignation against vice and crime is recognized as an essential element of human goodness. We expect people to be outraged by gross injustice and cruelty. The noted Greek exegete Richard Trench said, "There [can be no] surer and sadder token of an utterly prostrate moral condition than . . . not being able to be angry with sin—and sinners" (Synonyms of the New Testament [Grand Rapids: Eerdmans, 1983], p. 134). God is perfectly so all the time with a holy fury.

THE TIMING OF GOD'S WRATH

is revealed (1:18b)

Second, the timing of God's wrath is seen in the fact that it **is revealed,** a better rendering being "constantly revealed." God's wrath is continually being revealed, perpetually being manifested. *Apokaluptō* (**revealed**) has the basic meaning of uncovering, bringing to light, or making known.

God's wrath has always been revealed to fallen mankind and is repeatedly illustrated throughout Scripture. It was first revealed in the Garden of Eden, when Adam and Eve trusted the serpent's word above God's. Immediately the sentence of death was passed on them and on all their descendants. Even the earth itself was cursed. As already mentioned, God's wrath was revealed in the Flood, when God drowned the whole human race except for eight souls, in the destruction of Sodom and Gomorrah, and in the drowning of Pharaoh's army. It was revealed in the curse of the law upon every transgression and in the institution of the sacrificial system of the Mosaic covenant. Even the imperfect laws that men make to deter and punish wrongdoers reflect and thereby help to reveal the perfect and righteous wrath of God.

By far the surpassing revelation of God's wrath was that placed upon His own Son on the cross, when Jesus took to Himself the sin of the world and bore the full divine force of God's fury as its penalty. God hates sin so deeply and requires its penalty so that He allowed His perfect, beloved Son to be put to death as the only means by which fallen mankind might be redeemed from sin's curse.

The British commentator Geoffrey B. Wilson wrote, "God is no idle spectator of world events; He is dynamically active in human affairs. The conviction of sin is constantly punctuated by Divine judgment" (*Romans: A Digest of Reformed Comment* [London: Banner of Truth], p. 24). The historian J. A. Froude wrote, "One lesson, and only one, history may be said to repeat with distinctness; that the world is built somehow on moral foundations; that, in the long run, it is well with the good; in the long run, it is ill with the wicked" (*Short Studies on Great Subjects*, vol. 1, "The Science of History" [London: Longmans, Green and Co., 1915], p. 21).

We wonder, then, why so many wicked people prosper, seemingly doing evil with utter impunity. But if God's wrath is delayed, His bowl of wrath is all the while filling up, increasing judgment for increased sin. They are only storing up wrath for the coming day of wrath (Rom. 2:5).

Donald Grey Barnhouse recounts the story of a group of godly farmers in a Midwest community being irritated one Sunday morning by a neighbor's plowing his field across from their church. Noise from his tractor interrupted the worship service, and, as it turned out, the man had purposely chosen to plow that particular field on Sunday morning in order to make a point. He wrote a letter to the editor of the local paper, asserting that, although he did not respect the Lord or honor the Lord's Day, he had the highest yield per acre of any farm in the county. He asked the editor how Christians could explain that. With considerable insight and wisdom, the editor printed the letter and followed it with the simple comment, "God does not settle [all] His accounts in the month of October" (*Man's Ruin: Romans 1:1-32* [Grand Rapids: Eerdmans, 1952], p. 220).

THE SOURCE OF GOD'S WRATH

from heaven (1:18c)

God's wrath is rendered **from heaven**. Despite Satan's present power as prince of the air and of this world, the earth is ultimately dominated by **heaven**, the throne of God, from which His wrath is constantly and dynamically manifested in the world of men.

Paul frequently speaks about *the* wrath, indicating a specific time or type of wrath. Although the NASB rendering does not indicate it, there is a definite article before *wrath* in Romans 3:5, which should read, "who inflicts the wrath." In chapter 5 he speaks of our being "saved from the wrath of God through" Christ (v. 9), in chapter 12 of our leaving "room for the wrath of God" (v. 19), and in chapter 13 of believers being in subjection to God "not only because of wrath, but also for conscience' sake" (v. 5). In his letter to Thessalonica he assures believers that Jesus delivers them "from the wrath to come" (1 Thess. 1:10).

Heaven reveals God's wrath in two ways, through His moral order and through His personal intervention. When God made the world, He built in certain moral as well as physical laws that have since governed its operation. Just as a person falls to the ground when he jumps from a high building, so does he fall into God's judgment when he deviates from God's moral law. That is built-in wrath. When a person sins, there is a built-in consequence that inexorably works. In this sense God is not specifically intervening, but is letting the law of moral cause and effect work.

The second way in which God reveals His wrath is through His direct and personal intervention. He is not an impersonal cosmic force that set the universe in motion to run its own course. God's wrath is executed exactly according to His divine will.

Several Hebrew words which convey a highly personal character are used in the Old Testament to describe God's anger. *Ḥārâ* is used ninety-one times. It refers to becoming heated, to burning with fury, and is frequently used of God (see, e.g., Gen. 18:30). *Ḥārôn* is used forty-one times. It refers exclusively to divine anger and means "a burning, fierce wrath" (see, e.g., Ex. 15:7). *Qâtsaph,* which means bitter, is used thirty-four times, most of which refer to God (see, e.g., Deut. 1:34). The fourth term for wrath is *Ḥēmâh,* which also refers to a venom or poison, is frequently associated with jealousy and is used most often of God (see, e.g., 2 Kings 22:13). David declared that "God is a righteous judge, and a God who has indignation every day" (Ps. 7:11). "Indignation" translates *zā'am,* which means to foam at the mouth, and is used over twenty times in the Old Testament, often of God's wrath.

Whether the cause and effect wrath or the personal fury of God is meted out, the wrath originates in heaven.

THE EXTENT AND NATURE OF GOD'S WRATH

against all ungodliness and unrighteousness of men, (1:18*d*)

The fourth and fifth features of God's wrath concern its extent and its nature.

God's wrath is universal, being discharged **against all** who deserve it. No amount of goodwill, giving to the poor, helpfulness to others, or even service to God can exclude a person from the **all** Paul mentions here. As he later explains more explicitly, "both Jews and Greeks are all under sin, . . . all have sinned and fall short of the glory of God" (Rom. 3:9, 23). Obviously, some people are morally better than others, but even the most moral and upright person falls far short of God's standard of perfect righteousness. No one escapes.

Men's relative goodness compared to God's perfect standard can be illustrated by a hypothetical attempt to jump from the beach near Los Angeles to Catalina Island, a distance of some twenty-six miles. Some people could not manage to jump at all, many could jump a few feet, and a rare few could jump twenty or twenty-five feet. The longest conceivable jump, however, would cover only the smallest fraction of the distance required. The most moral person has as little chance of achieving God's righteousness in his own power as the best athlete has of making that jump to Catalina. Everybody falls short.

The second emphasis of this phrase is on the nature of God's wrath. It is not like the wrath of a madman who strikes out indiscriminately, not caring who is injured or killed. Nor is it like the sin-tainted anger of a person who seeks to avenge a wrong done to him. God's wrath is reserved for and justly directed at sin. *Asebia* (**ungodliness**) and *adikia* (**unrighteousness**) are synonyms, the first stressing a faulty personal relationship to God. God is angered because sinful men are His enemies (see Rom. 5:10) and therefore "children of wrath" (Eph. 2:3).

Ungodliness refers to lack of reverence for, devotion to, and worship of the true God, a failure that inevitably leads to some form of false worship. Although the details and circumstances are not revealed, Jude reports that Enoch, the righteous seventh-generation descendant of Adam, prophesied about God's coming "to execute judgment upon all, and to convict all the ungodly of all their ungodly deeds which they have done in an ungodly way, and of all the harsh things which ungodly sinners have spoken against Him" (Jude 14-15). Four times he uses the term *ungodly* to describe the focus of God's wrath upon sinful mankind.

Unrighteousness encompasses the idea of ungodliness but focuses on its result. Sin first attacks God's majesty and then His law. Men do not act righteously because they are not rightly related to God, who is the only measure and source of righteousness. **Ungodliness** unavoidably leads to **unrighteousness.** Because men's relation to God is wrong, their relation to their fellow men is wrong. Men treat other men the way they do because they treat God the way they do. Man's enmity with his fellow man originates with his being at enmity with God.

Sin is the only thing God hates. He does not hate poor people or rich people, dumb people or smart people, untalented people or highly skilled people. He only hates the sin that those people, and all others, naturally practice, and sin inevitably brings His wrath.

THE CAUSE OF GOD'S WRATH

who suppress the truth in unrighteousness, (1:18e)

"But how is it," we ask, "that God can hold everyone responsible for moral and spiritual failure, and be so angry when some people have so much less opportunity than others for hearing the gospel and coming to know God?" The answer is that, because of his sinful disposition, every person is naturally inclined to follow sin and resist God. This phrase could be rendered, "who are constantly attempting to suppress the truth by steadfastly holding to their sin." **Unrighteousness** is so much a part of man's nature that *every* person has a built-in, natural, compelling desire to **suppress** and oppose God's **truth**.

As Paul declares in the following verse, "That which is known about God is evident within them; for God made it evident to them" (v. 19). His point is that all people, regardless of their relative opportunities to know God's Word and hear His gospel, have internal, God-given evidence of His existence and nature, but are universally inclined to resist and assault that evidence. No matter how little spiritual light he may have, God guarantees that any person who sincerely seeks Him will find Him. "You will seek me and find Me," He promises, "when you search for Me with all your heart" (Jer. 29:13).

But men are not naturally inclined to seek God. That truth was proved conclusively in the earthly ministry of Christ. Even when face-to-face with God incarnate, the Light of the world, "men loved darkness rather than the light; for their deeds were evil. For everyone who does evil hates the light, and does not come to the light, lest his deeds should be exposed" (John 3:19-20). As David had proclaimed hundreds of years earlier, "The fool has said in his heart, 'There is no God.' They are corrupt, they have committed abominable deeds; there is no one who does good"

(Ps. 14:1). Sinful men oppose the idea of a holy God because they innately realize that such a God would hold them accountable for the sins they love and do not want to relinquish.

Every person, no matter how isolated from God's written Word or the clear proclamation of His gospel, has enough divine truth evident both within and around Him (Rom. 1:19-20) to enable him to know and be reconciled to God if his desire is genuine. It is because men refuse to respond to that evidence that they are under God's wrath and condemnation. "This is the judgment," Jesus said, "that . . . men loved the darkness rather than the light" (John 3:19). Thus God is angry with the wicked every day (Psa. 7:11).

Reasons for the Wrath of God— part 1

because that which is known about God is evident within them, for God made it evident to them. For since the creation of the world His invisible attributes, His eternal power and divine nature, have been clearly seen, being understood through what has been made, so that they are without excuse. For even though they knew God, they did not honor Him as God, or give thanks; but they became futile in their speculations, and their foolish heart was darkened. (1:19-21)

The head of the department of evangelism for a major denomination in America said, "We don't need to evangelize the people of the world who have never heard the message of salvation. We only need to announce to them that they're already saved."

That leader reflects the rising tide of universalism, the belief that, because God is too loving and gracious to send anyone to hell, everyone ultimately will go to heaven. If that were true, there obviously would be no place for judgment in the proclamation of the gospel. Just as obviously there would be no place for biblical evangelism, as the person just quoted contends.

Some years ago, an article in *The Times* of London reported that fourteen church study groups in Woodford looked at the Old Testament psalms and concluded that eighty-four of them were "not fit for Christians to sing" ("Psalms Chosen from New Testament" [23 August 1962], sec. 1, p. 10). They reasoned that the wrath and vengeance reflected in those psalms was not compatible with the Christian gospel of love and grace.

But Scripture makes clear that justice, wrath, and judgment are as much divine attributes as are love, mercy, and grace. In chapters 27-28 of Deuteronomy, more than fifty verses detail God's judgment on those who violate His commandments. In response to Jeremiah's plea for vengeance against his enemies, God said,

> "Behold, I am about to bring a calamity upon this place, at which the ears of everyone that hears of it will tingle. Because they have forsaken Me and have made this an alien place and have burned sacrifices in it to other gods that neither they nor their forefathers nor the kings of Judah had ever known, and because they have filled this place with the blood of the innocent and have built the high places of Baal to burn their sons in the fire as burnt offerings to Baal, a thing which I never commanded or spoke of, nor did it ever enter My mind; therefore, behold, days are coming," declared the Lord, "when this place will no longer be called Topheth or the valley of Ben-hinnom, but rather the valley of Slaughter. And I shall make void the counsel of Judah and Jerusalem in this place, and I shall cause them to fall by the sword before their enemies and by the hand of those who seek their life; and I shall give over their carcasses as food for the birds of the sky and the beasts of the earth." (Jer. 19:3-7)

Isaiah declared, "Behold, the day of the Lord is coming, cruel, with fury and burning anger, to make the land a desolation; and He will exterminate its sinners from it" (Isa. 13:9). Nahum testified that "a jealous and avenging God is the Lord; the Lord is avenging and wrathful. The Lord takes vengeance on His adversaries, and He reserves wrath for His enemies. The Lord is slow to anger and great in power, and the Lord will by no means leave the guilty unpunished" (Nah. 1:2-3).

As was noted in the previous chapter, lest some think that God's wrath and judgment are primarily Old Testament concepts, it should be noted that the New Testament has equally vivid portrayals of those divine attributes. When a group of Pharisees and Sadducees came to John the Baptist for baptism, he dismissed them with the scathing words, "You brood of vipers, who warned you to flee from the wrath to come? Therefore bring forth fruit in keeping with repentance" (Matt. 3:7-8). A short while later he said of Jesus, "He who is coming after me is mightier than I, and I am not fit to remove His sandals; He will baptize you with the Holy Spirit and fire. And His winnowing fork is in His hand, and He will thoroughly clear His threshing floor; and He will gather His wheat into the barn, but He will burn up the chaff with unquenchable fire" (vv. 11-12). On a later occasion John told some enquiring Jews, "He who believes in the Son has eternal life; but he who does not obey the Son shall not see life, but the wrath of God abides on him" (John 3:36).

Jesus was God incarnate and therefore love incarnate, but He spoke more about judgment and hell than anyone else in Scripture. He probably spoke more about those truths than everyone else in the New Testament combined. The Sermon on the Mount is replete with warnings about divine wrath and judgment. "I say to you that everyone who is angry with his brother shall be guilty before the court," Jesus said; "and whoever shall say to his brother, 'Raca,' shall be guilty before the supreme court; and whoever shall say, 'You fool,' shall be guilty enough to go in to the fiery hell" (Matt. 5:22). "And if your right eye makes you stumble," He said, "tear it out, and throw it from you; for it is better for you that one of the parts of your body perish, than for your whole body to be thrown into hell. And if your right hand makes you stumble, cut it off, and throw it from you; for it is better for you that one of the parts of your body perish, than for your whole body to go into hell" (vv. 29-30). He declared that "the sons of the kingdom [unbelieving Jews] shall be cast out into the outer darkness; in that place there shall be weeping and gnashing of teeth" (8:12).

As He sent out the Twelve to witness in Israel, Jesus told them, "Whoever does not receive you, nor heed your words, as you go out of that house or that city, shake off the dust of your feet. Truly I say to you, it will be more tolerable for the land of Sodom and Gomorrah in the day of judgment, than for that city" (Matt. 10:14-15). Later during that same time of instruction He said, "Do not fear those who kill the body, but are unable to kill the soul; but rather fear Him who is able to destroy both soul and body in hell" (v. 28). He warned the multitudes "that every careless word that men shall speak, they shall render account for it in the day of judgment. For by your words you shall be justified, and by your words you shall be condemned" (Matt. 12:36-37; cf. vv. 41-42; see also 13:40, 49; 16:26; 18:34-35; 22:13; 23:33; 24:50-51; 25:26-30).

Paul declared that it is because of "the fear of the Lord [that] we persuade men" (2 Cor. 5:11). In other words, it is because of God's fearful judgment on unbelieving mankind that we should be motivated to witness to God's provision of escape through Jesus Christ. Luke reports that when Paul began to speak about "righteousness, self-control and the judgment to come, Felix [the governor] became frightened" (Acts 24:25). Paul warned the Ephesian church: "Let no one deceive you with empty words, for because of these things the wrath of God comes upon the sons of disobedience" (Eph. 5:6). The same apostle warned unbelievers: "Because of your stubbornness and unrepentant heart you are storing up wrath for yourself in the day of wrath and revelation of the righteous judgment of God" (Rom. 2:5; cf. vv. 8-9, 16).

The author of Hebrews declared, "For if we go on sinning willfully after receiving the knowledge of the truth, there no longer remains a sacrifice for sins, but a certain terrifying expectation of judgment, and the fury of a fire which will consume the adversaries" (Heb. 10:26-27). "For if those did not escape when they refused him who warned them on earth," the writer says later, "much less shall we escape who turn away from Him who warns from heaven" (12:25).

In his vision from Patmos, the apostle John heard an angel warn unbelievers, "If anyone worships the beast and his image, and receives a mark on his forehead or upon his hand, he also will drink of the wine of the wrath of God, which is mixed in full strength in the cup of His anger; and he will be tormented with fire and brimstone in the presence of the holy angels and in the presence of the Lamb. And the smoke of their torment goes up forever and ever; and they have no rest day and night" (Rev. 14:9-11).

The New Testament ends with the somber warning from the Lord Himself:

> Blessed are those who wash their robes, that they may have the right to the tree of life, and may enter by the gates into the city. Outside are the dogs and the sorcerers and the immoral persons and the murderers and the idolaters, and everyone who loves and practices lying. . . . I testify to everyone who hears the words of the prophecy of this book: if anyone adds to them, God shall add to him the plagues which are written in this book; and if anyone takes away from the words of the book of this prophecy, God shall take away his part from the tree of life and from the holy city, which are written in this book. (Rev. 22:14-15, 18-19)

People today, as in times past, deny that God is wrathful, and those denials come in two basic forms. One teaches such ideas as soul sleep, the notion that an unbeliever simply goes into eternal sleep at death, without suffering any sort of conscious punishment. The other form of denial is universalism, which teaches that ultimately God will save everyone. But both of those heresies directly contradict God's Word.

Four cautions are in order in regard to spurious teachings about God's wrath. First, we should be aware of the great appeal to the natural man of such concepts as unconscious soul sleep and universalism, both of which deny God's judgment and wrath. Second, we should recognize the pervasive influence of Christian liberalism, which views God as being too loving to condemn anyone and necessarily denies the authenticity of the texts that state otherwise. Third, we should realize that religious groups that deny God's wrath are frequently cultic. And fourth, we should remember that denial of God's wrath removes the purpose and motivation for witnessing, namely, the God-glorifying salvation of unbelievers from sin and hell.

Bible teacher R. A. Torrey wisely wrote: "Shallow views of sin and of God's holiness, and of the glory of Jesus Christ and His claims upon us, lie at the bottom of weak theories of the doom of the impenitent. When we see sin in all its hideousness and enormity, the Holiness of God in all its perfection, and the glory of Jesus Christ in all its infinity, nothing but a doctrine that those who persist in the choice of sin, who love darkness rather than light, and who persist in the rejection of the Son of God, shall endure everlasting anguish, will satisfy the demands of our own moral intuitions. . . . The more closely men walk with God and the more devoted they become to His service, the more likely they are to believe this doctrine" (*What the Bible Teaches* [New York: Revell, 1898], pp. 311-13).

Throughout the history of the church, faithful men of God have understood and proclaimed the biblical truths that God is a God of justice and judgment and that His wrath is against all unbelief and ungodliness. That knowledge was the great motivation for their tireless service in winning the lost. John Knox pleaded before God, "Give me Scotland or I die." As the young Hudson Taylor contemplated the fate of the unreached multitudes of China, he earnestly prayed, "I feel that I cannot go on living unless I do something for China." Upon landing in India, Henry Martyn said, "Here I am in the midst of heathen midnight and savage oppression. Now, my dear Lord, let me burn out for Thee." Adoniram Judson, the famed missionary to Burma, spent long, tiresome years translating the Bible for that people. He was eventually put into prison because of his work, and while there his wife died. After being released, he contracted a serious disease that sapped what little energy he had left. Nevertheless he prayed, "Lord, let me finish my work. Spare me long enough to put the saving Word into the hands of the people." James Chalmers, a Scottish missionary to the South Sea Islands, was so burdened for the lost that someone wrote of him, "In Christ's service he endured hardness, hunger, shipwreck and exhausting toil, and did it all joyfully. He risked his life a thousand times and finally was clubbed to death, beheaded, and eaten by men whose friend he was and whom he sought to enlighten." Although he was unable to go overseas, Robert Arthington enabled countless others to go. By working hard and living frugally he managed to give over $500,000 to the work of foreign missions. He testified, "Gladly would I make the floor my bed, a box my chair, and another box my table, rather than that men should perish for want of the knowledge of Christ."

Those faithful saints, and many others like them, have clearly understood the wrath and the judgment of God and the consequent horror of men dying without Christ. Without such understanding there is no basis for evangelism. If men are not lost, hopeless, and incapable of glorifying God apart from Christ, there is no reason for them to be saved by Him.

The biblical order in any gospel presentation is always first the warning of danger and then the way of escape, first the judgment on sin and then the means of pardon, first the message of condemnation and then the offer of forgiveness, first the bad news of guilt and then the good news of grace. The whole message and purpose of the loving, redeeming grace of God offering eternal life through Jesus Christ rests upon the reality of man's universal guilt of abandoning God and thereby being under His sentence of eternal condemnation and death.

Consistent with that approach, the main body of Romans begins with 1:18, a clear affirmation of God's wrath "against all ungodliness and unrighteousness of men." As the apostle points out in his Ephesian letter, all unbelievers are "by nature children of wrath" (2:3), born unto God's wrath as their natural inheritance in fallen mankind. With the Fall, God's smile turned to a frown. Moses rhetorically asked God, "Who understands the power of Thine anger, and Thy fury, according to the fear that is due Thee?" (Ps. 90:11).

The Puritan writer Thomas Watson said, "As the love of God makes every bitter thing sweet, so the curse of God makes every sweet thing bitter" (*A Body of Divinity* [Carlisle, Pa.: Banner of Truth, 1983 reprint], p. 151). A more contemporary writer, George Rogers, said that God's "righteous anger never rises, never abates: it is always at flood tide in the presence of sin because He is unchangeably and inflexibly righteous" (*Studies in Paul's Epistle to the Romans*, vol. 1 [Los Angeles: G. Rogers, 1936], p. 40).

How could One who delights only in what is pure and lovely not loathe what is impure and ugly? How could He who is infinitely holy disregard sin, which by its very nature violates that holiness? How could He who loves righteousness not hate and act severely against all unrighteousness? How could He who is the sum of all excellency look with complacency on virtue and vice equally? He *cannot* do those things, because He is holy, just, and good. Wrath is the only just response a perfectly holy God could make to unholy men. Righteous wrath therefore is every bit as much an element of God's divine perfection as any other of His attributes, as Paul makes quite clear in Romans 9:22-23 (see comments on that text).

Paul is determined for us to know that before we can understand the grace of God we must first understand His wrath, that before we can understand the meaning of the death of Christ we must first understand why man's sin made that death necessary, that before we can begin to comprehend how loving, merciful, and gracious God is we must first see how rebellious, sinful, and guilty unbelieving mankind is.

Tragically, even many evangelicals have come to soft-pedal the theme of God's wrath and judgment. Even so much as a minimum mention of hell has been quietly removed from much preaching. Wrath, when mentioned at all, is frequently depersonalized, as if somehow it is worked out automatically by some deistic operation in which God Himself is not directly involved.

Many are inclined to wonder if man really deserves such a harsh fate. After all, no person asks to be born. Why, then, they surmise, should a person who had nothing to do with his own birth spend eternity in hell for being born sinful? The question, "Why is *everyone* born under God's wrath and condemnation?" deserves attention. It is those very questions that Paul answers in Romans 1:19-23, where he explains why God is justified in His wrath against all sinful men.

Some people, even some pagans, have recognized God's right to be angry at man's sin. During the priesthood of Eli, while the young Samuel still served under him in the Temple, Israel had reached a low spiritual level. There was religious tokenism but little genuine faith or obedience. Thinking to use the ark of the covenant much as a magic charm to assure their victory, Israel took it into battle against the Philistines. But Israel not only lost 30,000 men in the battle but also lost the ark of the covenant to the enemy. After suffering numerous disastrous and embarrassing experiences with the ark, the Philistines decided to return it to Israel. When they returned it, they sent along a guilt offering to assuage the anger of God against them. Although their understanding of Israel's God was faulty and the offering they presented to Him was thoroughly pagan, they nevertheless recognized His power and His right to judge and punish them as being guilty of violating His honor (see 1 Sam. 4-6).

When Achan stole some of the booty from Jericho, all of which was to be given to the Tabernacle treasury, his sin caused Israel to be defeated at Ai. When his disobedience was exposed, he readily confessed, saying, "Truly, I have sinned against the Lord, the God Israel" (Josh. 7:20).

God is absolutely just, never condemning unless condemnation is deserved. Achan knew God's law given through Moses and he knew of God's special ban on taking the spoil from Jericho for personal use. The pagan Philistines, on the other hand, knew only of God's tremendous power. But Achan and the Philistines both knew they were guilty before God and deserved His wrath. In Romans 1:19-23, Paul gives four reasons why they, and every person born except Jesus Christ, fully deserve to be under God's wrath. Those reasons may be identified as God's revelation, man's rejection, man's rationalization, and man's religion.

GOD'S REVELATION

because that which is known about God is evident within them, for God made it evident to them. For since the creation of the world His invisible attributes, His eternal power and divine nature, have been clearly seen, being understood through what has been made, so that they are without excuse. (1:19-20)

First of all God is justified in His wrath against sinners because of the revelation of Himself to all mankind. Romans 1:18–2:16 pertains especially to Gentiles, who did not have the benefit of God's revealed Word as did Israel. Israel, of course, was doubly guilty, because she not only rejected God's natural, universal revelation of Himself in creation and conscience but even rejected His unique written revelation through Scripture.

THE GIFT OF REVELATION

because that which is known about God is evident within them, for God made it evident to them. (1:19)

Paul's point here is that, even apart from His written revelation, **that which is known about God is evident within** even pagan Gentiles, **for God made it evident to them.** The Lord testifies through Paul that His outward, visible manifestation of Himself is universally known by man. It **is evident within them** as well as without them. *All* men have evidence of God, and what their physical senses can perceive of Him their inner senses can understand to some extent. The Philistines both saw and acknowledged God's power, as did the Canaanites, the Egyptians, and every other people who have lived on earth. The rebels who built the tower of Babel both saw and acknowledged God's greatness, as did the wicked inhabitants of Sodom and Gomorrah. All men know something and understand something of the reality and the truth of God. They are responsible for a proper response to that revelation. Any wrong response is "inexcusable."

Theologian Augustus Strong wrote, "The Scriptures . . . both assume and declare that the knowledge that God is, is universal (Rom.

1:19-21, 28, 32; 2:15). God has inlaid the evidence of [that] fundamental truth in the very nature of man, so that nowhere is He without a witness" (*Systematic Theology* [Valley Forge, Pa.: Judson, 1979 reprint], p. 68). Unregenerate man has "no help and [is] without God in the world" (Eph. 2:12), not because he has no knowledge of God but because he naturally rebels against the knowledge of God that he has. As Paul has already attested (Rom. 1:18), sinful mankind naturally suppresses God's truth with his own unrighteousness.

No one can find God on his own initiative or by his own wisdom or searching. Yet God has never left man to his own initiative and understanding but has graciously provided abundant evidence of Himself. He has sovereignly and universally **made** Himself **evident to** men. No person, therefore, can plead ignorance of God, because, entirely apart from Scripture, God has *always* revealed Himself and continues to reveal Himself to man. God is perfectly just and therefore could not rightly condemn those who are totally ignorant of Him. As Paul unequivocally asserts here, no person can rightly claim ignorance of God, and therefore no person can rightly claim that God's wrath against him is unjust. Every person is accountable for the revelation of God that may lead one to salvation.

Tertullian, the prominent early church Father, said that it was not the pen of Moses that initiated the knowledge of the Creator. The vast majority of mankind, though they had never heard the name of Moses— to say nothing of his book—know the God of Moses nonetheless (cf. *An Answer to the Jews*, chap. 2).

A disease left Helen Keller as a very young girl without sight, hearing, and speech. Through Anne Sullivan's tireless and selfless efforts, Helen finally learned to communicate through touch and even learned to talk. When Miss Sullivan first tried to tell Helen about God, the girl's response was that she already knew about Him—just didn't know His name (Helen Keller, *The Story of My Life* [New York: Grosset & Dunlap, 1905], pp. 368-74).

That which is known could be rendered "that which is knowable." Obviously, finite man cannot know everything about God even with the perfect revelation of Scripture. Paul's point is that **that which is** capable of being **known about God** apart from special revelation is indeed known by fallen mankind. The characteristics of God that are reflected in His creation give unmistakable testimony to Him.

While ministering in Lystra, Paul told his Gentile audience about the God "who made the heaven and the earth and the sea, and all that is in them." He went on to explain that "in the generations gone by [God] permitted all the nations to go their own ways; and yet He did not leave Himself without witness, in that He did good and gave you rains from heaven and fruitful seasons, satisfying your hearts with food and gladness" (Acts 14:15-17). The very goodness of life testifies to the goodness of the God who provides it.

On his next journey Paul told the pagan philosophers on Mars Hill at Athens,

> While I was passing through and examining the objects of your worship, I also found an altar with this inscription, "TO AN UNKNOWN GOD." What therefore you worship in ignorance, this I proclaim to you.
> The God who made the world and all things in it, since He is Lord of heaven and earth, does not dwell in temples made with hands; neither is He served by human hands, as though He needed anything, since He Himself gives to all life and breath and all things; and He made from one, every nation of mankind to live on all the face of the earth, having determined their appointed times, and the boundaries of their habitation, that they should seek God, if perhaps they might grope for Him and find Him, though He is not far from each one of us; for in Him we live and move and exist. (Acts 17:23-28)

In other words, God controls the nations, their boundaries, and their destinies. He controls time, the seasons, and every other aspect both of heaven and earth. Even more remarkable than that, Paul says, because God has graciously chosen to make Himself known and approachable, "He is not far from each one of us."

John speaks of Jesus Christ as "the true light which, coming into the world, enlightens every man" (John 1:9). He was not speaking about the saving knowledge of God, which comes only through faith, but of the intellectual knowledge of God, which comes to every human being through God's self-manifestation in His creation. Every person has a witness of God, and therefore every person is accountable to follow the opportunity to respond to Him in faith.

THE CONTENT OF REVELATION

For since the creation of the world His invisible attributes, His eternal power and divine nature, have been clearly seen, being understood through what has been made, so that they are without excuse. (1:20)

Next Paul specifies the content of the revelation of Himself that God makes known to all mankind. **Since the creation of the world**, he declares, God has made His **invisible attributes** visible. The particular

attributes that man can perceive in part through his natural senses are God's **eternal power and** His **divine nature.** God's **eternal power** refers to His never-failing omnipotence, which is reflected in the awesome creation which that **power** both brought into being and sustains. God's **divine nature** of kindness and graciousness is reflected, as Paul told the Lystrans, in the "rains from heaven and fruitful seasons, satisfying your hearts with food and gladness" (Acts 14:17).

The noted theologian Charles Hodge testified, "God therefore has never left himself without a witness. His existence and perfections have ever been so manifested that his rational creatures are bound to acknowledge and worship him as the true and only God" (*Commentary on the Epistle to the Romans* [Grand Rapids: Eerdmans, 1983 reprint], p. 37).

God's natural revelation of Himself is not obscure or selective, observable only by a few perceptive souls who are specially gifted. His revelation of Himself through creation can be **clearly seen** by everyone, **being understood through what has been made.**

Even in the most ancient of times, long before the telescope and microscope were invented, the greatness of God was evident both in the vastness and in the tiny intricacies of nature. Men could look at the stars and discover the fixed order of their orbits. They could observe a small seed reproduce itself into a giant tree, exactly like the one from which it came. They could see the marvelous cycles of the seasons, the rain, and the snow. They witnessed the marvel of human birth and the glory of the sunrise and sunset. Even without the special revelation David had, they could see that "the heavens are telling of the glory of God; and their expanse is declaring the work of His hands" (Ps. 19:1).

Some birds are able to navigate by the stars. Even if hatched and raised in a windowless building, if shown an artificial sky, they immediately are able to orient themselves to the proper place to which to migrate. The archerfish is able to fire drops of water with amazing force and accuracy, knocking insects out of the air. The bombardier beetle separately produces two different chemicals, which, when released and combined, explode in the face of an enemy. Yet the explosion never occurs prematurely and never harms the beetle itself. No wonder David declared that "power belongs to God" (Ps. 62:11) and that Asaph (Ps. 79:11) and Nahum (1:3) spoke of the greatness of His power.

Robert Jastrow, an astrophysicist and director of NASA's Goddard Institute for Space Studies, has said:

> Now we see how the astronomical evidence supports the biblical view of the origin of the world. . . . The essential elements in the astronomical and biblical accounts of Genesis are the same. Consider the enormousness of the problem: Science has proved that the universe exploded into being

at a certain moment. It asks what cause produced this effect? Who or what put the matter and energy into the Universe? And science cannot answer these questions . . .

For the scientist who has lived by his faith in the power of reason, the story ends like a bad dream. He has scaled the mountains of ignorance; he is about to conquer the highest peak; as he pulls himself over the final rock, he is greeted by a band of theologians who have been there for centuries. (*God and the Astronomers* [New York: Norton, 1978], pp. 14, 114, 116)

With giant telescopes such as the 200 inch-diameter instrument at Mount Palomar in California astronomers can observe objects 4 billion light years away, a distance of more than 25 septillion miles! (James Reid, *God, the Atom, and the Universe* [Grand Rapids: Zondervan], 1968).

At any given time, there are an average of 1,800 storms in operation in the world. The energy needed to generate those storms amounts to the incredible figure of 1,300,000,000 horsepower. By comparison, a large earth-moving machine has 420 horsepower and requires a hundred gallons of fuel a day to operate. Just one of those storms, producing a rain of four inches over an area of ten thousand square miles, would require energy equivalent to the burning of 640,000,000 tons of coal to evaporate enough water for such a rain. And to cool those vapors and collect them in clouds would take another 800,000,000 horsepower of refrigeration working night and day for a hundred days.

Agricultural studies have determined that the average farmer in Minnesota gets 407,510 gallons of rainwater per acre per year, free of charge, of course. The state of Missouri has some 70,000 square miles and averages 38 inches of rain a year. That amount of water is equal to a lake 250 miles long, 60 miles wide, and 22 feet deep.

The U. S. Natural Museum has determined that there are at least 10 million species of insects, including some 2,500 varieties of ants. There are about 5 billion birds in the United States, among which some species are able to fly 500 miles non-stop across the Gulf of Mexico. Mallard ducks can fly 60 miles an hour, eagles 100 miles an hour, and falcons can dive at speeds of 180 miles an hour.

The earth is 25,000 miles in circumference, weighs 6 septillion, 588 sextillion tons, and hangs unsupported in space. It spins at 1,000 miles per hour with absolute precision and careens through space around the sun at the speed of 1,000 miles per minute in an orbit 580 million miles long.

The head of a comet may be from 10,000 to 1,000,000 miles long, have a tail 100,000,000 miles long, and travel at a speed of 350 miles per second. If the sun's radiated energy could be converted into horsepower, it would be the equivalent of 500 million, million, billion horsepower. Each second it consumes some 4 million tons of matter. To travel at the speed of light (ca. 186,281 miles per second) across the Milky Way, the galaxy in which our solar system is located, would take 125,000 years. And our galaxy is but one of millions.

The human heart is about the size of its owner's fist. An adult heart weighs less than half a pound, yet can do enough work in twelve hours to lift 65 tons one inch off the ground. A water molecule is composed of only three atoms. But if all the molecules in one drop of water were the size of a grain of sand, they could make a road one foot thick and a half mile wide that would stretch from Los Angeles to New York. Amazingly, however, the atom itself is largely space, its actual matter taking up only one trillionth of its volume.

Except to a mind willfully closed to the obvious, it is inconceivable that such power, intricacy, and harmony could have developed by any means but that of a Master Designer who rules the universe. It would be infinitely more reasonable to think that the separate pieces of a watch could be shaken in a bag and eventually become a dependable timepiece than to think that the world could have evolved into its present state by blind chance.

Even a pagan should be able to discern with the psalmist that surely the One who made the ear and the eye is Himself able to hear and to see (see Ps. 94:9). If we can hear, then whoever made us surely must understand hearing and seeing. If we, His creatures, can think, then surely the mind of our Creator must be able to reason.

Men are judged and sent to hell not because they do not live up to the light evidenced in the universe but because ultimately that rejection leads them to reject Jesus Christ. The Holy Spirit "will convict the world concerning sin, and righteousness, and judgment," Jesus said; "concerning sin, because they do not believe in Me" (John 16:8-9). But if a person lives up to the light of the revelation he has, God will provide for his hearing the gospel by some means or another. In His sovereign, predetermined grace He reaches out to sinful mankind. "As I live!" declared the Lord through Ezekiel, "I take no pleasure in the death of the wicked, but rather that the wicked turn from his way and live" (Ezek. 33:11). God does not desire "for any to perish but for all to come to repentance" (2 Pet. 3:9). He will give His elect the privilege of hearing the gospel and will bring them to Himself. "You will seek Me and find me," the Lord promised through Jeremiah, "when you search for Me with all your heart" (Jer. 29:13).

Because the Ethiopian eunuch was sincerely seeking God, the Holy Spirit sent Philip to witness to him. Upon hearing the gospel, he believed and was baptized (Acts 8:26-39). Because Cornelius, a Gentile centurion in the Roman army, was "a devout man, and one who feared

God with all his household, and gave many alms to the Jewish people, and prayed to God continually," God sent Peter to him to explain the gospel. "While Peter was still speaking, . . . the Holy Spirit fell upon all those who were listening to the message," and they were "baptized in the name of Jesus Christ" (Acts 10:2, 44, 48). Because Lydia was a true worshiper of God, when she heard the gospel, "the Lord opened her heart to respond to the things spoken by Paul" (Acts. 16:14).

MAN'S REJECTION

For even though they knew God, they did not honor Him as God, or give thanks; but they became futile in their speculations, and their foolish heart was darkened. (1:21)

God is also justified in His wrath and judgment because of man's willful rejection of Him. Paul explicitly declares that **though they knew God** through this natural, general revelation, unbelieving men still rejected Him. Although man is innately conscious of God's existence and power, he is just as innately and wickedly inclined to reject that knowledge. The natural tendency of unregenerate mankind is to "proceed from bad to worse, deceiving and being deceived" (2 Tim. 3:13). As Paul reminds believers, "We also once were foolish ourselves, disobedient, deceived, enslaved to various lusts and pleasures, spending our life in malice and envy, hateful, hating one another" (Titus 3:3).

A certain evolutionist said, "I refuse to believe in God, so what other alternative do I have but evolution?" The man was honest, but he gave clear testimony to the fact that it was not evidence for evolution that led him to disbelief in God but rather his disbelief in God that led him to embrace evolution.

Donald Grey Barnhouse made this potent observation:

> Will God give man brains to see these things and will man then fail to exercise his will toward that God? The sorrowful answer is that both of these things are true. God will give a man brains to smelt iron and make a hammer head and nails. God will grow a tree and give man strength to cut it down and brains to fashion a hammer handle from its wood. And when man has the hammer and the nails, God will put out His hand and let man drive nails through it and place Him on a cross in the supreme demonstration that men are without excuse. (*Romans,* vol. 1 [Grand Rapids: Eerdmans, 1953], p. 245)

In verse 21, Paul mentions four ways in which men exhibit their rejection of God: by dishonoring Him, by being thankless to Him, by being futile in their speculations concerning Him, and by being darkened in their hearts about Him.

First, man fails to **honor** God **as God.** This is the basic expression of the root sin of pride which is at the core of man's fallenness. *Doxazō* (**honor**) is probably better translated here as *glory,* as it is in numerous versions. The worst deed committed in the universe is failure to give God **honor,** or glory. Above everything else, God is to be glorified. To glorify God is to exalt Him, to recognize Him as supremely worthy of honor, and to acknowledge His divine attributes. Since the glory of God is also the sum of all the attributes of His being, of all He has revealed of Himself to man, to give God glory is to acknowledge His glory and extol it. We cannot give Him glory by adding to His perfection, but by praising His perfection. We glorify Him by praising His glory!

Scripture continually calls upon believers to glorify the Lord. David admonishes us: "Ascribe to the Lord glory and strength. Ascribe to the Lord the glory due to His name" (Ps. 29:1-2). "Whether, then, you eat or drink or whatever you do," Paul says, "do all to the glory of God" (1 Cor. 10:31). One day the twenty-four elders will fall down before Christ on His heavenly throne and declare, "Worthy art Thou, our Lord and our God, to receive glory and honor and power; for Thou didst create all things, and because of Thy will they existed, and were created" (Rev. 4:11).

As the *Westminster Shorter Catechism* eloquently declares, "The chief end of man is to glorify God and to enjoy Him forever." Man was created to glorify God (see Lev. 10:3; 1 Chron. 16:24-29; Ps. 148; Rom. 15:5-6), and for him to fail to give God glory is therefore the ultimate affront to his Creator.

After they were created in God's own image, Adam and Eve continually experienced God's presence and glory. They communed directly with Him and they praised Him and acknowledged His glory and honor. But when they sinned by disobeying God's command and seeking to gain glory and honor for themselves, they "hid themselves from the presence of the Lord God among the trees of the garden" (Gen. 3:8). Sin brought separation from God, and Adam and Eve no longer sought God's presence or yearned to bring Him glory. Ever since that time, fallen man has sought to avoid God and to deny His glory and even His very existence.

Throughout Scripture, God has revealed many elements of His glory. When Moses asked to see God's glory, the Lord manifested His *goodness, graciousness,* and *compassion,* saying, "I Myself will make all My goodness pass before you, and will proclaim the name of the Lord before you; and I will be gracious to whom I will be gracious, and will show compassion on whom I will show compassion" (Ex. 33:19). The Lord placed Moses in the cleft of the rock and covered him with His hand, lest he see His full glory and be consumed. He then allowed Moses to view Him partially from behind as He passed by. As God presented Himself before Moses, He also gave a litany of His divine attributes, declaring, "The Lord, the Lord God, *compassionate* and *gracious, slow to anger,* and abounding in *lovingkindness* and *truth;* who keeps lovingkindness for thousands, who *forgives* iniquity, transgression and sin" (Ex. 33:20–34:7; emphasis added).

Although He had delivered them from bondage in Egypt and given them His holy law by which to live, the people persistently rebelled against God and against His appointed leader, Moses. Yet God continued to manifest His glory to His chosen people. After the Tabernacle was built, the Lord filled it with His glory as the sign of His divine presence with His people (Ex. 40:34). As Israel moved about in the wilderness for forty years, God manifested His presence and His glory through the pillar of cloud that guided them by day and the pillar of fire that reassured them by night (vv. 36-38). After the Temple was built by Solomon, the cloud of the Lord's glory filled the holy place there (1 Kings 8:11). Yet Israel continued to rebel against the Lord through countless kinds of false worship (see Ezek. 8:4-18). When she persistently refused to turn from her sin, God's glory eventually departed from the Temple (Ezek. 11:22-23), and at that point the theocratic kingdom of Israel came to an end.

The glory of God did not return to earth until Messiah came. As the veiled incarnation of God's glory, Jesus Christ manifested divine glory through His *grace* and *truth* (John 1:14). On the Mount of Transfiguration, Jesus presented Himself before Peter, James, and John in a unique manifestation of His royal *splendor* (Matt. 17:2). Paul pointed up the *power* of God's glory when he declared that "Christ was raised from the dead through the glory of the Father," (Rom. 6:4). In less dramatic but just as certain ways, Jesus was a living testimony to God's glory through His miracles and through His *love, truth, mercy, kindness,* and *grace.*

The rest of the created world, however, has never revolted against God or sought to hide His glory as has man. As already cited, David exulted that "the heavens are telling of the glory of God, and their expanse is declaring the work of His hands" (Ps. 19:1). Psalm 148 calls on the entire universe to proclaim God's glory. The animals do just what God has created them to do. The flowers bloom just as God designed them to, and the butterfly gently and beautifully flies from place to place, testifying to God's beauty and order.

But recognizing God's glorious attributes and acts and glorifying Him for them is precisely what fallen men do *not* do. Millions upon millions of people have lived in the midst of God's wonderful universe and yet proudly refused to recognize Him as its Creator and to affirm His majesty and glory. And for that willful, foolish rejection they are without excuse as they stand under God's righteous judgment. The person who can live in the midst of God's marvelous creation and yet refuse to recognize Him as its Creator and affirm His majesty and glory is a fool indeed.

Through Jeremiah, the Lord warned His people, "Listen and give heed, do not be haughty, for the Lord has spoken. Give glory to the Lord your God, before He brings darkness and before your feet stumble on the dusky mountains, and while you are hoping for light He makes it into deep darkness, and turns it into gloom" (Jer. 13:15-16). When King Herod proudly accepted the crowd's acclamation that he spoke "with the voice of a god and not of a man, . . . immediately an angel of the Lord struck him because he did not give God the glory, and he was eaten by worms and died" (Acts 12:22-23).

When Christ returns to earth, "the sun will be darkened, and the moon will not give its light, and the stars will fall from the sky, and the powers of the heavens will be shaken" (Matt. 24:29). And at that moment, when all the natural lights of the universe are extinguished, the dazzling divine light of God's eternal glory in His Son will illumine the entire earth. "Then the sign of the Son of Man will appear in the sky, and then all the tribes of the earth will mourn, and they will see the Son of Man coming on the clouds of the sky with power and great glory" (v. 30).

Second, because man in his pride fails to honor and glorify God as Creator, he also fails to **give thanks** to Him for His gracious provision. His unbelief is made still worse by his ingratitude. Although God is the source of every good thing that men possess — giving rain, sun, and other natural blessings to the just and unjust alike (see Matt. 5:45; Acts 14:15-17) — the natural man fails to thank Him because he fails even to acknowledge His existence.

Third, as a consequence of their failing to honor and thank God, fallen men have become **futile in their speculations.** To reject God is to reject the greatest reality in the universe, the reality which gives the only true meaning, purpose, and understanding to everything else. Refusing to recognize God and to have His truth guide their minds, sinful men are doomed to **futile** quests for wisdom through various human **speculations** that lead only to falsehood and therefore to still greater unbelief and wickedness. The term **speculation** embraces all man's godless reasonings.

To forsake God is to exchange truth for falsehood, meaning for hopelessness, and satisfaction for emptiness. But an empty mind and soul is like a vacuum. It will not long remain empty but will draw in falsehood and darkness to replace the truth and light it has rejected. The history of fallen mankind is devolutionary, not evolutionary. The **foolish heart** that rejects and dishonors God does not become enlightened and freed, as sophisticated unbelievers like to claim, but rather becomes spiritually **darkened** and further enslaved to sin. The person who forsakes God forsakes truth, light, and eternal life, as well as meaning, purpose, and happiness. He also forsakes the foundation and motivation for moral righteousness.

Spiritual darkness and moral perversity are inseparable. When man forfeits God, he forfeits virtue. The godless philosophy of the world inescapably leads to moral perversion, because unbelief and immorality are inextricably intertwined. "See to it that no one takes you captive through philosophy and empty deception," Paul warned the Colossians, "according to the tradition of men, according to the elementary principles of the world, rather than according to Christ" (Col. 2:8).

When the incarnation of truth and light came into the world, unbelieving mankind would not have Him. Because Jesus was the light of the world, they rejected Him, because their deeds were evil and they loved darkness rather than light (John 3:19-20). For the very reason that Jesus spoke the truth, they would not believe Him (John 8:45). That is the legacy of man's refusal to glorify God.

Reasons for the Wrath of God— part 2

Professing to be wise, they became fools, and exchanged the glory of the incorruptible God for an image in the form of corruptible man and of birds and four-footed animals and crawling creatures. (1:22-23)

In Romans 1:19-23 Paul describes the character of fallen man. He gives four reasons why *everyone* is born under God's wrath and condemnation. The first two reasons, God's revelation and man's rejection, are presented in verses 19-21 and were discussed in the previous chapter. The third and fourth reasons, man's rationalization and man's religion, are presented in verses 22-23.

MAN'S RATIONALIZATION

Professing to be wise, they became fools, (1:22)

In rejecting God's clear revelation of Himself through His creation, men failed to honor and glorify God, failed to give Him thanks, became futile in their philosophical speculations, and became foolish and darkened in their hearts (vv. 19-21). Trying to justify themselves, they rationalized their sin, just as fallen mankind still does today. **Professing to be wise** about God, about the universe, and about themselves, **they became** still greater **fools** (see v. 21d).

Centuries earlier, David had declared that men who deny God and His truth are fools (Ps. 14:1; 53:1), and it is that very foolishness that deludes them into thinking they are **wise.** The natural man cannot think perfectly about anything. But his thinking is perverted most severely in the spiritual and divine realm, because that is where his sinful rebellion is centered. These things are also beyond his human perception and since he rejects revelation, he has no hope of coming to truth in himself. His foolish speculations therefore go the furthest astray when he philosophizes about his origin, purpose, and destiny and about the origin and meaning of the universe in which he lives.

The mind devoid of God's truth has no way to discriminate between truth and falsehood, between right and wrong, between the significant and the trivial, between the truly beautiful and the monstrous, or between the ephemeral and the eternal.

These dominating worldly speculations often infect the church. Because, for example, gifted and articulate unbelievers have so long and loudly touted evolution as scientific fact rather than philosophical theory, many Christians have been intimidated into accommodating their theology accordingly. In the name of theistic evolution or progressive creationism, they not only compromise scientific integrity but also, and infinitely more disastrously, compromise God's revelation. They accept the unfounded foolishness of unregenerate men above the flawless truth of God's Word.

In a similar approach, many Christians try to adapt God's revelation to men's speculations in the areas of the mind and soul. Intimidated by the ever-changing and mutually-conflicting theories of psychology, sociology, and anthropology, they foolishly modify or exchange the truths of God's revelation about man in favor of man's absurd conjectures about himself.

The late Martyn Lloyd Jones perceptively wrote, "The whole drift toward modernism that has blighted the church of God and nearly destroyed its living gospel may be traced to an hour when men began to turn from revelation to philosophy." Thinking they are wise, they have become fools because their own speculations can't replace the revelation they reject.

Institution after institution that once firmly stood on God's Word has progressively accommodated itself to the intellectual foolishness of the world system. In the name of man's wisdom they come to reflect the foolishness, and inevitably the godlessness, of the world system of Satan.

Because he knew that "the word of the cross is to those who are perishing foolishness," that "God [has] made foolish the wisdom of the world," and that "the foolishness of God is wiser than men," Paul "determined to know nothing among [those to whom he preached] except Jesus Christ, and Him crucified" (1 Cor. 1:18, 20, 25; 2:2).

The greatest fool in all the world is the person who exchanges God's wisdom of truth and light for man's wisdom of deceit and darkness.

MAN'S RELIGION

and exchanged the glory of the incorruptible God for an image in the form of corruptible man and of birds and four-footed animals and crawling creatures. (1:23)

The fourth reason why every person is born under God's wrath and condemnation is man-made religion, reflected in the countless systems he has devised to replace the truth and the worship of God.

Yet although fallen man is not naturally godly, he is very much naturally religious. According to the 1986 *World Almanac*, approximately 2.6 billion people in the world have an identifiable religious affiliation of some sort. Many more are said to have some form of unidentified religion.

Hindus have some 330 million gods, which amounts to about eight gods per family. They also revere cows and countless other animals that they consider to be sacred. A two-inch-long discolored tooth, claimed to have belonged to Buddha and to have been retrieved from his funeral pyre in 543 B.C., is venerated by millions of Buddhists. The tooth is set in a golden lotus blossom surrounded with rubies and enshrined in the Temple of the Tooth in Sri Lanka.

The beliefs and practices of ritualistic Christianity differ little from such pagan superstitions.

Many humanistic sociologists, philosophers, and theologians maintain that religion is a mark of man's upward climb from primitive chaos and ignorance, ascending through animism to polydemonism to polytheism and finally to monotheism. But the clear testimony of Scripture is that human religion of every sort, whether simple or highly sophisticated, is a downward movement away from God, away from truth, and away from righteousness. Contrary to much thinking, men's religions do not reflect their highest endeavors but their lowest depravity. The natural trend of religion throughout history has not been upward but downward. It has, in fact, descended from monotheism.

That truth is attested even by secular history. Herodotus, the famous Greek historian of the fifth century B.C., said that the earliest Persians had no pagan temples or idols (*The Histories*, 1:31). The first-century Roman scholar Varro reported that the Romans had no animal or human images of a god for 170 years after the founding of Rome (Augustine, *The City of God,* 4:31). Lucian, a second-century A.D. Greek writer, made similar statements concerning early Greece and Egypt (*The Syrian Goddess,* 34). The fourth-century Christian historian Eusebius declared that "the oldest peoples had no idols."

Even many ancient unbelievers recognized the absurdity of worshiping something fashioned by man's own hands. Horace, the Roman poet of the first century B.C., satirized the practice when he wrote, "I was a fig tree's trunk, a useless log. The workman wavered, 'Shall I make a stool or a god?' He chose to make a god, and thus a god I am."

The Apocrypha tells of a woodcutter felling a tree, stripping off its bark, and skillfully fashioning the wood into useful utensils and pieces of furniture. But the same woodcutter would take a gnarled leftover, of no practical value, and fashion it into the likeness of a man or animal, filling in defects with clay and painting over blemishes. After securing the figure to a wall or setting it in a niche so that it would not fall, he would then bow down and worship it, asking protection and health for himself and his family (see Wisdom, 13:11-19).

Even after the Fall, at first "men began to call upon the name of the Lord" (Gen. 4:26), because He was the only deity of which they had any knowledge. The next two chapters of Genesis make clear, however, that merely calling on the name of the true God did not prevent men from falling progressively into worse and worse sin. As ancient Israel proved repeatedly throughout her history, merely knowing about and claiming the true God did not protect her either from sin or from spiritual unbelief and divine judgment. As Jesus clearly asserted in the Sermon on the Mount, simply claiming allegiance to the Lord does not guarantee entrance into His kingdom (Matt. 7:21).

Yet despite the rebellious and unrepentant wickedness of the world before the Flood, there is no evidence that men at that time were idolatrous. The earliest instance of idolatry mentioned in the Bible is that of Abraham's family in Ur (Josh. 24:2). Idolatry had developed sometime previously among some of the descendants of Noah. There is no indication, however, that Noah and his family, as the only survivors of the Flood, even knew of the concept of idolatry when they began to replenish the earth.

But as mankind again turned away from the true God, they began to create substitute gods, probably first only in their imaginations and later with their hands. By the time God brought His people back into the land of Canaan, they discovered idolatry had become as rife there as it was in Egypt. The idolatry of the pagan inhabitants they had disobediently failed to destroy was a continuous threat to Israel until God allowed them to be taken captive to Babylon. Remarkably, however, by His sovereign protection, from that time until now even unbelieving Jews have never again manufactured idols in any significant numbers.

Before the Exile, Isaiah scathingly mocked the wicked foolishness of idolatry that had so corrupted his people:

> Those who fashion a graven image are all of them futile, and their precious things are of no profit; even their own witnesses fail to see or know, so that they will be put to shame. Who has fashioned a god or cast an idol to no profit? Behold, all his companions will be put to shame, for the craftsmen themselves are mere men. Let them all assemble themselves, let them stand up, let them tremble, let them together be put to shame. The man shapes iron into a cutting tool, and does his work over the coals, fashioning it with hammers, and working it with his strong arm. He also gets hungry and his strength fails, he drinks no water and becomes weary. Another shapes wood, he extends a measuring line; he outlines it with red chalk. He works it with planes, and outlines it with a compass, and makes it like the form of a man, like the beauty of man, so that it may sit in a house. Surely he cuts cedars for himself, and takes a cypress or an oak, and raises it for himself among the trees of the forest. He plants a fir, and the rain makes it grow. Then it becomes something for a man to burn, so he takes one of them and warms himself; he also makes a fire to bake bread. He also makes a god and worships it; he makes it a graven image, and falls down before it. Half of it he burns in the fire; over this half he eats meat as he roasts a roast, and is satisfied. He also warms himself and says, "Aha! I am warm, I have seen the fire." But the rest of it he makes into a god, his graven image. He falls down before it and worships; he also prays to it and says, "Deliver me, for thou art my god." (Isa. 44:9-17)

Along with the rebellious, proud, vain, foolish, and darkened Gentiles, many Jews had also **exchanged the glory of the incorruptible God for** that which is inglorious, shameful, and **corruptible**. They substituted the reality of the holy **God** for the vain **image** of every sort of His creatures.

In their spiritual blindness, intellectual darkness, and moral depravity, men are by nature inclined to reject the Holy Creator for the unholy creature. Because something even in their fallenness demands a god, but one they like better than the true God, they devise deities of their own making.

It is not incidental that the Ten Commandments begin with the admonition: "You shall have no other gods before Me. You shall not make for yourself an idol, or any likeness of what is in heaven above or on the earth beneath or in the water under the earth. You shall not worship them or serve them" (Ex. 20:3-5). Yet at the very time those and the other commandments and ordinances were being given to Moses, the children

of Israel were making a golden calf to worship (32:1-6).
Although the Lord continued to warn

> Israel and Judah, through all His prophets and every seer, saying, "Turn
> from your evil ways and keep My commandments, My statutes according to
> all the law which I commanded your fathers, and which I sent to you
> through My servants the prophets," . . . they rejected His statutes and His
> covenant which He made with their fathers, and His warnings with which
> He warned them. And they followed vanity and became vain, and went
> after the nations which surrounded them, concerning which the Lord had
> commanded them not to do like them. And they forsook all the command-
> ments of the Lord their God and made for themselves molten images. (2
> Kings 17:13-16)

Man's rejection of God and embracing of idols can be compared
to a son who murdered his father and then made a dummy figure that
he introduces to the world as his father. Yet what sinful mankind has
always done and continues to do with God is infinitely more wicked and
senseless than that.

The first creature man substitutes for God is himself, **an image
in the form of corruptible man.** Instead of glorifying and worshiping
God, he attempts to deify himself. Although he doubtlessly made this
alleged statement in derisive sarcasm, Voltaire was correct in observing:
"God made man in His own image and man returned the favor."

Every form of idolatry is a form of self-worship, just as every form
of idolatry is a form of demon, or Satan, worship. Whether his idols are
fashioned out of his own depraved thinking or are inspired by Satan,
every false god appeals to man's fallen nature and entices him to glorify
and indulge himself. In one way or another, all idolatry is worship of self
and service of Satan.

The epitome of human self-worship will be that of Antichrist, who
will demand that all the world worship him in the rebuilt Temple in
Jerusalem (2 Thess. 2:3-4). As Satan's supreme emissary on earth in the
last days, Antichrist's demand of worship will also testify that, despite his
self-glorification, his real god will be Satan—just as every idolater's real
god is Satan.

"The things which the Gentiles sacrifice, they sacrifice to demons,"
Paul declared (1 Cor. 10:20). In other words, even though a person may
make an idol of his own design and for his own purposes out of wood,
stone, or metal, demons take advantage of that ungodliness by imper-
sonating the characteristics the man-made god is supposed to have.
Supernatural happenings have been reliably reported in pagan cultures
throughout history and into modern times. Although Satan is limited in

his power over nature and even in his own supernatural realm, Scripture makes clear that he is able to produce his own kinds of miracles, as Pharaoh's sorcerers did before Moses and Aaron (Ex. 7:11, 22; 8:7). Just as Pharaoh's satanically-empowered sorcerers demonstrated enough supernatural ability to keep that ruler's heart hardened, Satan allows enough astrological predictions to come true and enough supernatural events to be manifested to keep his followers deluded (cf. 2 Thess. 2:9).

Nebuchadnezzar was perhaps the greatest monarch of the ancient world. But he became so enamored of his accomplishments that he ignored Daniel's warning and arrogantly declared, "Is this not Babylon the great, which I myself have built as a royal residence by the might of my power and for the glory of my majesty?" As Daniel goes on to report,

> while the word was in the king's mouth, a voice came from heaven, saying "King Nebuchadnezzar, to you it is declared: sovereignty has been removed from you, and you will be driven away from mankind, and your dwelling place will be with the beasts of the field. You will be given grass to eat like cattle, and seven periods of time will pass over you, until you recognize that the Most High is ruler over the realm of mankind, and bestows it on whomever He wishes." Immediately the word concerning Nebuchadnezzar was fulfilled; and he was driven away from mankind and began eating grass like cattle, and his body was drenched with the dew of heaven, until his hair had grown like eagles' feathers and his nails like birds' claws. (Dan. 4:31-33; cf. vv. 19-27)

By exalting himself virtually as a god, the proud king exceeded the limits of God's patience, and in an instant both his power and his sanity were forfeited for "seven periods of time" (see vv. 25, 32), meaning perhaps seven months or even seven years.

"At the end of that period," the king himself reported, "I, Nebuchadnezzar, raised my eyes toward heaven, and my reason returned to me, and I blessed the Most High and praised and honored Him who lives forever" (v. 34). It would seem that his chastisement brought him to believe in God, and he ended his confession with the words, "Now I Nebuchadnezzar praise, exalt, and honor the King of heaven, for all His works are true and His ways just, and He is able to humble those who walk in pride" (v. 37).

Belshazzar, Nebuchadnezzar's successor, learned nothing from his predecessor's experience. One night he gave a lavish banquet for his noblemen, and under the influence of much wine he ordered that the sacred gold vessels that his father had confiscated from the Temple in Jerusalem be used to drink from at the feast. As the revelers drank from those vessels, they "praised the gods of gold and silver, of bronze, iron, wood, and stone. Suddenly the fingers of a man's hand emerged and began writing opposite the lampstand on the plaster of the wall of the king's palace."When the conjurers and diviners of the terrified king could not decipher the message, he appealed to Daniel. After reminding him of Nebuchadnezzar's punishment by God, Daniel told the king, "Yet you, his son, Belshazzar, have not humbled your heart, even though you knew all this, but you have exalted yourself against the Lord of heaven. . . . But the God in whose hand are your life-breath and your ways, you have not glorified. . . . This is the interpretation of the message: 'MENE'—God has numbered your kingdom and put an end to it. 'TEKEL'—you have been weighed on the scales and found deficient. 'PERES'—your kingdom has been divided and given over to the Medes and Persians" (Dan. 5:1-29).

Belshazzar deliberately and openly sinned against the knowledge of God that he had. He even flagrantly blasphemed God by profaning the sacred vessels from His Temple and worshiping man-made idols instead of God. Typical of all sinful men, the king's natural inclination was to turn from the knowledge he had of the true God and to turn to false gods of his own choosing.

A. W. Tozer wisely observed that idolatry begins in the mind when we pervert or exchange the idea of God for something other than what He really is (*The Knowledge of the Holy* [N.Y.: Harper & Row, 1961], pp. 9-10).

An even more ludicrous form of idolatry noted by Paul is the worship **of birds and four-footed animals and crawling creatures.** Among the many **birds** worshiped in the ancient world were the eagle in Rome, and the stork and hawk in Egypt. It was because eagles were often deified by Romans that the Jews so vehemently opposed their being displayed in any form in Israel, especially in the holy city of Jerusalem. Some American Indians still worship various birds, as seen in their totem poles. The stylized Indian thunderbird has become a popular symbol in modern society.

Ancient idols in the form of **four-footed animals** were almost too numerous to count. The Egyptians worshiped the bull-god Apis, the cat-goddess Bubastis, the cow-goddess Hathor, the hippopotamus-goddess Opet, and the wolf-god Ophois. As already noted, even the ancient Israelites were guilty of fashioning and then worshiping a golden calf, which was intended to represent the true God! Many Egyptians and Canaanites worshiped bulls, some of which were buried with great riches just as were the pharaohs. Artemis, or Diana, a popular Greek goddess in New Testament times (see Acts 19:27), did not have the form of a beautiful woman but rather that of a gross, ugly female beast with countless nipples hanging beneath her, supposedly enough to suckle the world. Other ancient idols were in the form of such diverse objects as mice and rats, elephants, crocodiles, monkeys, and the sun and moon.

We also know from secular sources as well as from Scripture about many kinds of **crawling creatures** that were worshiped, many of which are still deified in parts of the world today. Among their many idols, the ancient Egyptians worshiped the scarab beetle, likenesses of which are sold as souvenirs in that country today. The insect lives in manure piles and is commonly referred to as the dung beetle. The Assyrians became fond of worshiping snakes, as did many Greeks.

The name of the Canaanite god Baal-zebub (2 Kings 1:2), or Beelzebul (Matt. 10:25), means "Lord of the flies." Because so much pagan worship was associated with flies, many superstitious Jews believed that no fly would dare enter God's Temple in Jerusalem (cf. Avot 5:5 in the Talmud). Modern Hindus refuse to kill or harm most animals and insects, because the creatures might be either a deity or the reincarnated form of a human being who is transmigrating from one stage of his karma to another.

Lest we think that contemporary, sophisticated man has risen above such crude foolishness, we have only to consider the monumental increase in astrology and other occultic practices during the last few decades in the United States and western Europe. Many leading world figures, including noted scientists, are said to consult their horoscopes or occult advisers for information from star movement or tea leaves before making major decisions or taking extended trips.

There have always been people who worship the idols of wealth, health, pleasure, prestige, sex, sports, education, entertainment, celebrities, success, and power. And at no time in history have those forms of idolatry been more pervasive and corrupting than in our own day.

Countless books, magazines, games, movies, and videos glorify sexual promiscuity, incest, rape, homosexuality, brutality, deceit, manipulation of others to one's own advantage, and every other form of immorality and ungodliness. Many of those things are specifically occultic—involving magic, spell casting, witchcraft, sex rites, human sacrifice, and even demon and Satan worship. Moral and spiritual pollution is pandemic in modern society and is a degenerative and addictive form of idolatry. Tragically, it is being packaged and marketed to reach younger and younger ages.

Many years ago J. H. Clinch wrote the provocative and powerful lines,

> And still from Him we turn away,
>   And fill our hearts with worthless things;
> The fires of greed melt the clay,
>   And forth the idol springs!
> Ambition's flame, and passions's heart,
>   By wondrous alchemy transmute earth's dross
> To raise some gilded brute to fill Jehovah's seat.

When man rejects God's revelation, whatever the form of that revelation might be, he regresses through rationalization and false religion ultimately to reprobation, which, in Romans 1:24-32, Paul proceeds to relate.

Abandoned by God

Therefore God gave them over in the lusts of their hearts to impurity, that their bodies might be dishonored among them. For they exchanged the truth of God for a lie, and worshiped and served the creature rather than the Creator, who is blessed forever. Amen

For this reason God gave them over to degrading passions; for their women exchanged the natural function for that which is unnatural, and in the same way also the men abandoned the natural function of the woman and burned in their desire toward one another, men with men committing indecent acts and receiving in their own persons the due penalty of their error.

And just as they did not see fit to acknowledge God any longer, God gave them over to a depraved mind, to do those things which are not proper, being filled with all unrighteousness, wickedness, greed, evil; full of envy, murder, strife, deceit, malice; they are gossips, slanderers, haters of God, insolent, arrogant, boastful, inventors of evil, disobedient to parents, without understanding, untrustworthy, unloving, unmerciful; and, although they know the ordinance of God, that those who practice such things

are worthy of death, they not only do the same, but also give hearty approval to those who practice them. (1:24-32)

As Paul illustrates in these verses, and develops theologically through the end of chapter 4, man is not basically good but evil. His nature is innately bent toward sin. "There is none righteous, not even one; . . . there is none who does good, there is not even one. . . . all have sinned and fall short of the glory of God" (Rom. 3:10, 12, 23). Those who ignore God's provision for dealing with sin and seek to improve themselves by their own power invariably commit the most heinous sin of all, which is self-righteousness and pride. Only God can graciously remove sin or produce righteousness, and the person who tries to eliminate his own guilt or achieve his own righteousness merely drives himself deeper into sin and further from God.

Like an untended garden, when man is left to himself the bad always chokes out the good, because that is the inclination of his fallen nature. Man has no capacity in himself to restrain the weeds of his sinfulness or to cultivate the good produce of righteousness. Man's natural development is not upward but downward; he does not evolve but devolve. He is not ascending to God but descending from God. He has continued a downward spiral of depravity throughout history, getting worse and worse, and when the restraints of the Holy Spirit are removed during the final Tribulation period, all hell will break loose on earth as evil reaches its ultimate stage (see 2 Thess. 2:3-9; Rev. 9:1-11).

Man cannot stop this slide because he is innately a slave to sin (Rom. 6:16-20), and the more he pursues his deceiving efforts at self-reformation apart from God the more he becomes enslaved to sin, whose ultimate end is eternal death (Rom. 6:16-23). As C. S. Lewis perceptively observes in his book *The Problem of Pain,* "[The lost] enjoy forever the horrible freedom they have demanded, and are therefore self-enslaved" ([New York: Macmillan, 1962], pp. 127-28).

The major point of Romans 1:24-32 is that when men persistently abandon God, God will abandon them (see vv. 24, 26, 28). Even when God's own people ignore and disobey Him, He may temporarily abandon them. "But My people did not listen to My voice," the psalmist wrote in behalf of the Lord, "and Israel did not obey Me. So I gave them over to the stubbornness of their heart, to walk in their own devices" (Ps. 81:11-12). Hosea reports the same tragic reality concerning the unfaithfulness of the northern kingdom, represented by Ephraim, to whom God said: "Ephraim is joined to idols; let him alone" (Hos. 4:17).

In his message to the high priest and other religious leaders in Jerusalem, Stephen reminded them that when the ancient Israelites rejected the Lord and erected and worshiped the golden calf while Moses was on Mount Sinai, "God turned away and delivered them up to serve the host of heaven," that is, the demon-inspired deities they had made (Acts 7:38-42). Paul declared to a pagan crowd in Lystra, "In the generations gone by [God] permitted all the nations to go their own ways" (Acts 14:16).

When God abandons men to their own devices, His divine protection is partially withdrawn. When that occurs, men not only become more vulnerable to the destructive wiles of Satan but also suffer the destruction that their own sin works in and through them. "You have forsaken Me and served other gods," the Lord said to Israel. "Therefore I will deliver you no more" (Judg. 10:13). When God's Spirit came upon Azariah, He told Judah, "The Lord is with you when you are with Him. And if you seek Him He will let you find Him; but if you forsake Him, He will forsake you" (2 Chron. 15:2). Through "Zechariah, the son of Jehoiada the priest," God again said to Judah, "Why do you transgress the commandments of the Lord and do not prosper? Because you have forsaken the Lord, He has also forsaken you" (2 Chron. 24:20).

Romans 1:24-32 vividly portrays the consequences of God's abandonment of rebellious mankind, showing the essence (vv. 24-25), the expression (vv. 26-27), and the extent (vv. 28-32) of man's sinfulness. Each of those progressively more sobering sections is introduced with the declaration "God gave them over."

The Essence of Man's Sinfulness

Therefore God gave them over in the lusts of their hearts to impurity, that their bodies might be dishonored among them. For they exchanged the truth of God for a lie, and worshiped and served the creature rather than the Creator, who is blessed forever. Amen. (1:24-25)

Therefore refers back to the reasons Paul has just set forth in verses 18-23. Although God revealed himself to man (vv. 19-20), man rejected God (v. 21) and then rationalized his rejection (v. 22; cf. v. 18b) and created substitute gods of his own making (v. 23). And because man abandoned God, God abandoned men—He **gave them over.** It is that divine abandonment and its consequences that Paul develops in verses 24-32, the most sobering and fearful passage in the entire epistle.

Paradidōmi (**gave . . . over**) is an intense verb. In the New Testament it is used of giving one's body to be burned (1 Cor. 13:3) and three times of Christ's giving Himself up to death (Gal. 2:20; Eph. 5:2, 25). It is used in a judicial sense of men's being committed to prison (Mark 1:14; Acts 8:3) or to judgment (Matt. 5:25; 10:17, 19, 21; 18:34) and of rebellious angels being delivered to pits of darkness (2 Pet. 2:4). It is also used of Christ's committing Himself to His Father's care (1 Pet. 2:23) and of the Father's delivering His own Son to propitiatory death (Rom. 4:25; 8:32).

God's giving over sinful mankind has a dual sense. First, in an *indirect* sense God **gave them over** simply by withdrawing His restraining and protective hand, allowing the consequences of sin to take their inevitable, destructive course. Sin degrades man, debases the image of God in which he is made, and strips him of dignity, peace of mind, and a clear conscience. Sin destroys personal relationships, marriages, families, cities, and nations. It also destroys churches. Thomas Watson said, "Sin . . . puts gravel in our bread [and] wormwood in our cup" (*A Body of Divinity* [Carlisle, Pa.: Banner of Truth, 1983 reprint], p. 136).

Fallen men are not concerned about their sin but only about the pain from the unpleasant consequences sin brings. Someone has well said that sin would have fewer takers if the consequences were immediate. Many people, for example, are greatly concerned about venereal disease but resent the suggestion of avoiding it by restraining sexual promiscuity and perversions. Instead of adhering to God's standards of moral purity, they attempt to remove the consequences of their impurity. They turn to counseling, to medicine, to psychoanalysis, to drugs, to alcohol, to travel, and to a host of other means to escape what cannot be escaped except by the removal of their sin.

It is said that an ermine would rather die than defile its beautiful coat of fur; the animal will go to incredible lengths to protect it. Man does not have such an inclination concerning the defilement of sin. He cannot keep himself pure and has no natural desire to do so.

Not all of God's wrath is future. In the case of sexual promiscuity— perhaps more specifically and severely than in any other area of morality— God has continually poured out His divine wrath by means of venereal disease. In regard to countless other manifestations of godlessness, He pours out His wrath in the forms of the loneliness, frustration, meaning-lessness, anxiety, and despair that are so characteristic of modern society. As sophisticated, self-sufficient mankind draws further and further away from God, God gives them over to the consequences of their spiritual and moral rebellion against Him. Commentator Alan F. Johnson said, "Without God there are no abiding truths, lasting principles, or norms, and man is cast upon a sea of speculation and skepticism and attempted self-salvation" (*The Freedom Letter* [Chicago: Moody, 1974], p. 41).

The divine abandonment of men to their sin about which Paul speaks here is not eternal abandonment. As long as sinful men are alive, God provides opportunity for their salvation. That is the marvelous good news of God's grace, which Paul develops later in the epistle. Like her Old Testament namesake, the Jezebel who was misleading the church at Thyatira was the embodiment of idolatrous, immoral godlessness, yet the

Lord graciously gave her opportunity to repent (see Rev. 2:20-21). Despite His righteous wrath against sin, God is patient toward sinners, "not wishing for any to perish but for all to come to repentance" (2 Pet. 3:9).

After giving a list of sins similar to that in Romans 1:29-31, Paul reminded the Corinthian believers, "And such were some of you; but you were washed, but you were sanctified, but you were justified in the name of the Lord Jesus Christ, and in the Spirit of our God" (1 Cor. 6:11). It is sin that makes the gospel of salvation necessary and that makes God's offer of salvation through Christ so gracious.

In a second, *direct* sense God **gave . . over** rebellious mankind by specific acts of judgment. The Bible is replete with accounts of divine wrath being directly and supernaturally poured out on sinful men. The flood of Noah's day and the destruction of Sodom and Gomorrah, for example, were not indirect natural consequences of sin but were overt supernatural expressions of God's judgment on gross and unrepented sin.

God often allows men to go deeper and deeper into sin in order to drive them to despair and to show them their need of Him. Often He punishes men in order to heal and restore (Isa. 19:22).

It was because **the lusts of their hearts** were for **impurity** that God abandoned men to their sin. Men's lostness is not determined by the outward circumstances of their lives but by the inner condition of their **hearts**. A person's sin begins within himself. "For out of the heart," Jesus said, "come evil thoughts, murders, adulteries, fornications, thefts, false witness, slanders. These are the things which defile the man" (Matt. 15:19-20). Jeremiah had proclaimed the same basic truth: "The heart is more deceitful than all else and is desperately sick" (Jer. 17:9; cf. Prov. 4:23).

Used metaphorically in Scripture, "the heart" does not represent the emotions or feelings, as it generally does in modern usage, but rather the whole thinking process, including especially the will and man's motivation. In its broadest sense, the heart represents the basic nature of a person, his inner being and character.

In our day, the basic ungodliness of man is nowhere more clearly exposed than in the popular admonition to do one's own thing. Man's "own thing" is sin, which characterizes his whole natural being. Self-will is the essence of all sin. Although Satan was responsible for their being tempted to sin, it was the voluntary placing of their own wills above God's that caused Adam and Eve to commit the first sin.

Men reject God because their preferences, their **lusts**, are for their own way rather than God's. **Lusts** translates *epithumia,* which can refer to any desire but was most often used of carnal desire for that which was sinful or forbidden.

Speaking about believers as well as unbelievers, James declared that "each one is tempted when he is carried away and enticed by his own lust" (James 1:14). Because even Christians are tempted to desire their own sin above God's holiness, Paul warned the Thessalonians about falling into the lustful passions that characterized pagan Gentiles (1 Thess. 4:5). He reminded the Ephesians that "we too all formerly lived in the lusts of our flesh, indulging the desires of the flesh and of the mind, and were by nature children of wrath, even as the rest" (Eph. 2:3).

Akatharsia (**impurity**) was a general term for uncleanness and was often used of decaying matter, especially the contents of a grave, which were considered by Jews to be both physically and ceremonially unclean. As a moral term, it usually referred to or was closely associated with sexual immorality. Paul lamented over the Corinthians "who [had] sinned in the past and not repented of the impurity, immorality and sensuality which they [had] practiced" (2 Cor. 12:21). He used the same three terms to introduce the list of "deeds of the flesh" that are in perpetual conflict with "the fruit of the Spirit" (Gal. 5:19-23). He exhorted the Ephesians: "Do not let immorality or any impurity or greed even be named among you, as is proper among saints" (Eph. 5:3; cf. 1 Thess. 4:7).

The effect of men's rebellious, self-willed **impurity** was **that their bodies might be dishonored.** When men seek to glorify their own ways and to satisfy their bodies through shameful indulgence in sexual and other sins, their **bodies,** along with their souls, are instead **dishonored.** When man seeks to elevate himself for his own purposes and by his own standards, he inevitably does the opposite. The way of fallen mankind is always downward, never upward. The more he exalts himself, the more he declines. The more he magnifies himself the more he diminishes. The more he honors himself, the more he becomes **dishonored.**

No society in history has given more attention to caring for the body than has the modern Western world. Yet no society has caused more degradation of the body. The more human life is exalted for its own sake, the more it is debased. In tragic irony, the same society that glorifies the body has no regard for the body, the same society that exalts man incessantly degrades him. The world echoes with demands for men's rights; yet books, movies, and television often portray brutality and murder as all but normal, and sexual promiscuity and perversion are constantly glamorized.

Because humanism rejects God, it has no basis for man's dignity. And therefore in the name of humanism, humanity is dehumanized. While lamenting man's inhumanity to man, fallen men refuse to recognize that in rejecting God they reject the only source and measure of man's dignity. Therefore, while loudly proclaiming the greatness of man, modern society abuses man at every turn. We sexually abuse one another, economically abuse one another, criminally abuse one another, and verbally abuse one another. Because they reject the God who made them and would redeem them, "the hearts of the sons of men are full of evil, and insanity is in their hearts throughout their lives" (Eccles. 9:3).

The well-known founder of a contemporary pornographic empire is said to have commented: "Sex is a biological function like eating and drinking. So let's forget all the prudery about it and do whatever we feel like doing." That such thinking is not the modern invention of a sophisticated "world come of age" is clearly seen in the fact that Paul confronted precisely the same thinking in Corinth nearly 2,000 years ago. A common saying in that day was "Food is for the stomach, and the stomach is for food," and the apostle intimates that it was used even by some Christians to justify sexual immorality, comparing eating to sexual indulgence. Both were claimed to be merely biological functions, which could be used however one might choose. Paul's stinging reply to that perverted reasoning was, "The body is not for immorality but for the Lord; and the Lord is for the body" (1 Cor. 6:13).

As the apostle goes on to explain in that passage, sexual immorality not only is sin against the Lord but is sin against one's own body (v. 18). That is his point of the present passage. The body that indulges in sexual impurity is itself **dishonored**; it is debased, disgraced, and degraded.

Newspapers abound with reports of senseless beatings for no other purpose than the perverted fun of it. Brutal wife and child abuse have become epidemic. *The Indianapolis Star* reported that child molesters have their own national organization called NAMBLA (National American Man Boy Love Association) that publishes a newsletter for members (Tom Keating, "Molesters Have Own Organization" [15 April 1981], p. 17). One of the shocking things the article mentioned was that at a large seminar to discuss prevention of child pornography and related crimes, a man interrupted the proceedings and loudly defended his and other men's rights to indulge in such perversion. Lately NAMBLA has been in the news again because it is becoming more bold and open about its activities.

That is the legacy of those who have **exchanged the truth of God for a lie.** Having suppressed God's truth in unrighteousness (Rom. 1:18), rebellious man submits himself to untruth, **a lie.** The basic divine truth that fallen man suppresses is that of God's very existence and therefore His right and demand to be honored and glorified as sovereign Lord (see vv. 19-21). Scripture often speaks of God as being the truth, as Jesus declared of Himself (John 14:6). Isaiah described a pagan who held an idol in his hand but was too spiritually blind to ask what should have been an obvious question: "Is there not a lie in my right hand?" (Isa. 44:20). Through Jeremiah, the Lord declared to apostate Judah, "You have forgotten Me and trusted in falsehood" (Jer. 13:25). To forsake God is to forsake truth and become a slave to falsehood. To reject God, the Father of truth, is to become vulnerable to Satan, the father of lies (John 8:44).

Tragically, as in the Corinthian church of Paul's day, many people who claim the name of Christ today have succumbed to the world's self-oriented view of morality. An advice columnist to singles received a letter asking how Christian singles can deal with their sexual desires and still uphold their Christian beliefs. The columnist referred to a woman on her staff who conducts Christian singles retreats, who replied that such decisions were up to each couple to make for themselves. If having sex before marriage would harm their relationship or compromise their personal value systems, they should refrain, she said. Otherwise, "sex in a loving relationship is all right without the sanction of marriage" (Joan Keeler, "The Single Experience," *Glendale News-Press* [13 August 1981], p. 10).

When men turned from God and His truth, Paul goes on to say, they then **worshiped and served the creature rather than the Creator.** As the apostle had just pointed out, they found themselves foolishly and wickedly worshiping lifeless images of their own making, "in the form of corruptible man and of birds and four-footed animals and crawling creatures" (v. 23).

Perhaps unable to continue discussing such vile things without "coming up for air," as it were, Paul inserts a common Jewish doxology about the true God, **the Creator, who is blessed forever. Amen.** Paul could not resist adding that refreshing thought in the sea of filth he was describing. That word of praise to the Lord served, by utter contrast, to magnify the wickedness of idolatry and all other ungodliness.

The Expression of Man's Sinfulness

For this reason God gave them over to degrading passions; for their women exchanged the natural function for that which is unnatural, and in the same way also the men abandoned the natural function of the woman and burned in their desire toward one another, men with men committing indecent acts and receiving in their own persons the due penalty of their error. (1:26-27)

For this reason, Paul declares—that is, because of man's rejecting the true God for false gods of his own making, for worshiping the creature rather than the Creator—**God gave them over to degrading passions.** For the second time (see v. 24) the apostle mentions God's abandonment of sinful mankind. He abandoned them not only to idolatry, the ultimate sexual expression of man's spiritual degeneracy, but also **to degrading passions,** which he identifies in these two verses as homosexuality, the ultimate expression of man's moral degeneracy.

To illustrate the **degrading passions** that rise out of the fallen human heart, Paul uses homosexuality, the most **degrading** and repulsive of all **passions**. In their freedom from God's truth men turned to perversion and even inversion of the created order. In the end their humanism resulted in the dehumanization of each of them. Perversion is the illicit and twisted expression of that which is God-given and natural. Homosexuality, on the other hand, is inversion, the expression of that which is neither God-given nor natural. When man forsakes the Author of nature, he inevitably forsakes the order of nature.

Some **women** of ancient times and throughout history have **exchanged the natural function for that which is unnatural.** Paul does not use *gunē*, the usual term for **women,** but rather *thēleia,* which simply means female. In most cultures women have been more reluctant than men to become involved either in sexual promiscuity or homosexuality. Perhaps Paul mentions **women** first because their practice of homosexuality is especially shocking and dismaying. In commenting on this verse, theologian Charles Hodge wrote, "Paul first refers to the degradation of females among the heathen, because they are always the last to be affected in the decay of morals, and their corruption is therefore proof that all virtue is lost" (*Commentary on the Epistle to the Romans* [Grand Rapids: Eerdmans, 1983 reprint], p. 42).

Chrēsis (**function**) was commonly used of sexual intercourse, and in this context the term could refer to nothing other than intimate sexual relations. Even most pagan societies have recognized the clearly obvious fact that homosexuality is abnormal and **unnatural.** It is also an abnormality that is unique to man.

And in the same way also the men, Paul says, again using a Greek term that simply denotes gender, in this case, males. The usual Greek terms for women and men, like corresponding terms in most languages, imply a certain dignity, and Paul refused to ascribe even an implied dignity to those who degenerate into homosexuality.

Those males, says Paul, **abandoned the natural function of the woman and burned in their desire toward one another, men with men committing indecent acts.** There is a burning level of lust among homosexuals that beggars description and is rarely known among heterosexuals. The homosexuals of Sodom were so passionately consumed with their lust that they ignored the fact that they had been made blind and "wearied themselves trying to find the doorway" into Lot's house in order to pursue their vile passion (Gen. 19:11). Those ancient people were so morally perverse that in Scripture the name *Sodom* became a byword for immoral godlessness, and *sodomy,* a term derived from that name, became throughout history a synonym for homosexuality and other forms of sexual deviation.

In the United States and many other western countries it is not uncommon for homosexual males to have 300 partners a year. Even when relationships are on a friendly basis, the most bizarre acts imaginable are committed, and mutilation is common. In his biography (*Where Death*

Delights, by Marshall Houts [New York: Coward-McCann, 1967]), the New York City forensic expert Dr. Milton Helpern, who makes no claim of being a Christian and avoids making moral judgments about homosexuality, nevertheless comments that, after having performed thousands of autopsies, he would warn anyone who chooses a homosexual lifestyle to be prepared for the consequences: "When we see . . . brutal, multiple wound cases in a single victim . . . we just automatically assume that we're dealing with a homosexual victim and a homosexual attacker. . . . I don't know why it is so, but it seems that the violent explosions of jealousy among homosexuals far exceed those of the jealousy of a man for a woman, or a woman for a man. The pent-up charges and energy of the homosexual relationship simply cannot be contained. When the explosive point is reached, the result is brutally violent. . . . But this is the 'normal' pattern of these homosexual attacks, the multiple stabbings, the multiple senseless beatings that obviously must continue long after the victim dies" (pp. 269-70).

A San Francisco coroner estimated that ten percent of his city's homicides were probably related to sado-masochistic sex among homosexuals (cf. Bob Greene, "Society's Been Given Far Too Much Rope," the *Chicago Tribune* [19 March 1981], sec. 2, p. 1). Yet in spite of such impartial and damning evidence, many people, including a large number of psychologists and other social professionals, persist in maintaining there is no scientific proof that homosexuality is abnormal or harmful to society. Some even assert that attempts to convert homosexuals to heterosexuals are ethically questionable. The city government of San Francisco has even conducted workshops to teach homosexuals how to avoid serious bodily harm while engaging in sado-masochistic sex— although by definition, both sadism and masochism are destructive! The very purpose of both deviations is to inflict pain and harm, sadism on others and masochism on oneself. Many mass murderers seem to be homosexuals.

Unimaginably, many church denominations in the United States and elsewhere have ordained homosexuals to the ministry and even established special congregations for homosexuals. One denominational group claims that homosexuality is no more abnormal than left-handedness. An official church organization for homosexuals is called *Dignity.*

Instead of trying to help their children become free of sexual deviation, many parents of homosexuals have banded together to defend their children and to coerce society, government, and churches to recognize and accept homosexuality as normal. In many cases, religions that hold homosexuality to be a sin are blamed for the tragic results that homosexuals bring on themselves and on their families and friends. Evangelical Christianity in particular is often made the culprit and is accused of persecuting innocent people who cannot help being what they are.

But in both testaments God's Word condemns homosexuality in the strongest of terms. Under the Old Covenant it was punishable by death. Paul declares unequivocally that, although homosexuality can be forgiven and cleansed just as any other sin, no unrepentant homosexual will enter heaven, just as will no unrepentant fornicator, idolater, adulterer, effeminate person, thief, covetous person, drunkard, reviler, or swindler (1 Cor. 6:9-11; cf. Gal. 5:19-21; Eph. 5:3-5; 1 Tim. 1:9-10; Jude 7).

All people are born in sin, and individuals have varying tendencies and temptations toward certain sins. But no one is born a homosexual, any more than anyone is born a thief or a murderer. A person who becomes a habitual and unrepentant thief, murderer, adulterer, or homosexual does so of his own choice.

Any attempt at all to justify homosexuality is both futile and wicked, but to attempt to justify it on biblical grounds, as do many misguided church leaders, is even more futile and vile. To do that is to make God a liar and to love what He hates and justify what He condemns.

God so abhors homosexuality that He determined that the disgraceful, shameful acts that women commit with women and men commit with men would result in their **receiving in their own persons the due penalty of their error.** They would be judged by the self-destructiveness of their sin. The appalling physical consequences of homosexuality are visible evidence of God's righteous condemnation. Unnatural vice brings its own perverted reward. AIDS is frightening evidence of that fatal promise.

THE EXTENT OF MAN'S SINFULNESS

And just as they did not see fit to acknowledge God any longer, God gave them over to a depraved mind, to do those things which are not proper, being filled with all unrighteousness, wickedness, greed, evil; full of envy, murder, strife, deceit, malice; they are gossips, slanderers, haters of God, insolent, arrogant, boastful, inventors of evil, disobedient to parents, without understanding, untrustworthy, unloving, unmerciful; and, although they know the ordinance of God, that those who practice such things are worthy of death, they not only do the same, but also give hearty approval to those who practice them. (1:28-32)

Because fallen mankind **did not see fit to acknowledge God any longer, God gave them over** in still another way, in this case **to a**

depraved mind. The godless mind is **a depraved mind,** whose predetermined and inevitable disposition is **to do those things which are not proper.**

The basic meaning of *adokimos* (**depraved**) is that of not standing the test, and the term was commonly used of metals that were rejected by refiners because of impurities. The impure metals were discarded, and *adokimos* therefore came to include the ideas of worthlessness and uselessness. In relation to God, the rejecting mind becomes a rejected mind and thereby becomes spiritually **depraved,** worthless and useless. Of unbelievers, Jeremiah wrote, "They call them rejected silver, because the Lord has rejected them" (Jer. 6:30). The mind that finds God worthless becomes worthless itself. It is debauched, deceived, and deserving only of God's divine wrath.

The sinful, **depraved mind** says to God, "Depart from us! We do not even desire the knowledge of Thy ways. Who is the Almighty, that we should serve Him, and what would we gain if we entreat Him?" (Job 21:14-15). Although godless people think they are wise, they are supremely foolish (Rom. 1:22). Regardless of their natural intelligence and their learning in the physical realm, in the things of God they are devoid even of "the beginning of knowledge," because they lack reverential fear of Him. They are merely "fools [who] despise wisdom and instruction" (Prov. 1:7; cf. v. 29).

Even God's chosen people, the Jews, fell into that foolishness when they rejected or neglected the revelation and blessings He had showered on them so uniquely and abundantly. "For My people are foolish, they know Me not," the Lord declared through Jeremiah; "they are stupid children, and they have no understanding. They are shrewd to do evil, but to do good they do not know" (Jer. 4:22; cf. 9:6). Those who reject the true God are wholly vulnerable to "the god of this world [who] has blinded the minds of the unbelieving, that they might not see the light of the gospel of the glory of Christ, who is the image of God" (2 Cor. 4:4).

The catalog of sins Paul proceeds to mention in Romans 1:29-31 is not exhaustive, but it is representative of the virtually endless number of vices with which the natural man is **filled.**

The first two terms in the NASB text, **all unrighteousness** and **wickedness,** are comprehensive and general, synonyms that encompass the entire range of the particular sins that follow. Some versions include *fornication* between those first two terms, but that word is not found in the best Greek manuscripts. The idea is certainly not inappropriate to the context, however, because fornication is universally condemned in Scripture and is frequently included by Paul in lists of vices (see 1 Cor. 6:9; Gal. 5:19; Col. 3:5). Fornication is implied in the sin of impurity, which has already been mentioned in the present passage (1:24).

The sins mentioned in the rest of the list are basically self-explanatory: **greed, evil; full of envy, murder, strife, deceit, malice; they are gossips, slanderers, haters of God, insolent, arrogant, boastful, inventors of evil, disobedient to parents, without understanding, untrustworthy, unloving, unmerciful.** The Greek term behind **untrustworthy** means literally to break a covenant, as reflected in some translations. **Unloving** relates especially to unnatural family relationships, such as that of a parent who abandons a young child or a grown child who abandons his aging parents.

Reiterating the fact that rebellious, ungodly men are without excuse, Paul declares that **they know the ordinance of God, that those who practice such things are worthy of death.** The apostle has already established that, since the creation of the world, God has made Himself known to every human being (vv. 19-21). People do not recognize God because they do not *want* to recognize Him, because they willingly "suppress the truth in unrighteousness" (v. 18). "This is the judgment," Jesus said, "that the light is come into the world, and men loved the darkness rather than the light; for their deeds were evil. For everyone who does evil hates the light, and does not come to the light, lest his deeds should be exposed" (John 3:19-20).

Whether they recognize it or not, even those who have never been exposed to the revelation of God's Word are instinctively aware of His existence and of His basic standards of righteousness. "They show the work of the Law written in their hearts, their conscience bearing witness, and their thoughts alternately accusing or else defending them" (Rom. 2:15).

In most societies of the world, even in those considered uncivilized, most of the sins Paul lists here are considered wrong, and many are held to be crimes. Men inherently know that such things as greed, envy, murder, deceit, arrogance, disobedience, and mercilessness are wrong.

The absolute pit of wickedness is reached, Paul says, when those who are themselves involved in evils **also give hearty approval to** others **who practice them.** To justify one's own sin is wicked enough, but to approve and encourage others to sin is immeasurably worse. Even the best of societies have had those within them who were blatantly wicked and perverse. But a society that openly condones and defends such evils as sexual promiscuity, homosexuality, and the rest has reached the deepest level of corruption. Many of the most socially advanced societies of our own day are in that category. Sexually promiscuous celebrities are glamorized and the rights of homosexuals are ardently defended. These acts of sin are in direct contradiction to the revealed will of God.

A certain species of ants in Africa builds its nests in deep subterranean tunnels, where its young and its queen live. Although they may be great distances from the nest foraging for food, worker ants of that species are able to sense when the queen is being molested and they become extremely nervous and uncoordinated. If she is killed, they become frantic and rush around aimlessly until they die.

What better illustration could there be of fallen man. Even in his sinful rejection and rebellion, he cannot function properly apart from God and is destined only for death.

Principles of God's Judgment—part 1

Therefore you are without excuse, every man of you who passes judgment, for in that you judge another, you condemn yourself; for you who judge practice the same things. And we know that the judgment of God rightly falls upon those who practice such things. And do you suppose this, O man, when you pass judgment upon those who practice such things and do the same yourself, that you will escape the judgment of God? Or do you think lightly of the riches of His kindness and forbearance and patience, not knowing that the kindness of God leads you to repentance? But because of your stubbornness and unrepentant heart you are storing up wrath for yourself in the day of wrath and revelation of the righteous judgment of God, (2:1-5)

After reading Paul's severe condemnation of those who have abandoned God and plummeted into the gross sins mentioned in 1:29-31, one naturally wonders about how God deals with the more upright, moral, and religious person who has a sense of right and wrong, and leads an outwardly virtuous life.

Many such ethically upright people would heartily concur with Paul's assessment of the flagrantly immoral people he has just described.

They obviously deserve God's judgment. Throughout history many pagan individuals and societies have held high standards of conduct. As F. F. Bruce points out, the Roman philosopher Seneca, a contemporary of Paul,

> might have listened to Paul's indictment and said, "Yes, that is perfectly true of great masses of mankind, and I concur in the judgment which you pass on them—but there are others, of course, like myself, who deplore these tendencies as much as you do."
>
> Paul imagines someone intervening in terms like these, and he addresses the supposed objector. . . . How apt this reply would have been to a man like Seneca! For Seneca could write so effectively on the good life that Christian writers of later days were prone to call him "our own Seneca." Not only did he exalt the great moral virtues; he exposed hypocrisy, he preached the equality of all men, he acknowledged the pervasive character of evil, . . . he practiced and inculcated daily self-examination, he ridiculed vulgar idolatry, he assumed the role of a moral guide. But too often he tolerated in himself vices not so different from those which he condemned in others—the most flagrant instance being his connivance at Nero's murder of his mother Agrippina. (*Romans* [London: Tyndale, 1967], pp. 86, 87)

Most Jews of Paul's day believed in the idea that performing certain moral and religious works produced righteousness. Specifically, they could earn God's special favor and therefore eternal life by keeping the Mosaic law and the traditions of the rabbis. Many even believed that if they failed in the works effort, they might forfeit some earthly reward but were still exempt from God's judgment simply because they were Jews, God's chosen people. They were firmly convinced that God would judge and condemn pagan Gentiles because of their idolatry and immorality but that no Jew would ever experience such condemnation. They loved to repeat such sayings as, "God loves Israel alone of all the nations," and "God will judge the Gentiles with one measure and the Jews with another." Some taught that Abraham sat outside the gates of hell in order to prevent even the most wicked Jew from entering.

In his *Dialogue with Trypho*, the second-century Christian Justin Martyr reports his Jewish opponent as saying, "They who are the seed of Abraham according to the flesh shall in any case, even if they be sinners and unbelieving and disobedient towards God, share in the eternal kingdom."

Even the unregenerate have the basic knowledge of good and evil built into them and into society. Consequently, many people today recognize and seek to uphold the moral standards of Scripture and profess to be Christians. But also like Seneca, because they are not true believers in God, they lack the spiritual resources to maintain that divine morality in their lives and are unable to restrain their sinfulness. They trust in their baptism, in their church membership, in their being born into a Christian family, in the sacraments, in high ethical standards, in orthodox doctrine, or in any number of other outward ideas, relationships, or ceremonies for spiritual and even eternal safety.

But no one can understand or appropriate salvation apart from recognizing that he stands guilty and condemned before God, totally unable to bring himself up to God's standard of righteousness. And no person is exempt. The outwardly moral person who is friendly and charitable but self-satisfied is, in fact, usually harder to reach with the gospel than the reprobate who has hit bottom, recognized his sin, and given up hope. Therefore, after showing the immoral pagan his lostness apart from Christ, Paul proceeds with great force and clarity to show the moralist that, before God, he is equally guilty and condemned.

In doing so, he presents six principles by which God judges sinful men: knowledge (v. 1), truth (vv. 2-3), guilt (vv. 4-5), deeds (vv. 6-10), impartiality (vv. 11-15), and motive (v. 16).

KNOWLEDGE

Therefore you are without excuse, every man of you who passes judgment, for in that you judge another, you condemn yourself; for you who judge practice the same things. (2:1)

Therefore refers to what Paul has just said in the last half of chapter 1, and specifically to the introductory statement: "For the wrath of God is revealed from heaven against all ungodliness and unrighteousness of men, who suppress the truth in unrighteousness, because that which is known about God is evident within them; for God made it evident to them, . . . so that they are without excuse" (vv. 18-20).

Addressing the new group of moral people, the apostle says, **you** also **are without excuse, every man of you who passes judgment.** As becomes clear in verse 17, he was speaking primarily to Jews, who characteristically passed **judgment** on Gentiles, thinking them to be spiritually inferior and even beyond the interest of God's mercy and care. But **every man of you** encompasses all moralists, including professing Christians, who think they are exempt from God's judgment because they have not sunk into the pagan, immoral extremes Paul has just mentioned.

Paul's initial argument is simple. **In that you judge another,** he points out, **you condemn yourself,** because you obviously have a criterion by which to judge, meaning that you know the truth about what is right and wrong before God. Even the Gentiles know the basic truth of God's "eternal power and divine nature" through natural revelation (1:20). They also have a sense of right and wrong by conscience (2:15). The Jew, however, not only had both of those means of knowing God's truth but also had the great advantage of having received His special revelation through Scripture (3:2; 9:4). Not only that, but almost all Jews of Paul's day would have known something of Jesus Christ and of His teaching and claims even though they would not have believed He was the promised Messiah. Such knowledge would have made them still more inexcusable, in that their greater knowledge of God's truth would have made them more accountable to it (see Heb. 10:26-29).

If relatively unenlightened pagans know basic truths about God and realize they deserve His punishment (1:19-20, 32), Paul was saying, how much more should Jews? The same principle applies to Christians, both nominal and true. Because they have greater knowledge of God's truth they are more accountable to it and more inexcusable when they self-righteously judge others by it. James gave a special warning to those who aspire to be Christian teachers, reminding them that, because of their greater knowledge of God's truth, they will be judged more strictly by Him (James 3:1). And the fact is, the moralists who condemn others' sins are filled with their own iniquities which demand judgment by the same standard.

But it was not simply that those who are judgmental are wrong in assessing the moral standing of others but that they also are wrong in assessing their *own* moral standing. **You who judge practice the same things,** Paul insists. The self-righteous make two grave errors: they underestimate the height of God's standard of righteousness, which encompasses the inner as well as the outer life (the theme of the Sermon on the Mount), and they underestimate the depth of their own sin. It is a universal temptation to exaggerate the faults of others while minimizing one's own, to notice a small speck in someone's eye but not the log in one's own eye (see Matt. 7:1-3).

Many self-sanctified, blind Jews who read these words of Paul would immediately have concluded that what he said did not apply to them. Like the rich young ruler (Luke 18:21), they were convinced they had done a satisfactory job of keeping God's commandments (cf. also Matt. 15:1-3). It was that self-righteous spirit that Jesus repeatedly undermined in the Sermon on the Mount. After declaring, "unless your righteousness surpasses that of the scribes and Pharisees, you shall not enter the kingdom of heaven," He charged that the person who is angry at or insults his brother is as surely worthy of punishment as the murderer and that the person who lusts is guilty of adultery or fornication just as surely as the person who physically commits those immoral acts (Matt. 5:20-22, 27-28). Many Jewish men tried to legalize their adultery by formally divorcing their wives and then marrying the woman they preferred. Because divorce had become easy and commonplace, some men repeatedly divorced and remarried. But Jesus warned: "I say to you that everyone who divorces his wife, except for the cause of unchastity, makes her commit adultery; and whoever marries a divorced woman commits adultery" (v. 32). If one has enough knowledge to judge others, he is thus self-condemned, for he has enough to judge his own true condition.

TRUTH

And we know that the judgment of God rightly falls upon those who practice such things. And do you suppose this, O man, when you pass judgment upon those who practice such things and do the same yourself, that you will escape the judgment of God? (2:2-3)

Know translates *oida*, which carries the idea of awareness of that which is commonly known and obvious. As Paul has already pointed out, even the pagan Gentiles acknowledge that "those who practice such things [the sins listed in 1:29-31] are worthy of death" (v. 32). Surely then, the more spiritually enlightened Jews **know that the judgment of God rightly falls upon those who practice such things.**

Everything God does is, by nature, right and according to the truth. Paul declares, "Let God be found true, though every man be found a liar," (Rom. 3:4), and, "There is no injustice with God, is there? May it never be!" (9:14). God is not capable of doing that which is not right or saying that which is not true. David declared that the Lord "dost sit on the throne judging righteously. . . . He will judge the world in righteousness; He will execute judgment for the peoples with equity" (Ps. 9:4, 8). Another psalmist exulted that God "will judge the world in righteousness, and the people in His faithfulness" (Ps. 96:13; cf. 145:17; cf. also Isa. 45:19). There is always distortion in human perception, but never any in God's.

Men are so used to God's blessings and mercy that they take them for granted, not realizing that they receive those things purely because of God's longsuffering and grace. God would be perfectly just to blot out any person or all persons. But human nature trades on God's grace, believing that everything will work out all right in the end because God is too good and merciful to send anyone to hell. As someone astutely observed, "There is some kind of a still little voice in everybody that constantly convinces them that in the end it's going to be OK." That little voice speaks from a person's fallen nature, which constantly seeks to justify itself.

Paul sternly warns against such false confidence. Although he was conscious of no specific unconfessed sin in his life, even he knew better than to rely on his imperfect human judgment, declaring, "I am not by this acquitted; but the one who examines me is the Lord" (1 Cor. 4:3-4). He knew that every person's discernment is hopelessly distorted and cannot make a proper evaluation even of his own spiritual health, much less that of someone else. "Therefore do not go on passing judgment before the time," the apostle goes on to say, "but wait until the Lord comes who will both bring to light the things hidden in the darkness and disclose the motives of men's hearts; and then each man's praise will come to him from God" (v. 5).

Man's judgment never squares completely with the truth, because he never knows the complete truth. When the proud moralist judges and condemns others, while thinking he himself is acceptable to God, it is only because he is judging by his own perverted perspective, which fallen human nature always skews to its own advantage. But God's perspective and judgment are always perfect. The writer of Hebrews therefore warns, "There is no creature hidden from His sight, but all things are open and laid bare to the eyes of Him with whom we have to do" (Heb. 4:13). Every sin that every individual has ever committed flashes on a life-sized screen before God, as it were, with no detail missing from His view.

The secret hope of the hypocrite is that God will somehow judge him by a standard lower than perfect truth and righteousness. He knows enough to recognize the wickedness of his heart, but he hopes vainly that God will judge him in the same superficial way that most others judge him and that he judges himself. He plays a kind of religious charade, wanting to be judged by his appearance rather than by his true character. And because most men accept him for what he pretends to be, as most hypocrites he assumes God will do the same. But as God cautioned Samuel, "Do not look at his [Eliab's] appearance or at the height of his stature, . . . for God sees not as man sees, for man looks at the outward appearance, but the Lord looks at the heart" (1 Sam. 16:7).

And do you suppose this, O man, when you pass judgment upon those who practice such things and do the same yourself, that you will escape the judgment of God? *Logizomai* (**suppose**) carries the idea of calculating or estimating. (It is related to the English term *logic*.). The moralist falsely calculates his own sinfulness and guilt.

Donald Grey Barnhouse gives a contemporary and forceful paraphrase of this verse: "You dummy—do you really figure that you have doped out an angle that will let you go up against God and get away with it? You don't have a ghost of a chance." Dr. Barnhouse continues by commenting, "There is no escape. Do you understand? No escape—ever. And this means you—the respectable person, sitting in judgment upon another fellow creature, and remaining unrepentant yourself" (*Expositions of Bible Doctrines*, vol. 2, *God's Wrath* [Grand Rapids: Eerdmans, 1953], p. 18).

The hypocritical, self-righteous **man** who passes **judgment upon those who practice** the sinful **things** that he himself practices brings greater judgment on himself. God not only judges him for those evil practices but also for his hypocrisy in the self-righteous judgment of others. Such people "are like whitewashed tombs which on the outside appear beautiful, but inside they are full of dead men's bones and all uncleanness" (Matt. 23:27). "You are foolish and self-deceived," Paul says, "if you think **that you will escape the judgment of God.**"

If a man cannot escape his own judgment, how can he escape divine judgment? If we are forced to condemn ourselves, how much more will the infinitely Holy God condemn us?

Comparing the ancient Israelites (who heard God speak through Moses from Mount Sinai) to those who hear the gospel of Christ (which comes from heaven), the writer of Hebrews declares:

> See to it that you do not refuse Him who is speaking. For if those did not escape when they refused him who warned them on earth, much less shall we escape who turn away from Him who warns from heaven. And His voice shook the earth then, but now He has promised, saying, "Yet once more I will shake not only the earth, but also the heaven." And this expression, "Yet once more," denotes the removing of those things which can be shaken, as of created things, in order that those things which cannot be shaken may remain. Therefore, since we receive a kingdom which cannot be shaken, let us show gratitude, by which we may offer to God an acceptable service with reverence and awe; for our God is a consuming fire." (Heb. 12:25-29)

Because the Israelites refused to listen to God when He spoke to them on earth in regard to His law, that generation perished in the wilderness. How much more accountable, then, will those be who disregard the infinitely greater message of the gospel? "If the word spoken through angels," that is, the Mosaic law (see Acts 7:53), "proved unalterable, and every transgression and disobedience received a just recompense, how shall we escape if we neglect so great a salvation" as that offered by God's own Son, Jesus Christ (Heb. 2:2-3)?

The only way any person, no matter how outwardly moral and religious, can escape God's judgment is to receive Jesus Christ as Lord and Savior, receiving in faith the provision He made on the cross by His paying the penalty all deserve.

It has been told that nomadic tribes roamed ancient Russia much as American Indians once roamed North America. The tribe that controlled the choicest hunting grounds and natural resources was led by an exceptionally strong and wise chief. He ruled not only because of his superior physical strength but because of his utter fairness and impartiality.

When a rash of thefts broke out, he proclaimed that if the thief were caught he would be punished by ten lashes from the tribal whip master. As the thefts continued, he progressively raised the number of lashes to forty, a punishment that everyone knew he was the only one strong enough to endure. To their horror, the thief turned out to be the chief's aged mother, and speculation immediately began as to whether or not he would actually sentence her to the announced punishment. Would he satisfy his love by excusing her or would he satisfy his law by sentencing her to what would surely be her death? True to his integrity, the chief sentenced his mother to the forty lashes. But true also to his love for his mother, just before the whip came down on her back he surrounded her frail body with his own, taking upon himself the penalty he had prescribed for her.

In an infinitely greater way, Christ took the penalty of all men's sin upon Himself.

GUILT

Or do you think lightly of the riches of His kindness and forbearance and patience, not knowing that the kindness of God leads you to repentance? But because of your stubbornness and unrepentant heart you are storing up wrath for yourself in the day of wrath and revelation of the righteous judgment of God, (2:4-5)

Here the Holy Spirit, through Paul, affirms that God judges on the basis of a person's true guilt, guilt that is common to every human being, including those, such as ancient Jews, who considered themselves exempt because of their high moral standing, their religious affiliation, or any other external reason.

The apostle first warns his readers not to **think lightly of the riches of** God's **kindness and forbearance and patience.** The famous commentator Matthew Henry wrote, "There is in every willful sin a contempt for the goodness of God." Every intentional sin takes **lightly** and presumes upon God's **kindness and forbearance and patience.**

Think lightly of translates *kataphroneō*, which literally means "to think down on" something or someone and to underestimate the true value. It therefore often had the connotation of disregarding or even despising.

Through the prophet Hosea, God proclaimed His great love for His people, saying, "When Israel was a youth I loved him, and out of Egypt I called My son. . . . I who taught Ephraim to walk, I took them in My arms; . . . I led them with cords of a man, with bonds of love, and I became to them as one who lifts the yoke from their jaws; and I bent down and fed them" (Hos. 11:1, 3-4). But "My people are bent on turning from Me," the Lord lamented. "Though they call them to the One on high, none at all exalts Him" (v. 7). It seemed that the more gracious God was to Israel, the more she presumed upon or spurned His grace.

Without exception, every person who has ever lived has experienced the **kindness and forbearance and patience** of God. Every breath a person takes and every bite of food he eats is by the kind provision of God. God is the only source of goodness, and therefore everything good and worthwhile a person has is from the gracious hand of God.

God's own **kindness** is reflected in His children and is one among the fruit of the Spirit that believers are to manifest (Gal. 5:22). **Forbearance** comes from *anochē,* which means "to hold back," as of judgment. It was sometimes used to designate a truce, which involves cessation of hostilities between warring parties. God's **forbearance** with mankind is a kind of temporary divine truce He has graciously proclaimed. **Patience** translates *makrothumia,* which was sometimes used of a powerful ruler who voluntarily withheld vengeance on an enemy or punishment of a criminal.

Until the inevitable moment of judgment, God's **kindness and forbearance and patience** are extended to all mankind, because He does not wish "for any to perish but for all to come to repentance" (2 Pet. 3:9). **Kindness** refers to the benefits God gives, **forbearance** refers to the judgment He withholds, and **patience** to the duration of both. For long periods of time the Lord is kind and forbearing. That is God's common grace or providence that He bestows on all of fallen mankind.

The psalmists rejoiced that "the earth is full of the lovingkindness of the Lord" (Ps. 33:5), that "the lovingkindness of God endures all day long" (52:1), that He gives "His wonders to the sons of men" (107:8), that the Lord is "good and doest good" (119:68), and that "the Lord is good to all, and His mercies are over all His works" (145:9).

Strangely, most people do not perceive of God as being totally good. Instead of recognizing His gracious provision, patience, and His mercy, they accuse Him of being insensitive and unloving for letting certain things happen. "How could God allow that little child to die?" they ask, or, "Why does God allow that good person to suffer pain and poor health and permit a scoundrel to enjoy health and wealth?" Such people judge God from an incomplete and distorted human perspective, failing to acknowledge that, if it were not for God's gracious goodness and patience, *no* human being would be alive. It is only His grace that allows any person to take another breath (Job 12:10).

Before God destroyed the world in the Flood, He waited 120 years for men to repent while Noah was building the ark and calling them to repentance through his preaching of righteousness (2 Pet. 2:5). Despite

His many warnings and Israel's continued rebellion, the Lord waited some 800 years before sending His people into captivity.

Rather than asking why God allows bad things to happen to seemingly good people, we should ask why He allows seemingly good things to happen to obviously bad people. We could ask why He does *not* strike down many other people for their sins, including Christians, as He did with Ananias and Sapphira (Acts 5:1-10). We should wonder why does God not cause the earth to swallow up apostate Christendom as He did with the rebellious Korah and his followers (Num. 16:25-32)? The reason is that God "endured with much patience vessels of wrath prepared for destruction, . . . in order that He might make known the riches of His glory upon vessels of mercy, which He prepared beforehand for glory" (Rom. 9:22-23).

The purpose of the **kindness of God** is not to excuse men of their sin but to convict them of it and lead them **to repentance.** *Metanoia* (**repentance**) has the basic meaning of changing one's mind about something. In the moral and spiritual realm it refers to changing one's mind about sin, from loving it to renouncing it and turning to God for forgiveness (1 Thess. 1:9).

The person who, because of **stubbornness and** an **unrepentant heart,** presumes on God's kindness, forbearance, and patience, is simply **storing up wrath for** himself **in the day of wrath and revelation of the righteous judgment of God.**

Stubbornness translates *sklērotēs*, which literally refers to hardness and is the word from which we get the medical term *sclerosis*. Arteriosclerosis refers to hardening of the arteries. Such physical hardening is an ideal picture of the spiritual condition of hearts that have become unresponsive and insensitive to God. But the spiritual condition is immeasurably worse than the physical. Hardening of the arteries may take a person to the grave, but hardening of his spiritual heart will take him to hell.

Scripture is replete with warnings about spiritual hardness, an affliction which ancient Israel suffered almost continually. Through Ezekiel, God promised His people that one day "I will give you a new heart and put a new spirit within you; and I will remove the heart of stone from your flesh and give you a heart of flesh" (Ezek. 36:26). Jesus reminded His Jewish hearers that "because of your hardness of heart, Moses permitted you to divorce your wives" (Matt. 19:8). When the self-righteous, legalistic Jewish leaders were waiting for Jesus to heal on the Sabbath and thereby give them an excuse to accuse Him of breaking the law, He looked "around at them with anger, grieved at their hardness of heart" (Mark 3:5; cf. 6:52; 8:17; John 12:40). In each instance quoting the Old Testament, the writer of Hebrews three times warns against hardening one's heart to God (Heb. 3:8, 15; 4:7).

To stubbornly and unrepentantly refuse God's gracious pardon of sin through Jesus Christ is the worst sin of all. To do so is to greatly magnify one's guilt by rejecting God's goodness, presuming on His kindness, abusing His mercy, ignoring His grace, and spurning His love. The person who does that increases the severity of God's **wrath** upon him in **the day of** God's **judgment.** When God's goodness is persistently taken lightly, the result is certain and proportionate **judgment.**

The day of wrath and revelation of the righteous judgment of God doubtless refers to the great white throne judgment, at which the wicked of all times and from all places will be cast into the lake of fire, where they will join Satan and all his other evil followers (Rev. 20:10-15).

The German philosopher Heine presumptuously declared, "God will forgive; after all it's His trade." Many people share that presumption although they might not state it so bluntly. They take everything good from God that they can and continue sinning, thinking He is obliged to overlook their sin.

Modern man looks askance at the Old Testament, finding it impossible from his purely human perspective to explain the seemingly brutal and capricious acts on the part of God that are recorded there. Commenting on the release of the *New English Bible* some years ago, Lord Platt wrote to the London *Times* (March 3, 1970): "Perhaps, now that it is written in a language all can understand, the Old Testament will be seen for what it is, an obscene chronicle of man's cruelty to man, or worse perhaps, his cruelty to woman, and of man's selfishness and cupidity, backed up by his appeal to his god; a horror story if ever there was one. It is to be hoped that it will at last be proscribed as totally inappropriate to the ethical instruction of school-children."

Superficial study of the Old Testament seems to confirm that sentiment. Why, many people ask, did God destroy the whole world through the Flood, except for eight people? Why did God turn Lot's wife into a pillar of salt simply because she turned back to look at Sodom? Why did He command Abraham to sacrifice his son Isaac? Why did He harden Pharaoh's heart and then punish him for his hardness by slaying all the male children in Egypt? Why did God in the Mosaic law prescribe the death penalty for some thirty-five different offenses? Why did He command His chosen people to completely eradicate the inhabitants of Canaan? Why did God send two bears to kill forty-two teens for mocking the prophet Elisha? Why did He instantly slay Uzzah for trying to keep the Ark of the Covenant from falling to the ground, while at the same time allowing many grossly immoral and idolatrous Israelites to live? Why did God send fire to devour Aaron's two sons, Nadab and Abihu, for making an improper sacrifice while allowing many other ungodly priests to live to old age? Why did He not take David's life for committing murder and adultery, both of which were capital offenses under the law?

We wonder about such things only if we compare His justice with His mercy rather than with His law. The Old Testament must be understood from the perspective of the creation. God declared to Adam, "From any tree of the garden you may eat freely; but from the tree of the knowledge of good and evil you shall not eat, for in the day that you eat from it you shall surely die" (Gen. 2:16-17). From the beginning, therefore, *all* sin was a capital offense.

God sovereignly created man in His own image. He made man to glorify Himself and to radiate His image and manifest His character. When man rebelled by trusting Satan's word above God's, God had every right to take life back from man. Man is God's creature. He did not create himself and he cannot preserve himself. Everything he has is by God's gracious provision.

Although by justice they deserved to die for eating the forbidden fruit, Adam and Eve instead experienced God's mercy. And at that moment the plan of salvation was activated, because it became necessary for someone to bear the death penalty that Adam and Eve deserved and every subsequent sinner has deserved. In light of that provision it becomes clear that demanding the death penalty for only about thirty-five transgressions, as in the Mosaic law, was not cruel and unusual punishment but an amazing reduction in the severity of God's judgment.

Compared to the original created standard, the Old Testament is full of God's patience and mercy, with Gentiles as well as with His chosen people, Israel. Even in the case of the specified capital offenses, God frequently did not demand their enforcement. When adultery became commonplace in Israel, instead of demanding that every adulterer be put to death, God permitted divorce as a gracious alternative (Deut. 24:1-4). And even a cursory reading of the Old Testament clearly reveals that God graciously spared many more sinners than He executed (people like David). Periodically, God did dramatically take someone's life to remind men of what all sinners deserve. Such incidents seem capricious because they were not clearly related to certain sins or degrees of sinning, but showed, by example, what all sins and degrees of sinning deserve.

Even under the Old Covenant, God's people became so accustomed to God's grace that they came to take it for granted. They became so accustomed to not being punished in the way they deserved that they came to think they were above being punished at all. In much the same way, Christians sometimes become offended when God is not as beneficent as they think He should be and are scandalized at the idea of His actually punishing them for their sin.

If God did not occasionally exercise deserved judgment instead of undeserved mercy, it is hard to imagine how much more we would trade on His goodness and abuse His grace. If He did not give periodic reminders of the consequences of sin, we would go on blissfully presuming on His grace. Paul soberly reminded the Corinthian believers,

> For I do not want you to be unaware, brethren, that our fathers were all under the cloud, and all passed through the sea; and all were baptized into Moses in the cloud and in the sea; and all ate the same spiritual food; and all drank the same spiritual drink, for they were drinking from a spiritual rock which followed them; and the rock was Christ. Nevertheless, with most of them God was not well-pleased; for they were laid low in the wilderness. Now these things happened as examples for us, that we should not crave evil things, as they also craved. And do not be idolaters, as some of them were; as it is written, "The people sat down to eat and drink, and stood up to play." Nor let us act immorally, as some of them did, and twenty-three thousand fell in one day. Nor let us try the Lord, as some of them did, and were destroyed by the serpents. Nor grumble, as some of them did, and were destroyed by the destroyer. Now these things happened to them as an example, and they were written for our instruction. (1 Cor. 10:1-11)

Every day we live we should thank the Lord for being so patient and merciful with us, overlooking the many sins for which, even as His children, we deserve His just punishment. The crucial question is not "Why do certain people suffer or die?," but "Why does anyone live?"

When some Jews asked Jesus "about the Galileans, whose blood Pilate had mingled with their sacrifices," He replied, "Do you suppose that these Galileans were greater sinners than all other Galileans, because they suffered this fate? I tell you, no, but, unless you repent, you will all likewise perish. Or do you suppose that those eighteen on whom the tower in Siloam fell and killed them, were worse culprits than all the men who live in Jerusalem? I tell you, no, but, unless you repent, you will all likewise perish" (Luke 13:1-5).

Obviously those who questioned Jesus thought that the worshipers who were slaughtered by Pilate and the men who were killed in the tower accident were exceptionally wicked sinners and were being punished by God. Jesus plainly contradicted their presupposition, however, telling them that those unfortunate victims were no more sinful than other Jews. More than that, He warned His questioners that *all* of them were guilty of death and would indeed ultimately suffer that punishment if they did not repent and turn to God.

Principles of God's Judgment—part 2

who will render to every man according to his deeds: to those who by perseverance in doing good seek for glory and honor and immortality, eternal life; but to those who are selfishly ambitious and do not obey the truth, but obey unrighteousness, wrath and indignation. There will be tribulation and distress for every soul of man who does evil, of the Jew first and also of the Greek, but glory and honor and peace to every man who does good, to the Jew first and also to the Greek. For there is no partiality with God. For all who have sinned without the Law will also perish without the Law; and all who have sinned under the Law will be judged by the Law; for not the hearers of the Law are just before God, but the doers of the Law will be justified. For when Gentiles who do not have the Law do instinctively the things of the Law, these, not having the Law, are a law to themselves, in that they show the work of the Law written in their hearts, their conscience bearing witness, and their thoughts alternately accusing or else defending them, on the day when, according to my gospel, God will judge the secrets of men through Christ Jesus. (2:6-16)

Paul here continues to talk about "the day of wrath and revelation of the righteous judgment of God" (v. 5). As mentioned in the previous chapter, "the day of wrath" refers to God's final judgment of sinful mankind. Peter refers to it as "the day of judgment and destruction of ungodly men" (2 Pet. 3:7), and Jude as "the judgment of the great day" (v. 6). Paul explains that it will occur at the second coming of Jesus Christ, "who is to judge the living and the dead, and by His appearing and His kingdom" (2 Tim. 4:1). At that time "the Lord Jesus shall be revealed from heaven with His mighty angels in flaming fire, dealing out retribution to those who do not know God and to those who do not obey the gospel of our Lord Jesus" (2 Thess. 1:7-8).

This final judgment is described in some detail by John:

> I saw a great white throne and Him who sat upon it, from whose presence earth and heaven fled away, and no place was found for them. And I saw the dead, the great and the small, standing before the throne, and books were opened; and another book was opened, which is the book of life; and the dead were judged from the things which were written in the books, according to their deeds. And the sea gave up the dead which were in it, and death and Hades gave up the dead which were in them; and they were judged every one of them according to their deeds. And death and Hades were thrown into the lake of fire. This is the second death, the lake of fire. And if anyone's name was not found written in the book of life, he was thrown into the lake of fire. (Rev. 20:11-15)

Jesus declared that at that time "the Son of Man will send forth His angels, and they will gather out of His kingdom all stumbling blocks, and those who commit lawlessness, and will cast them into the furnace of fire; in that place there shall be weeping and gnashing of teeth. Then the righteous will shine forth as the sun in the kingdom of their Father" (Matt. 13:41-43). All of history is moving inexorably toward that awful day, when the sinful of all ages will "fall into the hands of the living God" (Heb. 10:31).

The story is told of an ancient Roman ruler named Brutus the Elder who discovered that his two sons were conspiring to overthrow the government, an offense that carried the death penalty. At the trial the young men tearfully pleaded with their father, calling him by endearing names and appealing to his paternal love. Most of the crowd who had gathered at court also pleaded for mercy. But because of the severity of the crime, and perhaps because being the ruler's sons made the men even more accountable and guilty of worse treason, the father ordered and then witnessed their execution. As someone has commented about the incident, "The father was lost in the judge; the love of justice overcame all the fondness of the parent."

God offers Himself as a Father to fallen mankind. He pleads with them to come to Him for salvation through His Son, because He does not want "any to perish but for all to come to repentance" (2 Pet. 3:9). But one day the opportunity for repentance will end. At that time God will execute His perfect judgment even more inexorably than that Roman ruler.

The first three of the six criteria God will employ in final judgment were discussed in the previous chapter. The second three are deeds (Rom. 2:6-10), impartiality (vv. 11-15), and motive (v. 16).

Deeds

who will render to every man according to his deeds: to those who by perseverance in doing good seek for glory and honor and immortality, eternal life; but to those who are selfishly ambitious and do not obey the truth, but obey unrighteousness, wrath and indignation. There will be tribulation and distress for every soul of man who does evil, of the Jew first and also of the Greek, but glory and honor and peace to every man who does good, to the Jew first and also to the Greek. (2:6-10)

Although it is simple and straightforward, this passage embraces several truths that are easily misinterpreted if not studied carefully.

In the text from Revelation 20 quoted above, we are twice told that men will be judged "according to their deeds" (vv. 12-13). That is the same truth Paul emphasizes in Romans 2:6-10, declaring plainly that God **will render to every man according to his deeds.**

Judgment by deeds, or works, is clearly taught in the Old Testament. The Lord instructed Isaiah to declare, "Say to the righteous that it will go well with them, for they will eat the fruit of their actions. Woe to the wicked! It will go badly with him, for what he deserves will be done to him" (Isa. 3:10-11). Through Jeremiah, God proclaimed even more specifically, "I, the Lord, search the heart, I test the mind, even to give to each man according to his ways, according to the results of his deeds" (Jer. 17:10).

Jesus reiterated that principle of judgment, teaching that "the Son of Man is going to come in the glory of His Father with His angels; and will then recompense every man according to his deeds" (Matt. 16:27). On another occasion He said, "Do not marvel at this; for an hour is coming, in which all who are in the tombs shall hear His voice, and shall come forth; those who did the good deeds to a resurrection of life, those who committed the evil deeds to a resurrection of judgment" (John 5:28-29).

Paul, the great apostle of salvation by grace alone through faith alone, consistently taught that God's judgment of believers as well as unbelievers will be based on works. "He who plants and he who waters are one; but each will receive his own reward according to his own labor" (1 Cor. 3:8). He goes on to explain,

> No man can lay a foundation other than the one which is laid, which is Jesus Christ. Now if any man builds upon the foundation with gold, silver, precious stones, wood, hay, straw, each man's work will become evident; for the day will show it, because it is to be revealed with fire; and the fire itself will test the quality of each man's work. If any man's work which he has built upon it remains, he shall receive a reward. If any man's work is burned up, he shall suffer loss; but he himself shall be saved, yet so as through fire. (1 Cor. 3:11-15)

Again speaking to believers Paul writes, "We must all appear before the judgment seat of Christ, that each one may be recompensed for his deeds in the body, according to what he has done, whether good or bad" (2 Cor. 5:10). Even in that wondrous epistle of grace Paul declares, "Do not be deceived, God is not mocked; for whatever a man sows, this he will also reap. For the one who sows to his own flesh shall from the flesh reap corruption, but the one who sows to the Spirit shall from the Spirit reap eternal life. And let us not lose heart in doing good, for in due time we shall reap if we do not grow weary" (Gal. 6:7-9).

God does not judge on the basis of religious profession, religious relationships, or religious heritage. But among other standards, He judges on the basis of the products of a person's life. An issue on the day of judgment will not be whether a person is a Jew or Gentile, whether he is a heathen or orthodox, whether he is religious or irreligious, or whether he attends church or does not. An issue will be whether or not his life has manifested obedience to God. On that day "each one of us shall give account of himself to God" (Rom. 14:12).

The subjective criterion for salvation is faith alone, with nothing added. But the objective reality of that salvation is manifested in the subsequent godly works that the Holy Spirit leads and empowers believers to perform. For that reason, good deeds are a perfectly valid basis for God's judgment.

A person's actions form an infallible index to his character. "You will know them by their fruits," Jesus twice declared in the Sermon on the Mount (Matt. 7:16, 20). The works of a person's life are one of the unchanging bases upon which God will judge men. Every man will one day face the divine Judge, who has a comprehensive record of that man's deeds, and by that record, the man's eternal destiny will be determined.

It must be made clear, of course, that although Scripture, both Old and New Testaments, teaches that *judgment* is by works, it nowhere teaches that *salvation* is by works. "Not to us, O Lord, not to us, but to Thy name give glory because of Thy lovingkindness, because of Thy truth" (Ps. 115:1). Whatever good a person has or does comes by God's gracious provision, and only He should be given credit and praise for those things. "For My own sake, for My own sake, I will act," the Lord declared through Isaiah. "For how can My name be profaned? And My glory I will not give to another" (Isa. 48:11). God will save whom He will save, and His sovereign grace completely excludes works righteousness.

Speaking of the New Covenant in His Son, Jesus Christ, God promised ancient Israel:

> Behold, days are coming . . . when I will make a new covenant with the house of Israel and with the house of Judah, not like the covenant which I made with their fathers in the day I took them by the hand to bring them out of the land of Egypt, My covenant which they broke, although I was a husband to them. . . . But this is the covenant which I will make with the house of Israel after those days, . . . I will put My law within them, and on their heart I will write it; and I will be their God, and they shall be My people. (Jer. 31:31-33)

The essence of the New Covenant is God's extension of mercy and grace to unworthy people. The work of salvation is entirely by God's sovereign and gracious will and power. "It is a trustworthy statement, deserving full acceptance," Paul said, "that Christ Jesus came into the world to save sinners, among whom I am foremost of all. And yet for this reason I found mercy, in order that in me as the foremost, Jesus Christ might demonstrate His perfect patience" (1 Tim. 1,15-10). To all believers the apostle says, "For by grace you have been saved through faith; and that not of yourselves, it is the gift of God; not as a result of works, that no one should boast" (Eph. 2:8-9).

But if salvation is wholly by faith, then how do works enter the picture? Paul continues his great statement in Ephesians 2 by saying, "For we are His workmanship, created in Christ Jesus for good works, which God prepared beforehand, that we should walk in them" (v. 10). The same apostle admonished the Philippian believers to "work out your salvation with fear and trembling; for it is God who is at work in you, both to will and to work for His good pleasure" (Phil. 2:12-13). In other words, the life that is saved by faith is to give evidence of that salvation by doing God's work. Outward godly works are the evidence of inner faith.

Salvation is not *by* works, but it will assuredly *produce* works. The presence of genuinely good deeds in a person's life reveals that he has truly been saved, and in God's infallible eyes those deeds are a perfectly reliable indicator of saving faith. In the same way, the absence of genuinely good deeds reveals the absence of salvation. In both cases, deeds become a trustworthy basis for God's judgment. When God sees works that manifest righteousness, He knows if they have come from a regenerated heart. And when He sees works that manifest unrighteousness, He knows if they come from an unregenerated heart.

In Romans 2:1-16 Paul is not talking about the basis for salvation but the basis for judgment. He does not begin discussing salvation as such until chapter three. In the present passage he is talking about deeds as one of the elements, or principles, God employs in judgment. He is discussing the *evidences* of salvation, not the means or basis of it. He is saying that if a person is truly saved, there will be outward evidence of it in his life. If he is not saved, there will be no such evidence. Every believer falls short of God's perfect righteousness and sometimes will fall into disobedience. But a life that is completely barren of righteous deeds can make no claim to being redeemed.

In Romans 2:7-10 Paul draws a clear line between two classes of people, the only two classes that exist: the saved and the unsaved. He focuses first on the determinative deeds of the redeemed (v. 7), next on the determinative deeds of the unredeemed (vv. 8-9), and then again on the deeds of the redeemed (v. 10).

THE DEEDS OF THE REDEEMED

to those who by perseverance in doing good seek for glory and honor and immortality, eternal life; (2:7)

True salvation is manifested in a believer's **perseverance in doing good,** and the highest good he can do is to **seek for glory, and honor and immortality.** Although those three terms seem to be used here almost as synonyms, they carry distinct meanings. Together they describe a believer's heavenly perspective and aspirations.

First, the highest and most wonderful desire of a believer is **glory,** above all, God's glory. A person who does not have such a desire deep within him cannot be a true believer. "Whether, then, you eat or drink or whatever you do, do all to the glory of God," Paul admonishes (1 Cor. 10:31). To live to the glory of God is to manifest the very nature of God as a willing vehicle for His own divine working.

A believer also seeks **glory** for himself, not in the fleshly, self-seeking way that is common to fallen human nature, but by looking forward to his sharing God's own glory some day when his salvation is perfected (see Rom. 8:21, 30; 2 Thess. 2:14; cf. Ps. 17:15). We know that any "momentary, light affliction is producing for us an eternal weight of glory far beyond all comparison" (2 Cor. 4:17) and that "when Christ, who is our life, is revealed, then [we] also will be revealed with Him in glory" (Col. 3:4). In seeking this heavenly glory it is really a seeking of Christlikeness. Paul had it in mind when he penned Philippians 3:10-14, 20, 21:

> that I may know Him, and the power of His resurrection and the fellowship of His sufferings, being conformed to His death; in order that I may attain to the resurrection from the dead. Not that I have already obtained it, or have already become perfect, but I press on in order that I may lay hold of that for which also I was laid hold of by Christ Jesus. Brethren, I do not regard myself as having laid hold of it yet; but one thing I do: forgetting what lies behind and reaching forward to what lies ahead, I press on toward the goal for the prize of the upward call of God in Christ Jesus.
>   . . . For our citizenship is in heaven, from which also we eagerly wait for a Savior, the Lord Jesus Christ; who will transform the body of our humble state into conformity with the body of His glory, by the exertion of the power that He has even to subject all things to Himself.

Second, a true believer seeks **honor,** again not the worldly honor that most men long for but the honor that comes from God, the honor of His saying, "Well done, good and faithful slave; you were faithful with a few things, I will put you in charge of many things, enter into the joy of your master" (Matt. 25:21).

Third, a true believer seeks **immortality,** the day when his perishable body "must put on the imperishable, and this mortal must put on immortality" (1 Cor. 15:53).

Paul is not discussing how a person comes to salvation or *how* God produces Christlikeness in him. He is describing what the life of a true believer is like, pointing out that those divinely-bestowed qualities will eventuate in the final glory of the divinely-bestowed **eternal life.** John beautifully states that basic truth at the end of his first epistle: "We know that the Son of God has come, and has given us understanding, in order that we might know Him who is true, and we are in Him who is true, in His Son Jesus Christ. This is the true God and eternal life" (1 John 5:20).

Eternal life is not simply a quantity of life, although by definition it lasts through eternity. But even the unsaved will have eternal *existence,* an existence which will be everlasting death and punishment (2 Thess. 1:9; Rev. 14:9-11). **Eternal life,** however, is first of all a quality of life, the life of God in the soul of man. Speaking of his own eternal life, Paul said, "It is no longer I who live, but Christ lives in me; and the life which I now live in the flesh I live by faith in the Son of God, who loved me, and delivered Himself up for me" (Gal. 2:20).

Paul's point in the present passage is that a person who possesses the life of God will reflect the true character of God, and that it is on the basis of that reflected godly character that he will be judged. It is just as impossible for a person having eternal life to indefinitely fail to reflect something of God's character as it would be for him to indefinitely hold his breath. Eternal life induces spiritual breathing just as surely as physical life induces bodily breathing. John Murray succinctly noted that "works without redemptive aspiration are dead works. Aspiration without good works is presumption."

Justification by faith alone does not negate works of righteousness in the believer's life. Scripture makes clear that just as surely as we are saved by our faith we will be judged by our works. When in sovereign grace God receives a sinner at the time of his conversion, He asks nothing but that he believe in Jesus Christ and submit to Him. But from that moment on, the believer enters into a responsibility of obedience, and the mark of his new spiritual life becomes his obedience to God. Faith in Christ does not produce freedom to sin and to do as we please but freedom *from* sin and a new, God-given desire and capacity to do what pleases Him.

James makes the relationship between faith and works explicitly clear:

> What use is it, my brethren, if a man says he has faith, but he has no works? Can that faith save him? If a brother or sister is without clothing and in need of daily food, and one of you says to them, "Go in peace, be warmed and be filled," and yet you do not give them what is necessary for their body, what use is that? Even so faith, if it has no works, is dead, being by itself. But someone may well say, "You have faith, and I have works; show me your faith without the works, and I will show you my faith by my works." You believe that God is one. You do well; the demons also believe, and shudder. But are you willing to recognize, you foolish fellow, that faith without works is useless? . . . For just as the body without the spirit is dead, so also faith without works is dead. (James 2:14-20, 26)

In Romans 2:7 Paul is focusing on the completed, fulfilled **eternal life** that comes after the final judgment, when the eternal state begins. This completed eternal life will be rendered according to the salvation evidenced by those good deeds a believer has manifested during his life on earth (v. 6).

THE DEEDS OF THE UNREDEEMED

but to those who are selfishly ambitious and do not obey the truth, but obey unrighteousness, wrath and indignation. There will be tribulation and distress for every soul of man who does evil, of the Jew first and also of the Greek, (2:8-9)

Here Paul contrasts those who prove by their good deeds that they belong to God with those who similarly prove by their bad deeds that they do not belong to Him. Those who do not belong to God manifest many evil characteristics, three of the general underlying ones Paul mentions in verse 8.

The first characteristic of the unredeemed is that they are **selfishly ambitious,** a phrase that translates the single Greek word *eritheia,* the root meaning of which may have been that of a hireling. The idea is of a mercenary, who does his work simply for money, without regard for the issues or any harm he may be doing. Everything he does is for the purpose of serving and pleasing self. Certainly this fits the Bible's emphasis that the basic problem of unregenerate man is his being totally wrapped up in himself and having no place in his life for God.

The second and consequent characteristic of the unredeemed is that they **do not obey the truth.** The person who seeks his own way above all else naturally resists any other way, including God's, which is the way of **truth.** Disobedience of **the truth** is synonymous with rebellion, and spiritual rebellion is what the Fall was all about and what fallen human nature is all about. The unredeemed are rebels by nature, the enemies of God (Rom. 8:7; cf. 5:10; Col. 1:21).

The third characteristic of the unredeemed is that they **obey unrighteousness.** No person lives in a moral and spiritual vacuum. He is either godly or ungodly, righteous or unrighteous. Jesus declared categorically that "no one can serve two masters; for either he will hate the one and love the other, or he will hold to one and despise the other" (Matt. 6:24). And it can be deduced that no man serves no master. It is either God or another. And when man does not serve God, all other masters lead him to sin. Serving God means obeying God's will! Serving another master means obeying sin.

The road to hell is here very simply defined as the spirit of antagonism against the lordship of Jesus Christ. The unsaved person is by nature **selfishly ambitious,** and his enmity against God leads him to disobey God's truth and instead to **obey unrighteousness.**

To such people God will render (see v. 6) **wrath and indignation.** *Orgē* (**wrath**) signifies the strongest kind of anger, that which reaches fever pitch, when God's mercy and grace are fully exhausted. It will mark the end of God's patience and tolerance with unregenerate, unrepentant mankind in the swelling of His final, furious anger which He will vent on those whose works evidence their persistent and unswerving rebellion against Him.

Thumos (**indignation**) represents an agitated, vehement anger that rushes along relentlessly. The root meaning has to do with moving rapidly and was used of a man's breathing violently while pursuing an enemy in great rage. It is used by the writer of Hebrews to describe Pharaoh's murderous fury at Moses (Heb. 11:27; cf. Ex. 10:28). It is used by Luke to describe the fury of the Jews in the synagogue at Nazareth who wanted to throw Jesus off a cliff (Luke 4:28-29). It is used of the pagan Ephesians who resented Paul's preaching the gospel and especially his claim that their idols "made with hands [were] no gods at all" (Acts 19:26-28). On the final day of judgment God's **indignation** will explode like a consuming fire upon all rebellious mankind.

Consequently, **there will be tribulation and distress for every soul of man who does evil.** *Thlipsis* (**tribulation**) has the root meaning of exerting extreme pressure, and is sometimes translated as *affliction, anguish,* or *persecution.* It is used of the persecution of the early church by the Jews in Palestine (Acts 11:19) and of the tribulation of the saints in general (John 16:33; Acts 14:22; Rom. 5:3; 2 Thess. 1:4). Paul used it to describe his persecution in the province of Asia (2 Cor. 1:8), and it is used of the crushing of the grapes of wrath during the great battle of Armageddon (Rev. 14:18-20).

Stenochōria (**distress**) literally means "a narrow place" and came metaphorically to refer to severe confinement or constriction, and hence the idea of anguish or severe **distress.** Besides capital punishment, solitary confinement has long been considered the worst form of punishment, being the absolute, lonely confinement of a prisoner who is already strictly confined. Part of hell's torment will be its absolute, isolated, lonely, and eternal confinement, with no possible hope of release or escape.

Paul uses the phrase **the Jew first and also the Greek** twice in this passage, and it is significant that the first instance relates to those who are *condemned* by God. Jews were used to thinking of themselves as being first in God's sight. The typical Jew, in fact, believed that, with perhaps a very few exceptions such as Rahab and Ruth, Gentiles were by nature beyond the reach of God's care and redemption.

God had indeed chosen Israel above other peoples to be His elect nation. "You only have I chosen among all the families of the earth," He declared to Israel (Amos 3:2*a*). But He immediately went on to say, "Therefore, I will punish you for all your iniquities" (v. 2*b*). Israel will receive severer punishment because she was given greater light and greater blessing. As Paul here makes clear, **the Jew first** means that being first in salvation opportunity also means being first in judgment responsibility.

The righteous deeds that God requires and for which men will be judged are, of course, impossible even for a believer to produce in his own power. He is no more able to keep his salvation by good works than he was able to attain it by goods works. Like salvation itself, the good works it produces are made possible by God's sovereign grace alone and empowered by His Holy Spirit working within the life. The only way to produce righteous deeds is to possess the righteousness of Christ, which comes by trusting in Him as Lord and Savior, to possess the Holy Spirit who empowers those works, and to consciously seek to obey the Word of God!

In His infinite justice as well as His infinite grace, God will be certain that the **glory and honor** that is sought by **every man who does good** will indeed be his reward. This **peace** that God divinely imparts is perhaps used by Paul as a synonym for the immortality the true believer seeks along with glory and honor (see v. 7). Everything divine that the saint of God seeks he will receive.

Again the apostle points out that the order of judgment will be that of **the Jew first** and then **the Greek**. The unbelieving Jew will be the first to be condemned (v. 9). Only after God has dealt with His chosen people will He deal with **the Greek**, that is, the Gentile.

IMPARTIALITY

For there is no partiality with God. For all who have sinned without the Law will also perish without the Law; and all who have sinned under the Law will be judged by the Law; for not the hearers of the Law are just before God, but the doers of the Law will be justified. For when Gentiles who do not have the Law do instinctively the things of the Law, these, not having the Law, are a law to themselves, in that they show the work of the Law written in their hearts, their conscience bearing witness, and their thoughts alternately accusing or else defending them, (2:11-15)

A fifth element related to God's judgment is His impartiality. *Prosōpolēmptēs* (**partiality**) means literally "to receive a face," that is, to give consideration to a person because of who he is. That exact idea is seen in the popular symbolic statue of justice as a woman blindfolded, signifying that she is unable to see who is before her to be judged and therefore is not tempted to be partial either for or against the accused.

Sometimes she is also pictured with her hands tied, suggesting she cannot receive a bribe.

Unfortunately, there is partiality even in the best of human courts, but there will be none in God's day of judgment. Because of His perfect knowledge of every detail and because of His perfect righteousness, it is not possible for His justice to be anything but perfectly impartial. Such things as position, education, influence, popularity, or physical appearance will have absolutely no bearing on God's decision concerning a person's eternal destiny.

The most magnificent and exalted creature God made was Lucifer, the "star of the morning, son of the dawn." But because of his prideful ambition to raise himself even above his Creator, to make himself "like the Most High," even the high-ranking, majestic Lucifer was cast out of heaven by God to Sheol (Isa. 14:12-15). The most exalted became the most debased. If ever there was a being whose position merited special favor before God it was Lucifer. But his high position instead made him more accountable for his evil rebellion and he therefore will receive the greatest punishment of any creature in hell.

When Peter saw how God was working in the life of Cornelius, he was finally able to surmount his Jewish prejudice against Gentiles and confess, "I most certainly understand now that God is not one to show partiality" (Acts 10:34). Like his Lord, Paul was not impressed by a person's elevated religious position (Gal. 2:6). That quality of justice is also implied in the apostle's declaration that "God is not mocked; for whatever a man sows, this he will also reap" (Gal. 6:7). Who a person is will have no bearing at all on what he reaps at God's judgment. "The one who sows to his own flesh shall from the flesh reap corruption, but the one who sows to the Spirit shall from the Spirit reap eternal life" (v. 8).

In warning masters to be considerate of their slaves, Paul reminds them that "both their Master and yours is in heaven, and there is no partiality with Him" (Eph. 6:9). "He who does wrong will receive the consequences of the wrong which he has done," the apostle assured the Colossians, "and that without partiality" (Col. 3:25). Peter admonished his readers, "If you address as Father the One who impartially judges according to each man's work, conduct yourselves in fear during the time of your stay upon earth" (1 Pet. 1:17).

God's impartiality does not exclude His taking into account the varying spiritual light that people have. Paul mentions two distinct groups of sinners: those who have not had opportunity to know God's **Law** and those who have had such opportunity. He is speaking, of course, about **the Law** given through Moses to the people of Israel. Those **without the Law** are therefore the Gentiles.

It is not that Gentiles have no awareness of God or sense of right and wrong. The apostle has already established that, through the evidence of creation, all men have witness of God's "eternal power and divine nature" (1:20). Gentiles **who have sinned without the law will** therefore **also perish without the Law,** that is, they will be judged according to their more limited knowledge of God. That, of course, includes the vast majority of humanity of all times. Even with the increased ability to distribute God's Word in the various languages of the world, and the remarkable new techniques and media for preaching the gospel, most people in the world today have never heard clear teaching from the Bible, much less grasped clear knowledge of its saving truths.

But because they have God's natural revelation in creation, as well as the witness of right and wrong in their hearts and consciences (v. 15), they are guilty and accountable. They will therefore **perish without the Law.** *Apollumi* (**perish**) pertains to destruction but not annihilation. It basically has to do with that which is ruined and is no longer usable for its intended purpose. That is the term Jesus used to speak of those who are thrown into hell (Matt. 10:28). As He makes clear elsewhere, hell is not a place or state of nothingness or unconscious existence, as is the Hindu Nirvana. It is the place of everlasting torment, the place of eternal death, where there will be "weeping and gnashing of teeth" (see Matt. 13:42, 50). All people are created by God for His glory, but when they refuse to come to Him for salvation they lose their opportunity for redemption, for becoming what God intends for them to be. They are then fit only for condemnation and destruction.

The lost Gentile will just as surely **perish** as the lost Jew, but, as Paul has already intimated (v. 9), their eternal tribulation and distress will be less than that of the Jews, who have had the immeasurable advantage of possessing God's law. Jesus stated the principle clearly. Using the illustration of the slaves of a master who returned after a long journey, He said, "That slave who knew his master's will and did not get ready or act in accord with his will, shall receive many lashes, but the one who did not know it, and committed deeds worthy of a flogging, will receive but few. And from everyone who has been given much shall much be required; and to whom they entrusted much, of him they will ask all the more" (Luke 12:47-48).

It is Jews, those to whom the Lord had entrusted much, whom the apostle addresses next, declaring that **all who have sinned under the Law will be judged by the Law.** The person who has not had the benefit of knowing God's **Law** will be judged according to his limited knowledge of God. But the person who has access to God's **Law** will be judged according to his greater knowledge about the Lord.

Those who have knowledge not only of the Old Testament law but also of the New Testament gospel are also included in this second category of those who are judged. And because they have even greater knowledge of God than the ancient Jews, they will be held still more accountable.

They will be like the Jewish cities of Chorazin, Bethsaida, and Capernaum, which had heard Jesus' teaching and witnessed His miracles but had rejected Him as their Messiah and King. They not only had God's law but had been privileged to meet God's only Son. The Lord scathingly told them it would therefore be better on the day of judgment for the pagan cities of Tyre, Sidon, and Sodom than for them (Matt. 11:20-23).

Though all unbelievers will be there, the hottest part of hell will be reserved for those who have wasted the greatest spiritual opportunity. That is why it is such a fearful thing to be an apostate, one who has known and even acknowledged God's truth but ultimately turned his back on it. Of such people the writer of Hebrews says, "For in the case of those who have once been enlightened and have tasted of the heavenly gift and have been made partakers of the Holy Spirit, and have tasted the good word of God and the powers of the age to come, and then have fallen away, it is impossible to renew them again to repentance, since they again crucify to themselves the Son of God, and put Him to open shame" (Heb. 6:4-6). Hebrews 10:26-31 adds:

> For if we go on sinning willfully after receiving the knowledge of the truth, there no longer remains a sacrifice for sins, but a certain terrifying expectation of judgment, and the fury of a fire which will consume the adversaries. Anyone who has set aside the Law of Moses dies without mercy on the testimony of two or three witnesses. How much severer punishment do you think he will deserve who has trampled under foot the Son of God, and has regarded as unclean the blood of the covenant by which he has been sanctified, and has insulted the Spirit of grace? For we know Him who said, "Vengeance is Mine, I will repay." And again, "The Lord will judge His people." It is a terrifying thing to fall into the hands of the living God.

Although those who have the opportunity to hear God's Word have a great advantage above those who do not have such opportunity, if they fail to heed His Word they are much worse off than those others.

For not the hearers of the Law are just before God, Paul says, **but the doers of the Law will be justified.** Just as James does in his warning about those who hear God's Word but do not do it (James 1:22-23), Paul here does not use the usual Greek term for hearing (*akouō*) but the word *akroatēs*, which was used of those whose business it is to listen.

The idea is much like that of a college student. His primary purpose in class is to listen to the teacher's instruction. Normally, he also has the responsibility of being accountable for what he hears and is tested on it. If he is simply auditing, however, he is required only to attend the class sessions. He takes no tests and receives no grade. In other words, he listens without being held accountable for what he hears.

In many synagogues during Paul's time, teaching did not focus on Scripture but on the system of man-made traditions that the rabbis had developed over the centuries since the Exile. Frequently, God's Word in the Old Testament was merely read and listened to, without explanation or application. Most Jews, therefore, were simply "auditing the course," **hearers of the Law** and nothing more.

But God recognizes no mere "auditors" of His Word. The more a person hears His truth, the more he is responsible for believing and obeying it. Unless there is obedience, the greater the hearing, the greater the judgment.

People who only think they are Christians merely because they do such things as attend church, listen to sermon tapes, participate in a neighborhood Bible study, and listen to Christian music "delude themselves," James warns. "For if anyone is a hearer of the word and not a doer, he is like a man who looks at his natural face in a mirror; for once he has looked at himself and gone away, he has immediately forgotten what kind of person he was" (James 1:23-24). In other words, the person who is satisfied with superficially knowing God's Word is living a spiritual illusion, thinking he is saved when he is not. By looking in a mirror, he judges himself by himself rather than by the Word of God that he knows much about but does not take to heart. His failure to obey what he hears proves he does not believe it or accept it. His disobedience proves he does not trust in the God whose Word he hears. And the more he hears without obeying the more he piles up guilt against himself for the day of judgment. Our Lord certainly had this on His mind when he preached the conclusion of the Sermon on the Mount. Matt. 7:24-27 records His words:

> Therefore everyone who hears these words of Mine, and acts upon them, may be compared to a wise man, who built his house upon the rock. And the rain descended, and the floods came, and the winds blew, and burst against that house; and yet it did not fall, for it had been founded upon the rock. And everyone who hears these words of Mine, and does not act upon them, will be like a foolish man, who built his house upon the sand. And the rain descended, and the floods came, and the winds blew, and burst against that house; and it fell, and great was its fall.

The **doers of the Law,** on the other hand, are those who come to God in repentance and faith, realizing that His **Law** is impossible for them to keep apart from Him and that knowledge of it places them under greater obligation to obey it. The true **doers** of God's law are those who come to Jesus Christ in faith, because the purpose of the law is to lead men to Him (Gal. 3:24). And after they have come to Him in faith, their obedient lives give evidence of their saving relationship to Him and of the fact that they **will be justified.** The idea here is not that obeying the law will produce justification, because Scripture makes clear that justification *comes* only through faith (Rom. 3:24, 28). But they will be demonstrated to be the just by the evidence of their doing of God's holy law.

Again Paul is pointing to the same truth as James in regard to the relationship between faith and works, and, also like James, is using justification in the sense of completed or perfected salvation. The person who genuinely obeys God's Word proves by his divinely-empowered obedience that he is saved and thereby **will be** recognized as **justified** on the day of judgment (cf. James 2:20-26).

Does that mean, then, that Gentiles are excused from eternal judgment and punishment because they have not had the advantage of **the Law** and therefore had no basis for obedient living? No, because as Paul has already established, **the Gentiles,** that is, those **who do not have the Law,** have God's general, or natural, revelation of Himself in creation and know instinctively that they are guilty and worthy of death (1:18-32). But does not Paul say later in this epistle that "where there is no law, neither is there violation" (4:15), that "until the Law sin was in the world; but sin is not imputed when there is no law" (5:13), and "I would not have come to know sin except through the Law" (7:7)?

Anticipating such questions, Paul here states that **Gentiles who do not have the Law do instinctively the things of the Law,** being a **law to themselves.** Explaining further, the apostle says, **They show the work of the Law written in their hearts, their conscience bearing witness, and their thoughts alternately accusing or else defending them.**

There are four reasons why the heathen are lost. First, as already noted, their rejection of their knowledge of God available through His *creation* condemns them.

Second, as the apostle now points out, their *conduct,* based on the knowledge **of the Law written in their hearts,** condemns them. Throughout history there have been many unbelievers who have been honest in business, respectful of their parents, faithful to their wives or husbands, caring of their children, and generous to those in need—all of which good things God's Word commends. God's standard of justice is reflected in many secular judicial systems, wherein stealing, murder, and various other forms of immorality are considered wrong and made illegal. Many pagan philosophies, both ancient and modern, teach certain standards of ethics that closely parallel those in Scripture.

The Bible reports many good deeds done by pagans such as Darius (Dan. 6:25-28), the city clerk of Ephesus (Acts 19:35-41), the Roman military officers who protected Paul (Acts 23:10, 17-35), and the natives of Malta who befriended Paul and his shipmates (Acts 28:10). The fact that such people did good things, *knowing they were ethically good,* proves they had knowledge of God's **Law written in their hearts.** Therefore if those people never come to trust in the true God, their good deeds will actually witness against them on the day of judgment.

Third, the heathen are condemned because of *conscience*. Gentiles who do not have the privilege of knowing God's law nevertheless have a **conscience bearing witness** to His law. *Suneidēsis* (**conscience**) literally means "knowledge with," or "co-knowledge." Synonyms of that term, most with the same root meaning, are found in many ancient languages. The very idea behind the word testifies to the fact that men recognize they have an instinctive, built-in sense of right and wrong that activates guilt.

It is reported that a tribe in Africa had an unusual but effective way to test the guilt of an accused person. A group of suspects would be lined up and the tongue of each would be touched with a hot knife. If saliva was on the tongue the blade would sizzle but cause little pain. But if the tongue was dry, the blade would stick and create a vicious, searing burn. The tribe knew that a sense of guilt tends to make a person's mouth dry, and a seared tongue therefore was taken as proof of guilt. The making of such a dry mouth is, of course, the work of the conscience.

Consciences vary in sensitivity, depending on the degree of one's knowledge of and feeling about right and wrong. The person who has considerable knowledge of God's Word will have a more sensitive conscience than someone who has never had opportunity to know Scripture.

But consciences also vary in sensitivity depending on whether they are obeyed or resisted. Some years ago it was discovered that, contrary to long-held medical thinking, the gross disfiguration of the extremities that is so common in lepers is not caused directly by the disease. Leprosy does not deteriorate or eat at the flesh but rather desensitizes the nerves. Unprotected by the warning signals of pain, the leper wears down his extremities or suffers cuts, burns, and infections without knowing he is being injured.

In much the same way, the neglected and resisted conscience becomes more insensitive and eventually may stop giving warning signals about wrongdoing. Paul speaks of heretics and apostates in the last days whose consciences will be desensitized as if cauterized by a hot iron because of their persistent opposition to God and His truth (1 Tim. 4:2).

God uses the consciences of His children as vehicles for His guidance. Paul therefore makes many appeals for believers to be faithful to the leading of their own consciences and to respect the consciences of other believers (see Rom. 13:5; 1 Cor. 8:7, 12; 10:25, 29; 2 Cor. 5:11). Consistent with his own teaching, the apostle was careful to obey his own conscience (Acts 23:1; 24:16; Rom. 9:1).

Fourth, the heathen are lost because of their *contemplation,* **their thoughts alternately accusing or else defending them**. This natural faculty obviously is closely related to conscience. Building on the instinctive knowledge of right and wrong that the conscience provides, even unbelievers have the obvious ability to determine that certain things are basically right or wrong.

Many ardent crime fighters and advocates for the poor, for example, do not get their motivation from Scripture or from a saving relationship to Jesus Christ. As human beings they simply cannot help but know that opposing crime and helping the poor are good things to do. Even the most godless society becomes incensed when a child or elderly person is brutally attacked or murdered. Even pagans, agnostics, and atheists are able to discern basic right and wrong.

For those four profound reasons, no person can stand guiltless before God's judgment. The fact that they do not turn to God proves they do not live up to the light God has given them. Jesus declared categorically, "If any man is willing to do His will, he shall know the teaching, whether it is of God, or whether I speak from Myself" (John 7:17). Paul assured his pagan listeners in Athens that God "made from one, every nation of mankind to live on all the face of the earth, having determined their appointed times, and the boundaries of their habitation, that they should seek God, if perhaps they might grope for Him and find Him, though He is not far from each one of us" (Acts 17:26-27). The person who genuinely seeks to know and follow God is divinely assured he will succeed. "You will seek Me and find Me," the Lord says, "when you search for Me with all your heart" (Jer. 29:13).

A man of my acquaintance is an excellent illustration of God's honoring a genuine quest to find Him. This man grew up in one of the most primitive tribes in Africa. Because he was ill-behaved and incorrigible as a child, he was frequently made to stay outside when the family had guests. Although he was severely punished by the tribe as well as by his mother, he persisted in acts of pointless mischief and even cruelty. He reports that he felt guilty and heartsick even while doing the mischief but could not seem to help himself. He knew something was very wrong with his life and would often go into the forest and pound his head against a tree, crying, "What's wrong with me? Why do I do such things?" More than once he considered suicide.

One day one of his friends returned from a visit to the coast. Among the many fascinating stories he told was that of some people who met together every Sunday to sing and talk. When the boy asked his friend why those people met together, he was told they were singing about and praying to the God who had created the whole world. They called their God *Father* and believed He heard and answered their prayers.

With that small bit of knowledge about the Lord, the boy over whom the tribe had despaired decided to pray to this God himself. "I had never heard anyone pray," he recounts, "but I decided I would just talk to this God like He was my father. I can't explain what happened but it was an exciting experience. I wanted to know more about this God but there was no one in our village who knew anything about Him. So for two years I kept praying by myself on Sundays, hoping that some day someone would come along who could tell me about Him."

While working on a government road project, he visited his cousin in the village where he had been born and discovered to his great surprise and delight that a group of people met there on Sundays to sing and pray to the God he had heard about. "How excited I was," he says. "I could hardly wait for Sunday. That morning I sat in the back. I listened to a man tell about God for the first time in my life. I found He was far more wonderful than I had ever imagined. The preacher said that God loved the world so much that He sent His only Son named Jesus to take away my sins. I wondered if He knew how terrible I was. I wondered if He knew the awful things I had done back in my village. But the preacher said no matter what I had done, God would forgive me and make my heart clean. I knew it was all true."

Because that young man had been genuinely seeking God, when he finally heard the gospel the Holy Spirit confirmed its truth to his yearning heart. He knew that God had heard his prayers and had sent him to a place where he could hear the message of salvation. "I gave my heart to God that morning," he testifies, "and it was nice to know He had a Son, too. He was really a Father, just like I had been praying to."

MOTIVE

on the day when, according to my gospel, God will judge the secrets of men through Christ Jesus. (2:16)

A sixth principle of God's judgment is that of motive. Here Paul makes clear that he is speaking about the *final* judgment, **the day when, according to my gospel, God will judge.**

Motive is a valid basis for judgment only because God is able to **judge the secrets of men through Jesus Christ.** Because the Lord infallibly knows every person's motives for doing the things he does, He can infallibly judge whether or not those deeds are truly good or bad, whether they come from the flesh or from the Spirit.

David counseled his son Solomon to serve God "with a whole heart and a willing mind; for the Lord searches all hearts, and understands every intent of the thoughts" (1 Chron. 28:9). In one of his most beautiful psalms David confessed, "O Lord, Thou hast searched me and known me. Thou dost know when I sit down and when I rise up; Thou dost understand my thought from afar. Thou dost scrutinize my path and my

lying down, and art intimately acquainted with all my ways" (Ps. 139:1-
3). Through Jeremiah God said, "I, the Lord, search the heart, I test the
mind, even to give to each man according to his ways, according to the
results of his deeds" (Jer. 17:10). Three times in the Sermon on the Mount
Jesus said, "Your Father who sees in secret will repay you" (Matt. 6:4, 6,
18).

There is obviously such a thing as relative human goodness. Many
unbelievers live on a high moral plane compared to most people. But that
is not the kind of goodness that satisfies God, because nothing is truly
good that is done from any motive other than His glory and done in any
power but His own. Everything that is done in the flesh can only serve
the flesh and is by nature tainted with imperfection and self-interest. It
cannot be done out of the only right motive, that of pleasing and glorifying
God. Whether done to impress others with one's goodness, to react to
peer pressure, to alleviate guilt feelings, or simply to feel better about
oneself, anything that is not done for God and through His power is
basically sinful and unacceptable to Him—no matter how outwardly
good and self-sacrificial it may appear to be.

David committed terrible sins while he served as God's anointed
king of God's chosen nation. As noted in the previous chapter, many of
his sins, such as his adultery with Bathsheba and the murder of her
husband Uriah, were capital offenses for which God could justly have
demanded David's life. But the basic motivation and direction of David's
life were not selfish ambition and unrighteousness but the service and
worship of God. He readily acknowledged and confessed his sins before
God, throwing himself on the Lord's mercy and grace. Judas, on the other
hand, although outwardly upright and religious and a professed follower
of Christ, was thoroughly self-centered. Inwardly he came to have
contempt for Christ and His gospel of grace. The heart desires that moved
those two men were open books to the Lord, and their respective guilt
and deeds will be judged for what they truly were and not for the way
they appeared to other men.

If Romans 2:6-16 teaches anything, it teaches that a redeemed life
will produce holy living and that a life that reflects no holy living has no
claim on eternal life. Right living, which can only come from right
motivation, is the God-given evidence of genuine salvation. Lack of right
living is just as certain evidence of lostness.

False Security

But if you bear the name "Jew," and rely upon the Law, and boast in God, and know His will, and approve the things that are essential, being instructed out of the Law, and are confident that you yourself are a guide to the blind, a light to those who are in darkness, a corrector of the foolish, a teacher of the immature, having in the Law the embodiment of knowledge and of the truth, you, therefore, who teach another, do you not teach yourself? You who preach that one should not steal, do you steal? You who say that one should not commit adultery, do you commit adultery? You who abhor idols, do you rob temples? You who boast in the Law, through your breaking the Law, do you dishonor God? For "the Name of God is blasphemed among the Gentiles because of you," just as it is written. For indeed circumcision is of value, if you practice the Law; but if you are a transgressor of the Law, your circumcision has become uncircumcision. If therefore the uncircumcised man keeps the requirements of the Law, will not his uncircumcision be regarded as circumcision? And will not he who is physically uncircumcised, if he keeps the Law, will he not judge you who though having the letter of the Law and circumcision are a transgressor of the Law? For he is not a Jew who is one outwardly;

neither is circumcision that which is outward in the flesh. But he is a Jew who is one inwardly; and circumcision is that which is of the heart, by the Spirit, not by the letter; and his praise is not from men, but from God. (2:17-29)

People long for economic security, job security, marital security, national security, health security, home security, security of social position, and many other kinds of security. It is the natural impulse of self-preservation to want security. Yet, despite the claims of independence and self-sufficiency that many people make, they know instinctively that, in themselves, they are not completely secure.

A measure of economic security can be had from such things as having a long-term work contract, working for or owning a business that has proven to do well even in hard times, or by having a diversified portfolio of investments. A measure of home security can be achieved by burglar alarms, high fences, or watch dogs. A measure of national security can be had from a well-trained, well-equipped military force. But history and personal experience have proved over and over again that such things cannot guarantee absolute security.

When they bother to think about it, most people hope for some form of *eternal* security. If they do not believe in heaven and hell, they hope death will be the end of existence, that it will usher them into an impersonal, unconscious nothingness, or recycle them through another lifetime in an endless linking chain of lives better than the ones before.

But Paul has already declared unequivocally that, whether they realize or admit it or not, *all* men, even the most pagan reprobates, know something of God's "invisible attributes, His eternal power and divine nature" (Rom. 1:18-21). Every person, Jew and Gentile alike, has the witness of heart and conscience, by which he is able to discern basic right from wrong (2:14-15). And all people know to some degree that those who do not live up to God's standards of righteousness are "worthy of death" (1:32). Most have this gnawing fear that God is going to judge their sin, that one day they will be held accountable for the way they have lived. And Scripture says they will live and die only once, "and after this comes judgment" (Heb. 9:27).

Therefore instinctively people hope that, in some way or another, they can escape that judgment. Whether consciously or unconsciously, religiously or irreligiously, they understand deep within themselves that they need to deal with their spiritual insecurity. They want the assurance that they will not be punished for their evil. In the attempt to do that, men have devised countless false ideas and philosophies to try to escape the punishment they innately know they deserve.

Some people build up a false sense of spiritual security by trying to convince themselves they are basically good and that a just God could not condemn good people to hell. They believe that their good works and intentions outweigh their bad ones and that, in the balance, they are pleasing and acceptable to God. Others believe that God is too loving to send anyone to hell and will ultimately save even the most wicked of sinners. Still others insist that there is no God and that the idea of a final divine judgment is therefore ludicrous. These beliefs are so common that those who put their security in them can find reassurance in the large numbers of other people doing the same. They even design religions to affirm these views.

Far from being cruel and insensitive, the Christian who exposes such false ideas of spiritual security does a great service to those he warns. If a person is to be commended for warning a family that their house is on fire or that a bridge they are about to cross might collapse under them, how much more is a believer to be commended when he warns the unsaved of their lostness and condemnation apart from Jesus Christ. No greater kindness can possibly be offered a person than that of showing him the way of salvation. But before he can have motivation for being saved, he obviously must be convinced that he is lost.

As the forerunner of Jesus Christ, John the Baptist preached a sobering message of repentance from sin (Matt. 3:2). Jesus began His own ministry preaching the same message (Matt. 4:17). Perhaps more than anything else, the Sermon on the Mount is an extended series of warnings about such false spiritual security. In that message the Lord declares unequivocally that men's righteousness, attitudes, good works, relationships, professions, prayers, fasting, ceremonies, and generosity can never measure up to the standard of perfect holiness to which God holds them accountable (Matt. 5:48).

Jesus stripped naked the hypocritical and legalistic false securities of the Judaism of that day. He declared that those who trust in outward substitutes for true righteousness will one day say to Him, "Lord, Lord, did we not prophesy in Your name, and in Your name cast out demons, and in Your name perform many miracles?" But to such false disciples Jesus will say, "I never knew you; depart from Me, you who practice lawlessness" (Matt. 7:22-23). The person who builds his religious house on any self-made foundation is certain to have it washed away by the storm of God's judgment (vv. 26-27).

Having shown how both the moral Jew and the moral Gentile alike will be brought before God's great tribunal in the end times and have no basis for any sense of well-being and security (Rom. 2:1-16), Paul now focuses exclusively on the Jews, the covenant people of God. They had far greater light and blessings than the Gentiles. But as the apostle now points out, that greater privilege made them more accountable to God, not less, as most of them supposed. Before he explains the way of salvation through faith in Jesus Christ, he shatters the idea of false spiritual security that most Jews had in their heritage (2:17a), in their knowledge (vv. 17b-24), and in their ceremony (v. 25-29).

THE FALSE SECURITY OF HERITAGE

But if you bear the name "Jew," (2:17a)

The chosen people of God took great pride in the name **Jew.** In centuries past they had been referred to as Hebrews, so called because of the language they spoke. They also had long been called Israelites, after the land God had promised and given to them according to His covenant with Abraham. But by the time of Christ, the most common name they had was that of **Jew.** The term was derived from *Judah,* the name of one of the twelve tribes as well as the name of the southern kingdom after the division following Solomon's death. But during and after the Babylonian captivity, it had come to refer to the whole race that descended from Abraham through Isaac.

The name represented both their racial and religious heritage, and in their own minds it denoted their distinctiveness from all other peoples of the world. Despite the bondage and oppression they had suffered at the hands of Gentiles for hundreds of years, and were presently still suffering, they wore the name **Jew** as a badge of great honor and pride. The name marked them off as the unique and specially favored people of God. The root meaning of *Judah,* and therefore of **Jew,** is "praised," and the Jews of Paul's day considered that to be a well-deserved title and description of themselves.

Jews had long since lost sight of the purpose of their unique divine calling, however, which was to be the channel through which "all the families of the earth shall be blessed" (Gen. 12:3). They had no desire to share their God-given truths and blessings with the rest of the world, much less be used by the Lord as the means through which He would draw all nations to Himself. Jonah's reluctance to preach in Nineveh because he feared they would believe in God and be spared judgment (Jonah 4:2) typified the attitude of many Jews toward Gentiles.

Instead of viewing those divine truths and blessings as a trust from a gracious and forgiving God, they viewed them as their right by merit. They believed they were specially blessed not because of God's grace but because of their own goodness. They felt superior and proud. Instead of boasting in their great God and in His gracious revelation of Himself to them, they boasted in their own supposed greatness for having received it. John Murray observed that such an attitude "demonstrates . . . how close lies the grossest vice to the highest privilege and how the best can be prostituted to the service of the worst."

The minor prophets repeatedly warned their fellow countrymen about arrogant boasting in their heritage as God's chosen people, which caused many of them to think they could sin with impunity. As the heirs of God's promise to Abraham, they believed they were automatically protected from judgment. But Micah declared that wicked, corrupt Jews who presumptuously said, "Is not the Lord in our midst? Calamity will not come upon us," would one day find their holy city of Jerusalem "plowed as a field" and left "a heap of ruins" (Mic. 3:11-12).

Pride in their being the chosen people of God made some Jews absolutely blind to reality, not only religiously but politically. On one occasion when Jesus was teaching "those Jews who had believed Him," He said, "If you abide in My word, then you are truly disciples of Mine; and you shall know the truth, and the truth shall make you free" (John 8:31-32). When some of the unbelieving Jewish leaders heard those words, they were greatly offended. They were so self-deluded about their superiority and independence that they retorted, "We are Abraham's offspring, and have never yet been enslaved to anyone; how is it that You say, 'You shall become free'" (v. 33). As the Lord explained, they completely missed His point. "Truly, truly, I say to you," He said, "everyone who commits sin is the slave of sin" (v. 34).

Even if Jesus had been speaking politically, as those leaders assumed, their response would have been ludicrous. For the past 100 years they had been brutally subjugated to Rome, and immediately before that to Greece. And during more than a thousand years before that they had been in periodic bondage to Egypt, Assyria, and Babylon.

The Jewish leaders' main confusion, however, was spiritual. Being Abraham's physical descendants did not make Jews his spiritual descendants. "If you are Abraham's children," Jesus told them, "do the deeds of Abraham. But as it is, you are seeking to kill Me, a man who has told you the truth, which I heard from God; this Abraham did not do. You are doing the deeds of your father." When they replied indignantly, "We have one Father, even God," Jesus responded, "If God were your Father, you would love Me; for I proceeded forth and have come from God. . . . You are of your father the devil, and you want to do the desires of your father. . . . Abraham rejoiced to see My day, and he saw it and was glad" (John 8:40-42, 44, 56). If the Jewish leaders had been spiritual heirs of Abraham and true children of God, they would joyously have received Jesus as their Messiah and King. Instead of receiving Him in faith, however, they sought to kill Him, reflecting the murderous character of Satan, their spiritual lord and father.

Infuriating the leaders still more, Jesus said, "Truly, truly, I say to you, before Abraham was born, I am" (v. 58). The root meaning of Jehovah, or Yahweh, is "I am" (see Ex. 3:14). Jesus therefore not only claimed to have existed before Abraham was born, some 2,000 years earlier, but even applied the covenant name of God to Himself. Because they rejected Jesus' claims to messiahship, the Jews considered His words to be inconceivably blasphemous, and "therefore they picked up stones to throw at Him; but Jesus hid Himself, and went out of the temple" (John 8:59).

Jesus utterly undermined the Jews' imagined security of racial and religious heritage. John the Baptist had done the same thing. While he was baptizing repentant Jews at the Jordan River, a group of Pharisees and Sadducees came to him for baptism. But John scathingly rebuked them, saying, "You brood of vipers, who warned you to flee from the wrath to come? Therefore bring forth fruit in keeping with repentance." Well aware that those religious leaders believed that merely being Jews protected them from God's judgment, John added, "And do not suppose that you can say to yourselves, 'We have Abraham for our father'; for I say to you, that God is able from these stones to raise up children to Abraham" (Matt. 3:7-9).

In a similar way, countless people since the time of Christ have considered themselves safe from God's judgment simply because they have been born into a Christian family or have been baptized or belong to a church or have made a profession of faith. Some people consider themselves Christians virtually by default. In European countries that have been thought of as Christian for centuries, many citizens who do not specifically belong to another religion consider themselves Christians simply by virtue of their national heritage. Even in some countries of the Middle East, many citizens who are not Muslim think they are therefore Christian, simply because the other historically prominent religion in the country is the Eastern Orthodox brand of Christianity to which their ancestors adhered.

The Swiss Reformer Ulrich Zwingli took the position that if a child of believers died while in infancy it was within the Christian covenant, in other words, it was saved. He did not believe, however, that children of unbelievers were saved if they died in infancy. With an illogic that was not typical of his thinking, the great Puritan John Owen believed that infant salvation could be passed down two generations, from grandparent to grandchild, sometimes skipping the intervening generation. One wonders how the in-between parents, being themselves children of believers, could escape being saved.

The Roman Catholic church believes that infant baptism actually confers salvation. As one Catholic writer has said, "The faith which the infant lacks is replaced by the faith of the church." Some Protestant denominations, though denying that infant baptism in itself has power to save, nevertheless maintain that the ritual has direct spiritual benefit for the child. Martin Luther, for instance, believed that through this sacrament God miraculously grants saving faith to the infant, who itself is incapable of believing. Others view infant baptism as a confirmation of the child's salvation by virtue of its being born into a Christian family and thereby into the New Covenant of Jesus Christ.

According to Scripture, however, a person who is raised in a Christian home and trained in a Christian environment is not saved by such a heritage, valuable as it is. Nor does baptism, or any other Christian rite in itself, possess or bestow any spiritual benefit. Apart from true faith held by the person receiving it, no ritual or ceremony has any spiritual value whatsoever. Baptism is not a sacrament and, without faith, it becomes a sacrilege.

Such ideas about covenant transferral of salvation and about the spiritual efficacy of baptism are merely extensions of the kind of thinking that caused the common Jewish belief in New Testament times that a person was saved simply by being a circumcised descendant of Abraham through the line of Isaac.

THE FALSE SECURITY OF KNOWLEDGE

and rely upon the Law, and boast in God, and know His will, and approve the things that are essential, being instructed out of the Law, and are confident that you yourself are a guide to the blind, a light to those who are in darkness, a corrector of the foolish, a teacher of the immature, having in the Law the embodiment of knowledge and of the truth, you, therefore, who teach another, do you not teach yourself? You who preach that one should not steal, do you steal? You who say that one should not commit adultery, do you commit adultery? You who abhor idols, do you rob temples? You who boast in the Law, through your breaking the Law, do you dishonor God? For "the Name of God is blasphemed among the Gentiles because of you," just as it is written. (2:17b-24)

The second false religious security Paul mentions is knowledge of God's **Law**, which in this context represented what we now refer to as the Old Testament. This **Law** represented not only the Pentateuch, the five books of the Mosaic law, but also what were called the writings (Psalms, Proverbs, etc.) and the prophets. This **Law** encompassed all of God's revelation until that time: His revelation about His covenants, His blessings, His cursings, His warnings, His promises, His rites and ceremonies, His moral standards, and His teaching about Himself and about man and the plan of redemption.

In regard to the Jews' knowledge of that divine revelation, the apostle mentions four aspects: what they learned of the **Law** (vv. 17b-18), what they taught about it (vv. 19-20), what they did in light of it (vv. 21-22), and what they caused by breaking it (vv. 23-24).

WHAT THEY LEARNED ABOUT THE LAW

and rely upon the Law, and boast in God, and know His will, and approve the things that are essential, being instructed out of the Law, (2:17b-18)

Taken by itself, this statement by Paul might seem to have been a commendation. But as he soon makes clear (see vv. 21-25), it was a strong indictment, because the Jews did not live up to the **Law** they knew so well and praised so highly. Most Jews of that day were proud and self-righteous about their heritage and had come to **rely upon** their knowledge of **the Law and** their boasting **in God** as means of satisfying the Lord. They loved to recite such passages as, "[God] declares His words to Jacob, His statutes and His ordinances to Israel. He has not dealt thus with any nation; and as for His ordinances, they have not known them" (Ps. 147:19-20).

But since it was impossible for anyone to keep all of God's law perfectly, some of the rabbis began teaching that merely *learning* the facts of the **Law** was sufficient to please God. Weakening the purpose of the law still further, some taught that the mere *possession* of it, in the form of written scrolls, was sufficient. Still others taught that Jews were safe from God's judgment simply because, as a people, they were the specially chosen *recipients and custodians* of God's **Law.**

The Old Testament makes its purpose quite clear, however, and it repeatedly warns against Jews placing their trust in outward ceremonies and objects, even those, such as the priestly sacrifices and the Temple, which God had ordained. Through Jeremiah, the Lord said,

> Amend your ways and your deeds, and I will let you dwell in this place. Do not trust in deceptive words, saying, "This is the temple of the Lord, the temple of the Lord, the temple of the Lord." For if you truly amend your ways and your deeds, if you truly practice justice between a man and his neighbor, if you do not oppress the alien, the orphan, or the widow, and do not shed innocent blood in this place, nor walk after other gods to your own ruin, then I will let you dwell in this place, in the land that I gave to your fathers forever and ever. (Jer. 7:3-7)

In other words, spiritual safety and security was not in the Temple but in God Himself and in faithful obedience to the divine truth and righteousness which His Temple represented.

When ungodly Jews would **boast in God** it was really a means of boasting in themselves, in the unique privileges and blessings they thought were theirs by right rather than by grace.

Self-righteous, presumptuous Jews were satisfied simply to **know His will,** without obeying it. They knew what God required and what He forbade, what He commanded and what He prohibited, what He approved and what He disapproved, what He rewarded and what He punished. But rather than saving them, that knowledge became a judgment against them, because they refused to live by it and refused to accept the remedy for such failure.

They were also willing to **approve the things that are essential.** *Dokimazō* (**approve**) carried the idea of testing in order to prove the value of something, such as precious metals. In other words, the Jews had the means not only to know what was right and wrong but to discern what was the most important part of God's law.

Jews were also continually **being instructed out of the Law.** *Katēcheō* (**being instructed**) is the term from which *catechism* is derived. It had the general meaning of oral instruction of any sort but was especially associated with teaching by repetition. Both at home and in the synagogues, Jewish boys in particular were systematically and thoroughly **instructed out of the Law.** Not only rabbis but also many other Jewish men memorized large portions of the Old Testament, which they often recited in public as a demonstration of piety.

It is ironic that ancient Jews considered wisdom to consist of acting according to the knowledge one had, whereas the ancient Greeks simply equated wisdom with knowledge. By New Testament times, however, many Jews, especially the religious leaders, had, in practice, accepted the Greek view of wisdom. Whether they did so intentionally or not, the consequence was that they felt content with merely knowing God's law and had little desire or motivation to obey it. They knew much but obeyed little.

WHAT THEY TAUGHT ABOUT THE LAW

and are confident that you yourself are a guide to the blind, a light to those who are in darkness, a corrector of the foolish, a teacher of the immature, having in the Law the embodiment of knowledge and of the truth, (2:19-20)

The Jews not only felt secure in what they knew but also in what they taught. Considering themselves to be the most religiously wise, they naturally thought themselves to be the most competent teachers of the spiritually unwise, namely the Gentiles, who did not have the benefit of God's written revelation.

But Israel's continued unfaithfulness to God and disobedience of His Word disqualified her as an example and teacher to the unenlightened Gentiles. And when Jews made an occasional convert to Judaism, they made him worse off than he was before. "Woe to you, scribes and Pharisees, hypocrites," Jesus said, "because you travel about on sea and land to make one proselyte; and when he becomes one, you make him twice as much a son of hell as yourselves" (Matt. 23:15). Instead of leading Gentiles to trust in the true God and become obedient to His will, the Jewish leaders engulfed converts in the vast rabbinical system of man-made, legalistic traditions.

In Romans 2:19-20, Paul mentions four specific areas in which many Jews considered themselves to be spiritually superior teachers.

First, Paul said, "You **are confident that you yourself are a guide to the blind.**" Jews in general, and the scribes and Pharisees in particular, considered themselves to be superior mentors of the community in spiritual and moral matters. They saw themselves as religious guides to their unlearned Jewish brethren and especially to the spiritually **blind** Gentile pagans. But because of their arrogant pride and blatant hypocrisy, Jesus charged them with being "blind guides" (see Matt. 23:24-28). Far from being qualified to guide others, they were themselves in desperate need of guidance.

Second, Paul notes that most Jews considered themselves to be **a light to those who are in darkness.** Actually that was precisely the role God had intended for Israel. He had called His people to be a spiritual light to the Gentiles (Isa. 42:6). As noted above, it was through them that "all the families of the earth shall be blessed" (Gen. 12:3).

Jesus declares His disciples to be "the light of the world" and charges them to put their light on a lampstand, where it can be seen and will do some good. "Let your light shine before men in such a way that they may see your good works, and glorify your Father who is in heaven," He said (Matt. 5:14-16). That has always been God's intention for His people. He gives them light not only for their own spiritual benefit but also for the spiritual benefit of the rest of the world, before whom they are His witnesses.

Third, the self-righteous Jew prided himself as being **a corrector of the foolish.** Again the primary focus was on the Gentiles, even the wisest of whom most Jews considered to be **foolish** in the area of religion.

Fourth, the self-righteous Jew thought of himself as **a teacher of the immature.** The idea is that of teaching very small children, in this case, children in the Jewish faith. In light of the context, it is likely that the term **immature** here represents Gentile proselytes to Judaism, who needed special instruction. They not only needed to learn God's law but also needed to rid themselves of the many pagan ideas and practices in which they had been brought up.

Through God's unique revelation of Himself and of His will to Israel, Jews had **in the Law the embodiment of knowledge and of the truth.** *Morphōsis* (**embodiment**) has the basic meaning of an outline or sketch. It therefore seems better to translate the word here as "semblance" or "appearance," because throughout this passage Paul emphasizes the religious superficiality of most of the Jews of his day. He uses the same word in 2 Timothy 3:5, where he warns of men in the last days who will hold "a form [*morphōsis*] of godliness, although they [will] have denied its power."In both passages the idea of counterfeit is implied.

The Jews did indeed through **the Law** have the revelation of divine **knowledge and . . . truth,** but their understanding, teaching, and exemplifying of it had become so encrusted with rabbinical tradition that God's true **Law** was generally unknown and disregarded.

WHAT THEY DID IN RELATION TO THE LAW

you, therefore, who teach another, do you not teach yourself? You who preach that one should not steal, do you steal? You who say that one should not commit adultery, do you commit adultery? You who abhor idols, do you rob temples? (2:21-22)

A third area of false security was related to what most Jews did in response to the law they claimed to know and teach. Paul here contends that their understanding and teaching not only fell far short of God's law but that they themselves disobeyed it. Even when they taught the truth, they taught it hypocritically. Just as Satan sometimes disguises himself as an angel of light (2 Cor. 11:14), false teachers sometimes teach the truth for their own selfish and perverse ends.

In theological terms, their preaching reflects orthodoxy (right doctrine), but their living does not reflect orthopraxy (right practice). They are much like corrupt police officials or judges, whose lives are in direct contradiction of the laws they have sworn to uphold and enforce. And because of their greater responsibility, they bring upon themselves greater punishment when they break those laws.

The psalmist sternly warned ungodly men who presume to teach in God's name. "To the wicked God says, 'What right have you to tell of My statutes, and to take My covenant in your mouth? For you hate discipline, and you cast My words behind you. When you see a thief, you are pleased with him, and you associate with adulterers. You let your mouth loose in evil, and your tongue frames deceit. You sit and speak against your brother; you slander your own mother's son'" (Ps. 50:16-20).

Even teachers who are true believers are held especially account-able for living out what they teach. James therefore gives the somber caution: "Let not many of you become teachers, my brethren, knowing that as such we shall incur a stricter judgment" (James 3:1).

Like the wicked teachers the psalmist castigated, the hypocritical Jew of Paul's day would often **teach another** person the truths of God's Word but would fail to **teach** them to himself. Even less would he *obey* those truths himself. Such men were typified by the scribes and Pharisees, of whom Jesus said, "They say things, and do not do them" (Matt. 23:3).

Paul mentions three areas of their spiritual and moral hypocrisy: stealing, adultery, and sacrilege. **You who preach that one should not steal, do you steal?** he asks. Despite the clear pronouncements of the Mosaic law against theft, it was very common in ancient Judaism. Isaiah rebuked those who "turned to their own way, each one to his unjust gain" (Isa. 56:11). Ezekiel denounced those who "have taken bribes to shed blood; . . . taken interest and profits, and . . . injured [their] neighbors for gain by oppression" (Ezek. 22:12). Amos wrote of those who stole by making "the bushel smaller and the shekel bigger" and by cheating "with dishonest scales" (Amos 8:5). Malachi accused his fellow Jews even of robbing God by withholding some of the tithes and offerings owed to Him (Mal. 3:8-9).

When Jesus cleansed the Temple during the last week of His earthly ministry, He censured the money changers and sacrifice merchants for making His Father's house "a robbers' den" (Matt. 21:13; cf. John 2:16). On another occasion He scathingly condemned the scribes and Pharisees—the self-appointed authorities on righteousness—for devouring "widows' houses" under the pretense of serving God (Matt. 23:14).

The second area of hypocrisy related to sexual sin. **You who say that one should not commit adultery, do you commit adultery?** As with stealing, the clear implication is that they practiced the very evil they condemned in others. Many Jewish men tried to circumvent the Mosaic command against adultery by divorcing their wives and marrying another woman to whom they were attracted. But Jesus declared that divorce and remarriage on any ground other than sexual infidelity results in adultery just as surely as if no divorce is involved (Matt. 5:32; 19:9). Adultery can even be committed without the physical act. "Everyone who looks on a woman to lust for her," He said, "has committed adultery with her already in his heart" (Matt. 5:28).

The third area of hypocrisy related to sacrilege. **You who abhor idols, do you rob temples?** The root word behind *bdelussō* (**abhor**) means "to stink, to reek." Although Israel had fallen into idolatry repeatedly during the period of the monarchies, since the Babylonian exile Jews have never practiced that evil to any significant degree. During the Greek and Roman occupations after their return from Babylon, Jews developed a strong abhorrence for anything remotely resembling idolatry. Because some caesars had declared themselves to be gods, Jews even loathed handling Roman coins, because Caesar's image was inscribed on them (see Matt. 22:19-21).

To **rob temples** may have referred to Jews who robbed their own Temple in Jerusalem. As noted above, they often robbed God by withholding part of their tithes and offerings. According to the Jewish historian Josephus, some Jews also robbed the Temple in other devious ways. He reports that on one occasion a group of Jewish men enticed a wealthy Roman woman into giving a large sum of money to the Temple. But instead of putting the money in the Temple treasury, they divided it among themselves.

But Paul's reference to abhorring **idols** suggests that he had something else in mind in regard to temple robbery. The Mosaic law strictly forbade Israelites from making personal gain from the idols they seized after conquering pagan enemies. "The graven images of their gods you are to burn with fire; you shall not covet the silver or the gold that is on them, nor take it for yourselves, lest you be snared by it, for it is an abomination to the Lord your God" (Deut. 7:25).

Although by New Testament times the nation of Israel had long since ceased conquering Gentile territories, it is possible that individual rogue Jews plundered pagan temples for purely mercenary reasons. The statement by the town clerk at Ephesus that Paul and his associates were not robbers of temples (Acts 19:37) suggests that it was not uncommon for Jews to be guilty of that offense. It is possible that, despite the clear Mosaic prohibition, the offending Jews rationalized such theft by thinking they were doing God a favor by striking a blow at paganism. But Paul condemns their hypocrisy. Their motive was not religious, but mercenary.

WHAT THEY CAUSED BY BREAKING GOD'S LAW

You who boast in the Law, through your breaking the Law, do you dishonor God? For "the Name of God is blasphemed among the Gentiles because of you," just as it is written. (2:23-24)

The indictment of verse 24 makes clear that the question in verse 23 was rhetorical. Many hypocritical Jews were blatantly **breaking the** divine **Law** they so proudly boasted in, and in doing so, they brought **dishonor** to **God**.

Every sin dishonors God. David confessed, "Against Thee, Thee only, I have sinned, and done what is evil in Thy sight" (Ps. 51:4). Sin committed by those who claim God's name dishonors Him the most. Quoting Isaiah 52:5, Paul strongly rebuked hypocritical Jews by declaring that **"the name of God is blasphemed among the Gentiles because of you,"** just as it is written.

The principle applies even more strongly to Christians, because they not only have greater spiritual light through the New Testament but have greater spiritual resources to obey that light through the indwelling Holy Spirit. When a believer falls into sin, his witness is ruined and the name of His Lord is sullied before the world. Those who claim to be Christians but persistently live in sin give evidence that they carry the name of Christ in vain. And because there is no difference between their standard of living and that of the world, the Lord's name is **blasphemed.**

The Lord lamented to Ezekiel,

> Son of man, when the house of Israel was living in their own land, they defiled it by their ways and their deeds; their way before Me was like the uncleanness of a woman in her impurity. Therefore, I poured out My wrath on them for the blood which they had shed on the land, because they had defiled it with their idols. Also I scattered them among the nations, and they were dispersed throughout the lands. According to their ways and their deeds I judged them. When they came to the nations where they went, they profaned My holy name, because it was said of them, "These are the people of the Lord." (Ezek. 36:17-20)

When those who go by God's name are openly sinful, or are exposed as being privately sinful, God and His Word are understandably ridiculed by the world. The unbeliever has no reason to repent of his sins and turn to God for salvation if he sees professed believers committing the same sins.

Unfortunately, God's name is also ridiculed when the world sees His people being chastised for their sins, as in the case of ancient Israel just cited. Failing to comprehend the purpose of the chastening, the world reasons, "If God makes His own people suffer in that way, why should anyone want to believe in and serve Him?"

And on the other hand, when God chooses to withhold chastening for a time, the world may conclude that He is either too impotent to control and correct His people or that He approves their sinful acts and is therefore Himself evil. In that way His name is **blasphemed** worst of all.

It would be better for many Christians, true believers as well as false, to hide their religious profession. Their living is such an obvious contradiction of Scripture that the cause of Christ is mocked and scorned by the world.

Because of the Jews' exclusive self-righteousness, many defamatory legends grew up about them in Gentile lands where they lived. They were accused of sometimes sacrificing a Gentile in their religious rites and of being descended from a band of leper slaves who managed to escape the rock quarries of Egypt. Unfounded as such stories were, their origin is understandable. The Gentiles were simply returning in kind the contempt that most Jews had for them.

THE FALSE SECURITY OF CEREMONY

For indeed circumcision is of value, if you practice the Law; but if you are a transgressor of the Law, your circumcision has become uncircumcision. If therefore the uncircumcised man keeps the requirements of the Law, will not his uncircumcision be regarded as circumcision? And will not he who is physically uncircumcised, if he keeps the Law, will he not judge you who though having the letter of the Law and circumcision are a transgressor of the Law? For he is not a Jew who is one outwardly; neither is circumcision that which is outward in the flesh. But he is a Jew who is one inwardly; and circumcision is that which is of the heart, by the Spirit, not by the letter; and his praise is not from men, but from God. (2:25-29)

Proceeding to a third type of false security (**circumcision**) in which many Jews placed their trust, Paul clarifies the true significance of that rite.

God had instituted **circumcision** as a mark of His covenant with Abraham and his descendants, declaring that "every male among you who is eight days old shall be circumcised throughout your generations" (Gen. 17:10-12). Centuries later, when for some reason Moses failed to circumcise one of his sons, his wife, Zipporah, performed the rite herself, thereby protecting Moses from the Lord's wrath (Ex. 4:24-26).

No doubt this surgery was symbolic of the sinfulness of man that was passed from generation to generation. The very procreative organ needed to be cleansed of a covering. So man at the very center of his nature is sinful and needs cleansing of the heart. This graphic symbol of the need for removing sin became the sign of being a Jew.

But as important as circumcision was as an act of obedience to God and as a reminder to Jews of their covenant relation to Him, the rite had no spiritual power. **Circumcision is of value,** Paul explains, only **if you practice the Law,** that is, live in obedience to God's will. To the faithful, obedient Jew, **circumcision** was a symbol of God's covenant, His blessings, His goodness, and His protection of His chosen people.

But if you are a transgressor of the Law, Paul warned, **your circumcision has become uncircumcision,** that is, valueless. A Jew who continually transgressed God's law proved that he had no more saving relationship to God than a pagan Gentile, whom Jews often referred to as the uncircumcised.

Important as it was, **circumcision** was only an outward symbol. And rather than freeing Jews from God's law, **circumcision** made them even more responsible for obeying it, because that ritual testified to their greater knowledge of their sin, of God, and of His will in regard to them.

Circumcision was, in fact, more a mark of judgment and obligation than of salvation and freedom. It was a constant reminder to Jews of their sinfulness and of their obligation to obey God's law. Speaking about the Judaizers, who were corrupting the church by teaching that Christians were obligated to keep the Mosaic law, Paul wrote, "I testify again to every man who receives circumcision, that he is under obligation to keep the whole Law" (Gal. 5:3). Circumcision was a mark of legal obligation.

Long before Paul's day the rite of circumcision had become so shrouded in superstition that ancient rabbis formulated sayings such as "No circumcised Jewish man will see hell" and "Circumcision saves us from hell." The Midrash includes the statement "God swore to Abraham that no one who was circumcised would be sent to hell. Abraham sits before the gate of hell and never allows any circumcised Israelite to enter."

But the prophets had made clear that mere physical circumcision had no spiritual power or benefit. " 'Behold the days are coming,' declares the Lord, 'that I will punish all who are circumcised and yet uncircum-cised—Egypt, and Judah, and Edom, and the sons of Ammon, and Moab, and all those inhabiting the desert who clip the hair on their temples; for all the nations are uncircumcised, and all the house of Israel are uncircumcised of heart' " (Jer. 9:25-26). Disobedience to God put the circumcised Israelites in the same category of judgment as the uncircum-cised Gentiles.

On the other hand, Paul continues, **If the uncircumcised man keeps the requirement of the Law, will not his uncircumcision be regarded as circumcision? And will not he who is physically uncircumcised, if he keeps the Law, will he not judge you who though having the letter of the Law and circumcision are a transgressor of the Law?**

The apostle's point is that the substance of pleasing God is obedience to His will, of which circumcision is but a symbolic reminder. Sincerely keeping **the requirement of the Law** because it is God's will is of great value, whereas circumcision without obedience is of absolutely no value. **If the uncircumcised man,** that is, a Gentile, **keeps the requirement of the Law,** God will look on him just as favorably as on a circumcised Jew who keeps His law—counting the believing Gentile's **uncircumcision** as if it were true **circumcision.**

Paul's next devastating salvo at the Jew who had false trust in his Jewish privileges was the declaration that the obedient Gentile who is **physically uncircumcised** not only pleases God but figuratively will sit in judgment on disobedient Jews, **who though having the letter of the Law and** physical **circumcision are a transgressor of the Law.** It is not that such Gentiles will perform the actual judgment, which is God's prerogative alone, but that their faithful obedience will stand as a rebuke to the faithless disobedience of hypocritical Jews. To the Philippian Gentile church Paul said that the unsaved and disobedient Jews who rejected the gospel of grace were "dogs, . . . evil workers, . . . [and] false circumcision" (Phil. 3:2).

Theologian Charles Hodge wrote, "Whenever true religion declines, the disposition to lay undo stress on external rites is stressed. The Jews when they lost their spirituality supposed that circumcision had the power to save them." Apostasy always moves the religious focus from the inward to the outward, from humble obedience to empty formality.

In verses 28-29 Paul summarizes his demolition of false trust. First, he reiterates that Jewish heritage, wonderful as it was, had absolutely no spiritual benefit if it stood alone: **He is not a Jew who is one outwardly.** As John the Baptist had pronounced many years earlier, God could raise up *physical* descendants of Abraham from stones if He so chose (Matt. 3:9). Making much the same point, later in his epistle Paul contends that "they are not all Israel who are descended from Israel" (Rom. 9:6). Second, Paul reemphasizes the truth that ceremony is of no value in itself, saying, **neither is circumcision that which is outward in the flesh.**

Putting those two truths together, the apostle says that the true child of God, epitomized by the faithful **Jew,** is the person **who is one inwardly.** The true mark of God's child is not an outward symbol, such as **circumcision,** but a godly condition **of the heart.**

Third, Paul restates the truth that knowledge of God's law has no power to save a person. Salvation comes **by the Spirit** of God Himself working in a believer's heart, not by the mere **letter** of His Word, true as it is.

The **praise** that the true Jew, the true believer, receives **is not from men,** who are more inclined to ridicule God's people than to praise them. The true believer's reward of praise comes directly **from God,** his heavenly Father.

The Advantage of Being Jewish

Then what advantage has the Jew? Or what is the benefit of circumcision? Great in every respect. First of all, that they were entrusted with the oracles of God. What then? If some did not believe, their unbelief will not nullify the faithfulness of God, will it? May it never be! Rather, let God be found true, though every man be found a liar, as it is written, "That Thou mightest be justified in Thy words, and mightest prevail when Thou art judged." But if our unrighteousness demonstrates the righteousness of God, what shall we say? The God who inflicts wrath is not unrighteous, is He? (I am speaking in human terms.) May it never be! For otherwise how will God judge the world? But if through my lie the truth of God abounded to His glory, why am I also still being judged as a sinner? And why not say (as we are slanderously reported and as some affirm that we say), "Let us do evil that good may come"? Their condemnation is just. (3:1-8)

Looking at the rather tragic history of the Jewish people, one is not inclined to think there has been any advantage in being a Jew. In spite of the reality that they are such a noble strain of humanity and chosen by God, their history has been a saga of slavery, hardship, warfare, persecution, slander, captivity, dispersion, and humiliation.

They were menial slaves in Egypt for some 400 years, and after God miraculously delivered them, they wandered in a barren wilderness for forty years, until an entire generation died out. When they eventually entered the land God had promised them, they had to fight to gain every square foot of it and continue to fight to protect what they gained. After several hundred years, civil war divided the nation. The northern kingdom eventually was almost decimated by Assyria, with the remnant being taken captive to that country. Later, the southern kingdom was conquered and exiled in Babylon for seventy years, after which some were allowed to return to Palestine.

Not long after they rebuilt their homeland, they were conquered by Greece, and the despotic Antiochus Epiphanes revelled in desecrating their Temple, corrupting their sacrifices, and slaughtering their priests. Under Roman rule they fared no better. Tens of thousands of Jewish rebels were publicly crucified, and under Herod the Great scores of male Jewish babies were slaughtered because of his insane jealousy of the Christ child. In the year A.D. 70, the Roman general Titus Vespasian carried out Caesar's order to utterly destroy Jerusalem, its Temple, and most of its citizens. According to Josephus, over a million Jews of all ages were mercilessly butchered, and some 100,000 of those who survived were sold into slavery or sent to Rome to die in the gladiator games. Two years previously, Gentiles in Caesarea had killed 20,000 Jews and sold many more into slavery. During that same period of time, the inhabitants of Damascus cut the throats of 10,000 Jews in a single day.

In A.D. 115 the Jews of Cyrene, Egypt, Cyprus, and Mesopotamia rebelled against Rome. When they failed, Emperor Hadrian destroyed 985 towns in Palestine and killed at least 600,000 Jewish men. Thousands more perished from starvation and disease. So many Jews were sold into slavery that the price of an able-bodied male slave dropped to that of a horse. In the year 380 Emperor Theodosius I formulated a legal code that declared Jews to be an inferior race of human beings—a demonic idea that strongly permeated most of Europe for over a thousand years and that even persists in many parts of the world in our own day.

For some two centuries the Jews were oppressed by the Byzantine branch of the divided Roman empire. Emperor Heroclitus banished them from Jerusalem in 628 and later tried to exterminate them. Leo the Assyrian gave them the choice of converting to Christianity or being banished from the realm. When the first crusade was launched in 1096 to recapture the Holy Land from the Ottoman Turks, the crusaders slaughtered countless thousands of Jews on their way to Palestine, brutally trampling many to death under their horses' hooves. That carnage, of course, was committed in the name of Christianity.

In 1254 King Louis IX banished all Jews from France. When many later returned to that country, Philip the Fair expelled 100,000 of them again in 1306. In 1492 the Jews were expelled from Spain even as Columbus began his first voyage across the Atlantic, and four years later they were expelled from Portugal as well. Soon most of western Europe was closed to them except for a few areas in northern Italy, Germany, and Poland. Although the French Revolution emancipated many Jews, vicious anti-Semitism continued to dominate most of Europe and parts of Russia. Thousands of Jews were massacred in the Ukraine in 1818. In 1894, because of growing anti-Semitism in the French army, a Jewish officer named Dreyfus was falsely accused of treason, and that charge was used as an excuse to purge the military of all Jews of high rank.

When a number of influential Jews began to dream of reestablishing a homeland in Palestine, the Zionist movement was born, its first congress being convened in Basel, Switzerland, in 1897. By 1914, some 90,000 Jews had settled in Palestine. In the unparalleled Nazi holocaust of the early 1940s at least 6,000,000 Jews were exterminated, this time for racial rather than religious reasons.

Although in our society anti-Semitism is seldom expressed so openly, Jews in many parts of the world still suffer for no other reason than their Jewishness. From the purely historical perspective, therefore, Jews have been among the most continuously and harshly disadvantaged people of all time.

Not only have Jews historically had little social or political security, but in Romans 2:17-20 Paul declares that, although they are God's specially chosen and blessed people, Jews did not even have guaranteed *spiritual* security—either by physical lineage or religious heritage. Being born a descendant of Abraham, knowing God's law, and being circumcised did not assure them a place in heaven. In fact, rather than protecting Jews from God's judgment, those blessings made them all the more accountable for obedience to the Lord.

After having demolished the false securities on which most Jews relied, Paul anticipated the strong objections his Jewish readers would make. The truths he sets forth in the book of Romans he had taught many times before in many places, and he knew what the most common objections in Rome would be.

Paul had confronted Jewish objectors from the beginning of his ministry when he took the four Jewish Christians into the Temple to fulfill a vow, for example. The leaders seized him and cried out to the crowd that had gathered, "Men of Israel, come to our aid! This is the man who preaches to all men everywhere against our people, and the Law, and this place" (Acts 21:28). It was because Paul had a reputation for teaching such things that the Christian elders in Jerusalem persuaded him to take the men into the Temple for purification, thinking such an act would convince the leaders that Paul had not forsaken the teaching of Moses (see vv. 21-24).

In his defense before King Agrippa, Paul said,

> I did not prove disobedient to the heavenly vision, but kept declaring both to those of Damascus first, and also at Jerusalem and then throughout all the region of Judea, and even to the Gentiles, that they should repent and turn to God, performing deeds appropriate to repentance. For this reason some Jews seized me in the temple and tried to put me to death. And so, having obtained help from God, I stand to this day testifying both to small and great, stating nothing but what the Prophets and Moses said was going to take place. (Acts 26:19-22)

The apostle did not teach that Jewish heritage and the Mosaic law ceremonies were not important. Because they were God-given, they had tremendous importance. But they were not in Paul's day, and had never been, the means of satisfying the divine standard of righteousness. They offered Jews great spiritual advantages, but they did not provide spiritual security.

After his conversion, Paul continued to worship in the Temple when he was in Jerusalem and faithfully practiced the moral teachings of the Mosaic law. He personally circumcised Timothy, who was Jewish on his mother's side, as a concession to the Jews in the region of Galatia (Acts 16:1-3). He even continued to follow many of the ceremonial customs and the rabbinical patterns in order not to give undue offense to legalistic Jews, as noted in Acts 21:24-26.

But the essence of his preaching was that none of those outward acts have any saving benefit and that a person can become right with God only through trust in His Son Jesus Christ. It was that truth of salvation only by God's grace working through man's faith that the unbelieving Jews found intolerable, because it exposed the worthlessness of their traditions and the hypocrisy of their ostentatious devotion to God.

Self-righteous, self-satisfied Jews could not stand any attack on their supposed Abrahamic security and their man-made legalism. The apostle had learned from all these experiences that unbelieving Jews would always accuse him of teaching against God's chosen people, against God's promises to His people, and against God's purity. It is therefore those three objections that he confronts in Romans 3:1-8.

THE OBJECTION THAT PAUL ATTACKED GOD'S PEOPLE

Then what advantage has the Jew? Or what is the benefit of

circumcision? Great in every respect. First of all, that they were entrusted with the oracles of God. (3:1-2)

Paul's accusers continually charged him with teaching that the Lord's calling of Israel to be His special people was meaningless. If that were so, the apostle blasphemed the very character and integrity of God.

Paul knew the questions that some Jews in Rome would ask after they read or hear about the first part of his letter. "If our Jewish heritage, our knowing and teaching the Mosaic law, and our following Jewish rituals such as circumcision do not make a Jew righteous before God," they would wonder, **"then what advantage has the Jew? Or what is the benefit of circumcision?"**

Many Scripture passages would have come to their minds. Just before God presented Israel with the Ten Commandments, He told them, "You shall be to Me a kingdom of priests and a holy nation" (Ex. 19:6). Moses wrote of Israel, "Behold, to the Lord your God belong heaven and the highest heavens, the earth and all that is in it. Yet on your fathers did the Lord set His affection to love them, and He chose their descendants after them, even you above all peoples" (Deut. 10:14-15). In the same book Moses wrote, "You are a holy people to the Lord your God; and the Lord has chosen you to be a people for His own possession out of all the peoples who are on the face of the earth" (14:2). The psalmist exulted, "The Lord has chosen Jacob for Himself, Israel for His own possession" (Ps. 135:4). Through Isaiah, the Lord declared of Israel, "The people whom I formed for Myself, will declare My praise" (Isa. 43:21).

Because of those and countless other Old Testament passages that testify to Israel's unique calling and blessing, many Jews concluded that, in itself, being Jewish made them acceptable to God. But as Paul has pointed out, being *physical* descendants of Abraham did not qualify them as his *spiritual* descendants. If they did not have the mark of God's Spirit within their hearts, the outward mark of circumcision in their flesh was worthless (Rom. 2:17-29).

Nevertheless, Paul continues, the advantage of being Jewish was **great in every respect.** Although it did not bring salvation, it bestowed many privileges that Gentiles did not have. Later in the epistle, Paul tells his readers, doubtlessly with tears in his eyes as he wrote, "For I could wish that I myself were accursed, separated from Christ for the sake of my brethren, my kinsmen according to the flesh, who are Israelites, to whom belongs the adoption as sons and the glory and the covenants and the giving of the Law and the temple service and the promises, whose are the fathers, and from whom is the Christ according to the flesh" (9:3-5).

The Jews as a people had been adopted by God as His children, with whom He had made several exclusive covenants. He had given them

His holy law and promised that through their lineage the Savior of the world would come. The Jewish people were indeed special in God's eyes. They were blessed, protected, and delivered as no other nation on earth.

But most Jews paid little attention to the negative side of God's revelation to them. He proclaimed of Israel, "You only have I chosen among all the families of the earth," but immediately went on to say, "therefore, I will punish you for all your iniquities" (Amos 3:2). With high privilege also came high responsibility.

In the parable of the wedding feast, Jesus compared the kingdom of heaven to a feast given by a king to celebrate his son's marriage. Several times he sent messengers to the invited guests telling them that the feast was ready, but each time they ignored the invitation. Some of them even beat and killed the messengers. The enraged king sent his soldiers to destroy the murderers and set their cities on fire. The king then sent other messengers to invite everyone in the kingdom to the feast, regardless of rank or wealth (Matt. 22:1-9).

That parable pictures Israel as the first and most privileged guests who were invited to celebrate the coming of God's Son to redeem the world. But when the majority of Jews rejected Jesus as the Messiah, God opened the door to Gentiles, those whom the king's messengers found along the highways and in the streets. I believe that the guests who attended the feast represent the church, people in general who acknowledge Christ as God's Son and received Him as Lord and Savior.

Through Isaiah, the Lord lamented of Israel, "What more was there to do for My vineyard that I have not done in it? Why, when I expected it to produce good grapes did it produce worthless ones?" (Isa. 5:4). The answer, of course, was that there was nothing more that God could have done for His people. He had bestowed on them every conceivable blessing and advantage.

Becoming more specific regarding their benefits, Paul said to his hypothetical Jewish objectors, "You **were entrusted with the oracles of God.**" *Logion* (**oracles**) is a diminutive of *logos,* which is most commonly translated *word. Logion* generally referred to important sayings or messages, especially supernatural utterances.

Although **oracles** is a legitimate translation (see also Acts 7:38; Heb. 5:12), because of the term's association with pagan rites, that rendering seems unsuitable in this context. In many pagan religions of that day, mediums and seers gave occultic predictions of the future and other messages from the spirit world through supernatural "oracles." By observing the movements of fish in a tank, the formation of snakes in a pit, or listening to the calls of certain birds, fortune-tellers would purport to predict such things as business success or failure, military victory or defeat, and a happy or tragic marriage.

Such a connotation could not have been further from Paul's use of *logion* in this passage. His point was that the Jews **were entrusted with** the very *words* of the one and only true **God**, referring to the entire Old Testament (cf. Deut. 4:1-2; 6:1-2). God's revelation of Himself and of His will had been **entrusted** to the Jews, and that gave them unimaginably great privilege as well as equally immense responsibility.

As the poet William Cowper wrote,

> They, and they only, amongst all mankind,
> Received the transcript of the Eternal Mind;
> Were trusted with His own engraven laws,
> And constituted guardians of His cause;
> Theirs were the prophets, theirs the priestly call,
> And theirs, by birth, the Saviour of us all.

Tragically, however, Jews had focused much attention on their privileges but little on their responsibilities. During one period of their history they misplaced and lost the written record of God's law. Only when a copy of it was found by Hilkiah the high priest during the restoration of the Temple did Judah begin again to honor the Lord's commandments and observe His ceremonies for a brief time under the godly King Josiah (see 2 Chron. 34:14-33).

For many centuries before the time of Paul, beginning during the Babylonian Captivity, the Jews' reverence for her man-made rabbinical traditions and interpretations had come to far outweigh her reverence for God's written Word.

The religious leaders of Jesus' day prided themselves as being experts in the Scriptures. But when the Sadducees tried to maneuver Jesus into a corner by asking a hypothetical question about marriage in heaven, He rebuked them by saying, "Is this not the reason you are mistaken, that you do not understand the Scriptures, or the power of God?" (Mark 12:24).

To a crowd of unbelieving Jews in Jerusalem the Lord declared, "You search the Scriptures, because you think that in them you have eternal life; and it is these that bear witness of Me" (John 5:39). In the story of the rich man and Lazarus, the rich man died and went to hell. From there he cried out to Abraham to send a special messenger to tell his brothers the way of salvation. But Abraham replied, "They have Moses and the Prophets; let them hear them" (Luke 16:29). In other words, the Old Testament contained all the truth that any Jew (or any Gentile, for that matter) needed to be saved. Jews who truly believed the Scriptures recognized Jesus as the Son of God, because He is the focus of the Old Testament as well as the New. But most Jews preferred to follow the traditions of the rabbis and elders rather than "the sacred writings which are able to give . . . the wisdom that leads to salvation through faith which is in Christ Jesus" (2 Tim. 3:15).

That same attitude has characterized much of Christianity throughout its history. The teachings and standards of a denomination or of an exclusive group or sect have frequently overshadowed, and often completely contradicted, God's own revelation in the Bible.

Belonging to a Christian church is much like it was to be a Jew under the Old Covenant. Outward identity with those who claim to be God's people, even when they are genuine believers, is in itself of no benefit to an unbeliever. But such a person does have a great advantage above other unbelievers if in a church he is exposed to the sound teaching of God's Word. If he does not take advantage of that privilege, however, he makes his guilt and condemnation worse than if he had never heard the gospel. "For if we go on sinning willfully after receiving the knowledge of the truth, there no longer remains a sacrifice for sins, but a certain terrifying expectation of judgment" (Heb. 10:26-27; cf. 4:2-3).

THE OBJECTION THAT PAUL ATTACKED GOD'S PROMISES

What then? If some did not believe, their unbelief will not nullify the faithfulness of God, will it? May it never be! Rather, let God be found true, though every man be found a liar, as it is written, "That Thou mightest be justified in Thy words, and mightest prevail when Thou art judged." (3:3-4)

The next objection Paul anticipated and confronted was that his teaching abrogated God's promises to Israel. As any student of the Old Testament knows, God's promises to His chosen people are numerous. How, then, could Paul maintain that it was possible for a Jew not to be secure in those promises?

Paul's answer reflected both the explicit and implicit teaching of the Jewish Scriptures themselves. God had never promised that any individual Jew, no matter how pure his physical lineage from Abraham, or from any of the other great saints of the Old Testament, could claim security in God's promises apart from repentance and personal faith in God, resulting in obedience from the heart. Isaiah 55:6-7 provides a good illustration of an invitation to such obedient faith: "Seek the Lord while He may be found; call upon Him while He is near. Let the wicked forsake his way, and the unrighteous man his thoughts; and let him return to the Lord, and He will have compassion on him; and to our God, for He will abundantly pardon."

As in the passage from Amos 3:2 mentioned above, many of God's greatest promises were accompanied by the severest warnings. And most of the promises were conditional, based on His people's faith and obedience. The few unconditional promises He made were to the nation of Israel as a whole, not to individual Jews (see, e.g., Gen. 12:3; Isa. 44:1-5; Zech. 12:10).

The apostle therefore agreed in part with his accusers, saying, **What then? If some did not believe, their unbelief will not nullify the faithfulness of God, will it?** His opponents were perfectly right in defending the Lord's integrity. No matter how men respond to His promises, He is absolutely faithful to keep His word.

Though certainly not intentionally, the idea in covenant theology that the church has replaced Israel in God's plan of redemption assumes God's faithlessness in keeping His unconditional promises to Israel. Because of Israel's rejection of Jesus Christ as her Messiah, God has postponed the fulfillment of His promise to redeem and restore Israel as a nation. But He has not (and because of His holy nature He *could not*) reneged on that promise. His prediction, for example, that He will one day "pour out on the house of David and on the inhabitants of Jerusalem, the Spirit of grace and of supplication, so that they will look on Me whom they have pierced" (Zech. 12:10) could not possibly apply to the church. And because such a renewal has never happened in the history of Israel, either the prediction is false or it is yet to be fulfilled.

Later in the epistle Paul strongly affirms that God has not rejected His people Israel (Rom. 11:1). A few verses later he declares, "For I do not want you, brethren, to be uninformed of this mystery, lest you be wise in your own estimation, that a partial hardening has happened to Israel until the fulness of the Gentiles has come in; and thus all Israel will be saved; just as it is written, 'The Deliverer will come from Zion, He will remove ungodliness from Jacob. And this is My covenant with them, when I take away their sins.'" Lest he be misunderstood as referring to the church as the new Israel, Paul adds, "From the standpoint of the gospel they [Jews] are enemies for your [Christians'] sake, but from the standpoint of God's choice they are beloved for the sake of the fathers; for the gifts and the calling of God are irrevocable" (vv. 25-29).

The national salvation of Israel is as inevitable as God's promises are irrevocable. But that future certainty gives *individual* Jews no more present guarantee of being saved than the most pagan Gentile.

The mistake of Paul's accusers was in believing that God's unconditional promises to Israel applied to all individual Jews at all times. But as Paul shows earlier in 9:6-7, when he writes: "But it is not as though the word of God has failed. For they are not all Israel who are descended from Israel; neither are they all children because they are Abraham's descendants, but: 'through Isaac your descendants will be named.'"

The accusers were right in contending that God cannot break His word. If the blessings of a promise failed to materialize it was because

His *people* **did not believe** and obey the conditions of the promise. But **their unbelief** could not prevent the salvation which God would ultimately bring to the promised nation.

But an even deeper truth was that, contrary to the thinking of most Jews, salvation was *never* offered by God on the basis of the heritage, ceremony, good works, or any basis other than that of faith. Paul therefore asks rhetorically, "The fact that Jews who **did not believe** forfeited their personal right to God's promised blessings and barred themselves from the inheritance of God's kingdom **will not nullify the faithfulness of God, will it?**" His salvation will come to Israel some day, when all Israel will be saved.

Answering his own question, he exclaims, **May it never be!** The phrase *mē genoito* (**may it never be**) was the strongest negative Greek expression and usually carried the connotation of impossibility. "Of course God cannot be unfaithful in His promises or in any other way," Paul was saying.

Rather, let God be found true, though every man be found a liar. If every human being who ever lived declared that God is faithless, **God** would **be found true** and **every man** who testified against Him would **be found a liar.**

Summoning Scripture as he regularly did, Paul quotes from the great penitential psalm of David, Israel's most illustrious and beloved king, from whose throne the Messiah Himself would some day reign. **As it is written, "That Thou mightest be justified in Thy words, and mightest prevail when Thou art judged"** (see Ps. 51:4). Because God is perfect and is Himself the measure of goodness and truth, His Word is its own verification and His judgment its own justification. It is utter folly to suppose that the Lord of heaven and earth might not **prevail** against the sinful, perverted judgment that either man or Satan could make against Him.

THE OBJECTION THAT PAUL ATTACKED GOD'S PURITY

But if our unrighteousness demonstrates the righteousness of God, what shall we say? The God who inflicts wrath is not unrighteous, is He? (I am speaking in human terms.) May it never be! For otherwise how will God judge the world? But if through my lie the truth of God abounded to His glory, why am I also still being judged as a sinner? And why not say (as we are slanderously reported and as some affirm that we say), "Let us do evil that good may come"? Their condemnation is just. (3:5-8)

The third objection Paul anticipated was that his teaching attacked the very purity and holiness of God. The argument of his accusers would have been something like this:

> If God is glorified by the sins of Israel, being shown faithful Himself despite the unfaithfulness of His chosen people, then sin glorifies God. In other words, Paul, you are saying that what God strictly forbids actually brings Him glory. You are saying that God is like a merchant who displays a piece of expensive gold jewelry on a piece of black velvet so the contrast makes the gold appear even more elegant and beautiful. You are charging God with using man's sin to bring glory to Himself, and that is blasphemy. You are impugning the righteous purity of God. Not only that, but if man's **unrighteousness demonstrates the righteousness of God, what shall we say** about God's judgment? If what you say is true, why does God punish sin? **The God who inflicts wrath is not unrighteous, is He?**

Again lest his readers conclude that he was expressing his own thinking, Paul immediately adds the parenthetical explanation that he was **speaking in human terms,** that is, according to the **human** logic of the natural mind. He was saying, in effect, "Don't think for a minute that I believe such perverted nonsense. I am only paraphrasing the charges that are often made against me."

To intensify the disclaimer, Paul says again, **"May it never be!** Obviously God does not encourage or condone sin in order to glorify Himself, **for otherwise how will God judge the world?"**

If Jews understood anything about the nature of God it was that He is a perfect judge. From the earliest part of the Old Testament He is called "the Judge of all the earth" (Gen. 18:25). The psalmists repeatedly refer to Him as a judge (see, e.g., Pss. 50:6; 58:11; 94:2). A major theme of virtually all the prophets is that of God's judgment—past as well as present, imminent as well as in the distant future. Paul's very obvious point is that God would have no basis for equitable, righteous, pure judgment if He condoned sin.

In verses 7 and 8 the apostle reiterates the false charges against him in somewhat different terms. "You claim that I say, **'If through my lie the truth of God abounded to His glory, why am I also still being judged a sinner?'"**

That was clearly a charge of antinomianism (disregard of God's law) of the worst sort. The critics were accusing Paul of teaching that the more wicked a person is, the more he glorifies God; the more faithless a person is, the more faithful he makes God appear; the more a person lies, the more he exalts God's truthfulness.

Those were not hypothetical misrepresentations, as Paul makes clear in his next statement: **"And why not say (as we are slanderously**

reported and as some affirm that we say), 'Let us do evil that good may come'?" Paul's enemies obviously had repeatedly charged that his gospel of salvation by grace through faith alone not only undermined God's law but granted license to sin with impunity. In effect, they accused him of saying that, in God's eyes, sin is as acceptable as righteousness, if not more so.

Although the scribes and Pharisees were themselves sinful and hypocritical to the core, they loved to condemn others for breaking the Mosaic law and the rabbinical traditions even in the smallest degree. Their religion was legalism personified, and the idea of divine grace was therefore anathema to them, because it completely undermined the works righteousness in which their hope was founded.

The same legalism characterized the Judaizers, supposed Jewish converts to Christianity who insisted that Christians had to maintain all the Mosaic laws and ceremonies. Their charges against Paul's gospel of grace were virtually identical to those of the scribes and Pharisees. The apostle therefore was attacked in much the same way both from within and without the church. It is therefore probable that Paul was addressing his arguments both to the Jewish leaders without and to the Judaizers within.

One of the most obvious characteristics of fallen human nature is its amazing ability to rationalize sin. Even small children are clever at giving a good reason for doing a wrong thing. That, essentially, was what Paul's opponents charged him with doing—rationalizing sin on the basis that it glorified God.

Later in the epistle Paul deals in detail with this same issue. After saying that "where sin increased, grace abounded all the more," he quickly counters the false conclusion he knew many people would jump to. "What shall we say then? Are we to continue in sin that grace might increase? May it never be!" (Rom. 5:20–6:1-2). With all the forcefulness he could muster, the apostle denounced the charge that he condoned any kind of sin. Least of all would he presume to justify sin by the spurious and vile argument that it brought glory to God.

It is possible, of course, that some of Paul's accusers wrongly associated his teachings with that of libertines in the church, such as those who were a blotch on the church at Corinth. Jude wrote of "certain persons [who had] crept in unnoticed, those who were long beforehand marked out for this condemnation, ungodly persons who turn the grace of our God into licentiousness and deny our only Master and Lord, Jesus Christ" (Jude 4).

For a professed Christian to live in continual, unrepentant sin is a certain mark that he is not saved. To be a Christian is to be under the lordship of Jesus Christ and genuinely desire to serve Him. As Jude makes indisputably clear, the person who tries to justify his sin by presuming on God's grace is ungodly and denies Christ (v. 4).

Paul's final response to his slanderous critics was short but pointed. Although he was not the least guilty of teaching antinomianism, he fully concurred that for those who do teach it, **their condemnation is just.**

The Guilt of All Men

What then? Are we better than they? Not at all; for we have already charged that both Jews and Greeks are all under sin; as it is written, "There is none righteous, not even one; there is none who understands, there is none who seeks for God; all have turned aside, together they have become useless; there in none who does good, there is not even one. Their throat is an open grave, with their tongues they keep deceiving, the poison of asps is under their lips; whose mouth is full of cursing and bitterness; their feet are swift to shed blood, destruction and misery are in their paths, and the path of peace have they not known. There is no fear of God before their eyes."

Now we know that whatever the Law says, it speaks to those who are under the Law, that every mouth may be closed, and all the world may become accountable to God; because by the works of the Law no flesh will be justified in His sight; for through the Law comes the knowledge of sin. (3:9-20)

Men like to believe they are basically good and that belief is continually reinforced by psychologists, counselors, and a great many religious leaders.

But deep in his heart man knows there is a problem with the way he is, that something is wrong. No matter whom or what he may try to blame for that feeling, he cannot escape it. He feels guilt, not only about things he has done that he knows are wrong but also about the kind of person he is on the inside.

A popular newspaper advice columnist wrote, "One of the most painful, self-mutilating, time- and energy-consuming exercises in the human experience is guilt. . . . It can ruin your day—or your week or your life—if you let it. It turns up like a bad penny when you do something dishonest, hurtful, tacky, selfish, or rotten. . . . Never mind that it was the result of ignorance, stupidity, laziness, thoughtlessness, weak flesh, or clay feet. You did wrong and the guilt is killing you. Too bad. But be assured," she concluded, "the agony you feel is normal. . . . Remember guilt is a pollutant and we don't need any more of it in the world" (*The Ann Landers Encyclopedia* [New York: Doubleday, 1978], pp. 514-17). With that, she went on to another subject.

The ancient Roman philosopher Seneca wrote that every guilty person is his own hangman. No matter how often a man tells himself he is good, he inevitably sees that he cannot help thinking, saying, and doing wrong things and feeling guilty about it. Guilt drives people to alcohol, drugs, despair, insanity, and more and more frequently to suicide. After playing psychological games about blaming his environment or other people or society in general, man still cannot escape the feeling of his own guilt. In fact, societies with sophisticated psychological services seem even more guilt ridden. People want to get rid of their guilty feelings but they do not know how. And the more they probe for solutions, the more guilty they feel.

Men *feel* guilty because they *are* guilty. The guilt feeling is only the symptom of the real problem, which is sin. All of the psychological counseling in the world cannot relieve a person of his guilt. At best it can only make him feel better, superficially and temporarily, by placing the blame on someone else or something else. That, of course, only intensifies the guilt, because it adds dishonesty to the sin that caused the guilt feeling in the first place.

Man's guilt has only one cause—his own sin—and unless his sin is removed, his guilt cannot be. That is why the first element of the gospel is confronting men with the reality of their sin. The word *gospel* means "good news." But the good news it offers is the way of salvation from sin, and until a person is convicted of his sin, the gospel has nothing to offer. The gospel therefore begins by declaring that all men are fundamentally sinful and that the greatest need of their lives is to have that sin removed through trust in the Lord Jesus Christ.

As Paul has already forcefully declared in the first two chapters of Romans, both the pagan Gentile and the religious Jew are sinful and stand condemned before a holy God. But human nature strongly resists that truth. Dr. Donald Grey Barnhouse said, "It is only stubborn self-pride that keeps man from the confession to God that would bring release, but that way he refuses to take. Man stands before God today like a little boy who swears with crying and tears that he has not been anywhere near the jam jar, and who with an air of outraged innocence, pleads the justice of his position, in total ignorance of the fact that a good spoonful of the jam has fallen on his shirt under his chin and is plainly visible to all but himself" (*God's Wrath: Romans 2—3:1-20* [Grand Rapids: Eerdmans, 1953], p. 191).

The apostle Paul was well aware of man's disposition to deny his sin. Therefore, from creation, from history, from reason and logic, and from conscience, Paul has already presented powerful testimony of man's sinfulness. Now he presents the ultimate testimony, the testimony of Scripture. Beginning with verse 10 and continuing through verse 18, Paul introduces before the court, as it were, the testimony of God's own Word as revealed in the Old Testament. Verses 9-20 summarize God's divine and perfect view of man and they continue in a trial motif: the arraignment (v. 9), the indictment (vv. 10-17), the motive (v. 18), and the verdict (vv. 19-20).

THE ARRAIGNMENT

What then? Are we better than they? Not at all; for we have already charged that both Jews and Greeks are all under sin; (3:9)

The charge begins with two questions. The first is simply, **What then?** The idea is, "What is the point of further testimony?" Paul has already condemned the immoral pagan, the moral pagan, and then both the moral and immoral Jew. Anticipating what some of his readers would think, his second question asks rhetorically, **Are we better than they?** That is, "Do we have a **better** basic nature than those who have just been shown to be condemned? Are we made from a different mold, cut from a different piece of cloth than they?"

The ones to whom **we** refers is not absolutely clear. Some commentators believe Paul is speaking of his fellow Jews. But he has already dealt in verses 1-8 with the question most Jews would ask, declaring that they do indeed have a spiritual advantage above Gentiles by having been "entrusted with the oracles of God," that is, the Old Testament Scriptures. He had previously pointed out, however, that their greater advantage also brought greater accountability (2:17-25). Nowhere else in the epistle does Paul identify himself with his fellow Jews by the use of *we.*

It seems better to take this **we** to refer to himself and his fellow believers in Rome, both Jew and Gentile. The question would then mean, "Are we Christians, in ourselves, **better than** the other groups of people already shown to be condemned before God? Are we intrinsically superior to those others? Were we saved because our basic human nature was on a higher plane than theirs?"

Immediately answering his own question, Paul unequivocally asserts, **Not at all.** "No, we are not in ourselves any better than others," he says. He has already pointed out the condemnation of everyone, from the most reprobate, vice-ridden pagan to the most outwardly moral and upright Jew. In other words, the entire human race, with absolutely no exceptions, is arraigned before God's court of justice: **For we have already charged that both Jews and Greeks are all under sin.**

Proaitiaomai (**already charged**) was often used as a legal term to designate a person previously indicted for a given offense. *Hupo* (**under**) was a common Greek term that frequently meant not simply to be beneath but to be totally under the power, authority, and control of something or someone. That is obviously the sense Paul has in mind here: Every human being, **both Jews and Greeks are all under,** completely subservient and in bondage to, the dominion of **sin.**

Such an idea was preposterous to most Jews. In his rebuke of Peter for succumbing to the Judaizers, Paul referred to the common belief of Jews that they were righteous before God simply by virtue of being Jewish, members of His chosen race. On the other hand, Jews believed just as strongly that Gentiles—commonly called **Greeks** because of the prevalence of Greek culture and language even under Roman rule—were naturally sinful simply by virtue of being *non*-Jewish (see Gal. 3:15).

If a Jew was poverty stricken, handicapped, or otherwise seriously afflicted, it was assumed that either he or his parents had committed some unusually heinous sin, for which, for a generation or so, they forfeited their normally high standing before God. That belief is reflected in the story of the blind man whom Jesus and the disciples passed just outside the Temple one day. Noticing the man's condition, the disciples asked the Lord, "Rabbi, who sinned, this man or his parents, that he should be born blind?" (John 9:2). After Jesus corrected the disciples' wrong assumption, He restored the man's sight. When the man was talking with the Pharisees a short while later, they vehemently voiced the same wrong assumption the Twelve had expressed. When the man said to them of Jesus, "If this man were not from God, He could do nothing," the Pharisees were greatly offended and replied, "You were born entirely in sins, and are you teaching us?" (vv. 33-34).

People who are very religious tend to think of themselves as being inherently better than others and favored by God because of their goodness and religiosity. Even Christians are sometimes tempted to think that God saved them because they were somehow more deserving of salvation than others. But if a person ever becomes right before God it is never because he is innately better than anyone else or because he has managed to bring his life up to God's standards or because he zealously observes certain religious practices. It is only because he has acknowledged his sin and helplessness and prostrated himself in humble faith before the Lord Jesus Christ for forgiveness and cleansing.

Despite great differences in outward behavior and attitudes among people, *every* Christless person is sinful in nature and is under the dominion and control of Satan. The entire unredeemed world, John declares, "lies in the power of the evil one" (1 John 5:19) and is therefore arraigned, as it were, before God's bar of justice.

THE INDICTMENT

as it is written, "There is none righteous, not even one; there is none who understands, there is none who seeks for God; all have turned aside, together they have become useless; there is none who does good, there is not even one. Their throat is an open grave, with their tongues they keep deceiving, the poison of asps is under their lips; whose mouth is full of cursing and bitterness; their feet are swift to shed blood, destruction and misery are in their paths, and the path of peace have they not known." (3:10-17)

Paul now presents an appalling thirteen-count indictment against fallen mankind. To reinforce the inclusiveness of the indictment, he reiterates the fact that *all* of fallen humanity, Jew and Gentile alike, is under sin (see v. 9). In verses 10-18, he uses the term **none** (and its equivalent, **not even one**) six times in referring to man's absolute lack of righteousness before God.

The indictment comes directly from Old Testament Scripture, to which **it is written** refers. Both Jesus and Satan used that phrase to introduce quotations from the Old Testament during the temptation in the wilderness (Matt. 4:4, 6-7, 10). **It is written** translates the Greek perfect tense, indicating the continuity and permanence of what was **written** and implying its divine authority, which every faithful Jew and every faithful Christian, whether Jew or Gentile, acknowledged.

The thirteen charges of the indictment are presented in three categories—the first concerning the character (vv. 10-12), the second concerning the conversation (vv. 13-14), and the third concerning the conduct (vv. 15-17) of the accused.

THE CHARACTER OF THE ACCUSED

"There is none righteous, not even one; there is none who understands, there is none who seeks for God; all have turned aside, together they have become useless; there is none who does good, there is not even one. (3:10-12)

Under the heading of what could be called character, Paul lists the first six of the thirteen charges. Because of their fallen natures, men are universally evil (v. 10*b*), spiritually ignorant (v. 11*a*), rebellious (v. 11*b*), wayward (v. 12*a*), spiritually useless (v. 12*b*), and morally corrupt (v. 12*c*).

First, mankind is universally evil, there being absolutely no exceptions. Quoting from the Psalms, Paul declares, **There is none righteous, not even one.** The full text of Psalm 14:1 is, "The fool has said in his heart 'There is no God.'They are corrupt, they have committed abominable deeds; there is no one who does good."

Righteousness is a major theme of the book of Romans, appearing in one form or another more than thirty times. Other terms from the same Greek root are usually translated "justified," "justification," or the like. Together they are used more than sixty times in the book of Romans. It is not surprising, therefore, that the first first charge Paul makes in his indictment is that of mankind's unrighteousness.

Paul is using the term **righteous** in its most basic sense of being right before God, of being as God created man to be. Obviously, people are able to do many things that are morally right. Even the most vile person may occasionally do something commendable. But the apostle is not speaking of specific acts or even general patterns of behavior, but of man's inner character. His point is that **there is** not a single person who has ever lived, apart from the sinless Lord Jesus (cf. 2 Cor. 5:21), whose innermost being could be characterized as **righteous** by God's standard. To prevent some people from thinking that they might be exceptions, Paul adds, **not even one.**

As already noted, there are obviously vast differences among people as to their kindness, love, generosity, honesty, truthfulness, and the like. But **not even one** person beside Christ has come remotely close to **righteous** perfection, which is the only standard acceptable to God. God's standard of righteousness for men is the righteousness that He Himself possesses, which was manifest in Christ. "You are to be perfect," Jesus declared, "as your heavenly Father is perfect" (Matt. 5:48).

In other words, a person who is not as good as God is not acceptable to God. As Paul makes clear later in the epistle, and as the New Testament teaches throughout, men can become perfectly righteous, when the righteousness of Christ is imputed to them. The very truth that makes the gospel the "good news" is that God has provided a way for men to become perfect, divinely perfect. But that perfection comes entirely by God's grace in response to faith in His Son, Jesus Christ.

Paul is here speaking of men, *all* men, who are apart from Christ. In God's sight, there are no levels of righteousness as far as salvation is concerned. There is either perfect righteousness in Christ or perfect sinfulness apart from Christ.

As mentioned above, from man's perspective there are vast moral and spiritual differences among people. But men's achieving God's standard of righteousness on their own may be compared to a group of people trying to jump from the shore of a south seas island to the United States. A good athlete could jump twenty-five feet or more. Many could jump ten or fifteen feet, and a few might be in such poor shape that they could barely jump five. Measured against each other, therefore, their efforts would be considerably different. But measured against the distance from those islands to the United States, the differences among them would be undetectable and their efforts would be equally futile. Almost as if commenting on such a contest, Paul declares a few verses later: "All have sinned and fall short of the glory of God" (3:23).

Second, man not only is universally evil but also spiritually ignorant. Quoting again from the Psalms, Paul says, **There is none who understands** (see Pss. 14:2; 53:3). Even if men somehow had the ability to achieve God's perfect righteousness, they would not know what it is or how to go about attaining it. To use the south seas island example again, they would have no idea as to which way to jump.

Man has no innate ability to fully comprehend God's truth or His standard of righteousness. From God's magnificent creation, man has sufficient evidence of His "invisible attributes, His eternal power and divine nature" to make every person "without excuse" for not honoring and glorifying God (Rom. 1:20). But apart from the ability to see that general revelation of His power and majesty, man has no spiritual capacity to know or understand God, because the "natural man does not accept the things of the Spirit of God; for they are foolishness to him, and he cannot understand them, because they are spiritually appraised" (1 Cor. 2:14).

In his letter to the Ephesians, the apostle points out that man's spiritual ignorance is not due to unfortunate outward circumstances or lack of opportunity. It is due solely to his own innate sinful nature that does not *want* to know and understand, much less obey and serve God. Unsaved persons are "darkened in their understanding, excluded from the life of God, because of the ignorance that is in them, because of the hardness of their heart" (Eph. 4:18). Men are not sinful and hardened against God because they are ignorant of Him, but, to the contrary, they are ignorant of Him because of their sinful and hardened disposition. People have a certain sense about God through the testimony of creation, as already noted, and also through the witness of their consciences (Rom. 2:15). But their willfully sinful nature blocks out that testimony and witness. The natural man is thereby hardened in his heart and darkened in his mind. He not only does not understand God but has no inclination to do so.

Some years ago a fascinating but pathetic story of a duck in a Toronto park made headlines for several days (*Toronto Star*, Nov. 4-13, 1971). The duck, who came to be called Ringo, made her home at the park lake. One day she accidentally poked her bill through the ring of a pull tab from a pop can and was not able to extricate herself. She was, of course, unable to eat and would soon starve to death. When her plight was noticed by some park visitors, she became something of a celebrity. Park personnel and animal experts tried numerous ways to catch Ringo so she could be helped. They even called in a champion duck caller. People tried luring her with food but without success. Unfortunately, the frightened Ringo mistook all the efforts to help her as being threats. The rescuers lost sight of her and never did catch her. It is not known if Ringo eventually dislodged the pull tab before she died.

Fallen and condemned man, trapped in his sin, is similarly confused. Because he sees it as a threat to his life-style rather than an eternal blessing, he makes every effort to escape the gospel, which the Lord has so graciously provided for his salvation.

Third, in addition to being universally evil and spiritually ignorant, fallen man is rebellious. **There is none who seeks for God**, Paul declares, alluding again to Psalm 14:2. Judging from the vast number of religions in the world with millions of zealous adherents, one would think that a great many people are diligently seeking after God. But Scripture makes clear, in this passage and in many others, that all religious systems and efforts are, in reality, attempts to escape the true God and to discover or manufacture false gods of one's own liking.

God has given the absolute assurance that anyone who seeks Him with his heart will find Him (Jer. 29:13). Jesus offers the divine promise that everyone who sincerely asks of Him will receive, that everyone who sincerely seeks Him will find Him, and that everyone who sincerely knocks on the door of heaven will have it opened to him (Matt. 7:8). But the Lord knows that man's sinful inclination is *not* to seek Him, and He therefore seeks individuals out to draw them to Himself.

During the council at Jerusalem in the early days of the church, James reminded the gathering of apostles and elders of God's ancient promises that "after these things I will return, and I will rebuild the Tabernacle of David which has fallen, and I will rebuild its ruins, and I will restore it, in order that the rest of mankind may seek the Lord" (Acts 15:16-17). Peter gives assurance in the clearest possible words that the

Lord does not wish "for any to perish but for all to come to repentance" (2 Pet. 3:9).

But man-made religions are demon-inspired efforts to escape from God, not to find Him. Every person who comes to Jesus Christ for salvation has been sent to Him through the divine initiative of God the Father (John 6:37). "No one can come to Me," Jesus goes on to say, "unless the Father who sent Me draws him" (v. 44). The only person, therefore, who seeks God is the person who has responded positively to God's seeking him.

The person who truly **seeks for God** is like David, who declared, "I have set the Lord continually before me" (Ps. 16:8). Such a person seeks first the kingdom of God and His righteousness (Matt. 6:33). God becomes the focus of everything, the source of everything, the beginning and end of everything. To truly seek for God is to respect and adore His sovereign majesty and to feed on the truth of His Word. It is to obey His commandments, to speak to Him in prayer, to live consciously in His presence with a desire to please Him. No one can do such things naturally, but only by the Spirit of God working through him. The natural inclination of men is to "seek after their own interests" (Phil. 2:21).

Fourth, Paul charges that men are naturally wayward. Continuing to quote from the Psalms (14:3), he declares that **all have turned aside** from God. The person who is naturally evil, naturally ignorant of God's truth, and naturally rebellious against God, will inevitably naturally live apart from God's will.

Turned aside is from *ekklinō,* and has the basic meaning of leaning in the wrong direction. In a military context it referred to a soldier's running the wrong way, in other words deserting in the midst of battle.

Speaking of the universal human inclination to go against God's way, Isaiah wrote, "All of us like sheep have gone astray, each of us has turned to his own way" (Isa. 53:6). In the early church the gospel was sometimes called "the Way" (Acts 9:2), and Christians were often referred to as followers of the Way. Jesus said of Himself, "I am the way, and the truth, and the life" (John 14:6). Even the demon who had given a certain slave girl the power of divination acknowledged through her that Paul and his companions were "bond-servants of the Most High God, who are proclaiming to you the *way* of salvation" (Acts 16:17, emphasis added). Luke referred to some Jewish opponents of Paul's ministry in Ephesus as men who were "speaking evil of the Way" (Acts 19:9), and because of that opposition, "there arose no small disturbance concerning the Way" (v. 23). In his defense before the governor Felix, Paul said, "This I admit to you, that according to the Way which they call a sect I do serve the God of our fathers, believing everything that is in accordance with the

Law, and that is written in the Prophets" (Acts 24:14). The writer of Hebrews spoke of Christ's atoning work as "a new and living way which He inaugurated for us through the veil, that is, His flesh" (Heb. 10:20). Peter spoke of false teachers who had infiltrated the church as those who had forsaken "the right way" of the true gospel, which is "the way of righteousness" (2 Pet. 2:15, 21).

On the other hand, the basic pattern of living of the natural man is characterized as "the evil way" (Prov. 8:13), the "way which seems right to a man, but [whose] end is the way of death" (Prov. 14:12).

The great evangelist Dwight L. Moody told of being asked by the warden of a large prison in New York City to speak to the inmates. Because there was no chapel or other suitable or safe place to speak to the group, he preached from a gangway at one end of a large tier of cells, unable to see the face of a single prisoner. After the message he asked permission to talk face-to-face with some of the men through the bars of their cells. He soon discovered that most of the men had not even been listening to his message. When Moody would ask an inmate why he was in prison, the man almost invariably declared his innocence. He would insist that a false witness testified against him, or that he was mistaken for the person who really committed the crime, or that the judge or jury was prejudiced against him, or he would give some other reason he was unjustly incarcerated. "I began to get discouraged," Moody said, "but when I had gotten almost through I found one man with his elbows on his knees and two streams of tears running down his cheeks. I looked in at the little window and said, 'My friend, what is your trouble?' He looked up with despair and remorse on his face and said, 'My sins are more than I can bear.' I said, 'Thank God for that.'" The evangelist was thankful because he knew that no man is open to God's way until he forsakes his own way, that he will not seek salvation until he admits he is lost.

Fifth, Paul charges that the natural man is spiritually worthless. **Together,** that is, all of fallen mankind, **they have become useless.** The Hebrew equivalent of the Greek term translated here as **useless** was often used to describe milk that had turned sour and rancid, thereby becoming unfit to drink or to be used to make butter, cheese, or anything else edible. In ancient Greek literature the word was even used of the senseless laughter of a moron.

Apart from a saving relationship to Jesus Christ, a person is a spiritually dead branch, totally unable to produce any fruit. As such, it is lifeless and worthless, fit only to be thrown into the fire to be burned (John 15:6). Paul's letter to Titus emphasizes the same tragic reality when it reflects on the utter worthlessness of even religious men (Titus 1:16). The natural man is useless for the purposes of God and, much like the worthless dead branch, is destined for the fires of hell.

Sixth, the natural man is charged with being corrupt, which is both a repetition of the first charge and something of a summary of the previous five charges. **There is none who does good,** Paul says, **there is not even one.**

Chrēstotēs (**does good**) refers to what is upright, specifically to what is morally upright. Measured by God's perfect standard of righteousness, the natural man has no ability to do anything upright and **good.** As already mentioned, relative to other human beings, some people obviously are better behaved. But no human being has within himself either the desire or the capacity for the **good** that is holy, perfect, and God-glorifying by the divine standard.

The story is told of a man in Scotland who was walking through a park one Saturday afternoon, carrying a small New Testament in a leather case. Thinking the case contained a camera, a group of young people asked him to take their picture. In response, he said, "I already have it." When the astonished youths asked him where and when he had taken it, he took out the Testament and read Romans 3:9-23. After saying, "That is your picture," he took the opportunity to witness to them about Christ.

THE CONVERSATION OF THE ACCUSED

Their throat is an open grave, with their tongues they keep deceiving, the poison of asps is under their lips; whose mouth is full of cursing and bitterness; (3:13-14)

A person's character will inevitably manifest itself in his conversation. Jesus declared that "the mouth speaks out of that which fills the heart. The good man out of his good treasure brings forth what is good; and the evil man out of his evil treasure brings forth what is evil" (Matt 12:34-35). On another occasion He taught the same truth in slightly different words: "The things that proceed out of the mouth come from the heart" (15:18). The writer of Proverbs said, "The mouth of the righteous flows with wisdom, but the perverted tongue will be cut out. The lips of the righteous bring forth what is acceptable, but the mouth of the wicked, what is perverted" (Prov. 10:31-32). He also wrote, "The tongue of the wise makes knowledge acceptable, but the mouth of fools spouts folly. . . . The heart of the righteous ponders how to answer, but the mouth of the wicked pours out evil things" (Prov. 15:2, 28).

Continuing to quote from the Psalms, Paul illustrates the truths about a person's character as they are reflected in his conversation. In doing so, he adds four more charges to the divine indictment against the unregenerate man.

Commenting on Paul's use of human anatomy to illustrate how

man's evil character manifests itself, one writer paraphrased the psalmist's and the apostle's words in this way: "His tongue is tipped with fraud, his lips are tainted with venom, his mouth full of gall [bitterness], . . . his tongue a sword to run men through, and his throat a sepulchre in which to bury them."

The seventh charge of Paul's indictment is that by nature fallen mankind is spiritually dead, demonstrated by the metaphor of **their throat** being **an open grave** (cf. Ps. 5:9). A spiritually dead heart can generate only spiritually dead words.

The **throat** is to the heart as **an open grave** is to the corpse within it. Where embalming is not available, a corpse is placed in the ground and then covered up—not only to show respect for the deceased but also to protect passersby from viewing the disfigurement and smelling the stench of decay. But the natural man keeps his throat wide open, and in so doing continually testifies to his spiritual death by the foulness of his words.

The eighth charge is that by nature fallen mankind is deceitful: **with their tongues they keep deceiving.** *Dolioō,* from which **keep deceiving** is derived, has the basic meaning of luring and was used of baiting a hook by covering it with a small piece of food to disguise its danger. When a fish bites the food, thinking he will get a meal, he instead becomes a meal for the fisherman. The imperfect Greek tense of the verb indicates continual, repetitive deceit. For the natural man, lying and other forms of deceit are a habitual and normal part of his life.

Psalm 5:9 describes flatterers, whose words of praise are really a means of serving themselves rather than the one they are praising. And because praise appeals to human nature, it also leads the flattered person into pride and false self-confidence. A flatterer therefore both uses and abuses others.

David declares that man's sinfulness can also lead to self-deceit and self-flattery. "Transgression speaks to the ungodly within his heart; there is no fear of God before his eyes. For it flatters him in his own eyes, concerning the discovery of his iniquity and the hatred of it. The words of his mouth are wickedness and deceit" (Ps. 36:1-3).

Isaiah wrote, "Behold, the Lord's hand is not so short that it cannot save; neither is His ear so dull that it cannot hear." But he follows those comforting words with the awesome declaration: "But your iniquities have made a separation between you and your God, and your sins have hidden His face from you, so that He does not hear. For your hands are defiled with blood, and your fingers with iniquity; your lips have spoken falsehood, your tongue mutters wickedness" (Isa. 59:1-3).

Jeremiah also exposed man's natural deceitfulness, saying of the wicked, " 'They bend their tongue like their bow; lies and not truth prevail in the land; for they proceed from evil to evil, and they do not know Me,' declares the Lord. 'Let everyone be on guard against his neighbor, and do not trust any brother; because every brother deals craftily, and every neighbor goes about as a slanderer. And everyone deceives his neighbor, and does not speak the truth, they have taught their tongue to speak lies'" (Jer. 9:3-5).

The ninth charge in Paul's indictment of the unconverted man is closely related to the previous one. Quoting from part of Psalm 140:3, he says of ungodly men that **the poison of asps is under their lips.** The psalmist precedes that charge with the observation that "they sharpen their tongues as a serpent." Because of the spiritually damning false doctrines and the deceitful character of most of the religious leaders in Jesus' day, both He and John the Baptist described them as broods of vipers (Matt. 3:7; 12:34).

In describing **asps,** one writer says, "The fangs of such a deadly snake ordinarily lie folded back in the upper jaw, but when the snake throws his head to strike, these hollow fangs drop down, and when the snake bites, the fangs press a sac of deadly poison hidden under the lips, ejecting venom into the victim."

I remember reading about a man who found a baby rattlesnake and decided to make a pet of it. He kept it in the house and played with it for a week or so, but then it disappeared for several months and could not be found. One day the man reached behind a piece of furniture to retrieve something he had dropped. When he felt a sharp stab of pain, he pulled back his hand, with the rattler hanging from it by its fangs. Man's sinful nature is equally untameable.

Even those who belong to the Lord can succumb to terrible deceit. David, the divinely anointed king of Israel and a man after God's own heart, became enamored of Bathsheba when he happened to see her bathing. Although he was told she was married, he nevertheless summoned her to the palace and had sexual relations with her. When she became pregnant and notified David, the king flashed the fangs of deceit by inviting her husband, Uriah, to a sumptuous banquet, giving the impression that this man was a valued friend. But David was determined to have Bathsheba for his own wife, and the next morning he sent her husband to the battlefront with a sealed note to the commander that contained Uriah's own death warrant (see 2 Sam. 11:1-15).

The tenth charge in the indictment continues the imagery of speaking, describing the ungodly as those **whose mouth is full of cursing and bitterness** (see Ps. 10:7).

Ara (**cursing**) carries the idea of intense malediction, of desiring the worst for a person and making that desire public through open criticism and defamation. *Pikria* (**bitterness**) was not used so much in regard to physical taste as to describe openly-expressed emotional hostility against an enemy. Such is the obvious meaning in this context.

David described cursing, bitter persons as those who "have sharpened their tongue like a sword . . . aimed bitter speech as their arrow, to shoot from concealment at the blameless; suddenly they shoot him, and do not fear" (Ps. 64:3-4). Every age of mankind, our own certainly included, has been characterized by people who use their tongues as vicious weapons. Their attacks not only are against those they know well enough to hate but sometimes, as David seems to intimate, even against strangers, simply for the perverse pleasure of venting their anger and hatred.

THE CONDUCT OF THE ACCUSED

their feet are swift to shed blood, destruction and misery are in their paths, and the path of peace have they not known. (3:15-17)

The last three charges in Paul's indictment relate to the conduct of the natural man. The eleventh charge is that the ungodly are innately murderous: **their feet are swift to shed blood.**

The cannibalism that still exists in a few primitive tribes and the mass executions of innocent civilians that have taken place in numerous "developed" countries in modern times are but extreme manifestations of the basically destructive disposition of fallen mankind. The nineteenth-century Scottish evangelist Robert Haldane wrote, "The most savage animals do not destroy so many of their own species to appease their hunger, as man destroys of his fellows', to satiate his ambition, his revenge, or his cupidity [greed]" (*An Exposition of the Epistle to the Romans* [MacDill AFB, Fla.: MacDonald, 1958], p. 120).

Even in the United States, with its Christian heritage, since the turn of the twentieth century twice as many of its citizens have been slain in private acts of murder than have been killed in all the wars of its entire history. According to researcher Arnold Barnett of the Massachusetts Institute of Technology, a child born today in any one of the fifty largest cities in the United States has the chance of one in fifty of being murdered. Dr. Barnett estimated that a baby born in the 1980s is more likely to be murdered than an American soldier in World War II was of being killed in combat.

Whether in peace or in war, man kills man. The mass exterminations by Nazis and Marxists in our own century have their counterparts in past history. The notorious terrorist Chang Hsien-chung in seventeenth-century China killed practically all the people in the Szechwan province. During that same century in Hungary, a certain countess systematically tortured and murdered more than six hundred young girls.

Obviously most people are far from possessing such extreme

brutality. But Scripture makes clear that the seed of murder is one of a multitude of evil seeds that are universally found in the human heart and that, to some degree, inevitably grow and bear fruit.

The twelfth charge in the overall indictment, and the second one that is manifested in man's conduct, is that of general destructiveness. **Destruction and misery are in their paths.** *Suntrimma* (**destruction**) is a compound word that denotes breaking in pieces and completely shattering, causing total devastation.

The manifestation of wanton **destruction** is becoming more and more evident in much of modern society. Victims are often robbed or raped and then beaten or murdered for no reason other than sheer brutality. The terms "abused children" and "abused wives" have become common in contemporary vocabularies. Special divisions of many police departments and social service agencies are devoted specifically to dealing with the crimes and victims that those terms relate to.

Misery is a general term that denotes the resulting harm that is always in the wake of man's acts of destruction against his fellow man. His destructiveness inevitably leaves a trail of pain and despair.

The thirteenth and last of the charges in Paul's indictment of condemned man is that of his peacelessness: **And the path of peace have they not known.** The apostle is not speaking of the lack of inner peace—although that is certainly a characteristic of the ungodly person— but of man's essential inclination *away* from peace. This charge is therefore something of a counterpart to the previous one.

Peace has never been more highly extolled than in our own day. But few would argue that peace, whether personal or international, actually characterizes our times. Nevertheless, as in Jeremiah's day, many modern leaders are trying to heal the brokenness of their people superficially, crying, "Peace, peace," when obviously there is no peace (see Jer. 6.14).

God's Word gives much counsel as to what makes for peace, and those individuals and societies who have chosen to follow His guidance have experienced relative times of peacefulness. But Scripture makes clear that peace will never dominate human society until the Prince of Peace returns to establish His kingdom on earth.

Note this gripping description of sin:

> It is a debt, a burden, a thief, a sickness, a leprosy, a plague, poison, a serpent, a sting; everything that man hates it is; a load of curses, and calamities beneath whose crushing most intolerable pressure, the whole creation groaneth. . . .
>
> Who is the hoary sexton that digs man a grave? Who is the painted temptress that steals his virtue? Who is the murderess that destroys his life? Who is this sorceress that first deceives, and then damns his soul?—Sin.

Who with icy breath, blights the fair blossoms of youth? Who breaks the hearts of parents? Who brings old men's grey hairs with sorrow to the grave?—Sin.

Who, by a more hideous metamorphosis than Ovid even fancied, changes gentle children into vipers, tender mothers into monsters and their fathers into worse than Herods, the murderers of their own innocents?—Sin.

Who casts the apple of discord on household hearts? Who lights the torch of war, and bears it blazing over trembling lands? Who by divisions in the church, rends Christ's seamless robe?—Sin.

Who is this Delilah that sings the Nazirite asleep and delivers up the strength of God into the hands of the uncircumcised? Who with winning smiles on her face, honey flattery on her tongue, stands in the door to offer the sacred rites of hospitality and when suspicion sleeps, treacherously pierces our temples with a nail? What fair siren is this who seated on a rock by the deadly pool smiles to deceive, sings to lure, kisses to betray, and flings her arm around our neck to leap with us into perdition?—Sin.

Who turns the soft and gentlest heart to stone? Who hurls reason from her lofty throne, and impels sinners, mad as Gadarene swine, down the precipice, into a lake of fire?—Sin. (Cited in Elon Foster's *New Cyclopedia of Prose Illustrations* [New York: T. Y. Crowell, 1877], p. 696)

THE MOTIVE

There is no fear of God before their eyes." (3:18)

The motive for man's sinfulness is his built-in godlessness. The basic sinful condition of men and of their spiritual deadness is evidenced by the fact that, for the unsaved, **there is no fear of God before their eyes.** The full text of Psalm 36:1, from which Paul here quotes, reads: "Transgression speaks to the ungodly within his heart; there is no fear of God before his eyes." Because men's ears are attuned to the lies of sin rather than to the truth of righteousness, they have an inadequate concern about and **no fear of God.**

Fearing God has both positive and negative elements. In a positive way, every true believer has reverential fear of God—an awesome awareness of His power, His holiness, and His glory. Proper worship always includes that kind of fear of the Lord. Reverential fear of God is the beginning of spiritual wisdom (Prov. 9:10). That kind of fear is a necessary element in one's being led to salvation, as with Cornelius (Acts 10:2), and motivates new believers in their spiritual growth.

The negative aspect of the **fear of God** has to do with dread and terror. Even believers should have a measure of that kind of fear, which acts as a protection from sinning. The writer of Proverbs observed, "By the fear of the Lord one keeps away from evil" (16:6). For the very reason they are God's children, believers are subject to His chastisement (see Heb. 12:5-11). Sometimes His dealing with disobedient believers can be severe, as with Ananias and Sapphira, who lost their lives for lying to the Holy Spirit. God used that punishment to produce godly fear and obedience within the early church (see Acts 5:1-11). Some of the believers in the church at Corinth also died or became ill by the direct infliction of God's chastisement for their sin (1 Cor. 11:30).

Ideally, Christians should live holy lives out of love for God and gratitude for His grace and blessings. But it often takes God-given hardship and pain to pry believers from a sin, or it takes the prospect of punishment to keep them from getting into it in the first place.

Unbelievers, however, should have **fear of God** in its most intense and terrifying sense. The Old Testament is replete with stories of the Lord wreaking destruction and death as punishment for sins of all kinds. He destroyed Sodom and Gomorrah because of their indescribable immorality and turned Lot's wife into a pillar of salt for simply looking back disobediently on that horrifying scene. Because of its unrelenting wickedness, God destroyed the whole human race through the Flood, saving only eight people. He drowned the entire Egyptian army when it tried to capture the children of Israel and bring them back to slavery in Egypt. The Lord ordered Moses to have the Levites slay some three thousand Israelite men who had erected and worshiped a golden calf while Moses was on the mountain receiving the tablets of the law from God.

On one occasion a group of Jews asked Jesus, in effect, why God had allowed Pilate to kill some Galileans and mingle their blood with their sacrifices and why eighteen people were killed when a tower at Siloam toppled over on them. He replied that those people did not die because they were more wicked than others, and then proceeded to warn His inquirers, "Unless you repent, you will all likewise perish" (Luke 13:1-5).

I once heard of a minister who was known for his emphasis on worship and had even written a book on the subject. One day when some members of his congregation were helping him move his office, they discovered a large box filled with pornographic magazines. One wonders if such a man could be a Christian; but it was obvious that he had little real fear of God's righteous judgment or reverence for His honor and glory.

Robert Haldane, mentioned above, wrote,

> It is astonishing that men, while they acknowledge that there is a God, should act without any fear of His displeasure. Yet this is their character. They fear a worm of the dust like themselves, but disregard the Most High. . . . They are more afraid of man than of God—of his anger, his contempt,

or ridicule. The fear of man prevents them from doing many things from which they are not restrained by the fear of God. . . . They love not His character, not rendering to it that veneration which is due; they respect not His authority. Such is the state of human nature while the heart is unchanged. (*Exposition of Romans,* p. 121)

THE VERDICT

Now we know that whatever the Law says, it speaks to those who are under the Law, that every mouth may be closed, and all the world may become accountable to God; because by the works of the Law no flesh will be justified in His sight; for through the Law comes the knowledge of sin. (3:19-20)

Here Paul declares God's verdict on fallen, unrepentant mankind.

Oida (**know**) refers to knowledge that is certain and complete. **We know** with absolute certainty, Paul was saying, **that whatever the Law says, it speaks to those who are under the Law, that every mouth may be closed, and all the world may become accountable to God.** That declaration allows no exceptions. Every unredeemed human being, Jew or Gentile, is **under the Law** of God and **accountable to God.**

As Paul has already declared, the Jew is under God's written law, delivered through Moses, and the Gentile is under the equally God-given law written in his heart (Rom. 2:11-15). God is the Creator, Sustainer, and Lord of the entire universe, and it is therefore impossible for anyone or anything to be outside His control or authority.

The final verdict, then, is that unredeemed mankind has no defense whatever and is guilty of all charges. The defense must rest, as it were, before it has opportunity to say anything, because the omniscient and all-wise God has infallibly demonstrated the impossibility of any grounds for acquittal.

Absolute silence is the only possible response, just as there will be utter silence in heaven when the Lord Jesus Christ will one day break the seventh seal and release the seven trumpet judgments upon the condemned earth (see Rev. 8:1-6).

In anticipation of the argument that perhaps a few exceptionally zealous people might live up to the perfect standard of God's law, the apostle adds: **by the works of the Law no flesh will be justified in His sight.** There is no salvation through the keeping of God's law, because sinful man is utterly incapable of doing so. He has neither the ability nor the inclination within himself to obey God perfectly.

As Paul goes on to say, *apart from the law,* through the grace of God acting through the sacrifice of His Son, salvation and eternal life are made possible (Rom. 3:21-22). But *under* the law there can be no sentence but death.

How to Be Right with God

But now apart from the Law the righteousness of God has been manifested, being witnessed by the Law and the Prophets, even the righteousness of God through faith in Jesus Christ for all those who believe; for there is no distinction; for all have sinned and fall short of the glory of God, being justified as a gift by His grace through the redemption which is in Christ Jesus; whom God displayed publicly as a propitiation in His blood through faith. (3:21-25a)

Job asked the most important question it is possible to ask: "How can a man be in the right before God?" (Job 9:2) He then said,

> If one wished to dispute with Him, He could not answer Him once in a thousand times. Wise in heart and mighty in strength, who has defied Him without harm? It is God who removes the mountains, they know not how, when He overturns them in His anger; who shakes the earth out of its place, and its pillars tremble; who commands the sun not to shine, and sets a seal upon the stars; who alone stretches out the heavens, and tramples down the waves of the sea; who makes the Bear, Orion, and the Pleiades, and the chambers of the south; who does great things, unfathomable, and

wondrous works without number. Were He to pass by me, I would not see Him; were He to move past me, I would not perceive Him. Were He to snatch away, who could restrain Him? Who could say to Him, "What art Thou doing?" God will not turn back His anger; beneath Him crouch the helpers of Rahab. How then can I answer Him, and choose my words before Him? For though I were right, I could not answer; I would have to implore the mercy of my judge. If I called and He answered me, I could not believe that He was listening to my voice. For He bruises me with a tempest, and multiplies my wounds without cause. He will not allow me to get my breath, but saturates me with bitterness. If it is a matter of power, behold, He is the strong one! And if it is a matter of justice, who can summon Him? Though I am righteous, my mouth will condemn me; though I am guiltless, He will declare me guilty. (vv. 3-20)

Because God is the kind of God He is, Job wondered how a person could ever hope to approach Him, much less become right and acceptable before Him. Can a mere human being have a right relationship with a God who is perfectly holy, infinite, and mighty? Bildad echoed Job's question, saying, "How then can a man be just with God?" (Job 25:4).

Upon hearing John the Baptist's fearful warnings about God's judgment, "the multitudes were questioning him, saying, 'Then what shall we do?'" (Luke 3:10). The crowd that Jesus had miraculously fed the day before asked Him, "What shall we do, that we may work the works of God?" (John 6:27-28). The rich young ruler asked Jesus, "Teacher, what good thing shall I do that I may obtain eternal life?" (Matt. 19:16). After hearing Peter's sobering message at Pentecost, some of the listeners said to him "and the rest of the apostles, 'Brethren, what shall we do?'" (Acts 2:37). As he lay blinded on the road to Damascus, Saul cried out to Jesus, "What shall I do, Lord?" (Acts 22:10). The Philippian jailor asked Paul and Silas, "Sirs, what must I do to be saved?" (Acts 16:30).

Throughout history men have asked much the same questions as did Job and the others. The very reason that religion is so universally common to mankind reflects man's attempts to answer such questions. As noted in the last chapter, people cannot escape feelings of guilt, not only for doing things they know are wrong but for being the way they are. Man's sense of lostness, loneliness, emptiness, and meaninglessness is reflected in the literature and archaeological remains of every civilization. So are his fear of death, of existence, if any, beyond the grave, and of divine punishment. Nearly every religion is a response to those fears and seeks to offer a way of reaching and satisfying deity. But every religion except Christianity is man-made and works-centered, and for that reason, none of them can succeed in leading a person to God.

Scripture makes clear that there is indeed a way to God, but that it is not based on anything men themselves can do to achieve or merit it. Man can be made right with God, but not on his own terms or in his own power. In that basic regard Christianity is distinct from every other religion. As far as the way of salvation is concerned, there are therefore only two religions the world has ever known or will ever know—the religion of divine accomplishment, which is biblical Christianity, and the religion of human achievement, which includes all other kinds of religion, by whatever names they may go under.

When threatened by the fierce and powerful Babylonians, the people of Judah asked Jeremiah to intercede for them before God, "that the Lord your God may tell us the way in which we should walk and the thing that we should do." To reinforce their seeming sincerity, they then "said to Jeremiah, 'May the Lord be a true and faithful witness against us, if we do not act in accordance with the whole message with which the Lord your God will send you to us. Whether it is pleasant or unpleasant, we will listen to the voice of the Lord our God.'" But when Jeremiah brought them God's answer, which was to stay in their own land and trust Him to save them, they rejected His word and went to Egypt (Jer. 42:1–43:7).

Their response is typical of myriads of people who ask how to get right with God. They seem very sincere, but when they hear about the true and only way, which is through trust in Jesus Christ, they are unwilling to comply. Their response makes it evident that they are seeking salvation on their own terms, not God's.

All men are equally incapable of coming to God in their own power. They can be saved only by the provision of God's grace. Since Adam and Eve fell, faith responding to the offer of God's grace has always been the only means of salvation, of providing a right relationship to God. Man cannot be saved even by God's own divine law given through Moses. That law was never, under any covenant or dispensation, a means of salvation. Its purpose was to show how impossible it is to measure up to God's standards by human effort. The moral standards commanded and the ceremonies prescribed in the Mosaic covenant were never intended and were never able to save. A sincere desire to obey the law and a proper observance of the rituals were pleasing to God, but only as they reflected faith in Him.

One of the major and repeated themes of the book of Romans is righteousness. As mentioned in the previous chapter, the common Greek root behind *righteousness, justification,* and their various verb and adjectival forms is found more than sixty times in Romans. The present passage (3:21-25a) is one of many in the epistle that focus on God's righteousness, by which all righteousness is measured.

The only righteousness man possesses or attains within himself is unrighteousness, because that is the character and substance of his fallen nature. Man's "righteous deeds," Isaiah declares, "are like a filthy garment," referring to a menstrual cloth (Isa. 64:6).

The light of righteousness comes only from above. Zacharias, the father of John the Baptist, prophesied of Jesus that He would be "the Sunrise from on high [who] shall visit us, to shine upon those who sit in darkness and the shadow of death" (Luke 1:78-79). As the godly Simeon held the infant Jesus in his arms, he declared, "My eyes have seen Thy salvation, which Thou hast prepared in the presence of all peoples, a light of revelation to the Gentiles, and the glory of Thy people Israel" (Luke 2:30-32). John describes the Lord Jesus Christ as "the true light which, coming into the world enlightens every man" (John 1:9). Jesus Christ was God incarnate, bringing in His own self the light of salvation to the world.

Ancient Greek and Roman poets loved to write overly dramatic tragedies in which the hero or heroine was rescued from impossible situations by the last-minute intervention of a god (the *deus ex machina* literary device). However, the more reputable among them opted not to bring a god onto the stage unless the problem were one that deserved a god to solve it.

The supreme human tragedy is man's sin, and only the true God can solve it. Only the perfectly righteous God Himself can provide the righteousness that men need to be acceptable to Him.

God's righteousness is different from all other kinds of righteousness in many ways. First of all, it is different because of its *source,* which is God Himself. "Drip down, O heavens, from above, and let the clouds pour down righteousness; let the earth open up and salvation bear fruit, and righteousness spring up with it. I, the Lord, have created it" (Isa. 45:8).

Second, God's righteousness is different in *essence.* It is a comprehensive righteousness that fulfills both the precept and the penalty of God's law, under which all men stand judged. The precept of God's law is the perfect fulfillment of it, in other words sinless perfection, which only the man Christ Jesus has ever fulfilled. He kept every requirement of God's law without even the most minute deviation or shortcoming. Although He endured every temptation to which man is subject, He was completely without sin (Heb. 4:15). Yet, in order to fulfill the penalty of the law for sinful mankind, God "made Him who knew no sin to be sin on our behalf, that we might become the righteousness of God in Him" (2 Cor. 5:21). "He Himself bore our sins in His body on the cross, that we might die to sin and live to righteousness" (1 Pet. 2:24; cf. Heb. 9:28).

Third, God's righteousness is unique in its *duration.* His righteousness is everlasting righteousness, existing from eternity to eternity. Throughout Scripture His righteousness is referred to as everlasting (see, e.g., Ps. 119:142; Isa. 51:8; Dan. 9:24). The person, therefore, who receives God's righteousness receives everlasting righteousness.

In the *Iliad* of Homer, the great Trojan warrior Hector was preparing to fight Achilles and the invading Greeks. As he was about to leave home, Hector wanted to hold his young son Astyanax in his arms and bid him farewell for what ended up being the last time. But Hector's armor so frightened the infant that he shrank back to his nurse's caress. The father, laughing out loud, then removed his bronze helmet and took up his little child in his arms. The boy discovered the father of his love behind all that armor.

That is akin to what Paul does in his letter to the Romans, beginning with 3:21. After having shown God the judge and executioner, as it were, he now shows the God of love, who reaches out His arms to sinful men in the hope that they will come to Him and be saved.

In 3:21-25a Paul gives seven additional elements of the righteousness that God divinely imparts to those who trust in His Son, Jesus Christ. It is apart from legalism (v. 21a), built on revelation (v. 21b), acquired by faith (v. 22a), provided for all (vv. 22b-23), given freely through grace (v. 24a), accomplished by redemption (v. 24b), and paid for by atoning sacrifice (v. 25a).

RIGHTEOUSNESS IS APART FROM LEGALISM

But now apart from the Law the righteousness of God has been manifested, (3:21a)

But translates an adversative, indicating a contrast, in this instance a wonderful and marvelous contrast—between man's total depravity and inability to please God and God's own provision of a way to Himself. Except for the introduction (1:1-18), the epistle has portrayed an utterly dark picture of man's wickedness and hopelessness apart from God. In that introduction Paul gave a brief glimpse of light when he spoke "of the gospel, [which] is the power of God for salvation to everyone who believes, to the Jew first and also to the Greek. For in it the righteousness of God is revealed from faith to faith; as it is written, 'But the righteous man shall live by faith'" (1:16-17).

Now, after backing all sinful mankind, Jew and Gentile alike, into the totally dark and seemingly inescapable corner of God's wrath (1:18–3:20), Paul begins to open the window of divine grace that lets in the glorious light of salvation through the righteousness that God Himself has provided.

First of all, Paul says, the righteousness that God imparts to believers is **apart from the Law.** *Nomos* (**Law**) is used in the New Testament in a number of senses, much like its English equivalent. In a negative sense, it sometimes refers to legalism, the strict, self-dependent trust in one's own efforts to perform to the level of divine morality (see Luke 18:9). Sometimes it refers to the commandments and ceremonial rituals prescribed by God in the Old Covenant through Moses. Sometimes it refers simply to divine standards in general. Sometimes it refers to the entire body of Scripture that God had revealed before the time of Christ, what we now call the Old Testament. Sometimes it is a synonym for a general principle or rule. In interpeting the New Testament, therefore, the specific meaning must be determined from the context.

Because they capitalize **Law** in this passage, it is evident that the translators of the *New American Standard Bible* understood *nomos* to refer to God's divine revelation, either in the narrower sense of the Mosaic law or the wider sense of the entire Old Testament. But I believe that in this passage Paul primarily has in mind the sense of legalism, of men's attempt to become acceptable to God by means of their own human efforts.

But the apostle's main point is the same, whichever of those senses he had in mind for **Law.** He is declaring that the righteousness God gives to believers is entirely **apart from** obedience to *any* law, even God's own revealed law. God's righteousness is in no way based on human achievement, on anything that man can do in his own power.

The Jews' own Scriptures did not teach salvation by obedience to God's law, much less by obedience to the many man-made laws and traditions that had been devised by the rabbis and elders during the several hundred years before Christ. Nevertheless, members of the Jewish majority in Jesus' and Paul's day placed their trust in those man-made regulations. In fact, most of them had more faith in rabbinical traditions than in God's divinely revealed law in Scripture. Before his conversion, Paul was himself the epitome of Jewish legalism (see Phil. 3:4-6).

The spirit of legalism was carried over into the church by many Jews who had taken on the name of Christ. They were referred to as Judaizers, because they attempted to add to the gospel the legalistic requirements of the Old Testament, such as circumcision and obedience to the Sabbath laws. Paul admonished believers in Colossae, "Let no one act as your judge in regard to food or drink or in respect to a festival or a new moon or a Sabbath day" (Col. 2:16). He reminded the believers in Galatia that they were "justified by faith in Christ, and not by the works of the Law; since by the works of the Law shall no flesh be justified" (Gal. 2:16). Later in that epistle he wrote, "It was for freedom that Christ set us free; therefore keep standing firm and do not be subject again to a yoke of slavery. Behold I, Paul, say to you that if you receive circumcision, Christ will be of no benefit to you . . . For in Christ Jesus neither circumcision nor uncircumcision means anything" (Gal. 5:1-2, 6). To the Romans he declared, "We maintain that a man is justified by faith apart from works of the Law" (Rom. 3:28).

Even under the Old Covenant, good works based on God's own standards were worthless as far as salvation was concerned. Paul says, "David also speaks of the blessing upon the man to whom God reckons righteousness apart from works" (Rom. 4:6) and then proceeds to quote from Psalm 32:1-2.

God holds before men the standards of His righteousness in order to demonstrate the impossibility of keeping them by human effort. Because of that inability, "the Law brings about wrath" (Rom. 4:15), God's judgment on man's sin. "For as many as are of the works of the Law are under a curse; . . . Now that no one is justified by the Law before God is evident; for, 'The righteous man shall live by faith'" (Gal. 3:10-11). "By grace you have been saved," Paul told the Ephesians; "and that not of yourselves, it is the gift of God; not as a result of works" (Eph. 2:8-9). Countless other New Testament passages (see, e.g., Phil. 3:9; 2 Tim. 1:9; Titus 3:5) repeat the basic gospel truth that rightness with God can never be achieved by human effort.

Whether the law of God is the Mosaic law of the Jews or the law written in the hearts and consciences of all men, including Gentiles (Rom. 2:11-15), obedience to it can never be perfect and therefore can never save. That is a devastating truth to everyone who seeks to please God on his own terms and in his own power—which is why the gospel is so offensive to the natural man.

Now, however, Paul declares that **the righteousness of God,** the divine and eternal righteousness by which men *can* be made right with God, **has been manifested.** As he will explain in the following verse, that righteousness has been manifested "in Jesus Christ for all those who believe" (v. 22).

RIGHTEOUSNESS IS BUILT ON REVELATION

being witnessed by the Law and the Prophets, (5:21b)

Before he presents the means for men to receive God's manifested righteousness, however, Paul declares that it not only is apart from legalism but is also divinely revealed, **being witnessed by the Law and the Prophets.**

That truth was obviously directed primarily at Jews, whose whole religion centered in **the Law and the Prophets,** a phrase commonly used to encompass all of God's written Word, what we now call the Old Testament. In other words, the apostle was not speaking about a new kind of righteousness but about the divine righteousness that is spoken of throughout the Jewish Scriptures.

Not only do **the Law and Prophets** proclaim God's perfect righteousness but they affirm what Paul has just stated—that, without exception, men are unable to achieve that righteousness in their own way or power.

The Jews had great reverence for their Scriptures, but most of them failed to realize that, although divinely revealed, those Scriptures in themselves had no power to save. "You search the Scriptures," Jesus told a group of Jewish listeners, "because you think that in them you have eternal life; and it is these that bear witness of Me" (John 5:39). In other words, **the Law and the Prophets** did not show men how to achieve their own righteousness but pointed to the coming Messiah, the Savior and Son of God, who Himself would *provide* the righteousness that God demands of men. Although the full revelation of salvation through Christ was not given in the Old Testament, that had *always* been the way of salvation to which that testament pointed.

The Mosaic laws were not given as a means of achieving righteousness but of describing God's righteousness and showing the impossibility of men's living up to it. The Mosaic sacrifices were not prescribed as a means of atoning for sin but of symbolically pointing to Jesus Christ, who Himself became the sacrifice for the sins of the whole world. The commandments, rituals, sacrifices, and godly principles taught in the Old Testament were, and still are, a part of His divinely inspired Word. But they could never remove sin, forgive sin, atone for sin, or give a new and righteous life to a sinner—no matter how zealously and sincerely he tried to abide by them.

RIGHTEOUSNESS IS ACQUIRED BY FAITH

even the righteousness of God through faith in Jesus Christ (3:22a)

To avoid any possible misunderstanding, Paul mentions again that he is speaking of the absolute and perfect **righteousness of God**, not the relative and imperfect righteousness of human achievement.

His point here is that the perfect, saving **righteousness of God** not only is received apart from legalism and built on revelation, but is also acquired only by **faith.** That has always been the only way of salvation as far as man's part is concerned. The very point of Hebrews 11 is to show that there has *never* been a means of salvation other than **faith** in the true God.

That is also a repeated theme of Paul's Roman epistle. In chapter 4 he says, "To the one who does not work, but believes in Him who justifies the ungodly, his faith is reckoned as righteousness" (v. 5), and, "The promise to Abraham or to his descendants that he would be heir of the world was not through the Law, but through the righteousness of faith" (v. 13; cf. v. 20). He begins chapter 5 by declaring that "having been justified by faith, we have peace with God through our Lord Jesus Christ."

There is, of course, such a thing as false faith, even in the name of Christ. John reports that many people who had a superficial faith in Jesus did not have saving faith. "Jesus therefore was saying to those Jews who had believed Him, 'If you abide in My word, then you are truly disciples of Mine'" (John 8:31). In other words, obedience to His Word is evidence of true faith, whereas continual disobedience is evidence of false faith. "Faith, if it has no works, is dead, being by itself," James declared (James 2:17). In other words, disobedient faith is spurious faith. It is "by itself," that is, unrelated to faith in God. False faith may be faith in good works, faith in ritual, faith in a religious experience or system, faith in one's own goodness, or simply a nebulous faith in faith that is so common in our day.

A person is saved **through faith in Jesus Christ** alone, apart from anything else. But Scripture makes clear that saving faith is immeasurably more than simply making a verbal declaration of believing about Him.

The late A. W. Tozer perceptively commented:

> Something has happened to the doctrine of justification. . . . The faith of Paul and Luther was a revolutionizing thing. It upset the whole life of the individual and made him into another person altogether. It laid hold on the life and brought it unto obedience to Christ. It took up its cross and followed along after Jesus with no intention of going back. It said good-bye to its old friends as certainly as Elijah when he stepped into the fiery chariot and went away in the whirlwind. It had a finality about it. It snapped shut on a man's heart like a trap; it captured the man and made him from that moment forward a happy love-servant of his Lord. (*The Root of the Righteous* [Harrisburg, Pa.: Christian Publications , 1955], pp. 45-46)

The saving **faith in Jesus Christ** that the New Testament teaches is much more than a simple affirmation of certain truths about Him. Even the demons acknowledged many facts about Him. One of the demons who possessed the man from Gadara said to Jesus, "What do I have to do with You, Jesus, Son of the Most High God?" (Mark 5:7). The demon who gave the slave girl the power of divination described Paul and his friends as "bond-servants of the Most High God, who are proclaiming to you the way of salvation" (Acts 16:17).

Saving faith is a placing of oneself totally in submission to the Lord Jesus Christ, and it has certain indispensable elements that the New Testament clearly teaches.

Saving **faith in Jesus Christ** involves the exercise of *will*. Paul told the Roman believers, "Thanks be to God that though you were slaves of sin, you became obedient from the heart to that form of teaching to which you were committed" (Rom. 6:17). Salvation begins (from the human standpoint) with a person's willful obedience in turning from sin to follow the Lord Jesus Christ.

Saving **faith** also involves the *emotions,* because, as in the verse just mentioned above, it must come from the heart as well as from the mind. A person cannot be saved by good feelings about Christ, and many people throughout the ages and in our own day have substituted good feelings about Christ for saving faith in Him. But on the other hand, a person whose life is transformed by Christ will be affected in his emotions in the deepest possible way.

Saving **faith** also involves the *intellect.* No one can think his way into heaven, but neither can he receive Jesus Christ as Lord and Savior without some comprehension of the truth of the gospel (see Rom. 10:17ff.).

Jesus Christ is the very embodiment of God's righteousness, and it is because of that truth that He can impart divine righteousness to those who trust in Him. During His earthly incarnation, Jesus demonstrated God's righteousness by living a sinless life. In His death Christ also demonstrated God's righteousness by paying the penalty for the unrighteous lives of every human being.

The seventeenth-century English minister Joseph Alleine wrote:

> All of Christ is accepted by the sincere convert; he loves not only the wages, but the work of Christ; not only the benefits, but the burden of Christ; he is willing not only to tread out the corn, but to draw under the yoke; he takes up the command of Christ, yea, the cross of Christ.
>
> The unsound closeth by halves with Christ: he is all for the salvation of Christ, but he is not for sanctification; he is for the privileges, but appropriates not the person of Christ; he divides the offices and benefits of Christ. This is an error in the foundation. Whoso loveth life, let him beware here; it is an undoing mistake, of which you have been often warned, and yet none is more common.
>
> Jesus is a sweet name, but men "love not the Lord Jesus in sincerity." They will not have him as God offers, "to be a Prince and a Saviour." They divide what God has joined, the king and the priest; yea, they will not accept the salvation of Christ as he intends it; they divide it here.
>
> Every man's vote is for salvation from suffering; but they desire not to be saved from sinning; they would have their lives saved, but withal would have their lusts. Yea, many divide here again; they would be content to have some of their sins destroyed, but they cannot leave the lap of Delilah, or divorce the beloved Herodias; they cannot be cruel to the right eye or right hand; the Lord must pardon them in this thing. O be carefully scrupulous here; your soul depends upon it.
>
> The sound convert takes a whole Christ, and takes him for all intents and purposes, without exceptions, without limitations, without reserve. He

is willing to have Christ upon any terms; he is willing to have the dominion of Christ, as well as deliverance by Christ; he saith, with Paul, "Lord, what wilt thou have me to do?" Any thing, Lord. He sends the blank to Christ, to set down his own conditions. (*The Alarm to Unconverted Sinners* [Grand Rapids: Baker, 1980 reprint], pp. 46-48)

John Wesley went to heaven on March 2, 1791, at the age of eighty-eight, after having preached the gospel for about sixty-five years. One of his favorite hymns to sing on his deathbed was:

> I'll praise my Maker while I've breath
> And when my voice is lost in death
> Praise shall employ my nobler powers.
> My days of praise shall ne'er be past
> While life, and thought, and being last,
> Or immortality endures.

RIGHTEOUSNESS IS PROVIDED FOR ALL

for all those who believe; for there is no distinction; for all have sinned and fall short of the glory of God, (3:22b-23)

The provision of salvation and the righteousness it brings is granted **for all those who believe.** Anyone will be saved who believes in Jesus Christ as Lord and Savior, **for there is no distinction.**

Preaching in the synagogue in Pisidian Antioch, Paul declared, "Through Him [Christ] everyone who believes is freed from all things, from which you could not be freed through the Law of Moses" (Acts 13:39). In his letter to the church at Galatia, the apostle said, "A man is not justified by the works of the Law but through faith in Christ Jesus" (Gal. 2:16).

Jesus Himself said, "The one who comes to me I will certainly not cast out" (John 6:37). Anyone who believes in Jesus Christ—whether a murderer, prostitute, thief, rapist, homosexual, religious hypocrite, false teacher, pagan, or anything else—will be saved. Just as no one is good enough to be saved, no one is so evil that he cannot be saved.

That is the wonderful point of Romans 3:22. **All those who believe** will be saved, because in God's sight **there is no distinction.** Just as everyone apart from Christ is equally sinful and rejected by God, everyone who is in Christ is equally righteous and accepted by Him. Even the "foremost of all" sinners, as Paul called himself (1 Tim. 1:15), was not too wicked to be saved.

There is no distinction among those who are saved, because there is no distinction among those who are lost, **for all have sinned and fall short of the glory of God.** *Hustereō* (**fall short**) has the basic meaning of being last or inferior. Every human being comes in last as far as **the glory of God** is concerned.

RIGHTEOUSNESS IS GIVEN FREELY THROUGH GRACE

being justified as a gift by His grace (3:24a)

By the same token, no one is ahead of anyone else as far as salvation is concerned. **Being justified** refers back to the "alls" of the previous two verses—*all* those who have believed, of whom *all* were sinful. Just as there is no distinction among those who need salvation, there is no distinction among those who receive it, because they all are **justified as a gift by His grace.**

Dikaioō (**justified**) means to declare the rightness of something or someone. Justification is God's declaration that all the demands of the law are fulfilled on behalf of the believing sinner through the righteousness of Jesus Christ. Justification is a wholly forensic, or legal, transaction. It changes the judicial *standing* of the sinner before God. In justification, God *imputes* the perfect righteousness of Christ to the believer's account, then declares the redeemed one fully righteous. Justification must be distinguished from sanctification, in which God actually *imparts* Christ's righteousness to the sinner. While the two must be distinguished, justification and sanctification can never be separated. God does not justify whom He does not sanctify.

Yet God justifies believers **as a gift by His grace**, not because of any good thing in the one who is justified.

By definition, **a gift** is something given freely, unearned and unmerited by the recipient. God's greatest of all gifts is that of salvation through His Son, given completely out of **His** divine **grace.** "If righteousness comes through the Law," that is, through human fulfillment of God's divine standard, Paul declares, "then Christ died needlessly" (Gal. 2:21).

The law reveals God's righteousness and exposes man's unrighteousness. **Grace**, on the other hand, not only reveals God's righteousness but actually *gives* His righteousness to those who trust in His Son. That **gift** of **grace** cost God the suffering and death of His own Son on the cross, so that, for the believer, there is nothing left to pay.

RIGHTEOUSNESS IS ACCOMPLISHED BY REDEMPTION

through the redemption which is in Christ Jesus; (3:24b)

Apolutrōsis (**redemption**) is a strengthened form of *lutrōsis*, which carries the idea of delivering, especially by means of paying a price. It was commonly used of paying a ransom to free a prisoner from his captors or paying the price to free a slave from his master.

Because of man's utter sinfulness and inability to bring himself up to the standard of God's righteousness, **the redemption** of a sinner could come only by that **which is in Christ Jesus.** Only the sinless Savior could pay the price to redeem sinful men.

RIGHTEOUSNESS WAS PAID BY ATONING SACRIFICE

whom God displayed publicly as a propitiation in His blood through faith. (3:25a)

Because man cannot become righteous on his own, God graciously provided for his redemption through the atoning sacrifice of His own Son, Jesus Christ.

That sacrifice was not made in the dark or even in the hidden and holy recesses of the sacred Temple, but openly on the hill of Calvary for all the world to see. **God displayed** His Son **publicly as a propitiation.**

Hilastērion (**propitiation**) carries the basic idea of appeasement, or satisfaction. In ancient pagan religions, as in many religions today, the idea of man's appeasing a deity by various gifts or sacrifices was common. But in the New Testament **propitiation** always refers to the work of God, not of man. Man is utterly incapable of satisfying God's justice except by spending eternity in hell.

The only satisfaction, or **propitiation,** that could be acceptable to God and that could reconcile Him to man had to be made by God. For that reason, God in human flesh, Jesus Christ, "gave Himself as a ransom for all" (1 Tim. 2:6). He appeased the wrath of God.

That ransoming **propitiation** made by Christ was paid **in His** own divine **blood.** To believers scattered throughout the Roman Empire, Peter wrote, "You were not redeemed with perishable things like silver or gold from your futile way of life inherited from your forefathers, but with precious blood, as of a lamb unblemished and spotless, the blood of Christ" (1 Pet. 1:18-19).

The Hebrew equivalent of *hilastērion* is used in the Old Testament in reference to the Mercy Seat in the Holy of Holies, where the high priest went once a year, on the Day of Atonement, to make a sacrifice on behalf of his people. On that occasion he sprinkled blood on the Mercy Seat, symbolizing the payment of the penalty for his own sins and the sins of the people.

But that yearly act, although divinely prescribed and honored, had no power to remove or pay the penalty for a single sin. It could only point

to the true and effective "offering of the body of Jesus Christ once for all.
. . . For by one offering He has perfected for all time those who are
sanctified" (Heb. 10:10, 14).

Those who are sanctified by the offering of Christ are those who
receive that sanctification **through faith** in Him. To the Colossian
believers Paul wrote,

> In Him [Christ] you were also circumcised with a circumcision made
> without hands, in the removal of the body of the flesh by the circumcision
> of Christ; having been buried with Him in baptism, in which you were also
> raised up with Him through faith in the working of God, who raised Him
> from the dead. And when you were dead in your transgressions and the
> uncircumcision of your flesh, He made you alive together with Him, having
> forgiven us all our transgressions, having canceled out the certificate of debt
> consisting of decrees against us and which was hostile to us; and He has
> taken it out of the way, having nailed it to the cross. (Col. 2:11-14)

In his beautiful hymn, Horatius Bonar wrote,

> Not what my hands have done
> Can save my guilty soul;
> Not what my toiling flesh has borne
> Can make my spirit whole.
> Not what I feel or do
> Can give me peace with God;
> Not all my prayers and sighs and tears
> Can bear my awful load.
> Thy grace alone, O God,
> To me can pardon speak;
> Thy power alone, O Son of God,
> Can this sore bondage break.
> No other work save thine,
> No other blood will do;
> No strength save that which is divine
> Can bear me safely through.

How Christic Died for God

This was to demonstrate His righteousness, because in the for-bearance of God He passed over the sins previously committed; for the demonstration, I say, of His righteousness at the present time, that He might be just and the justifier of the one who has faith in Jesus. Where then is boasting? It is excluded. By what kind of law? Of works? No, but by a law of faith. For we maintain that a man is justified by faith apart from works of the Law. Or is God the God of Jews only? Is He not the God of Gentiles also? Yes, of Gentiles also, since indeed God who will justify the circumcised by faith and the uncircumcised through faith is one.

Do we then nullify the Law through faith? May it never be! On the contrary, we establish the Law. (3:25b-31)

Among the most obvious characteristics of modern society is selfism, manifested in self-centeredness, selfishness, self-gratification, and self-fulfillment. People are absorbed in their own feelings, their own desires, their own possessions, and their own welfare.

Sadly, selfism has found its way into Christianity and has almost become a hallmark of some purportedly evangelical churches and organizations. Christ is portrayed as the answer to all problems, the source of peace and joy, success and happiness, the One who makes life worth living and saves from hell.

In the right biblical perspective, Christ *is* the answer to man's needs, the first of which is salvation from sin. And it is certainly true, of course, that life in Him is the only escape from hell. Obviously salvation involves man, and just as obviously it is the greatest blessing a human being can receive—the single great blessing apart from which no others have any permanent value.

But in Scripture, salvation does not focus on man but on God. God's Word makes clear that the foremost purpose of salvation is to glorify God. "All things have been created by Him and for Him," Paul reminds us (Col. 1:16). The psalmist declared, "Not to us, O Lord, not to us, but to Thy name give glory because of Thy lovingkindness, because of Thy truth" (Ps. 115:1). That should be the continual heart cry of every believer.

Since God is the one and only true God, the Creator and Sustainer of the universe, the source and measure of all things, He alone has the right to be glorified. He alone has the right to man's worship and adoration.

Through Isaiah, God said, "I am the Lord, and there is no other; besides Me there is no God. . . . There is no other God besides Me, a righteous God and a Savior; there is none except Me. Turn to Me, and be saved, all the ends of the earth; for I am God, and there is no other. I have sworn by Myself, the word has gone forth from My mouth in righteousness and will not turn back, that to Me every knee will bow, every tongue will swear allegiance" (Isa. 45:5, 21-23).

Because God is our sovereign Lord, Paul admonishes believers to honor and glorify Him in even the smallest and most mundane things we do. "Whether, then, you eat or drink or whatever you do, do all to the glory of God" (1 Cor. 10:31). Our very reason for existence is to glorify God. Instead of being consumed by our own interests and feelings and welfare, we should be lost in the wonderful privilege of living to give God praise and adoration. In everything we do, we are to seek first the kingdom of God and His righteousness (Matt. 6:33).

In his book *Our Guilty Silence,* John Stott says that the best example he knew of a person consumed with glorifying God was Henry Martyn:

> Although a Senior Wrangler [a mathematics expert] of Cambridge University, and then a Fellow of St. John's College, he turned his back on an academic career and entered the ministry. Two years later, on July 16th, 1805, he sailed for India. "Let me burn out for God," he cried in Calcutta, as he lived in an abandoned Hindu temple. And as he watched the people prostrating

themselves before their images, he wrote: "this excited more horror in me than I can well express."

Later he moved to Shiraz, and busied himself with the translation of the New Testament into Persian. Many Muslim visitors came to see him and to engage him in religious conversation. His customary serenity was only disturbed when anybody insulted his Lord. On one occasion the sentiment was expressed that "Prince Abbas Mirza had killed so many Christians that Christ from the fourth heaven took hold of Mahomet's [Muhammad's] skirt to entreat him to desist." It was a dramatic fantasy. Here was Christ kneeling before Mahommed. How would Martyn react? "I was cut to the soul at this blasphemy." Seeing his discomfiture, his visitor asked what it was that was so offensive. Martyn replied: "I could not endure existence if Jesus was not glorified; it would be hell to me, if He were to be always thus dishonoured." His Muslim visitor was astonished and again asked why. "If anyone pluck out your eyes," he answered, "there is no saying *why* you feel pain;—it is feeling. It is because I am one with Christ that I am thus dreadfully wounded." ([Grand Rapids: Eerdmans, 1969], pp. 21-22)

Here was a man who could live in the most uncomfortable of circumstances without complaint but was heartbroken over a pagan society that dishonored his Lord.

Doubtless David was a man after God's own heart because he could truthfully declare, "I have set the Lord continually before me" (Ps. 16:8). Despite his sins and shortcomings, the major focus of his life was always on God.

The worldly spirit of selfism is perhaps the major reason most Christians are not aggressive in witnessing to the lost. It is the reason the church, for the most part, is not moving out into the world with the gospel of Jesus Christ. The Christian who is primarily concerned about his own comfort and blessings, even his spiritual blessings, does not have his focus on God. Consequently, his life will not be directed toward fulfilling God's Great Commission.

In the summer of 1865, Hudson Taylor became tremendously burdened for the land of China. His biographer reports that he also became greatly troubled about the church he was attending in Brighton, England. As he looked around the congregation he saw

pew upon pew of prosperous bearded merchants, shopkeepers, visitors; demure wives in bonnets and crinolines, scrubbed children trained to hide their impatience; the atmosphere of smug piety sickened him. He seized his hat and left.

"Unable to bear the sight of a congregation of a thousand or more Christian people rejoicing in their own security, while millions were perishing for lack of knowledge, I wandered out on the sands alone, in great spiritual agony." And there on the beach he prayed for "twenty-four willing skilful labourers." (Stott, p. 24)

Out of that prayer eventually came the China Inland Mission. Due to that ministry and others like it, there are reportedly twenty-five million to perhaps fifty million believers in China today, despite its officially atheistic government.

God could use men such as Henry Martyn and Hudson Taylor because their attention was not focused on their own interests but on God's.

Salvation is first and foremost a way of glorifying God. The fact that it saves men from hell and gives them eternal life, marvelous and wonderful as that is, is secondary to the glory of God. The cross of Jesus Christ had the most dramatic effect on mankind in providing the way of redemption. But Jesus' death on the cross was primarily to glorify God. He glorified God during His earthly ministry, enabling Him to say to His heavenly Father, "I glorified Thee on earth, having accomplished the work which Thou hast given Me to do" (John 17:4).

Speaking to every believer, the apostle Paul writes,

> Have this attitude in yourselves which was also in Christ Jesus, who, although He existed in the form of God, did not regard equality with God a thing to be grasped, but emptied Himself, taking the form of a bond-servant, and being made in the likeness of men. And being found in appearance as a man, He humbled Himself by becoming obedient to the point of death, even death on a cross. Therefore also God highly exalted Him, and bestowed on Him the name which is above every name, that at the name of Jesus every knee should bow, of those who are in heaven, and on earth, and under the earth, and that every tongue should confess that Jesus Christ is Lord, to the glory of God the Father. (Phil. 2:5-11)

Even when we think about heaven, we have a tendency to focus on the great blessings and joy *we* will have there. But the Lord brings believers to heaven first of all in order that they might glorify Him forever. That is the purpose for which man was created, and that will be the eternal purpose of all who are re-created by God's grace through faith in His Son.

On his deathbed David Brainerd said, "My heaven is to please God and glorify Him, and give all to Him, and to be wholly devoted to His glory. I do not go to heaven to be advanced, but to give honor to God. It is no matter where I shall be stationed in heaven, whether I have a high or low seat there, but to live and please and glorify God" (Jonathan

Edwards, *The Life of David Brainerd* [Grand Rapids: Baker, 1980 reprint], pp. 330-31).

There will, of course, be bliss beyond description in heaven, but even that bliss will itself be an eternal testimony to the grace and glory of God.

The theme of the book of Romans, and the heart of the gospel message, is the doctrine of justification by faith alone in response to God's grace. It is a doctrine that has been lost and found again and again throughout the history of the church. It has suffered from understatement, from overstatement, and, perhaps most often, simply from neglect. It was the central message of the early church and the central message of the Protestant Reformation, under the godly leadership of men such as Martin Luther and John Calvin. It is still today the central message of every church that is faithful to God's Word. Only when the church understands and proclaims justification by faith can it truly present the gospel of Jesus Christ.

One of the most significant passages that teaches that truth is the present text (Rom. 3:25b-31). At first reading this passage seems terribly intricate, complicated, and baffling. But its basic truth is simple, while also being the most profound truth in all of Scripture: Justification for sinful mankind was made possible by God's grace through the death of His Son Jesus Christ on the cross, and it is appropriated by men when they place their trust in Him as Lord and Savior.

The cross affects those who trust in Jesus by giving them eternal life. Through His death and resurrection, God "delivers us from the wrath to come" (1 Thess. 1:10). As Paul testifies later in Romans, "God demonstrates His own love toward us, in that while we were yet sinners, Christ died for us. Much more then, having now been justified by His blood, we shall be saved from the wrath of God through Him" (5:8-9; cf. 2 Cor. 5:18; Titus 2:14).

The cross affected Satan by breaking his power and dominion over the earth. The writer of Hebrews declares that through His death, Jesus Christ rendered "powerless him who had the power of death, that is, the devil" (Heb. 2:14). In doing that, Jesus "delivered us from the domain of darkness, and transferred us to the kingdom of His beloved Son, in whom we have redemption, the forgiveness of sin" (Col. 1: 13-14).

The cross obviously affected Jesus Christ Himself. In obedience to His Father's will, He suffered the agony of taking sin upon Himself and of paying its death penalty, and He was resurrected in order that He might return to the never-again-to-be-broken presence of His heavenly Father (John 14:28).

The cross also affected God the Father and the Holy Spirit, because of their perfect oneness with the Son.

In Romans 3:25*b*-31, Paul directs our thought specifically to four ways in which the cross of Jesus Christ glorifies God—by revealing God's righteousness (vv. 25*b*-26), by exalting God's grace (vv. 27-28), by revealing God's universality (vv. 29-30), and by confirming God's law (v. 31).

THE CROSS REVEALS GOD'S RIGHTEOUSNESS

This was to demonstrate His righteousness, because in the forbearance of God He passed over the sins previously committed; for the demonstration, I say, of His righteousness at the present time, that He might be just and the justifier of the one who has faith in Jesus. (3:25*b*-26)

As explained in the previous chapter, **righteousness,** *justification,* and their verb and adjective forms are from the same Greek root. As those two English words indicate, the basic meaning relates to what is right and just.

A look at ethnology and the history of religion shows that, without exception, pagan gods were, as they still are, made in the likeness of men. Their only difference from men is in their presumed power. Otherwise, they reflect the same moral deficiencies and frailties. They are capricious, inconsistent, and totally unpredictable. In the Greek and Roman pantheons, the fabricated deities were continually competing among themselves and were jealous of one another and even of human beings who demonstrated unusual intelligence, skill, and power. Some of the gods supposedly demanded a high standard of conduct from human beings but were themselves whimsical and often grossly immoral.

That is exactly what one would expect. Man-made gods can never be more than larger-than-life images of men. Many ancient men and women, in fact, lived on a much higher moral plane than their gods reportedly did. Men would frequently accuse a particular god of unfairness and wrongdoing and appeal to another god or gods to rectify the wrong of the erring deity.

Men have even been quick to judge the true God in much the same way. Unbelievers frequently point to what they consider capricious, unjust, and even brutal acts on God's part. "If your God is so holy and just," they ask, "why does He let His own people suffer so much and let wicked people, including the enemies and persecutors of His people, get by with terrible sins? And why does He let innocent people suffer because of the wickedness of others?"

Many things that God is reported in Scripture to have done *do* seem, from the human perspective, to be unjust and unrighteous. Why, for instance, did God not let Abraham actually inherit the land promised to Him? Why did He allow His people to stay and suffer so long in Egypt before He delivered them? The Hebrews who were delivered were no better than their ancestors who came there in the first place. They were, if anything, much worse, having picked up many pagan beliefs and practices from their Egyptian masters. After God gave possession of the Promised Land to Israel, why did He frequently use ungodly and fiercely wicked pagan nations to conquer, persecute, and scatter His own chosen people? The punishers were worse than those they were used to punish.

In human systems of justice, a judge or other high official in public office who commits a given crime often receives greater punishment than would an ordinary citizen. Their high office demands a higher standard. "Why, then, should the highest of all gods," people have wondered, "not Himself be held accountable to man's highest standards of righteousness and justice?"

The prophet Habakkuk doubtless understood with Moses that the Lord is "The Rock! His work is perfect, for all His ways are just; a God of faithfulness and without injustice, righteous and upright is He" (Deut. 32:4). Yet the godly Habakkuk could not understand why the Lord would let His own people suffer while pagan nations prospered. "Thine eyes are too pure to approve evil, and Thou canst not look on wickedness with favor," He prayed. "Why dost Thou look with favor on those who deal treacherously? Why art Thou silent when the wicked swallow up those more righteous than they?" (Hab. 1:13).

Certain Jews in Malachi's day were concerned about the same thing, but unlike the humble Habakkuk they presumed to judge God, saying impiously, "Everyone who does evil is good in the sight of the Lord, and He delights in them." Others asked, "Where is the God of justice?" (Mal. 2:17).

Anticipating such questions, the Holy Spirit led Paul to declare that, through the cross, God not only allowed but planned before the foundation of the world what would be the most unjust act that men could commit—the putting to death of His own sinless Son. But through that heinous act on men's part, God not only *manifested* His divine righteousness by offering His own Son but also used that act of divine grace **to demonstrate His** divine **righteousness.** Through that incomparable sacrifice, God provided punishment for sin sufficient to forgive and blot out every sin that would ever be committed by fallen mankind— including the supreme sin of crucifying His own Son, for which *every* unregenerate person shares the guilt (Heb. 6:6).

That greatest of all acts of God's grace was further demonstrated by His divine **forbearance, as He passed over the sins previously committed.** God is not unaware of nor does He condone even the smallest sin. His **forbearance** is therefore not a sign of injustice but of His patient and loving grace. "The Lord is not slow about His promise," Peter assures us, "but is patient toward you, not wishing for any to perish but for all to come to repentance" (2 Pet. 3:9).

God's justice and grace are on a perfect and infinitely grander scale than human wisdom can perceive or comprehend. Because of His justice, no sin will ever go unpunished; yet because of His grace, no sin is beyond forgiveness. Therefore every sin will be paid for by the sinner himself in the form of eternal death and punishment in hell or it will be paid for him because he has placed his faith in the sacrifice of Jesus Christ on his behalf.

Paresis (**passed over**) does not carry the idea of remission, as the King James Version renders it, but refers to passing by or overlooking. In the context of God's **forbearance**, the meaning is therefore that of a temporary passing over sin and of withholding judgment on it for a certain period of time. After the Fall, when God could have justly destroyed Adam and Eve, and therefore the human race, He **passed over** the **sins** of fallen mankind. Even in the Flood the Lord saved eight people, not because they were perfectly righteous but because they trusted in Him. In the same way, the many subsequent judgments of God recorded in Scripture were never universal, but were rendered upon specific individuals, groups, or nations.

The psalmist Asaph understood something of why God allows many wicked people to live and thrive, often at the expense of those who are less sinful. He wrote that God, "being compassionate, forgave their iniquity, and did not destroy them; and often He restrained His anger, and did not arouse all His wrath. Thus He remembered that they were but flesh, a wind that passes and does not return" (Ps. 78:38-39).

In his discourse before the Epicurean and Stoic philosophers on the Areopagus (Mars Hill) just outside Athens, Paul said, "Having overlooked the times of ignorance, God is now declaring to men that all everywhere should repent, because He has fixed a day in which He will judge the world in righteousness through a Man whom He has appointed, having furnished proof to all men by raising Him from the dead" (Acts 17:30-31).

From the beginning, God had demonstrated "His eternal power and divine nature" for all men to see (Rom. 1:20). Through the incarnation, death, and resurrection of Christ, God gave mankind the ultimate revelation of Himself—the ultimate **demonstration . . . of His righteousness at the present time.**

That is why the God of perfect holiness could be both **just** as well as **the justifier of the** sinful and unworthy **one who has faith in Jesus.** Though he could not have known the full truth of what he wrote, the ancient psalmist beautifully pictured Jesus' sacrifice on the cross: "Loving-kindness and truth have met together; righteousness and peace have kissed each other" (Ps. 85:10).

The real "problem," as it were, with salvation was not the matter of getting sinful men to a holy God but of getting a holy God to accept sinful men without violating His justice. It was only through the cross that God could provide a just redemption for sinful men. But of immeasurably more importance was that the cross demonstrates forever that God is both supremely just and supremely gracious. First and foremost, Christ died that the world might see that neither God's holiness nor His justice have been abrogated. God has perfect and absolute integrity. The cross was the ultimate vindication of God's justice and righteousness. The most unfathomable of all spiritual mysteries is that of the holy and just God providing redemption for sinful men and in that gracious act, not violating any attribute of His nature, but bringing supreme glory to Himself.

Just as the primary purpose of salvation is to glorify God, so is the confession of sin by those who are saved. When God chastens His children and they confess their sin, they testify to their heavenly Father's justice and righteousness and therefore to His glory. It is as if a person saw a father spanking his child and the child told the onlooker that he was being rightly punished for something wrong he had done. Just as such a confession by a human child honors and vindicates his human father, so the confession of sin by God's children honors, vindicates, and glorifies their heavenly Father.

Joshua understood that truth, and when Achan's sin was exposed, Joshua told him, "My son, I implore you, give glory to the Lord, the God of Israel, and give praise to Him; and tell me now what you have done. Do not hide it from me" (Josh. 7.19).

Two beautiful and beloved hymns express something of the faithful believer's awesome awareness of God's justice, righteousness, and grace.

From the pen of the nineteenth-century poet Elizabeth C. Clephane came "The Ninety and Nine," which includes these lines:

> "Lord, Thou hast here Thy ninety and nine,
> Are they not enough for Thee?"
> But the Shepherd made answer, "This of mine
> Has wandered away from me;
> And though the road be rough and steep,
> I go to the desert to find my sheep."
> But none of the ransomed ever knew
> How deep were the waters crossed;

> Nor how dark was the night
> That the Lord passed through
> Ere He found His sheep that was lost.

Isaac Watts wrote in his famous hymn:

> When I survey the wondrous cross,
> On which the Prince of glory died,
> My richest gain I count but loss,
> And pour contempt on all my pride.
>
> Were the whole realm of nature mine,
> That were an offering far too small;
> Love so amazing, so divine,
> Demands my soul, my life, my all.

THE CROSS EXALTS GOD'S GRACE

Where then is boasting? It is excluded. By what kind of law? Of works? No, but by a law of faith. For we maintain that a man is justified by faith apart from works of the Law. (3:27-28)

The cross proves the utter futility of man's coming to God in his own way and power. **Where then** is man's **boasting?** Paul asks. In answer to his own question, he declares unequivocally, **It is excluded.**

Because the power of salvation is in the cross of Christ alone, man has no cause for self-congratulation or self-satisfaction—much less for the self-exaltation that is now so widely proclaimed under the guise of the gospel.

Paul reminded the Corinthian believers: "Consider your calling, brethren, that there were not many wise according to the flesh, not many mighty, not many noble" (1 Cor. 1:26). Paul was, of course, using those descriptions purely on the human level, because in God's sight and by His standard, no person is wise, mighty, or noble. He goes on to say, "But God has chosen the foolish things of the world to shame the wise, and God has chosen the weak things of the world to shame the things which are strong, and the base things of the world and the despised, God has chosen the things that are not, that He might nullify the things that are, that no man should boast before God" (vv. 27-29).

By what kind of law is boasting excluded, Paul asks. Is it on the basis **of works?** Again answering his own question, he declares, **No, but by a law of faith.** Not even Abraham, the father of God's chosen people, was justified by works (Rom. 4:2). "For by grace you have been saved through faith," Paul declared to the church at Ephesus; "and that not of yourselves, it is the gift of God; not as a result of works, that no one should boast" (Eph. 2:8-9).

The attitude of true faith is exemplified by the tax-gatherer in the Temple, who "was even unwilling to lift up his eyes to heaven, but was beating his breast, saying, 'God be merciful to me, the sinner!'" (Luke 18:13).

The greatest lie in the world, and the lie common to all false religions and cults, is that, by certain works of their own doing, men are able to make themselves acceptable to God. The greatest error in that belief is its sheer impossibility. But the greatest evil of that belief is that it robs God of His glory.

Paul completely cuts the ground out from under works righteousness by declaring, **For we maintain that a man is justified by faith apart from works,** even the good works done in response to God's own Law.

What, then, is this saving **faith** that is completely **apart from works**? First we will consider some things that neither prove nor disprove true faith. Although they will be evident to some degree or another in true believers, they can also be evidenced, sometimes to a high degree, in unbelievers.

First is visible morality. A person can be outwardly moral and yet not be saved. Some pagans and cultists put many Christians to shame by their high standards of behavior. When a certain young man came to Jesus and asked, "Teacher, what good thing shall I do that I may obtain eternal life?" Jesus told him to keep the commandments and then proceeded to list some of the major ones. When the man responded, "All these things I have kept," Jesus did not challenge his sincerity. According to outward appearance and his own human perception of obedience, the man probably was speaking the truth. But when Jesus told him to sell all his possessions and give the proceeds to the poor and then "come, follow Me," the man "went away grieved; for he was one who owned much property" (Matt. 19:16-22). By his refusal to obey Christ, the man demonstrated that his outward obedience to the law was not done out of love for God or for the purpose of His glory but was done out of self-love and for the purpose of his own self-interest. When commanded to give all of his possessions as well as all of himself to Christ, he refused. And by that refusal, even his seemingly good works were exposed as spiritually worthless works, because they were done out of selfish motivation.

Second, intellectual knowledge of God's truth is not necessarily a proof of saving faith. It is possible to have a great deal of knowledge about God's Word and yet be unsaved. Like the scribes and Pharisees of Jesus' day, many scholars throughout the centuries have devoted their lives to careful study of Scripture. But because they did not believe or obey the truths they studied, those truths became a judgment against them, and they remained as lost as the primitive tribesman who is unaware that there *is* such a thing as Scripture. To his self-confident brothers in the flesh Paul said, "You bear the name 'Jew,' and rely upon the Law, and boast in God, . . . [but] through your breaking the Law, do you dishonor God? For 'the name of God is blasphemed among the Gentiles because of you,' just as it is written" (Rom. 2:17, 23-24; cf. Ezek. 36:20-23).

Third, religious involvement is not necessarily a proof of saving faith. In the Old Testament, the Lord repeatedly condemned the Israelites for their meticulous outward observance of the Mosaic ordinances and ceremonies while having no trust in Him. The ten virgins in Jesus' parable had the same outward dress and carried the same kind of lamps. The fact that all ten women were spoken of as virgins suggests that outwardly they were all morally pure and religiously faithful. But five of them had no oil in their lamps, and because they lacked the oil of saving faith, they were disqualified from meeting the bridegroom, who represented Christ (see Matt. 25:1-13).

Fourth, active ministry in Christ's name is no certain proof of saving faith. Outwardly, Judas was as active as the other disciples, witnessed by the fact that he served as their trusted treasurer. And obviously he considered himself a follower of Christ. But Jesus sternly warned, "Not everyone who says to Me, 'Lord, Lord,' will enter the kingdom of heaven; but he who does the will of My Father who is in heaven. Many will say to Me on that day, 'Lord, Lord, did we not prophesy in Your name, and in your name cast out demons, and in Your name perform many miracles?' And then I will declare to them, 'I never knew you; depart from Me, you who practice lawlessness'" (Matt. 7:21-23).

Fifth, even conviction of sin does not necessarily demonstrate saving faith. Mental institutions throughout the world are filled with people who are so burdened by the knowledge of their sinfulness that they cannot function in society. Their sense of guilt became so overpowering that it drove them to insanity—but it did not drive them to Jesus Christ. Others who are convicted of their sin determine to reform themselves. Many people who have been long and deeply enslaved by a particular sin have been able, sometimes through sheer will power, to rid themselves of it. But successfully forsaking that particular sin in their own power makes them even more susceptible to other sins, especially pride. They are like the man who managed to rid himself of an evil spirit. But after a while the spirit returned and found the man's life "unoccupied, swept, and put in order. Then it goes and takes along with it seven other spirits more wicked than itself, and they go in and live there; and the last state of that man becomes worse than the first" (Matt. 12:43-45). Self-reformation drives a person further from God's grace and therefore further from salvation.

Sixth, assurance of salvation is not an infallible mark of saving faith. The world is filled with people who are sincerely convinced in their own minds that they are right with God and that their place in heaven is secured. If being persuaded that we *are* Christians makes us Christians indeed, we would need no warnings about being deceived by false hopes. If it were not possible to believe oneself saved when one is not, Satan would have no way to deceive people about their salvation. Yet Scripture is full of warnings to unsaved people who think they are saved (Matt. 7:21-23; James 1:22).

Seventh, the experience of a past "decision" for Christ does not necessarily prove saving faith. If no evidence of godly living results from that event, no matter how strong and genuine the profession seemed to be, it is no proof of salvation.

There *are*, however, some reliable proofs of saving faith. God does not leave His children in uncertainty about their relationship to Him.

The first reliable evidence of saving faith is *love for God.* "The mind set on the flesh is hostile toward God," Paul says (Rom. 8:7). The unsaved person cannot love God and has no desire to love Him. The true child of God, however, despite his often failing his heavenly Father, will have a life characterized by delight in God and His Word (Ps. 1:2). "As the deer pants for the water brooks," so his soul pants and thirsts for God (Ps. 42:1-2). Jesus declared, "He who loves father or mother more than Me is not worthy of Me, and he who loves son or daughter more than Me is not worthy of Me" (Matt. 10:37). The true believer will proclaim with Asaph, "Whom have I in heaven but Thee? And besides Thee, I desire nothing on earth" (Ps. 73:25). Love for God will be the direction of the true believer's life, if not the perfection of it. Peter declares, "Unto you therefore which believe He is precious" (1 Pet. 2:7, KJV).

A second reliable evidence of saving faith is *repentance from sin and the hatred of it* that always accompanies true contrition. This second mark of saving faith is the reverse side of the first. The person who genuinely loves God will have a built-in hatred of sin. It is impossible to love two things that are contradictory of one another. "No one can serve two masters," Jesus declared categorically; "for either he will hate the one and love the other, or he will hold to one and despise the other" (Matt. 6:24). To love the holy and righteous God is, almost by definition, to have a deep abhorrence of sin.

"He who conceals his transgressions will not prosper," the writer of Proverbs declares, "but he who confesses and forsakes them will find compassion" (Prov. 28:13). This verse links the two inseparable parts of true repentance: the confession and forsaking of sin.

When confronted by Nathan concerning his sins of adultery with Bathsheba and the murder of her husband Uriah, David's repentance was genuine, as reflected in Psalm 51. "Be gracious to me, O God, according to Thy lovingkindness; according to the greatness of Thy compassion blot out my transgressions," he prayed. "Wash me thoroughly from my iniquity, and cleanse me from my sin. For I know my transgressions, and my sin is ever before me. Against Thee, Thee only, I have sinned, and done what is evil in Thy sight" (vv. 1-4).

The true believer often hates sin even while he is doing it and *always* after he has done it, because it is completely contrary to his new nature in Christ. Even though a believer's humanness sometimes draws him into sin and, like Paul, he does the very thing he knows he ought not to do (Rom. 7:16), he will have no peace of conscience until he repents of it.

True repentance is more than simply sorrow for sin. Judas became bitterly sorry for His sin of betraying Jesus, to the extreme of committing suicide; but he did not repent of his betrayal or ask Jesus' forgiveness. Paul commended the Corinthian believers for being "made sorrowful to the point of repentance; for you were made sorrowful according to the will of God" (2 Cor. 7:9). True repentance always involves *godly* sorrow, sorrow that one has disobeyed and offended his Lord.

No Christian becomes completely sinless until he goes to meet the Lord. "If we say that we have no sin," John says, "we are deceiving ourselves and the truth is not in us." But he goes on to give the beautifully encouraging word that "if we confess our sins, He is faithful and righteous to forgive us our sins and to cleanse us from all unrighteousness" (1 John 1:8-9).

If a person's sin does not bother him and increasingly put him under conviction about it, that person's salvation is questionable. The test for true repentance is not simply sorrow for the way sin harms oneself (as it always does), but sorrow for the sin's offense against the holy Lord, which above all else leads a believer to implore God's forgiveness.

Someone has written, "When God touches a life, He breaks the heart. Where He pours out the spirit of grace, there are not a few transient sighs that agitate the breast, there are heart-rending pangs of sorrow."

A third reliable evidence of true faith is *genuine humility*. A person cannot be saved as long as he trusts in and exalts himself. Salvation begins by confessing one's poverty of spirit (Matt. 5:3) and the willingness to deny self and take up the cross of Christ (Matt. 16:24). Like the prodigal son, the true believer who sins will eventually come "to his senses," his spiritual senses that convict him of sin. He will then, again like the prodigal, go to his heavenly Father and humbly confess his sin and his unworthiness of forgiveness, while pleading for it on the basis of his Father's grace (see Luke 15:17-21).

A fourth reliable evidence of true faith is *devotion to God's glory*, which is closely related to the love of God and repentance of sin. The true believer will say with Paul, "My earnest expectation and hope [is] that I shall not be put to shame in anything, but that with all boldness, Christ shall even now, as always, be exalted in my body, whether by life or by death" (Phil. 1:20). As already noted, although that desire will not be seen in perfection in the true believer's life, it will always be evidenced in the direction of his life.

A fifth reliable evidence of true faith is *prayer*. "Because you are sons," Paul told the Galatian believers, "God has sent forth the Spirit of His Son into our hearts, crying, 'Abba! Father!'" (Gal. 4:6). The heart of a genuine Christian cannot help calling out to God, who is his heavenly Father and whose own Spirit is within him to generate that yearning.

Every genuine Christian will freely admit that he does not pray as often or as earnestly and persistently as he should. But in his innermost being, communion with his heavenly Father will be the desire of his heart. As Jonathan Edwards succinctly observed, "Hypocrites [are] deficient in the duty of prayer," which is also the title of two great sermons on the topic (*The Works of Jonathan Edwards*, vol. 2 [Carlisle, Pa.: Banner of Truth, 1986 reprint], pp. 71-77).

A sixth mark of saving faith is *selfless love*, not only for God, as in the first mark, but also for other people, especially fellow Christians. "The one who says he is in the light and yet hates his brother is in the darkness until now. The one who loves his brother abides in the light and there no cause for stumbling in him" (1 John 2:9-10). Later in that letter John said, "We know that we have passed out of death into life, because we love the brethren. He who does not love abides in death" (3:14). The person who does not sincerely care for the welfare of true believers is himself *not* a true believer, but still abides in spiritual death. Again in that letter John says, "Beloved, let us love one another, for love is from God; and every one who loves is born of God and knows God. The one who does not love does not know God, for God is love" (4:7-8).

A seventh mark of saving faith is *separation from the world*. Believers are called to be in the world but not of it. They are in the world to testify to Christ, a central testimony of which is not to reflect the world's standards and ways (see John 17:15-18). "If anyone loves the world, the love of the Father is not in him. For all that is in the world, the lust of the flesh and the lust of the eyes and the boastful pride of life, is not from the Father, but is from the world" (1 John 2:15-16). On the other hand, "Whatever is born of God overcomes the world; and this is the victory that has overcome the world—our faith. And who is the one who overcomes the world, but he who believes that Jesus is the Son of God?" (1 John 5:4-5). The person who has saving faith has "received, not the spirit of the world, but the Spirit who is from God" (1 Cor. 2:12).

An eighth mark of saving faith is *spiritual growth*. The central truth of the parable of the soils (Matt. 13:3-23) is that true believers will always grow spiritually to varying degrees, because by faith they have genuinely received the seed of the gospel. "The kingdom of God is like a man who casts seed upon the soil," Jesus said on another occasion; "and [he] goes to bed at night and gets up by day, and the seed sprouts up and grows—how, he himself does not know. The soil produces crops by itself; first the blade, then the head, then the mature grain in the head" (Mark 4:26-28). Like the farmer and his crops, the believer does not understand *how* he grows spiritually, but he knows that because he has spiritual life within him he *will* grow (see also Eph. 4:13; Phil. 1:6).

The ninth and final mark of saving faith is *obedient living*. "By this we know that we have come to know Him [Christ]," John says, "if we keep His commandments. The one who says, 'I have come to know Him,' and does not keep His commandments, is a liar, and the truth is not in him; but whoever keeps His word, in him the love of God has truly been perfected. By this we know that we are in Him" (1 John 2:3-5; cf. 3:10). Although no one is saved *by* his good works, those who are truly saved will produce good works, because "we are [God's] workmanship, created in Christ Jesus for good works, which God prepared beforehand, that we should walk in them" (Eph. 2:10).

THE CROSS REVEALS GOD'S UNIVERSALITY

Or is God the God of Jews only? Is He not the God of Gentiles also? Yes, of Gentiles also, since indeed God who will justify the circumcised by faith and the uncircumcised through faith is one. (3:29-30)

Pagan religions almost invariably have many gods. Frequently there is a supreme god who is more powerful than the rest, but he shares with them a common form of "deity."

The fundamental truth of Judaism, however, has always been "The Lord is our God, the Lord is one!" (Deut. 6:4). That truth is repeated in one form or another throughout the Old Testament. Through His prophet Isaiah, God Himself declared, "I am the Lord, and there is no other; besides Me there is no God" (Isa. 45:5). There is only *one* God, the Creator, Sustainer, and Lord of the entire universe. There are no "lesser gods," only false gods that have been created by man's imagination and often are demonically inspired and empowered.

Yet despite the central truth of their faith that there is only one God, many Jews in biblical times believed that Gentiles somehow were outside the domain of "their" God. Instead of considering themselves as belonging to God, they virtually considered God as belonging only to them.

Jonah resisted going to Nineveh not because he thought his witness might fail but because he feared it would succeed. He confessed to the Lord, "Please Lord, was not this what I said while I was still in my own country? Therefore, in order to forestall this I fled to Tarshish, for I knew that Thou art a gracious and compassionate God, slow to anger and abundant in lovingkindness" (Jonah 4:2). He tried to flee to Tarshish because he knew his preaching might cause the pagan Ninevites to trust in God and become acceptable to Him. He confessed, in effect, that although he knew he belonged to God and was His servant, he did not want to be *like* God in His love and grace.

From their own Scripture the Jews knew that many Gentiles had found favor with God. They knew that Rahab, not only a pagan Gentile but also a prostitute, found favor with God. They knew that Ruth, a Moabitess, was the great-grandmother of David, their greatest king. They knew that the prophet Elisha graciously volunteered to heal Naaman, a captain in the army of Syria, of his leprosy. Yet many Jews persisted in their deep prejudice against, and often hatred of, Gentiles.

Probably having had such prejudice and hatred himself before his conversion, Paul anticipated the question many Jews would ask in regard to justification by faith. He therefore asked rhetorically, **Or is God the God of Jews only? Is He not the God of Gentiles also?** The obvious answer, even for a prejudiced Jew, would have to be, **Yes, of Gentiles also**. If there is only one God, then He had to be **the God of Gentiles** as well as of Jews. If there is only one God, He has to be the God of everyone.

As far as men's religions are concerned, there are, of course, many "so-called gods whether in heaven or on earth, as indeed there are many gods and many lords," Paul says; "yet for us there is but one God, the Father, from whom are all things, and we exist for Him; and one Lord, Jesus Christ, by whom are all things, and we exist through Him" (1 Cor. 8:5-6).

Having established that the Jews had God's law given through Moses, that the Gentiles had His law written on their hearts and consciences (2:11-15), and that there is only one true God, Paul makes his argument irrefutable: The **God who will justify the circumcised**, that is, Jews, **by faith and the uncircumcised**, that is, Gentiles, **through faith is one.** Just as there is only one God, there is only one way of salvation—faith in Jesus Christ.

In his letter to Timothy, Paul reminded his young protégé, "This is good and acceptable in the sight of God our Savior, who desires all men to be saved and to come to the knowledge of the truth. For there is one God, and one mediator also between God and men, the man Christ

Jesus, who gave Himself as a ransom for all" (1 Tim. 2:3-6).

Just as all men are equally condemned by God for their sin (Rom. 3:19), they are equally offered God's gracious salvation through faith in His Son. As the apostle declared near the opening of the letter, "I am not ashamed of the gospel, for it is the power of God for salvation to everyone who believes, to the Jew first and also to the Greek [the Gentile]" (Rom. 1:16).

As Paul later demonstrates in this letter, salvation by faith has always been the *only* way of salvation, under the covenant of Moses and before that even for their first and greatest patriarch, Abraham (4:1-3). Hebrews 11 makes clear that God's way of salvation by faith alone extended back to the Fall, when the need for salvation began.

THE CROSS CONFIRMS GOD'S LAW

Do we then nullify the Law through faith? May it never be! On the contrary, we establish the Law. (3:31)

The next question Paul knew his readers would ask was, **Do we then nullify the Law through faith?** "If men have never been saved on any other basis than faith in God," they would argue, "then the law not only is useless now but was always useless."

Again Paul responds with the powerful repudiation, **May it never be!** (see 3:4, 6). "A thousand times no," is the idea. The cross of Jesus Christ, through which justification by faith was made possible, not only does not **nullify the Law** but confirms it. **On the contrary,** Paul says, **we establish the Law.**

As far as salvation is concerned, the gospel does not replace the law, because the law was never a means of salvation. The law was given to show men the perfect standards of God's righteousness and to show that those standards are impossible to meet in man's own power. The purpose of the law was to drive men to faith in God. In the Sermon on the Mount, Jesus declared God's perfect standards to be higher even than those of the Old Covenant. A person breaks God's law, He said, not only by killing but even by hating (Matt. 5:21-22), not only by committing adultery but by having lustful thoughts (5:27-28). If it is impossible to fulfill perfectly the Mosaic law, how much more impossible is it to keep the standards set forth by Christ in His earthly ministry.

The cross establishes, or confirms, the law in three ways. First, it establishes the law by paying the penalty of death, which the law demanded for failing to fulfill perfectly and completely its righteous requirements. When Jesus said that He had come not to abolish the law or the prophets but to fulfill them (Matt. 5:17), He was speaking not only of His sinless earthly life but of His sin-bearing death.

Second, the cross establishes the law by fulfilling its purpose of driving men to faith in Jesus Christ. Paul had already declared that "by the works of the Law no flesh will be justified" (3:20). "Whoever keeps the whole law and yet stumbles in one point," James says, "he has become guilty of all" (James 2:10). "The Law has become our tutor," Paul told the Galatians, "to lead us to Christ, that we may be justified by faith" (Gal. 3:24).

Third, the cross establishes the law by providing believers the potential for fulfilling it. "For what the Law could not do, weak as it was through the flesh, God did: sending His own Son in the likeness of sinful flesh and as an offering for sin, He condemned sin in the flesh, in order that the requirements of the Law might be fulfilled in us" (Rom. 8:3-4).

Abraham—
Justified by Faith

17

What then shall we say that Abraham, our forefather according to the flesh, has found? For if Abraham was justified by works, he has something to boast about; but not before God. For what does the Scripture say? "And Abraham believed God, and it was reckoned to him as righteousness." Now to the one who works, his wage is not reckoned as a favor, but as what is due. But to the one who does not work, but believes in Him who justifies the ungodly, his faith is reckoned as righteousness, just as David also speaks of the blessing upon the man to whom God reckons righteousness apart from works: "Blessed are those whose lawless deeds have been forgiven, and whose sins have been covered. Blessed is the man whose sin the Lord will not take into account. (4:11-18)

If there is any doctrine that the chief enemy of man and of God desires to undercut and distort, it is the doctrine of salvation. If Satan can cause confusion and error in regard to that doctrine, he has succeeded in keeping men in their sin and under divine judgment and condemnation, which the unredeemed will one day share with Satan and his demonic angels in the eternal torment of hell.

Every false religion of the world—whether a heretical branch of

Christianity, a highly developed pagan religion, or primitive animism—is founded on some form of salvation by works. Without exception, they teach that, by one means or another, man can become right with deity by attaining righteousness in his own power.

The entire fourth chapter of Romans is devoted to Abraham, whom Paul uses as an illustration of the central biblical truth that man can become right with God only by faith in response to His grace, and never by works. Verses 6-8 pertain to David, but Paul is simply using David as an illustration to substantiate what he is teaching about Abraham.

We can assume several reasons for Paul's choosing Abraham as the supreme example of salvation by faith. First, Abraham lived about 2,000 years before Paul wrote this letter, demonstrating that the principle of salvation by faith rather than by works was not new in Judaism. Abraham was the first and foremost Hebrew patriarch. He lived more than six hundred years before the Old Covenant was established through Moses. He therefore lived long before the law was given and obviously could not have been saved by obedience to it.

Second, Paul used Abraham as an example of salvation by faith simply because he was a human being. Until this point in Romans, Paul has been speaking primarily about theological truths in the abstract. In Abraham he gives a flesh and blood illustration of justification by faith.

The third, and doubtless most important, reason Paul used Abraham as the example of justification by faith was that, although rabbinical teaching and popular Jewish belief were contrary to Scripture as far as the *basis* of Abraham's righteousness was concerned, they agreed that Abraham was the Old Testament's supreme example of a godly, righteous man who is acceptable to the Lord. He is the biblical model of genuine faith and godliness.

The majority of Jews in Paul's day believed that Abraham was made right with God because of his own righteous character. They believed God chose Abraham to be the father of His people Israel because Abraham was the most righteous man on earth during his time. Like many cults today, they took certain scriptural passages and twisted or interpreted them out of context in order to support their preconceived ideas.

The rabbis, for example, pointed out that the Lord told Isaac, "I will multiply your descendants as the stars of heaven, and will give your descendants all these lands; and by your descendants all the nations of the earth shall be blessed; because Abraham obeyed Me and kept My charge, My commandments, My statutes and My laws" (Gen. 26:4-5). They pointed out that the Lord called Abraham "My friend" (Isa. 41:8). Habakkuk 2:4 was often rendered, "The just shall live by his faithfulness," rather than "by his faith." Instead of understanding faithfulness as being a fruit of faith, they had the notion that justification could be earned through one's efforts to be faithful. In the same way, the rabbis interpreted Genesis 15:6 as referring to Abraham's faithfulness rather than to his faith.

Several Jewish apocryphal books taught that Abraham was justified by keeping God's law. In *Ecclesiasticus* (also known as *The Wisdom of Sirach*), Abraham is said to have become right with God because of his obedience (44:19-21). *The Prayer of Manasseh* even asserted Abraham's sinlessness: "Therefore thou, O Lord, God of the righteous, hast not appointed repentance for the righteous, for Abraham, Isaac, and Jacob, who did not sin against thee" (v. 8). In *The Book of Jubilees* the writer says, "Abraham was perfect in all his deeds with the Lord, and well-pleasing in righteousness all the days of his life" (23:10). Some rabbinical writings claimed that Abraham was so inherently good that he began serving God when he was three years old and that he was one of seven righteous men who had the privilege of bringing back the Shekinah glory to the Tabernacle.

By using Abraham as the supreme scriptural example of justification, or salvation, by *faith alone,* Paul was storming the very citadel of traditional Judaism. By demonstrating that Abraham was not justified by works, the apostle demolished the foundation of rabbinical teaching—that man is made right with God by keeping the law, that is, on the basis of his own religious efforts and works. If Abraham was not and could not have been justified by keeping the law, then no one could be. Conversely, if Abraham was justified solely on the basis of his faith in God, then everyone else must be justified in the same way, since Abraham is the biblical standard of a righteous man.

ABRAHAM WAS NOT JUSTIFIED BY HIS WORKS

What then shall we say that Abraham, our forefather according to the flesh, has found? For if Abraham was justified by works, he has something to boast about; but not before God. (4:1-2)

Paul begins by asking, **What then shall we say that Abraham, our forefather according to the flesh, has found?** He was asking, in effect, "Because we agree that **Abraham** is the peerless example of a justified man in God's sight, why don't we look at him carefully in order to determine the basis of his justification?"

In this context **what then** is the equivalent of *therefore,* tying the discussion of Abraham to all that Paul has said in the preceding chapter. As noted above, after asserting that both Jew and Gentile are justified by faith (3:30), the apostle brings **Abraham** into the picture because he knew that this greatest of Jewish patriarchs, their **forefather according**

to the flesh, was used by the rabbis as the ultimate example of man's being justified by works. Paul will demonstrate that, to the contrary, Scripture clearly teaches that Abraham was saved by his faith alone.

Abraham was the human **forefather** of God's first covenant with His chosen people. He was therefore, **according to the flesh,** the human standard of a genuine Jew and of a man who is right before God. The whole Hebrew race came from his loins, and what was true regarding his relationship to God must therefore be true of all his descendants.

According to the flesh refers first of all to physical lineage. But in this context it also suggests human effort in regard to justification. Paul has already asserted that Jew and Gentile alike are justified by faith (3:30) and in 4:2 he refers to the traditional Jewish idea of Abraham's justifying himself by good works. Therefore, **according to the flesh** could refer to reliance on human works.

In a hypothetical syllogism, Paul says, **For if Abraham was justified by works, then he has something to boast about.** The major premise is that, if a man could be justified before God by his own human efforts, then he has ground for boasting in himself. The minor premise is that Abraham, as a man, was justified by works. The necessary conclusion would be that Abraham therefore **has something to boast about.**

The major premise is true: If a man *could* be **justified by works,** he would indeed have something **to boast about,** because he would have merited his own salvation. But, as Paul goes on to demonstrate, the minor premise is *not* true. Consequently, the conclusion is untrue. Abraham did **not** have anything in himself to boast about **before God.**

ABRAHAM WAS JUSTIFIED BY HIS FAITH

For what does the Scripture say? "And Abraham believed God, and it was reckoned to him as righteousness." Now to the one who works, his wage is not reckoned as a favor, but as what is due. But to the one who does not work, but believes in Him who justifies the ungodly, his faith is reckoned as righteousness, (4:3-5)

On the positive side of his argument, Paul first appeals to **Scripture,** the divine and infallible truth upon which all of his arguments are based. Quoting Genesis 15:6, he declares, **And Abraham believed God, and it was reckoned to him as righteousness.** Early in the Genesis account of Abraham, which begins with chapter 12, Moses was inspired to write of the patriarch that he was made right with God *only* because of his faith. Because **Abraham believed God,** and on no other basis, his belief **was reckoned to him** by God **as righteousness.**

In his letter to the Galatian churches, the apostle cites the same verse from Genesis and then goes on to say, "Therefore, be sure that it is those who are of faith who are sons of Abraham" (Gal. 3:6-7). Several verses later he refers to the patriarch as "Abraham, the believer" (v. 9). Because Abraham was the quintessential man of faith, he is in that sense "the father of all who believe" (Rom. 4:11). Through his faith in God, "Abraham rejoiced to see My day," Jesus said, "and he saw it and was glad" (John 8:56).

The writer of Hebrews describes the faith by which Abraham was declared righteous by God: "By faith, Abraham, when he was called, obeyed by going out to a place which he was to receive for an inheritance; and he went out, not knowing where he was going. By faith he lived as an alien in the land of promise, as in a foreign land, dwelling in tents with Isaac and Jacob, fellow heirs of the same promise; for he was looking for the city which has foundations, whose architect and builder is God" (Heb. 11:8-10).

Like Paul, who wrote this epistle to Rome, Abraham was sovereignly and directly chosen by God. Neither Abraham nor Paul was searching for God when they were divinely called and commissioned. Abraham had probably never heard of the true God, whereas Paul knew a great deal about Him. Abraham was seemingly content with his idolatrous paganism, and Paul was content with his traditional, but false, Judaism.

When Abraham was first called by God, he lived in Ur of Chaldea (Gen. 11:31; 15:7), a thoroughly pagan and idolatrous city. Archaeologists have estimated that it consisted of perhaps 300,000 inhabitants during Abraham's time. It was an important commercial city, located in Mesopotamia on the lower Euphrates River, a little more than a hundred miles northwest of the Persian Gulf. The people of Ur were highly educated, being proficient in such diverse areas as math, agriculture, weaving, engraving, and astronomy. Contrary to the claims of liberal scholars of the nineteenth and early twentieth centuries, it has been proved that by Abraham's time the Chaldeans had developed a system of writing.

The Chaldeans were polytheistic, having a multitude of gods, the foremost of which was called Nanna, the moon god. Because his father, Terah, was an idolater (Josh. 24:2), Abraham obviously was reared in paganism.

When God called Abraham, or Abram, which was his original name, He gave no reason for selecting that pagan from the millions of others in the world. Nowhere in Scripture is the reason given. God chose Abraham because that was His divine will, which needs no justification or explanation.

After commanding Abraham to leave his country and his relatives and to go to the land that would be shown to him, God sovereignly and unconditionally promised, "I will make you a great nation, and I will bless you, and make your name great; and so you shall be a blessing; and I will bless those who bless you, and the one who curses you I will curse. And in you all the families of the earth shall be blessed" (Gen. 12:2-3).

With no guarantee but God's word, Abraham left his business, his homeland, his friends, most of his relatives, and probably many of his possessions. He abandoned his temporal security for a future uncertainty, as far as his human eyes could see or his human mind could comprehend. The land he was promised to inherit was inhabited by pagans perhaps even more wicked and idolatrous than those of his home country. Abraham may have had only a remote idea of where the land of Canaan was, and it is possible that he had never heard of it at all. But when God called him to go there, Abraham obeyed and began the long journey.

Because he only partly obeyed God, however, bringing along his father and his nephew Lot, Abraham wasted fifteen years in Haran, where the group lived until Terah died (Gen. 11:32). By that time Abraham was seventy-five years old, and as he continued the journey to Canaan, he also continued to obey God only partly by taking Lot with him (12:4).

When Abraham, Sarah, and Lot reached Shechem in Canaan, Abraham received another sovereign and unconditional promise from God: "The Lord appeared to Abram and said, 'To your descendants I will give this land'. So he built an altar there to the Lord who had appeared to him" (Gen. 12:7). As Abraham continued his journey through Canaan, he built another altar "to the Lord and called upon the name of the Lord" (v. 8).

But Abraham's faith was not perfect, just as no believer's faith is perfect. The first test he had to face was a famine in Canaan, and Abraham went to Egypt for help instead of to God. That disobedience put him in a compromising situation with the pharaoh. He claimed that his beautiful wife was his sister, fearing that the pharaoh might kill him in order to have her for himself. In so doing, Abraham dishonored the Lord and caused plagues to come upon the pharaoh's family (Gen. 12:10-17).

The Lord gave repeated assurances to Abraham, and Abraham responded in faith, which God "reckoned . . . to him as righteousness" (Gen. 15:6). But again, when testing came, he relied on his own judgment rather than the Lord's word. When Sarah was getting beyond normal childbearing age and remained barren, Abraham took her foolish advice and took matters into his own hands. He committed adultery with Hagar, Sarah's maid, in the hope of having a male heir by her. But as always, his disobedient act backfired and again caused misery to the innocent (see Gen. 16:1-15). He also brought future misery to his own descendants, with whom the Arab descendants of Ishmael, the son by Hagar, would be in continuous conflict, as they are to this day.

Despite his spiritual imperfection, Abraham always came back to the Lord in faith, and the Lord honored that faith and continued to renew his promises to Abraham. God miraculously caused Sarah to bear a son in her old age, the son whom God had promised to give Abraham. And when the greatest test of all came, Abraham did not waver in his trust of the Lord. When God commanded him to sacrifice Isaac, the only human means through which the promise could be fulfilled, Abraham responded with immediate obedience, and God responded by providing a substitute for Isaac (Gen. 22:118). The writer of Hebrews declared that it was "by faith [that] Abraham, when he was tested, offered up Isaac; and he who had received the promises was offering up his only begotten son; it was he to whom it was said, 'In Isaac your descendants shall be called.' He [that is, Abraham] considered that God is able to raise men even from the dead; from which he also received back as a type" (Heb. 11:17-19).

Neither Abraham nor his most immediate heirs—his son Isaac and his grandson Jacob—ever owned any land in Canaan, except for a small field near Mamre in which the cave of Machpelah was located. Abraham bought this plot from Ephron, a Hittite, for the burial of Sarah (see Gen. 23:3-11). Abraham himself and Isaac, Rebekah, and Leah were also buried there (49:31). Many years later, according to Jacob's request, his body was brought back from Egypt by Joseph and his brothers for burial alongside Jacob's father and grandfather (Gen. 50:13-14).

As is always the case with true belief, the Holy Spirit enlightened Abraham's mind and heart to recognize the true and only God, and enabled him to respond in faith. Abraham saw the Promised Land and wandered through it as a nomad, but he never possessed it. Even his descendants did not possess the land until more than a half century after the promise of it was first given.

Just as Abraham trusted God's word to give him a land he had never seen, he trusted God's power to raise Isaac from the dead, if necessary, by a divine miracle he had never seen. It was in response to Abraham's faith in God that it **was reckoned to him as righteousness.**

Was reckoned is from *logizomai,* which carried the economic and legal meaning of crediting something to another's account. The only thing God received from Abraham was his imperfect faith, but by His divine grace and mercy, He **reckoned** it to Abraham's spiritual account **as righteousness.** That gracious reckoning reflects the heart of God's redemptive revelation and is the focus of both the Old and New Testaments. God has never provided any means of justification except through faith in Him.

Even though Abraham's repeated disobedience was sinful and brought harm to himself and others, God even used that disobedience to glorify Himself. Those acts of disobedience testify that, contrary to rabbinical teaching, Abraham was sovereignly chosen by God for His own divine reasons and purposes, *not* because of Abraham's faithfulness or righteousness. Abraham was chosen by God's sovereign, elective grace, not because of his works or even because of his faith. His faith was acceptable to God only because God graciously **reckoned,** or counted, it **as righteousness.** It was not the greatness of Abraham's faith that saved him but the greatness of the gracious Lord in whom he placed his faith.

Faith is never the *basis* or the *reason* for justification, but only the *channel* through which God works His redeeming grace. Faith is simply a convicted heart reaching out to receive God's free and unmerited gift of salvation.

What was true in regard to Abraham's faith is true in regard to every believer's faith. **Now to the one who works, his wage is not reckoned as a favor, but as what is due,** Paul declares. **But to the one who does not work, but believes in Him who justifies the ungodly, his faith is reckoned as righteousness.**

Although faith is required for salvation, it has no power in itself to save. It is the power of God's redemptive grace alone, working through the atoning work of His Son on the cross, that has power to save. Faith is not, as some claim, a type of work. Paul here makes clear that saving faith is completely apart from *any* kind of human **works.**

If man were able to save himself by his own **works,** then salvation would be apart from God's grace, and Christ's sacrifice on the cross would have been in vain. If such righteous **works** were attainable by men, then salvation would not be a gift of God's grace but would be a **wage** that **is due.** Not only would works righteousness obviate God's grace, it would also rob Him of glory, for which all creation was made. "For from Him and through Him and to Him are all things," Paul reminded the Roman believers later in this epistle. "To Him be the glory forever. Amen" (Rom. 11:36). The primary purpose of the gospel is not to save men but to glorify God. In another beautiful benediction in the middle of his letter to the Ephesians, Paul exulted, "Now to Him who is able to do exceeding abundantly beyond all that we ask or think, according to the power that works within us, to Him be the glory in the church and in Christ Jesus to all generations forever and ever. Amen" (Eph. 3:20-21).

There are many reasons why sinful man cannot save himself by his own works. First, because of his sin he is incapable of reaching the divine standard of righteousness, which is absolute perfection. Second, no matter how generous, sacrificial, and beneficent his works might be, they could not atone for his sins. Even if God recognized all of a person's works as being good, the worker would still be under the divine penalty of death for his sins. Third, as noted above, if men were able to save themselves, Christ's atoning death was useless. Fourth, as also already noted, if man could save himself, God's glory would be eclipsed by man's.

God only saves the person **who does not** trust in his **work, but believes in Him who justifies the ungodly.** Until a person confesses that he is **ungodly,** he is not a candidate for salvation, because he still trusts in his own goodness. That is what Jesus meant when He said, "I have not come to call the righteous but sinners to repentance" (Luke 5:32). Those who are righteous in their own eyes have no part in God's redemptive work of grace.

In the parable of the vineyard Jesus illustrated God's impartial grace. From a human perspective, the men who had worked all day deserved more than those who worked only the last hour. But Jesus' point was that the landowner, representing God, had the right to do as he willed. He did not defraud the all-day workers, but paid them exactly what he had promised and they had agreed to.

By God's standard, every person's work falls far short of earning the redemption He provides. On the divine scale of perfect righteousness, even the most devoted and longserving Christian is not a hair's breadth closer to earning his salvation than is the most vile criminal who accepts Christ on his deathbed.

Even genuine faith does not in itself merit or produce the perfect righteousness apart from which no man can come to God. **His faith is** rather **reckoned as** that required **righteousness.**

The "reckoning" Paul speaks of here is justification, that forensic act of God whereby He imputes Christ's perfect righteousness to the sinner's account, then declares His verdict that the forgiven one is fully just. In his book *Redemption Accomplished and Applied,* John Murray wrote, "God cannot but accept into His favour those who are invested with the righteousness of his own Son. While his wrath is revealed from heaven against all unrighteousness and ungodliness of men, his good pleasure is also revealed from heaven upon the righteousness of his well-beloved and only-begotten" ([Grand Rapids: Eerdmans, 1955], p. 124).

God thus **justifies the ungodly,** not by simply disregarding their sin—but having imputed our sin to Christ, who paid the penalty in full, He now reckons Christ's righteousness to us. "Surely our griefs He Himself bore, and our sorrows He carried; yet we ourselves esteemed Him stricken, smitten of God, and afflicted. But He was pierced through for our transgressions, He was crushed for our iniquities; the chastening for our well-being fell upon Him, and by His scourging we are healed" (Isa. 53:4-5).

Because God credits the believer's sin to Christ's account, He can credit Christ's righteousness to the believer's account. God could not have justly credited righteousness to Abraham had not Abraham's sin, like every believer's sin, been paid for by the sacrifice of Christ's own blood.

Before the cross, the believer's sin was paid in anticipation of Christ's atoning sacrifice, and since the cross the believer's sin has been paid in advance.

Commenting on God's reckoning righteousness to believers, Arthur Pink wrote,

> It is called "the righteousness *of God*" (Rom. 1:17; 3:21) because He is the appointer, approver, and imputer of it. It is called "the righteousness *of God and our Saviour Jesus Christ*" (II Peter 1:1) because He wrought it out and presented it unto God. It is called "the righteousness *of faith*" (Rom. 4:13) because faith is the apprehender and receiver of it. It is called *man's* righteousness (Job 33:26) because it was paid for him and imputed to him. All these varied expressions refer to so many aspects of that one perfect obedience unto death which the Saviour performed for His people. (*The Doctrines of Election and Justification* [Grand Rapids: Baker, 1974], p. 188)

God's reckoning a believer's faith as His own divine righteousness is an incomprehensible but incontrovertible truth. It thrills the heart of those who place their faith in Jesus Christ as Lord and Savior.

When a penitent sinner is confronted by the majesty, power, and justice of God, he cannot help seeing his own lostness and the worthlessness of his own works. By divinely-given insight he realizes he is worthy only of God's condemnation. But God gives divine assurance that, through a sinner's faith in Jesus Christ, He not only will save him from condemnation but will also fill him with His own eternal righteousness.

The truly penitent sinner cries out with the prophet Micah, who confessed, "With what shall I come to the Lord and bow myself before the God on high? Shall I come to Him with burnt offerings, with yearling calves? Does the Lord take delight in thousands of rams, in ten thousand rivers of oil? Shall I present my first-born for my rebellious acts, the fruit of my body for the sin of my soul?" (Mic. 6:6-7).

A simple acrostic, using the letters of the word *faith,* may help in understanding the elements of saving faith. "F" could represent *facts.* Faith is not based on a blind leap into the unknown and unknowable, as many liberal and neoorthodox theologians would have us believe. It is based on the facts of God's redeeming work through His Son Jesus Christ.

In his first letter to the church at Corinth, Paul declared,

> Now I make known to you, brethren, the gospel which I preached to you, which also you received, in which also you stand, by which also you are saved, if you hold fast the word which I preached to you, unless you believed in vain. For I delivered to you as of first importance what I also

received that Christ died for our sins according to the Scriptures, and that He was buried, and that He was raised on the third day according to the Scriptures, and that He appeared to Cephas, then to the twelve. After that He appeared to more than five hundred brethren at one time, most of whom remain until now, but some have fallen asleep; then He appeared to James, then to all the apostles; and last of all, as it were to one untimely born, He appeared to me also. (1 Cor. 15:1-8)

To further show the importance of the fact of Jesus' resurrection, Paul went on to say, "If Christ has not been raised, then our preaching is vain, your faith also is vain. . . . and if Christ has not been raised, your faith is worthless; you are still in your sins" (vv. 14, 17).

The letter "A" could represent *agreement*. It is one thing to know the truth of the gospel; it is quite another to agree with it. The believing heart affirms the truth it receives from God's Word.

The letter "I" could represent *internalization*, the inner desire of a believer to accept and apply the truth of the gospel to his own life. Speaking of Christ, the apostle John wrote, "He came to His own, and those who were His own did not receive Him. But as many as received Him, to them He gave the right to become children of God, even to those who believe in His name, who were born not of blood, nor of the will of the flesh, nor of the will of man, but of God" (John 1:11-13). Internalization also involves the genuine desire to obey Christ as Lord. "If you abide in My word," Jesus said, "then you are truly disciples of Mine" (John 8:31).

The letter "T" could represent *trust*. In some ways and in some contexts, trust is a synonym for faith. But trust also carries the idea of having unreserved confidence in God, of trusting Him to keep His promises to never forsake us as His children and to provide all our needs. The parables of the hidden treasure and of the pearl of great price (Matt. 13:44-46) both teach the necessity of a believer's surrendering all he has for the sake of Christ, of affirming and trusting in His lordship and His grace.

Genuine trust involves turning away from sin and self and turning to God. That turning is called repentance, apart from which no person can be saved. Repentance is so much a part of the gospel that it is sometimes equated with salvation. Peter declared, "The Lord is not slow about His promise, as some count slowness, but is patient toward you, not wishing for any to perish but for all to come to repentance: (2 Pet. 3:9).

The letter "H" could represent *hope*. Every believer is saved in the hope of going to live eternally with God in heaven, although he has never seen heaven or seen the Lord in whom he believes. When Thomas refused to believe Jesus was raised from the dead until he touched his Lord's body, Jesus said, "Blessed are they who did not see, and yet believed" (John 20:29). The vast majority of those who have trusted in Christ over the centuries have never seen Him. Even those who saw Him after the resurrection and witnessed His ascent to heaven had only the hope, and not yet the reality, of their joining Him one day in heaven. Until he meets the Lord through death or by rapture, every believer must live in hope of that which he has not yet fully received.

Justification Brings Blessing

just as David also speaks of the blessing upon the man to whom God reckons righteousness apart from works: "Blessed are those whose lawless deeds have been forgiven, and whose sins have been covered. Blessed is the man whose sin the Lord will not take into account." (4:6-8)

Paul here cites David in order to establish that the greatest king of Israel understood and taught that justification is by faith alone. **The blessing** David is speaking about is salvation, God's supreme **blessing** offered to fallen mankind. The only ones who can receive it are those for **whom God reckons righteousness apart from works.**

In Psalm 32 the man after God's own heart declared: **"Blessed are those whose lawless deeds have been forgiven, and whose sins have been covered. Blessed is the man whose sin the Lord will not take into account."**

David clearly understood God's grace. In his great penitential psalm written after Nathan confronted him with his adultery with Bathsheba and the murder of her husband, David cast himself entirely on God's grace. "Be gracious to me, O God," he pleaded, "according to Thy lovingkindness; according to the greatness of Thy compassion blot out my transgressions." He confessed, "Against Thee, Thee only, I have sinned, and done what is evil in Thy sight, so that Thou art justified when Thou dost speak, and blameless when Thou dost judge." David knew that only God could purify and wash away his sins and blot out all his iniquities. Only God could create in him a pure heart and deliver him from guilt and from the sin that produced it (Ps. 51:1-14).

The person of genuine faith is **blessed,** David proclaims, because by God's gracious provision his **lawless deeds have been forgiven,** because his many particular **sins have been covered,** and because the basic **sin** and depravity of his fallen nature **the Lord will not take into account.**

Abraham was justified only by faith, David was justified only by faith, and every believer before and after them has been justified only by faith. A sinner's faith is graciously accepted by God and counted for him as righteousness for Christ's sake.

The story is told of a poor farmer who had saved his money for years in order to buy an ox to pull his plow. When he thought he had enough saved, he traveled a great distance to the nearest town to shop for an ox. He soon discovered, however, that the paper money he had been saving had been replaced by a new currency and that the date for exchange from the old to the new had long since passed. Because he was illiterate, the man asked a neighbor school boy to write a letter to the president of their country, explaining his dire situation and asking for an exemption. The president was touched by the letter and wrote back to the farmer: "The law must be followed, because the deadline for exchanging bills has already passed. The government can no longer change your bills for the new ones. Even the president is not exempt from this rule. However," the president continued, "because I believe that you really worked hard to save this money, I am changing your money for new money from my own personal funds so that you will be able to buy your ox."

Before God, every person's good works are as worthless as that farmer's outdated money. But God Himself, in the Person of His Son, has paid the debt. And when a confessed sinner casts himself on God's mercy and accepts in faith the Lord's atoning work in his behalf, he can stand forgiven and divinely righteous before Him.

With the following touching lines from his hymn "It Is Finished," James Proctor captured the essence of justification by faith apart from works:

> Nothing, either great or small —
>   Nothing, sinner, no;
> Jesus did it, did it all,
>   Long, long ago.
>
> When He, from His lofty throne,
>   Stooped to do and die,
> Everything was fully done:
>   Hearken to His cry!
>
> Weary, working, burdened one,
>   Wherefore toil you so?
> Cease your doing; all was done
>   Long, long ago.
>
> 'Till to Jesus' work you cling
>   By a simple faith,
> "Doing" is a deadly thing —
>   "Doing" ends in death.

Cast your deadly "doing" down
  Down at Jesus' feet;
Stand in Him, in Him alone,
  Gloriously complete.

"It is finished!" yes indeed,
  Finished every jot;
Sinner, this is all you need,
  Tell me, is it not?

(Copyright 1922. Hope Publishing Co., owner; in *Choice Hymns of the Faith*
[Fort Dodge, Iowa: Walterick, 1944], #128.)

Abraham— Justified by Grace

Is this blessing then upon the circumcised, or upon the uncircumcised also? For we say, "Faith was reckoned to Abraham as righteousness." How then was it reckoned? While he was circumcised, or uncircumcised? Not while circumcised, but while uncircumcised; and he received the sign of circumcision, a seal of the righteousness of the faith which he had while uncircumcised, that he might be the father of all who believe without being circumcised, that righteousness might be reckoned to them, and the father of circumcision to those who not only are of the circumcision, but who also follow in the steps of the faith of our father Abraham which he had while uncircumcised. For the promise to Abraham or to his descendants that he would be heir of the world was not through the Law, but through the righteousness of faith. For if those who are of the Law are heirs, faith is made void and the promise is nullified; for the Law brings about wrath, but where there is no law, neither is there violation. For this reason it is by faith, that it might be in accordance with grace, in order that the promise may be certain to all the descendants, not only to those who are of the Law, but also to those who are of the faith of Abraham, who is the father of us all, (as it is written, "A father of

many nations have I made you") in the sight of Him whom he believed, even God, who gives life to the dead and calls into being that which does not exist. (4:9-17)

It is a terribly sad and oppressing experience to visit Catholic holy sites such as the Shrine of Guadalupe in Mexico. The shrine is built over the place where Mary supposedly appeared on one occasion. In the hope of her interceding for them with her Son, Jesus Christ, every year myriads of pilgrims crawl on their hands and knees for a quarter of a mile or so to the shrine. They then enter and light candles, one for each friend or relative for whom they seek to reduce the stay in purgatory.

Some years ago a missionary to India visited my office and showed me a recent copy of the major English-language Indian news magazine. The feature story was on a great Hindu religious festival called Maha Kumbh Mela, which is celebrated every twelve years at the confluence of the Ganga (Ganges) and Yamuna rivers, called the fabled waters of the Sangam. It is claimed to be the world's largest single religious event.

Disregarding the difficult journey, the great expense, and the chilling waters, multitudes of the faithful are drawn to the celebration. Caste and economic class are temporarily set aside. The festival is led by a group of stark naked holy men who lead a procession of millions of pilgrims down to the water. Fakirs sit on beds of nails and walk over broken glass and lie down on hot coals. A common sight is to see worshipers taking long knives and piercing their tongues in order to sentence themselves to eternal silence as a way to appease their myriad gods. Some worshipers will stare at the sun until they are blinded. Others intentionally cause their limbs to atrophy in gestures of worship. One man had held his arm upright for eight years. Although his arm muscles had long since atrophied, his uncut fingernails had continued to grow and descended some two and a half feet below his hands.

One Hindu holy book declares, "Those who bathe at the conflux of the black and white river, the Ganga and the Yamuna, go to heaven." Another sacred writing says that "the pilgrim who bathes at this place wins absolution for his whole family, and even if he has perpetrated a hundred crimes, he is redeemed the moment he touches the Ganga, whose waters wash away his sins."

At this festival the waterfront is lined with countless shaving booths, in which the devoted strip themselves bare and have every hair on their bodies shaved off, including their eyebrows and eyelashes. Every shaved hair is collected and all the hair is then thrown into the filthy water. Hindu writings assure pilgrims that "for every hair thus thrown in, you are promised a million years residence in heaven."

The article closed with the comment: "Millions who come with spiritual hunger depart with peace in their hearts and renewed faith."

What a hellish, damning deception of Satan! But it perfectly illustrates the works-centered systems of religion that men create under Satan's inspiration, all of which seek to convince people that they can be made right with God and guaranteed a place in heaven by performing certain rites and ceremonies. Some religions are much more sophisticated and humanly attractive than others, but all share the common false belief in works righteousness in some form or the other. The natural man instinctively believes that somehow he can make himself right with God by his own efforts.

Continuing his assault against works righteousness and establishing that Abraham, the supreme example of a godly man, was saved by faith rather than by works (Rom. 4:1-8), Paul next establishes that Abraham was saved through God's grace and not by being circumcised or by keeping the law. His argument was that if Abraham, the greatest man in the old dispensation, was saved through faith by God's grace, then every other person must be justified on the same basis. And, contrarily, if Abraham could not be justified by being circumcised or by keeping the law, then neither could any another person.

In Romans 4:9-17 Paul demonstrates three closely related truths: Abraham's justifying faith did not come by his circumcision (vv. 9-12); it did not come by his keeping the law (vv. 13-15); but rather it came solely by God's grace (vv. 16-17).

ABRAHAM WAS NOT JUSTIFIED BY CIRCUMCISION

Is this blessing then upon the circumcised, or upon the uncircumcised also? For we say, "Faith was reckoned to Abraham as righteousness." How then was it reckoned? While he was circumcised, or uncircumcised? Not while circumcised, but while uncircumcised; and he received the sign of circumcision, a seal of the righteousness of the faith which he had while uncircumcised, that he might be the father of all who believe without being circumcised, that righteousness might be reckoned to them, and the father of circumcision to those who not only are of the circumcision, but who also follow in the steps of the faith of our father Abraham which he had while uncircumcised. (4:9-12)

Paul anticipated the question that Jews would be asking at this point in his argument: "If Abraham was justified by his faith alone, why did God demand circumcision of Abraham and all his descendants?"

Most Jews in New Testament times were thoroughly convinced that circumcision was not only the unique mark that set them apart from all other men as God's chosen people but was also the means by which they became acceptable to God.

The Jewish apocryphal *Book of Jubilees* declares:

> This law is for all generations for ever, and there is no circumcision of the time, and no passing over one day out of the eight days; for it is an eternal ordinance, ordained and written on the heavenly tables. And every one that is born, the flesh of whose foreskin is not circumcised on the eighth day, belongs not to the children of the covenant which the Lord made with Abraham, for he belongs to the children of destruction; nor is there moreover any sign on him that he is the Lord's but (he is destined) to be destroyed and slain from the earth. (15:25ff.)

Many Jews believed that salvation was based on their obedience to God in being circumcised, and that, therefore, their eternal security rested in that rite. In his commentary on the *Book of Moses,* Rabbi Menachem wrote, "Our Rabbins [rabbis] have said that no circumcised man will ever see hell" (fol. 43, col. 3). Circumcision was considered such a mark of God's favor that it was taught that if a Jew had practiced idolatry his circumcision must first be removed before he could go down to hell. Since it is humanly impossible to remove circumcision, presumably that would be accomplished by a direct act of God.

The *Jalkut Rubem* taught that "Circumcision saves from hell" (num. 1), and the Midrash Millim that "God swore to Abraham that no one who was circumcised should be sent to hell" (fol. 7, col. 2). The book *Akedath Jizehak* taught that "Abraham sits before the gate of hell, and does not allow that any circumcised Israelite should enter there" (fol. 54, col. 2).

Such beliefs were so strong in Judaism that many of them were carried over into Christianity by Jewish converts in the early church. Circumcision and following the law of Moses became such issues that a special council of the apostles and elders was called in Jerusalem to settle the matter. The unanimous decision, expressed in a letter sent to all the churches, was that obedience to Mosaic ritual, including circumcision, was not necessary for salvation (see Acts 15:19-29).

Paul had come out of a strongly legalistic Jewish background, being "circumcised the eighth day, . . . a Hebrew of Hebrews; as to the Law, a Pharisee" (Phil. 3:5). Yet the Holy Spirit had revealed to him, and the Jerusalem council had acknowledged, that neither circumcision nor any other ceremony or human act, no matter how divinely ordained, could bring salvation. Circumcision had never saved a Jew and it could never save a Gentile (Rom. 2:25-29). Paul therefore warned his fellow Christians, especially Jewish believers, to "beware of the dogs, beware of the evil workers, beware of the false circumcision; for we are the true circumcision, who worship in the Spirit of God and glory in Christ Jesus and put no confidence in the flesh" (Phil. 3:2-3). He gave a similar warning to believers in Galatia:

> It was for freedom that Christ set us free; therefore keep standing firm and do not be subject again to a yoke of slavery. Behold I, Paul, say to you that if you receive circumcision, Christ will be of no benefit to you. And I testify again to every man who receives circumcision, that he is under obligation to keep the whole Law. You have been severed from Christ, you who are seeking to be justified by law; you have fallen from grace. (Gal. 5:1-4)

A person who trusts in circumcision, or in any other ceremony or work, nullifies the work of Christ on his behalf. He places himself under the law, and a person under the law must obey it with absolute perfection, which is humanly impossible. "For in Christ Jesus neither circumcision nor uncircumcision means anything, but faith working through love" (Gal. 5:6).

In the region of Phrygia, which bordered Galatia, the dominant pagan religion involved the worship of Cybele. The Cybelene priests normally castrated themselves as an act of sacrificial devotion, and that is perhaps the mutilation to which Paul refers in Galatians 5:12. If so, he was suggesting, in effect, that if the Judaizers thought the act of circumcision was such a religiously meritorious act, why did they not continue to the extreme self-mutilation of the Cybelene priests?

The Judaizers—those who claimed that a Christian, Gentile as well as Jew, had to keep the law of Moses in order to be saved (see Acts 15:5)—were such a persistent and powerful threat to the Galatian churches that in his closing words to them Paul reiterated his previous warnings. "Those who desire to make a good showing in the flesh try to compel you to be circumcised, simply that they may not be persecuted for the cross of Christ" (Gal. 6:12). In other words, even many of the Judaizers were hypocrites about circumcision, using it as a means of escaping persecution from fellow Jews.

Genesis 17:10-14 makes clear that the act of circumcision was a God-given mark of His covenant with Abraham and his descendants, the Jews. It was on the basis of that passage that the rabbis taught, and most Jews believed, that obedience to that rite was the means of pleasing God and becoming right with Him. But Paul uses that very passage to demonstrate that, to the contrary, Abraham was *not* made righteous before God by his circumcision but that when he was given the command of circumcision he had *already* been declared righteous.

Paul begins by asking, **Is this blessing then upon the circumcised, or upon the uncircumcised also? For we say, "Faith was**

reckoned to Abraham as righteousness." How then was it reckoned? While he was circumcised, or uncircumcised?

The relevance of this basic truth for our own day is great. Although few people, even Jews, now believe that circumcision brings salvation, countless millions firmly trust in some other form of religious ceremony or activity to make them right with God.

Among those claiming the name of Christ, the Roman Catholic church is by far the greatest offender. Throughout its history it has taught salvation by human works, made effective through the mediation of the Catholic priesthood.

In his book *Fundamentals of Catholic Dogma* (St. Louis: B. Herder, 1962), Dr. Ludwig Ott explains the cardinal teachings of Roman Catholicism in regard to salvation and spiritual blessing.

Ott defines a sacrament by the Roman Catechism (II I,8) as "a thing perceptible to the senses, which on the ground of Divine institution possesses the power of effecting and signifying sanctity and righteousness" (p. 326). He goes on to say that the sacraments confer grace immediately without the mediation of a person's faith (p. 326) and that the sacraments confer sanctifying grace on the receivers (p. 332). Since sacramental rites confer regeneration, forgiveness, the Holy Spirit, and eternal life, "for the dispensing of this grace it is necessary that the minister accomplish the Sacramental Sign in the proper manner" (p. 343). Roman Catholicism maintains that neither orthodox belief nor moral worthiness on the part of the recipient is necessary for the validity of a sacrament (p. 345).

In the mid-sixteenth century the Council of Trent issued a statement that declared, "If anyone denies that by the grace of our Lord Jesus Christ which is conferred in Baptism, the guilt of original sin is remitted; or even asserts that the whole of that which has the true and proper nature of sin is not taken away . . . let him be anathema" (p. 354).

Quoting from the apocryphal *Letter of Barnabas,* Ott reports that Catholics believe "we descend into the water [of baptism] full of sins and filth and we arise from it bearing fruit as we have in our hearts the fear of God, and our spirit hope in Jesus" (p. 355). Catholics teach that according to Scripture baptism has the power both of eradicating sin and effecting inner sanctification. "Baptism effects the forgiveness of all punishment of sin, both of the eternal and the temporal" (p. 355), and that baptism is "necessary for all men, without exception, for salvation" (p. 356).

Roman Catholicism holds that the sacrament of confirmation imparts the Holy Spirit to a person and increases sanctifying grace (p. 365). The sacrament of the Eucharist (the mass) unites the recipient with Christ (p. 390). As spiritual food, the mass "preserves and increases the supernatural life of the soul" (p. 395). Consequently, if a faithful Catholic in any part of the world is asked if he has received Christ, he will likely answer that he received Him at the last mass, and at every other mass he has attended.

The sacraments of penance, holy orders, marriage, and extreme unction also are claimed to impart, in and of themselves, other spiritual benefits of divine grace.

Some Protestant groups hold similar doctrines, believing, for example, that baptism places a person into the New Covenant, apart from any knowledge or faith on his own part. Consequently, the baptism of an infant is as valid as the baptism of a mature, professing adult.

But all such doctrines are forms of magic, in which neither the recipient nor the source of the desired result needs to be consciously involved. The result is conferred solely on the basis of the appropriate words being spoken or actions being performed. Even God is not involved directly in the efficacy of the sacraments. They operate not only without the recipients having faith but also without God directly imparting His grace. The power is in the formula of the rite.

That is exactly the kind of power the Jews of Paul's day attached to circumcision. And because they believed that what was true for Abraham in regard to justification was true of every person, especially every Jew, Paul continues to use that patriarch as his model. Answering his own question about the time of Abraham's being declared righteous, the apostle declares that it was **not while circumcised, but while uncircumcised.**

The obvious chronology of Genesis proves it. When Abraham was circumcised, Ishmael was thirteen years old and Abraham was ninety-nine (see Gen. 17:23-25). But when Abraham was declared righteous by God (15:6), Ishmael had not yet been born or even conceived (16:2-4). When Ishmael was born, Abraham was eighty-six (see 16:16). Therefore Abraham was declared righteous by God at least fourteen years before he was circumcised.

Abraham was in God's covenant and under His grace long before he was circumcised, whereas Ishmael, although circumcised, was never in the covenant. Circumcision *became* a mark of the covenant relationship between God and His people, but the covenant was not established on the basis of circumcision. When Abraham was first given the covenant promise, he was only seventy-five (Gen. 12:1-4). Circumcision came not only at least fourteen years after Abraham was declared righteous but also twenty-four years after he first entered into a covenant relationship with God. In addition to that, because there were no Jews at that time, when Abraham was declared righteous he was, as it were, an uncircumcised Gentile.

The natural question to be asked, therefore, would be, "Why circumcision? Why did God make that rite a binding law on all of Abraham's descendants?" First of all, Paul says, circumcision was a sign.

Abraham **received the sign of circumcision.** Circumcision was the physical, racial mark of identity for His people. Even under the New Covenant, Paul had no objection to a Jew being circumcised, as long as the act was seen in this light. In fact Paul personally circumcised Timothy, who was only half Jewish, in order that Timothy might have better opportunity to witness to Jews near his home area who knew him (Acts 16:3).

Circumcision was also a mark of God's covenant, setting Abraham's descendants apart as uniquely His chosen people, the Hebrews, or Jews as they became known during the Babylonian Exile. During the wilderness wanderings in Sinai, circumcision was not performed by that disobedient generation, whom God allowed to die out before they could enter the Promised Land. But when God readied His people to enter the land, the mark of circumcision was reinstituted by Joshua under direct command from God (Josh. 5:2).

Second, circumcision was **a seal of the righteousness of the faith which he,** that is, Abraham, **had while uncircumcised.** In other words, every time circumcision was performed God's people were to be reminded of God's **righteousness** that Abraham had, and all other believers have, through **faith,** completely apart from circumcision.

Although they convey similar ideas, a sign points to something, whereas a seal guarantees it. When an official seal was stamped on a letter or decree, for instance, its authenticity was guaranteed. In that sense, circumcision was the authentication that God's covenant promises would be fulfilled. It pointed to the fact that God wanted to circumcise, that is, place His authenticating seal upon, His people's hearts, not simply their bodies.

That was always God's intent, and the Jews should have known it long before Paul pointed it out in his Roman letter. Moses had declared, "Moreover the Lord your God will circumcise your heart and the heart of your descendants, to love the Lord your God with all your heart and with all your soul, in order that you may live" (Deut. 30:6). God had always wanted first of all to cut away the sin that covered the heart. "For thus says the Lord to the men of Judah and to Jerusalem," Jeremiah wrote, "Break up your fallow ground, and do not sow among thorns. Circumcise yourselves to the Lord and remove the foreskins of your heart, men of Judah and inhabitants of Jerusalem, lest My wrath go forth like fire and burn with none to quench it, because of the evil of your deeds" (Jer. 4:3-4). Through that same prophet the Lord declared,

> "Let him who boasts boast of this, that he understands and knows Me, that I am the Lord who exercises lovingkindness, justice, and righteousness on earth; for I delight in these things," declares the Lord. "Behold, the days are

coming," declares the Lord, "that I will punish all who are circumcised and yet uncircumcised—Egypt, and Judah, and Edom, and the sons of Ammon, and Moab, and all those inhabiting the desert who clip the hair on their temples; for all the nations are uncircumcised, and all the house of Israel are uncircumcised of heart" (Jer. 9:24-26).

Every male child of Israel was a testimony that men's hearts need spiritual circumcision, or cleansing.

In a similar way, baptism symbolizes a believer's death and resurrection with Christ. Communion symbolizes His redemptive act on our behalf, which we are to commemorate until He comes again. Neither rite has any merit in itself, and the elements of water, bread, and wine certainly have no merit or power in themselves. Both baptism and communion are outward demonstrations and reminders of the inner reality of salvation through Jesus Christ.

As Paul had already made clear in this epistle, "For he is not a Jew who is one outwardly; neither is circumcision that which is outward in the flesh. But he is a Jew who is one inwardly; and circumcision is that which is of the heart, by the Spirit, not by the letter; and his praise is not from men, but from God" (Rom. 2:28-29).

Contrary to the teaching in some churches today, infant baptism does not correspond to the circumcision of Jewish male infants. Even if it did, however, baptism would no more provide salvation than did circumcision.

The Passover meal, which has been celebrated by Jews for some three and one-half millennia, has never been considered a means of deliverance but only the symbol and reminder of it. For the Jew, Passover is a collective symbol of deliverance and circumcision is an individual symbol of justification. For the Christian, communion is the collective, corporate symbol of our relationship to Christ; baptism is the individual symbol of it.

Abraham received circumcision *after* he was reckoned righteous in order **that he might be the father of all who believe without being circumcised, that righteousness might be reckoned to them, and the father of circumcision to those who not only are of the circumcision, but who also follow in the steps of the faith of our father Abraham which he had while uncircumcised.**

Racially, Abraham is the father of all Jews; spiritually, he is the father of both believing Gentiles, **who believe without being circumcised,** and of believing Jews, **who . . . are of the circumcision.** Both groups of believers are reckoned righteous because of their **faith** in God through Jesus Christ, and they **also follow in the steps of the faith of our father Abraham which he had while uncircumcised.**

253

ABRAHAM WAS NOT JUSTIFIED BY THE LAW

For the promise to Abraham or to his descendants that he would be heir of the world was not through the Law, but through the righteousness of faith. For if those who are of the Law are heirs, faith is made void and the promise is nullified; for the Law brings about wrath, but where there is not law, neither is there violation. (4:13-15)

Paul's second point in this passage is that Abraham not only was not justified by the rite of circumcision but also was justified by keeping the Mosaic law. Again the chronology of the Jewish Scriptures proves his point. As every Jew well knew, the law was not revealed to Moses until more than five hundred years after Abraham lived, and that patriarch obviously had no way of knowing what the law required.

Man has never been able to come to God by means of an outward ceremony or standard of conduct. When Abraham was declared right with God, he was neither circumcised nor in possession of the Mosaic law. Circumcision had not yet been required by God and the law had not yet been revealed by God. Therefore, **the promise to Abraham or to his descendants that he would be heir of the world was not through the Law, but through the righteousness of faith.**

The promise to Abraham was embodied in God's covenant with Abraham, in which the patriarch was told that **his descendants** would be heirs **of the world** (Gen. 12:3; 15:5; 18:18; 22:18). In analyzing God's promise to Abraham, four significant factors emerge.

First, the **promise** involved *a land* (see Gen. 15:18-21) in which Abraham would live but that would not be possessed until some five centuries later, when Joshua led the Israelites in their conquest of Canaan.

Second, the **promise** also involved *a people,* who would be so numerous that they could not be numbered, like the dust of the earth and the stars in the sky (Gen. 13:16; 15:5). Eventually, Abraham would become the "father of many nations" (Gen. 17:5; cf. Rom. 4:17).

Third, the **promise** involved *a blessing* of the entire world through Abraham's descendants (Gen. 12:3).

Fourth, the **promise** would be fulfilled in the giving of *a Redeemer,* who would be a descendant of Abraham through whom the whole world would be blessed by the provision of salvation. That promise to Abraham was, in essence, a preaching to him of the gospel (Gal. 3:8). Abraham believed that gospel, and even when Isaac, the sole divinely-promised heir, was about to be offered as a sacrifice, Abraham trusted that somehow God would "provide for Himself the lamb for the burnt offering" (Gen. 22:8). Through the writer of Hebrews, the Lord gives a beautiful revelation of the extent of Abraham's understanding and faith. "By faith Abraham, when he was tested, offered up Isaac; and he who had received the promises was offering up his only begotten son; it was he to whom it was said, 'In Isaac your descendants shall be called.' He considered that God is able to raise men even from the dead; from which he also received him back as a type" (Heb. 11:17-19).

Jesus told the unbelieving Jewish religious leaders, "Your father Abraham rejoiced to see My day, and he saw it and was glad" (John 8:56). In a way that is not explained, Abraham foresaw the coming of the Messiah, who would be born as one of his promised descendants. It was through that descended Messiah, the Christ, that Abraham would bless the entire world and be **heir of the world.** Referring to the Hebrew text of Genesis 22:17 and 18, Paul gives God's exegesis of His own Word, declaring that "the promises were spoken to Abraham and to his seed. He does not say, 'And to seeds,' as referring to many, but rather to one, 'And to your seed,' that is Christ" (Gal. 3:16). Later in that same chapter the apostle says of *all* believers, Gentile as well as Jew, "If you belong to Christ, then you are Abraham's offspring, heirs according to promise" (v. 29). In Him they become part of that single spiritual seed, "that is, Christ."

All believers are one in Jesus Christ, "one spirit with Him" (1 Cor. 6:17). Because they are identified with God's only begotten Son, believers become themselves children of God. "The Spirit Himself bears witness with our spirit, that we are children of God," Paul declares later in the book of Romans, "and if children, heirs also, heirs of God and fellow heirs with Christ, if indeed we suffer with Him in order that we may also be glorified with Him" (Rom. 8:16-17).

It is not human descent from Abraham but spiritual descent from him, by following his example of faith, that makes a believer an heir both with Abraham and with Christ. As Paul reminded the Corinthian believers, most of whom doubtless were Gentiles, human descent means nothing as far as a person's standing before God is concerned. "So then let no one boast in men. For all things belong to you, whether Paul or Apollos or Cephas or the world or life or death or things present or things to come; all things belong to you, and you belong to Christ; and Christ belongs to God" (1 Cor. 3:21-23). On the other hand, Jesus told the unbelieving Jewish leaders that, although they physically descended from Abraham, spiritually they were sons of their "father the devil" (John 8:44).

Justification has never been through the Law, just as it has never been through circumcision. The Greek of that phrase is anarthrous, that is, it has no definite article, the being inserted by translators. Paul therefore was speaking not only of the Mosaic law but of God's Law in its broadest sense, referring to all of God's commandments and standards. He was also speaking of the general principle of human lawkeeping, in which many Jews trusted for their salvation.

As Paul clarifies later in the epistle, God's law "is holy, and the commandment is holy and righteous and good" (Rom. 7:12; cf. Gal. 3:21). But the law was never given as a means of salvation, even for Jews. "For as many as are of the works of the Law," that is, seek to justify themselves on the basis of keeping the law, "are under a curse; for it is written, 'Cursed is everyone who does not abide by all things written in the book of the law, to perform them'" (Gal. 3:10). The person who trusts in his ability to save himself by lawkeeping is cursed because of the impossibility of perfectly keeping God's law. Paul counted his own previous efforts at lawkeeping as spiritual debits, as loss and rubbish (Phil. 3:7-8).

The purpose of **the Law** was to reveal God's perfect standards of righteousness and to show men that they are unable in their own power to live up to those standards. Awareness of that inability should drive men to God in faith. The law was given as a "tutor to lead us to Christ, that we may be justified by faith" (Gal. 3:24).

God has never recognized any righteousness but **the righteousness of faith** in Him, and that righteousness, like His imparted and imputed righteousness, comes by means of His own gracious provision. Jesus Christ not only is the object of our faith but is also its "author and perfecter" (Heb. 12:2).

Abraham was justified because he believed God's promise, and, as Paul has already declared in this epistle, that belief "was reckoned to him as righteousness" (Rom. 4:3; cf. Gen. 15:6). In exactly the same way, when a person believes God's promise of salvation through trust in His Son Jesus Christ, that act of faith is reckoned to him as Christ's own righteousness (1 Cor. 1:30; 2 Cor. 5:21).

Abraham's trust was not in what he possessed but in what he was promised.

> By faith Abraham, when he was called, obeyed by going out to a place which he was to receive for an inheritance; and he went out, not knowing where he was going. By faith he lived as an alien in the land of promise, as in a foreign land, dwelling in tents with Isaac and Jacob, fellow heirs of the same promise; for he was looking for the city which has foundations, whose architect and builder is God. (Heb. 11:8-10)

Abraham's **faith** was exemplified in his willingness to go to a land he had never seen, which was a promised inheritance he would never possess. Abraham journeyed to that land and was satisfied to live there as an alien, because his ultimate hope was in the inheritance of "the city which has foundations, whose architect and builder is God."

Paul continues to explain, **For if those who are of the Law are**

heirs, faith is made void and the promise is nullified. If men were able to keep God's **Law** perfectly they would indeed be **heirs** of God. That, of course, is impossible, but if it were true it would make **faith . . . void** and would make God's **promise . . . nullified.**

Faith is able to receive anything God promises. If, on the other hand, God's promise is only to be received through obedience to a law which neither Abraham nor his children could keep, then faith is cancelled. In other words, to predicate a promise on an impossible condition is to nullify the promise.

The law cannot save because **the Law brings about wrath.** The more a person seeks to justify himself by keeping God's **Law,** the more he proves his inability to do so because of his sinfulness and the more judgment and **wrath** he brings upon himself. Just as surely as the law reveals God's righteousness so it also exposes man's sinfulness.

As Paul comments later in Romans,

> What shall we say then? Is the Law sin? May it never be! On the contrary, I would not have come to know sin except through the Law; for I would not have known about coveting if the Law had not said, "You shall not covet." But sin, taking opportunity through the commandment, produced in me coveting of every kind; for apart from the Law sin is dead. And I was once alive apart from the Law; but when the commandment came, sin became alive, and I died; and this commandment, which was to result in life, proved to result in death for me; for sin, taking opportunity through the commandment, deceived me, and through it killed me. (Rom. 7:7-11)

"Why the law then?" Paul rhetorically asked the Galatian believers. "It was added," he explains, "because of transgressions, having been ordained through angels by the agency of a mediator, until the seed should come to whom the promise had been made" (Gal. 3:19). As already noted, the law was not given to save us but to be "our tutor to lead us to Christ, that we may be justified by faith" (Gal. 3:24).

ABRAHAM WAS JUSTIFIED BY GOD'S GRACE

For this reason it is by faith, that it might be in accordance with grace, in order that the promise may be certain to all the descendants, not only to those who are of the Law, but also to those who are of the faith of Abraham, who is the father of us all, (as it is written, "A father of many nations have I made you") in the sight of Him whom he believed, even God, who gives life to the dead and calls into being that which does not exist. (4:16-17)

The crux of this passage is verse 16. God reckons the believer's **faith** as righteousness in order that salvation **might be in accordance with grace**. Were it not for God's sovereign **grace** providing a way of salvation, even a person's faith could not save him. That is why **faith** is not simply another form of human works, as some theologians throughout the centuries have maintained. The power of salvation, or justification, is in God's **grace**, not in man's **faith.** Abraham's faith was not *in itself* righteousness but was *reckoned* to him as righteousness on the basis of the One who would Himself graciously provide for believers, including Abraham, the righteousness they could never attain by themselves.

Grace is the divine power that brings justification **in order that the promise may be certain to all the descendants**. That Paul is here speaking of spiritual, not physical, **descendants,** is made clear by his going on to say, **not only to those who are of the Law,** that is, Jews, **but also to those who are of the faith of Abraham, who is the father of us all.**

As noted above, when Abraham was called in Ur of the Chaldeans, he was an idolatrous pagan. Before God's covenant with Abraham, there were no Jews and therefore no Gentiles, strictly speaking. But Paul's point here is that God reckoned Abraham's faith as righteousness before any such distinctions were made. It was for that reason that Abraham's faith was a universal faith that applies to all mankind, not merely to Jews, those **who are of the Law.** And it was for that reason that **Abraham** became **the father of us all,** that is, of all who trust in Jesus Christ, regardless of racial or religious heritage. **Abraham** was the spiritual prototype of every genuine believer. He was a pagan, idolatrous, ungodly sinner who trusted not in his own efforts but in God's gracious promise.

As always, Paul's defense is scriptural. **As it is written,** refers to Genesis 17:5, which Paul here renders as, **"A father of many nations have I made you."** The promise to Abraham was fulfilled **in the sight of Him whom he believed, even God.** Lest there be any doubt about what **God** he was speaking about, Paul gives two qualifications. First, this God is the one **who gives life to the dead.** Abraham had experienced first-hand that power of God. He was miraculously given Isaac, the son of promise, long after Sarah had passed her child-bearing years and after Abraham was "as good as dead" as far as his fathering a child was concerned (Heb. 11:11-12).

Second, this God is the one who **calls into being that which does not exist.** Paul here obviously refers to God's power as expressed through creation, in which "what is seen was not made out of things which are visible" (Heb. 11:3). He is the one true **God** who calls people, places, and events into existence solely by His divine and sovereign determination.

Salvation by Divine Power, Not by Human Effort

In hope against hope he believed, in order that he might become a father of many nations, according to that which had been spoken, "So shall your descendants be." And without becoming weak in faith he contemplated his own body, now as good as dead since he was about a hundred years old, and the deadness of Sarah's womb; yet, with respect to the promise of God, he did not waver in unbelief, but grew strong in faith, giving glory to God, and being fully assured that what He had promised, He was able also to perform. Therefore also it was reckoned to him as righteousness. Now not for his sake only was it written, that it was reckoned to him, but for our sake also, to whom it will be reckoned, as those who believe in Him who raised Jesus our Lord from the dead, He who was delivered up because of our transgressions, and was raised because of our justification. (4:18-25)

This passage concludes Paul's illustration of Abraham as the supreme Old Testament example of saving faith. It makes clear the fact that although man's faith and God's grace are both involved in salvation, they are in no way equal components. Even man's faith is included with the provision of God's gracious salvation, as the apostle declares to the

Ephesians: "For by grace you have been saved through faith; and that not of yourselves, it is the gift of God; not as a result of works, that no one should boast. For we are His workmanship" (Eph. 2:8-10a).

Abraham's original name was Abram (see Gen. 11:26ff.), which means "father of many." Yet when God called him while he was living in Ur of the Chaldeans (Gen. 11:28, 31; cf. Acts 7:2-4), the patriarch was childless. By the time he left Haran, after the death of his father, Terah, Abraham was seventy-five years old (Genesis 12:4) and still without children. Yet by faith he began the last part of his journey to the land God had promised.

In His initial call, God promised that He would make of Abram a great nation (Gen. 12:1-2). And when the promise was reiterated some years later, the Lord promised Abram that his descendants would be as innumerable as the stars in the heavens (15:5; cf. 22:17), although the patriarch and his wife Sarah were still childless. It was at that time that Abram "believed in the Lord; and He reckoned it to him as righteousness" (15:6). Yet it is evident from the preceding passages in Genesis that Abraham's response to God had previously been that of sincere, unconditional faith.

We do not know what Abram's thoughts were when he was originally called in Ur or when he first entered Canaan, the Promised Land. We do not know how God convinced Abram, an idolatrous pagan (see Josh. 24:2), that He was indeed the true and only God or how He persuaded Abram to place his trust in Him. But we do know that the same God who made the call prompted the faith to respond to it.

Abram's faith was truly astounding. For some forty years before it was fulfilled, Abram believed God's promise to give him an heir. For the century that he lived in Canaan (see Gen. 25:7), Abram owned none of it, except for the small parcel of ground he bought for a burial site for Sarah and himself (23:16-20). Abram trusted God to make him the father of a great nation and of a multitude of people, although there would not be a nation in the usual sense of that term until nearly 600 years later, when Joshua would lead the Israelites back into Canaan to possess it.

After Abram arrived in Canaan he was immediately faced with a number of severe tests of his faith. He encountered famine (Gen. 12:10), a potentially hostile pharaoh (12:14-20), a conflict with his nephew Lot (13:5-9), and apparently a struggle with fear (see 15:1). Yet through all that testing he remained faithful to the God who had called him.

In his commentary on Romans, Donald Grey Barnhouse writes insightfully of Abram:

> Now Abram was an Oriental. He was used to the palaver of the Orientals. Furthermore, he was strategically located athwart the roads of

the camel caravans that carried the commerce of the ancient world between Egypt and the North and East. He owned the wells, and his flocks and herds were great. The Scripture says that "Abram was very rich in cattle, in silver, and in gold" (Gen. 13:2). When the caravans of the rich merchants came into the land, either from the north or from the south, they stopped at Abram's wells. The servants of Abram took good care of the needs of the camels and the servants of the traders. Food was sold to the travellers. And in the evening time the merchants would have come to Abram's tent to pay their respects. The questions would have followed a set pattern. How old are you? Who are you? How long have you been here? When the trader had introduced himself, Abram would be forced to name himself: Abram, father of many.

It must have happened a hundred times, a thousand times, and each time more galling than the time before. "Oh, Father of many! Congratulations! And how many sons do you have?" And the answer was so humiliating to Abram: "None." And, many a time there must have been the half concealed snort of humor at the incongruity of the name and the fact that there were no children to back up such a name. Abram must have steeled himself for the question and the reply, and have hated the situation with great bitterness.

. . . Father of many—father of none. The possibilities were varied, and I believe that it is possible to detect in the psychology of the narrative the fact that there was much gossip about it. The servants who heard the jokes and who saw Abram's embarrassment repeated the details with embroidered variations. It was a world of cloth and goat skins, where all lived in tents, and where there was little privacy from the eyes and none in the realm of the ears. There must have been many conversations on the subject—who was sterile, Abram or Sarah? Was he really a full man? Oh, he was the patriarch; his word was law; he had the multitude of cattle and the many servants, but—he had no children, and his name was "father of many." (*God's Remedy: Romans 3:21–4:25* [Grand Rapids: Eerdmans, 1954], pp. 311-12)

Such pressure undoubtedly was a strong contribution to Sarah's suggestion that Abram have a son by her Egyptian maid, Hagar (Gen. 16:2). It is quite possible that the servants overheard that proposal and knew that in desperation Abram consented. When Hagar became pregnant, everyone knew that it was Sarah who was sterile. Sarah soon regretted her rash suggestion and became envious of Hagar and treated her with considerable cruelty.

When Hagar gave birth to Ishmael, Abram at last had an heir, but it was an heir of his own sinful contriving and human virility, not the divinely-promised and divinely-provided heir to whom only Sarah could give birth. Thirteen years later, when Abram was ninety-nine years old, the merciful Lord appeared to him again and repeated the promise of multiplying Abram's descendants. He also changed Abram's name saying,

No longer shall your name be called Abram, but your name shall be
Abraham; for I will make you the father of a multitude of nations. And I
will make you exceedingly fruitful, and I will make nations of you, and
kings shall come forth from you. And I will establish My covenant between
Me and you and your descendants after you throughout their generations
for an everlasting covenant, to be God to you and to your descendants after
you. And I will give to you and to your descendants after you, the land of
your sojournings, all the land of Canaan, for an everlasting possession; and
I will be their God. (Gen. 17:5-8)

But if Abram was embarrassed by his former name, he was even
more embarrassed by his new one. Because he could not perceive how
the promise could be fulfilled through a son by Sarah, who was now 90
years old and past the normal time of childbearing, Abraham asked the
Lord that Ishmael might become the promised heir (Gen. 17:18). But the
Lord replied, "No, but Sarah your wife shall bear you a son, and you shall
call his name Isaac; and I will establish My covenant with him for an
everlasting covenant for his descendants after him" (Gen. 17:19). God
now told Abraham explicitly that he would indeed bear a son by Sarah,
that the birth would occur one year later, and that the son's name was to
be Isaac (v. 21).

It is a profound lesson to learn that God's promises can only be
fulfilled by God's power, and human efforts to effect His will, no matter
how sincere or clever those efforts might be, are doomed to failure, and
bring God dishonor rather than glory. Human effort, even for the purpose
of keeping God's commandments or of fulfilling His promises, is futile
and is a form of works righteousness. In warning the Galatian believers
against the legalistic Judaizers (those teaching that Christians must conform
to the Mosaic law as well as believe in Jesus in order to be saved) Paul
said, "Tell me, you who want to be under law, do you not listen to the
law? For it is written that Abraham had two sons, one by the bondwoman
and one by the free woman. But the son by the bondwoman was born
according to the flesh, and the son by the free woman through the
promise" (Gal. 4:21-23).

Ishmael illustrates the product of legalistic human self-effort,
whereas Isaac illustrates the product of God's sovereign and gracious
provision. Paul reminded the Galatian believers that, because of their trust
in Jesus Christ, they were, "like Isaac, children of promise" (4:28). They
were God's children by the working of His divine grace, not by the
working of their own human efforts.

Just as God would not recognize Ishmael as the son of His promise
to Abraham because that son was naturally conceived, He will not
recognize as His spiritual children those who trust in their own goodness
and accomplishments.

After showing that salvation comes by faith not works (Rom. 4:1-8) and from grace not law (vv. 9-17), Paul concludes the chapter (vv. 18-25) by showing that faith also comes by divine power, not by human effort. In this passage the apostle points out three realities of saving faith: its analysis (vv. 18-21), its answer (v. 22), and its application (vv. 23-25).

THE ANALYSIS OF ABRAHAM'S FAITH

In hope against hope he believed, in order that he might become a father of many nations, according to that which had been spoken, "So shall your descendants be." And without becoming weak in faith he contemplated his own body, now as good as dead since he was about a hundred years old, and the deadness of Sarah's womb; yet, with respect to the promise of God, he did not waver in unbelief, but grew strong in faith, giving glory to God, and being fully assured that what He had promised, He was able also to perform. (4:18-21)

In this passage Paul lists seven key characteristics of Abraham's faith and of all faith that is God given, the only kind of faith that results in salvation.

First, the apostle declares of Abraham that **in hope against hope he believed.** The terms *hope* and *faith* are related, but they are not the same. **Hope,** in this case, is the desire for something that might be true or might happen, whereas faith is the firm confidence that it *is* true or *will* happen. The ancient patriarch had **hope** when, from the human vantage point, there was absolutely no basis or justification for **hope.** Yet despite the seeming impossibility hoped for, **he believed** it would happen as God said.

The object of Abraham's faith was God, and in particular His promise that **he,** that is, Abraham, **might become a father of many nations, according to that which had been spoken, "So shall your descendants be."** When the Lord had taken Abraham "outside and said, 'Now look toward the heavens, and count the stars, if you are able to count them,' and He said to him, 'So shall your descendants be,' then [Abraham] believed in the Lord; and He reckoned it to him as righteousness" (Gen. 15:5-6).

Second, Paul declares that Abraham believed God **without becoming weak in faith.** To become **weak in faith** is to allow doubt to cloud and partly undermine belief. Abraham had been trusting God for 25 years, acknowledging, as Paul had just intimated, that "God . . . gives life to the dead and calls into being that which does not exist" (Rom. 4:17). As far as we know, Abraham had witnessed no miracle of God. He had never seen God raise a person from the dead or call anything or anyone into being who did not already exist. Yet he firmly believed that the Lord was easily capable of doing such things. Commenting on that characteristic of Abraham's faith, the writer of Hebrews said, "By faith Abraham, when he was tested, offered up Isaac; and he who had received the promises was offering up his only begotten son; it was he to whom it was said, 'In Isaac your descendants shall be called.' He considered that God is able to raise men even from the dead; from which he also received him back as a type" (Heb. 11:17-19).

Third, Paul tells us that Abraham's faith prevented him from becoming discouraged by his own natural weakness. Because Abraham's faith in God was strong and unwavering, his own ignorance and weakness were no obstacles to his trust. He therefore did not falter when **he contemplated his own body, now as good as dead since he was about a hundred years old.** Abraham's natural procreative power was now gone, **as good as dead,** yet that physiological fact did not diminish his faith. Natural impotence was no problem to Abraham, because his faith was in the supernatural God who had created him in the first place.

Many generations before the time of Abraham, Noah had demonstrated similar unwavering faith in God. When the Lord commanded Noah to build an ark, he had never seen rain, because all the earth's necessary moisture came from mist and dew. Yet for 120 long years Noah faithfully continued to build the ark, for no other reason than that it was God's will. In obedience to God, he gathered the animals exactly according to the Lord's instruction and led them into the ark before it started to rain, a phenomenon unknown until God then sovereignly opened the floodgates of the heavens.

"By faith Noah being warned by God about things not yet seen, in reverence prepared an ark" (Heb. 11:7). Noah did not build the ark because he saw a need for it but solely because that was his divine commission. Not only did he build the ark because of his faith in the Lord, but while he built he was also a faithful "preacher of righteousness" (2 Pet. 2:5) to the unbelieving multitudes around him, who doubtless ridiculed him incessantly about his seemingly foolish and pointless construction project. That is the kind of undaunted faith that Noah's descendant Abraham had.

Fourth, Abraham did not doubt God's promise when the circumstances around him seemed to make its fulfillment impossible. When God repeated the specific promise that Isaac would be born to Abraham and Sarah the following year, both "Abraham and Sarah were old, advanced in age; Sarah was past childbearing" (Gen. 18:11-14; cf. 17:21). But **the deadness of Sarah's womb** was no more a hindrance to Abraham's faith than was the impotence of his own body.

Fifth, **with respect to the promise of God**, Abraham **did not**

waver in unbelief. He did not vacillate between faith and doubt as many believers frequently do. When from the human viewpoint things are going well, it is easy to trust God. But when things seem impossible, it is even easier to distrust Him. Sarah was a woman of faith, and "she considered Him faithful who had promised" (Heb. 11:11). But before her faith came to that point of unqualified trust, she had laughed at the promise she overheard the Lord making to her husband (Gen. 18:12).

It would seem from the Genesis narratives that Paul was mistaken about Abraham's unwavering faith. When "the word of the Lord came to Abram in a vision, saying, 'Do not fear, Abram, I am a shield to you; your reward shall be very great,'. . . Abram said, 'O Lord God, what wilt Thou give me, since I am childless, and the heir of my house is Eliezer of Damascus? . . . Since Thou hast given no offspring to me, one born in my house is my heir'" (Gen. 15:1-3). Abraham openly admitted before God that he could not understand how the divine promise of an heir, much less of a multitude of nations, could be fulfilled. The only heir he could see was his chief servant, Eliezer, who would have received Abraham's inheritance had no son been born to him by Sarah.

But struggling faith is not doubt, just as temptation to sin is not itself sin. The very fact that Abraham was trying to understand how God's promise could be fulfilled indicates he was *looking* for a way of fulfillment, although he could not yet *see* a way. Weaker faith might have simply succumbed to doubt. Sincere struggling with spiritual problems comes from strong, godly faith. Such faith refuses to doubt and trusts in God's promises, even when no way of fulfillment is humanly imaginable. God's testing of His children's faith is designed to strengthen their trust, and they should thank Him for it, hard as it seems to be at the time (see James 1:2-4). When Abraham was tested by God, he **grew strong in faith.**

John Calvin wisely observed that believers "are never so enlightened that there are no remains of ignorance, nor is the heart so established that there are no misgivings." A Christian who claims to understand all of God's truth and to envision the fulfillment of all His promises is not demonstrating great faith but great presumption. Godly faith is not full understanding but full trust, "the assurance of things hoped for, the conviction of things not seen" (Heb. 11:1).

Sixth, Paul says that Abraham's faith was characterized by his **giving glory to God.** Godly faith glorifies God; the One who gives faith receives all the credit. Conversely, any faith that does *not* glorify God is not of or from Him. Faith in God, because it affirms His trustworthy character, is the supreme way that men glorify Him, while without faith, any attempt to worship, praise, or honor Him is a worthless, self-righteous sham. John makes the sobering declaration that "the one who does not believe God has made Him a liar, because he has not believed in the witness that God has borne concerning His Son" (1 John 5:10).

When King Nebuchadnezzar ordered Shadrach, Meshach, and Abednego to worship the golden image under threat of death, they calmly replied, "O Nebuchadnezzar, we do not need to give you an answer concerning this. If it be so, our God whom we serve is able to deliver us from the furnace of blazing fire; and He will deliver us out of your hand, O king. But even if He does not, let it be known to you, O king, that we are not going to serve your gods or worship the golden image that you have set up" (Dan. 3:16-18). The overriding concern of those three young men was to honor, obey, and glorify God, just as their forefather Abraham had done.

As they sailed across the Mediterranean Sea on their way to Rome, Paul and his fellow travelers encountered a fierce storm that threatened to tear the ship apart. Even after throwing all the ship's cargo and tackle overboard, they continued to founder, and everyone but Paul gave up hope of survival. Luke reports that

> when they had gone a long time without food, then Paul stood up in their midst and said, "Men, you ought to have followed my advice and not to have set sail from Crete, and incurred this damage and loss. And yet now I urge you to keep up your courage, for there shall be no loss of life among you, but only of the ship. For this very night an angel of the God to whom I belong and whom I serve stood before me, saying, 'Do not be afraid, Paul; you must stand before Caesar; and behold, God has granted you all those who are sailing with you.' Therefore, keep up your courage, men, for I believe God, that it will turn out exactly as I have been told." (Acts 27:21-25)

Not even the most hazardous of circumstances could weaken Paul's trust in his heavenly Father, and it is through such trust that His children glorify and honor Him the most.

Seventh, Abraham was fully persuaded that God's promise was certain and His power sufficient, **being fully assured that what He had promised, He was able also to perform.** This statement sums up the fact that his faith in God was complete and unqualified.

THE ANSWER TO ABRAHAM'S FAITH

Therefore also it was reckoned to him as righteousness. (4:22)

The heart of this entire passage, in fact of the whole chapter, is that in response to Abraham's faith, God graciously **reckoned** it **to him as righteousness.** In his sinful flesh, Abraham was totally unable to meet God's standard of perfect **righteousness.** But the good news of salvation, "the gospel of God" (Rom. 1:1), is that the Lord will take the faith that He Himself has enabled a person to possess and count that faith as divine **righteousness** on the believing sinner's behalf.

It is not that faith merits salvation but that faith accepts salvation from God's gracious hand. Through that acceptance comes the **righteousness** that only God can impart.

THE APPLICATION OF ABRAHAM'S FAITH

Now not for his sake only was it written, that it was reckoned to him, but for our sake also, to whom it will be reckoned, as those who believe in Him who raised Jesus our Lord from the dead, He who was delivered up because of our transgressions, and was raised because of our justification. (4:23-25)

The marvelous thing about Abraham's faith being reckoned as righteousness is that the same divine principle applies to every person who trusts in God's Son. The Holy Spirit inspired that truth to be **written . . . for our sake also, to whom it will be reckoned** just as it was for Abraham.

No part of Scripture was given only for the time in which it was written. The psalmist declares, "For [God] established a testimony in Jacob, and appointed a law in Israel, which He commanded our fathers, that they should teach them to their children, that the generation to come might know, even the children yet to be born, that they may arise and tell them to their children, that they should put their confidence in God, and not forget the works of God, but keep His commandments" (Ps. 78:5-7). Paul expresses the same truth later in the book of Romans: "For whatever was written in earlier times was written for our instruction, that through perseverance and the encouragement of the Scriptures we might have hope" (Rom. 15:4).

The story of Abraham and of his faith is important to us today because men are now saved on exactly the same basis on which Abraham was saved—trust in God. Even the sacrificial work of Jesus was the provision for Abraham's sin by which God saved him. Men today have much greater divine revelation than Abraham had. During his lifetime, and for many centuries afterward, there was no written Word of God. Yet Jesus declared categorically to the disbelieving Jewish leaders that "Abraham rejoiced to see My day, and he saw it and was glad" (John 8:56).

From the human side, the key phrase in Romans 4:24 is **who believe in Him.** Faith is the necessary condition for salvation. As the eleventh chapter of Hebrews makes clear, the only persons who have ever been received by God are those who have received Him by faith.

If, despite his limited revelation, Abraham could anticipate the Savior and believe that God could raise the dead, how much more reason do men today have to believe that the Father did indeed raise **Jesus our Lord from the dead,** in order that those who believe "in Him should not perish, but have eternal life" (John 3:16)?

Jesus **was delivered up because of our transgression, and was raised because of our justification. Delivered up** was a judicial term, referring to the commitment of a criminal to his punishment. Jesus Christ **was delivered up** to serve the sentence of death that **our transgressions** deserve, and He **was raised up** to provide the **justification** before God that we could never attain in our own power or merit.

The great nineteenth-century theologian Charles Hodge wrote,

> With a dead Saviour, a Saviour over whom death had triumphed and held captive, our justification had been for ever impossible. As it was necessary that the high priest, under the old economy, should not only slay the victim at the altar, but carry the blood into the most holy place, and sprinkle it upon the mercy-seat; so it was necessary not only that our great High Priest should suffer in the outer court, but that he should pass into heaven to present his righteousness before God for our justification. Both, therefore, as the evidence of the acceptance of his satisfaction on our behalf, and as a necessary step to secure the application of the merits of his sacrifice, the resurrection of Christ was absolutely essential, even for our justification. (*Commentary on the Epistle to the Romans* [Grand Rapids: Eerdmans, 1983 reprint], p. 129)

Despite his claims of scientific objectivism, modern man has become enthralled by the supernatural and by the prospect of extraterrestrial beings. Eastern mysticism, in many forms and degrees, is sweeping the intellectually "enlightened" world as never before in history. Many men and women of great prominence would not think of making a major decision or taking an extended trip without consulting their horoscopes.

This demonstrates that it is not that modern, educated, sophisticated man is beyond belief in the supernatural or the miraculous. It is rather that, like unbelieving men of all ages, he inherently resists the supernatural and miraculous work of Jesus Christ. For *that* supernatural, miraculous work to be effective, a person must confess and renounce his **transgressions,** which is the supreme offense to man's depraved nature. But only by such confession and repentance, which always accompany true faith, can a person receive the **justification,** the reckoning of undeserved righteousness to his account, that the sacrifice of Christ makes possible.

The Security of Salvation

Therefore having been justified by faith, we have peace with God through our Lord Jesus Christ, through whom also we have obtained our introduction by faith into this grace in which we stand; and we exult in hope of the glory of God. And not only this, but we also exult in our tribulations, knowing that tribulation brings about perseverance; and perseverance, proven character; and proven character, hope; and hope does not disappoint, because the love of God has been poured out within our hearts through the Holy Spirit who was given to us. For while we were still helpless, at the right time Christ died for the ungodly. For one will hardly die for a righteous man; though perhaps for the good man someone would dare even to die. But God demonstrates His own love toward us, in that while we were yet sinners, Christ died for us. Much more then, having now been justified by His blood, we shall be saved from the wrath of God through Him. For if while we were enemies, we were reconciled to God through the death of His Son, much more, having been reconciled, we shall be saved by His life. And not only this, but we also exult in God through our Lord Jesus Christ, through whom we have now received the reconciliation. (Rom. 5:1-11)

One of Satan's primary tactics against believers is that of making them doubt that salvation is secure forever or that it is real in their personal case. Perhaps for that reason, Paul describes one of the key parts of a Christian's armor as "the helmet of salvation" (Eph. 6:17; cf. 1 Thess. 5:8), provided to surround and protect his mind against doubt and insecurity concerning his redemption. This is both objective and subjective. First, salvation can be shown by the objective testimony of Scripture to be eternally secure for all the saved.

The issue of eternal security, or "once saved, always saved," has been hotly debated throughout much of church history. Everyone agrees that the truth or falsehood of that doctrine is of immense importance. But it is also crucial to the believer to recognize the evidence that he actually has that real salvation. Once security is established as a fact of salvation, then assurance must be maintained in the heart of the Christian subjectively.

If, as some maintain, a person is saved by faith in Jesus Christ but can sin his way out of God's grace, Christians must live in continual uncertainty about their spiritual destiny on both counts. That which they received on the basis of God's work must be maintained on the basis of their own work; the divine righteousness they received from God as a gift must be maintained by the righteousness they themselves achieve. According to that doctrine, salvation is received by faith but maintained by works, given by God's power but maintained by man's power. It is therefore a form of works righteousness. It teaches that if a believer's life does not measure up to God's standards, his salvation is forfeited and he is again lost in his sin. One day he can be spiritually alive and the next be spiritually dead again. One day he can be a child of God and the next be back in Satan's family. Obviously, if there is no eternal security (objective), then there can be reason for fear from lacking assurance in the heart that one is saved (subjective).

In chapters 3 and 4 of Romans, Paul establishes unequivocally that salvation comes only on the basis of God's grace working through man's faith. Man's only part in becoming saved is to receive forgiveness and reconciliation freely in faith from God's gracious hand. The person who trusts in anything else, including obedience to God's own law, cannot be saved. In regard to that aspect of salvation, it should be noted, even most of those who deny security fully concur.

The apostle has established the fact that faith has *always* been the only way to salvation. Abraham, the physical progenitor of all Jews and their supreme example of a man right with God, did not accomplish that relationship through his good works but only through his faith. Quoting Genesis 15:6, Paul declares that "Abraham believed God, and it was reckoned to him as righteousness" (Rom. 4:3).

But that truth had long been lost by most Jews of Paul's day. It had been replaced by a system of works-righteousness based on partial conformity to the Old Testament law as well as on a multitude of traditions developed by the rabbis. In that respect, popular Judaism was no different from other man-made religions, all of which are built on the principle of man's pleasing and appeasing deity on the basis of human goodness and accomplishment. Because of the spiritual blindness and pride caused by sin, fallen man has always been convinced he is able to lift himself up by his own spiritual bootstraps. If he believes in God at all, he believes either that he is inherently good enough to please God or that he can make himself acceptable to God through his own efforts. (Paul comments on this further in 10:1-4.)

In Romans 3-4, Paul's arguments are specifically directed to Jews (see, e.g., 3:1, 9, 29; 4:1, 13), and it seems likely they continue to be his primary audience in chapter 5. As he often does in this epistle, the great apostle anticipates the typical arguments that would be raised against his inspired teaching, many of which arguments he doubtless had already encountered during his ministry.

The questions and objections Paul now addresses pertain to how salvation is maintained. "Granted that a person is made right with God only by 'being justified as a gift by His grace through the redemption which is in Christ Jesus'" (3:24; cf. 4:24), some of Paul's readers would say. "Under what conditions then is redemption preserved? If a person is saved only through his faith, apart from any good works he may achieve, does that mean he can henceforth live just as he pleases because his right relationship with God is eternally secure? Or is salvation preserved by one's good works?"

Paul answered the second question when he countered the spurious charge that the doctrine of salvation by grace through faith encourages a believer to sin. In response to the apostle's teaching that our unrighteousness demonstrates the righteousness of God" (3:5), some of his opponents accused him of promoting sin, of teaching that Christians should do "evil that good may come" (3:8). Now he counters the somewhat opposite idea that, although salvation is received by faith, it must be preserved by good works.

If the preservation of salvation depends on what believers themselves do or do not do, their salvation is only as secure as their faithfulness, which provides no security at all. According to that view, believers must protect by their own human power what Christ began by His divine power.

To counteract such presumption and its consequent hopelessness, Paul assured the Ephesian church with these comforting words: "I pray that the eyes of your heart may be enlightened, so that you may know what is the hope of His calling, what are the riches of the glory of His inheritance in the saints, and what is the surpassing greatness of His power toward us who believe. These are in accordance with the working of the strength of His might which He brought about in Christ, when He raised Him from the dead, and seated Him at His right hand in the heavenly places" (Eph. 1:18-20). As the apostle points out in that passage, it is of great importance for Christians to be aware of the security they *now have and forever will have* in Christ, a security that does not depend on their own sinful and futile efforts but on the "surpassing greatness of His power toward us" and on "the strength of His might." That truth is the cornerstone of the feeling of assurance.

Our hope is not in ourselves but in our great God, who, even "if we are faithless, He remains faithful; for He cannot deny Himself" (2 Tim. 2:13). Isaiah described God's faithfulness as "the belt about His waist" (Isa. 11:5). David declared that the Lord's "faithfulness reaches to the skies" (Ps. 36:5), and Jeremiah praised Him with the exclamation, "Great is Thy faithfulness" (Lam. 3:23). The writer of Hebrews admonishes Christians with the words: "Let us hold fast the confession of our hope without wavering, for He who promised is faithful" (Heb. 10:23). While continued faith is necessary, our being able to hold fast is founded upon the Lord's faithfulness, not our own.

In developing his argument in the book of Romans against the destructive notion that believers must live in uncertainty about the completion of their salvation, Paul presents six "links" in the chain of truth that binds a true believer eternally to his Savior and Lord, completely apart from any effort or merit on the believer's part. Those links are: the believer's peace with God (5:1), his standing in grace (v. 2a), his hope of glory (vv. 2b-5a), his possession of divine love (vv. 5b-8), his certainty of deliverance (vv. 9-10), and his joy in the Lord (v. 11).

THE BELIEVER'S PEACE WITH GOD

Therefore having been justified by faith, we have peace with God through our Lord Jesus Christ, (5:1)

The first link in the unbreakable chain that eternally binds believers to Christ is their peace with God.

The term **therefore** connects Paul's present argument with what he has already said, especially in chapters 3 and 4. In those chapters the apostle established that, as believers, we have **been justified by faith.** Because of our justification **by faith, we have peace with God through our Lord Jesus Christ.**

The verb translated **we have** is in the present tense, indicating something that is already possessed. Many of a believer's blessings must await his resurrection and glorification, but **peace with God** is established the moment he places his trust in the **Lord Jesus Christ.**

The **peace** that Paul is speaking about here is not subjective but objective. It is not a feeling but a fact. Apart from salvation through **Jesus Christ,** every human being is at enmity with God, spiritually at war with Him (see v. 10; cf. 8:7), regardless of what his feelings about God may be. In the same way, the person who is justified by faith in Christ is at **peace** with God, regardless of how he may feel about it at any given moment. Through his trust in **Jesus Christ,** a sinner's war with God is ended for all eternity.

Most unsaved people do not think of themselves as enemies of God. Because they have no conscious feelings of hatred for Him and do not actively oppose His work or contradict His Word, they consider themselves, at worst, to be "neutral" about God. But no such neutrality is possible. The mind of every unsaved person is at peace only with the things of the flesh, and therefore by definition is "hostile toward God" and cannot be otherwise (Rom. 8:7).

After the famous missionary David Livingstone had spent several years among the Zulus of South Africa, he went with his wife and young child into the interior to minister. When he returned, he discovered that an enemy tribe had attacked the Zulus, killed many of the people, and taken the chief's son captive. The Zulu chief did not want to make war with the other tribe, but he poignantly asked Dr. Livingstone, "How can I be at peace with them while they hold my son prisoner?"

Commenting on that story, Donald Grey Barnhouse wrote, "If this attitude is true in the heart of a savage chief, how much more is it true of God the Father toward those who trample under foot His Son, who count the blood of the covenant wherewith they were set apart as an unholy thing, and who continue to despise the Spirit of grace (Heb. 10:29)?" (*God's River: Romans 5:1-11* [Grand Rapids: Eerdmans, 1959], p. 26).

Not only are all unbelievers enemies of God but God is also the enemy of all unbelievers, to the degree that He is angry with them every day (cf. Ps. 7:11) and condemns them to eternal hell. God is the enemy of the sinner, and that enmity cannot end unless and until the sinner places his trust in **Jesus Christ.** Every person who is not a child of God is a child of Satan (see John 8:44), and every person who is not a citizen of God's kingdom is a citizen of Satan's. As Paul declared near the opening of this letter, "the wrath of God is revealed from heaven against all ungodliness and unrighteousness of men, who suppress the truth in unrighteousness" (Rom. 1:18).

Apart from personal trust in God, even members of His chosen race Israel were not exempt from divine enmity and wrath. "My anger will be kindled, and I will kill you with the sword," God warned ancient Israel soon after He delivered her from Egypt (Ex. 22:24). During the subsequent wilderness wanderings, the Lord declared of unbelieving, unfaithful Israelites: "They have made Me jealous with what is not God; they have provoked Me to anger with their idols. So I will make them jealous with those who are not a people; I will provoke them to anger with a foolish nation, for a fire is kindled in My anger, and burns to the lowest part of Sheol, and consumes the earth with its yield, and sets on fire the foundations of the mountains" (Deut. 32:21-22). Shortly after Israel entered the Promised Land, God warned: "When you transgress the covenant of the Lord your God, which He commanded you, and go and serve other gods, and bow down to them, then the anger of the Lord will burn against you, and you shall perish quickly from off the good land which He has given you" (Josh. 23:16; cf. 2 Kings 22:13; Isa. 5:25; 13:9; Nah. 1:2).

To those who foolishly think God is too loving to send anyone to hell, Paul declared, "Let no one deceive you with empty words, for because of these things [the sins listed in v. 5] the wrath of God comes upon the sons of disobedience" (Eph. 5:6).

I once heard a professional football coach say during a pre-game devotional service I held for his team: "I don't know if there is a God, but I like having these chapels, because if there is one I want to be sure He's on my side." Sentiments such as that are frequently expressed by unbelievers who think that the Creator and Sustainer of the universe can be cajoled into doing one's bidding by giving Him superficial lip service. God is *never* on the side of unbelievers. He is their enemy, and His wrath against them can only be placated by their trust in the atoning work of His Son, Jesus Christ.

But on the cross, Christ took upon Himself all the fury of God's wrath that sinful mankind deserves. And those who trust in Christ are no longer God's enemies and no longer under His wrath, but are at peace with Him.

Paul assured the Colossian believers: "For it was the Father's good pleasure for all the fulness to dwell in Him [Christ], and through Him to reconcile all things to Himself, having made peace through the blood of His cross; through Him, I say, whether things on earth or things in heaven. And although you were formerly alienated and hostile in mind, engaged in evil deeds, yet He has now reconciled you in His fleshly body through death, in order to present you before Him holy and blameless and beyond reproach" (Col. 1:19-22).

The most immediate consequence of justification is reconciliation, which is the theme of Romans 5. Reconciliation with God brings peace with God. That peace is permanent and irrevocable, because Jesus Christ, through whom believers receive their reconciliation, "always lives to make intercession for them" (Heb. 7:25). "For I will be merciful to their iniquities," the Lord says of those who belong to Him, "and I will remember their sins no more" (Heb. 8:12; cf. 10:17). If anyone is ever to be punished in the future for the sins of believers, it would have to be the One who took them on Himself—Jesus Christ. And that is impossible, because He has already paid the penalty in full.

When a person embraces Jesus Christ in repentant faith, the sinless Son of God who made perfect satisfaction for all our sins makes that person eternally at peace with God the Father. In fact, Christ not only *brings* peace to the believer but "He Himself is our peace" (Eph. 2.14). This all points out how crucial it is to understand the nature and extent of the atoning work of Jesus the Lord as the basis for assurance.

Although the peace of which Paul is speaking in this passage is the objective peace of being reconciled to God, awareness of that objective truth gives the believer a deep and wonderful subjective peace as well. To know that one is a child of God, a brother of Jesus Christ, cannot but give Christians what Charles Hodge called the "sweet quiet of the soul" (*Commentary on the Epistle to the Romans* [Grand Rapids: Eerdmans, 1974 reprint], p. 132).

But awareness of our peace with God through Jesus Christ is meant to give us far more than feelings of gratitude and warmth, wonderful as those are. When a Christian is convinced he is eternally secure in Christ, he is freed from focusing on his own goodness and merit and is able to serve the Lord with the unqualified confidence that nothing can separate him from his heavenly Father. He can say with Paul, "I am convinced that neither death, nor life, nor angels, nor principalities, nor things present, nor things to come, nor powers, nor height, nor depth, nor any other created thing, shall be able to separate us from the love of God, which is in Christ Jesus our Lord" (Rom. 8:38-39).

The peace that a believer has in the knowledge that he is secure forever in Christ not only strengthens his faith but strengthens his service. The knowledge that we are eternally at peace with God prepares us to wage effective spiritual warfare in Christ's behalf and in His power. When engaged in battle, a Roman soldier wore boots with spikes in the bottom to give him a firm footing while fighting. Because Christians have their feet shod with "the gospel of peace" (Eph. 6:15), they have the confidence to stand firmly for Christ without the spiritual slipping and emotional sliding that uncertainty about salvation inevitably brings, knowing God is on their side!

THE BELIEVER'S STANDING IN GRACE

through whom also we have obtained our introduction by faith into this grace in which we stand; (5:2a)

A second link in the unbreakable chain that eternally binds believers to Christ is their standing in God's grace.

Through whom refers, of course, to the Lord Jesus Christ (v. 1). Because of our reconciliation to God the Father through our trust in His Son, **we have obtained our introduction by faith into this grace.** *Prosagōgē* (**introduction**) is used only three times in the New Testament, and in each instance it is used of the believer's access to God through Jesus Christ (see also Eph. 2:18; 3:12).

For Jews, the idea of having direct access, or **introduction,** to God was unthinkable, because to see God face to face was to die. When God gave His law to Israel at Sinai, He "said to Moses, 'Behold, I shall come to you in a thick cloud, in order that the people may hear when I speak with you, and may also believe in you forever'" (Ex. 19:9). But after the people had cleansed themselves according to His instruction, "the Lord came down on Mount Sinai, to the top of the mountain; and the Lord called Moses to the top of the mountain, and Moses went up. Then the Lord spoke to Moses, 'Go down, warn the people, lest they break through to the Lord to gaze, and many of them perish'" (vv. 20-21).

After the Tabernacle was built, and later the Temple, strict boundaries were set. A Gentile could only go into the outer confines and no farther. Jewish women could go beyond the Gentile limit but not much farther. And so it was with the men and the regular priests. Each group could go nearer the Holy of Holies, where God's divine presence was manifested, but none could actually enter there. Only the high priest could enter, and that only once a year and very briefly. And even he could lose his life if he entered unworthily. Bells were sewn on the special garments he wore on the Day of Atonement, and if the sound of the bells stopped while he was ministering in the Holy of Holies, they knew he had been struck dead by God (Ex. 28:35).

But Christ's death ended that. Through His atoning sacrifice, He made God the Father accessible to any person, Jew or Gentile, who trusts in that sacrifice. The writer of Hebrews encourages believers to "draw near with confidence to the throne of grace, that we may receive mercy and may find grace to help in time of need" (Heb. 4:16).

To make this truth graphic, when Jesus was crucified, "the veil of the temple was torn in two from top to bottom" by God's power (Matt. 27:51). His death forever removed the barrier to God's holy presence that the Temple veil represented. Commenting on that amazing truth, the writer of Hebrews says, "Since therefore, brethren, we have confidence to enter the holy place by the blood of Jesus, by a new and living way which He inaugurated for us through the veil, that is, His flesh, and since we have a great priest over the house of God, let us draw near with a sincere heart in full assurance of faith, having our hearts sprinkled clean from an evil conscience and our bodies washed with pure water" (Heb. 10:19-22).

Predicting the new relationship that believers would have with God under the New Covenant, the prophet Jeremiah wrote, "And they shall be My people, and I will be their God; . . . And I will make an everlasting covenant with them that I will not turn away from them, to do them good; and I will put the fear of Me in their hearts so that they will not turn away from Me" (Jer. 32:38, 40).

On the basis of our **faith** in Him, Jesus Christ brings believers **into this grace in which we stand.** *Histēmi* (**stand**) here carries the idea of permanence, of standing firm and immovable. Although faith is necessary for salvation, it is God's **grace,** not the believer's faith, that has the power to save and to keep saved. We are not saved by divine grace and then preserved by human effort. That would be a mockery of God's grace, meaning that what God begins in us He is either unwilling or unable to preserve and complete. Paul unequivocally declared to the Philippian believers: "For I am confident of this very thing, that He who began a good work in you will perfect it until the day of Christ Jesus" (Phil. 1:6). Emphasizing that same sublime truth, Jude speaks of Christ as "Him who is able to keep you from stumbling, and to make you stand in the presence of His glory blameless with great joy" (Jude 24). We do not begin in the Spirit to be perfected by the flesh (Gal. 3:3).

Believers will often fall into sin, but their sin is not more powerful than God's grace. They are the very sins for which Jesus paid the penalty. If no sin a person commits before salvation is too great for Christ's atoning death to cover, surely no sin he commits after salvation is too great to be covered. Later in this same chapter the apostle declares, "For if while we were enemies, we were reconciled to God through the death of His Son, much more, having been reconciled, we shall be saved by His life" (Rom. 5:10). If a dying Savior could bring us to God's grace, surely a living Savior can keep us in His grace. Still later in the chapter Paul affirms the truth again: "The Law came in that the transgression might increase," he writes; "but where sin increased, grace abounded all the more" (Rom. 5:20). Standing in **grace,** we are in the sphere of constant forgiveness.

Bible expositor Arthur Pink wrote graphically, "It is utterly and absolutely impossible that the sentence of the divine Judge should ever be revoked or reversed. Sooner shall the lightnings of omnipotence shiver the Rock of Ages than those sheltering in Him again be brought under condemnation" (*The Doctrines of Election and Justification* [Grand Rapids: Baker, 1974], pp. 247-48).

To Timothy, his beloved son in the faith, Paul asserted with the utmost confidence: "I know whom I have believed and I am convinced that He is able to guard what I have entrusted to Him until that day" (2 Tim. 1:12). With equal certainty he wrote: "What then shall we say to these things? If God is for us, who is against us? He who did not spare His own Son, but delivered Him up for us all, how will He not also with Him freely give us all things? Who will bring a charge against God's elect? God is the one who justifies; who is the one who condemns? Christ Jesus is He who died, yes, rather who was raised, who is at the right hand of God, who also intercedes for us" (Rom. 8:31-34).

If God sovereignly declares those who believe in His Son to be forever just, who can overturn that verdict? What higher court can overrule that divine acquittal? There is, of course, no higher court and no greater judge. Jesus Christ is the divine judge of all mankind, and He gives His true disciples the unspeakably comforting promise that "all that the Father gives Me shall come to Me, and the one who comes to Me I will certainly not cast out" (John 6:37).

It is not so that believers may be free to sin that their salvation is secured. The very purpose and effect of salvation is to free men *from* sin, not to free them to do it. "Having been freed from sin, you became slaves of righteousness," Paul reminds the Roman believers later in this letter (Rom. 6:18). A professing Christian who persistently and consistently sins proves that he does not belong to the Lord. As the apostle John said of certain apostates in the early church, "They went out from us, but they were not really of us; for if they had been of us, they would have remained with us; but they went out, in order that it might be shown that they all are not of us" (1 John 2:19). Later in that epistle John wrote: "No one who is born of God practices sin . . . . Anyone who does not practice righteousness is not of God" (3:9-10). The true believer will begin, from salvation on, a new pattern of righteousness springing from his new nature which hates sin and loves God. He will not be perfect, but his desires will be different and so will his patterns of behavior. That new development toward holiness is God's work as we shall see in coming chapters.

Scripture repeatedly details the sinfulness, frailty, and weakness of men, including believers, and a sensible and honest person can see those self-evident truths for himself. Therefore, only self-delusion can lead a Christian to believe that, in his own weakness and imperfection, he can preserve the great gift of spiritual life that could only be bought by the precious, sinless blood of God's own Son.

For a believer to doubt his security is to bring into question both God's integrity and His power. It is also to add the merit of men's work to the gracious, unmerited work of God. It is to add self-trust to trust in our Lord, because if salvation can be lost by anything that we can or cannot do, our ultimate trust obviously must be in ourselves rather than in God.

The saintly Scottish poet and preacher Horatius Bonar penned these beautiful lines in a hymn entitled "The Sin-Bearer" (*Hymns of Faith and Hope* [London: James Nisbett, 1872], pp. 100-102):

Thy bonds, not mine, O Christ,
    Unbind me of my chain,
And break my prison-doors,
    Ne'er to be barred again.

Thy righteousness, O Christ,
    Alone can cover me;
No righteousness avails
    Save that which is of Thee.

Thy righteousness alone
    Can clothe and beautify;
I wrap it round my soul;
    In this I'll live and die.

THE BELIEVER'S HOPE OF GLORY

and we exult in hope of the glory of God. And not only this, but we also exult in our tribulations, knowing that tribulation brings about perseverance; and perseverance, proven character; and proven character, hope; and hope does not disappoint, (5:2b-5a)

A third link in the unbreakable chain that eternally binds believers to Christ and gives them reason to **exult** is their **hope of the glory of God.** Since every aspect of it is solely the work of God, salvation cannot possibly be lost. And the end of that marvelous divine work is the ultimate glorification of every believer in Jesus Christ. Those "whom [God] foreknew, He also predestined to become conformed to the image of His Son, that He might be the first-born among many brethren; and whom He predestined, these He also called; and whom He called, these He also justified; and whom He justified, these He also glorified" (Rom. 8:29-30).

As the apostle has already established, salvation is anchored in the *past* because Christ has made peace with God for all those who trust in Him (5:1). It is anchored in the *present* because, by Christ's continual intercession (Heb. 7:25), every believer now stands securely in God's grace (v. 2a). Next he proclaims that salvation is also anchored in the *future,* because God gives every one of His children the unchangeable promise that one day they will be clothed with the glory of His own Son.

Kauchaomai (**exult**) denotes jubilation and rejoicing. The Christian has no reason to fear the future and every reason to rejoice in it, because he has the divinely-secured **hope** that his ultimate destiny is to share in the very **glory of God.** Jesus Christ guarantees the believer's hope because He Himself *is* our hope (1 Tim. 1:1). In His beautiful high priestly prayer, Jesus said to His heavenly Father, "And the glory which Thou hast given Me I have given to them; that they may be one, just as We are one" (John 17:22). A believer does not earn his future glory in heaven but will receive it from God's gracious hand, just as he received redemption when he first trusted in Christ and sanctification since.

You know "that you were not redeemed with perishable things like silver or gold from your futile way of life inherited from your forefathers," Peter reminds us, "but with precious blood, as of a lamb unblemished and spotless, the blood of Christ. For He was foreknown before the foundation of the world, but has appeared in these last times for the sake of you who through Him are believers in God, who raised Him from the dead and gave Him glory, so that your faith and hope are in God" (1 Pet. 1:18-21; cf. Col. 3:4; Heb. 2:10). And when our own perishable and mortal bodies one day are raised imperishable and immortal (1 Cor. 15:53-54), they will be fit to receive and to display God's divine glory. "For our citizenship is in heaven, from which also we eagerly wait for a Savior, the Lord Jesus Christ; who will transform the body of our humble state into conformity with the body of His glory, by the exertion of the power that He has even to subject all things to Himself" (Phil. 3:20-21).

The Holy Spirit is also Himself a guarantee of the believer's security. "In Him [Christ], you also, after listening to the message of truth, the gospel of your salvation—having also believed, you were sealed in Him with the Holy Spirit of promise, who is given as a pledge of our inheritance, with a view to the redemption of God's own possession, to the praise of His glory" (Eph. 1:13-14).

As Paul explains to the Corinthian believers, our glorification begins, in part, even in our present earthly life: "But we all, with unveiled face beholding as in a mirror the glory of the Lord, are being transformed into the same image from glory to glory, just as from the Lord, the Spirit" (2 Cor. 3:18).

Because our human understanding is so imperfect, it is impossible for us to comprehend the wonder and magnitude of **the glory of God**. Nevertheless, we have the Lord's own assurance that one day we not only will behold His divine glory but will partake of it. The **glory** of His own divine holiness and majestic perfection will radiate in us and through us for all eternity. We will share God's own glory because we are "predestined to become conformed to the image of His Son" (Rom. 8:29; cf. 1 Cor. 2:7). God has so predestined us, Paul explains later in the epistle, "in order that He might make known the riches of His glory upon vessels of mercy, which He prepared beforehand for glory" (Rom. 9:23). In other words, God's own glory is manifested through His grace, through His sharing His divine glory with those who deserve only destruction (v. 22).

Although their security rests entirely in the finished work of Christ and the sustaining power of Christ's Spirit, a Christian's outward living will testify to his inward spiritual life. Obedience to the Lord does not preserve salvation, but it *is* an evidence of it. Our perseverance in the faith does not maintain our salvation, but it is an outward proof of it. Those who renounce Christ—whether by heretical words or by persistent ungodly living—prove they never belonged to Him in the first place (see 1 John 2:19).

The writer of Hebrews declares that "Christ was faithful as a Son over His house whose house we are, if we hold fast our confidence and the boast of our hope firm until the end." A few verses later he adds, "For we have become partakers of Christ, if we hold fast the beginning of our assurance firm until the end" (Heb. 3:6, 14). He is not saying that our spiritual security rests in our own ability to hold fast to Christ but that our God-given ability to hold fast is evidence that we belong to Christ. It is only His holding us fast that enables us to hold Him fast. The two sides of Christian perseverance are this: from the divine perspective, God holds believers; from the human perspective, they hold on to Him, because of the strength His Holy Spirit provides.

In addition to exulting in our certain hope of the glory of God, **we also exult in our tribulations**. This is because they contribute to a present blessing and ultimate glory. *Thlipsis* (**tribulations**) has the underlying meaning of being under pressure and was used of squeezing olives in a press in order to extract the oil and of squeezing grapes to extract the juice.

The **tribulations** of which Paul is speaking are not the troubles that are common to all mankind but the troubles that Christians suffer for the sake of their Lord. One of the less attractive promises that Scripture gives believers is that those who are faithful can be certain of being under pressure from Satan and from the present world system that is under his control. "All who desire to live godly in Christ Jesus will be persecuted," Paul assured Timothy (2 Tim. 3:12). The last beatitude, which is as long as all the others together, contains the promise that persecution brings God's blessing (see Matt. 5:10-12). Perhaps because that beatitude is humanly so unappealing, it is given twice (vv. 10, 11) and is accompanied by the admonition to "rejoice, and be glad" when persecution comes (v. 12).

Persecution for Christ's sake in this life is itself an earnest or guarantee of our future glory. "For momentary, light affliction," Paul assures us, "is producing for us an eternal weight of glory far beyond all comparison" (2 Cor. 4:17). Persecution for Christ's sake is evidence that we are living Christlike lives. "Remember the word that I said to you," Jesus reminded His disciples, "'A slave is not greater than his master.' If they persecuted Me, they will also persecute you" (John 15:20; cf. Matt. 10:24-25).

"Let those also who suffer according to the will of God," says

Peter, "entrust their souls to a faithful Creator in doing what is right" (1 Pet. 4:19). Christians have no reason to despair in this present life, no matter how great their suffering may be or how hopeless their plight may appear from the human perspective. We should always be able to say with Paul's unreserved confidence: "For I consider that the sufferings of this present time are not worthy to be compared with the glory that is to be revealed to us" (Rom. 8:18). As the apostle continues to reveal, even "the creation itself also will be set free from its slavery to corruption into the freedom of the glory of the children of God. . . . And not only this, but also we ourselves, having the first fruits of the Spirit, even we ourselves groan within ourselves, waiting eagerly for our adoption as sons, the redemption of our body" (vv. 21, 23).

Christians not only should rejoice in **tribulations** because those hardships are evidence of faithful living which is blessed and rewarded, but also because of the spiritual benefits they produce. **Tribulation brings about perseverance; and perseverance, proven character; and proven character, hope; and hope does not disappoint.** Our afflictions for Christ's sake produce ever-increasing blessings. It should not seem strange, then, that God's children are *destined* for affliction in this life (1 Thess. 3:3).

Verses 3-5a of Romans 5 are a synopsis of Christian maturity and sanctification, which, as every other aspect of salvation, is accomplished by God's gracious power. In his beautiful benediction at the end of his first letter to Thessalonica, Paul prays, "Now may the God of peace Himself sanctify you entirely; and may your spirit and soul and body be preserved complete, without blame at the coming of our Lord Jesus Christ. Faithful is He who calls you, and He also will bring it to pass" (1 Thess. 5:23-24).

Hupomonē (**perseverance**) is often translated "patience," as it is in the King James Version. It also carries the idea of endurance, the ability to continue working in the face of strong opposition and great obstacles.

Perseverance, in turn, produces **proven character.** The Greek term (*dokimē*) translated **proven character** simply means "proof," which in the present context obviously refers to Christian **character.** The term was used of testing precious metals such as silver and gold to demonstrate their purity. When Christians experience tribulations that demand perseverance, that perseverance, in turn, produces in them **proven** spiritual **character.** Just as a metalsmith uses intense heat to melt silver and gold in order to cleanse them of physical impurities, so does God use tribulations to cleanse His children of spiritual impurities. "Blessed is a man who perseveres under trial," James assures believers; "for once he has been approved, he will receive the crown of life, which the Lord has promised to those who love Him" (James 1:12).

Coming full circle, as it were, Paul says that godly hope produces godly hope. Our "hope of the glory of God" (v. 2) is increased and strengthened by our heavenly Father through the process of tribulation, perseverance, and proven character, the end product of which is **hope** that **does not disappoint.** The more a believer pursues holiness, the more he is persecuted and troubled and the greater will be his hope as he is sustained through it all by God's powerful grace.

THE BELIEVER'S POSSESSION OF DIVINE LOVE

because the love of God has been poured out within our hearts through the Holy Spirit who was given to us. For while we were still helpless, at the right time Christ died for the ungodly. For one will hardly die for a righteous man; though perhaps for the good man someone would dare even to die. But God demonstrates His own love toward us, in that while we were yet sinners, Christ died for us. (5:5b-8)

A fourth marvelous link in the unbreakable chain that eternally binds believers to Christ is their possession of the divine **love of God,** which **has been poured out within our hearts through the Holy Spirit who was given to us.** When a person receives salvation through Jesus Christ, he enters a spiritual love relationship with God that lasts throughout all eternity.

As the apostle makes unambiguous in verse 8, **love of God** does not here refer to our love for God but to His love for us. The most overwhelming truth of the gospel is that God loved sinful, fallen, rebellious mankind, so much "that He gave His only begotten Son, that whoever believes in Him should not perish, but have eternal life" (John 3:16). And as the apostle proclaims in verse 9 of this present chapter, if God loved us with so great a love before we were saved, when we were still His enemies, how much more does He love us now.

As if that were not enough, God even graciously imparts His love to us. For those who accept His offer of salvation, God takes His indescribable and undeserved **love** and pours it **out within** the **hearts** of those who believe, **through** His own **Holy Spirit who** he gives to them. Taking the truth of eternal security out of the objective area of the mind, Paul now reveals that, in Christ, we are also given subjective evidence of permanent salvation, evidence that God Himself implants within our deepest being, in that we love the One who first loved us (1 John 4:7-10; cf. 1 Cor. 16:22).

Poured out refers to lavish outpouring to the point of overflowing. Our heavenly Father does not proffer His **love** in measured drops but in immeasurable torrents. The very fact that God gives His **Holy Spirit** to indwell believers is itself a marvelous testimony to His love for us, because He would hardly indwell those whom He did not love. And it is only because of the indwelling Spirit that His children are able to truly love Him. Speaking to His disciples about the Holy Spirit, Jesus said, "He who believes in Me, as the Scripture said, 'From his innermost being shall flow rivers of living water'" (John 7:38; cf. v. 39). Those rivers of blessing can flow *out* of believers only because of the divine rivers of blessing, including the blessing of divine **love,** that God has **poured** *into* them.

In the same way, our spiritual security is not in our ability to live godly but in the power of the indwelling **Holy Spirit** to *make* us godly. Only God can make men godly, and the Spirit's leading us into godliness is one of the great evidences of salvation. "For all who are being led by the Spirit of God," Paul declares, "these are sons of God" (Rom. 8:14).

With the longing to love, even the genuine desire to be godly is produced by the Holy Spirit. Whenever we sincerely aspire to righteous living, whenever we have an earnest desire to pray, whenever we yearn to study God's Word, whenever we long to worship the Lord Jesus Christ with all our hearts, we know we are being led by the Holy Spirit. Whenever we experience the awesome awareness that God is indeed our heavenly Father, it is "the Spirit Himself [who] bears witness with our spirit that we are children of God, and if children, heirs also, heirs of God and fellow heirs with Christ" (Rom. 8:16-17). The natural man has no such desires or experiences, and even Christians would not have them apart from being indwelt and led by the **Holy Spirit.**

Because acknowledging His promises with the mind does not necessarily bring personal confidence to the heart, God makes provision for the emotional encouragement as well as the mental enlightenment of His children. When the Lord is given free reign in our lives, the Holy Spirit will bear fruit in and through us, the first fruit of which is love (Gal. 5:22). But when we grieve Him through our disobedience (Eph. 4:30), He cannot produce what He intends. Therefore, when we live in disobedience, we not only will not feel loving toward God but will not feel His love for us.

With perhaps that truth in mind, Paul prayed for the Ephesian believers: "For this reason, I bow my knees before the Father, from whom every family in heaven and on earth derives its name, that He would grant you, according to the riches of His glory, to be strengthened with power through His Spirit in the inner man; so that Christ may dwell in your hearts through faith; and that you, being rooted and grounded in love, may be able to comprehend with all the saints what is the breadth and length and height and depth, and to know the love of Christ which surpasses knowledge, that you may be filled up to all the fulness of God" (Eph. 3:14-19). The Holy Spirit strengthens the inner man and enables him "to know the love of Christ which surpasses knowledge." By the gracious work of the Spirit within us, our hearts are able to experience a depth of love that our minds are unable to grasp, "the love of Christ which surpasses knowledge."

Knowing that his readers would want to know more about the quality and character of the divine love that filled them, Paul reminds them of the greatest manifestation of God's love in all history, perhaps in all eternity: **For while we were still helpless, at the right time Christ died for the ungodly.** While men were utterly **helpless** to bring themselves to God, He sent His only begotten Son, Jesus **Christ,** to die for us, notwithstanding the fact that we were **ungodly** and completely unworthy of His love. When we were powerless to escape from our sin, powerless to escape death, powerless to resist Satan, and powerless to please Him in any way, God amazingly sent His Son to die on our behalf.

Natural human love is almost invariably based on the attractiveness of the object of love, and we are inclined to love people who love us. Consequently, we tend to attribute that same kind of love to God. We think that His love for us is dependent on how good we are or on how much we love Him. But as Jesus pointed out, even traitorous tax collectors were inclined to love those who loved them (Matt. 5:46). And as theologian Charles Hodge observed, "If [God] loved us because we loved him, he would love us only so long as we love him, and on that condition; and then our salvation would depend on the constancy of our treacherous hearts. But as God loved us as sinners, as Christ died for us as ungodly, our salvation depends, as the apostle argues, not on our loveliness, but on the constancy of the love of God" (*Commentary on the Epistle to the Romans* [Grand Rapids: Eerdmans, 1974 reprint], pp. 136-37).

God's immense love is supremely demonstrated by Christ's dying for **the ungodly,** for totally unrighteous, undeserving, and unlovable mankind. In the human realm, by contrast, Paul observes that **one will hardly die for a righteous man; though perhaps for the good man someone would dare even to die.** Paul is not contrasting a **righteous man** with a **good man,** but is simply using those terms synonymously. His point is that it is uncommon for a person to sacrifice his own life in order to save the life even of someone of high character. Still fewer people are inclined to give their lives to save a person they know to be a wicked scoundrel. But God was so inclined, and in that is our security and assurance. Saved, we can never be as wretched as we were before salvation—and He loved us totally then.

But God demonstrates His own love toward us, in that while we were yet sinners, Christ died for us. That sort of selfless, undeserved love is completely beyond human comprehension. Yet that is the **love** that the just and infinitely holy God had **toward us** even **while we were yet sinners.** The God who hates every sinful thought and every sinful deed nevertheless loves the **sinners** who think and do those things, even while they are still hopelessly enmeshed in their sin. Even when men openly hate God and do not have the least desire to give up their sin, they are still the objects of God's redeeming **love** as long as they live. Only at death does an unbeliever cease to be loved by God. After that, he is eternally beyond the pale of God's love and is destined irrevocably for His wrath. In Christ, we are forever linked to God by His love, demonstrated in (positive) blessings and (negative) mercy.

THE BELIEVER'S CERTAINTY OF DELIVERANCE

Much more then, having now been justified by His blood, we shall be saved from the wrath of God through Him. For if while we were enemies, we were reconciled to God through the death of His Son, much more, having been reconciled, we shall be saved by His life. (5:9-10)

As if the first four were not enough to completely overwhelm us with assurance, there is a fifth link in the unbreakable chain that eternally binds believers to Christ, which is their certainty of deliverance from God's judgment.

The phrase **much more then** indicates that what follows is even more overwhelming and significant than what has preceded, astounding and wonderful as that is. **Having been justified by His blood** refers to the initial aspect of salvation, which for believers is past. In light of the fact that we already have **been justified,** Paul is saying, we are assured of being **saved from the wrath of God through Him,** that is, through Christ. Because we are now identified with Christ and are adopted as God's children through Him, we are no longer "children of wrath" (Eph. 2:3). As part of His atoning work, Jesus delivered us "from the wrath to come" (1 Thess. 1:10; cf. 5:9), because on the cross He took upon Himself the penalty and suffered the wrath that we deserve.

Paul's next thought is closely related to the previous one (v. 9) and is the central message of this passage: **For if while we were enemies, we were reconciled to God through the death of His Son, much more, having been reconciled, we shall be saved by His life.** If God had the power and the will to redeem us in the first place, how **much more,** does He have the power and the will to keep us redeemed? In other words, if God brought us to Himself **through the death of His Son** when **we were** His **enemies,** how **much more,** now that we are His **reconciled** children, will He keep us **saved by** the **life** of His Son? If the dying Savior reconciled us to God, surely the living Savior can and will keep us reconciled.

The thrust of this truth for believers is that our Savior not only delivered us from sin and its judgment, but also delivers us from uncertainty and doubt about that deliverance. If God has already made sure our rescue from sin, death, and future judgment, how could our present spiritual life possibly be in jeopardy? How can a Christian, whose past and future salvation are secured by God, be insecure during the time between? If sin was no barrier to the beginning of our redemption, how can it become a barrier to its completion? If sin in the greatest degree could not prevent our becoming reconciled, how can sin in lesser degree prevent our staying reconciled? If God's grace covers the sins even of His enemies, how much more does it cover the sins of His children?

Paul here reasons from the greater to the lesser. It is a greater work of God to bring sinners to grace than to bring saints to glory, because sin is further from grace than grace is from glory.

Every blessing a Christian has comes from Christ. Through Him we have peace with God (Rom. 5:1), grace and the hope of glory (v. 2), perseverance, proven character, and hope (vv. 3-4), God's love poured into our hearts by His Spirit, who is Himself the Savior's gift to us (v. 5), deliverance from sin by His atoning death (vv. 6-8), deliverance from God's wrath (v. 9), reconciliation with God the Father (v. 10*a*), and preservation during this present life (v. 10*b*).

THE BELIEVER'S JOY IN GOD

And not only this, but we also exult in God through our Lord Jesus Christ, through whom we have now received the reconciliation. (5:11)

A sixth and final link in the unbreakable chain that eternally binds believers to Christ is their joy, their great exultation, in God. This may not be the most important or the most profound evidence of our security in Christ, but it is perhaps the most beautiful. And although this divine evidence is subjective, it is none the less real. Why do we **exult in God through our Lord Jesus Christ** who gave us access to Him? Because from Him we **received the reconciliation.** He gave it as a gift to us.

The abundant joy that **God** gives His children **through the Lord Jesus Christ** includes grateful joy in their salvation and simply in who God is.

Surely one of the reasons David was a man after God's own heart was his rejoicing in the Lord for the Lord's own sake. "O magnify the Lord with me," he declared, "and let us exalt His name together" (Ps. 34:3). Other psalmists echoed that same joy. One wrote, "For our heart rejoices in Him, because we trust in His holy name" (Ps. 33:21), and another, "Then I will go to the altar of God, to God my exceeding joy; and upon the lyre I shall praise Thee, O God, my God" (Ps. 43:4).

Perhaps nowhere outside of Scripture has this deepest level of Christian joy been expressed more beautifully than in the following stanzas from Charles Wesley's magnificent hymn "O for a Thousand Tongues to Sing."

> O for a thousand tongues to sing
>   My great Redeemer's praise,
> The glories of my God and King,
>   The triumphs of His grace!
>
> Hear Him ye deaf; His praise, ye dumb,
>   Your loosened tongues employ;
> Ye blind, behold your Savior come;
>   And leap ye lame for joy!

Where these six links bind the believer to the Lord, there is true eternal salvation and every reason for full assurance of it.

Adam and the Reign of Death

Therefore, just as through one man sin entered into the world, and death through sin, and so death spread to all men, because all sinned—for until the Law sin was in the world; but sin is not imputed when there is no law. Nevertheless death reigned from Adam until Moses, even over those who had not sinned in the likeness of the offense of Adam, who is a type of Him who was to come. (5.12-14)

Many people consider Romans 5:12-21, of which the present text is the introduction, to be the most difficult passage in the epistle. At first reading it seems complex and enigmatic, and in one sense it is. As will be discussed later, as far as complete human comprehension is concerned, the truths of this passage are beyond reach. But on the other hand, the truths themselves are wonderfully simple and clear when accepted in humble faith as God's Word. Just as it is possible to accept and live in accordance with the law of gravity without fully understanding it, so it is possible for believers to accept and live according to God's truth without fully understanding it.

Verses 12-14 lay the foundation for the remainder of the chapter by pointing out the obvious truth that death is universal to the human race. In these three verses Paul focuses on Adam and the reign of death that his sin engendered. In the remainder of the chapter (vv. 15-21) he focuses on Christ and the reign of life.

As the apostle makes clear later in the letter, the destruction caused by sin affects *all* creation (see Rom. 8:19-22). But his present focus is on the universal destruction of human life that sin brought upon the world—the death of those whom God created in His own image.

No truth is more self-evident than the inevitability of death. The earth is pock-marked with graves, and the most incontestable testimony of history is that all men, whatever their wealth, status, or accomplishments, are subject to death. Since Creation, every person but two, Enoch and Elijah, have died. And were it not for Christ's rapture of His church, all men would continue to die.

The painful reality of death touches mankind without interruption and without exception. According to an Oriental proverb, "The black camel death kneeleth once at each door and each mortal must mount to return nevermore." The very term *mortal* means "subject to death."

The eighteenth-century poet Thomas Gray wrote these haunting lines in his *Elegy Written in a Country Churchyard:*

> The boast of heraldry, the pomp of pow'r,
>   And all that beauty, all that wealth e'er gave,
> Awaits alike th' inevitable hour,
>   The paths of glory lead but to the grave.

In Shakespeare's *King Richard II*, the king wisely observes (III.II.195):

> Within the hollow crown
> That rounds the mortal temples of a king
> Keeps death his court, and there the antick sits,
> Scoffing his state and grinning at his pomp,
> Allowing him a breath, a little scene,
> To monarchize, be fear'd, and kill with looks,
> Infusing him with self and vain conceit
> As if this flesh, which walls about our life
> Were brass impregnable; and humour'd thus
> Comes at the last, and with a little pin
> Bores through his castle wall, and farewell king!

The seventeenth-century poet James Shirley wrote in *The Contention of Ajax and Ulysses,*

> The glories of our birth and state
>> Are shadows, not substantial things;
> There is no armour against fate;
>> Death lays his icy hands on kings:
>>> Sceptre and crown
>>> Must tumble down,
> And in the dust be equal made
> With the poor crooked scythe and spade.

In view of the universality of mortality the questions come to mind, "Why does death reign in the world? Why must everyone die, whether at the end of a long life or at its beginning? How did death become the undisputed victor over mankind?"

Paul gives the answer to those questions in the present text. And although the basic truths he presents are in themselves rather simple, his argument in defense of them is not. His divinely-inspired reasoning plunges the reader deep into mysteries that we will never fully understand until we one day see our Lord face to face. The primary purpose of this passage, however, is not to explain why all people die. Paul brings in the subject of death merely to establish the principle that one person's deeds can inexorably affect many other people. Paul's primary objective in this chapter is to show how one Man's death provided salvation for many, and to do so the apostle first shows the reasonableness of that truth since one man's sin produced condemnation for many.

Paul's analogy of Adam and Christ clarifies several truths about God's plan of redemption, but it by no means clarifies every aspect of that marvelous provision. It is not that any of God's truths are unexplainable but that the explanations of many of them are beyond human comprehension. Our responsibility is to accept in faith both what is clear and what is not, what is comprehensible and what remains a mystery.

After describing the appalling sin and lostness of all mankind (1:18–3:20), Paul has revealed how Christ, by His justifying death on the cross, provided the way of salvation for everyone who comes to God in faith (3:21–5:11). The inevitable question that then arises is, "How could what one man did at one time in history have such an absolute effect on mankind?"

The analogy of Adam and Christ is antithetical, an analogy of opposites. Because of Adam's sin, all men are condemned; because of Christ's obedience, many are pardoned. Adam is therefore analogous to Christ only in regard to the common principle that what one man did affected countless others.

Paul's argument in verses 12-14 is comprised of four logical elements or phases: sin entered the world through one man (v. 12a);

death entered the world through sin (v. 12*b*); death spread to all men because all sinned (v. 12*c*); and history proves that death reigns over all men (vv. 13-14).

SIN ENTERED THE WORLD THROUGH ONE MAN

Therefore, just as through one man sin entered into the world, (5:12*a*)

Therefore connects what follows with what has just been declared, namely, that as believers we have been reconciled to God by the sacrifice of His Son Jesus Christ (vv. 8-11). Now Paul begins the analogy of Christ with Adam, the common principle being that, in each case, a far-reaching effect on countless others was generated **through one man.**

In the case of Adam, it was **through one man** that **sin entered into the world.** It is important to note that Paul does not say that sin originated with Adam but only that sin in **the world,** that is, in the human realm, began with Adam. Sin originated with Satan, who "has sinned from the beginning" (1 John 3:8). John does not specify when that beginning was, but it obviously was before the creation of Adam and Eve, because they were tempted by Satan.

After He placed Adam in the Garden of Eden, "the Lord God commanded the man, saying, 'From any tree of the garden you may eat freely; but from the tree of the knowledge of good and evil you shall not eat, for in the day that you eat from it you shall surely die'" (Gen. 2:15-17). Adam was given but one, simple prohibition by God, yet the consequence for disobedience of that prohibition was severe.

After Eve was created from Adam and joined him in the garden as his wife and helper, Satan tempted her to doubt and to disobey the command of God. She, in turn, induced her husband to disobey, and they sinned together. But although Eve disobeyed first, the primary responsibility for the sin was Adam's, first of all because it was to him that God had directly given the command, and second because he had headship over Eve and should have insisted on their mutual obedience to God rather than allow her to lead him into disobedience.

The one command was the only point of submission to God required of Adam. Except for that single restriction, Adam had been given authority to subjugate and rule the entire earth (Gen. 1:26-30). But when Adam disobeyed God, sin entered into his life and generated a constitutional change in his nature, from innocence to sinfulness, an innate sinfulness that would be transmitted to every one of his descendants.

Paul's argument begins with the assertion that, through Adam, **sin entered into the world.** He does not speak of sins, plural, but of

sin, singular. In this sense, **sin** does not represent a particular unrighteous act but rather the inherent propensity to unrighteousness. It was not the many other sinful acts that Adam eventually committed, but the indwelling **sin** *nature* that he came to possess because of his first disobedience, that he passed on to his posterity. Just as Adam bequeathed his physical nature to his posterity, he also bequeathed to them his spiritual nature, which henceforth was characterized and dominated by **sin.**

God made men a procreative race, and when they procreate they pass on to their children, and to their children's children, their own nature—physical, psychological, and spiritual.

John Donne wrote these well-known lines in his *Meditation XVII,*

> No man is an Island, entire of itself; every man is a piece of the Continent, a part of the main; if a clod be washed away by the sea, Europe is the less, as well as if a promontory were, as well as if a manor of thy friends or of thine own were; any man's death diminishes me, because I am involved in Mankind; And therefore never send to know for whom the bell tolls; It tolls for thee.

Mankind is a single entity, constituting a divinely ordered solidarity. Adam represents the entire human race that is descended from him, no matter how many subgroups there may be. Therefore when Adam sinned, all mankind sinned, and because his first sin transformed his inner nature, that now depraved nature was also transmitted to his posterity. Because he became spiritually polluted, all his descendants would be polluted in the same way. That pollution has, in fact, accumulated and intensified throughout the ages of human history. Instead of evolving, as humanists insist, man has devolved, degenerating into greater and greater sinfulness.

Ancient Jews understood well the idea of corporate identity. They never thought of themselves as isolated personalities or as a mass of separate individuals who happened to have the same bloodline as their families and fellow Jews. They looked at all other races in the same way. A given Canaanite or Edomite or Egyptian was inextricably connected to all others of his race. What one of them did affected all the others, and what the others did affected him—in a way that is difficult for modern, individual-oriented man to comprehend.

It was on that basis that God frequently punished or blessed an entire tribe, city, or nation because of what a few, or even just one, of its members did. It was in light of that principle that Abraham asked the Lord to spare Sodom if only a few righteous people could be found there (Gen. 18:22-33). It was also on the basis of that principle that God held all Israel accountable and eventually destroyed Achan's family along with him because of that one man's disobedience in keeping for himself some of the booty from Jericho (see Josh. 7:1-26).

The writer of Hebrews knew that his Jewish readers would understand his statement about the tithes that Levi paid to Melchizedek. "Without any dispute," he declared, "the lesser is blessed by the greater. And in this case mortal men receive tithes, but in that case one receives them, of whom it is witnessed that he lives on. And, so to speak, through Abraham even Levi, who received tithes, paid tithes, for he was still in the loins of his father when Melchizedek met him" (Heb. 7:7-10; cf. vv. 1-3; Gen. 14:18-20). In other words, although Melchizedek lived many years before Levi, the father of the priestly tribe, was born, along with all other descendants of Abraham, Levi, by being in the seed in Abraham's loins, shared in the tithe paid to the ancient king.

In the same way, although with enormously greater consequences, the sin of Adam was passed on to all of his descendants. When he sinned in the Garden of Eden, he sinned not only as *a* man but as *man*. When he and his wife, who were one flesh (Gen. 2:24), sinned against God, all of their descendants—that is, the entire human race in their loins—would share in that sin and the alienation from God and subjection to death that were its consequence. "In Adam all die," Paul explained to the Corinthians (1 Cor. 15:22). As far as guilt is concerned, every human being was present in the garden with Adam and shares in the sin he committed there.

The fact that Adam and Eve not only were actual historical figures but were the original human beings from whom all others have descended is absolutely critical to Paul's argument here and is critical to the efficacy of the gospel of Jesus Christ. If a historical Adam did not represent all mankind in sinfulness, a historical Christ could not represent all mankind in righteousness. If all men did not fall with the first Adam, all men could not be saved by Christ, the second and last Adam (see 1 Cor. 15:20-22, 45).

DEATH ENTERED THE WORLD THROUGH SIN

and death through sin (5:12*b*)

The second element of Paul's argument is that, because sin entered the world through one man, so also **death,** the consequence of sin, entered the world **through** that one man's **sin.**

God did not create Adam as a mortal being, that is, as subject to death. But He explicitly warned Adam that disobedience by eating the fruit of the knowledge of good and evil would make him subject to death (Gen. 2:17). And, contrary to Satan's lie (3:4), that was indeed the fate that Adam suffered for his disobedience. Even before human sin existed, God had ordained that its wages would be death (Rom. 6:23; cf. Ezek.

18:4). Death is the unfailing fruit of the poison that entered Adam's heart and the heart of every one of his descendants.

Even tiny babies can die, not because they have committed sins but because they have a sin nature, the ultimate consequence of which is death. A person does not become a sinner by committing sins but rather commits sins because he is by nature a sinner. A person does not become a liar when he tells a lie; he tells a lie because his heart is already deceitful. A person does not become a murderer when he kills someone; he kills because his heart is already murderous. "For out of the heart," Jesus said, "come evil thoughts, murders, adulteries, fornications, thefts, false witness, slanders" (Matt. 15:19).

Sin brings several kinds of **death** to men. Death is separation, and Adam's first death was *spiritual* separation from God, which Adam experienced immediately after his disobedience.

"You were dead in your trespasses and sins," Paul reminded the Ephesian believers, "in which you formerly walked according to the course of this world, according to the prince of the power of the air, of the spirit that is now working in the sons of disobedience" (Eph. 2:1-2). The unsaved are "darkened in their understanding, excluded from the life of God, because of the ignorance that is in them, because of the hardness of their heart" (Eph. 4:18). The unregenerate are very much alive to the world, but they are dead to God and to the things of God.

A second, and obvious, kind of death that sin brings is *physical,* separation from fellow human beings. Although Adam did not immediately lose his physical life, he became subject to physical death the moment he sinned.

A third kind of death that sin brings is *eternal,* an immeasurably worse extension of the first. Referred to in Scripture as the second death (Rev. 21:8), this death not only brings eternal separation from God but also eternal torment in hell

The unbeliever has reason to fear all three deaths. Spiritual death prevents his earthly happiness; physical death will bring an end to opportunity for salvation; and eternal death will bring everlasting punishment. But no kind of death should be feared by believers. They are saved permanently by Christ from spiritual and eternal death, and their physical death (or rapture) will usher them into His divine presence. For believers Christ has removed the fear of death (Heb. 2:14, 15).

DEATH SPREAD TO ALL MEN BECAUSE ALL SINNED

and so death spread to all men, because all sinned— (5:12c)

A third element of Paul's argument is that **death** was transmitted to **all men,** without exception. No human being has ever escaped death.

Enoch and Elijah, who escaped physical and eternal death, nevertheless were spiritually dead before they trusted in the Lord. Even Jesus died, not because of His own sin but because of the world's sin that He vicariously took upon Himself. And when He took sin upon Himself, He also took upon Himself sin's penalty.

Sinned translates a Greek aorist tense, indicating that at one point in time **all** men **sinned.** That, of course, was the time that Adam first sinned. His sin became mankind's sin, because **all** mankind were in his loins.

Men have learned to identify certain physical and mental characteristics in human genes, but we will never discover a way to identify the spiritual depravity that has been transmitted from generation to generation throughout man's history. We know of that legacy only through the revelation of God's Word.

Paul does not attempt to make his explanation wholly understandable to his readers, and he himself did not claim to have full comprehension of the significance of what the Lord revealed to and through him. He simply declared that Adam's sin was transmitted to **all** his posterity because that truth was revealed to him by God.

Natural human depravity is not the result but the cause of man's sinful acts. An infant does not have to be taught to disobey or be selfish. It is born that way. A young child does not have to be taught to lie or steal. Those are natural to his fallen nature, and he will express them as a matter of course unless prevented.

"Behold, I was brought forth in iniquity," David confessed, "and in sin my mother conceived me" (Ps. 51:5). That condition was not unique to David, and in another psalm he testified that "the wicked are estranged from the womb; these who speak lies go astray from birth" (Ps. 58:3). Jeremiah declared that "the heart is more deceitful than all else and is desperately sick; who can understand it?" (Jer. 17:9). Eliphaz asked Job rhetorically: "What is man, that he should be pure, or he who is born of a woman, that he should be righteous?" (Job 15:14).

Every person who is not spiritually reborn through Christ (John 3:3) is a child of Satan. Jesus told the unbelieving Jewish leaders: "You are of your father the devil, and you want to do the desires of your father. He was a murderer from the beginning, and does not stand in the truth, because there is no truth in him. Whenever he speaks a lie, he speaks from his own nature; for he is a liar, and the father of lies" (John 8:44).

As already noted, although Eve disobeyed God's command first, Adam was more accountable for his disobedience, because "it was not Adam who was deceived, but the woman being quite deceived, fell into transgression" (1 Tim. 2:14). Adam had no excuse at all. Without being deceived, and fully aware of what he was doing, he deliberately disobeyed God.

Some object to the idea that they sinned in Adam, arguing that they not only were not there but did not even exist when he sinned. But by the same token, we were not physically at the crucifixion when Christ died, but as believers we willingly accept the truth that, by faith, we died with Him. We did not literally enter the grave with Christ and were not literally resurrected with Him, but by faith we are accounted to have been buried and raised with Him. If the principle were not true that **all sinned** in Adam, it would be impossible to make the point that all can be made righteous in Christ. That is the truth Paul makes explicit later in this letter (5:15-19) and in his first letter to Corinth: "For as in Adam all die, so also in Christ all shall be made alive" (1 Cor. 15:22).

Others argue that it is not fair to be born guilty of Adam's sin. "We did not asked to be born," they argue, "nor did our parents or their parents or grandparents before them." But neither was it "fair" that the sinless Son of God suffered the penalty of sin on behalf of all mankind. If God were only fair, Adam and Eve would have been destroyed immediately for their disobedience, and that would have been the end of the human race. It is only because God is gracious and forgiving, and not merely just, that men can be saved. The magnitude of Paul's analogy is mind-boggling, and its significance cannot be fully comprehended but only accepted by faith.

Habakkuk had great difficulty understanding the Lord. At first he could not understand why God did not bring revival to His chosen people Israel. He cried out, "How long, O Lord, will I call for help, and Thou wilt not hear? I cry out to Thee, 'Violence!' Yet Thou dost not save" (Hab. 1:2). Even less could he understand why God would punish His own people through the hands of the Chaldeans, who were pagans and immeasurably more wicked than the Israelites. "Thine eyes are too pure to approve evil," the prophet reminded the Lord, "and Thou canst not look on wickedness with favor. Why dost Thou look with favor on those who deal treacherously? Why art Thou silent when the wicked swallow up those more righteous than they?" (1:13).

Finally realizing that the Lord's ways are beyond human comprehension, Habakkuk testifies, "Though the fig tree should not blossom, and there be no fruit on the vines, though the yield of the olive should fail, and the fields produce no food, though the flock should be cut off from the fold, and there be no cattle in the stalls, yet I will exult in the Lord, I will rejoice in the God of my salvation. The Lord God is my strength" (3:17-19).

Habakkuk learned that when we cannot understand the Lord's ways, we must avoid the quicksand of human reason and stand in faith on the rock of God's righteous character.

It may, however, help to understand something of God's purpose for offering salvation to fallen mankind by considering the angels. Unlike man, they were not created in God's image or as procreative beings (Matt. 22:30), and when they fell with Lucifer (Rev. 12:7-9), they fell individually and were immediately damned to hell forever, with no opportunity for redemption.

God created the angels to serve Him and give Him glory. Because they were created holy, they fully understood such things as God's holiness, righteousness, and majesty. But they had no comprehension of His grace, mercy, compassion, or forgiveness, because those characteristics have meaning only where there is the guilt feeling of sin. It is perhaps for that reason that the holy angels long to look into the gospel of salvation (1 Pet. 1:12). It is impossible even for the holy angels to fully praise God, because they cannot fully comprehend His greatness.

For His own divine reasons, however, God created man to be procreative. And when Adam fell, and thereby brought his own condemnation and the condemnation of all his descendants, God in mercy provided a way of salvation in order that those who would experience His grace would then have cause to praise Him for it. Paul declares that it is through redeemed saints, saved human beings, "that the manifold wisdom of God might now be made known through the church to the rulers and the authorities in the heavenly places," that is, to His heavenly angels (Eph. 3:10).

Because the purpose of creation is to glorify God, it is fitting that God would fill heaven with creatures who have received His grace and His mercy, and have been restored to His divine likeness to give Him eternal praise.

HISTORY PROVES THAT DEATH REIGNS OVER ALL MEN

for until the Law sin was in the world; but sin is not imputed when there is no law. Nevertheless death reigned from Adam until Moses, even over those who had not sinned in the likeness of the offense of Adam, who is a type of Him who was to come. (5:13-14)

A fourth element of Paul's argument is that history verifies that death is universal.

The apostle points out that before God gave **the Law** on Mount Sinai, **sin was** already **in the world.** But men's failure to meet the standards of **the Law** was **not imputed** against them because during that period they had **no law.** Yet, because **death reigned from Adam to Moses,** that is, death was universal even though there was no law, it is obvious that men were still sinful. It was not because of men's *sinful acts* in breaking the Mosaic Law, which they did not yet have, but because of their *sinful nature* that all men **from Adam until Moses** were subject to death.

Because Adam and Eve were evicted from the Garden of Eden after they sinned, they had no more opportunity to disobey God's single prohibition. They no longer had access to the forbidden fruit of the tree of the knowledge of good and evil, nor have any of their descendants. Consequently, it has been impossible for any human being, either before or after Moses, to have **sinned in the likeness of the offense of Adam.**

But in regard to the principle of human solidarity, Adam was **a type of** Jesus Christ. That truth becomes Paul's transition to the glorious gospel of salvation from sin and death that God offers fallen mankind through His beloved Son, **Him who was to come.**

Christet and the Reign of Life

But the free gift is not like the transgression. For if by the transgression of the one the many died, much more did the grace of God and the gift by the grace of the one Man, Jesus Christ, abound to the many. And the gift is not like that which came through the one who sinned; for on the one hand the judgment arose from one transgression resulting in condemnation, but on the other hand the free gift arose from many transgressions resulting in justification. For if by the transgression of the one, death reigned through the one, much more those who receive the abundance of grace and of the gift of righteousness will reign in life through the One, Jesus Christ. So then as through one transgression there resulted condemnation to all men, even so through one act of righteousness there resulted justification of life to all men. For as through the one man's disobedience the many were made sinners, even so through the obedience of the One the many will be made righteous. And the Law came in that the transgression might increase; but where sin increased, grace abounded all the more, that, as sin reigned in death, even so grace might reign through righteousness to eternal life through Jesus Christ our Lord. (5:15-21)

Paul continues his analogy of Adam and Christ, showing how the life that was made possible for all men by Christ's atoning sacrifice is illustrated antithetically by the death that was made inevitable for all men by Adam's sin. It is the truth the apostle summarizes in his first letter to Corinth: "For as in Adam all die, so also in Christ all shall be made alive" (1 Cor. 15:22).

As noted in the previous chapter, the only truly analogous factor between Adam and Christ is that of one man/one act. That is, just as the one man Adam's sin brought sin to all mankind, so the one man Jesus Christ's one sacrifice made salvation available to all mankind.

In the present passage, as if to examine every facet of this marvelous analogy, Paul explores five essential areas of contrast between the condemning act of Adam and the redemptive act of Christ. Those acts were different in their effectiveness (v. 15), in their extent (v. 16), in their efficacy (v. 17), in their essence (vv. 18-19), and in their energy (vv. 20-21).

THE CONTRAST IN EFFECTIVENESS

But the free gift is not like the transgression. For if by the transgression of the one the many died, much more did the grace of God and the gift by the grace of the one Man, Jesus Christ, abound to the many. (5:15)

The first contrast is clearly stated as being between **the free gift** of Christ and **the transgression** of Adam, acts that were totally opposite.

By definition, all gifts are free, but *charisma* (**free gift**) refers to something given with special graciousness and favor, and therefore could also be appropriately rendered "grace gift." When used of what is given *to* God, the term refers to that which is right and acceptable in His sight; when used of that which is given *by* God, as here, it refers to that which is given completely apart from human merit. In regard to Jesus' atoning sacrifice, both meanings are involved. Going to the cross was Jesus' supreme act of obedience to His Father and therefore was wholly acceptable to the Father. His going to the cross was also the supreme act of divine grace, His free gift offered to sinful mankind.

Transgression is from *paraptōma*, which has the basic meaning of deviating from a path, or departing from the norm. By extension, it carries the idea of going where one should not go, and therefore is sometimes translated "trespass." The one sin of Adam that was bequeathed to all his posterity and that brought the reign of death on the world was a **transgression** from the one command, from the single norm for obedience, that God had given.

The impact of **the free gift** and of **the transgression** are distinct to themselves. **By the transgression of the one,** that is, Adam, **the many died.** Perhaps for the sake of parallelism, Paul uses **many** in two different senses in this verse. As will be seen below, he uses the term *all* with similarly distinct meanings in verse 18. In regard to Adam's act, **many** is universal and inclusive, corresponding to the "all" in verse 12. Because *all* men, without exception, bear in themselves the nature and mark of sin, they are *all*, without exception, under the sentence of death (as he has made clear in earlier chapters).

By eating of the fruit of the tree of the knowledge of good and evil, Adam departed from God's standard and entered a divinely-forbidden realm. And instead of becoming more like God, as Satan had promised, man became more unlike His Creator and separated from Him. Instead of bringing man into the province of God, Adam's **transgression** delivered him and all his posterity to the province of Satan.

The heart of Paul's comparison, however, is that Christ's one act of salvation had immeasurably greater impact than Adam's one act of damnation. **Much more,** he says, **did the grace of God and the gift by the grace of the one Man, Jesus Christ, abound to the many.** The divine provision of redemption not only is an expression of **the grace of God** the Father but of **the grace of** God the Son, **the one Man, Jesus Christ.**

The sin of Adam brought death. But **the gift by the grace of the one Man, Jesus Christ,** did more than simply provide the way for fallen mankind to be restored to the state of Adam's original innocence. **Jesus Christ** not only reversed the curse of death by forgiving and cleansing from sin but provided the way for redeemed men to share in the full righteousness and glory of God.

John Calvin wrote, "Since the fall of Adam had such an effect as to produce ruin of many, much more efficacious is the grace of God to the benefit of many; inasmuch as it is admitted, that Christ is much more powerful to save, than Adam was to destroy" (*Commentaries on the Epistle of Paul the Apostle to the Romans* [Grand Rapids: Baker, 1979], p. 206). God's grace is greater than man's sin. Not only is it greater than the one original sin of Adam that brought death to all men but it is greater than all the accumulated sins that men have ever or will ever commit.

It might be said that Adam's sinful act, devastating as it was, had but a one-dimensional effect—it brought death to everyone. But the effect of Christ's redemptive act has facets beyond measure, because He not only restores man to spiritual life but gives him the very life of God. Death by nature is static and empty, whereas life by nature is active and full. Only life can **abound.**

Contrary to its use in the beginning of this verse regarding Adam, the term **many** now carries its normal meaning, applying only to those for whom Christ's gracious gift of salvation is made effective through their faith in Him. Although Paul does not mention that qualifying truth at this point, He has just declared that believers are "justified by faith" and are introduced "by faith into this grace in which we stand" (5:1-2). That, of course, is the cardinal truth of the gospel as far as man's part is concerned; it is the focus of Paul's teaching in this epistle from 3:21–5:2.

Many of the Puritans and Reformers ended their sermons or commentary chapters with a statement about the passage's "practical use." The practical truth of Romans 5:15 is that the power of sin, which is death, can be broken, but the power of Christ, which is salvation, *cannot* be broken. "Our Savior Christ Jesus," Paul declared to Timothy, "abolished death, and brought life and immortality to light through the gospel" (2 Tim. 1:10).

Jesus Christ broke the power of sin and death, but the converse is not true. Sin and death cannot break the power of Jesus Christ. The condemnation of Adam's sin is reversible, the redemption of Jesus Christ is not. The effect of Adam's act is permanent only if not nullified by Christ. The effect of Christ's act, however, is permanent for believing individuals and not subject to reversal or nullification. We have the great assurance that once we are in Jesus Christ, we are in Him forever.

THE CONTRAST IN EXTENT

And the gift is not like that which came through the one who sinned; for on the one hand the judgment arose from one transgression resulting in condemnation, but on the other hand the free gift arose from many transgressions resulting in justification. (5:16)

The second contrast between the one act of Adam and the one act of Christ is in regard to extent. In that regard, just as in effectiveness, Christ's justification is far greater than Adam's condemnation.

In verse 15 Paul speaks of "the transgression of the one," whereas in verse 16 he speaks of **the one who sinned,** that is, the one who transgressed. In the first case the emphasis is on the sin, in the second it is on the sinner. But the basic truth is the same. It was the *one sin* by the *one man* at the *one time* that brought God's **judgment** and its **resulting . . . condemnation.**

But **the gift** of God's grace through Jesus Christ **is not like that.** God's **judgment** on Adam and his posterity **arose from** but **one transgression. On the other hand,** however, **the free gift arose** not simply because of that single transgression but **from many transgressions,** and its result is not simply restoration but **justification.**

John Murray offers a helpful observation: "The one trespass demanded nothing less than the condemnation of all. But the free gift unto justification is of such a character that it must take the many trespasses into its reckoning; it could not be the free gift of justification unless it blotted out the many trespasses. Consequently, the free gift is conditioned as to its nature and effect by the many trespasses just as the judgment was conditioned as to its nature and effect by the one trespass alone" (*The Epistle to the Romans* [Grand Rapids: Eerdmans, 1965], p. 196).

This verse contains two very practical truths that are closely related. The first is that God hates sin so much that it took only one sin to condemn the entire human race and separate them from Him. It was not that Adam's first sin was worse than others he committed or worse than men have committed since. It was simply that his first sin *was sin*. At the time, eating the forbidden fruit was the only sin that Adam and Eve could have committed, because God had placed but one restriction on them. But had it been possible, any other sin would have had the same effect. In the same way, any sin that any man has ever committed would be sufficient to damn the whole human race, just as Adam's one sin did. A sobering thought, indeed.

The other truth in verse 16 is still more amazing and incomprehensible, and is as heartening as the first is sobering. Greater even than God's hatred of sin is His love for the sinner. Despite the fact that God hates sin so much that any one sin could damn the human race, His loving grace toward man is so great that He provides not only for the redemption of one man from one sin but for the redemption of all men from all sins. Jesus Christ took upon Himself the sins of the whole world. "God was in Christ reconciling the world to Himself, not counting their trespasses against them" (2 Cor. 5:19).

THE CONTRAST IN EFFICACY

For if by the transgression of the one, death reigned through the one, much more those who receive the abundance of grace and of the gift of righteousness will reign in life through the One, Jesus Christ. (5:17)

The third contrast between the one act of Adam and the one act of Christ is in regard to efficacy, the capacity to produce a desired result.

As Paul has already pointed out, the one sin of the one man Adam brought the reign of death (vv. 12-14). It is to that truth that the **if**—which here carries the idea of "because"—refers. It has been established that Adam's one act of sin brought the reign of death. But that was hardly the *intent* of the first sin. Neither Adam nor Eve sinned because they wanted to die; they sinned because they expected to become like God. Their sin produced the very opposite result from that which they desired and emphasized the deception of the tempter. As noted above, instead of becoming more like God, they became more *unlike* Him.

The one act of the one Man, Jesus Christ, however, produced precisely the desired result. The divine intent of Jesus' sacrifice of Himself on the cross was that **those who receive the abundance of** that unmatched act of **grace and of the gift of righteousness** would **reign in life through the One** who died for them, namely, **Jesus Christ**.

The one-dimensional result of Adam's one act was death, whereas the result of Christ's one act is life, which is multidimensional. Christ not only offers **life** but abundant life, life that abounds (v. 15; cf. John 10:10). The redeemed in Christ not only *receive* abundant life but are given **righteousness** as a **gift** (cf. 2 Cor. 5:21). They **reign in** that righteous **life** with their Lord and Savior. They possess the very righteous, glorious, and eternal **life** of God Himself.

The "practical use" of this great truth is that the One who has granted us spiritual **life** will fulfill that life in us. "For I am confident of this very thing," Paul assured the Philippian believers, "that He who began a good work in you will perfect it until the day of Christ Jesus" (Phil. 1:6). God is the great transformer and fulfiller of life. "Therefore if any man is in Christ, he is a new creature; the old things passed away; behold, new things have come" (2 Cor. 5:17).

To **reign in life** through Christ is also to have power over sin. Later in this letter Paul says, "Thanks be to God that though you were slaves of sin, you became obedient from the heart to that form of teaching to which you were committed, and having been freed from sin, you became slaves of righteousness" (6:17-18). As believers, we know from experience as well as from Scripture that we are still plagued with sin, still clothed in the sinful rags of the old self (see Eph. 4:22). But sin is no longer the nature or the master of the believer. In Christ we are no longer victims of sin but victors over sin (1 Cor. 15:57).

The Contrast in Essence

So then as through one transgression there resulted condemnation to all men, even so through one act of righteousness there resulted justification of life to all men. For as through the one man's disobedience the many were made sinners, even so through the obedience of the One the many will be made righteous. (5:18-19)

The fourth contrast between the one act of Adam and the one act of Christ is in regard to essence. These two verses summarize the analogy of Adam and Christ.

As with *the many* in verse 15, Paul apparently uses **all** in verse 18 for the sake of parallelism, although the two occurrences of the term carry different meanings. Just as "the many died" in verse 15 refers inclusively to all men, so **life to all men** here refers exclusively to those who trust in Christ. This verse does not teach universalism, as some have contended through the centuries. It is abundantly clear from other parts of this epistle, including the first two verses of this chapter, that salvation comes only to those who have faith in Jesus Christ (see also 1:16-17; 3:22, 28; 4:5, 13).

Paul's primary teaching in these two verses is that the essence of Adam's **one transgression** (v. 18*a*) was **disobedience** (v. 19*a*), whereas the essence of Christ's **one act of righteousness** (v. 18*b*) was **obedience** (v. 19*b*). When God commanded Adam not to eat of the forbidden fruit, Adam disobeyed and brought death. When God sent His only begotten Son into the world to suffer and die, the Son obeyed and brought life.

Made translates *kathislēmi* and here carries the idea of constituting, or establishing. The guilt of Adam's **disobedience** was imputed to all his descendants. They were thus **made sinners**—in the sense that they became legally guilty in God's sight. In the same way, but with the exact opposite effect, Christ's **obedience** causes those who believe in Him to be **made righteous** in God's sight. The consequence of His perfect **obedience**—an unblemished, impeccable righteousness—is imputed to their account, making them legally righteous.

From beginning to end, Jesus' earthly life was characterized by perfect obedience to His heavenly Father. Even at the age of twelve, He reminded His parents that He had to be about His Father's business (Luke 2:49). Jesus' sole purpose on earth was to do His Father's will (John 4:34; 5:30; 6:38; cf. Matt. 26:39, 42). In His incarnation, "He humbled Himself by becoming obedient to the point of death, even death on a cross" (Phil. 2:8).

Christ's **obedience** to the divine commandments is often called "active obedience," and His death on the Cross is called "passive obedience." Though He obeyed the law perfectly in His life, He also submitted to the penalty of the law in all its horrible fulness. Both active and passive obedience are included in the perfect righteousness of Christ that is imputed to believers. It is therefore a righteousness that satisfies all the demands of the law, including the law's penal requirements. **The obedience of the One** thus secured redemption for **the many** who **will be made righteous** in God's sight. God—"who justifies the ungodly" (Rom. 4:5)—can therefore declare still-sinful believers fully righ-

teous without any taint on His righteousness. he is *both* "just and the justifier of the one who has faith in Jesus" (Rom. 3:26).

The "practical use" of this truth is that genuine believers can truly
sing with H. G. Spafford in his great hymn:

> My sin, O the bliss of this glorious thought,
> My sin, not in part but the whole,
> Is nailed to the cross and I bear it no more
> It is well, it is well with my soul.

THE CONTRAST IN ENERGY

**And the Law came in that the transgression might increase; but
where sin increased, grace abounded all the more, that, as sin
reigned in death, even so grace might reign through righteousness to eternal life through Jesus Christ our Lord.** (5:20-21)

The fifth and last contrast between the one act of Adam and the
one act of Christ is in regard to energy.

As Paul explains more fully in chapter 7, the energizing force
behind man's sin is **the Law,** which **came in that the transgression
might increase.** Knowing that he would be charged with being antinomian and with speaking evil of something God Himself had divinely
revealed through Moses, Paul states unequivocally that "the Law is holy,
and the commandment is holy and righteous and good" (Rom. 7:12).
Nevertheless, God's own Law had the effect of causing man's **transgression** to **increase.**

It should be noted here that God's law—ceremonial, moral, or
spiritual—has never been a means of salvation during any age or dispensation. The divinely-ordained place it had in God's plan was temporary.
As the biblical scholar F. F. Bruce has stated, "The Law has no permanent
significance in the history of redemption" (*The Letter of Paul to the
Romans* [Grand Rapids: Eerdmans, 1985], p. 121). Paul has already
declared that Abraham was justified by God solely on the basis of his
faith—completely apart from any good works he accomplished and several years before he was circumcised and many centuries before the law
was given (4:1-13).

The Law was a corollary element in God's plan of redemption,
serving a temporary purpose that was never in itself redemptive. Disobedience to the law has never damned a soul to hell, and obedience to the
law has never brought a soul to God. Sin and its condemnation were in
the world long before the law, and so was the way of escape from sin and
condemnation.

God gave **the Law** through Moses as a pattern for righteousness but not as a means of righteousness. The law has no power to produce righteousness, but for the person who belongs to God and sincerely desires to do His will, it is a guide to righteous living.

The law identifies particular transgressions, so that those acts can more easily be seen as sinful and thereby cause men to see themselves more easily as sinners. For that reason **the Law** also has power to incite men to unrighteousness, not because **the Law** is evil but because men are evil.

The person who reads a sign in the park that forbids the picking of flowers and then proceeds to pick one demonstrates his natural, reflexive rebellion against authority. There is nothing wrong with the sign; its message is perfectly legitimate and good. But because it places a restriction on people's freedom to do as they please, it causes resentment and has the effect of leading some people to do what they otherwise might not even think of doing.

The Law is therefore a corollary both to righteousness and to unrighteousness. For the lawless person it stimulates him to the disobedience and unrighteousness he already is inclined to do. For the person who trusts in God, the law stimulates obedience and righteousness.

Again focusing on the truth that Christ's one act of redemption is far greater than Adam's one act of condemnation, Paul exults, **But where sin increased, grace abounded all the more.** God's **grace** not only surpasses Adam's one sin but all the sins of mankind.

Like a master weaver, Paul pulls all the threads together in his tapestry of redemptive truth, declaring: **As sin reigned in death, even so grace might reign through righteousness to eternal life through Jesus Christ our Lord.**

Dying to Live

What shall we say then? Are we to continue in sin that grace might increase? May it never be! How shall we who died to sin still live in it? Or do you not know that all of us who have been baptized into Christ Jesus have been baptized into His death? Therefore we have been buried with Him through baptism into death, in order that as Christ was raised from the dead through the glory of the Father, so we too might walk in newness of life. For if we have become united with Him in the likeness of His death, certainly we shall be also in the likeness of His resurrection, knowing this, that our old self was crucified with Him, that our body of sin might be done away with, that we should no longer be slaves to sin; for he who has died is freed from sin. Now if we have died with Christ, we believe that we shall also live with Him, knowing that Christ, having been raised from the dead, is never to die again; death no longer is master over Him. For the death that He died, He died to sin, once for all; but the life that He lives, He lives to God. (Rom. 6:1-10)

In his early teens, John Newton ran away from England and joined the crew of a slave ship. Some years later he himself was given to the black wife of a white slave trader in Africa. He was cruelly mistreated and lived on leftovers from the woman's meals and on wild yams he dug from the ground at night. After escaping, he lived with a group of natives for a while and eventually managed to become a sea captain himself, living the most ungodly and profligate life imaginable. But after his miraculous conversion in 1748, he returned to England and became a selfless and tireless minister of the gospel in London. He left for posterity many hymns that are still among the most popular in the world. By far the best-known and best-loved of those is "Amazing Grace." He became the pastor of a church in England, and to this day the churchyard carries an epitaph that Newton himself wrote (*Out of the Depths: An Autobiography* [Chicago, Moody, n.d.], p. 151):

> John Newton, Clerk,
> once an infidel and libertine,
> A servant of slaves in Africa,
> was, by the rich mercy of our Lord and Saviour,
> Jesus Christ,
> Preserved, restored, pardoned,
> And appointed to preach the faith
> He had long labored to destroy.

How could such a debauched, self-proclaimed enemy of the faith eventually be able to say with Paul, "I thank Christ Jesus our Lord, who has strengthened me, because He considered me faithful, putting me into service; even though I was formerly a blasphemer and a persecutor and a violent aggressor. And yet I was shown mercy" (1 Tim. 1:12-13)? How could that apostle have addressed the Corinthian believers as "those who have been sanctified in Christ Jesus, saints by calling" (1 Cor. 1:2) and yet say to them, "Do you not know that the unrighteous shall not inherit the kingdom of God? Do not be deceived; neither fornicators, nor idolaters, nor adulterers, nor effeminate, nor homosexuals, nor thieves, nor the covetous, nor drunkards, nor revilers, nor swindlers, shall inherit the kingdom of God. *And such were some of you*" (6:9-11a; emphasis added)? Paul immediately gives the answer, reminding them that they "were justified in the name of the Lord Jesus Christ, and in the Spirit of our God" (v. 11b).

It is those and similar vital concerns that Paul deals with in chapters 6-8 of Romans. At this point in the epistle he begins a new development in his teaching about salvation and its practical effect on those who are saved. After extensive discussions of man's sin and of his redemption through Christ, he now moves to the subject of the believer's holiness—the life of righteousness that God demands of and provides for

His children, the life of obedience to His Word lived in the power of His Spirit.

In his letter to the Galatian churches Paul gives a brief and beautiful summary of the divine principle that makes transformed life and transformed living possible: "I have been crucified with Christ; and it is no longer I who live, but Christ lives in me; and the life which I now live in the flesh I live by faith in the Son of God, who loved me, and delivered Himself up for me" (Gal. 2:20).

In Romans 6:1-10, Paul links three elements in his opening defense of the believer's holy life: the antagonist (v. 1), the answer (v. 2), and the argument explaining and defending that answer (vv. 3-10).

THE ANTAGONIST

What shall we say then? Are we to continue in sin that grace might increase? (6:1)

As he frequently does, Paul anticipates the major objections of his critics. Well before the time he wrote this epistle, he and Barnabas in particular—but doubtless the other apostles, teachers, and prophets as well—had already encountered considerable opposition against the preaching of salvation by grace through faith alone. The typical religious Jew of that day could not comprehend pleasing God apart from strict adherence to the Mosaic and rabbinic law. To them, conformity to such law was the embodiment of godliness.

While Paul and Barnabas were preaching in Antioch of Syria, some Jewish men who professed faith in Christ "came down from Judea and began teaching the brethren, 'Unless you are circumcised according to the custom of Moses, you cannot be saved.' And when Paul and Barnabas had great dissension and debate with them, the brethren determined that Paul and Barnabas and certain others of them should go up to Jerusalem to the apostles and elders concerning this issue" (Acts 15:1-2). When the two men arrived in Jerusalem, some other Jews who claimed to be Christians, a group of legalistic Pharisees, also opposed their teaching, "saying, 'It is necessary to circumcise them [Gentile converts], and to direct them to observe the Law of Moses'" (Acts 15:5). During the ensuing council of Jerusalem, Peter boldly declared that God "made no distinction between us [Jews] and them [Gentiles], cleansing their hearts by faith. Now therefore why do you put God to the test by placing upon the neck of the disciples a yoke which neither our fathers nor we have been able to bear? But we believe that we are saved through the grace of the Lord Jesus, in the same way as they also are" (Acts 15:9-

11). After further comments by Paul and Barnabas and a summary by James, the council unanimously agreed that obedience to the Mosaic law contributes nothing to salvation and should not be made binding on any believer, Gentile or even Jew (see vv. 12-29).

Some years later, after returning to Jerusalem from collecting offerings from largely Gentile churches on behalf of needy believers in Judea, Paul sought to conciliate immature Jewish believers—as well as defuse some of the opposition from unbelieving Jews—by going to the Temple to make a vow. When some unbelieving Jews from Asia saw him in the Temple, they falsely assumed he had defiled the Temple by bringing Gentiles into the restricted area. They nearly caused a riot in the city when they cried out, "Men of Israel, come to our aid! This is the man who preaches to all men everywhere against our people, and the Law, and this place; and besides he has even brought Greeks into the temple and has defiled this holy place" (Acts 21:28-36).

Paul also knew that, at the opposite extreme, some readers would misinterpret his assertion that "where sin increased, grace abounded all the more" (5:20). They would foolishly accuse him of teaching that sin itself glorifies God by causing His grace to increase. If that were true, they reasoned, then men not only are free to sin but are *obligated* to sin in order to enable God to expand His grace. If salvation is all of God and all of grace, and if God is glorified in the dispensing of grace, the sinful heart may be inclined to reason: "The more sin, the more grace; therefore, men should sin with abandon." Or as others might put it, "If God delights in justifying the ungodly, as Romans 4:5 clearly states, then the doctrine of grace puts a premium on ungodliness, because it gives God more opportunity to demonstrate His grace."

That is exactly the perverted interpretation taught by the infamous Rasputin, religious adviser to the ruling Romanov family of Russia in the late nineteenth and early twentieth centuries. He taught and exemplified the antinomian view of salvation through repeated experiences of sin and false repentance. He believed that the more you sin, the more God gives you grace. So the more you sin with abandon, the more you give God the opportunity to glorify Himself. Rasputin declared that if you are simply an ordinary sinner, you are not giving God an opportunity to show His glory, so you need to be an *extraordinary* sinner.

Paul had already countered a similar hypothetical charge: "If our unrighteousness demonstrates the righteousness of God, what shall we say? The God who inflicts wrath is not unrighteous, is He? (I am speaking in human terms.)" The apostle answers his own question with an emphatic, "May it never be! For otherwise how will God judge the world?" (Rom. 3:5-6). He then proceeds to roundly condemn those who would teach the depraved idea of "Let us do evil that good may come" (v. 8).

Legalistic Jews would charge the apostle with just that sort of antinomianism, of contradicting the laws of God and advocating moral and spiritual license to do as one pleases—presumably justified on the grounds that such living actually glorifies God. Those opponents had an especially hard time accepting the idea of salvation on the basis of faith alone, apart from any works. To add to that doctrine the idea that increased sin somehow increases God's grace would be to compound anathema with still worse anathema. In trying to protect the faith from that danger, however, they injected another danger: the idea that salvation as well as spirituality—even for believers in Christ—is produced by conformity to external law.

Throughout church history, some Christian groups have fallen into the same kind of error, insisting that conformity to countless man-made regulations and ceremony is necessary for true godliness. Whether in the form of extreme ritualism or of strictly prescribed codes of conduct, men have presumed to protect and bolster the pure gospel of grace working through faith alone by adding legalistic requirements of their own making.

The church also has always been in danger of contamination by false believers who wickedly use the freedom of the gospel as a justification for sin. As Jude declared, "For certain persons have crept in unnoticed, those who were long beforehand marked out for this condemnation, ungodly persons who turn the grace of our God into licentiousness and deny our only Master and Lord, Jesus Christ" (Jude 4).

Here Paul deals a death blow to that kind of antinomianism, yet he does so without yielding an inch of ground to those who would deny that God's grace is sufficient for salvation. Under the leadership of the Holy Spirit, the apostle avoided the extreme of legalism on the one hand and of libertinism on the other. He would neither abandon God's grace to accommodate the legalists nor abandon God's righteousness to accommodate the libertines.

As Scripture makes plain throughout its pages, from Genesis through Revelation, a saving relationship with God is inextricably linked to holy living, and a holy life is lived by the power of God working in and through the heart of the true believer. In God's redemptive act in a person's heart, true holiness is as much a gift of God as is the new birth and the spiritual life it brings. The life that is not basically marked by holiness has no claim to salvation. It is true that no believer will be sinless until he goes to be with the Lord by death or by rapture, but a professed believer who persistently disregards Christ's lordship and His standards of righteousness by disobedience has no claim on Christ's saviorhood. It is that cardinal gospel truth that Paul forcefully defends in Romans 6–7.

In light of the pervasive antinomianism of our own day, there is no more important truth for believers to understand than the inseparable connection between justification and sanctification as salvation components, between new life in Christ and the living of that life in the holiness Christ demands and provides. By their unbiblical teachings of easy believism and the worldly lifestyles of both leaders and members, many churches who go under the banner of evangelicalism give little evidence either of redemption or of the holiness that necessarily accompanies saving grace.

"What shall we say then to such foolish assertions?" the apostle asks, adding rhetorically, **"Are we to continue in sin that grace might increase?"** *Epimenō* (**to continue**) carries the idea of habitual persistence. It was sometimes used of a person's purposely living in a certain place and of making it his permanent residence. It is the word that John used of the determined Jewish leaders who persisted in trying to induce Jesus to contradict the law of Moses (John 8:7).

Paul was not speaking of a believer's occasional falling into sin, as every Christian does at times because of the weakness and imperfection of the flesh. He was speaking of intentional, willful sinning as an established pattern of life.

Before salvation, **sin** *cannot* be anything but the established way of life, because sin at best taints everything the unredeemed person does. But the believer, who has a new life and is indwelt by God's own Spirit, has no excuse to **continue** habitually **in sin.** Can he then possibly live in the same submissive relationship to sin that he had before salvation? Put in theological terms, can justification truly exist apart from sanctification? Can a person receive a new life and continue in his old way of living? Does the divine transaction of redemption have no continuing and sustaining power in those who are redeemed? Put still another way, can a person who persists in living as a child of Satan have been truly born again as a child of God? Many say yes. Paul says no, as verse 2 emphatically states.

THE ANSWER

May it never be! How shall we who died to sin still live in it? (6:2)

Immediately answering his own question, Paul exclaims with obvious horror, **May it never be!** *Mē genoito* is literally and accurately translated **May it never be,** and it was the strongest idiom of repudiation in New Testament Greek. It is used some fourteen times in Paul's letters alone. The apostle has already used it three times in chapter 3 of Romans (vv. 4, 6, 31) and will use it another six times before he concludes (see 6:15; 7:7, 13; 9:14; 11:1, 11). It carries the sense of outrage that an idea of this kind could ever be thought of as true.

The very suggestion that sin could in any conceivable way please and glorify God was abhorrent to Paul. The falsehood is almost too self-evident to be given the dignity of detailed refutation. Instead it deserves only condemnation.

But lest his readers think he might be evading a difficult problem, the apostle seems almost to shout why the notion that sin brings glory to God is repugnant and preposterous. At this point he does not respond with reasoned argument but with a brief and arresting rhetorical question: **How shall we who died to sin still live in it?**

Paul does not recognize his antagonists' assertion as having the least credence or merit. He does not now argue the truth but merely declares it. The person who is alive in Christ has **died to sin,** and it is inconceivable and self-contradictory to propose that a believer can henceforth **live in** the sin from which he was delivered by death. God's grace is given for the very purpose of saving from sin, and only the most corrupt mind using the most perverted logic could argue that continuing in the sin from which he has supposedly been saved somehow honors the holy God who sacrificed His only Son to deliver men from all unrighteousness.

By simple reason it must be admitted that the person who has **died** to one kind of life cannot still **live in it.** The apostle Paul was not speaking of the present state of the believer as daily dying to sin but the past act (*apothnēskō*, second aorist active) of being dead to sin. Paul is saying it is impossible for a Christian to remain in a constant state of sinfulness. The act is in this sense once and for all.

Again by definition, a person does not continually die. If his death is real, it is permanent. The person who has truly **died to sin** cannot possibly **still live in it.** Both in the spiritual as well as the physical realms, death and life are incompatible. Both logically and theologically, therefore, spiritual life cannot coexist with spiritual death. The idea that a Christian can continue to live habitually in sin not only is unbiblical but irrational. Christians obviously are able to commit many of the sins they committed before salvation, but they are *not* able to live perpetually in those sins as they did before. "No one who is born of God practices sin," John declares, "because His seed abides in him; and he cannot sin, because he is born of God" (1 John 3:9). It is not merely that Christians *should not* continue to live in the realm and dimension of sin but that they *cannot.*

The apostle does not equivocate about the superabundance of God's grace. But the truth that "where sin increased, grace abounded all the more" (5:20*b*) obviously focuses on and magnifies God's grace, not man's sin. It declares that no single sin is too great for God to forgive and that even the collective sins of all mankind for all ages—past, present, and future—are more than sufficiently covered by the measureless abundance of God's grace activated in the atonement.

Paul goes on to declare with equal unequivocation that a genuinely justified life both *is* and will *continue to be* a sanctified life. For the purposes of systematic theology and to make God's work of redemption somewhat more comprehensible to finite human minds, we often speak of sanctification as following justification. There is, of course, a sense in which it does, in that justification involves what is often called a forensic, or legal, declaration of righteousness that is immediate, complete, and eternal. But justification and sanctification are not separate stages in salvation; rather, they are different aspects of the unbroken continuum of God's divine work of redemption in a believer's life by which He not only declares a person righteous but recreates him to become righteous. Holiness is as much a work of God in the believer as any other element of redemption. When a person is redeemed, God not only declares him righteous, but also begins to develop Christ's righteousness in him. Thus salvation is not merely a legal transaction, but results inevitably in a miracle of transformation.

Growing in the Christian life is always a process, not to be perfected "until the day of Christ Jesus" (Phil. 1:6). But there is no such thing as a true convert to Christ in whom justification has been accomplished but in whom sanctification, both forensic and practical, has not already begun. In other words, there is *never* a cleavage between justification and sanctification. There *is,* however, always and inevitably a total and permanent cleavage between the old self and the new self. In Christ, the old self has been made a corpse; and a corpse, by definition, has in it no remaining vestige of life.

The old man, the old self, is the unregenerate person. He is not part righteous and part sinful, but totally sinful and without the slightest potential *within himself* for becoming righteous and pleasing to God. The new man, on the other hand, is the regenerate person. He is made pleasing to God through Jesus Christ and his new nature is *entirely godly and righteous.* He is not yet perfected or glorified, but he *is* already spiritually alive and holiness is at work in him. The new man *will continue* to grow in that holiness, no matter how slowly or falteringly, because, by its very nature, life grows. Dr. Donald Grey Barnhouse wrote, "Holiness starts where justification finishes, and if holiness does not start, we have the right to suspect that justification never started either" (*Romans,* vol. 3 [Grand Rapids: Eerdmans, 1961], 2:12).

There is therefore simply no such thing as justification without sanctification. There is no such thing as divine life without divine living. The truly saved person lives a new and godly life in a new and godly realm. He now and forever lives in God's realm of grace and righteousness and can never again live in Satan's realm of self and sin. As the natural, sinful, unregenerate man cannot restrain the manifestation of what he is, neither can the regenerate man.

Again, salvation not only is a transaction but a transformation, not only forensic but actual. Christ died not only for what we did but for what we are. Paul tells believers: "For you have died and your life is hidden with Christ in god" (Col. 3:3). even more explicitly he declares that "if any man is in Christ, he is a new creature; the old things passed away; behold, new things have come" (2 Cor. 5:17).

And so the phrase **died to sin** expresses the fundamental premise of this entire chapter in Romans, the rest of which is essentially an elaboration of the cardinal reality. It is impossible to be alive in Christ and also still be alive to sin. It is not that a believer at any moment before going to be with Christ is totally separated from the controlling power of sin, the sin life from which Christ died to deliver him. The sense in which this crucial fact is true unfolds in the following text.

THE ARGUMENT

Or do you not know that all of us who have been baptized into Christ Jesus have been baptized into His death? Therefore we have been buried with Him through baptism into death, in order that as Christ was raised from the dead through the glory of the Father, so we too might walk in newness of life. For if we have become united with Him in the likeness of His death, certainly we shall be also in the likeness of His resurrection, knowing this, that our old self was crucified with Him, that our body of sin might be done away with, that we should no longer be slaves to sin; for he who has died is freed from sin. Now if we have died with Christ, we believe that we shall also live with Him, knowing that Christ, having been raised from the dead, is never to die again; death no longer is master over Him. For the death that He died, He died to sin, once for all; but the life that He lives, He lives to God. (6:3-10)

The idea that a believer can glorify God by continuing in sin apparently was pervasive in the Roman churches and elsewhere, or Paul would not have given it such attention. In a series of four logical and sequential principles, he reasons from his basic point made in verse 2 that the person who has died to sin cannot continue to live in it.

WE ARE BAPTIZED INTO CHRIST

Or do you not know that all of us who have been baptized into Christ Jesus (6:3a)

The first principle is that all true Christians **have been baptized into Christ Jesus.**

When John the Baptist baptized in water for repentance of sin, the clear and obvious intent was a turning to righteousness. In receiving John's baptism, the sinner renounced his sin and through symbolic cleansing henceforth identified himself with the Messiah and His righteousness. Baptism uniquely represented identification.

Kenneth S. Wuest defines this particular use of *baptizō* (to be **baptized**) as "the introduction or placing of a person or thing into a new environment or into union with something else so as to alter its condition or its relationship to its previous environment or condition" (*Romans in the Greek New Testament* [Grand Rapids: Eerdmans, 1955], pp. 96-97).

In his first letter to Corinth, Paul spoke of Israel's being baptized into Moses (1 Cor. 10:2), symbolizing the people's identity or solidarity with Moses as God's spokesman and leader and the placing of themselves under his authority. By that identity and submission they participated in the leadership and consequent blessings and honor of Moses. The faithful Israelite was, as it were, fused with Moses, who was fused with God. In a similar but infinitely more profound and permanent way, **all of us,** that is, all Christians, **have been baptized into Christ Jesus,** thus permanently being immersed into Him, so as to be made one with Him. It should be noted here that the Greek term as well as the concept call for water baptism being by immersion in order to symbolize this reality properly.

In other passages, Paul affirmed the importance of water baptism in obedience to the Lord's direct command (see 1 Cor. 1:13-17 and Eph. 4:5). But that is only the outward symbol of the baptism to which he refers here. He is speaking metaphorically of the spiritual immersion of believers into Christ through the Holy Spirit, of the believer's intimate oneness with his divine Lord. It is the truth of which Jesus spoke when He said, "Lo, I am with you always, even to the end of the age" (Matt. 28:20), and which John describes as "our fellowship . . . with the Father, and with His Son Jesus Christ" (1 John 1:3). In 1 Corinthians Paul speaks of it as the believer's being one spirit with Christ (1 Cor. 6:17), and he explains to the Galatian believers that "all of you who were baptized into Christ have clothed yourselves with Christ" (Gal. 3:27). In each instance, the idea is that of being totally encompassed by and unified with Christ.

It is in light of that incomprehensible truth that Paul so strongly rebukes the sexual immorality of some of the Corinthian believers, exclaiming incredulously, "Do you not know that your bodies are members of Christ? Shall I then take away the members of Christ and make them members of a harlot? May it never be!" (1 Cor. 6:15).

As noted above and throughout this volume on Romans, salvation not only is God's reckoning a sinner as righteous but of *granting* him a new, righteous disposition or nature. The believer's righteousness in Christ is an earthly as well as a heavenly reality, or else it is not a reality at all. His new life is a divine life. That is why it is impossible for a true believer to continue to live in the same sinful way in which he lived before being saved.

Many people interpret Paul's argument in Romans 6:3-10 as referring to water baptism. However, Paul is simply using the physical analogy of water baptism to teach the spiritual reality of the believer's union with Christ. Water baptism is the outward identification of an inward reality—faith in Jesus' death, burial, and resurrection. Paul was not advocating salvation by water baptism; that would have contradicted everything he had just said about salvation by grace and not works in Romans 3-5, which has no mention of water baptism.

Water baptism was a public symbol of faith in God. The apostle Peter said baptism is a mark of salvation because it gives outward evidence of an inward faith in Christ (1 Pet. 3:21). Titus says the same thing in Titus 3:4-5: "But when the kindness of God our Savior and His love for mankind appeared, He saved us, not on the basis of deeds which we have done in righteousness, but according to His mercy, by the washing of regeneration and renewing by the Holy Spirit." Paul says in Acts 22:16, "And now why do you delay? Arise, and be baptized, and wash away your sins, calling on His name." Those verses are not saying a person is saved by water but that water baptism is a symbol of genuine saving faith.

The Roman believers were well aware of the symbol of baptism. When Paul says **do you not know**, he is in effect saying, "Are you ignorant of the meaning of your own baptism? Have you forgotten what your baptism symbolized?" They were unaware that water baptism symbolizes the spiritual reality of being immersed into Jesus Christ. The tragedy is that many mistake the symbol of water baptism as the means of salvation rather than the demonstration of it. To turn a symbol into the reality is to eliminate the reality, which in this case is salvation by grace through faith in Christ alone.

WE ARE IDENTIFIED IN CHRIST'S DEATH AND RESURRECTION

have been baptized into His death? Therefore we have been buried with Him through baptism into death, in order that as Christ was raised from the dead through the glory of the Father, so we too might walk in newness of life. For if we have become united with Him in the likeness of His death, certainly we shall be also in the likeness of His resurrection, (6:3b-5)

The second principle Paul emphasizes is an extension of the first.

All Christians not only are identified with Christ but are identified with Him specifically in His death and resurrection.

The initial element of the second principle is that all true believers **have been baptized into His** [Christ's] **death.** That is a historical fact looking back to our union with Him on the cross. And the reason **we have been buried with Him through baptism into death is that as Christ was raised from the dead through the glory of the Father, so we too might walk in newness of life.** That is a historical fact looking back to our union with Him in resurrection.

That truth is far too wondrous for us to understand fully, but the basic and obvious reality of it is that we died with Christ in order that we might have life through Him and live like Him. Again Paul emphasizes not so much the immorality but the impossibility of our continuing to live the way we did before we were saved. By trusting in Jesus Christ as Lord and Savior, we were, by an unfathomable divine miracle, taken back 2,000 years, as it were, and made to participate in our Savior's **death** and to be **buried with Him,** burial being the proof of death. The purpose of that divine act of bringing us through **death** (which paid the penalty for our sin) and resurrection with Christ was to enable us henceforth to **walk in newness of life.**

The noble theologian Charles Hodge summarized, "There can be no participation in Christ's life without a participation in his death, and we cannot enjoy the benefits of his death unless we are partakers of the power of his life. We must be reconciled to God in order to be holy, and we cannot be reconciled without thereby becoming holy? (*Commentary on the Epistle to the Romans* [Grand Rapids: Eerdmans, 1983 reprint], p. 195).

As Christ's resurrection life was the certain consequence of His death as the sacrifice for our sin, so the believer's holy life in Christ is the certain consequence of his death to sin in Christ.

Newness translates *kairos,* which refers to newness of quality and character, not *neos,* which refers merely to newness in point of time. Just as sin characterized our old life, so righteousness now characterizes our new life. Scripture is filled with descriptions of the believer's new spiritual life. We are said to receive a new heart (Ezek. 36:26), a new spirit (Ezek. 18:31), a new song (Ps. 40:3), and a new name (Rev. 2:17). We are called a new creation (2 cor. 5:17), a new creature (Gal. 6:15), and a new self (Eph. 4:24).

Continuing to affirm the truth that this union with Christ in His death brings new life and also inevitably brings a new way of living, Paul says, **For if we have become united with Him in the likeness of His death, certainly we shall be also in the likeness of His resurrection.** In other words, as an old life died, so a new one was necessarily born.

Bishop Handley Moule graphically asserted,

We have "received the reconciliation" that we may now walk, not away from God, as if released from a prison, but with God, as His children in His Son. Because we are justified, we are to be holy, separated from sin, separated to God; not as a mere indication that our faith is real, and that therefore we are legally safe, but because we were justified for this very purpose, that we might be holy. . . .

The grapes upon a vine are not merely a living token that the tree is a vine and is alive; they are the product for which the vine exists. It is a thing not to be thought of that the sinner should accept justification—and live to himself. It is a moral contradiction of the very deepest kind, and cannot be entertained without betraying an initial error in the man's whole spiritual creed. (*The Epistle to the Romans* [London: Pickering & Inglis, n.d.], pp. 160-61)

OUR BODY OF SIN HAS BEEN DESTROYED

knowing this, that our old self was crucified with Him, that our body of sin might be done away with, that we should no longer be slaves to sin; for he who has died is freed from sin. (6:6-7)

The third principle Paul stresses is that the old sinful self has been killed. The phrase **knowing this** obviously is an appeal to what should be common knowledge among believers, those to and of whom Paul is speaking. "You should be well aware," he was saying, "that in Christ you are not the same people you were before salvation. You have new life, a new heart, a new spiritual strength, a new hope, and countless other new things that had no part in your former life." When Christ redeemed us, **our old self was crucified,** that is, put to death and destroyed.

Old does not translate *archaios,* which simply refers to chronological age, but rather *palaios,* which refers to something that is completely worn out and useless, fit only for the scrap heap. For all practical purposes it is destroyed. In a passage quoted above from Colossians, Paul declares "I have been crucified with Christ,"—that is, my old "I" is dead and no longer exists—"and it is no longer I who live, but Christ lives in me" (Gal. 2:20). In other words, our new life as Christians is not a made-over old life but a new divinely-bestowed life that is Christ's very own.

When Scripture is compared with Scripture, which responsible study of it always includes, it becomes clear that the "old self" to which Paul refers in Romans 6 is none other than the unregenerate, in-Adam man described in chapter 5, the person who is apart from divine redemption and the new life it brings.

The dualistic view that a Christian has two natures uses unbiblical terminology and can lead to perception that is extremely destructive of holy living. Some who hold such views go to the perverted extreme of the Gnostics in Paul's day, claiming that because the evil self cannot be controlled or changed and because it is going to be destroyed in the future anyway, it does not much matter what you let it do. It is only "spiritual" things, such as your thoughts and intentions, that are of significance. It is not surprising that in congregations where such a philosophy reigns, immoral conduct among the membership as well as the leadership is common and church discipline is usually nonexistent.

Paul asserts that such a perverted view of Christian liberty is known by well-taught believers to be false and destructive and that it should be condemned out-of-hand in the church. In Romans 6:6 Paul mentions three marvelous truths that should protect believers from such false views about the old and new natures.

The first truth is that **our old self was crucified with Him,** that is, with Christ. Crucifixion does not simply produce extreme suffering; it produces death. To be crucified is to die. The **old . . . self** of every believer **was crucified with** his Lord, or else he has not been saved. There is no such thing as a true Christian who has not died with Christ.

In Ephesians, Paul writes in some detail about the **old self,** or the old man. He tells believers: "But you did not learn Christ in this way, if indeed you have heard Him and have been taught in Him, just as truth is in Jesus, that, in reference to your former manner of life, you lay aside the old self, which is being corrupted in accordance with the lusts of deceit, and that you be renewed in the spirit of your mind, and put on the new self, which in the likeness of God has been created in righteousness and holiness of the truth" (Eph. 4:20-24). The Christian's *new self* is actually in God's own likeness!

As John Murray and other New Testament scholars have pointed out, both "lay aside" (v. 22) and "put on" (v. 24) translate Greek infinitives that in this context should be rendered as infinitives of result. In other words, Paul is not giving an admonition or command but rather a statement of fact about what has already been accomplished, finished. Murray therefore translates verse 22 as, "So that ye have put off according to the former manner life the old man" (*Principles of Conduct* [Grand Rapids: Eerdmans, 1957], see pp. 211-19).

Another scholar, Bishop Handley Moule, translated that verse as, "Our old man, our old state, as out of Christ and under Adam's headship, under guilt and in moral bondage, was crucified with Christ" (*The Epistle to the Romans* [London: Pickering & Inglis, n.d.], p. 164). Still another expositor and commentator, the late Martyn Lloyd-Jones, rendered the verse: "Do not go on living as if you were still that old man, because that old man has died. Do not go on living as if he was still there" (*Romans: An Exposition of Chapter 6* [Grand Rapids: Zondervan, 1972], p. 64).

Even if verse 22 is taken as a command, it would not be a

command to reject the dictates of our old self—which the apostle has just declared has been crucified and is now dead, and therefore cannot dictate to us anymore. It would rather be a command for us not to follow the remaining memories of its sinful ways, as if we were still under its evil mastery.

Declaring again that true believers have already been removed from the presence and control of the old sinful self, Paul tells the Galatian church, "Those who belong to Christ Jesus *have crucified* the flesh with its passions and desires" (Gal. 5:24; emphasis added).

In a somewhat parallel passage in Colossians, Paul clearly states that a believer's putting off the old self is a fait accompli, something that has already and irreversibly been accomplished. "Do not lie to one another," he says, "since you laid aside the old self with its evil practices, and have put on the new self who is being renewed to a true knowledge according to the image of the One who created him" (Col. 3:9-10). It was not that every Colossian believer was fully mature and had managed to gain complete mastery over the residual old self. Paul was saying rather that *every* believer, at any level of maturity, can claim that his old self *already has been* laid aside "with its evil practices." In exactly the same way, his new self in Christ is already "being renewed" into conformity with the very image of the God who has recreated him.

The second great truth Paul gives in verse 6 about the old and new dispositions is that **our body of sin might be done away with.** The phrase **might be** does not here carry the idea of possibility but is simply an idiomatic way of stating an already existing fact. In other words, our historical death to sin at the cross in Christ results in our **sin** being **done away with.** Those truths are so nearly synonymous that verse 6 is almost a tautology. Sin that is dead (**crucified**) is obviously **done away with.** Paul states the truth in those two different ways in order to make his point more understandable and to remove any possible ambiguity.

Both the NASB (**done away with**) and the King James ("destroyed") can suggest that **our body of sin** is annihilated. But *katargeō* (**done away with**) literally means "to render inoperative or invalid," to make something ineffective by removing its power of control. That meaning is seen clearly in the term's rendering in such other passages in Romans as 3:3, 31 ("nullify"), 4:14 ("nullified"), 7:2 ("released from").

As every mature Christian learns, the more he grows in Christ, the more he becomes aware of sin in his life. In many places, Paul uses the terms *body* and *flesh* to refer to sinful propensities that are intertwined with physical weaknesses and pleasures (see, e.g., Rom. 8:10-11, 13, 23). New birth in Christ brings death to the sinful self, but it does not bring death to the temporal flesh and its corrupted inclinations until the future glorification. Obviously, a Christian's body is potentially good and is intended to do only good things, else Paul would not have commanded believers to present their bodies to God as "a living and holy sacrifice, acceptable to God" (Rom. 12:1). It can respond to the new holy disposition, but does not always do so.

As Paul explains more fully in chapter 7 of this letter, a believer's unredeemed humanness—of which he uses his own as example—remains with him until he is transformed to heavenly glory. And, as both Scripture and experience clearly teach, the remaining humanness somehow retains certain weaknesses and propensities to sin. The tyranny and penalty of sin both in and over the Christian's life have been broken, but sin's potential for expression in his life has not yet been fully removed. His human weaknesses and instincts make him capable of succumbing to Satan's temptations when he lives apart from the Spirit's Word and power. He is a new, redeemed, holy creation incarcerated in unredeemed flesh.

To combat that remaining weakness in regard to sin, the apostle admonishes believers later in the present chapter: "Just as you presented your members as slaves to impurity and to lawlessness, resulting in further lawlessness, so now present your members as slaves to righteousness, resulting in sanctification" (Rom. 6:19).

The third great truth Paul gives in verse 6 about the old and new natures is that **we should no longer be slaves to sin**. Again, the translation leaves the meaning somewhat ambiguous. But as the apostle makes unequivocal a few verses later, "Thanks be to God that though you were slaves of sin, you *became obedient* from the heart to that form of teaching to which you were committed, *having been freed from sin,* you *became slaves of righteousness*" (Rom. 6:17-18; emphasis added). All the verbs in those two verses make clear that a believer's slavery under sin has already been broken by Christ and is henceforth a thing of the past. Several verses later, Paul reiterates the truth that the believer's new enslavement to righteousness is made possible because he *is now* enslaved to God (v. 22; emphasis added).

In other words, the immediate context of **should no longer be slaves of sin** carries the more precise—and extremely significant—meaning that believers *can* **no longer be slaves of sin**. As already noted, Paul does not teach that a Christian is no longer *capable* of committing sin but that he no longer is under the compulsion and tyranny of sin, nor will he dutifully and solely obey sin as he formerly did. For all genuine Christians, *slavery* to sin no longer exists.

The reason, of course, is that **he who has died is freed from sin**. Because the old life **has died,** what characterized the old life has died with it, most importantly slavery to **sin,** from which *all* the redeemed in Christ are once and forever **freed.**

In his first epistle, Peter strongly emphasizes that truth. "Therefore, since Christ has suffered in the flesh," he says, "arm yourselves also with the same purpose, because he who has suffered in the flesh has ceased from sin, so as to live the rest of the time in the flesh no longer for the lusts of men, but for the will of God" (1 Pet. 4:1-2). Peter is not, however, teaching sinless perfection in this present earthly life, because he goes on to give the severe warning: "By no means let any of you suffer as a murderer, or thief, or evildoer, or a troublesome meddler" (v. 15).

Martyn Lloyd-Jones offers a helpful illustration of the believer's relation to his old sinful disposition (*Romans: An Exposition of Chapter 6* [Grand Rapids: Zondervan, 1972], pp. 26-27). He pictures two adjoining fields, one owned by Satan and one owned by God, that are separated by a road. Before salvation, a person lives in Satan's field and is totally subject to his jurisdiction. After salvation, a person works in the other field, now subject only to God's jurisdiction. As he plows in the new field, however, the believer is often cajoled by his former master, who seeks to entice him back into the old sinful ways. Satan often succeeds in temporarily drawing the believer's attention away from his new Master and his new way of life. But he is powerless to draw the believer back into the old field of sin and death.

THE ONE DEATH OF CHRIST WAS A DEATH TO SIN

Now if we have died with Christ, we believe that we shall also live with Him, knowing that Christ, having been raised from the dead, is never to die again; death no longer is master over Him. For the death that He died, He died to sin, once for all; but the life that He lives, He lives to God. (6:8-10)

The fourth principle is that Christ's one death to sin brought not only the death of sin but the death of death for those who, by faith, have died with Him. These three verses are essentially a summary of what Paul has just been teaching about the believer's death to sin and his new life in Christ. He also stresses the permanence of that awesome and glorious truth.

The assurance that **we shall also live with Him** obviously applies to the believer's ultimate and eternal presence with Christ in heaven. But the context, which focuses on holy living, strongly suggests that Paul is here speaking primarily about our living **with Him** in righteousness in this present life. In Greek, as in English, future tenses often carry the idea of certainty. That seems to be the case with Paul's use of *suzaō* (or *sunzaō*), here rendered **shall also live.** As the apostle makes clear in verse 10 in regard to Christ, he is not merely speaking of existing in the presence of God but of living to God, that is, living a life fully consistent with God's holiness.

Building on that thought, Paul goes on to say, **knowing that**

**Christ, having been raised from the dead, is never to die again;
death no longer is master over Him.** The point is that, because *we*
have died and been raised with Christ (vv. 3-5), we, too, shall **never die
again.** The sin that made us subject to death is no longer master over us,
just as it **no longer is master over Him.** It also can never be our
executioner.

The climax of this section of chapter 6 is that **the death that He
died, He died to sin, once for all; but the life that He lives, He lives
to God.** Because death is the penalty of sin (Rom. 6:23), to break the
mastery of sin is to break the mastery of death.

Two extremely important truths in verse 10 should be emphasized.
The first is that Christ **died to sin.** Having lived a perfectly sinless life
during His incarnation, Christ obviously never had the same relationship
to sin that every other human being has. He not only was never mastered
by sin but never committed a sin of the least sort. How then, we wonder,
could *He* have **died to sin?** Yet it is clear from this verse that in whatever
way Christ died to sin, believers also have died to sin.

Some suggest that believers have died to sin in the sense of no
longer being sensitive to the allurements of sin. But that view is not borne
out by Christian experience, and it obviously could not apply to Christ,
who was never, in the first place, sensitive to sin's allurements. Others
suggest that Paul is teaching that believers *ought* to die to sin. But again,
such an interpretation could not apply to Christ. Nor could it mean that
Christ died to sin by becoming perfect, because He was always perfect.

It seems that Paul means two things in declaring that **Christ died
to sin.** First, He died to the *penalty* of sin by taking upon Himself the
sins of the whole world. He met sin's legal demand for all mankind who
would trust in Him. By their faith in Him, empowered by His divine and
limitless grace, believers have forensically died to sin. Second, Christ died
to the *power* of sin, forever breaking its power over those who belong to
God through their faith in His Son. Paul assured even the immature and
sin-prone believers in Corinth that God "made Him who knew no sin to
be sin on our behalf, that we might become the righteousness of God in
Him" (2 Cor. 5:21).

It was perhaps the twin truth that believers die both to the penalty
as well as to the power of sin that Augustus Toplady had in mind in the
beautiful line from his great hymn "Rock of Ages"—"Be of sin the double
cure, save from wrath and make me pure."

The second crucial emphasis in verse 10 is that Christ **died to
sin, once for all.** He achieved a victory that will never need repeating, a
profound truth that the writer of Hebrews stresses again and again (7:26-
27; 9:12, 28; 10:10; cf. 1 Pet. 3:18).

In addition to being actually identified with Christ in the ways
Paul mentions in this passage—namely, His death and resurrection, the

destruction of the body of sin, and the death to sin—believers are also analogically likened to their Lord in His virgin birth, in that both He in His physical birth and they in their spiritual births have been conceived by the Holy Spirit. He identified with our humanity in His incarnation; then through His circumcision He placed Himself temporarily under the authority of the Mosaic law in order to redeem those under the law (Col. 2:11). We also relate to our Lord in His sufferings, as we, like Paul, bear the marks of suffering for Him. In so many ways, believers are so completely and inextricably identified with the Lord Jesus Christ that He is not ashamed to call them brothers (Heb. 2:11).

Alive to God

Even so consider yourselves to be dead to sin, but alive to God in Christ Jesus.

Therefore do not let sin reign in your mortal body that you should obey its lusts, and do not go on presenting the members of your body to sin as instruments of unrighteousness; but present yourselves to God as those alive from the dead, and your members as instruments of righteousness to God. For sin shall not be master over you, for you are not under law, but under grace. (6:11-14)

After Lazarus had been dead for four days, Jesus called him forth from the grave. When he came out he was still wrapped from head to foot in his grave clothes, and Jesus instructed those standing nearby to "unbind him, and let him go" (John 11:44).

That story is a vivid picture of a believer's condition at the time of his conversion. He becomes fully alive spiritually when he trusts in Christ as Savior and Lord, but he is still bound, as it were, in some of the grave clothes of his old sinful life. The difference, of course, is that all of a believer's sinful old clothes do not come off immediately, as did those of Lazarus. Not only that, but believers are continually tempted to put the old clothes back on. It is that continuing battle with sin and Satan that Paul recognizes in Romans 6:11-14.

After reminding his readers that they have died to sin and been raised to new life with Christ, the apostle now turns their attention to taking off the old grave clothes and living the new life to the fullness of Christ's righteousness and to His glory.

In chapter 7, using himself as the example, Paul deals more fully with the believer's battle with the old sinful habits and inclinations. He confesses that, even as an apostle, he did not fully understand why, since he had died to sin, the battle against sin still raged within him. "For that which I am doing, I do not understand; for I am not practicing what I would like to do, but I am doing the very thing I hate" (Rom. 7:15). He does, however, know where the trouble lies, declaring a few verses later, "I know that nothing good dwells in me, that is, in my flesh; for the wishing is present in me, but the doing of the good is not" (v. 18).

In the present passage Paul again answers questions he knew his readers would wonder about: "If we have really been freed from sin by Christ (v. 7), why does it still give us so much trouble? If we are now holy before God, why are our lives so often unholy? If we *are* righteous, how can our lives better manifest that righteousness?" Three key words summarize the answers presented in 6:11-14: *know, consider,* and *yield.*

KNOW

Even so (6:11a)

The first key word (*know*) has to do with the mind and is implied in the transitional phrase **even so.** Those two words are crucial to Paul's explanation, referring back to the truths he has just given in the first ten verses of the chapter. The idea is, "You must *know and fully believe* what I have just said, or else what I am about to say will make no sense. The truth that you are spiritually dead to sin, and the reality that you are spiritually alive to Christ are not abstract concepts for your finite minds to attempt to verify. They are divinely-revealed, foundational axioms behind Christian living, apart from which you can never hope to live the holy lives your new Lord demands."

Realizing the importance of the truths he presents in verses 1-10, Paul uses forms of *know* and *believe* some four times (vv. 3, 6, 8, 9), and in other places he implies that his readers know about certain other truths (see, e.g., vv. 2, 5, 7).

Scriptural exhortation is *always* built on spiritual knowledge. Although God would have been perfectly justified simply to have given men a list of unexplained do's and don'ts, in His grace and compassion He did not choose to be autocratic. The basic reason He reveals as to why men are to live according to His standards was summarized in His declaration to ancient Israel:"Be holy; for I am holy" (Lev. 11:44). Quoting that very command, Peter admonishes Christians: "Like the Holy One who called you, be holy yourselves also in all your behavior; because it is written, 'You shall be holy, for I am holy' " (1 Pet. 1:15-16).

Scripture is replete with specific commands and standards for conduct, and behind all of them are divine truths, explicit or implicit, upon which those commands and standards are founded.

Paul has just declared that, as believers, we are united with Jesus Christ in His death and have through Him had the penalty paid for our sin. We have risen with our Lord Jesus Christ in His resurrection and therefore are able to walk in newness of life. Because Christ will never die again to sin, we will never die again to sin.

For a Christian to live out the fullness of his new life in Christ, for him to truly live as the new creation that he is, he *must* know and believe that he is not what he used to be. He *must* understand that he is not a remodeled sinner but a remade saint. He *must* understand that, despite his present conflict with sin, he is not longer under sin's tyranny and will never be again. the true understanding of his identity is essential.

Through Hosea the Lord lamented, "My people are destroyed for lack of knowledge. Because you have rejected knowledge, I also will reject you from being My priest. Since you have forgotten the law of your God I also will forget your children" (Hos. 4:6). Isaiah declared, "Listen, O heavens, and hear, O earth; for the Lord speaks, 'Sons I have reared and brought up, but they have revolted against Me. An ox knows its owner, and a donkey its master's manger, but Israel does not know, My people do not understand' " (Isa. 1:2-3) Paul admonished believers in Philippi, "Finally, brethren, whatever is true, whatever is honorable, whatever is right, whatever is pure, whatever is lovely, whatever is of good repute, if there is any excellence and if anything worthy of praise, let your mind dwell on these things" (Phil. 4:8). He reminded Colossian believers that they had "put on the new self who is being renewed to a true knowledge according to the image of the One who created him" (Col. 3:10). Faithful divine living without divine knowledge is impossible.

CONSIDER

consider yourselves to be dead to sin, but alive to God in Christ Jesus. (6:11b)

The second key word (consider) has more to do with what we would call the heart. In its literal sense, *logizomai* means simply to count or number something. Jesus used it of Himself during the Last Supper when He disclosed to the disciples that He was the One "numbered with transgressors" of whom Isaiah prophesied (Luke 22:37; cf. Isa. 53:12). But the word was commonly used metaphorically in the sense of fully affirming a truth, of having unreserved inner confidence in the reality of what the mind acknowledges. Though both aspects actually occur in the mind, we think of this matter in the sense of being "heart felt."

In the next chapter of this epistle Paul will illustrate from his own life how difficult it is for a Christian to realize experientially that he is free from sin's bondage. As we look honestly at our lives after salvation, it is more than obvious that sin's contamination is still very much with us. No matter how radical our outer transformation at the time of salvation may have been for the better, it is difficult to comprehend that we no longer have the fallen sin nature and that our new nature is actually divine. It is hard to realize that we are actually indwelt by the Holy Spirit and that God now calls us His children and deems us fit to live eternally with Him in His heaven.

To help us **consider**, it is advantageous to note that there are a number of reasons believers often find it difficult to comprehend that they are now free from sin's bondage. Many of them do not realize that marvelous truth simply because they have never heard of it. They assume, or perhaps have been wrongly taught, that salvation brings only transactional or forensic holiness—that because of their trust in Christ, God now *regards* them as holy but that their basic relationship to sin is the same as it always was and that it will not be changed until they go to be with Christ. That view of salvation often includes the idea that, although trust in Christ brings the believer a new nature, the old nature remains fully operative, and that the Christian life is essentially a battle between his two resident natures. This makes salvation "addition" rather than "transformation."

A second reason Christians often find it hard to believe they are actually free from the tyranny of sin is that Satan does not want them to believe it. If the enemy of our souls and the accuser of the brethren can make us think he still dominates our earthly lives, he weakens our resolve to live righteously by making it appear hopeless.

A third reason Christians often find it difficult to believe they are free from sin's compulsion is that the reality of the new birth in Christ is not experiential, it is not physically observable or verifiable. Redemption is a divine and spiritual transaction that may or may not be accompanied by physical or emotional experiences. A believer cannot perceive or experience in any *humanly* verifiable way the moment of his dying and resurrection with Christ.

A fourth and perhaps the most common reason why Christians find it hard to believe they are freed from sin's tyranny while they are still on earth is that their continued battle with sin seems almost constantly to contradict that truth. If they have a new holy disposition and sin's control has truly been broken, they wonder, why are they still so strongly tempted and why do they so often succumb?

Paul's answer follows, **Consider yourselves to be dead to sin, but alive to God in Christ Jesus.** He was not speaking of a psychological mind game, by which we keep affirming something over and over until we are convinced against our better judgment or even against reality that it is true. We know we are **dead to sin** and **alive to God in Christ Jesus** because God's Word declares it is so. In other words, those are truths of faith and they must be affirmed in faith.

David C. Needham wrote, "What could be more frustrating than being a Christian who thinks himself primarily a self-centered sinner, yet whose purpose in life is to produce God-centered holiness?" (*Birthright: Christian, Do You Know Who You Are?* [Portland: Multnomah, 1979], p. 69). Until a believer accepts the truth that Christ has broken the power of sin over his life, he cannot live victoriously, because in his innermost being he does not think it is possible.

Commentator Donald Grey Barnhouse said,

> Years ago, in the midst of a Latin-American revolution, an American citizen was captured and sentenced to death. But an American officer rushed before the firing squad and draped a large American flag entirely around the victim. "If you shoot this man," he cried, "you will fire through the American flag and incur the wrath of a whole nation!" The revolutionary in charge released the prisoner at once. (*Romans: God's Freedom* [Grand Rapids: Eerdmans, 1961], p. 118)

In a similar way, Christ's righteousness is draped over every believer, protecting him from sin's deadly attacks.

We believe we are in God's eternal purpose, plan, presence, and power because His Word assures us we are. Paul assured the Ephesian believers that God "chose us in Him [Christ Jesus] before the foundation of the world, that we should be holy and blameless before Him" (Eph. 1:4). And to the church at Philippi he wrote, "For I am confident of this very thing, that He who began a good work in you will perfect it until the day of Christ Jesus. . . . So then, my beloved, just as you have always obeyed, not as in my presence only, but now much more in my absence, work out your salvation with fear and trembling; for it is God who is at work in you, both to will and to work for His good pleasure" (Phil. 1:6; 2:12-13).

There are many important and practical results of our considering ourselves **dead to sin, but alive to God in Christ Jesus.** First, we can have confidence in the midst of temptation, knowing that with sin's tyranny broken we *can* successfully resist it in God's power. "No temptation has overtaken you but such as is common to man; and God is faithful, who will not allow you to be tempted beyond what you are able, but with the temptation will provide the way of escape also, that you may be able to endure it" (1 Cor. 10:13).

Second, we have confidence that we cannot sin our way out of God's grace. Just as we have been saved by God's power alone, we are kept by His power alone. "My sheep hear My voice," Jesus said, "and I know them, and they follow Me; and I give eternal life to them, and they shall never perish; and no one shall snatch them out of My hand. My Father, who has given them to Me, is greater than all; and no one is able to snatch them out of the Father's hand" (John 10:27-29).

Third, when we truly consider ourselves dead to sin and alive to Christ, we have confidence in the face of death. "I am the resurrection and the life," our Lord said; "he who believes in Me shall live even if he dies, and everyone who lives and believes in Me shall never die" (John 11:25-26; cf. Heb. 2:14).

Fourth, we know that, regardless of what happens to us in this life, no matter how disastrous it may be, God will use it not only for His glory but also for our blessing. "We know that God causes all things to work together for good to those who love God, to those who are called according to His purpose" (Rom. 8:28).

All of those things, and many more, are true because we are **alive to God in Christ Jesus.** No religion in the world can or does make such a claim. Even the most ardent Muslim does not claim to be *in* Mohammed or *in* Allah. Buddhists do not claim to be *in* Buddha or Hindus to be *in* any of their multitude of gods. As Christians, however, we know that God "has blessed us with *every spiritual blessing* in the heavenly places in Christ" (Eph. 1:3; emphasis added).

YIELD

Therefore do not let sin reign in your mortal body that you should obey its lusts, and do not go on presenting the members of your body to sin as instruments of unrighteousness; but present yourselves to God as those alive from the dead, and your members as instruments of righteousness to God. For sin shall not be master over you, for you are not under law, but under grace. (6:12-14)

The third key word is *yield,* or present (v. 13), which obviously has to do with the will. Because of the incomprehensible truths about his relationship to God that the believer knows with his mind and feels deeply committed to in his heart, he is **therefore** able to exercise his will successfully against **sin** and, by God's power, prevent its **reign in** his **mortal body.**

In this present life, **sin** will always be a powerful force for the Christian to reckon with. But it is no longer master, no longer lord, and it can and must be resisted. **Sin** is personified by Paul as a dethroned but still powerful monarch who is determined to **reign** in the believer's life just as he did before salvation. The apostle's admonition to believers, therefore, is for them to **not let sin reign,** because it now has no right to reign. It now has no power to control a believer unless the believer chooses to **obey its lusts.**

Peter makes a similar appeal. Because "you are a chosen race, a royal priesthood, a holy nation, a people for God's own possession," he says, "I urge you as aliens and strangers to abstain from fleshly lusts, which wage war against the soul" (1 Pet. 2:9, 11). The moment they are saved, Christians become citizens of God's kingdom of righteousness, and thereby aliens and strangers to Satan's realm of sin and death.

Because a believer is a new creature in Christ, his immortal soul is forever beyond sin's reach. The only remaining beachhead where sin can attack a Christian is in his **mortal body.** One day that body will be glorified and forever be out of sin's reach, but in the meanwhile it is still **mortal,** that is, subject to corruption and death. It still has sinful **lusts**— because the brain and the thinking processes are part of the **mortal body** and Satan uses those **lusts** to lure God's people back into sin in whatever ways he can.

Paul later declares in this letter, "For we know that the whole creation groans and suffers the pains of childbirth together until now. And not only this, but also we ourselves, having the first fruits of the Spirit, even we ourselves groan within ourselves, waiting eagerly for our adoption as sons, the redemption of our body" (Rom. 8:22-23). Teaching the same truth, he wrote the Philippian believers, "For our citizenship is in heaven, from which also we eagerly wait for a Savior, the Lord Jesus Christ, who will transform the body of our humble state into conformity with the body of His glory" (Phil. 3:20-21). And to the Corinthians he wrote, "For this perishable must put on the imperishable, and this mortal must put on immortality" (1 Cor. 15:53).

It is because our mortal bodies are still subject to sin that Paul says, **Do not go on presenting the members of your body to sin as instruments of unrighteousness.** He does not warn about sin reigning in our souls or our spirits, but only about its reigning in our bodies, because that is the only place in a Christian where sin can operate. That is why later in this epistle he laments, "For I know that nothing good dwells in me, that is, in my *flesh;* for the wishing is present in me, but the doing of the good is not. . . . For I joyfully concur with the law of God in the inner man, but I see a different law in the members of my *body,* waging war against the law of my mind, and making me a prisoner of the law of sin which is in my *members*" (Rom. 7:18, 22-23). He then concludes, "Wretched man that I am! Who will set me free from the *body* of this death? Thanks be to God through Jesus Christ our Lord! So then, on the one hand I myself with my mind am serving the law of God, but on the other, with my *flesh* the law of sin" (Rom. 7:24-25; emphasis added).

It is because the Christian's warfare with sin is waged in the body that the apostle also declared, "I urge you therefore, brethren, by the mercies of God, to present your *bodies* a living and holy sacrifice, acceptable to God, which is your spiritual service of worship" (Rom. 12:1), and "I buffet my *body* and make it my slave, lest possibly, after I have preached to others, I myself should be disqualified" (1 Cor. 9:27; emphasis added).

It is obvious that sin *can* reign in our bodies, else Paul's admonition would be pointless. But it is also obvious that sin does not *have to* reign there, or the warning would be equally pointless. He therefore commands: **Do not go on presenting the members of your body to sin as instruments of unrighteousness; but present yourselves to God as those alive from the dead, and your members as instruments of righteousness to God.**

By definition, a command presupposes a will in the one being commanded. The commands in God's Word are no exceptions. It is therefore the Christian's will that Paul is speaking about here. For a sin to have power over a child of God, that sin must first pass through his will. It is for that reason that Paul exhorts believers: "So then, my beloved, just as you have always obeyed, not as in my presence only, but now much more in my absence, work out your salvation with fear and trembling; for it is God who is at work in you, both to will and to work for His good pleasure" (Phil. 2:12-13). God's will can be active in our lives only as our wills are submissive to His.

When a believer yields **the members of** his **body to sin**, those members become **instruments of unrighteousness.** On the other hand, when in obedience to his heavenly Father he yields himself as one who is **alive from the dead** ways of sin and death, those same **members** become holy **instruments of righteousness to God.**

In verse 14, Paul changes from admonition to declaration, offering the assuring words: **For sin shall not be master over you, for you are not under law, but under grace.**

God's **law** "is holy, and the commandment is holy and righteous and good" (Rom. 7:12). But the **law** cannot break either sin's penalty or its power. It can only rebuke, restrain, and condemn. The Christian is no longer **under** the condemnation of God's **law** but is now **under** the redeeming power of His **grace.** It is in the power of that grace that the Lord calls him to live.

Free from Sin

What then? Shall we sin because we are not under law but under grace? May it never be! Do you not know that when you present yourselves to someone as slaves for obedience, you are slaves of the one whom you obey, either of sin resulting in death, or of obedience resulting in righteousness? But thanks be to God that though you were slaves of sin, you became obedient from the heart to that form of teaching to which you were committed, and having been freed from sin, you became slaves of righteousness. I am speaking in human terms because of the weakness of your flesh. For just as you presented your members as slaves to impurity and to lawlessness, resulting in further lawlessness, so now present your members as slaves to righteousness, resulting in sanctification. For when you were slaves of sin, you were free in regard to righteousness. Therefore what benefit were you then deriving from the things of which you are now ashamed? For the outcome of those things is death. But now having been freed from sin and enslaved to God, you derive your benefit, resulting in sanctification, and the outcome, eternal life. For the wages of sin is death, but the free gift of God is eternal life in Christ Jesus our Lord. (6:15-23)

Sin is the most devastating, debilitating, degenerating power that ever entered the human stream. Its evil, in fact, corrupted the entire creation, which "groans and suffers the pains of childbirth together until now" (Rom. 8:22).

Scripture characterizes sin and its effects in many ways. It refers to it as defiling, a pollution of the soul. It is to the human soul what corrosion is to a precious metal or smog is to a beautiful sky. Sin is called "an impure thing" (Isa. 30:22), and it is compared to "the venom of serpents, and the deadly poison of cobras" (Deut. 32:33). Even things that men consider to be righteous are like "a filthy garment" (lit., "menstrual cloth") in God's sight (Isa. 64:6; cf. Zech. 3:3-4). Paul refers to sin as "defilement of flesh and spirit" (2 Cor. 7:1) and to sinners as those whose minds and consciences are defiled (Titus 1:15).

Sin is rebellious, ignoring and even trampling on God's Word. Someone has called sin God's would-be murderer, because if sin had its way it would destroy God Himself along with His righteousness.

Sin is ungrateful, refusing to acknowledge God as the source of every good thing. The sinner indulges in God's gracious provisions that are all around him but fails to credit, much less thank, God for those things. He takes God's blessings and uses them to serve self and Satan. Every sinner is like Absalom, the undisciplined son of David who kissed his father while plotting to usurp his throne (see 2 Sam. 14:33—15:6).

Sin is incurable by man's own efforts and power. Even if fallen man wanted to rid himself of sin, he could not do it, any more than "the Ethiopian [could] change his skin or the leopard his spots" (Jer. 13:23). The Puritan writer John Flavel commented on the damning effect of sin by writing that if a sinner's penitential tears were as numberless as all the drops of rain that have fallen since the Creation, they could not wash away a single sin.

Sin is overpowering, hanging above fallen mankind like darkness over night. It dominates the mind (Rom. 1:21), the affections (John 3:19-21), and the will (Jer. 44:15-17).

Sin brings satanic control, because every sin serves the purposes of "the prince of the power of the air" (Eph. 2:2). Every unredeemed sinner is a spiritual child of the devil (John 8:44).

Although sin promises satisfaction, it instead brings misery, frustration, and hopelessness. Job lamented that "man is born for trouble, as sparks fly upward" (Job 5:7). In fact, because of sin, all "creation was subjected to futility" (Rom. 8:20).

Worst of all, sin damns the unredeemed soul to hell. In his vision on Patmos, the apostle John "saw the dead, the great and the small, standing before the throne, and books were opened; and another book was opened, which is the book of life; and the dead were judged from the things which were written in the books, according to their deeds. And the sea gave up the dead which were in it, and death and Hades gave up the dead which were in them; and they were judged, every one of them according to their deeds. And death and Hades were thrown into the lake of fire. This is the second death, the lake of fire. And if anyone's name was not found written in the book of life, he was thrown into the lake of fire" (Rev. 20:12-15).

With the single exception of Jesus Christ, every human being born into this world has been born with a sinful nature. The natural, unredeemed person is under the tyranny of sin. It controls his thoughts, words, actions—his total existence. Jesus declared that "everyone who commits sin is the slave of sin" (John 8:34), and because every unsaved person is unable to commit anything but sin, every unsaved person is a slave of sin.

As Paul notes in the present passage, the natural man is a *willing* slave of sin. Men prove that truth every day of their lives as they reject the light of God that they have. Although unregenerate persons often want desperately to escape the unpleasant and destructive consequences of their sins, they do not want to relinquish the cherished sins themselves.

It has often been noted that some black slaves willingly fought with their masters during the American Civil War. Not unlike sinners who oppose and reject the One who offers to save them, those slaves fought against the Union forces who wanted to emancipate them.

Paul began the major theological section of this epistle with the sobering declaration that "the wrath of God is revealed from heaven against all ungodliness and unrighteousness of men, *who suppress the truth* in unrighteousness, because *that which is known about God is evident within them;* for God made it evident to them. For since the creation of the world His invisible attributes, His eternal power and divine nature, *have been clearly seen, being understood* through what has been made, so that they are without excuse" (Rom. 1:18-20; emphasis added).

Sin is the terrible, life-wrecking, soul-damning reality that resides and grows in every unredeemed human heart like an incurable cancer. Even when men try to escape from sin, they cannot, and when they try to escape its guilt, they cannot. The greatest gift God could give to fallen mankind is freedom from sin, and it is that very gift that He offers through His Son, Jesus Christ. It is on that great, unsurpassable gift of redemption from sin that Paul now focuses his great inspired mind.

As he continues his discourse on sanctification, Paul first reminds his Christian readers of their own past enslavement to sin and then reminds them of their new enslavement to righteousness through their trust in Jesus Christ. His primary point in 6:15-23 is that believers in Jesus Christ should live in total subjection to Christ and His righteousness and not fall back into their former sins, which no longer have claim over them. Because they have died in Christ to sin and risen with Him to righteousness, they are no longer under the lordship of sin but are now under the lordship of righteousness. Because the Christian has a new relationship to God, he also has a new relationship to sin. For the first time, he is able *not* to live sinfully and able also for the first time to live righteously.

Paul's development of Romans 6:15-23 closely parallels that of verses 1-10 (see chap. 23 of this volume). He presents the antagonist (v. 15*a*), the answer (v. 15*b*), the axiom (v. 16), the argument (vv. 17-22), and the absolute (v. 23).

The Antagonist

What then? Shall we sin because we are not under law but under grace? (6:15*a*)

With his brief introductory question, **What then?** the apostle again anticipates the false conclusions his antagonists would derive from his declaration that believers "are not under law, but under grace" (v. 14*b*). To them, the idea of no longer being **under law but under grace** was tantamount to being free of all moral restraint. "If the **law** no longer needs to be obeyed, and if God's **grace** covers all sins," they would argue, "then believers are perfectly free to do as they please." Jewish legalists, on the other hand, believed obedience to God's law was the only way of salvation. To them, Paul exalted righteousness out of one side of his mouth, while in reality giving license to sin out of the other side. They accused Paul of condoning lawlessness in the name of God's **grace.**

The doctrine of grace has always been subject to that false charge, which the apostle first answers in the first half of chapter 6. But because the misunderstanding was so common and the issue so critical, he gives the answer again from a slightly different perspective. The doctrine of salvation by God's grace, working only through man's faith and apart from any works, is the furthest thing from a license to sin.

The Answer

May it never be! (6:15*b*)

Paul gives the same forceful and unambiguous denial he gave in verse 2. The idea is, "No, no, a thousand times no!" The mere suggestion that God's grace is a license to sin is self-contradictory, a logical as well as a moral and spiritual absurdity. The very purpose of God's grace is to free man from sin. How, then, could grace possibly justify continuing in sin?

Grace not only justifies but also transforms the life that is saved. A life that gives no evidence of moral and spiritual transformation gives no evidence of salvation.

THE AXIOM

Do you not know that when you present yourselves to someone as slaves for obedience, you are slaves of the one whom you obey, either of sin resulting in death, or of obedience resulting in righteousness? (6:16)

An axiom is a general truth that is so self-evident it needs no proof. **Do you not know?** is clearly rhetorical, implying that his readers would readily acknowledge the truth of what he was about to say if they gave it the least thought. What could be more obvious than the fact **that when you present yourselves to someone as slaves for obedience, you are slaves of the one whom you obey?** The phrase **present yourselves** indicates the *willing choice* of **obedience** to a master and makes Paul's point even more obvious. By definition, all **slaves,** particularly voluntary ones, are bound to total **obedience** to their master, **the one whom** they obey. A person who is not so bound is not a slave.

The apostle applies the axiom to the life-style of believers, the matter of sanctified living about which he has been teaching (vv. 1-14). In relation to God's will, a saved person has but two choices: **either** to **sin,** which is to disobey Him, **or of obedience.** A person's general pattern of living proves who his true master is. If his life is characterized by **sin,** which is opposed to God's will, then he is sin's slave. If his life is characterized by **obedience,** which reflects God's will, then he is God's slave. The end result of the first slavery is both physical and spiritual **death,** whereas that of the second slavery is **righteousness,** the inescapable mark of eternal *life.* Believers are God's "workmanship, created in Christ Jesus for good works, which God prepared beforehand, that we should walk in them" (Eph. 2:10). The habitually unrighteous life cannot be a Christian life.

In the previous chapter Paul described the same truth from the opposite perspective, that of the master. In the unregenerate life, the life in Adam, sin and death reign, whereas in the redeemed life, the life in Christ, righteousness and eternal life reign (5:12-21). There is no other alternative, no neutral ground. All men are either mastered by sin, which is to say they are under the lordship of Satan, or they are mastered by righteousness, which is to say they are under the lordship of Jesus Christ. As Matthew Henry observed, "If we would know to which of these two families we belong, we must inquire to which of these two masters we yield our obedience" (*Matthew Henry's Commentary on the Whole Bible,* vol. 6 [Old Tappan, N.J.: Revell, n.d.], p. 405).

Although the natural, freedom-seeking, rebellious mind recoils at the truth, no human being is his own master. The popular notion that a person can master his own life and destiny is a delusion that Satan has foisted on mankind ever since the Fall. It was by that lie, in fact, that Adam and Eve were drawn into the first sin. Warning against false teachers in the first century who proclaimed that attractive falsehood, Peter wrote: "For speaking out arrogant words of vanity they entice by fleshly desires, by sensuality, those who barely escape from the ones who live in error, promising them freedom while they themselves are slaves of corruption; for by what a man is overcome, by this he is enslaved" (2 Pet. 2:18-19). If the reality of man's situation is honestly acknowledged, it becomes obvious that human beings are not independent creatures. They are not and cannot be free in the sense in which the world defines and values freedom.

Many people resist the claims of Christ because they are afraid of having to give up their cherished freedoms. Actually, of course, they have no freedoms to lose. The unsaved person is not free to do good or evil as he chooses. He is bound and enslaved to sin, and the only thing he *can* do is to sin. His only choices have to do with when, how, why, and to what degree he will sin.

It should be just as self-evident that no human being can be the slave of two different masters. "No one can serve two masters," Jesus declared; "for either he will hate the one and love the other, or he will hold to one and despise the other. You cannot serve God and mammon" (Matt. 6:24).

Paul's point in the second half of Romans 6 is the same one that Jesus made in the above passage. A person cannot have two different and opposing natures at the same time, and he cannot live in two different and opposing spiritual worlds at the same time. He is either the slave of **sin,** which he is by natural birth, or he is the slave of **righteousness,** which he becomes by the new birth.

Paul is not speaking here of moral and spiritual obligation but of moral and spiritual reality. He is not saying that believers ought to admire righteousness or desire righteousness or practice righteousness, although they should, of course, do those things. He is not here teaching that a Christian *ought to be* a slave of **righteousness** but that every Christian, by divine creation, *is made* a slave of **righteousness** and cannot be anything else. Paul is saying exactly what John says in his first letter: "No one who is born of God practices sin, because His seed abides in him; and he cannot sin, because he is born of God. By this the children of God and the children of the devil are obvious: anyone who does not practice righteousness is not of God, nor the one who does not love his brother" (1 John 3:9-10).

"And although you were formerly alienated and hostile in mind, engaged in evil deeds," Paul tells the Colossian believers, "yet He [Jesus Christ, the Son] has now reconciled you in His fleshly body through death, in order to present you before Him [God the Father] holy and blameless and beyond reproach" (Col. 1:21-22). In other words, for the Christian, the life of unrighteousness, of alienation from and hostility toward God, is *past*. The old sinful way of life *cannot* continue to characterize a true Christian. Obedience to God in righteous living is a certainty in the life of a truly justified person. Because of temporary unfaithfulness, sinful disobedience may at times *appear* to dominate a Christian's life. But a true believer cannot continue indefinitely in disobedience, because it is diametrically opposed to his new and holy nature, which cannot indefinitely endure sinful living.

John emphasizes that truth repeatedly in his first epistle. "If we say that we have fellowship with Him and yet walk in the darkness, we lie and do not practice the truth; . . . The one who says, 'I have come to know Him,' and does not keep His commandments, is a liar, and the truth is not in him; . . . No one who is born of God practices sin, because His seed abides in him; and he cannot sin, because he is born of God" (1 John 1:6; 2:4; 3:9).

THE ARGUMENT—EXPLAINING THE TWO SLAVERIES

But thanks be to God that though you were slaves of sin, you became obedient from the heart to that form of teaching to which you were committed, and having been freed from sin, you became slaves of righteousness. I am speaking in human terms because of the weakness of your flesh. For just as you presented your members as slaves to impurity and to lawlessness, resulting in further lawlessness, so now present your members as slaves to righteousness, resulting in sanctification. For when you were slaves of sin, you were free in regard to righteousness. Therefore what benefit were you then deriving from the things of which you are now ashamed? For the outcome of those things is death. But now having been freed from sin and enslaved to God, you derive your benefit, resulting in sanctification, and the outcome, eternal life. (6:17-22)

Paul here explains and applies the principle he has just stated (v. 16), namely, that a person is a slave either to sin and Satan or to righteousness and God. In doing so, he contrasts the three aspects of each of those two domains of servanthood: their position, their practice, and their promise.

THEIR POSITION

But thanks be to God that though you were slaves of sin, you became obedient from the heart to that form of teaching to which you were committed, and having been freed from sin, you became slaves of righteousness. (6:17-18)

First the apostle gives **thanks . . . to God** that his believing readers were no longer subject to the slavery that leads to death. He does not thank or praise them for their own wisdom or intelligence or moral and spiritual determination, because none of those things had a part in their salvation. "No one can come to Me," Jesus said, "unless the Father who sent Me draws him, . . . [and] unless it has been granted him from the Father" (John 6:44, 65). Our thanks for salvation should always be to God alone, because it is God alone "who gives us the victory through our Lord Jesus Christ" (1 Cor. 15:57).

Believers are saved solely by the grace and power of **God.** And by His grace, habitual disobedience to Him is in the past tense. Formerly, Paul says, you **were slaves of sin,** but no more. **Were** translates an imperfect Greek tense, signifying an ongoing reality. In other words, the unregenerate person is under the continual, unbroken slavery of sin. That is the universal position of the natural man, with no exceptions. No matter how outwardly moral, upright, or benevolent an unsaved person's life may be, all that he thinks, says, and does emanates from a proud, sinful, ungodly heart. Quoting from Psalm 14, Paul had already made that truth clear. "As it is written, 'There is none righteous, not even one; there is none who understands, there is none who seeks for God; all have turned aside, together they have become useless; there is none who does good, there is not even one'" (Rom. 3:10-12).

That Paul is not speaking about merely outward righteousness is made clear from his declaration that **you became obedient from the heart.** God works His salvation in a person's innermost being. Through the grace provided by His Son, God changes men's very natures when they trust in Him. A person whose **heart** has not been changed has not been saved. Righteous living that issues from an **obedient . . . heart** is habitual. And just as God's grace operates only through a trusting heart, His righteousness operates only through an obedient heart.

Faith and obedience are inescapably related. There is no saving faith in God apart from obedience to God, and there can be no godly obedience without godly faith. As the beautiful and popular hymn admonishes, "Trust and obey, there's no other way." Our Lord "gave Himself for us," Paul says, not only to save us from hell and take us to heaven but to "redeem us from every lawless deed and purify for Himself a people for His own possession, zealous for good deeds" (Titus 2:14).

Salvation comes "according to the foreknowledge of God the Father, by the sanctifying work of the Spirit," Peter wrote to persecuted believers throughout the Roman world, in order that those who believe may "*obey Jesus Christ* and be sprinkled with His blood" (a symbol referring to a covenant of obedience, see Ex. 24:1-8). Later in the epistle he admonished: "Since you have in *obedience to the truth* purified your souls for a sincere love of the brethren, fervently love one another from the heart, for you have been born again not of seed which is perishable but imperishable, that is, through *the living and abiding word of God*" (1 Pet. 1:2, 22-23; emphasis added). Obedience to Jesus Christ and obedience to His truth are totally synonymous, and His truth is "the living and abiding word of God."

Obedience neither produces nor maintains salvation, but it is an inevitable characteristic of those who are saved. Belief itself is an act of obedience, made possible and prompted by God's sovereign grace, yet always involving the uncoerced will of the believer. A person is not transported passively from slavery in Satan's kingdom of darkness to slavery in God's kingdom of light. Salvation does not occur apart from an act of commitment on the believer's part. The life-changing work of salvation is by God's power alone, but it does not work apart from man's will. God has no unwilling children in His family, no unwilling citizens in His kingdom.

Genuine faith not only is in God's Son but in God's truth. Jesus said, "I am the way, and the truth, and the life; no one comes to the Father, but through Me" (John 14:6). Paul had confidence in the salvation of his readers in the church at Rome because they obeyed **to that form of teaching to which** [they] **were committed.** No believer, of course, comprehends all of God's truth. Even the most mature and faithful Christian only begins to fathom the riches of God's Word in this present life. But the desire to know and obey God's truth is one of the surest marks of genuine salvation. From its inception, the early church was characterized by its devotion "to the apostles' teaching" (Acts 2:42). And Jesus made it clear that those who obeyed His word were the true believers (see John 8:31; 14:21, 23, 24; 15:10; etc.).

Form translates *tupos,* which was used of the molds into which molten metal for castings was poured. **Committed** translates the aorist passive of *paradidōmi,* which carries the basic meaning of deliver over to. And because *eis* (**to**) can also be translated *into,* it seems that a more precise rendering of this phrase is "that form of teaching into which you were delivered." It is true, of course, that, through its reading and preaching, God's Word is delivered *to* believers. But Paul's point here seems to be that the true believer is also delivered *into* God's Word, His divine **teaching**. The idea is that when God makes a new spiritual creation of a believer, He casts him into the mold of divine truth. The J. B. Phillips rendering of Romans 12:1 uses the same figure: "Don't let the world around you squeeze you into its own mould, but let God re-mould your minds from within." In other words, "Do not let Satan's forces try to fit you back into the old sinful mold from which God delivered you. Let God continue to fashion you into the perfect image of His Son."

Throughout his epistles, Paul emphasizes the crucial relationship of God's truth to faithful Christian living. In his second letter to Timothy, he advised his young protégé in ministry to "retain the standard of sound words which you have heard from me, in the faith and love which are in Christ Jesus" (2 Tim. 1:13). He later warned him that "the time will come when [men] will not endure sound doctrine; but wanting to have their ears tickled, they will accumulate for themselves teachers in accordance to their own desires" (4:3). The apostle maintained that an overseer, or elder, in the church should hold "fast the faithful word which is in accordance with the teaching, that he may be able both to exhort in sound doctrine and to refute those who contradict" (Titus 1:9). Later in the same letter he admonished Titus to "speak the things which are fitting for sound doctrine" (2:1). The Christian who faithfully obeys God's Word becomes conformed to the truth of that Word, a living model of the gospel. The divine **teaching** to which a believer submits himself in Jesus Christ stamps him with the authentic image of his Savior and Lord.

A person does not become a Christian by claiming the name of Christ and then believing and doing whatever he himself wants. You cannot become a Christian by merely saying or doing certain things, even the godly things extolled in Scripture. But *after* genuine salvation a person will have the innate, Spirit-led desire to know and to obey God's truth.

After a businessmen's luncheon at which I spoke, a man said to me, "I've been in this group for a long time, and I'll tell you how I think you can get to God. You see, there is this long stairway, and at the top there is a door and behind it is this guy Jesus. What you really want to do is try to make it up the stairs and get through the door and then hope Jesus lets you in. As you're on your way up the stairs, you've got all these preachers and movements cheering you on, but you just continue going up the stairs your own way. I call it the stairway of hope. That's what I think the gospel is." With a heavy heart I replied, "Sir, you cannot be a Christian. What you just said has nothing to do with the gospel, and your stairway to heaven is hope*less*. You need to depend on Jesus Christ alone for your salvation. You have no idea of what it means to be saved, and you cannot be on your way to heaven."

A person cannot invent his own way to God, no matter how

sincere his efforts might be. God has established the only way to come to Him, and that is the way of faith in His Son, Jesus Christ. And saving faith in Jesus Christ is built on God's revelation about Him, not on men's ideas about Him. There is divinely-revealed content to the gospel, and the person who rejects or circumvents that content gives unmistakable evidence that he is not truly seeking God's kingdom and His righteousness.

Witness Lee, founder of the Local Church movement, wrote a book entitled *Christ Versus Doctrine,* the main thesis of which is that it is a personal relationship to Christ that matters and that doctrine actually interferes with that relationship. The book not only is unbiblical but, as one might guess from the title, is also self-contradictory. Doctrine is simply another word for teaching, and the purpose of Lee's book, of course, was to teach his *own* doctrine.

THEIR PRACTICE

I am speaking in human terms because of the weakness of your flesh. For just as you presented your members as slaves to impurity and to lawlessness, resulting in further lawlessness, so now present your members as slaves to righteousness, resulting in sanctification. (6:19)

It is difficult to put divine principles and truths into terms that finite human minds can comprehend. In saying, **I am speaking in human terms because of the weakness of your flesh,** Paul meant that the analogy of masters and slaves was used as an accommodation to his readers' humanness.

Flesh is here used as a synonym for humanness, or mortality, and is equivalent to "the members of your body" in verse 13 and **members** at the end of verse 19. The **flesh** is the human faculty influenced by sin and as long as believers remain in their mortal bodies, sin still has a beachhead, a place to launch its attacks. That is why Paul admonishes believers to present their *bodies* as "a living and holy sacrifice, acceptable to God" (Rom. 12:1). Although the inner person of a believer has been transformed into the likeness of Christ, the outer person, represented by **the flesh,** is still subject to the defilement of sin.

Paul here changes the focus from position to practice, admonishing believers to make their living correspond to their new natures. Although it is still possible for Christians to sin, they no longer are bound by sin. Now they are free *not* to sin, and they should exercise that divinely-provided ability in obedience to their new Lord and Master.

Before salvation, believers were like the rest of fallen mankind, having no other desire or ability but to follow their natural bent to

impurity and to lawlessness. Those two terms refer, respectively, to inward and outward sin. The unregenerate person is both internally and externally sinful, and as he lives out his sinfulness it results in still **further lawlessness.** Like a cancer that reproduces itself until the whole body is destroyed, sin reproduces itself until the whole person is destroyed.

After the brilliant writer Oscar Wilde's homosexuality and other deviant behavior was made public, he wrote, "I forgot that what a man is in secret he will some day shout aloud from the housetop." Another famous writer, Sinclair Lewis, was the toast of the literary world and received the Nobel Prize in literature in 1930. To mock what he considered the hypocrisy of Christianity, he wrote *Elmer Gantry,* the fictitious story of a Bible-pounding evangelist who was secretly an alcoholic, a fornicator, and a thief. Few people know, however, that Lewis himself died an alcoholic in a third-rate clinic outside Rome, a devastated victim of his own sinful life-style.

Because it is possible for them to resist sin and to live righteously, believers should **now present** their **members as slaves to righteousness.** And just as the life of sin leads to further sin, so the life of **righteousness** leads to further righteousness, whose ultimate end is complete **sanctification.**

The late Martyn Lloyd-Jones wrote, "As you go on living this righteous life, and practising it with all your might and energy, and all your time . . . you will find that the process that went on before, in which you went on from bad to worse and became viler and viler, is entirely reversed. You will become cleaner and cleaner, and purer and purer, and holier and holier, and more and more conformed unto the image of the Son of God" (*Romans: An Exposition of Chapter Six* [Grand Rapids: Zondervan, 1972], pp. 268-69).

No one stands still morally and spiritually. Just as unbelievers progress from sinfulness to greater sinfulness, a believer who is not growing in righteousness, though never falling back altogether out of righteousness, will slip further and further back into sin.

God's purpose in redeeming men from sin is not to give them freedom to do as they please but freedom to do as *He* pleases, which is to live righteously. When God commanded Pharaoh to let His people go, He also made clear His purpose for their deliverance: "that they may serve Me in the wilderness" (Ex. 7:16). God delivers men from enslavement to sin for the sole purpose of their becoming enslaved to Him and to His righteousness.

THEIR PROMISE

For when you were slaves of sin, you were free in regard to

righteousness. Therefore what benefit were you then deriving from the things of which you are now ashamed? For the outcome of those things is death. But now having been freed from sin and enslaved to God, you derive your benefit, resulting in sanctification, and the outcome, eternal life. (6:20-22)

Unsaved persons, who are **slaves of sin**, are **free in regard to righteousness.** That is, they have no connection to righteousness; it can make no demands on them since they possess neither the desire nor the ability to meet its requirements. They are controlled and ruled by sin, the master whom they are bound to serve. In that sense, they have no responsibility to righteousness, because they are powerless to meet its standards and demands. That is why it is foolish to preach reformation to sinners. They cannot reform their living until God transforms their lives.

Many unsaved people, of course, do not think their lives need reformation, much less transformation. The world is full of people who are decent, honest, law-abiding, helpful, and often very religious, who think their lives are exemplary. But Paul declares that apart from salvation through Jesus Christ, *all* people are **slaves of sin** and are **free in regard to,** that is, totally separated from and unrelated to, God's standard of **righteousness.** Paul described his own good works and religious accomplishments before salvation as rubbish, or dung (Phil. 3:8).

In God's sight, there is absolutely no **benefit** that men can derive from **the things** they do apart from salvation, things of which after salvation they become **ashamed.** The only possible **outcome of those things is death,** the second death, which is spiritual death and eternal torment in hell.

One of the marks of true salvation is a sense of being **ashamed** of one's life before coming to Christ. Whether the previous life was marked by sordid immorality or great propriety, by heinous crimes or sacrificial service to others, by extreme selfishness or extreme generosity, it is a life about which the true believer can be nothing but ashamed. No matter how it may appear before the world, the life apart from God is a life apart from righteousness.

John Calvin wrote,

> As soon as the godly begin to be enlightened by the Spirit of Christ and the preaching of the gospel, they freely acknowledge that the whole of their past life, which they lived without Christ, is worthy of condemnation. So far from trying to excuse it, they are in fact ashamed of themselves. Indeed, they go farther, and continually bear their disgrace in mind, so that the shame of it may make them more truly and willingly humble before God. (*The Epistles of Paul the Apostle to the Romans and to the Thessalonians* [Grand Rapids: Eerdmans, 1960], p. 135)

But for those who have **been freed from sin and enslaved to God** through faith in Jesus Christ, the **benefit** is **sanctification** and **the outcome** is **eternal life.** In salvation God not only frees us from sin's ultimate penalty but frees us from its present tyranny.

Freed from sin does not mean that a believer is no longer capable of sinning but that he is no longer enslaved to sin, no longer its helpless subject. The freedom from sin about which Paul is speaking here is not a long-range objective or an ultimate ideal but an already accomplished fact. Without exception, every person who trusts in Jesus Christ as Savior and Lord is **freed from sin and enslaved to God.** Obviously some believers are more faithful and obedient than others, but Christians are equally **freed from** bondage to **sin** and equally **enslaved to God**, equally granted **sanctification** and equally granted **eternal life.**

The Absolute

For the wages of sin is death, but the free gift of God is eternal life in Christ Jesus our Lord. (6:23)

This verse expresses two inexorable absolutes. The first is that **the wages of sin is death.** Spiritual **death** is earned. It is the just and rightful compensation for a life that is characterized by **sin,** which is *every* life apart from God.

The second inexorable absolute is that **the free gift of God is eternal life in Christ Jesus our Lord.** By definition, a gift is free, but lest anyone underestimate the magnitude of God's grace, Paul speaks of God's **free gift.** Salvation cannot be earned by works, by human goodness, by religious ritual, or by any other thing that man can do. "For by grace you have been saved through faith," the apostle reminded the Ephesian believers; "and that not of yourselves, it is the gift of God; not as a result of works, that no one should boast" (Eph. 2:8-9).

If a person wants what he deserves—eternal death—God will give that to him as his just **wages.** And if person wants what he does *not* deserve—**eternal life**—God offers that to him as well, but as a **free gift,** the only source of which is **Christ Jesus our Lord.**

That is Paul's great climax to chapter 6 of Romans: Jesus Christ is the *only* way from sin to righteousness, from damnation to salvation, from eternal death to eternal life.

As he stood before the Sanhedrin shortly after Pentecost, Peter boldly proclaimed that same truth, testifying that "there is salvation in no one else; for there is no other name under heaven that has been given among men, by which we must be saved" (Acts 4:12). To the unbelieving Pharisees, Jesus said, "Truly, truly, I say to you, I am the door of the sheep.

All who came before Me are thieves and robbers, but the sheep did not hear them. I am the door; if anyone enters through Me, he shall be saved, and shall go in and out, and find pasture" (John 10:7-9). During the Upper Room discourse, Jesus said, "I am the way, and the truth, and the life; no one comes to the Father, but through Me" (John 14:6).

The noted German pastor and theologian Dietrich Bonhoeffer was imprisoned for several years by the Nazis and was executed just before the close of World War II. In his book *The Cost of Discipleship,* he wrote the following insightful words about what he called the gospel of cheap grace:

> [Cheap grace] amounts to the justification of sin without the justification of the repentant sinner who departs from sin and from whom sin departs. Cheap grace is not the kind of forgiveness of sin which frees us from the toils of sin. . . . Cheap grace is grace without discipleship, grace without the cross, grace without Jesus Christ. . . .
>
> [Costly grace, on the other hand] is the call of Jesus Christ at which the disciple leaves his nets and follows him. . . . When [Martin Luther] spoke of grace, [he] always implied as a corollary that it cost him his own life, the life which was now subjected to the absolute obedience of Christ, . . . Happy are they who, knowing that grace, can live in the world without being of it, who by following Jesus Christ, are so assured of their heavenly citizenship that they are truly free to live their lives in this world. ([New York: Macmillan, 1959], pp. 47, 53, 60)

Only the Son of God could have paid the cost of salvation. But He calls His followers to pay the cost of discipleship. "If anyone wishes to come after Me," Jesus said, "let him deny himself, and take up his cross, and follow Me For whoever wishes to save his life shall lose it; but whoever loses his life for My sake shall find it" (Matt. 16:24-25).

Luke records the matter of dealing with the cost when he quotes Jesus in 14:26-33:

> If anyone comes to Me, and does not hate his own father and mother and wife and children and brothers and sisters, yes, and even his own life, he cannot be My disciple. Whoever does not carry his own cross and come after Me cannot be My disciple. For which one of you, when he wants to build a tower, does not first sit down and calculate the cost, to see if he has enough to complete it? Otherwise, when he has laid a foundation, and is not able to finish, all who observe it begin to ridicule him, saying, "This man began to build and was not able to finish." Or what king, when he sets out to meet another king in battle, will not first sit down and take counsel whether he is strong enough with ten thousand men to encounter the one coming against him with twenty thousand? Or else, while the other is still

far away, he sends a delegation and asks terms of peace. So therefore, no one of you can be My disciple who does not give up all his own possessions.

When our Lord gave the parables of the pearl and the treasure in the field (Matt. 13:44-46), in both cases, the man sold all he had to make the purchase.

Jesus Christ is not looking for people who want to add Him to their sin as insurance against hell. He is not looking for people who want to apply His high moral principles to their unregenerate lives. He is not looking for those who want only to be outwardly reformed by having their old nature improved.

Jesus Christ calls to Himself those who are willing to be inwardly transformed by Him, who desire an entirely new nature that is created in His own holy likeness. He calls to Himself those who are willing to exchange their sinfulness for His holiness. He calls to Himself those who are willing to die with Him in order to be raised with Him, who are willing to relinquish slavery to their sin for slavery to His righteousness. And when men come to Him on His terms, He changes their destiny from eternal death to eternal life.

Dead to the Law

Or do you not know, brethren (for I am speaking to those who know the law), that the law has jurisdiction over a person as long as he lives? For the married woman is bound by law to her husband while he is living; but if her husband dies, she is released from the law concerning the husband. So then if, while her husband is living, she is joined to another man, she shall be called an adulteress; but if her husband dies, she is free from the law, so that she is not an adulteress, though she is joined to another man. Therefore, my brethren, you also were made to die to the Law through the body of Christ, that you might be joined to another, to Him who was raised from the dead, that we might bear fruit for God. For while we were in the flesh, the sinful passions, which were aroused by the Law, were at work in the members of our body to bear fruit for death. But now we have been released from the Law, having died to that by which we were bound, so that we serve in newness of the Spirit and not in oldness of the letter. (7:1-6)

As you study the Old Testament, you cannot help being struck by the dignity and honor accorded the revealed law of God—also referred to by such names as His statutes, commandments, ordinances, and testimonies. God inspired Moses to write:

> Now this is the commandment, the statutes and the judgments which the Lord your God has commanded me to teach you, that you might do them in the land where you are going over to possess it, so that you and your son and your grandson might fear the Lord your God, to keep all His statutes and His commandments, which I command you, all the days of your life, and that your days may be prolonged. O Israel, you should listen and be careful to do it, that it may be well with you and that you may multiply greatly, just as the Lord, the God of your fathers, has promised you, in a land flowing with milk and honey. Hear, O Israel! The Lord is our God, the Lord is one! And you shall love the Lord your God with all your heart and with all your soul and with all your might. And these words, which I am commanding you today, shall be on your heart; and you shall teach them diligently to your sons and shall talk of them when you sit in your house and when you walk by the way and when you lie down and when you rise up. And you shall bind them as a sign on your hand and they shall be as frontals on your forehead. And you shall write them on the doorposts of your house and on your gates. (Deut. 6:1-9)

Solomon wrote, "The conclusion, when all has been heard, is: fear God and keep His commandments, because this applies to every person" (Eccles. 12:13). Psalm 119 uses some ten different synonyms for God's law. The writer declares:

> How blessed are those whose way is blameless, who walk in the law of the Lord (v. 1); Thou hast ordained Thy precepts, that we should keep them diligently (v. 4); Oh that my ways may be established to keep Thy statutes! (v. 5); Thy word I have treasured in my heart, that I may not sin against Thee (v. 11); Blessed art Thou, O Lord; teach me Thy statutes (v. 12); I shall delight in Thy statutes; I shall not forget Thy word (v. 16); Give me understanding, that I may observe Thy law, and keep it with all my heart (v. 34); O how I love Thy law! It is my meditation all the day (v. 97); The sum of Thy word is truth, and every one of Thy righteous ordinances is everlasting (v. 160); Those who love Thy law have great peace, and nothing causes them to stumble (v. 165); Let my tongue sing of Thy word, for all Thy commandments are righteousness (v. 172).

To his father-in-law Jethro, Moses explained that his primary purpose as the divinely-appointed leader of Israel was to "make known the statutes of God and His laws" (Ex. 18:16). Isaiah proclaimed, "The

Lord was pleased for His righteousness' sake to make the law great and glorious" (Isa. 42:21).

The great king David was inspired to pen this definitive declaration of the purpose, the eminence, and the grandeur of God's law: "The law of the Lord is perfect, restoring the soul; the testimony of the Lord is sure, making wise the simple. The precepts of the Lord are right, rejoicing the heart; the commandment of the Lord is pure, enlightening the eyes. The fear of the Lord is clean, enduring forever; the judgments of the Lord are true; they are righteous altogether. They are more desirable than gold, yes, than much fine gold; sweeter also than honey and the drippings of the honeycomb" (Ps. 19:7-10). The last command given by God in the Old Testament is "Remember the law of Moses My servant, even the statutes and ordinances which I commanded him in Horeb for all Israel" (Mal. 4:4).

God's law was so dominant in ancient Israel that many Jews had made it virtually an idol. In the Babylonian Talmud, the primary collection of ancient rabbinical commentary on the Torah (the Mosaic law), Rabbi Raba wrote, "The Holy One created man's evil inclination but created the Torah [the Mosaic law] to overcome it" (*Baba Bathra*, 16a). Although it clearly contradicts the divinely-revealed Torah itself, Raba's comment demonstrates how high the law was elevated in the minds of most Jews. Rabbi Judah, another noted talmudic commentator, said, "The nature of the Holy One differs from that of mortal men. When a man prescribes a remedy, it may benefit one individual but injure another. But God gave the Torah to Israel as a source of healing for all" (*Erubin*, 54a).

By the time of Christ, many Jews considered obedience to God's law to be not only the demonstration of salvation's godliness that God intended it to be but also the means of salvation, which God never intended. Faithfulness to the law came to supercede faith in the God who had given the law. As illustrated throughout the gospel accounts, such Jews often accused Jesus of contradicting and disobeying the Mosaic law.

Paul was vehemently criticized by his unbelieving Jewish opponents for supposedly disregarding the Mosaic law. When Paul returned from his third missionary journey, the elders in the Jerusalem church advised him to join a group of four other Jewish men in a Nazirite purification ceremony in the Temple. By participating in that rite he would demonstrate his respect for the law and perhaps defuse some of the false criticism. Because such an act would in no way compromise the gospel, the apostle willingly agreed (Acts 21:20-26). As it turned out, however, his actions were misinterpreted and misrepresented, and Jewish opposition against Paul was hardened still further (see vv. 27-30). Nevertheless, the incident clearly demonstrates the intense Jewish reverence for at least the external and ceremonial aspects of the law.

Before his conversion, Paul (then known as Saul) was the epitome of Jewish legalism. In his letter to the Philippian church he testifies to the trust he once had in his own human observance of the law. "If anyone else has a mind to put confidence in the flesh," he wrote, "I far more: circumcised the eighth day, of the nation of Israel, of the tribe of Benjamin, a Hebrew of Hebrews; as to the Law, a Pharisee; as to zeal, a persecutor of the church; as to the righteousness which is in the Law, found blameless" (Phil. 3:4-6).

The opposite view of the Old Testament law was also a problem during Jesus' ministry and in the early church. As in every age, many people were looking for a way to be religious without being hampered by a lot of restrictions. To them, the idea of salvation by grace through faith alone apart from the law seemed like a perfect way to have their cake and eat it too. They would simply "trust God" and then do as they pleased.

To make clear His own high regard for the divine law given through Moses, Jesus declared early in His ministry, "Do not think that I came to abolish the Law or the Prophets; I did not come to abolish, but to fulfill. For truly I say to you, until heaven and earth pass away, not the smallest letter or stroke shall pass away from the Law, until all is accomplished. Whoever then annuls one of the least of these commandments, and so teaches others, shall be called least in the kingdom of heaven; but whoever keeps and teaches them, he shall be called great in the kingdom of heaven" (Matt. 5:17-19).

Paul testifies that the oracles of God (Rom. 3:2; cf. Acts 7:38), which were delivered and ordained by God's own angels (Heb. 2:2; Acts 7:53), could not be anything but sacred and inviolable. The apostle had already testified: "Do we then nullify the Law through faith? May it never be! On the contrary, we establish the Law" (Rom. 3:31). He later asserts unequivocally that, despite its limitations and inability to save, "the Law is holy, and the commandment is holy and righteous and good" (7:12; cf. 1 Tim. 1:8).

Paul had also declared, however, that "by the works of the Law no flesh will be justified in His sight; for through the Law comes the knowledge of sin" (Rom. 3:19-20), and "the Law came in that the transgression might increase; but where sin increased, grace abounded all the more" (5:20). Christians are not saved by the law and "are not under law, but under grace" (6:14).

Knowing that his readers, especially Jewish believers, would still have a great many questions about the law in relation to their faith in Christ, Paul continues in the present passage to explain that critical relationship.

In the last part of Romans 6, he expounds the first truth of verse 14, namely, that believers are no longer under the law regarding its power to condemn. In chapter 7 he expounds the second truth in that verse, that believers are now under grace. Yet, in doing so, he refers to the law twenty-three times in this chapter, eight times in the first six verses. In his explanation he presents an axiom (v. 1), an analogy (vv. 2-3), an application (vv. 4-5), and an affirmation (v. 6).

THE AXIOM

Or do you not know, brethren (for I am speaking to those who know the law), that the law has jurisdiction over a person as long as he lives? (7:1)

The tactful and rhetorical question **Do you not know?** indicates the apostle is once again using a self-evident truth as the foundation of his argument. The term **brethren** refers to Paul's Jewish brethren (**those who know the law**). He may be emphasizing this term to assure Jewish believers of his sensitivity to their deep concern about his seeming denigration of the Mosaic **law**.

His primary point here, however, relates to *any* **law**, as indicated by the anarthrous construction (the absence of a definite article before a noun, in this case, **law**) in the Greek text. The literal translation is simply, "to those who know law." It should be obvious, he was saying, that any **law**—whether Roman, Greek, or even God-given biblical law—**has jurisdiction over a person** only **as long as he lives.** If a criminal dies, he is no longer subject to prosecution and punishment, no matter how numerous and heinous his crimes may have been. Lee Harvey Oswald, the accused assassin of President John F. Kennedy, was never brought to trial for that act because he himself was assassinated before his trial began. Law is binding only on the living.

THE ANALOGY

For the married woman is bound by law to her husband while he is living; but if her husband dies, she is released from the law concerning the husband. So then if, while her husband is living, she is joined to another man, she shall be called an adulteress; but if her husband dies, she is free from the law, so that she is not an adulteress, though she is joined to another man. (7:2-3)

Contrary to the confusing interpretations of some commentators, the apostle is not presenting a complex allegory, or an allegory of any kind. He is simply making an analogy to marriage law to illustrate the single point he has just mentioned, namely, that no law has jurisdiction over a person after he is dead. This passage has absolutely nothing to say about divorce and cannot legitimately be used as an argument from silence to teach that divorce is never justified for a Christian and, consequently, that only the death of a spouse gives the right to remarry. (Such a discussion requires treatment of other passages, such Matt. 5:31-32; 19:3-12; and 1 Cor. 7:10-15. For further study see the author's book *The Family* [Chicago: Moody, 1982].)

Paul is calling attention to the fact that marriage laws are binding only as long as both partners are alive. Being **joined to another man** while her husband is alive makes a woman **an adulteress**, an offender against the law. But to be joined in marriage to another man after **her husband dies** is perfectly legal and acceptable. A widow is absolutely **free from the law** that bound her to her former husband. Paul, in fact, encouraged young widows to remarry. As long as they were joined to a believer (see 1 Cor. 7:39), such widows, he says, should "get married, bear children, keep house, and give the enemy no occasion for reproach" (1 Tim. 5:14).

THE APPLICATION

Therefore, my brethren, you also were made to die to the Law through the body of Christ, that you might be joined to another, to Him who was raised from the dead, that we might bear fruit for God. For while we were in the flesh, the sinful passions, which were aroused by the Law, were at work in the members of our body to bear fruit for death. (7:4-5)

Therefore marks the transition from Paul's brief axiom and analogy to his application, and his adding **my** before a second use of **brethren** makes that term even gentler and more personal than in verse 1.

It is at this point that Paul begins his spiritual teaching in the passage. Just as the death of her husband frees a woman from the marriage that had bound them together, he declares, **you** (that is, Christians) **were made to die to the** Mosaic **Law. Were made to die** translates the aorist tense of *thanatoō*, which emphasizes the completeness and finality of death. The verb is also passive, indicating that believers do not die naturally or put themselves to death but have been **made to die** by the divine act of God in response to faith in His Son.

Though it was a result of Old Testament salvation by grace, obedience to the law was never a means of salvation (Rom. 3:20). The law has power only to condemn men to death for their sin (6:23), but no power to redeem them from it. Paul has already pointed out that God's grace extended by faith in Jesus Christ brings death to and freedom from sin (Rom. 6:3-7). He now declares that faith in Him also brings death to **the Law** and consequently freedom from the law's penalty.

Through the body of Christ, who suffered the penalty of death on their behalf, believers are freed from their relationship to the law, just as a widow is freed from her relationship to her former husband. And like that widow, believers are free to **be joined to another** husband, as it were, to Jesus Christ, **Him who was raised from the dead.** Salvation brings a complete change of spiritual relationship, just as remarriage after the death of a spouse brings a complete change of marital relationship. Believers are no longer married to the law but are now married to Jesus Christ, the divine Bridegroom of His church.

In Ephesians Paul gives a beautiful picture of that relationship: "But as the church is subject to Christ, so also the wives ought to be to their husbands in everything. Husbands, love your wives, just as Christ also loved the church and gave Himself up for her; that He might sanctify her, having cleansed her by the washing of water with the word, that He might present to Himself the church in all her glory, having no spot or wrinkle or any such thing; but that she should be holy and blameless" (Eph. 5:24-27). Using the same figure of marriage, the apostle lovingly told the Corinthian believers: "For I am jealous for you with a godly jealousy; for I betrothed you to one husband, that to Christ I might present you as a pure virgin" (2 Cor. 11:2).

The underlying emphasis of the book of Romans is that salvation produces total transformation. Through Jesus' death and resurrection, God "made Him who knew no sin to be sin on our behalf, that we might become the righteousness of God in Him" (2 Cor. 5:21). The purpose of our being joined to Christ is **that we might bear fruit for God.** "For we are His workmanship," Paul tells the Ephesians, "created in Christ Jesus for good works, which God prepared beforehand, that we should walk in them" (Eph. 2:10). He gives additional insight in his letter to Galatia: "For through the Law I died to the Law, that I might live to God. I have been crucified with Christ; and it is no longer I who live, but Christ lives in me; and the life which I now live in the flesh I live by faith in the Son of God, who loved me, and delivered Himself up for me" (Gal. 2:19-20). The transformed life *will* **bear fruit for God**.

The great theologian Charles Hodge wrote, "As far as we are concerned, redemption is in order to [produce] holiness. We are delivered from the law, that we may be united to Christ; and we are united to Christ, that we may bring forth fruit unto God. . . . As deliverance from the penalty of the law is in order to [produce] holiness, it is vain to expect that deliverance, except with a view to the end for which it is granted" (*Commentary on the Epistle to the Romans* [Grand Rapids: Eerdmans, n.d.], p. 220).

Godly **fruit** exists basically in two dimensions: attitude and action. The fruit of the Holy Spirit in a believer's life is manifested internally in his attitudes of "love, joy, peace, patience, kindness, goodness, faithfulness, gentleness, self-control" (Gal. 5:22-23). As far as godly *actions* are concerned, Jesus said, "I am the true vine, and My Father is the vinedresser. Every branch in Me that does not bear fruit, He takes away; and every branch that bears fruit, He prunes it, that it may bear more fruit" (John 15:1-2). The writer of Hebrews speaks of "the fruit of lips that give thanks to His name" (Heb. 13:15), and Paul prayed that Philippian believers would be prepared for the day of Christ by being "filled with the fruit of righteousness which comes through Jesus Christ, to the glory and praise of God" (Phil. 1:11).

In verse 5 Paul reminds his readers of four things that characterized their old lives as unbelievers. First, they **were in the flesh.** The unredeemed, unregenerate person can operate only in the area of **the flesh,** the natural and sinful sphere of fallen mankind.

In Scripture, the term **flesh** is used in several ways. It is used in a morally and spiritually neutral sense to describe man's physical being. In that sense, when He became God incarnate, the Lord Himself "became flesh, and dwelt among us" (John 1:14). In fact, one of the certain marks of a true believer is that he "confesses that Jesus Christ has come in the flesh" (1 John 4:2).

Flesh is also used in a moral and ethical sense, but always with an evil connotation. Paul repeatedly uses it in that way in Romans 8, Galatians 5, and Ephesians 2, and in every instance it refers to man's unredeemed humanness. A person who still lives in the realm of the flesh cannot belong to Christ. "You are not in the flesh but in the Spirit," Paul says of believers, "if indeed the Spirit of God dwells in you. But if anyone does not have the Spirit of Christ, he does not belong to Him" (Rom. 8:9). It is possible, of course, for a believer to fall back into some of the ways of the flesh, which he does whenever he sins. Although a believer can never again be in the flesh, the flesh is still able to manifest itself in the believer.

Second, the believer's old life was characterized by **sinful passions,** the impulses to think and to do evil that are generated in those who are in the flesh.

Third, the believer's old life was characterized by his sinful passions continually being **aroused by the Law.** One wonders how a good thing, such as the holy **Law** of God, can arouse that which is sinful. First of all it does so because, apart from knowledge of **the Law,** a person would not know good from evil (see 7:7). **The Law,** in declaring what is wrong, also arouses evil in the unregenerate person because his naturally rebellious nature makes him want to do the very things he learns are forbidden.

Fourth, the believer's old life was characterized by the unceasing **work** of his sinful passions **in the members of** his **body to bear fruit for death. Work** is from a Greek verb meaning to operate with power. We get our word *energy* from it. The phrase **members of our body** sums up the whole person in all his components as being the victim of **sinful passions** energized to produce the **fruit** of ultimate and eternal divine judgment in **death**.

THE AFFIRMATION

But now we have been released from the Law, having died to that by which we were bound, so that we serve in newness of the Spirit and not in oldness of the letter. (7:6)

The transitional phrase **but now** introduces the heart of this brief passage, which presents a radical contrast to the description just given (v. 5) of the unregenerate man. **We,** that is, believers in Jesus Christ (see v. 4), **have been released from** our old bondage to **the Law, having died to that by which we were** formerly **bound** in the flesh.

As Paul has just pointed out, "the law has jurisdiction over a person [only] as long as he lives" (v. 1). Therefore, when a person dies, he is discharged of all legal liabilities and penalties. Because we, as believers, died in Jesus Christ when He paid our sin debt on Calvary, we were thereby **released from** our moral and spiritual liabilities and penalties under God's **Law.** "Christ redeemed us from the curse of the Law, having become a curse for us—for it is written, 'Cursed is everyone who hangs on a tree'" (Gal. 3:13).

Paul has already declared as forcefully and unambiguously as possible that freedom from the law's bondage does *not* mean freedom to do what the law forbids (6:1, 15; cf. 3:31). Freedom from the law does not bring freedom to sin but just the opposite—freedom for the first time to do what is righteous, a freedom the unregenerate person does not and cannot have.

Paul's point is not simply that the redeemed person is *able* to do what is right but that he *will* do what is right. In response to their faith in His Son, Jesus Christ, God releases men from their bondage to the law **so that** they will **serve.** Many English renderings of *douleuō* (**serve**) are somewhat ambiguous and do not carry the full force of the Greek term. This verb does not describe the voluntary service of a hired worker, who is able to refuse an order and look for another employer if he so desires. It refers exclusively to the service of a bondslave, whose sole purpose for existence is to obey the will of his master.

Kenneth Wuest gives this accurate and beautiful rendering of verse

6: "But now, we were discharged from the law, having died to that in which we were constantly held down, insomuch that we are rendering habitually a bondslave's obedience" (*Wuest's Word Studies from the Greek New Testament,* vol. 1 [Grand Rapids: Eerdmans, 1973], p. 117).

Service to the Lord **in newness of the Spirit** rather than **in oldness of the letter** is the necessary fruit of redemption, not an option. As already noted, a fruitless Christian is not a genuine Christian and has no part in God's kingdom. "Every branch in Me that does not bear fruit," Jesus said, My Father "takes away; and every branch that bears fruit, He prunes it, that it may bear more fruit" (John 15:1-2).

The person who is justified by faith through the grace of Jesus Christ is secure (Romans 5), holy (chap. 6), free, fruitful, and serving (chap. 7). And the last four of those characteristics of the true believer are no more optional or conditional than the first. Although none of those divine marks of regeneration is ever perfect in its human manifestation, all of them are always present in a believer's life.

The law is still important to the Christian. For the first time, he is *able* to meet the law's demands for righteousness (which was God's desire when He gave it in the first place), because he has a new nature and God's own Holy Spirit to empower his obedience. And although he is no longer under the law's bondage or penalty, he is more genuinely eager to live by its godly standards than is the most zealous legalist. With full sincerity and joy, he can say with the psalmist, "O how I love Thy law!" (Ps. 119:97).

As believers, we are dead to the law as far as its demands and condemnation are concerned, but because we now live **in newness of the Spirit**, we love and serve God's law with a full and joyous heart. And we know that to obey His law is to do His will and that to do His will is to give Him glory.

Sin and the Law

What shall we say then? Is the Law sin? May it never be! On the contrary, I would not have come to know sin except through the Law; for I would not have known about coveting if the Law had not said, "You shall not covet." But sin, taking opportunity through the commandment, produced in me coveting of every kind; for apart from the Law sin is dead. And I was once alive apart from the Law; but when the commandment came, sin became alive, and I died; and this commandment, which was to result in life, proved to result in death for me; for sin, taking opportunity through the commandment, deceived me, and through it killed me. So then, the Law is holy, and the commandment is holy and righteous and good. Therefore did that which is good become a cause of death for me? May it never be! Rather it was sin, in order that it might be shown to be sin by effecting my death through that which is good, that through the commandment sin might become utterly sinful. (7:7-13)

Chapters 3-8 of Romans weave together in a remarkable way the various themes of faith, grace, sin, righteousness, and law. Especially important for Paul's Jewish readers was his comprehensive treatment of the law and its role in a person's coming to Christ and then living for Christ.

Paul has established that the law cannot save (Rom. 3-5), that it cannot sanctify (chap. 6), and that it can no longer condemn a believer (7:1-6). Now he establishes that the law can convict both unbelievers and believers of sin (7:7-13), and next that it cannot deliver from sin, either before or after salvation (7:14-25), and that it can be fulfilled by believers in the power of the indwelling Holy Spirit (8:1-4).

By New Testament times, Jewish rabbis had summed up scriptural law in 613 commandments, comprised of 248 mandates and 365 prohibitions. The mandates related to such things as worship, the Temple, sacrifices, vows, rituals, donations, sabbaths, animals used for food, festivals, community affairs, war, social issues, family responsibilities, judicial matters, legal rights and obligations, and slavery. The prohibitions related to such things as idolatry, historical lessons, blasphemy, Temple worship, sacrifices, the priesthood, diet, vows, agriculture, loans, business, slaves, justice, and personal relationships.

To those scriptural laws the rabbis had added countless adjuncts, conditions, and practical interpretations. The attempt to fulfill all the laws and traditions became a consuming way of life for legalistic Jews such as the Pharisees. At the Jerusalem Council, Peter described that extreme legalism as "a yoke which neither our fathers nor we have been able to bear" (Acts 15:10).

As far as the divinely-revealed laws were concerned, it is clear why faithful Jews tried to keep them in every detail. Through Moses, God had declared, "Cursed is he who does not confirm the words of this law by doing them" (Deut. 27:26). The next chapter of Deuteronomy specifies some of the severe consequences of disobedience, consequences that affected virtually every area of life:

> But it shall come about, if you will not obey the Lord your God, to observe to do all His commandments and His statutes with which I charge you today, that all these curses shall come upon you and overtake you. Cursed shall you be in the city, and cursed shall you be in the country. Cursed shall be your basket and your kneading bowl. Cursed shall be the offspring of your body and the produce of your ground, the increase of your herd and the young of your flock. Cursed shall you be when you come in, and cursed shall you be when you go out. The Lord will send upon you curses, confusion, and rebuke, in all you undertake to do, until you are destroyed and until you perish quickly, on account of the evil of your deeds, because you have forsaken Me. The Lord will make the pestilence cling to you until He has consumed you from the land, where you are entering to possess it. The Lord will smite you with consumption and with fever and with inflammation and with fiery heat and with the sword and with blight and with mildew, and they shall pursue you until you perish. (28:15-22)

As an apostle of Jesus Christ, Paul reiterated the truth that "for as many as are of the works of the Law are under a curse; for it is written, 'Cursed is everyone who does not abide by all things written in the book of the law, to perform them'" (Gal. 3:10; cf. Deut. 27:26). James declared that "whoever keeps the whole law and yet stumbles in one point, he has become guilty of all" (James 2:10).

Why, one wonders, did God give His chosen people a law that was impossible for them to keep? His purpose was not only to reveal the standard of righteousness by which the saved are to live but also to show them the impossibility of living it without His power and to show them the depth of their sinfulness when honestly measured against the law. The law was not given to show men how good they could be but how good they could not be. Following his quotation from Deuteronomy 27:26 mentioned above, Paul told the Galatians, "Now that no one is justified by the Law before God is evident" (Gal. 3:11a). To substantiate that truth he quoted another Old Testament passage that declared that "the righteous man shall live by faith" (v. 11b; cf. Hab. 2:4). The law was given to establish God's standard and to reveal to men the utter impossibility of their achieving that standard of righteousness and their consequent need for forgiveness and for trusting in God's goodness and mercy. As Hebrews 11 makes clear, both before and after the giving of the Mosaic law, those who became acceptable to God were those who trusted in His righteousness rather than their own.

Jesus condemned the Phariess for their failure to understand that truth (Luke 18:9). Paul, once the consummate Pharisee (Phil. 3:4-6), came to clearly understand that reality after his conversion. He testified to the Philippian believers: "Whatever things were gain to me, those things I have counted as loss . . . in order that I may gain Christ, and may be found in Him, not having a righteousness of my own derived from the Law, but that which is through faith in Christ, the righteousness which comes from God on the basis of faith" (Phil. 3:7-9).

After declaring that "while we [believers] were in the flesh, the sinful passions . . . were aroused by the Law," and that "now we have been released from the Law, . . . so that we serve in newness of the Spirit and not in oldness of the letter [of the Law]" (Rom. 7:5-6), Paul knew the next question his readers would ask would be, **What shall we say, then? Is the Law sin?** "Was the law given by God through Moses actually evil?" they would wonder. "And can Christians now disregard the standards of the law and live as they please?"

Paul responds by again using the strongest Greek negative, *mē genoito* (**May it never be!** See 3:4, 6, 31; 6:2, 15; 7:13). "Of course not! Of course not!" is the idea. The law not only is not sinful but continues to have great value for the Christian by convicting him of sin. In 7:7b-13, Paul gives four elements of the convicting work of God's law: it reveals sin (v. 7b), it arouses sin (v. 8), it ruins the sinner (vv. 9-11), and it reflects the absolute sinfulness of sin (vv. 12-13).

THE LAW REVEALS SIN

On the contrary, I would not have come to know sin except through the Law; for I would not have known about coveting if the Law had not said, "You shall not covet." (7:7b)

On the contrary, Paul says, just the opposite is true. It is outrageous and blasphemous even to suggest that anything God commands could be deficient in the least way, much less sinful.

By being perfect itself, however, God's law does *reveal* man's imperfection. **I would not have come to know sin,** Paul goes on to explain, **except through the Law.** In other words, because God has disclosed His divine standards of righteousness, men are able more accurately to identify **sin,** which is failure to meet those standards.

The apostle has already mentioned or alluded to that truth several times in the epistle: "Through the Law comes the knowledge of sin" (3:20); "the Law brings about wrath, but where there is no law, neither is there violation" (4:15); and "until the Law sin was in the world; but sin is not imputed when there is no law" (5:13).

Paul is not speaking of humanity's general awareness of right and wrong. Even pagan Gentiles who have never heard of God's revealed law nevertheless have His "Law written in their hearts, their conscience bearing witness, and their thoughts alternately accusing or else defending them" (Rom. 2:15). In the present passage the apostle is speaking about knowledge of the full extent and depravity of man's **sin.**

Throughout the rest of the chapter, Paul uses the first person singular pronouns *I* and *me,* indicating that he is giving his personal testimony as well as teaching universal truth. He is relating the conviction of sin that the Holy Spirit worked in his own heart through the law before and during his Damascus road encounter with Christ and the three days of blindness that followed (see Acts 9:1-18).

Although Christ's appearing to him and calling him to apostleship were sovereign acts of God, at some point Saul (as he was then known) had to confess his sins and trust in Christ for salvation. God forces no one into His kingdom against his will or apart from faith. In his testimony before King Agrippa, Paul recounted that, even while he was outwardly persecuting the followers of Christ, he was inwardly kicking "against the goads" of the Holy Spirit's convicting work in his heart (Acts 26:14).

Paul had been trained in Judaism since his early youth, had studied under the famous Gamaliel in Jerusalem, had tried to follow the law meticulously, and had considered himself to be zealous for God (Acts 22:3; Gal. 1:13-14; Phil. 3:5-6a). Before his conversion, he easily could have prayed the prayer of the self-satisfied Pharisee in the Temple who thanked God that he was not like other people (see Luke 18:11-12). He may have asserted with the rich young ruler that he had kept all the law since his youth (see Matt. 19:20; Phil. 3:6b).

Zealous Jews made such claims because rabbinical tradition had modified and externalized the law of God in order to make an acceptable lower lever of obedience humanly attainable. They did not take into account personal faith in God or the inner condition of the heart. To them, a person who lived up to the outward, observable demands of the rabbinical interpretations of the law became fully acceptable to God.

During his pre-salvation experience of conviction, Paul came to realize that the most important demands of God's revealed law were not external but internal and that he had failed to meet them. It is significant that the apostle chose the most obviously *internal* injunction of the Ten Commandments to illustrate his personal experience that the law reveals sin. **I would not have known about coveting,** he explains, **if the Law had not said, "You shall not covet."** It may have been the growing awareness of his own covetousness that finally broke his pride and opened his heart to the transforming work of the Spirit. Years after Paul's conversion, he told believers in Philippi, "We are the true circumcision, who worship in the Spirit of God and glory in Christ Jesus and put no confidence in the flesh" (Phil. 3:3).

The real battle with sin is internal, in the heart and mind. Counseling, therapy, or even strong willpower often can modify a person's behavior. People may stop drinking by faithfully following the plan of Alcoholics Anonymous or stop lying or cheating by submitting to psychotherapy. But only the transforming power of the Holy Spirit can take a sinful heart and make it pure and acceptable to God. The law's part in that transformation is to make a person aware of his sin and of his need for divine forgiveness and redemption and to set the standard of acceptable morality.

Charles Hodge wrote,

The law, although it cannot secure either the justification or sanctification of men, performs an essential part in the economy of salvation. It enlightens conscience and secures its verdict against a multitude of evils, which we should not otherwise have recognized as sins. It arouses sin, increasing its power, and making it, both in itself and in our consciousness, exceedingly sinful. It therefore produces that state of mind which is a necessary preparation for the reception of the gospel. . . . Conviction of sin, that is, an adequate knowledge of its nature, and a sense of its power over us, is an indispensable part of evangelical religion. Before the gospel can be embraced as a means of deliverance from sin, we must feel we are involved in corruption and misery. (*Commentary on the Epistle to the Romans* [Grand Rapids: Eerdmans, n.d.], p. 226)

Apart from the law, we would have no way of accurately judging our sinfulness. Only God's law reveals His divine standard of righteousness and thereby enables us to see how far short of His righteousness we are and how helpless we are to attain it by our own efforts.

The central theme of the Sermon on the Mount is that God demands perfect righteousness in the heart (Matt. 5:48), a righteousness that far surpasses the external and hypocritical righteousness typified by the scribes and Pharisees (Matt. 5:20). Following that declaration, Jesus gave a series of illustrations of God's standards of righteousness. In God's sight, the person who hates or denigrates his brother is as guilty of sin as the murderer (vv. 21-22), the person who lusts is as guilty of immorality as the adulterer (vv. 27-28), the person who divorces his or her spouse except on the grounds of unfaithfulness causes both of them, as well as any future spouses, to commit adultery (vv. 31-32; cf. also Matt. 19:3-12; Mark 10:11-12). Truth is truth, and falsehood is falsehood, Jesus declared, and an oath can neither justify a lie nor authenticate a truth (Matt. 5:33-37).

Jews had no excuse for failing to understand that God demands inner as well as outward righteousness. The Shema (from the Hebrew word for "hear") comprises the texts of Deuteronomy 6:4-9; 11:13-21; and Numbers 15:37-41, and it was recited twice daily by faithful Jews. The two texts from Deuteronomy were also among the four passages that were written on small pieces of parchment and placed in phylacteries worn on the foreheads and left arms of Jewish men during prayer. The same two texts were placed in mezuzahs, small boxes that Jews attached to their doorposts, following the instruction of Deuteronomy 6:9 and 11:20. Both phylacteries and mezuzahs are still used by many orthodox Jews today. The two texts from Deuteronomy include the repeated admonition to "love the Lord your God with all your heart and with all your soul and with all your might" (6:5; 11:13). When the Pharisees (who were the supreme authorities on the Mosaic law) asked Jesus to identify "the great commandment in the Law," He answered by citing Deuteronomy 6:5. He then said that the second greatest commandment "is like it, 'You shall love your neighbor as yourself,'" and declared that "on these two commandments depend the whole Law and the Prophets." Doubtless with great reluctance, His antagonists accepted His answer as correct (Matt. 22:34-40; Lev. 19:18). In a reverse situation, when Jesus asked a lawyer of the Pharisees to identify "what is written in the Law," the man immediately cited Deuteronomy 6:5 as the foremost commandment and, like Jesus, stated that the second great commandment was to love "your neighbor as yourself" (Luke 10:25-28).

It is clear, therefore, that despite the externality of their rabbinical traditions, which frequently contradicted Scripture (Matt. 15:3-6), the Jews of Jesus' and Paul's day knew that God's two *supreme* commandments had to do with inner motives rather than outward actions. Yet they continued to place their faith in their own outward achievements rather than in the God they professed to love with all their hearts.

THE LAW AROUSES SIN

But sin, taking opportunity through the commandment, produced in me coveting of every kind; for apart from the Law sin is dead. (7:8)

Paul once again (cf. v. 7) makes clear that the law itself is not sinful and is not responsible for sin. It is the **sin** that is already in a person's heart that takes **opportunity through the commandment** of the law to produce **coveting of every kind** as well as countless other specific sins.

Faithful preachers have always proclaimed the demands of God's law before proclaiming the grace of His gospel. A person who does not see himself as a lost and helpless sinner will see no need for a Savior. And the person who is not willing to be cleansed of his sin, even if he recognizes it, has no access to the Savior, because he refuses to be saved.

Bible commentator F. F. Bruce writes, "The villain of the piece is Sin; Sin seized the opportunity afforded it when the law showed me what was right and what was wrong" (*The Epistle of Paul to the Romans* [Grand Rapids: Eerdmans, 1963], p. 150). The problem is with sin, not with the law. "Is the Law then contrary to the promises of God?" Paul rhetorically asked the Galatians, and then answered with his favorite negative, "May it never be!" (Gal. 3:21).

Aphormē (**opportunity**) originally was used of the starting point or base of operations for an expedition. **Sin** uses **the commandment,** that is, God's law, as a beachhead from which to launch its evil work.

It is no secret that man has a natural rebellious streak that causes him almost reflexively to resent a command or prohibition. When people notice a sign that reads "Keep off the grass" or "Don't pick the flowers," for instance, there is often an impulse to do the very thing the sign forbids.

In his book *Principles of Conduct,* John Murray observes that the more the light of God's law shines into our depraved hearts, the more the enmity of our minds is aroused to opposition, proving that the mind of the flesh is not subject to the law of God ([Grand Rapids: Eerdmans, 1957], p. 185). When a person is confronted by God's law, the forbidden thing becomes all the more attractive, not so much for its own sake as for its furnishing a channel for the assertion of self-will.

In his rich allegory *Pilgrim's Progress,* John Bunyan paints a vivid word picture of sin's arousal by the law. A large, dustcovered room in Interpreter's house symbolizes the human heart. When a man with a broom, representing God's law, begins to sweep, the dust swirls up and all but suffocates Christian. That is what the law does to sin. It so agitates sin that it becomes stifling. And just as a broom cannot clean a room of dust but only stir it up, so the law cannot cleanse the heart of sin but only make the sin more evident and unpleasant.

The axiom of Paul's argument here is that **apart from the Law sin is dead.** It is not that sin has no existence apart from the law, because that is obviously not true. Paul has already stated that, long before the law was revealed, sin entered the world through Adam and then spread to all his descendants (Rom. 5:12). "Until the Law sin was in the world," he goes on to explain, "but sin is not imputed when there is no law" (v. 13). Paul's point in Romans 7:8 is that **sin is dead** in the sense that it is somewhat dormant and not fully active. It does not overwhelm the sinner as it does when **the Law** becomes known.

The Law Ruins the Sinner

And I was once alive apart from the Law; but when the commandment came, sin became alive, and I died; and this commandment, which was to result in life, proved to result in death for me; for sin, taking opportunity through the commandment, deceived me, and through it killed me. (7:9-11)

The law not only reveals and arouses sin but also ruins and destroys the sinner. Still recounting his own experience before salvation, Paul confesses that he had long been **alive apart from the Law.** As a highly-trained and zealous Pharisee, he was certainly not **apart from the law** in the sense of not knowing or being concerned about it. He was an expert on the law and considered himself to be blameless in regard to it, thus thinking he lived a life that pleased God (Phil. 3:6).

But throughout all his years of proud self-effort, Paul had served only the "oldness of the letter" of the law (Rom. 7:6). **But when** a true understanding of **the commandment came,** he began to see himself as he really was and began to understand how far short he came of the law's righteous standards. His **sin** then **became alive,** that is, he came to realize his true condition in its full evil and destructiveness. On the other hand, he **died** in the sense of his realizing that all his religious accomplishments were spiritual rubbish (Phil. 3:7-8). His self-esteem, self-satisfaction, and pride were devastated and in ruins. Paul **died**. That is, for the first time, he realized he was spiritually dead. When he saw the majesty and holiness of God's perfect law, he was broken and contrite. He was finally ready to plead with the penitent tax-gatherer, "God, be merciful to me, the sinner!" (Luke 18:13). He recognized himself as one of the helpless and ungodly for whom Christ had died (see Rom. 5:6).

In our day of great emphasis on God's love, often to the neglect of His wrath and judgment, it is especially important to evaluate the genuineness of salvation more by a person's regard for God's law than by his regard for God's love.

This commandment, representing all of God's law, **which was to result in life, proved** rather **to result in death for me,** Paul says. What he had considered to be a means of gaining eternal **life** had turned out to be the way of spiritual **death**.

God gave the law to provide blessing for those who love and serve Him. Throughout the Old Testament, the Lord gave His people such promises as, "How blessed are those whose way is blameless, who walk in the law of the Lord. How blessed are those who observe His testimonies, who seek Him with all their heart" (Ps. 119:1-2).

But the law, the **commandment,** cannot produce blessing and peace in the unbeliever, because he cannot fulfill the law's requirements and therefore stands under its sentence of **death**. The law cannot produce the **life** it was meant to produce because no man is able to meet the law's perfect standard of righteousness. If it were possible, perfect obedience to the law could bring life. But because such obedience is *not* possible for fallen, sinful man, the law brings him **death** rather than life.

As believers in Jesus Christ, we are saved and given eternal life because "*the requirement of the Law [is] fulfilled in us,* who do not walk according to the flesh, but according to the Spirit," and because Christ Himself indwells us through His own Spirit, "though the body is dead because of [our] sin, yet *[our] spirit is alive* because of [His] righteousness" (Rom. 8:4, 10; emphasis added).

Repeating what he has just said about **sin taking opportunity through the commandment** (cf. v. 8) and causing his death (**it killed me;** cf. vv. 9-10), Paul says that sin also **deceived** him. Deceit is one of sin's most subtle and disastrous evils. A person who is **deceived** into thinking he is acceptable to God because of his own merit and good works will see no need of salvation and no reason for trusting in Christ. It is doubtless for that reason that all false religions—including those that claim the name of Christ—in one way or another are built on a deceptive foundation of self-trust and self-effort. Self-righteousness is not righteousness at all but is the worst of sins. Both by the standard of the law and by the standard of grace, the very term *self-righteousness* is a self-contradiction.

Sometime before his encounter with Christ on the Damascus road, Paul came to recognize sin's deceit and the law's impossible demands and was convicted by the Holy Spirit of his own unrighteousness and spiritual helplessness.

THE LAW REFLECTS THE SINFULNESS OF SIN

So then, the Law is holy, and the commandment is holy and righteous and good. Therefore did that which is good become a cause of death for me? May it never be! Rather it was sin, in order that it might be shown to be sin by effecting my death through that which is good, that through the commandment sin might become utterly sinful. (7:12-13)

The apostle again answers the question, "Is the law sin?" (7:7). Now he declares that not only is the law not sin but that **the law is,** in fact, **holy, and the commandment is holy and righteous and good.** Throughout the remainder of the chapter Paul continues to praise and exalt God's law, calling it spiritual (v. 14), good (v. 16), and joyfully concurring in his "inner man" with its divine truth and standards (v. 22).

David highly exalted God's law, proclaiming:

> The law of the Lord is perfect, restoring the soul; the testimony of the Lord is sure, making wise the simple. The precepts of the Lord are right, rejoicing the heart; the commandment of the Lord is pure, enlightening the eyes. The fear of the Lord is clean, enduring forever; the judgments of the Lord are true; they are righteous altogether. They are more desirable than gold, yes, than much fine gold; sweeter also than honey and the drippings of the honeycomb. Moreover, by them Thy servant is warned; in keeping them there is great reward. (Ps. 19:7-11)

The fact that the law reveals, arouses, and condemns sin and brings death to the sinner does not make the law itself evil. When a person is justly convicted and sentenced for murder, there is no fault in the law or with those responsible for upholding it. The fault is in the one who broke the law.

Once again anticipating a question that would naturally come to mind in light of what he has said, Paul asks, **Therefore did that which is good become a cause of death for me?** And once again Paul answers his own question with a resounding, **May it never be!**

To use again the analogy of the murder trial, it is not the law against murder but the committing of murder that merits punishment. The law itself is good; it is the breaking of it that is evil. How much more is God's law **good,** and how much more evil is the breaking of it.

It is not the law that is the cause of spiritual death but **rather it is sin.** The law reveals and arouses sin **in order that it might be shown to be sin by effecting . . . death through that which is good.** Sin's deadly character is exposed under the pure light of God's law.

God has given His holy, righteous, and good law in order **that through the commandment sin might become utterly sinful.** As already noted, the preaching of the law is necessary to the preaching of the gospel. Until men see their sin for what it is, they will not see their need of salvation from it.

Paul's point here is that sin is so **utterly sinful** that it can even pervert and undermine the purpose of God's holy law. It can twist and distort the law so that instead of bringing life, as God intended, it brings death. It can manipulate the pure law of God to deceive and damn people. Such is the awful wretchedness of sin.

In his letter to the Galatian church, Paul gives additional insight on the place and purpose of the law.

> Why the Law then? It was added because of transgressions, having been ordained through angels by the agency of a mediator, until the seed should come to whom the promise had been made. Now a mediator is not for one party only; whereas God is only one. Is the Law then contrary to the promises of God? May it never be! For if a law had been given which was able to impart life, then righteousness would indeed have been based on law. But the Scripture has shut up all men under sin, that the promise by faith in Jesus Christ might be given to those who believe. (Gal. 3:19-22)

The ultimate purpose of the law was to drive men to faith in Jesus Christ, who fulfilled the demands of the law on behalf of sinners who trust in His righteousness instead of their own.

Although Robert Murray McCheyne died in 1843 at the age of thirty, he left God's people a great treasure is his memoirs and other writings. In the poem "Jehovah Tsidkenu," which means, "The Lord Our Righteousness," he testifies:

> I once was a stranger to grace and to God,
> I knew not my danger, and felt not my load;
> Though friends spoke in rapture of Christ on the tree,
> Jehovah Tsidkenu was nothing to me.
>
> I oft read with pleasure, to soothe or engage,
> Isaiah's wild measure and John's simple page;
> But even when they pictured the blood-sprinkled tree,
> Jehovah Tsidkenu seemed nothing to me.

Like tears from the daughters of Zion that roll,
I wept when the waters went over His soul,
Yet thought not that my sins had nailed to the tree
Jehovah Tsidkenu—'twas nothing to me.

When free grace awoke me by light from on high,
Then legal fears shook me, I trembled to die;
No refuge, no safety in self could I see—
Jehovah Tsidkenu my Savior must be.

My terrors all vanished before the sweet name;
My guilty fear banished, with boldness I came
To drink at the fountain, life-giving and free—
Jehovah Tsidkenu is all things to me.

Jehovah Tsidkenu! My treasure and boast,
Jehovah Tsidkenu! I ne'er can be lost;
In Thee shall I conquer by flood and by field—
My cable, my anchor, my breastplate and shield!

Even treading the valley, the shadow of death,
This "watchword" shall rally my faltering breath;
For while from life's fever my God sets me free,
Jehovah Tsidkenu my death-song shall be.

McCheyne experienced the same conviction of sin as did the apostle Paul. When he saw himself in the full light of God's law, he realized he was ruined and dead and had no hope but in the saving grace of the Lord Jesus Christ.

After salvation Christians still need continual exposure to the divine standards of God's law in order to see more clearly the sin in their lives and to confess it and experience the full blessing that belongs to His children. Then they can say with the psalmist, "Thy word I have treasured in my heart, that I may not sin against Thee" (Ps. 119:11) and can claim the promise that "if we confess our sins, He is faithful and righteous to forgive us our sins and to cleanse us from all unrighteousness" (1 John 1:9).

The Believer and Indwelling Sin

For we know that the Law is spiritual; but I am of flesh, sold into bondage to sin. For that which I am doing, I do not understand; for I am not practicing what I would like to do, but I am doing the very thing I hate. But if I do the very thing I do not wish to do, I agree with the Law, confessing that it is good. So now, no longer am I the one doing it, but sin which indwells me. For I know that nothing good dwells in me, that is, in my flesh; for the wishing is present in me, but the doing of the good is not. For the good that I wish, I do not do; but I practice the very evil that I do not wish. But if I am doing the very thing I do not wish, I am no longer the one doing it, but sin which dwells in me. I find then the principle that evil is present in me, the one who wishes to do good. For I joyfully concur with the law of God in the inner man, but I see a different law in the members of my body, waging war against the law of my mind, and making me a prisoner of the law of sin which is in my members. Wretched man that I am! Who will set me free from the body of this death? Thanks be to God through Jesus Christ our Lord! So then, on the one hand I myself with my mind am serving the law of God, but on the other, with my flesh the law of sin. (7:14-25)

This passage is obviously a poignant account of a person's inner conflict with himself, one part of him pulling one direction and another part pulling the opposite. The conflict is real and it is intense.

For perhaps as long as the church has known this text, however, interpreters have disagreed as to whether the person described is a Christian or a non-Christian. Whole movements have arisen to promote one of those views or the other. One side maintains that the person is too much in bondage to sin to be a believer, whereas the other side maintains that the person has too much love for the things of God and too much hatred of sin to be an unbeliever.

It is obviously important, therefore, to determine which sort of person Paul is talking about before any interpretation of the passage is attempted. It is also of some importance to determine whether Paul's first person singular refers to himself or whether that is simply a literary device he uses to identify more personally with his readers. The answer to those two questions will automatically answer a third: If Paul is speaking of himself, is he speaking of his condition before or after his conversion?

Those who believe Paul is speaking about an unbeliever point out that he describes the person as being "of flesh, sold into bondage" (v. 14), as having nothing good dwelling in him (v. 18), and as a "wretched man" trapped in a "body of . . . death" (v. 24). How then, it is argued, could such a person correspond to the Christian Paul describes in chapter 6 as having died to sin (v. 2), as having his old self crucified and no longer being enslaved to sin (v. 6), as being "freed from sin" (vv. 7, 18, 22), as considering himself dead to sin (v. 11), and as being obedient from the heart to God's Word (v. 17)?

Those who contend Paul is speaking about a believer in chapter 7 point out that this person desires to obey God's law and hates doing what is evil (vv. 15, 19, 21), that he is humble before God, realizing that nothing good dwells in his humanness (v. 18), and that he sees sin as in him, but not *all* there is in him (vv. 17, 20-22). He gives thanks to Jesus Christ as his Lord and serves Him with his mind (v. 25). The apostle has already established that none of those things characterize the unsaved. The unbeliever not only hates God's truth and righteousness but suppresses them, he willfully rejects the natural evidence of God, he neither honors nor gives thanks to God, and he is totally dominated by sin so that he arrogantly disobeys God's law and encourages others to do so (1:18-21, 32).

In Romans 6, Paul began his discussion of sanctification by focusing on the believer as a new creation, a completely new person in Christ. The emphasis is therefore on the holiness and righteousness of the believer, both imputed and imparted. For the reasons given in the previous paragraph, as well as for other reasons that will be mentioned later, it seems certain that in chapter 7 the apostle is still talking about the believer. Here, however, the focus is on the conflict a believer continues to have with sin. Even in chapter 6, Paul indicates that believers still must continually do battle with sin in their lives. He therefore admonishes them: "Do not let sin reign in your mortal body that you should obey its lusts, and do not go on presenting the members of your body to sin as instruments of unrighteousness" (Rom. 6:12-13).

Some interpreters believe that chapter 7 describes the carnal, or fleshly, Christian, one who is living on a very low level of spirituality. Many suggest that this person is a frustrated, legalistic Christian who attempts in his own power to please God by trying to live up to the Mosaic law.

But the attitude expressed in chapter 7 is not typical of legalists, who tend to be self-satisfied with their fulfillment of the law. Most people are attracted to legalism in the first place because it offers the prospect of living up to God's standards by one's own power.

It seems rather that Paul is here describing the most spiritual and mature of Christians, who, the more they honestly measure themselves against God's standards of righteousness the more they realize how much they fall short. The closer we get to God, the more we see our own sin. Thus it is immature, fleshly, and legalistic persons who tend to live under the illusion that they are spiritual and that they measure up well by God's standards. The level of spiritual insight, brokenness, contrition, and humility that characterize the person depicted in Romans 7 are marks of a spiritual and mature believer, who before God has no trust in his own goodness and achievements.

It also seems, as one would naturally suppose from the use of the first person singular (which appears forty-six times in Rom. 7:7-25), that Paul is speaking of himself. Not only is he the subject of this passage, but it is the mature and spiritually seasoned apostle that is portrayed. Only a Christian at the height of spiritual maturity would either experience or be concerned about such deep struggles of heart, mind, and conscience. The more clearly and completely he saw God's holiness and goodness, the more Paul recognized and grieved over his own sinfulness.

Paul reflects the same humility many places in his writings. In his first letter to the church at Corinth, he confessed, "I am the least of the apostles, who am not fit to be called an apostle, because I persecuted the church of God" (1 Cor. 15:9). Although he refers there to his attitude and actions before his conversion, he speaks of his apostleship in the present tense, considering himself still to be unworthy of that high calling. To the Ephesian believers he spoke of himself as "the very least of all saints" (Eph. 3:8), and to Timothy he marvelled that the Lord "considered me faithful, putting me into service" and refers to himself as the foremost of sinners (1 Tim. 1:12, 15). He knew and confessed that whatever he was in Christ was fully due to the grace of God (1 Cor. 15:10).

Only a new creation in Christ lives with such tension of sin against righteousness, because only a Christian has the divine nature of God within him. Because he is no longer in Adam but now in Christ, he possesses the Spirit-given desire to be conformed to Christ's own image and be made perfect in righteousness. But sin still clings to his humanness, although in his inner being he hates and despises it. He has passed from darkness to light and now shares in Christ's death, burial, resurrection, and eternal life, but as he grows in Christlikeness, he also becomes more and more aware of the continued presence and power of indwelling sin, which he loathes and longs to be rid of. It is such sensitivity that caused the fourth-century church Father John Chrysostom to say in his *Second Homily on Eutrophius* that he feared nothing but sin. The person depicted in Romans 7 has a deep awareness of his own sin and an equally deep desire to please the Lord in all things. Only a mature Christian could be so characterized.

The Puritan writer Thomas Watson observed that one of the certain signs of "sanctification is an antipathy against sin ... A hypocrite may leave sin, yet love it; as a serpent casts its coat, but keeps its sting; but a sanctified person can say he not only leaves sin, but loathes it." He goes on to say to the Christian, "God . . . has not only chained up sin, but changed thy nature, and made thee as a king's daughter, all glorious within. He has put upon thee the breastplate of holiness, which, though it may be shot at, can never be shot through" (*A Body of Divinity* [London: Banner of truth, rev. ed., 1965], pp. 246, 250).

The spiritual believer is sensitive to sin because he knows it grieves the Holy Spirit (Eph. 4:30), because it dishonors God (1 Cor. 6:19-20), because sin keeps his prayers from being answered (1 Pet. 3:12), and because sin makes his life spiritually powerless (1 Cor. 9:27). The spiritual believer is sensitive to sin because it causes good things from God to be withheld (Jer. 5:25), because it robs him of the joy of salvation (Ps. 51:12), because it inhibits spiritual growth (1 Cor. 3:1), because it brings chastisement from the Lord (Heb. 12:7), and because it prevents his being a fit vessel for the Lord to use (2 Tim. 2:21). The spiritual believer is sensitive to sin because it pollutes Christian fellowship (1 Cor. 10:21), because it prevents participating properly in the Lord's Supper (1 Cor. 11:28-29), and because it can even endanger his physical life and health (1 Cor. 11:30; 1 John 5:16).

As pointed out in the previous chapter of this volume, Paul uses past tense verbs in Romans 7:7-13, which doubtless indicates he was speaking of his preconversion life. Beginning in verse 14, however, and continuing throughout the rest of the chapter, he uses the present tense exclusively in reference to himself. That abrupt, obvious, and consistent change of tenses strongly supports the idea that in verses 14-25 Paul is describing his life as a Christian.

Beginning in verse 14 there is also an obvious change in the subject's circumstances in relation to sin. In verses 7-13 Paul speaks of sin as deceiving and slaying him. He gives the picture of being at sin's mercy and helpless to extricate himself from its deadly grasp. But in verses 14-25 he speaks of a conscious and determined battle against sin, which is still a powerful enemy but is no longer his master. In this latter part of the chapter Paul also continues to defend the righteousness of God's law and rejoice in the benefits of His law, which, although it cannot save from sin, can nevertheless continue to reveal and convict of sin in the believer's life, just as it did before salvation.

As long as a believer remains on earth in his mortal and corrupted body, the law will continue to be his spiritual ally. The obedient and Spirit-filled believer, therefore, greatly values and honors all the moral and spiritual commandments of God. He continues to declare with the psalmist, "Thy word I have treasured in my heart, that I may not sin against Thee" (Ps. 119:11), and that Word is more than ever a lamp to his feet and a light to his path (Ps. 119:105). God's Word is more valuable for believers under the New Covenant than it was for those under the Old Covenant, not only because the Lord has revealed more of His truth to us in the New Testament, but also because believers now have the fulness of His indwelling Holy Spirit to illumine and apply His truth. Therefore, although the law cannot save or sanctify, it is still holy, righteous, and good (Rom. 7:12), and obedience to it offers great benefits both to believers and unbelievers.

Paul is still teaching about the broader subject of justification by grace through faith. He has established that justification results in the believer's security (chap. 5), his holiness (chap. 6), and his freedom from bondage to the law (7:1-6). To that list of benefits the apostle now adds sensitivity to and hatred of sin.

In Romans 7:14-25 Paul gives a series of laments about his spiritual predicament and difficulties. The first three laments (vv. 14-17, 18-20, 21-23) follow the same pattern. Paul first describes the spiritual condition he is lamenting, then gives proof of its reality, and finally reveals the source of the problem. The final lament (vv. 24-25) also includes a beautiful exultation of gratitude to God for His Son Jesus Christ, because of whose gracious sacrifice believers in Him are no longer under condemnation, in spite of the lingering power of sin (8:1).

THE FIRST LAMENT

For we know that the Law is spiritual; but I am of flesh, sold into bondage to sin. For that which I am doing, I do not understand; for I am not practicing what I would like to do, but I am doing the very thing I hate. But if I do the very thing I do not wish to do, I

agree with the Law, confessing that it is good. So now, no longer am I the one doing it, but sin which indwells me. (7:14-17)

THE CONDITION

For we know that the Law is spiritual; but I am of flesh, sold into bondage to sin. (7:14)

The conjunction **for** carries the idea of *because* and indicates that Paul is not introducing a new subject but is giving a defense of what he has just said. He begins by again affirming **that the Law** is not the problem, because it **is spiritual.** Salvation by grace through faith does not replace or devalue **the Law,** because the law was never a means of salvation. As observed previously, Hebrews 11 and many other passages of Scripture make clear that the only means of salvation has always been the provision and power of God's grace working through the channel of man's faith.

"**But I,**" Paul continues, "**am** still **of the flesh.** I am still earth-bound and mortal." It is important to note that the apostle does not say he is still *in* **the flesh** but that he is still **of** it. He has already explained that believers are no longer "in the flesh" (7:5; cf. 8:8), no longer bound by and enslaved to its sinfulness as they once were. The idea is that, although believers are not still in the flesh, the flesh is still in them. In his first letter to the church at Corinth, Paul describes the Christians there as "men of flesh, . . . babes in Christ" (1 Cor. 3:1). As the apostle confesses later in the present passage, using the present tense, "I know that nothing good dwells in me, that is, in my flesh" (7:18). Even as an apostle of Jesus Christ he possessed a remnant of the sinfulness that characterizes all human beings, including those who, in Christ, are saved from its total mastery and its condemnation.

But the Christian's spirit, his inner self, has been completely and forever cleansed of sin. It is for that reason that, at death, he is prepared to enter God's presence in perfect holiness and purity. Because his spiritual rebirth has already occurred, his flesh, with its remaining sin, is left behind.

Every well-taught and honest Christian is aware that his life falls far short of God's perfect standard of righteousness and that he falls back into sin with disturbing frequency. He is no longer of his former father, the devil (John 8:44); he no longer loves the world (1 John 2:15); and he is no longer sin's slave—but he is still subject to its deceit and is still attracted by many of its allurements. Yet the Christian cannot be happy with his sin, because it is contrary to his new nature and because he knows that it grieves his Lord as well as his own conscience.

The story is told of an unbeliever who, when he heard of the gospel of salvation by grace alone, commented, "If I could believe that salvation is free and is received only by faith, I would believe and then take my fill of sin." The person witnessing to him wisely replied, "How much sin do you think it would take to fill a true Christian to satisfaction?" His point was that a person who has not lost his appetite for sin cannot be truly converted.

The phrase **sold into bondage to sin** has caused many interpreters to miss Paul's point and to take those words as evidence the person being talked about is not a Christian. But Paul uses a similar phrase in verse 23, where he makes clear that only his members, that is, his fleshly body, is "a prisoner of the law of sin." That lingering part of his unredeemed humanness is still sinful and consequently makes warfare against the new and redeemed part of him, which is no longer sin's prisoner and is now its avowed enemy.

Paul's strong words about his condition do not indicate he was only partially saved at the time but rather emphasize that sin can continue to have dreadful power in a Christian's life and is not to be trifled with. The believer's battle with sin is strenuous and life-long. And as Paul also points out later in this chapter, even a Christian can truthfully say, "I know that nothing good dwells in me, that is, in my flesh" (Rom. 7:18). *In himself*, that is, in his remaining fleshly being, a Christian is no more holy or sinless than he was before salvation.

Probably many years after he became a believer, David prayed, "Be gracious to me, O God, according to Thy lovingkindness; according to the greatness of Thy compassion blot out my transgressions. Wash me thoroughly from my iniquity, and cleanse me from my sin. For I know my transgressions, and my sin is ever before me" (Ps. 51:1-3). The rendering in the *New International Version* of verse 5 of that psalm gives helpful insight: "Surely I have been a sinner from birth, sinful from the time my mother conceived me." David well understood the truth the apostle John would later proclaim to believers: "If we say that we have no sin, we are deceiving ourselves, and the truth is not in us. If we confess our sins, He is faithful and righteous to forgive us our sins and to cleanse us from all unrighteousness. If we say that we have not sinned, we make Him a liar, and His word is not in us" (1 John 1:8-10).

It was in that humble spirit that Isaiah, although a prophet of God, confessed as he stood before the heavenly throne: "I am a man of unclean lips" (Isa. 6:5). Like Isaiah, the more a Christian draws near to God, the more clearly he perceives the Lord's holiness and his own sinfulness.

The commentator C. E. B. Cranfield observed, "The more seriously a Christian strives to live from grace and to submit to the discipline of the gospel, the more sensitive he becomes to . . . the fact that even his very best acts and activities are disfigured by the egotism which is still powerful within him—and no less evil because it is often more subtly disguised than formerly" (*A Critical and Exegetical Commentary on the Epistle to the Romans* [Edinburgh: T & T Clark, 1975], 1:358).

Thomas Scott, an evangelical preacher of the Church of England in the late eighteenth and early nineteenth centuries, wrote that when a believer "compares his actual attainments with the spirituality of the law, and with his own desire and aim to obey it, he sees that he is yet, to a great degree, carnal in the state of his mind, and under the power of evil propensities, from which (like a man sold for a slave) he cannot wholly emancipate himself. He is carnal in exact proportion to the degree in which he falls short of perfect conformity to the law of God" (cited in Geoffrey B. Wilson, *Romans: A Digest of Reformed Comment* [London: Banner of Truth, 1969], p. 121).

Sin is so wretched and powerful that, even in a redeemed person, it hangs on and contaminates his living and frustrates his inner desire to obey the will of God.

THE PROOF

For that which I am doing, I do not understand; for I am not practicing what I would like to do, but I am doing the very thing I hate. (7:15)

Paul's proof that sin still indwelt him was in the reality that **that which I am doing, I do not understand; for I am not practicing what I would like to do.**

Ginōskō (**understand**) has the basic meaning of taking in knowledge in regard to something or someone, knowledge that goes beyond the merely factual. By extension, the term frequently was used of a special relationship between the person who knows and the object of the knowledge. It was often used of the intimate relationship between husband and wife and between God and His people. Paul uses the term in that way to represent the relationship between the saved and the Savior: "Now that you have come to know God, or rather to be known by God, how is it that you turn back again to the weak and worthless elemental things, to which you desire to be enslaved all over again?" (Gal. 4:9). By further extension, the word was used in the sense of approving or accepting something or someone. "If anyone loves God," Paul says, "he is known [accepted] by Him" (1 Cor. 8:3).

That seems to be the meaning here and is consistent with the last half of the sentence. Paul found himself **doing** things he did not approve of. It was not that he was unable to do a particular good thing but that when he saw the fullness and grandeur of God's law, he was not able to measure up completely. It was not that he could never accomplish any good at all, nor that he could never faithfully obey God. The apostle was rather expressing an inner turmoil of the most profound kind, of sincerely desiring in his heart to fulfill the spirit as well as the letter of the law (see 7:6) but realizing that he was unable to live up to the Lord's perfect standards and his own heart's desire.

It was not Paul's conscience that was bothering him because of some unforgiven sin or selfish reluctance to follow the Lord. It was his inner man, recreated in the likeness of Christ and indwelt by His Spirit, that now could see something of the true holiness, goodness, and glory of God's law and was grieved at his least infraction or falling short of it. In glaring contrast to his preconversion self-satisfaction in thinking himself blameless before God's law (Phil. 3:6), Paul now realized how wretchedly short of God's perfect law he lived, even as a Spirit-indwelt believer and an apostle of Jesus Christ.

That spirit of humble contrition is a mark of every spiritual disciple of Christ, who cries out, "Lord, I can't be all you want me to be, I am unable to fulfill your perfect, holy, and glorious law." In great frustration and sorrow he painfully confesses with Paul, **I am not practicing what I would like to do**.

THE SOURCE

But if I do the very thing I do not wish to do, I agree with the Law, confessing that it is good. So now, no longer am I the one doing it, but sin which indwells me. (7:16-17)

Paul now deals with the reason, or the source, of his inability to perfectly fulfill the law, and he begins by staunchly defending the divine standard. "Whatever the reason for my doing **the very thing I do not wish to do**," he says, "it is not the law's fault. **I agree with the Law** in every detail. My new self, the new creation that placed God's incorruptible and eternal seed within me, is wholeheartedly **confessing** that the law **is good.** In my redeemed being I sincerely long to honor the law and to fulfill it perfectly."

Every true Christian has in his heart a sense of the moral excellence of God's **Law.** And the more mature he becomes in Christ, the more fully he perceives and lauds the law's goodness, holiness, and glory. The more profoundly he is committed to the direction of the Holy Spirit in his life, the deeper his love for the Lord Jesus Christ becomes, the deeper his sense of God's holiness and majesty becomes, and the greater will be his longing to fulfill God's law.

What then, is the problem? What is the source of our failure to live up to God's standards and our own inner desires? **"Now** it is **no longer I** who is **the one doing it,"** Paul explains, **"but sin which indwells me."**

Paul was not trying to escape personal responsibility. He was not mixing the pure gospel with Greek philosophical dualism, which later plagued the early church and is popular in some church circles today. The apostle was not teaching that the spirit world is all good and the physical world all evil, as the influential Gnostic philosophy of his day contended. Proponents of that ungodly school of thought invariably develop moral insensitivity. They justify their sin by claiming it is entirely the product of their physical bodies, which are going to be destroyed anyway, and that the inner, spiritual person remains innately good and is untouched by and unaccountable for anything the body does.

The apostle had already confessed his own complicity in his sin. "I am of flesh, sold into bondage to sin," he said of his present earthly life as a believer (7:14). If the "real" inner Christian were not responsible for sin in his life, he would have no reason to confess it and have it cleansed and forgiven. As noted above, John makes clear that a claim of sinlessness makes God a liar and proves that His Word is not in us (1 John 1:10). A true believer is continually recognizing and confessing his sin (v. 9).

Throughout this chapter Paul has spoken in personal, nontechnical terms. He has not been drawing precise theological distinctions between the old preconversion life of a believer and his new life in Christ. He was certainly not teaching that a Christian has two natures or two personalities. There is just one saved person, just as previously there was one lost person.

In verse 17, however, Paul becomes more technical and theologically precise in his terminology. There had been a radical change in his life, as there has been in the life of every Christian. *Ouketi* (**no longer**) is a negative adverb of time, indicating a complete and permanent change. Paul's new **I,** his new inner self, **no longer** approves of the sin that still clings to him through the flesh. Whereas before his conversion his inner self approved of the sin he committed, **now** his inner self, a completely new inner self, strongly disapproves. He explains the reason for that change in his letter to the Galatians: "I have been crucified with Christ; and it is no longer I who live, but Christ lives in me; and the life which I now live in the flesh I live by faith in the Son of God, who loved me, and delivered Himself up for me" (Gal. 2:20).

After salvation, sin, like a deposed and exiled ruler, no longer reigns in a person's life, but it manages to survive. It no longer resides in the innermost self but finds its residual dwelling in his flesh, in the unredeemed humanness that remains until a believer meets the Lord at the Rapture or at death. "For the flesh sets its desire against the Spirit, and the Spirit against the flesh," Paul further explained to the Galatians; "for these are in opposition to one another, so that you may not do the things that you please" (Gal. 5:17).

In this life, Christians are somewhat like an unskilled artist who beholds a beautiful scene that he wants to paint. But his lack of talent prevents him from doing the scene justice. The fault is not in the scene, or in the canvas, the brushes, or the paint but in the painter. That is why we need to ask the master painter, Jesus Christ, to place His hand over ours in order to paint the strokes that, independent of Him, we could never produce. Jesus said, "Apart from Me you can do nothing" (John 15:5). The only way we can live victoriously is to walk by Christ's own Spirit and in His power, in order not to "carry out the desire of the flesh" (Gal. 5:16).

THE SECOND LAMENT

For I know that nothing good dwells in me, that is, in my flesh; for the wishing is present in me, but the doing of the good is not. For the good that I wish, I do not do; but I practice the very evil that I do not wish. But if I am doing the very thing I do not wish, I am no longer the one doing it, but sin which dwells in me. (7:18-20)

The second lament follows the same pattern as the first: the condition, the proof, and the source.

THE CONDITION

For I know that nothing good dwells in me, that is, in my flesh; (7:18a)

In order that his readers will not misunderstand, the apostle explains that the **me** in whom **nothing good dwells** is not the same as the "I" he has just mentioned in the previous verse and which referred to his new, redeemed, incorruptible, Christlike nature. The part of his present being in which sin still **dwells** is his **flesh,** his old humanness, which has not yet been completely transformed.

Again he points out (see vv. 5, 14) that the only residence of sin in a believer's life is his **flesh,** his unredeemed humanness. As noted above, the **flesh** in itself is not sinful, but it is still subject to sin and furnishes sin a beachhead from which to operate in a believer's life.

THE PROOF

for the wishing is present in me, but the doing of the good is not. For the good that I wish, I do not do; but I practice the very evil that I do not wish. (7:18b-19)

Paul had a deep desire to do only good. The **wishing** to do God's will was very much **present** within his redeemed being. The **me** used here does not correspond to the *me* of the first half of this verse but to the *I* in verse 17. Unfortunately, however, the perfect **doing of the good** that his heart wished for was **not** present in his life. Slightly rephrasing the same truth, he says, **For the good that I wish, I do not do**.

As noted in regard to verse 15, Paul is not saying that he was totally incapable of doing anything that was good and acceptable. He is saying that he was incapable of *completely* fulfilling the requirements of God's holy law. "Not that I have . . . already become perfect," he explained to the Philippian church, "but I press on in order that I may lay hold of that for which also I was laid hold of by Christ Jesus. Brethren, I do not regard myself as having laid hold of it yet; but one thing I do: forgetting what lies behind and reaching forward to what lies ahead, I press on toward the goal for the prize of the upward call of God in Christ Jesus" (Phil. 3:12-14).

As a believer grows in his spiritual life, he inevitably will have both an increased hatred of sin and an increased love for righteousness. As desire for holiness increases, so will sensitivity to and antipathy toward sin.

The other side of the predicament, Paul says, is that **I practice the very evil that I do not wish**. Again, it is important to understand that this great inner struggle with sin is not experienced by the undeveloped and childish believer but by the mature man of God.

David was a man after God's own heart (1 Sam. 13:14) and was honored by having the Messiah named the Son of David. Yet no Old Testament saint seems a worse sinner or was more conscious of his own sin. Particularly in the great penitential psalms 32, 38, and 51, but in many other psalms as well, David agonized over and confessed his sin before God. He was so near to the heart of God that the least sin in his life loomed before his eyes as a great offense.

THE SOURCE

But if I am doing the very thing I do not wish, I am no longer the one doing it, but sin which dwells in me. (7:20)

Paul repeats what he said in verses 16-17, with only slight variation. **If I am doing the very thing I do not wish,** he argues with simple logic, then it follows that **I am no longer the one doing it.** The apostle again uses the phrase **no longer,** referring to the time before his conversion. Before salvation it was the inner **I** who sinned and agreed with the sin. An unsaved person cannot truthfully say he is not doing it. He has no moral or spiritual "no longers."

THE THIRD LAMENT

I find then the principle that evil is present in me, the one who wishes to do good. For I joyfully concur with the law of God in the inner man, but I see a different law in the members of my body, waging war against the law of my mind, and making me a prisoner of the law of sin which is in my members. (7:21-23)

The third lament is very much like the first two, both in substance and in order.

THE CONDITION

I find then the principle that evil is present in me, the one who wishes to do good. (7:21)

The continuing presence of **evil** in a believer's life is so universal that Paul refers to it not as an uncommon thing but as such a common reality as to be called a continually operating spiritual **principle.** Lingering sin does battle with every **good** thing a believer desires to do, every good thought, every good intention, every good motive, every good word, every good deed.

The Lord warned Cain when he became angry that Abel's sacrifice was accepted but his own was not: "Sin is crouching at the door; and its desire is for you, but you must master it" (Gen. 4:7). Sin continues to crouch at the door, even of believers, in order to lead people into disobedience.

THE PROOF

For I joyfully concur with the law of God in the inner man, but I see a different law in the members of my body, waging war against the law of my mind, (7:22-23a)

The first part of Paul's proof that sin is no longer his master and that he is indeed redeemed by God and made into the likeness of Christ is his being able to say, **I joyfully concur with the law of God in the inner man.** In other words, the apostle's justified **inner man** is on the side of **the law of God** and no longer on the side of sin, as is true of every unsaved person.

Psalm 119 offers many striking parallels to Romans 7. Over and over and in a multitude of ways, the psalmist praises and exalts the Lord and His Word: "I have rejoiced in the way of Thy testimonies, as much as in all riches" (v. 14), "I shall delight in Thy commandments, which I love" (v. 47), "Thy law is my delight" (v. 77), "Thy word is a lamp to my feet, and a light to my path" (v. 105), and "Thy word is very pure, therefore Thy servant loves it" (v. 140). It has always been true that the godly person's "delight is in the law of the Lord" (Ps. 1:2).

Paul's **inner man,** the deepest recesses of his redeemed person, the bottom of his heart, hungers and thirsts for God's righteousness (see Matt. 5:6) and seeks first His kingdom and His righteousness (see Matt. 6:33). "Though our outer man is decaying," Paul told the Corinthian believers, "yet our inner man is being renewed day by day" (2 Cor. 4:16). He prayed that Christians in Ephesus would "be strengthened with power through His Spirit in the inner man" (Eph. 3:16).

The second part of Paul's proof that sin is no longer his master and that he is indeed redeemed by God and made into the likeness of Christ involves a corresponding but opposite principle (cf. v. 21), **a different law,** which does not operate in the inner person but in **the members of** the believer's **body,** that is, in his unredeemed and still sinful humanness.

That opposing principle is continually **waging war against the law of** the believer's **mind,** a term that here corresponds to the redeemed inner man about whom Paul has been talking. Paul is not setting up a dichotomy between the mind and the body but is contrasting the inner man, or the redeemed "new creature" (cf. 2 Cor. 5:17), with the "flesh" (Rom. 7:25), that remnant of the old man that will remain with each believer until we receive our glorified bodies (8:23). Paul is not saying his mind is always spiritual and his body is always sinful. In fact, he confesses that, tragically, the fleshly principle undermines the law of his mind and temporarily makes him **a prisoner of the law of sin which is in** his **members**.

As Paul will explain in the following chapter, what he has just said of himself could not apply to an unbeliever, who is entirely, in his mind as well as in his flesh, "hostile toward God" (Rom. 8:7). Unbelievers do not want to please God and could not please Him if they wanted to (v. 8).

Psalm 119 also parallels Romans 7 on the down side, in regard to the believer's constant struggle with the sin that he hates and longs to be rid of. Like believers of every age, the psalmist sometimes was plagued by evil forces and people that warred against God and his own inner person. "My soul is crushed with longing after Thine ordinances at all times" (v. 20), he lamented, "My soul cleaves to the dust" (v. 25), and, "It is good for me that I was afflicted, that I may learn Thy statutes" (v. 71). He repeatedly pleads with God to revive him (vv. 25, 88, 107, 149, 154). With the deep humility that characterizes every mature believer, the writer ends by confessing, "I have gone astray like a lost sheep," by imploring God to "seek Thy servant," and finally by affirming again, "I do not forget Thy commandments" (v. 176).

THE SOURCE

and making me a prisoner of the law of sin which is in my members. (7:23b)

As Paul has already mentioned in the first part of this verse, the source of his sin is no longer the inner man, which is now redeemed and being sanctified. Like all believers while they are in this earthly life, Paul found himself sometimes to be **a prisoner of the law of sin**, the principle that evil was still present in him (7:21). But now **sin** was only in the **members** of his body, in his old self (Eph. 4:22), which was still "dead because of sin" (Rom. 8:10).

It is not that Paul's salvation was imperfect or in any way deficient. From the moment he receives Jesus Christ as Lord and Savior, the believer is completely acceptable by God and ready to meet Him. But as long as he remains in his mortal body, in his old unredeemed humanness, he remains subject to temptation and sin. "For though we walk in the flesh, we do not war according to the flesh," Paul explained to the Corinthian Christians (most of whom were spiritually immature and very much still fleshly), "for the weapons of our warfare are not of the flesh, but divinely powerful for the destruction of fortresses" (2 Cor. 10:3-4). In other words, although a Christian cannot avoid living *in* the flesh, he can and should avoid walking *according to* the flesh in its sinful ways.

THE FINAL LAMENT

Wretched man that I am! Who will set me free from the body of this death? Thanks be to God through Jesus Christ our Lord! So then, on the one hand I myself with my mind am serving the law of God, but on the other, with my flesh the law of sin. (7:24-25)

Paul's final lament is even more intense than the others. He cries out in utter anguish and frustration. **Wretched man that I am!** Because this person describes himself in such negative terms, many commentators believe he could not be speaking as a Christian, much less as an apostle. If Paul was speaking of himself, they argue, he must have been speaking about his preconversion condition.

But the Scottish commentator Robert Haldane wisely observed that men perceive themselves to be sinners in direct proportion as they have previously discovered the holiness of God and His law. In one of his penitential psalms, David expressed his great anguish of soul for not being all that he knew the Lord wanted him to be: "O Lord, rebuke me not in Thy wrath; and chasten me not in Thy burning anger. For Thine arrows have sunk deep into me, and Thy hand has pressed down on me. There is no soundness in my flesh because of Thine indignation; there is no health in my bones because of my sin. For my iniquities are gone over my head; as a heavy burden they weigh too much for me" (Ps. 38:1-4).

Another psalmist expressed distress over his sin in words that only a person who knows and loves God could ray: "Out of the depths I have cried to Thee, O Lord. Lord, hear my voice! Let Thine ears be attentive to the voice of my supplications. If Thou, Lord, shouldst mark iniquities, O Lord, who could stand? But there is forgiveness with Thee, that Thou mayest be feared. I wait for the Lord, my soul does wait, and in His word do I hope" (Ps. 130:1-5).

Paul next asks a question to which he well knows the answer: **Who will set me free from the body of this death?** He again makes clear that the cause of his frustration and torment is **the body of this death.** It is only a believer's **body** that remains subject to sin and **death.**

Rhuomai (**set . . . free**) has the basic idea of rescuing from danger and was used of a soldier's going to a wounded comrade on the battlefield and carrying him to safety. Paul longed for the day when he would be rescued from the last vestige of his old, sinful, unredeemed flesh.

It is reported that near Tarsus, where Paul was born (Acts 22:3), a certain ancient tribe sentenced convicted murderers to an especially gruesome execution. The corpse of the slain person was lashed tightly to the body of the murderer and remained there until the murderer himself died. In a few days, which doubtless seemed an eternity to the convicted man, the decay of the person he had slain infected and killed him. Perhaps Paul had such torture in mind when he expressed his yearning to be freed from t**he body of this death.**

Without hesitation, the apostle testifies to the certainty of his eventual rescue and gives thanks to his Lord even before he is set free: **Thanks be to God through Jesus Christ our Lord!** he exults. Later in the epistle he further testifies, "I consider that the sufferings of this present time are not worthy to be compared with the glory that is to be revealed to us" (Rom. 8:18). Frustrating and painful as a believer's present struggle with sin may be, that temporary earthly predicament is nothing compared with the eternal glory that awaits him in heaven.

Because Christians have a taste of God's righteousness and glory while they are still on earth, their longing for heaven is all the more acute: "We ourselves," Paul says, "having the first fruits of the Spirit, even we ourselves groan within ourselves, waiting eagerly for our adoption as sons, the redemption of our body" (Rom. 8:23; cf. 2 Cor. 5:4). On that great day, even our corruptible bodies will be redeemed and made incorruptible. "In a moment, in the twinkling of an eye," Paul assures us, "the dead will be raised imperishable, and we shall be changed. For this perishable must put on the imperishable, and this mortal must put on immortality. . . . The sting of death is sin, and the power of sin is the law; but thanks be to God, who gives us the victory through our Lord Jesus Christ" (1 Cor. 15:52-53, 56-57).

Paul's primary emphasis in the present passage, however, is not on the believer's eventual deliverance from sin's presence but on the conflict with sin that torments every spiritually sensitive child of God. He therefore ends by summarizing the two sides of that struggle: **So then, on the one hand I myself with my mind am serving the law of God, but on the other, with my flesh the law of sin.**

In the poem *Maud* (x. 5), one of Tennyson's characters yearns, "Ah for a new man to arise in me, that the man I am may cease to be!" The Christian can say that a new man has already arisen in him, but he also must confess that the sinful part his old man has not yet ceased to be.

Life in the Spirit— part 1
The Spirit Frees Us from Sin and Death and Enables Us to Fulfill the Law

There is therefore now no condemnation for those who are in Christ Jesus. For the law of the Spirit of life in Christ Jesus has set you free from the law of sin and of death. For what the Law could not do, weak as it was through the flesh, God did: sending His own Son in the likeness of sinful flesh and as an offering for sin, He condemned sin in the flesh, in order that the requirement of the Law might be fulfilled in us, who do not walk according to the flesh, but according to the Spirit. (8:1-4)

Although the Bible is a book offering the good news of salvation from sin, it is also a book that presents the bad news of condemnation for sin. No single book or collection of writings on earth proclaims so completely and vividly the totally desperate situation of man apart from God.

The Bible reveals that, since the Fall, every human being has been born into the world with a sin nature. What David said of himself can be said of everyone: "Surely I have been a sinner from birth, sinful from the time my mother conceived me" (Ps. 51:5, NIV). Earlier in his letter to the Romans, Paul declared, "All have sinned and fall short of the glory of God" (Rom. 3:23). Because of that universal and innate sinfulness, all unbelievers are under God's condemnation and are "by nature children of wrath" (Eph. 2:3).

Man is not simply influenced by sin but is completely overpowered by it, and no one can escape that dominance by his own effort. Sin is a defiling disease that corrupts every person, degrades every individual, disquiets every soul. It steals peace and joy from the heart and replaces them with trouble and pain. Sin is implanted in every human life, and its deadly force brings a universal depravity that no man can cure.

Sin places men under the power of Satan, the ruler of the present world system (John 12:31). They are under the control of "the prince of the power of the air" and "of the spirit that is now working in the sons of disobedience" (Eph. 2:2). As Paul went on to remind the Ephesian believers, all Christians were once a part of that evil system (v. 3). Jesus declared that Satan is the spiritual father of every unbeliever (John 8:41, 44), and that "the one who practices sin is of the devil; for the devil has sinned from the beginning" (1 John 3:8; cf. v. 10).

Because of sin, all of humankind is born in bondage to pain, disease, and death. One of Job's friends rightly observed that "Man is born for trouble, as sparks fly upward" (Job 5:7). Because of sin, all the rest of "creation was subjected to futility [and] . . . groans and suffers the pains of childbirth together until now" (Rom. 8:20, 22).

Because of sin, fallen men are heirs of God's judgment. "A certain terrifying expectation of judgment" awaits all unregenerate sinners, "and the fury of a fire which will consume [God's] adversaries" (Heb. 10:27). The sinner who lives in unconcern apart from God does so as if he were Damocles at Dionysius's banquet, with a sword hanging over his neck by a single horsehair, which at any moment could break and usher him into eternity.

Because of sin, there is a curse on the sinner's soul. Among the last words Jesus spoke on earth were: "He who has disbelieved shall be condemned" (Mark 16:16). Paul declared, "If anyone does not love the Lord, let him be accursed" (1 Cor. 16:22), and "For as many as are of the works of the Law are under a curse; for it is written, 'Cursed is everyone who does not abide by all things written in the book of the law, to perform them'" (Gal. 3:10; cf. 2 Thess. 1:8).

For at least three reasons, God is justified in His condemnation of sinners. First, He is justified because all men, through their lineage from Adam, share in the guilt of original sin and in the moral and spiritual depravity it produces. "For if by the transgression of the one, death reigned through the one," Paul has already explained in this epistle, "much more those who receive the abundance of grace and of the gift of righteousness will reign in life through the One, Jesus Christ. So then as through one transgression there resulted condemnation to all men, even so through one act of righteousness there resulted justification of life to all men" (Rom. 5:17-18).

Second, God is justified in condemning sinners because every person is born with an evil nature. "Among them we too all formerly lived in the lusts of our flesh," Paul reminded the Ephesian believers, "indulging the desires of the flesh and of the mind, and were by nature children of wrath, even as the rest" (Eph. 2:3).

Third, God is justified in condemning sinners because of the evil deeds their depraved natures inevitably produce. God "will render to every man according to his deeds: . . . to those who are selfishly ambitious and do not obey the truth, but obey unrighteousness, wrath and indignation" (Rom. 2:6, 8).

Because of sin, the unregenerate have no future to look forward to except eternal damnation in hell. That destiny is the sinner's second death, the lake of fire, judgment without mercy, pain without remission (Rev. 20:14). The lost will be in a place of "outer darkness," Jesus said, where "there shall be weeping and gnashing of teeth" (Matt. 8:12).

As already noted, the Bible is an extremely condemnatory book, and the book of Romans is far from being an exception. Paul has already established that the entire human race, Jews as well as Gentiles, is depraved and under sin. He declares that "there is none righteous, not even one," that "there is none who seeks for God," that "there is none who does good," that "with their tongues they keep deceiving," that "destruction and misery are in their paths," and that "there is no fear of God before their eyes" (Rom. 3:9-18).

Later in the epistle he declares that,

> just as through one man sin entered into the world, and death through sin, and so death spread to all men, because all sinned. . . . And the gift is not like that which came through the one who sinned; for on the one hand the judgment arose from one transgression resulting in condemnation, but on the other hand the free gift arose from many transgressions resulting in justification. . . . So then as through one transgression there resulted condemnation to all men, even so through one act of righteousness there resulted justification of life to all men. (Rom. 5:12, 16, 18)

Although God's revealed law is "holy and righteous and good" (Rom. 7:12) and is the standard by which men are to live and be blessed, the unsaved have neither the desire nor the ability to fulfill its demands. Because of man's depraved and rebellious nature, the holy law of God merely succeeds in arousing and aggravating the sin that is already present (7:5).

In his second letter to Thessalonica, the apostle reveals that "when the Lord Jesus shall be revealed from heaven with His mighty angels in flaming fire, [He will be] dealing out retribution to those who do not know God and to those who do not obey the gospel of our Lord Jesus.

And these will pay the penalty of eternal destruction, away from the presence of the Lord and from the glory of His power" (2 Thess. 1:7-9).

In itself, even the coming to earth of the Lord Jesus Christ, God incarnate, could not remove that condemnation. Jesus' perfect teaching and sinless life actually *increased* the condemnation of those who heard and saw Him. "And this is the judgment," Jesus said, "that the light is come into the world, and men loved the darkness rather than the light; for their deeds were evil. For everyone who does evil hates the light, and does not come to the light, lest his deeds should be exposed" (John 3:19-20). As the Lord had just explained, that was not God's desire: "For God did not send the Son into the world to judge the world, but that the world should be saved through Him" (John 3:17). But Christ's perfect teaching and perfect life had no more power in themselves to change men's hearts than had God's perfect law. Because Jesus' teaching was perfect and His living sinless, they demonstrated even more vividly than the law that fallen men cannot meet God's holy standards in their own power.

Such is the condition of every individual born into the world, and it is in light of that dreadful condition that Paul proclaims in Romans 8:1-4 the unspeakably wonderful truth about those who, by grace working through faith, belong to Jesus Christ. He proclaims to believers the thrilling promise that fills the heart with immeasurable consolation, joy, and hope. Some have called Romans 8:1 the most hopeful verse in Scripture. It is bewildering that any thinking mind or searching soul would not run with eagerness to receive such divine provision. But perhaps the greatest tragedy of sin is that it blinds the sinner to the life-giving promises of God and predisposes him to trust in the false and death-giving allurements of Satan.

In presenting God's salvation promise to believers, Paul focuses on its reality, no condemnation (v. 1a); its reason, justification (vv. 1b-2); its route, substitution (v. 3); and its result, sanctification (v. 4).

THE REALITY OF FREEDOM—NO CONDEMNATION

There is therefore now no condemnation (8:1a)

By simple definition, **therefore** introduces a result, consequence, or conclusion based on what has been established previously. It seems unlikely that Paul is referring to the immediately preceding text. He has just finished lamenting the continued problem of sin in a believer's life, including his own. It is surely not on the basis of *that* truth that he confidently declares that believers are no longer under divine **condemnation.** One might expect rather that any further sin would deserve some sort of further judgment. But Paul makes clear that such is not the case with our gracious God. It seems probable that **therefore** marks a consequent conclusion from the entire first seven chapters, which focus primarily on justification by faith alone, made possible solely on the basis of and by the power of God's grace.

Accordingly, chapter 8 marks a major change in the focus and flow of the epistle. At this point the apostle begins to delineate the marvelous results of justification in the life of the believer. He begins by explaining, as best as possible to finite minds, some of the cardinal truths of salvation (no condemnation, as well as justification, substitution, and sanctification).

God's provision of salvation came not through Christ's perfect teaching or through His perfect life but through His perfect sacrifice on the cross. It is through Christ's death, not His life, that God provides the way of salvation. For those who place their trust in Christ and in what He has done on their behalf **there is therefore now no condemnation**.

The Greek word *katakrima* (**condemnation**) appears only in the book of Romans, here and in 5:16, 18. Although it relates to the sentencing for a crime, its primary focus is not so much on the verdict as on the penalty that the verdict demands. As Paul has already declared, the penalty, or **condemnation,** for sin is death (6:23).

Paul here announces the marvelous good news that for Christians there will be **no condemnation,** neither sentencing nor punishment for the sins that believers have committed or will ever commit.

Ouketi (**no**) is an emphatic negative adverb of time and carries the idea of complete cessation. In His parable about the king who forgave one of his slaves an overwhelming debt (Matt. 18:23-27), Jesus pictured God's gracious and total forgiveness of the sins of those who come to Him in humble contrition and faith. That is the heart and soul of the gospel— that Jesus completely and permanently paid the debt of sin and the penalty of the law (which is **condemnation** to death) for every person who humbly asks for mercy and trusts in Him. Through the apostle John, God assures His children that "if anyone sins, we have an Advocate with the Father, Jesus Christ the righteous; and He Himself is the propitiation for our sins; and not for ours only, but also for those of the whole world" (1 John 2:1-2).

Jesus not only pays the believer's debt of sin but cleanses him "from all unrighteousness" (1 John 1:9). Still more amazingly, He graciously imputes and imparts to each believer His own perfect righteousness: "For by one offering He [Christ] has perfected for all time those who are sanctified" (Heb. 10:14; cf. Rom. 5:17; 2 Cor. 5:21; Phil. 3:9). More even than that, Jesus shares His vast heavenly inheritance with those who come to Him in faith (Eph. 1:3, 11, 14). It is because of such immeasurable divine grace that Paul admonishes Christians to be continually "giving thanks to the Father, who has qualified us to share in the inheritance of the saints in light" (Col. 1:12). Having been qualified by God the Father, we will never, under any circumstance, be subject to divine **condemnation**. How blessed to be placed beyond the reach of condemnation!

The truth that there can never be the eternal death penalty for believers is the foundation of the eighth chapter of Romans. As Paul asks rhetorically near the end of the chapter, "If God is for us, who is against us?" (v. 31), and again, "Who will bring a charge against God's elect? God is the one who justifies" (v. 33). If the highest tribunal in the universe justifies us, who can declare us guilty?

It is extremely important to realize that deliverance from condemnation is not based in the least measure on any form of perfection achieved by the believer. He does not attain the total eradication of sin during his earthly life. It is that truth that Paul establishes so intensely and poignantly in Romans 7. John declares that truth as unambiguously as possible in his first epistle: "If we say that we have no sin, we are deceiving ourselves, and the truth is not in us" (1 John 1:8). The Christian's conflict with sin does not end until he goes to be with the Lord. Nevertheless, there is still no condemnation—because the penalty for all the failures of his life has been paid in Christ and applied by grace.

It is also important to realize that deliverance from divine condemnation does not mean deliverance from divine discipline. "For those whom the Lord loves He disciplines, and He scourges every son whom He receives" (Heb. 12:6). Nor does deliverance from God's condemnation mean escape from our accountability to Him: "Do not be deceived, God is not mocked; for whatever a man sows, this he will also reap" (Gal. 6:7).

THE REASON FOR FREEDOM—JUSTIFICATION

for those who are in Christ Jesus. For the law of the Spirit of life in Christ Jesus has set you free from the law of sin and of death. (8:1b-2)

As noted at the beginning of the previous section, the *therefore* that introduces verse 1 refers back to the major theme of the first seven chapters of the epistle—the believer's complete justification before God, graciously provided in response to trust in the sacrificial death and resurrection of His Son.

The divine condemnation from which believers are exonerated (8:1a) is without exception or qualification. It is bestowed on **those who are in Christ Jesus,** in other words, on every true Christian. Justification completely and forever releases *every* believer from sin's bondage and its penalty of death (6:23) and thereby fits him to stand sinless before a holy God forever. It is that particular aspect of justification on which Paul focuses at the beginning of chapter 8.

Paul's use of the first person singular pronouns (*I* and *me*) in 7:7-25 emphasizes the sad reality that, in this present life, no Christian, not even an apostle, is exempt from struggles with sin. In the opening verses of chapter 8, on the other hand, Paul emphasizes the marvelous reality that *every* believer, even the weakest and most unproductive, shares in complete and eternal freedom from sin's condemnation. The holiest of believers are warned that, although they are no longer under sin's slavish dominion, they will experience conflicts with it in this present life. And the weakest of believers are promised that, although they still stumble and fall into sin's power in their flesh, they will experience ultimate victory over sin in the life to come.

The key to every aspect of salvation is in the simple but infinitely profound phrase **in Christ Jesus.** A Christian is a person who is **in Christ Jesus.** Paul has already declared that "all of us who have been baptized into Christ Jesus have been baptized into His death," and that "therefore we have been buried with Him through baptism into death, in order that as Christ was raised from the dead through the glory of the Father, so we too might walk in newness of life. For if we have become united with Him in the likeness of His death, certainly we shall be also in the likeness of His resurrection" (Rom. 6:3-5).

Being a Christian is not simply being outwardly identified with Christ but being *part* of Christ, not simply of being united with Him but united **in** Him. Our being in Christ is one of the profoundest of mysteries, which we will not fully understand until we meet Him face-to-face in heaven. But Scripture does shed light on that marvelous truth. We know that we are in Christ spiritually, in a divine and permanent union "For as in Adam all die, so also in Christ all shall be made alive," Paul explains (1 Cor. 15:22). Believers are also in Christ in a living, participatory sense. "Now you are Christ's body," Paul declares in that same epistle, "and individually members of it" (12:27). We are actually a part of Him and, in ways that are unfathomable to us now, we work when He works, grieve when He grieves, and rejoice when He rejoices. "For by one Spirit we were all baptized into one body," Paul assures us, "whether Jews or Greeks, whether slaves or free, and we were all made to drink of one Spirit" (1 Cor. 12:13). Christ's own divine life pulses through us.

Many people are concerned about their family heritage, about who their ancestors were, where they lived, and what they did. For better or worse, we are all life-linked physically, intellectually, and culturally to our ancestors. In a similar, but infinitely more important way, we are linked to the family of God because of our relationship to His Son, Jesus Christ. It is for that reason that every Christian can say, "I have been crucified with Christ; and it is no longer I who live, but Christ lives in me; and the life which I now live in the flesh I live by faith in the Son of God, who loved me, and delivered Himself up for me" (Gal. 2:20).

God's Word makes clear that every human being is a descendant of Adam and has inherited Adam's fallen nature. It makes just as clear that every true believer becomes a spiritual descendant of Jesus Christ, God's true Son, and is thereby adopted into the heavenly Father's own divine household as a beloved child. More than just being adopted, we inherit the very life of God in Christ.

Martin Luther said,

> It is impossible for a man to be a Christian without having Christ, and if he has Christ, he has at the same time all that is in Christ. What gives peace to the conscience is that by faith our sins are no more ours, but Christ's, upon whom God hath laid them all; and that, on the other hand, all Christ's righteousness is ours, to whom God hath given it. Christ lays His hand upon us, and we are healed. He casts His mantle upon us, and we are clothed; for He is the glorious Savior, blessed for ever. (Cited in Robert Haldane, *An Exposition of Romans;* [MacDill AFB, Fla.: McDonald, 1958], p. 312).

The relationship between God and His chosen people Israel was beautifully illustrated in the garment of the high priest. Over his magnificent robes he wore a breastplate in which twelve different precious stones were embedded, representing the twelve tribes of Israel. Each stone was engraved with the name of the tribe it represented. When the high priest entered the Holy of Holies once each year on the Day of Atonement, he stood before God with those visual representations of all His people.

That breastplate was a rich symbolism of Jesus Christ, our Great High Priest, standing before the Father making intercession on behalf of all those the Father has given Him (Heb. 7:24-25). In what is commonly called His high priestly prayer, Jesus prayed on behalf of those who belong to Him "that they may all be one; even as Thou, Father, art in Me, and I in Thee, that they also may be in Us; that the world may believe that Thou didst send Me" (John 17:21).

Luther also wrote,

> Faith unites the soul with Christ as a spouse with her husband. Everything which Christ has becomes the property of the believing soul; everything which the soul has, becomes the property of Christ. Christ possesses all blessings and eternal life: they are thenceforward the property of the soul. The soul has all its iniquities and sins: they become thenceforward the property of Christ. It is then that a blessed exchange commences: Christ

who is both God and man, Christ who has never sinned, and whose holiness is perfect, Christ the Almighty and Eternal, taking to Himself, by His nuptial ring of *faith,* all the sins of the believer, those sins are lost and abolished in Him; for no sins dwell before His infinite righteousness. Thus by faith the believer's soul is delivered from sins and clothed with the eternal righteousness of her bridegroom Christ. (Cited in Haldane, *Exposition of Romans,* p. 313)

The phrase "who walk not after the flesh, but after the Spirit" appears at the end of verse 1 in the King James, but it is not found in the earliest manuscripts of Romans or in most modern translations. It is probable that a copyist inadvertently picked up the phrase from verse 4. Because the identical wording appears there, the meaning of the passage is not affected.

The conjunction **for,** which here carries the meaning of because, leads into the reason there is no condemnation for believers: **the law of the Spirit of life in Christ Jesus has set you free from the law of sin and of death.**

Paul does not here use the term **law** in reference to the Mosaic law or to other divine commandments or requirements. He uses it rather in the sense of a principle of operation, as he has done earlier in the letter, where he speaks of "a law of faith" (3:27) and as he does in Galatians, where he speaks of "the law of Christ" (6:2). Those who believe in Jesus Christ are delivered from the condemnation of a lower divine law, as it were, by submitting themselves to a higher divine law. The lower law is the divine principle in regard to **sin,** the penalty for which is **death,** and the higher law is **the law of the Spirit,** which bestows **life in Christ Jesus.**

But it should not be concluded that the **law** Paul is speaking of in this passage has no relationship to obedience. Obedience to God cannot save a person, because no person in his unredeemed sinfulness wants to obey God and could not obey perfectly even if he had the desire. But true salvation will always produce true obedience—never perfect in this life but nonetheless genuine and always present to some extent. When truly believed and received, the gospel of Jesus Christ always leads to the "obedience of faith" (Rom. 16:25-26). The coming kingdom age of Christ that Jeremiah predicted and of which the writer of Hebrews refers is far from lawless. "For this is the covenant that I will make with the house of Israel after those days, says the Lord: I will put My laws into their minds, and I will write them upon their hearts" (Heb. 8:10; cf. Jer. 31:33). Release from the law's bondage and condemnation does not mean release from the law's requirements and standards. The higher law of the Spirit produces obedience to the lower law of duties.

The freedom that Christ gives is complete and permanent deliverance from sin's power and penalty (and ultimately from its presence). It also gives the ability to obey God. The very notion of a Christian who is free to do as he pleases is self-contradictory. A person who believes that salvation leads from law to license does not have the least understanding of the gospel of grace and can make no claim on Christ's saviorhood and certainly no claim on His lordship.

In speaking of **the Spirit of life in Christ Jesus,** Paul makes unambiguous later in this chapter that he is referring to the Holy **Spirit.** The Christian's mind is set on the things of the Spirit (v. 6) and is indwelt and given life by the Holy Spirit (vv. 9-11). Paul summarized the working of those two laws earlier in the epistle: "For the wages of sin is death, but the free gift of God is eternal life in Christ Jesus our Lord" (Rom. 6:23).

When Jesus explained the way of salvation to Nicodemus, He said, "Unless one is born of water and the Spirit, he cannot enter into the kingdom of God" (John 3:5). God "saved us, not on the basis of deeds which we have done in righteousness," Paul explains, "but according to His mercy, by the washing of regeneration and renewing by the Holy Spirit, whom He poured out upon us richly through Jesus Christ our Savior" (Titus 3:5-6). It is the Holy **Spirit** who bestows and energizes spiritual **life** in the person who places his trust **in Christ Jesus.** Paul could not be talking of any spirit but the Holy Spirit, because only God's Holy Spirit can bring spiritual life to a heart that is spiritually dead.

The truths of Romans 7 are among the most depressing and heart-rending in all of Scripture, and it is largely for that reason that many interpreters believe they cannot describe a Christian. But Paul was simply being honest and candid about the frustrating and discouraging spiritual battles that every believer faces. It is, in fact, the most faithful and obedient Christian who faces the greatest spiritual struggles. Just as in physical warfare, it is those on the front lines who encounter the enemy's most fierce attacks. But just as frontline battle can reveal courage, it can also reveal weaknesses and vulnerability. Even the most valiant soldier is subject to injury and discouragement.

During his earthly life, the Christian will always have residual weaknesses from his old humanness, the old fleshly person he used to be. No matter how closely he walks with the Lord, he is not yet completely free from sin's power. That is the discomfiting reality of Romans 7.

But the Christian is no longer a slave to sin as he once was, no longer under sin's total domination and control. Now he is free from sin's bondage and its ultimate penalty. Satan, the world, and his own humanness still can cause him to stumble and falter, but they can no longer control or destroy him, because his new life in Christ is the very divine life of God's own Spirit. That is the comforting truth of Romans 8.

The story is told of a man who operated a drawbridge. At a certain time each afternoon, he had to raise the bridge for a ferry boat and then lower it quickly for a passenger train that crossed at high speed a few minutes later. One day the man's young son was visiting his father at work and decided to go down below to get a better look at the ferry as it passed. Fascinated by the sight, he did not watch carefully where he was going and fell into the giant gears. One foot became caught and the boy was helpless to free himself. The father saw what happened but knew that if he took time to extricate his son, the train would plunge into to the river before the bridge could be lowered. But if he lowered the bridge to save the hundreds of passengers and crew members on the train, his son would be crushed to death. When he heard the train's whistle, indicating it would soon reach the river, he knew what he had to do. His son was very dear to him, whereas all the people on the train were total strangers. The sacrifice of his son for the sake of the other people was an act of pure grace and mercy.

   That story portrays something of the infinitely greater sacrifice God the Father made when He sent His only beloved Son to earth to die for the sins of mankind—to whom He owed nothing but condemnation.

THE ROUTE TO FREEDOM—SUBSTITUTION

For what the Law could not do, weak as it was through the flesh, God did: sending His own Son in the likeness of sinful flesh and as an offering for sin, He condemned sin in the flesh, (8:3)

   This verse is perhaps the most definitive and succinct statement of the substitutionary atonement to be found in Scripture. It expresses the heart of the gospel message, the wondrous truth that Jesus Christ paid the penalty on behalf of every person who would turn from sin and trust in Him as Lord and Savior.

   As in the previous verse, the conjunction **for** carries the meaning of *because* and gives an explanation for what has just been stated. Believers are set free from the law of sin and death and are made alive by the law of the Spirit of life because of what Jesus Christ has done for them.

   The Law can provoke sin in men and condemn them for it, but it cannot save them from its penalty. "For as many as are of the works of the Law are under a curse," Paul explained to the Galatians, "for it is written, 'Cursed is everyone who does not abide by all things written in the book of the law, to perform them'" (Gal 3:10). Later in that same chapter he says: "Is the Law then contrary to the promises of God? May it never be! For if a law had been given which was able to impart life, then righteousness would indeed have been based on law" (3:21). God's holy law can only set forth the standards of His righteousness and show men how utterly incapable they are in themselves of fulfilling those standards.

Paul has already explained that "this commandment [i.e., the law, v. 9], which was to result in life [if obeyed], proved to result in death for me; for sin, taking opportunity through the commandment, deceived me, and through it killed me" (Rom. 7:10-11). When God created man, sin had no place in His creation. But when man fell, the alien power of sin corrupted his very being and condemned him to death, both physical and spiritual. The whole human race was placed under the curse of God. Sin consigned fallen mankind to a divine debtor's prison, as it were, and the law became his jailer. The law, given as the standard for living under divine blessing and joy, became a killer.

Although it is "holy and righteous and good" (Rom. 7:12), **the Law could not** save men from sin because it was **weak . . . through the flesh.** The sinful corruption of **the flesh** made **the Law** powerless to save men. The law cannot make men righteous but can only expose their unrighteousness and condemn them for it. The law cannot make men perfect but can only reveal their great imperfection. As Paul explained in the synagogue at Antioch of Pisidia, through Jesus Christ "forgiveness of sins is proclaimed to you, and through Him everyone who believes is freed from all things, from which you could not be freed through the Law of Moses" (Acts 13:38-39).

During His incarnation, Jesus was the embodiment of the law of Moses. He alone of all men who have ever lived or will ever live perfectly fulfilled the law of God. "Do not think that I came to abolish the Law or the Prophets," He said; "I did not come to abolish, but to fulfill" (Matt. 5:17). During one of His discourses in the Temple, Jesus exposed the sinfulness of the self-righteous scribes and Pharisees, who, by their failure to throw stones at the woman taken in adultery, admitted they were not without sin (John 8:7-9). Later on that same occasion Jesus challenged His enemies to convict Him of any sin, and no one could do so or even tried (v. 46).

Some people, including many professing Christians, believe that they can achieve moral and spiritual perfection by living up to God's standards by their own power. But James reminds us that "whoever keeps the whole law and yet stumbles in one point, he has become guilty of all" (James 2:10). In other words, even a single sin, no matter how small and no matter when committed, is sufficient to disqualify a person for heaven.

On one occasion a young man came to Jesus and said to Him,

> "Teacher, what good thing shall I do that I may obtain eternal life?" And He said to him, "Why are you asking Me about what is good? There is only One who is good; but if you wish to enter into life, keep the commandments."

He said to Him, "Which ones?" And Jesus said, "You shall not commit murder; you shall not commit adultery; you shall not steal; you shall not bear false witness; honor your father and mother; and you shall love your neighbor as yourself." The young man said to Him, "All these things I have kept; what am I still lacking?" Jesus said to him, "If you wish to be complete, go and sell your possessions and give to the poor, and you shall have treasure in heaven; and come, follow Me." But when the young man heard this statement, he went away grieved; for he was one who owned much property. (Matt. 19:16-22)

This man was extremely religious. But he demonstrated that, despite his diligence in obeying the commandments, he failed to keep the two greatest commandments—to "love the Lord your God with all your heart, and with all your soul, and with all your mind" and to " 'love your neighbor as yourself.' On these two commandments," Jesus went on to say, "depend the whole Law and the Prophets" (Matt. 22:37-40). The young man who came to Jesus was self-centered, selfish, and materialistic. His love for himself surpassed his love for God and for his fellow man. Consequently, his meticulous religious living counted for absolutely nothing before God.

God's law commands righteousness, but it cannot provide the means to achieve that righteousness. Therefore, what the law was unable to do for fallen man, **God** Himself **did.** The law can condemn the sinner, but only God can condemn and destroy sin, and that is what He has done on behalf of those who trust in His Son—by His coming to earth **in the likeness of sinful flesh and as an offering for sin.**

Jesus said, "I am the living bread that came down out of heaven; if anyone eats of this bread, he shall live forever; and the bread also which I shall give for the life of the world is My flesh" (John 6:51). In His incarnation Jesus was completely a man, fully incarnated. But He was only **in the likeness of,** in the outward appearance of, **sinful flesh.** Although Paul does not here specifically mention Jesus' sinlessness, his phrasing carefully guards that profound truth.

Jesus was "tempted in all things as we are, yet without sin" (Heb. 4:15). If He had not been both fully human and fully sinless, He could not have offered an acceptable sacrifice to God for the sins of the world. If Jesus had not Himself been without sin, He not only could not have made a sacrifice for fallen mankind but would have needed to have a sacrifice made on His own behalf. Jesus resisted every temptation of Satan and denied sin any part in His earthly life. Sin was compelled to yield its supremacy in the **flesh** to the Victor, whereby Jesus Christ became sovereign over sin and its consequence, death.

Those who trust in Christ not only are saved from the penalty of sin but also are able for the first time to fulfill God's righteous standards.

The flesh of a believer is still weak and subject to sin, but the inner person is remade in the image of Christ and has the power through His Spirit to resist and overcome sin. No Christian will be perfected during his earthly life, but he has no excuse for sinning, because he has God's own power to resist sin. John assures believers that "greater is He [the Holy Spirit] who is in you than he [Satan] who is in the world" (1 John 4:4). As Paul has already declared, "For if while we were enemies, we were reconciled to God through the death of His Son, much more, having been reconciled, we shall be saved by His life," that is, be kept saved and protected from sin's domination (Rom. 5:10).

Speaking of His impending crucifixion, Jesus said, "Now judgment is upon this world; now the ruler of this world shall be cast out" (John 12:31). In other words, by His death on the cross Christ condemned and conquered both sin and Satan. He bore the fury of God's wrath on all sin, and in doing so broke sin's power over those whose trust is in His giving of Himself **as an offering for sin** on their behalf. By trusting in Jesus Christ, those who formerly were children of Satan become children of God, those who were targets of God's wrath become recipients of His grace. On the cross Jesus broke sin's power and assigned sin to its final destruction. God "made Him who knew no sin to be sin on our behalf, that we might become the righteousness of God in Him" (2 Cor. 5:21). Christ was "offered once to bear the sins of many" (Heb. 9:28).

Jesus' teaching, miracles, and sinless life were of great importance in His earthly ministry. But His supreme purpose in coming to earth was to be **an offering for sin.** Without the sacrifice of Himself for the sins of the world, everything else Jesus did would have left men in their sins, still separated from God.

To teach that men can live a good life by following Jesus' example is patronizing foolishness. To try to follow Jesus' perfect example without having His own life and Spirit within us is even more impossible and frustrating than trying to fulfill the Mosaic law. Jesus' example cannot save us but instead further demonstrates the impossibility of saving ourselves by our own efforts at righteousness.

The only hope men have for salvation from their sin is in their trust in the **offering for sin** that Christ Himself made at Calvary. And when He became that **offering,** He took upon Himself the penalty of death for the sins of all mankind. In his commentary on Romans, the nineteenth-century Scottish evangelist Robert Haldane wrote, "We see the Father assume the place of judge against His Son, in order to become the Father of those who were His enemies. The Father condemns the Son of His love, that He may absolve the children of wrath" (*Expostion of Romans,* p. 324).

Jesus Christ **condemned sin in the flesh.** Whereas sin once condemned the believer, now Christ his Savior condemns sin, delivering the believer from sin's power and penalty. The law condemns sin in the sense of exposing it for what it really is and in the sense of declaring its penalty of death. But the law is unable to condemn sin in the sense of delivering a sinner from his sinfulness or in the sense of overpowering sin and consigning it to its ultimate destruction. Only the Lord Jesus Christ was able to do that, and it is that amazing truth that inspired Paul to exult, "'O death, where is your victory? O death, where is your sting?' The sting of death is sin, and the power of sin is the law; but thanks be to God, who gives us the victory through our Lord Jesus Christ" (1 Cor. 15:55-57).

The prophet Isaiah eloquently predicted the sacrifice of the incarnate Christ, saying,

> Surely our griefs He Himself bore, and our sorrows He carried; Yet we ourselves esteemed Him stricken, smitten of God, and afflicted. But He was pierced through for our transgressions, He was crushed for our iniquities; the chastening for our well-being fell upon Him, and by His scourging we are healed. All of us like sheep have gone astray, each of us has turned to his own way; but the Lord has caused the iniquity of us all to fall on Him. He was oppressed and He was afflicted, yet He did not open His mouth; like a lamb that is led to slaughter, and like a sheep that is silent before its shearers, so He did not open His mouth. By oppression and judgment He was taken away; and as for His generation, who considered that He was cut off out of the land of the living, for the transgression of my people to whom the stroke was due? (Isa. 53:4-8)

THE RESULT OF FREEDOM—SANCTIFICATION

in order that the requirement of the Law might be fulfilled in us, who do not walk according to the flesh, but according to the Spirit. (8:4)

The believer's freedom from sin results in his present as well as in his ultimate sanctification. The true Christian has both the desire and the divinely-imparted ability to live righteously while he is still on earth. Because God sent His own Son to redeem mankind by providing the only sacrifice that can condemn and remove their sin (v. 3), **the requirement of the Law** is able to **be fulfilled in us,** that is, in believers.

Paul obviously is not speaking here of the justifying work of salvation but of its sanctifying work, its being lived out in the believer's earthly life. Apart from the working of the Holy Spirit through the life of a redeemed person, human efforts at righteousness are as contaminated and useless as filthy garments (Isa. 64:6). But because the Christian has been cleansed of sin and been given God's own divine nature within him, he now longs for and is able to live a life of holiness.

God does not free men from their sin in order for them to do as they please but to do as He pleases. God does not redeem men in order that they may continue sinning but **in order that** they may begin to live righteously by having **the requirement of the Law . . . fulfilled in** them.

Because they are no longer under law but are now under grace, some Christians claim that it makes little difference what they do, because just as nothing they could have done could have saved them, so nothing they now do can cause them to lose their salvation. But the Holy Spirit could never prompt a Christian to make such a foolish and ungodly statement. The spiritual Christian knows that God's law is holy, righteous, and good (Rom. 7:12) and that he has been saved in order to have that divine holiness, righteousness, and goodness **fulfilled** in him. And that is his desire. He has holy longings.

The phrase **who do not walk according to the flesh, but according to the Spirit** is not an admonition but a statement of fact that applies to all believers. As Paul explains several verses later, no person who belongs to Christ is without the indwelling Holy Spirit (v. 9). Being indwelt by the Spirit is not a mark of special maturity or spirituality but the mark of every true Christian, without exception.

In its figurative sense, *peripateō* (to **walk**) refers to an habitual way or bent of life, to a life-style. Luke describes Zacharias and Elizabeth, the parents of John the Baptist, as being "righteous in the sight of God, walking blamelessly in all the commandments and requirements of the Lord" (Luke 1:6). Paul counseled the Ephesian believers to "walk no longer just as the Gentiles also walk, in the futility of their mind" (Eph. 4:17). John declares that, "if we walk in the light as [God] Himself is in the light, we have fellowship with one another, and the blood of Jesus His Son cleanses us from all sin" (1 John 1:7).

Paul asserts that a true believer—whether young or old, immature or mature, well taught or poorly taught—does **not walk according to the flesh.** Just as categorically he declares that a true believer *does* walk **according to the Spirit.** There are no exceptions. Because every true believer is indwelt by the Spirit, every true believer will produce the fruit of the Spirit (Gal. 5:22-23). Jesus made clear "that unless your righteousness surpasses that of the scribes and Pharisees, you shall not enter the kingdom of heaven" (Matt. 5:20). At the end of that first chapter of the Sermon on the Mount, Jesus commanded, "You are to be perfect as your heavenly Father is perfect" (5:48).

Nothing is dearer to God's heart than the moral and spiritual excellence of those He has created in His own image—and nothing is dearer to them. He does not want them to have only imputed righteousness but practical righteousness as well. And that also is what they want. It is practical righteousness about which Paul speaks here, just as he does in the opening words of his letter to the church at Ephesus: "[God] chose us in [Christ] before the foundation of the world, that we should be holy and blameless before Him" (Eph. 1:4).

It is God's great desire that believers live out the perfect righteousness that He reckons to them when they are saved—that they live like His children and no longer like the children of the world and of Satan. Positional righteousness is to be reflected in practical righteousness. Christ does not want a bride who is only positionally righteous but one who is actually righteous, just as He Himself is righteous. And through His indwelling Spirit, He gives believers that desire.

The purpose of the gospel is not to make men happy but to make them holy. As the Beatitudes make clear, genuine happiness comes to those who belong to Christ and are obedient to His will. But true happiness comes only from holiness. God promises happiness, but He demands holiness, without which "no one will see the Lord" (Heb. 12:14).

In his book entitled *God's Righteous Kingdom*, Walter J Chantry writes,

> When preachers speak as if God's chief desire is for men to be happy, then multitudes with problems flock to Jesus. Those who have ill-health, marital troubles, financial frustration, and loneliness look to our Lord for the desires of their hearts. Each conceives of joy as being found in health, peace, prosperity or companionship. But in search of illusive happiness they are not savingly joined to Jesus Christ. Unless men will be holy, God is determined that they shall be forever miserable and damned. (Carlisle, Pa.: Banner of Truth, 1980, p. 67)

Righteousness is the very heart of salvation. It is for righteousness that God saves those who trust in His Son. "For I am not ashamed of the gospel," Paul declared at the beginning of the Roman epistle, "for in it the righteousness of God is revealed from faith to faith; as it is written, 'But the righteous man shall live by faith'" (Rom. 1:16-17). Peter admonishes believers, "Like the Holy One who called you, be holy yourselves also in all your behavior" (1 Pet. 1:15). Practical righteousness leads believers "to deny ungodliness and worldly desires and to live sensibly, righteously and godly in the present age" (Titus 2:11-12; cf. Gal. 5:24-25). As Augustine observed many centuries ago, grace was given for one reason, that the law might be fulfilled.

When a sinner leaves the courts of God and has received a pardon for sin by virtue of Christ's sacrifice, the work of God in his life has just begun. As the believer leaves the courtroom, as it were, God hands him the code of life and says, "Now you have in you My Spirit, whose power will enable you to fulfill My law's otherwise impossible demands."

Scripture is clear that, in some mystical way known only to God, a person begins to walk by the Spirit the moment he believes. But, on the other hand, he is also admonished to walk by the Spirit as he lives out his earthly life under the lordship of Christ and in the power of the Spirit. As with salvation itself, walking by the Spirit comes first of all by God's sovereign work in the believer's heart, but it also involves the exercise of the believer's will. Romans 8:4 is speaking of the first, whereas Galatians 5:25 ("let us . . . walk by the Spirit") is speaking of the second.

As far as a Christian's life is concerned, everything that is a spiritual reality is also a spiritual responsibility. A genuine Christian *will* commune with his heavenly Father in prayer, but he also has the responsibility to pray. A Christian *is* taught by the Holy Spirit, but he is also obligated to seek the Spirit's guidance and help. The Holy Spirit *will* produce spiritual fruit in a believer's life, but the believer is also admonished to bear fruit. Those truths are part of the amazing and seemingly paradoxical tension between God's sovereignty and man's will. Although man's mind is incapable of understanding such mysteries, the believer accepts them because they are clearly taught in God's Word.

We know little of the relationship between God and Adam before the Fall, except that it was direct and intimate. The Lord had given but one command, a command that was given for Adam and Eve's own good and that was easily obeyed. Until that one command was transgressed, they lived naturally in the perfect will of God. Doing His will was part of their very being.

The believer's relationship to God is much like that. Although Christians are drawn back to the old ways by the fleshly remnants of their life before salvation, their new being makes obedience to God the "natural" thing to do.

The Christian's obligations to God are not another form of legalism. The person who is genuinely saved has a new and divine nature that is, by definition, attuned to God's will. When he lives by his new nature in the power of the Spirit, his desire is God's desire, and no compulsion is involved. But because the believer is still clothed in the old self, he sometimes resists God's will. It is only when he goes against God's will and against his own new nature that the divine commands and standards seem burdensome. On the other hand, the faithful child of God who is obedient from the heart can always say with the psalmist, "O how I love Thy law!" (Ps. 119:97).

Life in the Spirit— part 2 The Spirit Changes Our Nature and Empowers Us for Victory

30

For those who are according to the flesh set their minds on the things of the flesh, but those who are according to the Spirit, the things of the Spirit. For the mind set on the flesh is death, but the mind set on the Spirit is life and peace, because the mind set on the flesh is hostile toward God; for it does not subject itself to the law of God, for it is not even able to do so; and those who are in the flesh cannot please God. However, you are not in the flesh but in the Spirit, if indeed the Spirit of God dwells in you. But if anyone does not have the Spirit of Christ, he does not belong to Him. And if Christ is in you, though the body is dead because of sin, yet the spirit is alive because of righteousness. But if the Spirit of Him who raised Jesus from the dead dwells in you, He who raised Christ Jesus from the dead will also give life to your mortal bodies through His Spirit who indwells you.

So then, brethren, we are under obligation, not to the flesh, to live according to the flesh—for if you are living according to the flesh, you must die; but if by the Spirit you are putting to death the deeds of the body, you will live. (8:5-13)

The spiritual richness, both theological and practical, of this chapter is beyond calculation and surpasses adequate comment. When read by a believer with an open mind and an obedient heart, it is incredibly enriching. It is one of the supreme life-changing chapters in Scripture. It moves along in an ever-ascending course, concluding in the marvelous paean of praise and assurance: "For I am convinced that neither death, nor life, nor angels, nor principalities, nor things present, nor things to come, nor powers, nor height, nor depth, nor any other created thing, shall be able to separate us from the love of God, which is in Christ Jesus our Lord" (Rom. 8:38-39).

The Holy Spirit is mentioned but once in the first seven chapters of Romans, but is referred to nearly twenty times in chapter 8. The Spirit is to a believer what God the Creator is to the physical world. Without God, the physical world would not exist. It has been created and is continually sustained by the omnipotent power of God. So the Holy Spirit—who also, of course, participated in the creation of the world—is to the Christian. The Holy Spirit is the divine agent who creates, sustains, and preserves spiritual life in those who place their trust in Jesus Christ. It is the Holy Spirit who ultimately will bring every believer into the full consummation of his salvation by granting him eternal glory in the presence of God.

It should be made clear that the Holy Spirit is not merely an influence or an impersonal power emanating from God. He is a person, the third member of the Trinity, equal in every way to God the Father and God the Son. The doctrine of God's being one essence, yet existing in three persons, is one of the most certain truths in Scripture. Yet the Holy Spirit is often not respected as every bit as much a divine person as the Father and the Son.

Among the many characteristics of personhood that the Holy Spirit possesses and manifests are: He functions with mind, emotion, and will; He loves the saints, He communicates with them, teaches, guides, comforts, and chastises them; He can be grieved, quenched, lied to, tested, resisted, and blasphemed. The Bible speaks of His omniscience, His omnipotence, His omnipresence, and His divine glory and holiness. He is called God, Lord, the Spirit of God, the Spirit of the Lord, the Spirit of Yahweh (or Jehovah), the Spirit of the Father, the Spirit of the Son, the Spirit of Jesus, and the Comforter and Advocate for believers.

Scripture reveals that the Holy Spirit was fully active with the Father and Son in the creation and that He has been with all believers and enabled and empowered them even before Pentecost. He has always been convicting men of sin, giving salvation to those who truly believed, and teaching them to worship, obey, and serve God rightly. The Holy Spirit has been the divine agent who uniquely came upon God's servants and inspired God's sovereignly-chosen men to pen God's Word. True believers have always served God not by human might or power but by the Holy Spirit (cf. Zech. 4:6). The Spirit was involved in Jesus' conception as a human being and in Jesus' baptism, anointing, temptation, teaching, miracles, death, and resurrection.

Since Pentecost, the Holy Spirit has, in His fulness, indwelt all believers, illuminating their understanding and application of God's Word as well as empowering them for sanctification in a greater way than had ever occurred before. He fills them, seals them, communes with them, fellowships with them, intercedes for them, comforts them, admonishes them, sanctifies them, and enables them to resist sin and to serve God.

In the present passage (Rom. 8:5-13), Paul continues to disclose the innumerable results of justification, specifically the marvelous, spirit-wrought benefits of freedom from condemnation. In verses 2-3 he has discussed the Spirit's freeing us from sin and death, and in verse 4 His enabling us to fulfill God's law. In verses 5-13 Paul reveals that the Spirit also changes our nature and grants us strength for victory over the unredeemed flesh.

THE HOLY SPIRIT CHANGES OUR NATURE

For those who are according to the flesh set their minds on the things of the flesh, but those who are according to the Spirit, the things of the Spirit. For the mind set on the flesh is death, but the mind set on the Spirit is life and peace, because the mind set on the flesh is hostile toward God; for it does not subject itself to the law of God, for it is not even able to do so; and those who are in the flesh cannot please God. However, you are not in the flesh but in the Spirit, if indeed the Spirit of God dwells in you. But if anyone does not have the Spirit of Christ, he does not belong to Him. And if Christ is in you, though the body is dead because of sin, yet the spirit is alive because of righteousness. But if the Spirit of Him who raised Jesus from the dead dwells in you, He who raised Christ Jesus from the dead will also give life to your mortal bodies through His Spirit who indwells you. (8:5-11)

In verse 4 Paul speaks of the believer's behavior, contending that he does "not walk according to the flesh, but according to the Spirit." As in verses 2 and 3, the conjunction **for** in verse 5 carries the meaning of because. The point is that a believer does not behave according to the flesh because his new heart and mind are no longer centered on the things of the flesh and ruled by sin.

In God's eyes, there are only two kinds of people in the world, those who do not belong to Him and those who do. Put another way, there are only **those who are according to the flesh** and **those who**

are according to the Spirit. As far as spiritual life is concerned, God takes no consideration of gender, age, education, talent, class, race, or any other human distinctions (Gal. 3:28). He differentiates people solely on the basis of their relationship to Him, and the difference is absolute.

Obviously there are degrees in both categories. Some unsaved people exhibit high moral behavior, and, on the other hand, many saints do not mind the things of God as obediently as they should. But every human being is completely in one spiritual state of being or the other; he either belongs to God or he does not. Just as a person cannot be partly dead and partly alive physically, neither can he be partly dead and partly alive spiritually. There is no middle ground. A person is either forgiven and in the kingdom of God or unforgiven and in the kingdom of this world. He is either a child of God or a child of Satan.

In this context, the phrase **according to** refers to basic spiritual nature. The Greek could be translated literally as **those** *being* **according to,** indicating a person's fundamental essence, bent, or disposition. **Those who are according to the flesh** are the unsaved, the unforgiven, the unredeemed, the unregenerate. **Those who are according to the Spirit** are the saved, the forgiven, the redeemed, the regenerated children of God. As the apostle points out a few verses later, the unsaved not only are according to the flesh but are *in* the flesh and are *not* indwelt by the Holy Spirit. The saved, on the other hand, not only are according to the Spirit but are *in* the Spirit and *indwelt* by Him (v. 9). Here in verse 5 Paul is speaking of the determinant spiritual *pattern* of a person's life, whereas in verses 8-9 he is speaking of the spiritual *sphere* of a person's life.

Phroneō, the verb behind **set their minds,** refers to the basic orientation, bent, and thought patterns of the mind, rather than to the mind or intellect itself (Greek *nous*). It includes a person's affections and will as well as his reasoning. Paul uses the same verb in Philippians, where he admonishes believers to "have this attitude [or, "mind"] in yourselves which was also in Christ Jesus" (2:5; see also 2:2; 3:15, 19; Col. 3:2).

The basic disposition of the unredeemed is to "indulge the flesh in its corrupt desires" (2 Pet. 2:10). The lost are those "whose end is destruction, whose god is their appetite, and whose glory is in their shame, who set their minds on earthly things" (Phil. 3:19). **The things of the flesh** includes false philosophies and religions, which invariably appeal, whether overtly or subtly, to **the flesh** through self-interest and self-effort.

But those who are according to the Spirit, Paul says, set their minds on **the things of the Spirit.** In other words, those who belong to God are concerned about godly things. As Jonathan Edwards liked to say, they have "holy affections," deep longings after God and sanctification. As Paul has made clear in Romans 7, even God's children sometimes falter in their obedience to Him. But as the apostle said of himself, they nevertheless "joyfully concur with the law of God in the inner man" (Rom. 7:22). Despite their many spiritual failures, their basic orientation and innermost concerns have to do with **the things of the Spirit.**

Phronēma (**the mind**) is the noun form of the verb in verse 5, and, like the verb, refers to the content or thought patterns of the mind rather than to the mind itself. It is significant that Paul does not say that **the mind set on the flesh** *leads* to **death,** but that it is death. The unsaved person is already dead spiritually. The apostle is stating a spiritual equation, not a spiritual consequence. The consequence involved in this relationship is the reverse: that is, because unredeemed men are already spiritually dead, their minds are inevitably **set on the flesh.** Paul reminded the Ephesian believers that, before salvation, they were all once "dead in [their] trespasses and sins" (Eph. 2:1).

There is, of course, a sense in which sin *leads* to death. "But your iniquities have made a separation between you and your God," Isaiah declared to Israel, "and your sins have hidden His face from you, so that He does not hear" (Isa. 59:2). Earlier in the book of Romans Paul explained that "the wages of sin is death" (6:23) and that "while we were in the flesh, the sinful passions, which were aroused by the Law, were at work in the members of our body to bear fruit for death" (7:5; cf. Gal. 6:8).

But Paul's emphasis in the present passage is on the state of death in which every unbeliever already exists, even while his body and mind may be very much alive and active. "A natural man does not accept the things of the Spirit of God," Paul explained to the Corinthian believers, "for they are foolishness to him, and he cannot understand them, because they are spiritually appraised" (1 Cor. 2:14).

Some years ago I conducted the funeral for a baby girl killed in an automobile accident. Before the service the mother kept reaching into the casket, taking the lifeless little body in her arms and caressing her and crying softly to her. The baby, of course, could no longer respond to anything in the physical realm, because there was no life there to respond.

The unsaved person is a spiritual corpse and consequently is completely unable, in himself, to respond to the things of God. Unless the Holy Spirit intervenes by convicting him of sin and enabling him to respond to God by faith and thus being made alive, the unsaved person is as insensitive to the things of God as that baby was to the caresses and cries of her mother.

But the mind set on the Spirit is life and peace. Again Paul sates an equation, not a consequence. **The mind set on the Spirit,** that is, on the things of God, equates **life and peace,** which equates being a Christian. **The mind set on the Spirit** is synonymous with Christian, a person who has been born again, given spiritual **life** by God's grace working through his faith.

The mind set on the Spirit is also synonymous with spiritual **peace,** that is, peace with God. The unsaved person, no matter how much he may claim to honor, worship, and love God, is God's enemy—a truth Paul has already pointed out in this epistle. Before we were saved, he states, we were all enemies of God (5:10). Only the person who has new **life** in God has **peace** with God.

The obvious corollary of that truth is that it is impossible to have a **mind set on the Spirit,** which includes having spiritual **life and peace,** and yet remain dead to the things of God. A professing Christian who has no sensitivity to the things of God, no "holy affections," does not belong to God. Nor does a merely professing Christian have a battle with the flesh, because he is, in reality, still naturally inclined toward the things of the flesh. He longs for the things of the flesh, which are normal to him, because he is still in the flesh and has his mind wholly set on the things of the flesh.

An unbeliever may be deeply concerned about not living up to the religious standards and code he has set for himself or that his denomination or other religious organization has set, and he may struggle hard in trying to achieve those goals. But his struggle is purely on a human level. It is a struggle not generated by the love of God but by self-love and the subsequent desire to gain greater favor with God or men on the basis of superior personal achievement. Whatever religious and moral struggles he may have are problems of flesh with flesh, not of Spirit against flesh, because the Holy Spirit is not in a fleshly person and a fleshly person is not in the Spirit.

As Paul has illustrated from his own life in Romans 7, a true Christian battles with the flesh because his mortal body still hangs on and tries to lure him back into the old sinful ways. But he is no longer *in* the flesh but *in* the Spirit. Speaking of true believers, Paul said, "For the flesh sets its desire against the Spirit, and the Spirit against the flesh; for these are in opposition to one another, so that you may not do the things that you please" (Gal. 5:17). But "if we live by the Spirit," he goes on to say, "let us also walk by the Spirit" (v. 25; cf. v. 16). In other words, because a believer's new nature is divine and is indwelt by God's own Spirit, he desires to behave accordingly.

It is important to note that, when he speaks of sin in a Christian's life, Paul is always careful to identify sin with the outer, corrupted body, not with the new, inner nature. A believer's flesh is not redeemed when he trusts in Christ. If that were so, all Christians would immediately become perfect when they are saved, which even apart from the testimony of Scripture is obviously not true. The sinful vestige of unredeemed humanness will not fall away until the Christian goes to be with the Lord. It is for that reason that the New Testament sometimes speaks of a Christian's salvation in the future tense (see Rom. 13:11). Referring to those who were already saved, Paul says later in this chapter, "Having the first fruits of the Spirit, even we ourselves groan within ourselves, waiting eagerly for our adoption as sons, the redemption of our body" (Rom. 8:23). As the apostle explains to the Corinthians, "It is sown a perishable body, it is raised an imperishable body; it is sown in dishonor, it is raised in glory; it is sown in weakness, it is raised in power; it is sown a natural body, it is raised a spiritual body. If there is a natural body, there is also a spiritual body" (1 Cor. 15:42-44).

No matter how self-sacrificing, moral, and sincere the life of an unredeemed person may be, his religious efforts are selfish because he cannot truly serve God, **because** his **mind, is set on the flesh.** Paul again (cf. v. 6) uses the term *phronēma* (**the mind**), which refers to the content, the thought patterns, the basic inclination and orientation of a person. This inclination, or bent, of **the flesh** is even more deep-seated and significant than actual disobedience, which is simply the outward manifestation of the inner, fleshly compulsions of an unregenerate person.

Every unredeemed person, whether religious or atheistic, whether outwardly moral or outwardly wicked, **is hostile toward God.** An unsaved person cannot live a godly and righteous life because he has no godly and righteous nature or resources. He therefore *cannot* have genuine love for God or for the things of God. His sinful, fleshly mind **does not subject itself to the law of God, for it is not even able to do so.** Even an unbeliever whose life seems to be a model of good works is not capable of doing anything truly good, because he is not motivated or empowered by God and because his works are produced by the flesh for self-centered reasons and can never be to God's glory. It clearly follows, then, that if the fleshly mind does not and cannot subject itself to the law of God, **those who are in the flesh cannot please God.**

Men were created for the very purpose of pleasing God. At the beginning of the practical section of this epistle Paul says, "I urge you therefore, brethren, by the mercies of God, to present your bodies a living and holy sacrifice, acceptable to God, which is your spiritual service of worship. And do not be conformed to this world, but be transformed by the renewing of your mind, that you may prove what the will of God is, that which is good and acceptable and perfect" (Rom. 12:1-2). In a similar way he admonished the Corinthians, "Whether at home or absent, to be pleasing to [God]" (2 Cor. 5:9; cf. Eph. 5:10; Phil. 4:18). He exhorted the believers at Thessalonica "to walk and please God (just as you actually do walk), that you may excel still more" (1 Thess. 4:1).

After describing the spiritual characteristics and incapacities of those who are in the flesh, Paul again addresses those who **are not in the flesh but in the Spirit.** As Jesus explained to Nicodemus, "That which is born of the flesh is flesh, and that which is born of the Spirit is spirit" (John 3:6). Sinful human flesh can only reproduce more sinful human flesh. Only God's Holy Spirit can produce spiritual life.

A test of saving faith is the indwelling presence of the Holy Spirit. "You can be certain of your salvation," Paul is saying, **"if indeed the Spirit of God dwells in you."** *Oikeō* (**dwells**) has the idea of being in one's own home. In a marvelous and incomprehensible way, the very **Spirit of God** makes His home in the life of every person who trusts in Jesus Christ.

The opposite of that reality is also true: **But if anyone does not have the Spirit of Christ, he does not belong to Him.** The person who gives no evidence of the presence, power, and fruit of God's Spirit in his life has no legitimate claim to Christ as Savior and Lord. The person who demonstrates no desire for the things of God and has no inclination to avoid sin or passion to please God is not indwelt by the Holy Spirit and thus does not belong to Christ. In light of that sobering truth Paul admonishes those who claim to be Christians: "Test yourselves to see if you are in the faith; examine yourselves! Or do you not recognize this about yourselves, that Jesus Christ is in you — unless indeed you fail the test?" (2 Cor. 13:5).

And if Christ is in you, Paul continues to say to believers, **though the body is dead because of sin, yet the spirit is alive because of righteousness.** In other words, if God's Spirit indwells us, our own **spirit is alive because of righteousness,** that is, because of the divinely-imparted righteousness by which every believer is justified (Rom. 3:21-26). In light of that perfect righteousness, all human attempts at being righteous are but rubbish (Phil. 3:8).

Summing up what he has just declared in verses 5-10, Paul says, **But if the Spirit of Him who raised Jesus from the dead dwells in you, He who raised Christ Jesus from the dead will also give life to your mortal bodies through His Spirit who indwells you.** It was again the Holy Spirit who was the divine agent of Christ's resurrection. And just as the Spirit lifted Jesus out of physical death and gave Him life in His mortal body, so the Spirit, who dwells in the believer, gives to that believer new life now and forever (cf. John 6:63; 2 Cor. 3:6).

THE HOLY SPIRIT EMPOWERS US FOR VICTORY OVER THE FLESH

So then, brethren, we are under obligation, not to the flesh, to live according to the flesh—for if you are living according to the flesh, you must die; but if by the Spirit you are putting to death the deeds of the body, you will live. (8:12-13)

In his often-republished book *The Reformed Pastor,* the seventeenth-century Puritan Richard Baxter wrote,

Take heed to yourselves, lest you live in those sins which you preach against in others, and lest you be guilty of that which daily you condemn. Will you make it your work to magnify God, and, when you have done, dishonour him as much as others? Will you proclaim Christ's governing power, and yet condemn it, and rebel yourselves? Will you preach his laws, and wilfully break them? If sin be evil, why do you live in it? If it be not, why do you dissuade men from it? If it be dangerous, how dare you venture on it? If it be not, why do you tell men so? If God's threatenings be true, why do you not fear them? If they be false, why do you needlessly trouble men with them, and put them into such frights without a cause? Do you "know the judgment of God, that they who commit such things are worthy of death;" and yet will you do them? "Thou that teachest another, teachest thou not thyself? Thou that sayest a man should not commit adultery," or be drunk, or covetous, art thou such thyself? "Thou that makest thy boast of the law, through breaking the law dishonourest thou God?" What! Shall the same tongue speak evil that speakest against evil? Shall those lips censure, and slander, and backbite your neighbour, that cry down these and the like things in others? Take heed to yourselves, lest you cry down sin, and yet do not overcome it; lest, while you seek to bring it down in others, you bow to it, and become its slaves yourselves: "For of whom a man is overcome, of the same is he brought into bondage." "To whom ye yield yourselves servants to obey, his servants ye are to whom ye obey, whether of sin unto death, or of obedience unto righteousness." O brethren! It is easier to chide at sin, than to overcome it. . . . Many a tailor goes in rags, that maketh costly clothes for others; and many a cook scarcely licks his fingers, when he hath dressed for others the most costly dishes. ([Carlisle, Pa.: Banner of Truth, 1974], pp. 67-68)

Paul has just made clear (vv. 5-11) that every genuine Christian is indwelt by God's own Spirit and that his new spiritual life therefore will not be characterized by worldly, fleshly concerns and activities but by the things of God. The apostle's emphasis then turns, in verses 12-13, to the believer's responsibility to eliminate sin in his life through the Indwelling Spirit.

By the phrase **so then**, Paul reminds his readers of the magnificent privileges of victory over sin that Christians have through the resident Holy Spirit. In the previous eleven verses of chapter 8, he has pointed out, among other things, that believers are no longer under God's condemnation, that they are set free from the law of sin and death, that they are no longer under the domination of sin, that they walk by the Spirit, that they have minds that are set on the Spirit, and that they have life and peace through the Spirit.

All biblical exhortations to believers are based on the blessings and promises they already have from the Lord. Without the provisions we have from Him, we would be unable to fulfill the commands we receive from Him. The children of Israel, for instance, were not com-

manded to take possession of the Promised Land until it was promised
to them by God and they were prepared by Him to conquer it. In this
letter to Rome, Paul's primary exhortations begin with chapter 12, after
he has given countless reminders to his readers of their great spiritual
privileges. In Ephesians he first gives three chapters that are largely a
listing of spiritual benefits. Just before his beautiful doxology at the end
of chapter 3, Paul prays that God "would grant you, according to the
riches of His glory, to be strengthened with power through His Spirit in
the inner man; so that Christ may dwell in your hearts through faith; and
that you, being rooted and grounded in love, may be able to comprehend
with all the saints what is the breadth and length and height and depth,
and to know the love of Christ which surpasses knowledge, that you may
be filled up to all the fulness of God" (Eph. 3:16-19). Only then does he
entreat fellow believers "to walk in a manner worthy of the calling which
you have been called" (4:1). Similar patterns are found in his letters to
Galatia, Philippi, Colossae, often noted by the word *therefore*.

Before the apostle gives the admonition in the present text, he
refers affectionately to his readers as **brethren**, identifying them as fellow
Christians, those to whom God promises victory over the flesh. He
chooses a term of esteem and equality, not of superiority or paternalism,
to refer to his brothers and sisters in Christ.

Paul then proceeds to set forth God's pattern for victory over the
flesh. As God's children indwelt by His Spirit, we have no **obligation . . .
to the flesh, to live according to the flesh. The flesh** is the ugly
complex of human sinful desires that includes the ungodly motives,
affections, principles, purposes, words, and actions that sin generates
through our bodies. **To live according to the flesh** is to be ruled and
controlled by that evil complex. Because of Christ's saving work on our
behalf, the sinful flesh no longer reigns over us, to debilitate us and drag
us back into the pit of depravity into which we were all born. For that
reason, **we are** no longer ruled by **the flesh** to **live** by its sinful ways.

Those who **are living according to the flesh . . . must die.**
The apostle is not warning genuine believers that they may lose their
salvation and be condemned to death if they fall back into some of the
ways of the flesh. He has already given the absolute assurance that "there
is therefore now no condemnation for those who are in Christ Jesus" (8:1).
He is rather saying that a person whose life is characterized by the things
of **the flesh** is not a true Christian and is spiritually dead, no matter what
his religious affiliations or activities may be. If he does not come to Christ
in true faith, he **must die** the second death under God's final judgment.

Paul next restates the reason genuine Christians are no longer
obligated to and bound by sin and are no longer under its condemnation.
Although there will always be some lingering influence of **the flesh** until
we meet the Lord, we have no excuse for sin to continue to corrupt our

lives. The Christian's obligation is no longer to the flesh but to the **Spirit**. We have the resources of the **Spirit** of Christ within us to resist and put **to death the deeds of the body**, which result from **living according to the flesh**.

Putting **to death the deeds of the body** is a characteristic of God's children. The Scottish theologian David Brown wrote, "If you don't kill sin, sin will kill you." Jesus said, "If your right eye makes you stumble, tear it out, and throw it from you; for it is better for you that one of the parts of your body perish, than for your whole body to be thrown into hell. And if your right hand makes you stumble, cut it off, and throw it from you; for it is better for you that one of the parts of your body perish, than for your whole body to go into hell" (Matt. 5:29-30). No action is too drastic in dealing with sin; no price is too great to pay in turning from sin to trust Jesus Christ and thereby escaping the damnation of eternal death in hell.

Paul here gives one of the many self-examination passages in Scripture. As noted above, the person who gives no evidence of the presence, power, and fruit of God's Spirit in his life has no legitimate claim to Christ as Savior and Lord. The obvious other side of that truth is that the person whose life is characterized by the sinful ways of the flesh is still in the flesh and is not in Christ. When Paul declares that believers are God's "workmanship, created in Christ Jesus for good works, which God prepared beforehand, that we should walk in them" (Eph. 2:10), he is stating a fact, not a wish.

Like many of the members of the church in Corinth, an immature and disobedient Christian will inevitably lapse into some of the ways of the flesh (see 1 Cor. 3:1). After he had been an apostle for many years, Paul himself confessed that even he was not yet spiritually flawless. "Not that I have already obtained it, or have already become perfect," he told the Philippians, "but I press on in order that I may lay hold of that for which also I was laid hold of by Christ Jesus. Brethren, I do not regard myself as having laid hold of it yet; but one thing I do: forgetting what lies behind and reaching forward to what lies ahead, I press on toward the goal for the prize of the upward call of God in Christ Jesus" (Phil. 3:12-14). Paul had not yet achieved perfect righteousness in Christ, although that was the supreme objective of his life. Although his flesh sometimes held him back and temporarily interrupted the full joy of his fellowship with Christ, his basic heart's desire was to obey and please his Lord.

If a professing Christian habitually lives in sin and shows no concern for repentance, forgiveness, worship, or fellowship with other believers, he proves that he claims the name of Christ in vain. Many false Christians in the church work hard at keeping their lives pure in appearance, because other people think more highly of them for it and because they feel prouder of themselves when they act morally and benevolently than when they do not. But feeling better about oneself, the popular psychological cure-all for many people in our times, is the very heart of the proud sinful flesh, man's unredeemed selfishness and godless humanness. Doing good for one's own sake rather than for God's is not doing good at all, but is merely a hypocritical projection of the sin of self-love.

It should not be surprising that, as the world more and more advocates self-love and self-fulfillment, the problems of sexual promiscuity, abuse, and perversion, of stealing, lying, murder, suicide, hopelessness, and all other forms of moral and social ills are multiplying exponentially.

The pattern of a true believer's life, on the other hand, will show that he not only professes Christ but that he lives his life **by** Christ's **Spirit** and is habitually **putting to death the** sinful and ungodly **deeds of the body.** Consequently, he **will live,** that is, possess and persevere to the fulness of eternal life given him in Christ.

When God ordered King Saul to destroy *all* of the Amalekites and their livestock, Saul did not completely obey, sparing king Agag and keeping the best of the animals. When the prophet Samuel confronted Saul, the king tried to defend his actions by claiming his people insisted on keeping some of the flocks and that those animals would be sacrificed to God. Samuel rebuked the king, saying, "Has the Lord as much delight in burnt offerings and sacrifices as in obeying the voice of the Lord? Behold, to obey is better than sacrifice, and to heed than the fat of rams" (1 Sam. 15:22). Despite the king's pleas for mercy, Samuel then proclaimed, "The Lord has torn the kingdom of Israel from you today, and has given it to your neighbor [David] who is better than you" (v. 28). Saul's failure to fully obey God cost him his throne.

God's people invariably fall back into sin when their focus turns away from the Almighty to themselves and to the things of the world. For that reason Paul admonished the believers at Colossae, "If then you have been raised up with Christ, keep seeking the things above, where Christ is, seated at the right hand of God. Set your mind on the things above, not on the things that are on earth. For you have died and your life is hidden with Christ in God" (Col. 3:1-3). He then gave a partial but representative list of sins that Christians should kill by considering themselves dead to: "immorality, impurity, passion, evil desire, and greed, which amounts to idolatry. For it is on account of these things that the wrath of God will come, and in them you also once walked, when you were living in them. But now you also, put them all aside: anger, wrath, malice, slander, and abusive speech from your mouth. Do not lie to one another, since you laid aside the old self with its evil practices, and have put on the new self who is being renewed to a true knowledge according to the image of the One who created him" (vv. 5-10).

Paul is not suggesting the "Let go and let God" philosophy that is promoted by groups and leaders who advocate a so-called deeper life, in which one progressively rises to higher and higher levels of spirituality until sin and even temptation are virtually absent. That is not the kind of spiritual life Paul promises or that he personally experienced, as he testifies so movingly in Romans 7. As long as a believer is in his earthly body, he will be subject to the perils of the flesh and will need to keep putting its sins to death. Only in heaven will his need for practical sanctification end. Until then, all believers are admonished to put sin to death and to live in and for their new Sovereign, the Lord Jesus Christ (cf. Rom. 6:3-11).

The Puritan John Owen warned that sin is never less quiet than when it seems to be most quiet, and its waters are for the most part deep when they are still (cf. *Sin and Temptation* [Portland, Ore.: Multnomah, 1983], p. xxi). Satan is likely to attach when a believer is most satisfied with his spiritual life. That is when pride, the chief of sins, easily sneaks into our lives unnoticed and leads us to believe that contentment with ourselves is contentment in God.

Scripture offers believers many helps for avoiding and killing sin in their lives. First, it is imperative to recognize the presence of sin in our flesh. We must be willing to confess honestly with Paul," I find then the principle that evil is present in me, the one who wishes to do good" (Rom. 7:21). If we do not admit to sin, we delude ourselves and become still more susceptible to its influence. Sin can become a powerful and destructive force in a believer's life if it is not recognized and put to death. Our remaining humanness is constantly ready to drag us back into the sinful ways of our life before Christ. Knowing that truth well, Peter admonishes, "Beloved, I urge you as aliens and strangers to abstain from fleshly lusts, which wage war against the soul" (1 Pet. 2:11). If Christians did not live in constant danger from sin, such advice would be pointless.

Because of the influence of our human weaknesses and limitations on our thinking, it is often difficult to recognize sin in our lives. It can easily become camouflaged, often under the guise of something that seems trivial or insignificant, even righteous and good. We must therefore pray with David, "Search me, O God, and know my heart; try me and know my anxious thoughts; and see if there be any hurtful way in me, and lead me in the everlasting way" (Ps. 139:23-24). Haggai's counsel to ancient Israel is helpful for believers in any age: "Consider your ways!" (Hag. 1:5, 7).

A second way for believers to kill sin in their lives is to have a heart fixed on God. David said to the Lord, "My heart is steadfast, O God, my heart is steadfast; I will sing, yes, I will sing praises!" (Ps. 57:7). Another psalmist testified, "O that my ways may be established to keep

Thy statutes! Then I shall not be ashamed when I look upon all Thy commandments" (Ps. 119:5-6). In other words, when we know and obey God's Word, we are building up both our defenses and offenses against sin.

A third way for believers to kill sin in their lives is to meditate on God's Word. Many of the Lord's truths become clear only when we patiently immerse ourselves in a passage of Scripture and give the Lord opportunity to give us deeper understanding. David gives us the example with these words: "Thy word I have treasured in my heart, that I may not sin against Thee" (Ps. 119:11).

A fourth way to destroy sin in our lives is to commune regularly with God in prayer. Peter calls us to "be of sound judgment and sober spirit for the purpose of prayer" (1 Pet. 4:7). When we are faithful in these disciplines we discover how interrelated they are. It is often difficult to tell where study of God's word ends and meditation on it begins, and where meditation ends and prayer begins.

It should be emphasized that true prayer must always have an element of confession. Although we have the assurance that we belong to God and are free from condemnation, we also know that we can never come before him completely sinless. "If we say that we have no sin, we are deceiving ourselves, and the truth is not in us," John warns believers. But "if we confess our sins, He is faithful and righteous to forgive us our sins and to cleanse us from all unrighteousness. If we say that we have not sinned, we make Him a liar, and His word is not in us" (1 John 1:8-10). The writer of Hebrews admonishes, "Let us therefore draw near with confidence to the throne of grace, that we may receive mercy and may find grace to help in time of need" (Heb. 4:16). We need to be cleansed every time we come to Him.

Sincere prayer has a way of unmasking sin's deceit. When God's children open their minds and hearts to their heavenly Father, He lovingly reveals sins that otherwise would go unnoticed.

A fifth way to put to death sin in our lives is to practice obedience to God. Doing His will and His will alone in all the small issues of life can be training in habits that will hold up in the severe times of temptations.

As Paul has already made plain by the testimony from his own life in chapter 7, putting sin to death is often difficult, slow, and frustrating. Satan is the great adversary of God's people and will make every effort to drag them down into sin. But as they conquer sin in their lives through the power of the indwelling Holy Spirit, they not only are brought nearer to their heavenly Father but attain ever increasing assurance that they are indeed His children and are eternally secure in Him.

When the New Testament speaks of such things as growing in grace, perfecting holiness, and renewing the inner man, it is referring to putting sin to death. Sin produced by the remaining flesh in which believers remain temporarily bound is all that stands between them and perfect godliness.

But Paul assures Christians that they have power for victory over the sinful flesh that still clings to them in this life. Apart from the Spirit's supernatural power, we could never succeed in putting to death the recurring sin in our lives. If we were left to our own resources, the struggle with sin would simply be flesh trying to overcome flesh, humanness trying to conquer humanness. Even as a Christian, Paul lamented, "For I know that nothing good dwells in me, that is, in my flesh; for the wishing is present in me, but the doing of the good is not" (Rom. 7:18). Without the Holy Spirit, a Christian would have no more power to resist and defeat sin than does an unbeliever.

The Holy Spirit is virtually synonymous with divine power. Just before His ascension, Jesus promised the apostles, "You shall receive power when the Holy Spirit has come upon you; and you shall be My witnesses both in Jerusalem, and in all Judea and Samaria, and even to the remotest part of the earth" (Acts 1:8). Later in his account of the early church, Luke reports: "You know of Jesus of Nazareth, how God anointed Him with the Holy Spirit and with power, and how He went about doing good, and healing all who were oppressed by the devil; for God was with Him" (Acts 10:38). In his gospel, Luke relates the angel's announcement to Mary concerning the divine conception and birth of Jesus: "The Holy Spirit will come upon you, and the power of the Most High will overshadow you; and for that reason the holy offspring shall be called the Son of God" (Luke 1:35).

The prophet Micah wrote, "I am filled with power—with the Spirit of the Lord—and with justice and courage to make known to Jacob his rebellious act, even to Israel his sin" (Mic. 3:8). Concerning the rebuilding of the Temple, an angel encouraged Zerubbabel through the prophet Zechariah: "This is the word of the Lord to Zerubbabel saying, 'Not by might nor by power, but by My Spirit,' says the Lord of hosts" (Zech. 4:6). In other words, the Spirit's divine power would undergird Zerubbabel and would far surpass the power of the wicked men who sought to thwart his work.

Paul reports later in this epistle that the salvation of many Gentiles through his ministry was accomplished only "in the power of the Spirit" (Rom. 15:19), and he prayed that believers in the Ephesian church would "be strengthened with power through His Spirit in the inner man" (Eph. 3:16).

Paul's main point in Romans 8:13 is that, by the power of **the Spirit** who **dwells in** them, Christians are able successfully to resist and destroy sin in their lives. "The weapons of our warfare are not of the flesh," Paul reminds us, "but divinely powerful for the destruction of

fortresses" (2 Cor. 10:4). It is such confidence in the power of the Holy
Spirit that gives hope to the frustration Paul expressed in Romans 7:24-
25, a frustration that every Christian faces from time to time.

Speaking of the believer's conflict with sin, Paul told the Galatians
that "the flesh sets its desire against the Spirit, and the Spirit against the
flesh; for these are in opposition to one another, so that you may not do
the things that you please" (Gal. 5:17). A few verses later he declares that
"those who belong to Christ Jesus have crucified the flesh with its passions
and desires. If we live by the Spirit, let us also walk by the Spirit" (vv. 24-
25). In other words, because our inner, spiritual lives are indwelt by the
Holy Spirit, our behavior should be according to His will and in His
power. Through the Holy Spirit who indwells him, every true Christian
has the divine resource to have victory over Satan, over the world, and
over sin.

In his letter to Ephesus, Paul refers to the believer's continual need
to rely on the Spirit's power, and he admonishes: "Do not get drunk with
wine, for that is dissipation, but be filled with the Spirit" (Eph. 5:18). A
more literal translation is, "keep being filled with the Spirit." The idea is,
"Always rely on the power of the Holy Spirit, who resides within you and
is always available to strengthen and protect you." To be filled with the
Spirit is to have one's mind completely under His divine control. This
requires the Word's dwelling richly in the believer (cf. Col. 3:16). And
when our minds are under God's control, our behavior inevitably will be
as well. It is not a matter of available power but of available will. By the
Spirit's power, all believers are able "to walk in a manner worthy of the
calling with which [they] have been called" (Eph. 4:1). Those who truly
"put on the Lord Jesus Christ" will "make no provision for the flesh in
regard to its lusts" (Rom. 13:14).

Being controlled by God's Spirit comes from being obedient to His
Word. The Spirit-filled life does not come through mystical or ecstatic
experiences but from studying and submitting oneself to Scripture. As a
believer faithfully and submissively saturates his mind and heart with
God's truth, his Spirit-controlled behavior will follow as surely as night
follows day. When we are filled with God's truth and led by His Spirit,
even our involuntary reactions—those that happen when we don't have
time to consciously decide what to do or say—will be godly.

Life in the Spirit— part 3 The Spirit Confirms Our Adoption

For all who are being led by the Spirit of God, these are sons of God. For you have not received a spirit of slavery leading to fear again, but you have received a spirit of adoption as sons by which we cry out, "Abba! Father!" The Spirit Himself bears witness with our spirit that we are children of God, (8:14-16)

This is one of the richest and most beautiful passages in all of Scripture. Using the figure of adoption, Paul explains the believer's intimate and permanent relationship to God as a beloved child.

In these verses, Paul continues to disclose the ways in which God confirms that believers are eternally related to Him as His children, testifying that we are led, given access to God, and granted inner assurance by His own Spirit. These three means of assurance are closely related and intertwined, but each presents a distinctive truth about the Spirit's work in the believer's life.

WE ARE LED BY THE SPIRIT

For all who are being led by the Spirit of God, these are sons of God. (8:14)

The first inner confirmation of adoption is the believer's **being led by the Spirit of God.** A person who is truly experiencing the leading hand of God at work in his life can be certain he is God's child.

It is important to note the tense Paul uses here. **Are being led** translates the present passive indicative of *agō,* indicating that which already exists. The phrase **are being led** does not, however, indicate uninterrupted leading by **the Spirit.** Otherwise the many New Testament admonitions and warnings to Christians would be meaningless. But the genuine believer's life is basically characterized by the Spirit's leading, just as it is basically characterized by Christ's righteousness.

A merely professing Christian does not and cannot be **led by the Spirit of God.** He may be moral, conscientious, generous, active in his church and other Christian organizations, and exhibit many other commendable traits. But the only accomplishments, religious or otherwise, he can make claim to are those of his own doing. His life may be outstandingly religious, but because he lives it in the power of the flesh, he can never be truly spiritual and he will never have the inner conviction of God's leading and empowering.

When someone confides in me that he has doubts about his salvation, I often respond by asking if he ever senses God's leading in his life. If he answers yes, I remind him of Paul's assurance in this verse: **All who are being led by the Spirit of God, these are sons of God.**

God's children are secure in Him even when they are not as responsive and obedient to His leading as they ought to be. But that is not to say that a child of God will always *feel* secure. The Christian who neglects study of Scripture, who neglects God in prayer, who neglects fellowship with God's people, and who is careless about His obedience to God will invariably have doubts about his salvation, because he is indifferent to God and the things of God. Even for the obedient child of God, doubts about his relationship to God can easily slip into the mind during times of pain, sorrow, failure, or disappointment. Satan, the great accuser of God's people, is always ready to take advantage of such circumstances to plant seeds of uncertainty.

But our heavenly Father wants His children to be certain at all times that they belong to Him and are secure in Him. As Paul has just stated (Rom. 8:13), a person who is succeeding in putting to death sin in his life is not doing so in his own power, that is, in the power of the flesh, but by the power of the Spirit. Those who see victory over sin in their lives, who see their sinful desires and practices diminishing, can be certain they **are sons of God,** because only God's **Spirit** can bring victory over sin. In the same way—when we begin to understand biblical truths that have long puzzled us, when we experience God's convicting our consciences, when we grieve for the Lord's sake when we sin—we have the divine assurance that we **are sons of God,** because only the indwelling

Spirit of God can instill such understanding, conviction, and godly sorrow.

Our finite minds cannot comprehend *how* the Spirit leads a believer, just as we cannot fully understand any of the supernatural work of God. We do, however, know that our heavenly Father does not force His will on His children. He seeks our willing obedience, which, by definition, cannot be coerced. It is when we are genuinely submissive to Him that our Lord supernaturally reshapes and redirects our will into voluntary conformity with His own.

God saves men through their faith in Him, and He leads those he saves through the same human channel of faith. "Trust in the Lord with all your heart, and do not lean on your own understanding," the writer of Proverbs counsels. "In all your ways acknowledge Him, and He will make your paths straight" (Prov. 3:5-6). The seeking, willing, and obedient heart is open to the Lord's leading. David prayed, "Make me know Thy ways, O Lord; teach me Thy paths. Lead me in Thy truth and teach me, for Thou art the God of my salvation; for Thee I wait all the day" (Ps. 25:4-5). Later in that psalm he reminds us that God "leads the humble in justice, and He teaches the humble His way" (Ps. 25:9). In another psalm he entreated the Lord, "Teach me to do Thy will, for Thou art my God; let Thy good Spirit lead me on level ground" (Ps. 143:10).

Isaiah assures us that if we truly seek the Lord's will, He is already standing beside us, as it were, ready to say, "This is the way, walk in it" (Isa. 30:21). The prophet was not speaking necessarily of an audible voice, but the voice of the believer's God-directed conscience, a conscience instructed by God's Word and attuned to His Spirit. Isaiah also assures us that the Lord is continually ready and eager to lead His people in the right way. Prophesying in the name of the preincarnate Christ, the prophet declared, "Come near to Me, listen to this: from the first I have not spoken in secret, from the time it took place, I was there. And now the Lord God has sent Me, and His Spirit. Thus says the Lord, your Redeemer, the Holy One of Israel; 'I am the Lord your God, who teaches you to profit, who leads you in the way you should go'" (Isa. 48:16-17). Jeremiah acknowledged, "I know, O Lord, that a man's way is not in himself; nor is it in a man who walks to direct his steps" (Jer. 10:23). Even the child of God cannot discern divine truth by his own intelligence or obey it in his own power.

God's Spirit sovereignly leads His children in many ways, sometimes in ways that are direct and unique. But the primary ways by which He promises to lead us are those of illumination and sanctification.

In the first way, God leads His children by illumination, by divinely clarifying His Word to make it understandable to our finite and still sin-tainted minds. As we read, meditate on, and pray over Scripture, the indwelling Spirit of God becomes our divine interpreter. This begins with the conviction of sin that leads through saving belief into the whole of the Christian life.

Although Joseph was not indwelt by the Holy Spirit as are believers under the New Covenant, even the pagan Egyptian ruler recognized him as a man "in whom is a divine spirit." Consequently, "Pharaoh said to Joseph, 'Since God has informed you of all this, there is no one so discerning and wise as you are'" (Gen. 41:38-39).

The Old Testament saint who wrote Psalm 119, which so eloquently glorifies God's Word, knew he needed the Lord's divine help both to understand and to obey that Word. Every believer should continually pray with the psalmist: "Make me walk in the path of Thy commandments, for I delight in it" (Ps. 119:35), and, "Establish my footsteps in Thy word, and do not let any iniquity have dominion over me" (Ps. 119:133).

During the Upper Room discourse, shortly before His betrayal and arrest, Jesus told the apostles, "These things I have spoken to you, while abiding with you. But the Helper, the Holy Spirit, whom the Father will send in My name, He will teach you all things, and bring to your remembrance all that I said to you" (John 14:25-26). That promise had special significance for the apostles, who would become Christ's uniquely authoritative witnesses to His truth after His ascension back to heaven. But the promise also applies in a general way to all believers after Pentecost. From that time on, *every* believer has been indwelt by Christ's own Holy Spirit, whose ministry to us includes that of shedding divine light on scriptural truths that otherwise are beyond our comprehension.

During one of His postresurrection appearances, Jesus said to the eleven remaining apostles, "'These are My words which I spoke to you while I was still with you, that all things which are written about Me in the Law of Moses and the Prophets and the Psalms must be fulfilled.' Then He opened their minds to understand the Scriptures" (Luke 24:44-45). Again Jesus' words had unique significance for the apostles, but in a similar way the Lord opens the minds of *all* His disciples "to understand the Scriptures."

On behalf of the Ephesian believers Paul prayed that "the God of our Lord Jesus Christ, the Father of glory, may give to you a spirit of wisdom and of revelation in the knowledge of Him. I pray that the eyes of your heart may be enlightened, so that you may know what is the hope of His calling, what are the riches of the glory of His inheritance in the saints, and what is the surpassing greatness of His power toward us who believe. These are in accordance with the working of the strength of His might" (Eph. 1:17-19). Later in that epistle Paul offered a similar prayer, asking that God "would grant you, according to the riches of His glory, to be strengthened with power through His Spirit in the inner man; so that Christ may dwell in your hearts through faith; and that you, being rooted and grounded in love, may be able to comprehend with all the saints what is the breadth and length and height and depth, and to know the love of Christ which surpasses knowledge, that you may be filled up to all the fulness of God" (3:16-19).

Paul assured the saints at Colossae that "we have not ceased to pray for you and to ask that you may be filled with the knowledge of His will in all spiritual wisdom and understanding" (Col. 1:9). His devotion to them was again expressed in the loving words: "Let the word of Christ richly dwell within you, with all wisdom teaching and admonishing one another with psalms and hymns and spiritual songs, singing with thankfulness in your hearts to God" (3:16).

Perhaps the most definitive passage on the illuminating work of the Holy Spirit is in Paul's first letter to Corinth. "A natural man does not accept the things of the Spirit of God," he asserts; "for they are foolishness to him, and he cannot understand them, because they are spiritually appraised. But he who is spiritual appraises all things, yet he himself is appraised by no man. For who has known the mind of the Lord, that he should instruct Him? But we have the mind of Christ" (1 Cor. 2:14-16). In other words, even God's own children could not understand their heavenly Father's Word apart from the illuminating work of His Spirit within them.

The second major way in which **the Spirit** leads God's children is by their sanctification. **The Spirit** not only illuminates our minds to understand Scripture but divinely assists us in obeying it, and that obedience becomes another testimony to our salvation. The humble child of God knows he cannot please his Lord in his own power. But he also knows that, when he sincerely labors in the Lord's work in accordance with the commands and principles of Scripture, the Holy Spirit will bless that work in ways far beyond what the believer's own abilities could have produced. It is then that our heavenly Father is deeply pleased with us, not for what we have accomplished but for what we have allowed Him to accomplish in and through us. It is not our work in itself but our spirit of obedience to Him and dependence on Him as we do His work that brings joy to our heavenly Father's heart. It is through our faithful obedience that we experience the gracious working of **the Spirit** in our lives. And, as with His divine illumination, His divine work of sanctification gives us assurance that we are indeed **sons of God.**

"I say, walk by the Spirit, and you will not carry out the desire of the flesh," Paul admonished the Galatians. "For the flesh sets its desire against the Spirit, and the Spirit against the flesh; for these are in opposition to one another, so that you may not do the things that you please" (Gal. 5:16-17). And because "we live by the Spirit," he goes on to say, "let us also walk by the Spirit" (v. 5:25).

As with illumination and all other divine works, we cannot

understand exactly *how* God accomplishes His sanctifying work in us. We simply know from His Word, and often from experience, that He performs spiritual works in and through us that are not produced by our own efforts or power. Often we become aware of the Spirit's activity only in retrospect, as we see His sanctifying power bearing fruit in our lives from seeds planted long beforehand. We also have the blessed assurance that, although we are not consciously *aware* of the Spirit's work in us at all times, He is nevertheless *performing* His divine work in us at all times. He not only gives and sustains our spiritual life, He *is* our spiritual life.

It is our heavenly Father's great desire for His children to submit to the leading of His Spirit, for the sake of His glory and for the sake of their spiritual fruitfulness, well-being, and peace.

WE ARE GIVEN ACCESS TO GOD BY THE SPIRIT

For you have not received a spirit of slavery leading to fear again, but you have received a spirit of adoption as sons by which we cry out, "Abba! Father!" (8:15)

A second way in which the Holy Spirit confirms our adoption as God's children is by freeing us from the **spirit of slavery** that inevitably leads us **to fear again.** Because God's "children share in flesh and blood," we are told by the writer of Hebrews, "He Himself [Christ] likewise also partook of the same, that through death He might render powerless him who had the power of death, that is, the devil; and might deliver those who through fear of death were subject to slavery all their lives" (Heb. 2:14-15).

No matter how cleverly they may manage to mask or deny the reality of it, sinful men are continually subject to fear because they continually live in sin and are therefore continually under God's judgment. Slavery to sin brings slavery to fear, and one of the gracious works of the Holy Spirit is to deliver God's children from both.

John Donne, the seventeenth-century English poet who later became pastor and dean of St. Paul's Cathedral in London, wrote in "A Hymn to God the Father" the following touching lines:

> Wilt Thou forgive that sin where I begun,
> Which was my sin, though it were done before?
> Wilt Thou forgive that sin, through which I run,
> And do run still, though still I do deplore?
> When Thou hast done, Thou hast not done;
> For I have more. . . .

> I have a sin of fear, that when I have spun
> My last thread, I shall perish on the shore;
> But swear by Thy self that at my death Thy Son
> Shall shine as he shines now and heretofore:
> And, having done that, Thou hast done,
> I fear no more.

Paul reminded Timothy that our heavenly Father "has not given us a spirit of timidity [or, fear], but of power and love and discipline" (2 Tim. 1:7). John assures us that "there is no fear in love; but perfect love casts out fear, because fear involves punishment, and the one who fears is not perfected in love" (1 John 4:18).

At this point in Romans, Paul is not so much emphasizing the transaction of **adoption** as the believer's assurance of it. Through the regenerating work of the Holy Spirit, we not only are truly and permanently adopted as children of God but are given **a spirit of adoption**. That is, God makes certain His children *know* they are His children. Because of His Spirit dwelling in our hearts, our **spirit** recognizes that we are always privileged to come before God as our beloved Father.

The term **adoption** is filled with the ideas of love, grace, compassion, and intimate relationship. It is the action by which a husband and wife decide to take a boy or girl who is not their physical offspring into their family as their own child. When that action is taken by the proper legal means, the adopted child attains all the rights and privileges of a member of the family.

The first adoption recorded in Scripture was that of Moses. When Pharaoh ordered all the male Hebrew children slain, Moses' mother placed him in a waterproof basket and set him in the Nile River among some reeds. When Pharaoh's daughter came to the river with her maids to bathe, she saw the basket and had one of her maids retrieve it. She immediately realized the infant was Hebrew but took pity on him. Moses' sister, Miriam, had been watching nearby and she offered to find a nursemaid for the child, as her mother had instructed. With the approval of Pharaoh's daughter, Miriam brought her own mother, who was then paid to take Moses home and nurse him. When Moses was a young boy, he was brought to the palace and adopted by Pharaoh's daughter (see Ex. 2:1-10).

Because Esther's parents had died, she was adopted by an older cousin named Mordecai, who loved her as a father and took special care to look after her welfare (see Esther 2:5-11).

Perhaps the most touching adoption mentioned in the Old Testament was that of Mephibosheth, the crippled son of Jonathan and the sole remaining descendent of Saul. When King David learned about

Mephibosheth, he gave him all the land that had belonged to his grandfather Saul and honored this son of his dearest friend, Jonathan, by having him dine regularly at the king's table in the palace at Jerusalem (see 2 Sam. 9:1-13).

Pharaoh's daughter adopted Moses out of pity and sympathy. And although Mordecai dearly loved Esther, his adoption of her was also prompted by family duty. But David's adoption of Mephibosheth was motivated purely by gracious love. In many ways, David's adoption of Mephibosheth pictures God's adoption of believers. David took the initiative in seeking out Mephibosheth and bringing him to the palace. And although Mephibosheth was the son of David's closest friend, he was also the grandson and sole heir of Saul, who had sought repeatedly to kill David. Being crippled in both feet, Mephibosheth was helpless to render David any significant service; he could only accept his sovereign's bounty. The very name Mephibosheth means "a shameful thing," and he had lived for a number of years in Lo-debar, which means "the barren land" (lit., "no pasture"). David brought this outcast to dine at his table as his own son and graciously granted him a magnificent inheritance to which he was no longer legally entitled.

That is a beautiful picture of the spiritual adoption whereby God graciously and lovingly seeks out unworthy men and women on His own initiative and makes them His children, solely on the basis of their trust in His true Son, Jesus Christ. Because of their adoption, believers will share the full inheritance of the Son. To all Christians God declares, "'I will welcome you, and I will be a father to you, and you shall be sons and daughters to Me,' says the Lord Almighty" (2 Cor. 6:17-18). Paul gives us the unspeakably marvelous assurance that God has "predestined us to adoption as sons through Jesus Christ to Himself, according to the kind intention of His will" (Eph. 1:5).

For some people today, the concept of adoption carries the idea of second-class status in the family. In the Roman culture of Paul's day, however, an adopted child, especially an adopted son, sometimes had greater prestige and privilege than the natural children. According to Roman law, a father's rule over his children was absolute. If he was disappointed in his natural sons' skill, character, or any other attribute, he would search diligently for a boy available for adoption who demonstrated the qualities he desired. If the boy proved himself worthy, the father would take the necessary legal steps for adoption. At the death of the father, a favored adopted son would sometimes inherit the father's title, the major part of the estate, and would be the primary progenitor of the family name. Because of its obvious great importance, the process of Roman adoption involved several carefully prescribed legal procedures. The first step totally severed the boy's legal and social relationship to his natural family, and the second step placed him permanently into his new family. In addition to that, all of his previous debts and other obligations were eradicated, as if they had never existed. For the transaction to become legally binding, it also required the presence of seven reputable witnesses, who could testify, if necessary, to any challenge of the adoption after the father's death.

Paul doubtless was well aware of that custom, and may have had it in mind as he penned this section of Romans. He assures believers of the wondrous truth that they are indeed God's adopted children, and that because of that immeasurably gracious relationship they have the full right and privilege to **cry out,** "**Abba!**" to God as their heavenly **Father,** just as every child does to his earthly father. The fact that believers have the compelling desire to cry out in intimate petition and praise to their loving Father, along with their longing for fellowship and communion with God, is evidence of the indwelling Holy Spirit, which indwelling proves one's salvation and gives assurance of eternal life.

Abba is an informal Aramaic term for **Father,** connoting intimacy, tenderness, dependence, and complete lack of fear or anxiety. Modern English equivalents would be Daddy, or Papa. When Jesus was agonizing in the Garden of Gethsemane as He was about to take upon Himself the sins of the world, He used that name of endearment, praying, "Abba! Father! All things are possible for Thee; remove this cup from Me; yet not what I will, but what Thou wilt" (Mark 14:36).

When we are saved, our old sinful life is completely cancelled in God's eyes, and we have no more reason to fear sin or death, because Christ has conquered those two great enemies on our behalf. In Him we are given a new divine nature and become a true child, with all the attendant blessings, privileges, and inheritance. And until we see our Lord face-to-face, His own Holy Spirit will be a ceaseless witness to the authenticity of our adoption into the family of God.

The idea of Christians being God's adopted children was clearly understood by Paul's contemporaries to signify great honor and privilege. In his letter to Ephesus, the apostle exults, "Blessed be the God and Father of our Lord Jesus Christ, who has blessed us with every spiritual blessing in the heavenly places in Christ, just as He chose us in Him before the foundation of the world, that we should be holy and blameless before Him. In love He predestined us to adoption as sons through Jesus Christ to Himself, according to the kind intention of His will" (Eph. 1:3-5). Countless ages ago, before He created the first human being in His divine image, God sovereignly chose every believer to be His beloved and eternal child!

It should be kept in mind that, marvelous as it is, the term **adoption** does not fully illustrate God's work of salvation. The believer is also cleansed from sin, saved from its penalty of death, spiritually reborn, justified, sanctified, and ultimately glorified. But those who are saved by their faith in Jesus Christ by the work of His grace have no higher title than that of adopted child of God. That name designates their qualification to share full inheritance with Christ. It is therefore far from incidental that Paul both introduces and closes this chapter with assurances to believers that they are no longer, and never again can be, under God's condemnation (see 8:1, 38-39).

WE ARE ASSURED BY THE SPIRIT

The Spirit Himself bears witness with our spirit that we are children of God, (8:16)

To give us even further assurance of our eternal relationship to Him, the Lord's Holy **Spirit Himself bears witness with our spirit that we are children of God.** As noted above, just as the witnesses to a Roman adoption had the responsibility of testifying to its validity, so the indwelling Holy **Spirit Himself** is constantly present to provide inner testimony to our divine adoption. He certainly does that through the inner work of illumination and sanctification, as well as through the longing for communion with God.

But here Paul does not have in mind just some mystical small voice saying we are saved. Rather, he may be referring to the fruit of the Spirit (Gal. 5:22-23), which, when the Spirit produces it, gives the believer assurance. Or, he may be thinking of the power for service (Acts 1:8), which when experienced is evidence of the Spirit's presence, thus assuring one of salvation.

When believers are compelled by love for God, feel deep hatred for sin, reject the world, long for Christ's return, love other Christians, experience answered prayer, discern between truth and error, long for and move toward Christlikeness, the work of the Holy Spirit is evidenced and those believers have witness that they truly **are children of God.**

The nineteenth-century British pastor Billy Bray seemed never to have lacked that inner testimony. He had been converted from a life of drunken debauchery while reading John Bunyan's *Visions of Heaven and Hell.* He was so continuously overjoyed by God's grace and goodness that he said, "I can't help praising the Lord. As I go along the street, I lift up one foot, and it seems to say, 'Glory.' And I lift up the other, and it seems to say, 'Amen.' And so they keep on like that all the time I am walking."

Whenever the world, other Christians, or we ourselves question that we are truly saved, we can appeal to the indwelling **Spirit** to settle the question in our hearts. Providing that assurance is one of His most precious ministries to us.

John offers the encouraging words, "Little children, let us not love with word or with tongue, but in deed and truth. We shall know by this that we are of the truth, and shall assure our heart before Him, in whatever our heart condemns us" (1 John 3:18-20a). That is objective evidence that we are truly God's children. John then reminds us of the subjective evidence our gracious Lord provides: "God is greater than our heart, and knows all things. Beloved, if our heart does not condemn us, we have confidence before God" (vv. 20b-21).

The Holy Spirit Guarantees Our Glory—part 1 The Incomparable Gain of Glory

and if children, heirs also, heirs of God and fellow heirs with Christ, if indeed we suffer with Him in order that we may also be glorified with Him.

For I consider that the sufferings of this present time are not worthy to be compared with the glory that is to be revealed to us. (8:17-18)

Whether consciously or not, every genuine Christian lives in the light and hope of glory. That hope is perhaps summed up best by John in his first epistle: "Beloved, now we are children of God, and it has not appeared as yet what we shall be. We know that, when He appears, we shall be like Him, because we shall see Him just as He is" (1 John 3:2). Because of our consummate trust in Jesus Christ as Lord and Savior, God graciously adopted us as His own children, and one day "we shall be like Him," like the perfect, sinless Son of God who took our sin upon Himself in order that we might share not only His righteousness but His glory!

In addition to freeing believers from sin and death (Rom. 8:2-3), enabling them to fulfill God's law (v. 4), changing their nature (vv. 5-11), empowering them for victory (vv. 12-13), and confirming their adoption as God's children (vv. 14-16), the Holy Spirit guarantees their ultimate glory (vv. 17-30). In verses 17-18 Paul focuses on believers' incomparable spiritual gain through the divine glory that they are guaranteed.

The various aspects and stages of salvation of which the Bible speaks—such as regeneration, new birth, justification, sanctification, and glorification—can be distinguished but never separated. None of those can exist without the others. They are inextricably woven into the seamless fabric of God's sovereign work of redemption.

There can therefore be no loss of salvation between justification and glorification. Consequently, there can never be justification without glorification. "Whom [God] predestined, these He also called; and whom He called, these He also justified; and whom He justified, these He also glorified" (Rom. 8:30). Justification is the beginning of salvation and glorification is its completion. Once it has begun, God *will not* stop it, and no other power in the universe *is able* to stop it. "Neither death, nor life, nor angels, nor principalities, nor things present, nor things to come, nor powers, nor height, nor depth, nor any other created thing, shall be able to separate us from the love of God, which is in Christ Jesus our Lord" (Rom. 8:38-39). During His earthly ministry, Jesus declared unequivocally: "All that the Father gives Me shall come to Me, and the one who comes to Me I will certainly not cast out. . . . And this is the will of Him who sent Me, that of all that He has given Me I lose nothing, but raise it up on the last day. For this is the will of My Father, that everyone who beholds the Son and believes in Him, may have eternal life; and I Myself will raise him up on the last day" (John 6:37, 39-40).

Because he was created in the image of God, man was made with a glorious nature. Before the Fall, he was without sin and, in a way that Scripture does not reveal, he radiated the glory of his Creator. But when Adam fell by disobeying the single command of God, man lost not only his sinlessness and innocence but also his glory and its attendant dignity and honor. It is for that reason that all men now "fall short of the glory of God" (Rom. 3:23).

Fallen men seem basically to know they are devoid of glory, and they often strive tirelessly to gain glory for themselves. The contemporary obsession with achieving self-esteem is a tragic reflection of man's sinful and futile efforts to regain glory apart from holiness.

The ultimate purpose of salvation is to forgive and to cleanse men of their sin and to restore to them God's glory and thereby bring to Him still greater glory through the working of that sovereign act of grace. The glory that believers are destined to receive through Jesus Christ, however, will far surpass the glory man had before the Fall, because perfection far exceeds innocence. Glorification marks the completion and perfection of salvation. Therefore, as the late British pastor and theologian Martyn Lloyd-Jones rightly observed in his exposition of our text, salvation cannot stop at any point short of entire perfection or it is not salvation. Pointing up that truth, Paul told the Philippian believers, "For I am confident of this very thing, that He who began a good work in you will perfect it until the day of Christ Jesus" (Phil. 1:6).

Salvation brings continual growth in divine glory until it is perfected in the likeness of Jesus Christ Himself. "But we all, with unveiled face beholding as in a mirror the glory of the Lord, are being transformed into the same image from glory to glory, just as from the Lord, the Spirit" (2 Cor. 3:18). As part of His ministry to us during our lives on earth, the Holy Spirit carries us from one level of glory to another.

In proclaiming the incomparable gain believers have in their divinely-bestowed glory, Paul focuses first on the heirs (8:17*a*), then on the source (v. 17*b*), the extent (v. 17*c*), the proof (v. 17*d*), and finally the comparison (v. 18).

THE HEIRS OF GLORY

and if children, heirs also, (8:17)

The emphasis in Romans 8:17-18 on believers' glory is closely related to their adoption as God's children (see vv. 14-16). As is clear from that preceding context, the **if** in verse 17 does not carry the idea of possibility or doubt but of reality and causality, and might be better translated "because." In other words, because *all* believers have the leading of the Holy Spirit (v. 14) and His witness (v. 16) that they are indeed **children** of God, they are thereby **heirs also.**

The heavenly angels not only serve God directly but also serve believers, because they are God's children and heirs. "Are they [angels] not all ministering spirits, sent out to render service for the sake of those who will inherit salvation?" the writer of Hebrews asks rhetorically (Heb. 1:14). Because of our faith in His Son Jesus Christ, God the Father "has qualified us to share in the inheritance of the saints in light" (Col. 1:12).

As explained in the last chapter, Paul's figure of adoption seems to correspond more to Roman law and custom than to Jewish. We might expect this, because Paul was writing to believers in Rome. And although many of them doubtless were Jewish, if their families had lived there for several generations, they would be as familiar with the Roman custom as the Jewish.

In Jewish tradition, the eldest son normally received a double portion of his father's inheritance. In Roman society, on the other hand, although a father had the prerogative of giving more to one child than to the others, normally all children received equal shares. And under Roman law, inherited possessions enjoyed more protection than those that were bought or worked for. Perhaps reflecting those Roman customs and laws, Paul's emphasis in this passage is on the equality of God's children and the security of their adoption.

Paul told the Galatians, "If you belong to Christ, then you are

Abraham's offspring, heirs according to promise" (Gal. 3:29; cf. 4:7). Here Paul is referring to spiritual heritage, citing Abraham, "the father of all who believe" (Rom. 4:11), as the human archetype of the adopted child and heir of God.

THE SOURCE OF GLORY

heirs of God, (8:17*b*)

The source of believers' incomparable glory is **God,** their heavenly Father, who has adopted them as His own children and **heirs.** Paul assured the Colossian Christians "that from the Lord you will receive the reward of the inheritance" (Col. 3:24). This inheritance is only God's to give, and He sovereignly bestows it, without exception, on those who become His children and heirs through faith in His divine Son, Jesus Christ.

In His description of the sheep and goats judgment in the last days, Jesus reveals the astounding truth that our inheritance with Him was ordained by God in eternity past! "Then the King will say to those on His right, 'Come, you who are blessed of My Father, inherit the kingdom prepared for you from the foundation of the world'" (Matt. 25:34). God does not adopt His children as an afterthought but according to His predetermined plan of redemption, which began before "the foundation of the world."

The value of an inheritance is determined by the worth of the one who bequeaths it, and the inheritance of Christians is from the Creator, Sustainer, and Owner of the world. **God** not only is the source of our inheritance but is Himself our inheritance. Of all the good things in the universe, the most precious is the Creator of the universe Himself. The psalmist declared, "Whom have I in heaven but Thee? And besides Thee, I desire nothing on earth" (Ps. 73:25). Jeremiah wrote, "'The Lord is my portion,' says my soul, 'Therefore I have hope in Him'" (Lam. 3:24). In his vision on the island of Patmos, John "heard a loud voice from the [heavenly] throne, saying, 'Behold, the tabernacle of God is among men, and He shall dwell among them, and they shall be His people, and God Himself shall be among them'" (Rev. 21:3). The greatest blessing God's children will have in heaven will be the eternal presence of their God.

THE EXTENT OF GLORY

and fellow heirs with Christ, (8:17*c*)

Many of us are heirs of those who have very little to bequeath in earthly possessions, and our human inheritance will amount to little, perhaps nothing. But just as God's resources are limitless, so our spiritual inheritance is limitless, because, as His **fellow heirs,** we share in everything that the true Son of God, Jesus **Christ,** inherits.

Paul exulted, "Blessed be the God and Father of our Lord Jesus Christ, who has blessed us with every spiritual blessing in the heavenly places in Christ, . . . also we have obtained an inheritance, having been predestined according to His purpose who works all things after the counsel of His will" (Eph. 1:3, 11). God the Father has appointed Jesus Christ the "heir of all things" (Heb. 1:2), and because we are **fellow heirs** with Him, we are destined to receive all that He receives!

In the arithmetic of earth, if each heir receives an equal share of an inheritance, each gets only a certain fraction of the whole amount. But heaven is not under such limits, and *every* adopted child of God will receive the *full* inheritance with the Son. Everything that **Christ** receives by divine right, we will receive by divine grace. The parable of the laborers in Matthew 20:1-16 illustrates this graciousness, showing that all who serve Christ will receive the same eternal reward, irrespective of differences in their service.

Believers one day will enter into the eternal joy of their Master (Matt. 25:21), who, for the sake of that joy, "endured the cross, despising the shame, and has sat down at the right hand of the throne of God" (Heb. 12:2). Believers will sit on the heavenly throne with Christ and rule there with Him (Rev. 3:21; cf. 20:4; Luke 22:30), bearing forever the very image of their Savior and Lord (1 Cor. 15:49; 1 John 3:2). In the infinite "grace of our Lord Jesus Christ, . . . though He was rich, yet for [our] sake He became poor, that [we] through His poverty might become rich" (2 Cor. 8:9). In His great high priestly prayer, Jesus spoke to His Father of the incredible and staggering truth that everyone who believes in Him will be one with Him and will share His full glory: "The glory which Thou hast given Me I have given to them; that they may be one, just as We are one" (John 17:22) We will not intrude on Christ's prerogatives, because, in His gracious will, He Himself bestows His glory on us and asks His Father to confirm that endowment.

It is not that believers will become gods, as some cults teach, but that we will receive, by our joint inheritance with Christ, all the blessings and grandeur that God has. We are "justified by His grace [in order that] we might be made heirs according to the hope of eternal life" (Titus 3:7). Jesus Christ "is the mediator of a new covenant, in order that since a death has taken place for the redemption of the transgressions that were committed under the first covenant, those who have been called may receive the promise of the eternal inheritance" (Heb. 9:15).

The Christian who is not eagerly looking for Christ's Second Coming and living his life in accordance with Christ's will is too tied to this earth. But according to God's Word, only those believers who have an eternal perspective, who are truly heavenly-minded, can be of service to Him on earth, because they are freed from the earthly desires and motivations that hinder the obedience of many of His children. Faithful believers are fruitful believers, and they know that their true citizenship is in heaven (Phil. 3:20) and that their inheritance is a promise of God (Heb. 6:12), who cannot lie and who is always faithful to fulfill His promises.

When Paul was caught up into the third heaven, he beheld sights and heard utterances that were beyond human description (2 Cor. 12:2-4). Even the inspired apostle was unable to depict the grandeur, majesty, and glory of heaven. Yet every believer some day not only will behold and comprehend those divine wonders but will share fully in them.

"And everyone who has this hope fixed on Him purifies himself, just as He is pure," John tells us (1 John 3:3). The hope and expectation of sharing in God's own glory should motivate every believer to dedicate himself to living purely while he is still on earth. Only a holy life is fully usable by God, and only a holy life is rightly prepared to receive the inheritance of the Lord.

One day everything on earth will perish and disappear, because the whole earth is defiled and corrupted. By great and marvelous contrast, however, one day every believer will "obtain an inheritance which is imperishable and undefiled and will not fade away, reserved in heaven for [him]" (1 Pet. 1:4). Our present earthly life as believers is merely an "introduction by faith into this grace in which we stand," and our ultimate hope and joy are "in hope of the glory of God" (Rom. 5:2). Because of his constant confidence in that ultimate inheritance, Paul could say, "I know how to get along with humble means, and I also know how to live in prosperity; in any and every circumstance I have learned the secret of being filled and going hungry, both of having abundance and suffering need" (Phil. 4:12). It was also in light of our ultimate divine inheritance that Jesus admonished, "Do not lay up for yourselves treasures upon earth, where moth and rust destroy, and where thieves break in and steal. But lay up for yourselves treasures in heaven, where neither moth nor rust destroys, and where thieves do not break in or steal; for where your treasure is, there will your heart be also" (Matt. 6:19-21).

THE PROOF OF GLORY

if indeed we suffer with Him in order that we may also be glorified with Him. (8:17*d*)

As in the beginning of the verse, **if** does not here connote possibility but actuality, and is better rendered "because," or "inasmuch."

Paul is declaring that, strange as it seems to the earthly mind, the present proof of the believer's ultimate glory comes through suffering on his Lord's behalf. Because **we suffer with Him,** we know that we will **also be glorified with Him.** Jesus closed the Beatitudes on the same note when He gave a double promise of blessing for those who are persecuted for righteousness' sake, that is, for His sake (Matt. 5:10-12).

Because the present world system is under the reign of Satan, the world despises God and the people of God. It is therefore inevitable that whether persecution comes in the form of mere verbal abuse at one extreme or as martyrdom at the other extreme, no believer is exempt from the possibility of paying a price for his faith. When **we suffer** mockery, scorn, ridicule, or any other form of persecution because of our relationship to Jesus Christ, we can take that affliction as divine proof we truly belong to Christ and that our hope of heavenly glory is not in vain, that ultimately we will **also be glorified with Him.**

Many of God's promises are not what we think of as "positive." Jesus promised, "A disciple is not above his teacher, nor a slave above his master. It is enough for the disciple that he become as his teacher, and the slave as his master. If they have called the head of the house Beelzebul, how much more the members of his household!" (Matt. 10:24-25). Paul promised that "all who desire to live godly in Christ Jesus will be persecuted" (2 Tim. 3:12; cf. 2:11). Peter implies the same promise of persecution in his first epistle: "And after you have suffered for a little while, the God of all grace, who called you to His eternal glory in Christ, will Himself perfect, confirm, strengthen and establish you" (1 Pet. 5:10). Suffering is an integral part of the process of spiritual maturity, and Peter assumes that every true believer will undergo some degree of suffering for the Lord's sake. Those who will reign with Christ in the life to come will enjoy the rewards for their suffering for Him during their life on earth.

Paul declares with confidence and joy, "We are afflicted in every way, but not crushed; perplexed, but not despairing; persecuted, but not forsaken; struck down, but not destroyed; always carrying about in the body the dying of Jesus, that the life of Jesus also may be manifested in our body. For we who live are constantly being delivered over to death for Jesus' sake, that the life of Jesus also may be manifested in our mortal flesh" (2 Cor. 4:8-11). Paul was willing to suffer for the sake of his fellow believers and for the sake of those who needed to believe, but his greatest motivation for suffering was the glory his suffering brought to God. "For all things are for your sakes," he went on to say, "that the grace which is spreading to more and more people may cause the giving of thanks to abound to the glory of God" (v. 15). Yet he also willingly suffered for his own sake, because he knew that his travail for the sake of Christ would accrue to his own benefit. "Therefore we do not lose heart," he said, "but

447

though our outer man is decaying, yet our inner man is being renewed day by day. For momentary, light affliction is producing for us an eternal weight of glory far beyond all comparison" (vv. 16-17).

The more a believer suffers in this life for the sake of his Lord, the greater will be his capacity for glory in heaven. Jesus made this relationship clear in Matthew 20:21-23, when He told James, John, and their mother that elevation to prominence in the future kingdom will be related to experiencing the depths of the cup of suffering through humiliation here and now. As with the relationship between works and rewards (see 1 Cor. 3:12-15), the spiritual quality of our earthly life will, in some divinely determined way, affect the quality of our heavenly life. It should be added that since the ultimate destiny of believers is to glorify God, it seems certain that our heavenly rewards and glory in essence will be capacities for glorifying Him.

The suffering in this life creates reactions that reflect the genuine condition of the soul. God allows suffering to drive believers to dependence on Him—an evidence of their true salvation.

Suffering because of our faith not only gives evidence that we belong to God and are destined for heaven but also is a type of preparation for heaven. That is why Paul was so eager to experience "the fellowship of [Christ's] sufferings, being conformed to His death" (Phil. 3:10) and was so determined to "press on toward the goal for the prize of the upward call of God in Christ Jesus" (v. 14).

The more we willingly suffer for Christ's sake on earth, the more we are driven to depend on Him rather than on our own resources and the more we are infused with His power. Suffering for Christ draws us closer to Christ. Our suffering for Him also enables us to better appreciate the sufferings He endured for our sakes during His incarnation. Whatever ridicule, rejection, ostracism, loss, imprisonment, physical pain, or type of death we may have to suffer for Christ is nothing compared to what we will gain. As already cited, these sufferings, no matter how severe they seem at the time, are no more than momentary, light afflictions which are "producing for us an eternal weight of glory far beyond all comparison" (2 Cor. 4:17).

Our being born again, our being given hope through Christ's resurrection, our obtaining an imperishable inheritance with Him, and our protection by God's power give us reason to "greatly rejoice" (1 Pet. 1:3-6a). The apostle then reminds his readers, however, that "now for a little while, if necessary, you have been distressed by various trials, that the proof of your faith, being more precious than gold which is perishable, even though tested by fire, may be found to result in praise and glory and honor at the revelation of Jesus Christ" (vv. 6b-7).

Our eternal capacity to glorify God in heaven will depend on our willingness to suffer for God while we are on earth. As mentioned above, persecution of some sort is not merely a possibility for true believers but an absolute certainty. "If the world hates you," Jesus assures His followers, "you know that it has hated Me before it hated you. If you were of the world, the world would love its own; but because you are not of the world, but I chose you out of the world, therefore the world hates you. Remember the word that I said to you, 'A slave is not greater than his master.' If they persecuted Me, they will also persecute you; if they kept My word, they will keep yours also. But all these things they will do to you for My name's sake, because they do not know the One who sent Me" (John 15:18-21).

To take a strong biblical stand for Christ is to guarantee some kind of opposition, alienation, affliction, and rejection by the world. Unfortunately, it also often brings criticism from those who profess to know God but by their deeds deny Him (Titus 1:16).

Yet we also have the Lord's wonderful assurance that nothing we suffer for His sake will do us any lasting harm, because "just as the sufferings of Christ are ours in abundance, so also our comfort is abundant through Christ" (2 Cor. 1:5). We have no greater privilege and no greater guarantee of glory than to suffer for Christ's sake.

The so-called health and wealth and prosperity gospels that abound today are not true to the gospel of Christ but reflect the message of the world. The world's seemingly good news offers temporary escape from problems and hardship. Christ's good news includes the promise of suffering for His sake.

THE COMPARISON OF GLORY

For I consider that the sufferings of this present time are not worthy to be compared with the glory that is to be revealed to us. (8:18)

Logizomai (to **consider**) refers literally to numerical calculation. Figuratively, as it is used here, it refers to reaching a settled conclusion by careful study and reasoning. Paul does not merely suggest, but strongly affirms, that any suffering for Christ's sake is a small price to pay for the gracious benefits received because of that suffering. **The sufferings of this present time,** that is, our time on earth, **are not worthy to be compared with the glory that is to be revealed to us.**

In the New Testament, *pathēma* (**sufferings**) is used both of Christ's sufferings and of believers' suffering for His sake. Resist Satan, Peter admonishes, "firm in your faith, knowing that the same experiences of suffering are being accomplished by your brethren who are in the world" (1 Pet. 5:9). Paul assured the Corinthian Christians, "If we are afflicted, it is for your comfort and salvation; or if we are comforted, it is for your comfort, which is effective in the patient enduring of the same sufferings which we also suffer; and our hope for you is firmly grounded, knowing that as you are sharers of our sufferings, so also you are sharers of our comfort" (2 Cor. 1:6-7).

Jesus Christ is the supreme and perfect example of suffering for righteousness' sake. "For it was fitting for Him, for whom are all things, and through whom are all things, in bringing many sons to glory, to perfect the author of their salvation through sufferings" (Heb. 2:10). Just as suffering was essential to Christ's obedience to His Father, so it is essential to our obedience to Christ.

Those who do not know Christ have no hope when they suffer. Whatever the reason for their affliction, it does not come upon them for Christ's sake, or righteousness's sake, and therefore cannot produce for them any spiritual blessing or glory. Those who live only for this life cannot look forward to any resolution of wrongs or to any comfort for their souls. Their pain, loneliness, and afflictions serve no divine purpose and bring no divine reward.

Christians, on the other hand, have great hope, not only that their afflictions eventually will end but that those afflictions actually will add to their eternal glory. Long before the incarnation of Christ, the prophet Daniel spoke of believers' glory as "the brightness of the expanse of heaven," and as being "like the stars forever and ever" (Dan. 12:3).

As followers of Christ, our suffering comes from men, whereas our glory comes from God. Our suffering is earthly, whereas our glory is heavenly. Our suffering is short, whereas our glory is forever. Our suffering is trivial, whereas our glory is limitless. Our suffering is in our mortal and corrupted bodies, whereas our glory will be in our perfected and imperishable bodies.

The Holy Spirit Guarantees Our Glory—part 2 The Inexpressible Groans for Glory

For the anxious longing of the creation waits eagerly for the revealing of the sons of God. For the creation was subjected to futility, not of its own will, but because of Him who subjected it, in hope that the creation itself also will be set free from its slavery to corruption into the freedom of the glory of the children of God. For we know that the whole creation groans and suffers the pains of childbirth together until now. And not only this, but also we ourselves, having the first fruits of the Spirit, even we ourselves groan within ourselves, waiting eagerly for our adoption as sons, the redemption of our body. For in hope we have been saved, but hope that is seen is not hope; for why does one also hope for what he sees? But if we hope for what we do not see, with perseverance we wait eagerly for it.

And in the same way the Spirit also helps our weakness; for we do not know how to pray as we should, but the Spirit Himself intercedes for us with groanings too deep for words; and He who searches the hearts knows what the mind of the Spirit is, because He intercedes for the saints according to the will of God. (8:19-27)

In his climactic presentation of the ministry of the Holy Spirit in securing the no-condemnation status of believers (see 8:1), Paul focuses on His securing us by guaranteeing our future glory (vv. 17-30). In he previous chapter of this volume we studied the incomparable gains that believers possess because of their God-promised glory (vv. 17-18).

In the present chapter Paul focuses our attention on the anticipation of that glory—the incomparable groans—of creation (vv. 19-22), of believers (vv. 23-25), and of the Holy Spirit Himself (vv. 26-27). A groan is an audible expression of anguish due to physical, emotional, or spiritual pain. These groanings bewail a condition that is painful, unsatisfying, and sorrowful—a cry for deliverance from a torturing experience.

THE GROANING OF CREATION

For the anxious longing of the creation waits eagerly for the revealing of the sons of God. For the creation was subjected to futility, not of its own will, but because of Him who subjected it, in hope that the creation itself also will be set free from its slavery to corruption into the freedom of the glory of the children of God. For we know that the whole creation groans and suffers the pains of childbirth together until now. (8:19-22)

The first groan is the personified lament coming from the created universe as it now exists in the corrupted condition caused by the Fall.

Apokaradokia (**anxious longing**) is an especially vivid word that literally refers to watching with outstretched head, and suggests standing on tiptoes with the eyes looking ahead with intent expectancy. The prefix *apo* adds the idea of fixed absorption and concentration on that which is anticipated. **The creation** is standing on tiptoes, as it were, as it **waits eagerly for the revealing of the sons of God.**

Jews were familiar with God's promise of a redeemed world, a renewed **creation.** On behalf of the Lord, Isaiah predicted, "For behold, I create new heavens and a new earth; and the former things shall not be remembered or come to mind" (Isa. 65:17). Jews anticipated a glorious time when all pain, oppression, slavery, anxiety, sorrow, and persecution would end and the Lord would establish His own perfect kingdom of peace and righteousness.

Even nonbiblical Jewish writings reflect that longing. The Apocalypse of Baruch describes an expected and long-awaited future utopia:

> The vine shall yield its fruit ten thousand fold, and on each vine there shall be a thousand branches; and each branch shall produce a thousand clusters; and each cluster produce a thousand grapes; and each grape a cor of wine.

And those who have hungered shall rejoice; moreover, also, they shall behold marvels every day. For winds shall go forth from before me to bring every morning the fragrance of aromatic fruits, and at the close of the day clouds distilling the dews of health. (29:5)

Jewish sections of Sibylline Oracles record similar expectations. "And earth, and all the trees, and the innumerable flocks of sheep shall give their true fruit to mankind, of wine and of sweet honey and of white milk and of corn, which to men is the most excellent gift of all" (3:620-33). Later in the oracles it says,

Earth, the universal mother, shall give to mortals her best fruit in countless store of corn, wine and oil. Yea, from heaven shall come a sweet draught of luscious honey. The trees shall yield their proper fruits, and rich flocks, and kine, and lambs of sheep and kids of goats. He will cause sweet fountains of white milk to burst forth. And the cities shall be full of good things, and the fields rich; neither shall there be any sword throughout the land or battle-din; nor shall the earth be convulsed any more, nor shall there be any more drought throughout the land, no famine, or hail to work havoc on the crops. (3:744-56)

Creation does not here include the heavenly angels, who, although created beings, are not subject to corruption. The term obviously does not include Satan and his host of fallen angels, the demons. They have no desire for a godly, sinless state and know they are divinely sentenced to eternal torment. Believers are not included in that term either, because they are mentioned separately in verses 23-25. Nor is Paul referring to unbelievers. The only remaining part of **creation** is the nonrational part, including animals and plants and all inanimate things such as the mountains, rivers, plains, seas, and heavenly bodies.

Jews were familiar with such a personification of nature. Isaiah had used it when he wrote that "The wilderness and the desert will be glad, and the Arabah will rejoice and blossom" (Isa. 35:1), and later that "the mountains and the hills will break forth into shouts of joy before you, and all the trees of the field will clap their hands" (55:12).

Waits eagerly translates a form of the verb *apekdechomai*, which refers to waiting in great anticipation but with patience. The form of the Greek verb gives the added connotations of readiness, preparedness, and continuance until the expected event occurs.

Revealing translates *apokalupsis*, which refers to an uncovering, unveiling, or revelation. It is this word from which the English name of the book of Revelation is derived (see Rev. 1:1). The world does not comprehend who Christians really are. In his first epistle, John explained to fellow believers: "See how great a love the Father has bestowed upon us, that we should be called children of God; and such we are. For this reason the world does not know us, because it did not know Him" (1 John 3:1).

In the present age, the world is unable to distinguish absolutely between Christians and nonbelievers. People who call themselves Christians walk, dress, and talk much like everyone else. Many unbelievers have high standards of behavior. On the other hand, unfortunately, many professing Christians give little evidence of salvation. But at the appointed time God will reveal those who are truly His.

At **the revealing of the sons of God,** "when Christ, who is our life, is revealed, then [believers] also will be revealed with Him in glory" (Col. 3:4). At that time, all believers will be eternally separated from sin and their unredeemed humanness, to be glorified with Christ's own holiness and splendor.

When Adam and Eve sinned by disobeying God's command, not only mankind but the earth and all the rest of the world was cursed and corrupted. After the Fall, God said to Adam,

> Because you have listened to the voice of your wife, and have eaten from the tree about which I commanded you, saying, "You shall not eat from it"; cursed is the ground because of you; in toil you shall eat of it all the days of your life. Both thorns and thistles it shall grow for you; and you shall eat the plants of the field; by the sweat of your face you shall eat bread, till you return to the ground, because from it you were taken; for you are dust, and to dust you shall return. (Gen. 3:17-19)

Before the Fall, no weeds or poisonous plants, no thorns or thistles or anything else existed that could cause man misery or harm. But after the Fall, **the creation was subjected to futility, not of its own will, but because of Him who subjected it.** *Mataiotēs* (**futility**) carries the idea of being without success, of being unable to achieve a goal or purpose. Because of man's sin, no part of nature now exists as God intended it to be and as it originally was. The verb **was subjected** indicates by its form that nature did not curse itself but was cursed by something or someone else. Paul goes on to reveal that the curse on nature was executed by its Creator. God Himself **subjected it** to futility.

Although various environmental organizations and government agencies today make noble attempts to protect and restore natural resources and regions, they are helpless to turn the tide of corruption that has continually devastated both man and his environment since the Fall. Such is the destructiveness of sin that one man's disobedience brought corruption to the entire universe. Decay, disease, pain, death, natural disaster, pollution, and all other forms of evil will never cease until the One who sent the curse removes it and creates a new heaven and a new earth (2 Pet. 3:13; Rev. 21:1).

No less a naturalist than John Muir was in serious error when he wrote that nature is "unfallen and undepraved" and that only man is a "blighting touch." The sentimental environmentalists of our time advocate living in some relaxed and easy "harmony with nature." Some are crying for the government to take us back to living in the Dark Ages, when, they assume, people and nature were in harmony. All the corruptions of this fallen environment were different in the past from what technology and industry have wrought—but perhaps even more deadly. Certainly disease and death, as well as exposure to the natural elements and disasters, were much greater in the past. And when people were supposedly living nearer nature, they had less comfort, more pain, harder times, more disease, and died younger. This is not a friendly earth but a violent and dangerous one. It is a ridiculous fantasy to think it is not cursed and that it naturally yields a comfortable life.

In spite of this curse, however, much of the beauty, grandeur, and benefits of the natural world remains. Although they all deteriorate, flowers are still beautiful, mountains are still grand, forests are still magnificent, the heavenly bodies are still majestic, food still brings nourishment and is a pleasure to eat, and water still brings refreshment and sustains life. Despite the terrible curse that He inflicted on the earth, God's majesty and gracious provision for mankind is still evident wherever one looks. It is for that reason that no person has an excuse for not believing in God: "Since the creation of the world His invisible attributes, His eternal power and divine nature, have been clearly seen, being understood through what has been made, so that they are without excuse" (Rom. 1:20).

Nature's destiny is inseparably linked to man's. Because man sinned, the rest of **creation** was corrupted with him. Likewise, when man's glory is divinely restored, the natural world will be restored as well. Therefore, Paul says, there is **hope** even for the natural creation itself, which **will be set free from its slavery to corruption into the freedom of the glory of the children of God.** In other words, just as man's sin brought corruption to the universe, so man's restoration to righteousness will be accompanied by the restoration of the earth and its universe to their divinely-intended perfection and glory.

In physics, the law of entrophy refers to the constant and irreversible degradation of matter and energy in the universe to increasing disorder. that scientific law clearly contradicts the theory of evolution, which is based on the premise that the natural world is inclined to continual self-improvement. But it is evident even in a simple garden plot that, when it is untended, it deteriorates. Weeds and other undesirable plants will choke out the good ones. The natural bent of the universe—whether of humans, animals, plants, or the inanimate elements of the earth and heavens—is obviously and demonstrably downward, not upward. It could not be otherwise while the world remains in **slavery to the corruption** of sin.

Yet despite their continual corruption and degeneration, neither man nor the universe itself will bring about their ultimate destruction. That is in the province of God alone, and there is no need to fear an independently initiated human holocaust. Men need fear only the God whom they rebelliously spurn and oppose. The destiny of earth is entirely in the hands of its Creator, and that destiny includes God's total destruction of the sin-cursed universe. "The day of the Lord will come like a thief, in which the heavens will pass away with a roar and the elements will be destroyed with intense heat, and the earth and its works will be burned up" (2 Pet. 3:10). That destruction will be on a scale infinitely more powerful than any man-made devices could achieve.

In his vision on Patmos, John "saw a new heaven and a new earth; for the first heaven and the first earth passed away, and there is no longer any sea. . . . and [God] shall wipe away every tear from their eyes; and there shall no longer be any death; there shall no longer be any mourning, or crying, or pain; the first things have passed away. And He who sits on the throne said, 'Behold, I am making all things new.' And He said, 'Write, for these words are faithful and true'" (Rev. 21:1, 4-5).

It is for that promised time of redemption and restoration that all nature groans in hope and expectation. As with "was subjected" in the previous verse, the verb **will be set free** is passive, indicating that nature will not restore itself but will be restored by God, who Himself long ago subjected it to corruption and futility.

Jesus referred to that awesome time as "the regeneration," a time when the old sinful environment will be radically judged and be replaced with God's new and righteous one. "Truly I say to you," He told the disciples, "that you who have followed Me, in the regeneration when the Son of Man will sit on His glorious throne, you also shall sit upon twelve thrones, judging the twelve tribes of Israel" (Matt. 19:28).

The freedom of the glory of the children of God refers to the time when all believers will be liberated from sin, liberated from the flesh, and liberated from their humanness. At that time we will begin to share eternally in God's own **glory,** with which **God** will clothe all His precious **children.** John reminds us, "Beloved, now we are children of God, and it has not appeared as yet what we shall be. We know that, when He appears, we shall be like Him, because we shall see Him just as He is" (1 John 3:2). In describing that glorious day, Paul wrote,

Behold, I tell you a mystery; we shall not all sleep, but we shall all be changed, in a moment, in the twinkling of an eye, at the last trumpet; for the trumpet will sound, and the dead will be raised imperishable, and we shall be changed. For this perishable must put on the imperishable, and this mortal must put on immortality. But when this perishable will have put on the imperishable, and this mortal will have put on immortality, then will come about the saying that is written, "Death is swallowed up in victory." (1 Cor. 15:51-54)

It is impossible for our finite minds to comprehend such divine mysteries. But by God's own Holy Spirit within us we can believe all of His revealed truth and rejoice with absolute and confident hope that our eternal life with our Father in heaven is secure. We acknowledge with Paul that "our citizenship is in heaven, from which also we eagerly wait for a Savior, the Lord Jesus Christ; who will transform the body of our humble state into conformity with the body of His glory, by the exertion of the power that He has even to subject all things to Himself" (Phil. 3:20-21).

We also acknowledge with the apostle that nature also awaits with hope for our redemption, a redemption it will share with us in its own way. But until that wonderful day and in anticipation of it, **the whole creation groans and suffers the pains of childbirth together until now.**

Stenazō (**groans**) refers to the utterances of a person who is caught in a dreadful situation and has no immediate prospect of deliverance. The term is used in its noun form by Luke to describe the desperate utterances of the Israelites during their bondage in Egypt (Acts 7:34). The verb is used by the writer of Hebrews to describe the frustration and grief of church leaders caused by immature and unruly members (13:17).

The groaning an suffering of the **creation** will one day cease, because God will deliver it from its corruption and futility. In the meanwhile, it endures **the pains of childbirth.** Like Eve, whose sin brought the curse of painful human childbirth (Gen. 3:16), nature endures its own kind of labor pains. But also like Eve and her descendants, nature's **pains of childbirth** presage new life.

Paul makes no mention of how or when the world will be made new. Nor does he give the phases of that cosmic regeneration or the sequence of events. Many other passages of Scripture shed light on the details of the curses being lifted (see Isa. 30:23-24; 35:1-7; etc.) and the ultimate creation of a new heaven and a new earth (2 Pet. 3:13; Rev. 21:1), but Paul's purpose here is to assure his readers in general terms that God's master plan of redemption encompasses the entire universe.

D. Martyn Lloyd-Jones wrote with deep insight:

I wonder whether the phenomenon of the Spring supplies us with a part answer. Nature every year, as it were, makes an effort to renew itself, to produce something permanent; it has come out of the death and the darkness of all that is so true of the Winter. In the Spring it seems to be trying to produce a perfect creation, to be going through some kind of birth-pangs year by year. But unfortunately it does not succeed, for Spring leads only to Summer, whereas Summer leads to Autumn, and Autumn to Winter. Poor old nature tries every year to defeat the "vanity," the principle of death and decay and disintegration that is in it. But it cannot do so. It fails every time. It still goes on trying, as if it feels things should be different and better; but it never succeeds. So it goes on "groaning and travailing in pain together until now." It has been doing so for a very long time . . . but nature still repeats the effort annually. (*Romans* [Grand Rapids: Zondervan, 1980], 6:59-60)

THE GROANING OF BELIEVERS

And not only this, but also we ourselves, having the first fruits of the Spirit, even we ourselves groan within ourselves, waiting eagerly for our adoption as sons, the redemption of our body. For in hope we have been saved, but hope that is seen is not hope; for why does one also hope for what he sees? But if we hope for what we do not see, with perseverance we wait eagerly for it. (8:23-25)

Not only does the natural creation groan for deliverance from the destructive consequences of sin into the promised new universe, **but also we ourselves**, that is, believers. It is the redemption of believers that is central to God's ultimate cosmic regeneration, because believers—as His own children, redeemed and adopted into His heavenly family in response to their faith in His beloved Son, Jesus Christ—are the heirs of His glorious, eternal, and righteous kingdom.

Every true believer agonizes at times over the appalling manifestations and consequences of sin—in his own life, in the lives of others, and even in the natural world. Because we have **the first fruits of the Spirit,** we are spiritually sensitized to the corruption of sin in and around us.

Because the Holy **Spirit** now indwells us, His work in us and through us is a type of spiritual **first fruits.** They are a foretaste of the glory that awaits us in heaven, when our corrupted and mortal bodies are exchanged for ones that are incorruptible and immortal. Although we will not be totally free of sin's power as long as we are in our present bodies, the Lord has given us complete victory over the dominion and bondage of sin. When we experience the Holy Spirit's empowering us to turn from iniquity and to truly worship, serve, obey, and love God, we have a taste of the future completed and perfected renewal He will work in us at the resurrection.

Because every genuine believer is indwelt by the Holy Spirit (Rom. 8:9), every genuine believer will to some degree manifest the fruit of the Spirit that Paul enumerates in Galatians 5:22-23, namely, "love, joy, peace, patience, kindness, goodness, faithfulness, gentleness, self-control." Every time we see Him working His righteousness in and through us, we yearn all the more to be freed of our remaining sin and spiritual weakness. Because of our divinely-bestowed sensitivity to sin, **we ourselves groan within ourselves** over the dreadful curse of sin that is still manifested by our remaining humanness.

Acknowledging his own sinfulness, David cried out, "My iniquities are gone over my head; as a heavy burden they weigh too much for me, . . . Lord, all my desire is before Thee; and my sighing is not hidden from Thee. My heart throbs, my strength fails me; and the light of my eyes, even that has gone from me" (Ps. 38:4, 9-10).

Paul grieved over the remnants of his humanness that clung to him like a rotten garment that could not be cast off. That reality brought him great spiritual frustration and anguish. "Wretched man that I am!" he lamented, "Who will set me free from the body of this death?" (Rom. 7:24). In another epistle he reminds all believers of their same plight: "For indeed while we are in this tent, we groan, being burdened, because we do not want to be unclothed, but to be clothed, in order that what is mortal may be swallowed up by life" (2 Cor. 5:4). As long as we are in the "tent" of our human body, we will never fully escape sin's corruption in our lives. That truth causes Christians to suffer times of deep inner distress over the debilitating sinfulness that still clings to them.

As believers, we therefore find ourselves **waiting eagerly** in anticipation of **our adoption as sons, the redemption of our body.** The New Testament speaks of believers as those who are already the adopted children of God, but whose adoption awaits ultimate perfection. Just as there is never salvation that is not completed, neither is there divine adoption that is never completed. A child of God need never fear that he might be cast out of his spiritual family or never enter his heavenly home.

Puritan pastor Thomas Watson said,

> The godly may act faintly in religion, the pulse of their affections may beat low. The exercise of grace may be hindered, as when the course of water is stopped. Instead of grace working in the godly, corruption may work; instead of patience, murmuring; instead of heavenliness, earthliness. . . . Thus lively and vigorous may corruption be in the regenerate; they may fall into enormous sins. . . . [But] though their grace may be drawn low, it is not drawn dry; though grace may be abated, it is not abolished. . . . Grace may

suffer an eclipse, not a dissolution. . . . a believer may fall from some degrees of grace, but not from the state of grace. (*A Body of Divinity* [reprint, Edinburgh: Banner of Truth, 1974], pp. 280, 284-85)

Scripture teaches that the believer's salvation is secured by God the Father, by the Son, and by the Holy Spirit. Referring to God the Father, Paul assured the Corinthians, "He who establishes us with you in Christ and anointed us is God, who also sealed us and gave us the Spirit in our hearts as a pledge" (2 Cor. 1:21-22; cf. 2 Tim. 2:19). The Father not only grants salvation to those who trust in His Son but also seals their salvation and gives the indwelling Holy Spirit as the guarantor. "Blessed be the God and Father of our Lord Jesus Christ," Peter declared, "who according to His great mercy has caused us to be born again to a living hope through the resurrection of Jesus Christ from the dead, to obtain an inheritance which is imperishable and undefiled and will not fade away, reserved in heaven for you, who are protected by the power of God through faith for a salvation ready to be revealed in the last time" (1 Pet. 1:3-5). Although persevering faith is indispensable to salvation, Peter emphasizes that, by God the Father's own initiative and power, He "caused us to be born again" and in that same power He sustains us toward the inheritance that our new birth brings, an inheritance that is "imperishable and undefiled and will not fade away." It is divinely "reserved in heaven" for each believer, who is divinely preserved to receive it. Whoever belongs to God belongs to Him forever.

In order to point up the absolute and incontrovertible security of those who trust in Jesus Christ, the writer of Hebrews declared, "In the same way God, desiring even more to show to the heirs of the promise the unchangeableness of His purpose, interposed with an oath, in order that by two unchangeable things, in which it is impossible for God to lie, we may have strong encouragement, we who have fled for refuge in laying hold of the hope set before us. This hope we have as an anchor of the soul, a hope both sure and steadfast and one which enters within the veil" (Heb. 6:17-19).

God the Son also secures the believer's salvation. "All that the Father gives Me shall come to Me," Jesus declared, "and the one who comes to Me I will certainly not cast out" (John 6:37). Paul assured the Corinthian church, which had more than its share of immature and disobedient believers, that "even as the testimony concerning Christ was confirmed in you, so that you are not lacking in any gift, awaiting eagerly the revelation of our Lord Jesus Christ, who shall also confirm you to the end, blameless in the day of our Lord Jesus Christ" (1 Cor. 1:6-8; cf. Col. 1:22). In other words, their relationship to Christ not only had been confirmed when they were justified but would remain confirmed by the Lord Himself until their glorification at His return (cf. 1 Thess. 3:13).

Later in that epistle Paul reminds us that "faithful is He who calls you, and He also will bring it to pass" (1 Thess. 5:24). The ongoing, mediatorial, intercessory work of Jesus Christ in heaven unalterably secures our eternal reward.

God the Spirit also secures the believer's salvation, by a work that Scripture sometimes refers to as the Spirit's sealing. In ancient times, the seal, or signet, was a mark of authenticity or of a completed transaction. The seal of a monarch or other distinguished person represented his authority and power. For example, when Daniel was thrown into the den of lions, King Darius had a large stone placed across the entrance and sealed "with his own signet ring and with the signet rings of his nobles, so that nothing might be changed in regard to Daniel" (Dan. 6:17). In an infinitely more significant and spiritual way, the Holy Spirit seals the salvation of every believer, which, by divine promise and protection, can never be altered.

Paul assured the Corinthian believers that "He who establishes us with you in Christ and anointed us is God, who also sealed us and gave us the Spirit in our hearts as a pledge" (2 Cor. 1:21-22). In similar words, he assured the Ephesians that "In Him [Christ], you also, after listening to the message of truth, the gospel of your salvation — having also believed, you were sealed in Him with the Holy Spirit of promise" (Eph. 1:13; cf. 4:30).

The ideas of partial or temporary salvation not only are foreign to the teaching of Scripture but completely contradict it. No true believer need ever fear loss of salvation. At the moment of conversion his soul is redeemed, purified, and eternally secured in God's family and kingdom.

Believers should be concerned about sin in their lives, but not because they might sin themselves out of God's grace. Because of God's promise and power, that is impossible. Until we are glorified and fully liberated from sin through **the redemption of our body**, we still have unredeemed bodies that make it very much possible for sin to harm us and to grieve our Lord. As the term is often used in the New Testament, **body** is not limited to a person's physical being but relates to the whole of his unredeemed humanness, in particular to the remaining susceptibility to sin.

It is only the **body**, the mortal humanness of a believer, that is yet to be redeemed. The inner person is already a completely new creation, a partaker of God's nature and indwelt by God's Spirit. "Therefore if any man is in Christ," Paul says, "he is a new creature; the old things passed away; behold, new things have come" (2 Cor. 5:17). Peter assures us that God's "divine power has granted to us everything pertaining to life and godliness, through the true knowledge of Him who called us by His own glory and excellence. For by these He has granted to us His precious and magnificent promises, in order that by them you might become partakers of the divine nature, having escaped the corruption that is in the world by lust" (2 Pet. 1:3-4).

Because believers are already new creatures possessing the divine nature, their souls are fit for heaven and eternal glory. They love God, hate sin, and have holy longings for obedience to the Word. But while on earth they are kept in bondage by their mortal bodies, which are still corrupted by sin and its consequences. Christians are holy seeds, as it were, encased in an unholy shell. Incarcerated in a prison of flesh and subjected to its weaknesses and imperfections, we therefore eagerly await an event that is divinely guaranteed but is yet to transpire—**the redemption of our body.**

Paul has already explained that "if we [believers] have become united with Him [Christ] in the likeness of His death, certainly we shall be also in the likeness of His resurrection, knowing this, that our old self was crucified with Him, that our body of sin might be done away with, that we should no longer be slaves to sin" (Rom. 6:5-6). The old man with his old sinful nature is dead, but the corrupted **body** in which he dwelt is still present. That is why, a few verses later, Paul admonishes believers not to "let sin reign in your mortal body that you should obey its lusts" and not to "go on presenting the members of your body to sin as instruments of unrighteousness; but present yourselves to God as those alive from the dead, and your members as instruments of righteousness to God" (vv. 12-13). Because we are still capable of sinning, we should be continually on guard to resist and overcome sin in the Spirit's power (vv. 14-17).

Paul also has already explained "that the Law is spiritual; but I am of flesh, sold into bondage to sin. For that which I am doing, I do not understand; for I am not practicing what I would like to do, but I am doing the very thing I hate" (Rom. 7:14-15). "But if I do the very thing I do not wish to do," he continues, "I agree with the Law, confessing that it is good. So now, no longer am I the one doing it, but sin which indwells me. For I know that nothing good dwells in me, that is, in my flesh; for the wishing is present in me, but the doing of the good is not" (vv. 16-18).

It is encouragingly hopeful for Christians to realize that their falling into sin does not have its source in their deepest inner being, their new and holy nature in Christ. When they sin, they do so because of the desires and promptings of the flesh—that is, their bodies, their remaining humanness—which they cannot escape until they go to be with the Lord. Summing up that vital truth, Paul said, "Thanks be to God through Jesus Christ our Lord! So then, on the one hand I myself with my mind am serving the law of God, but on the other, with my flesh the law of sin" (Rom. 7:25).

As noted above, our souls are already fully redeemed and are fit for heaven. But the fleshly, outer clothing of the old, sinful person is still corrupted and awaits redemption. "For our citizenship is in heaven," Paul explains, "from which also we eagerly wait for a Savior, the Lord Jesus Christ; who will transform the body of our humble state into conformity with the body of His glory, by the exertion of the power that He has even to subject all things to Himself" (Phil. 3:20-21).

It is hardly possible not to wonder what kind of resurrected and redeemed body believers will have in heaven, but it is foolish to speculate about it apart from what Scripture teaches. Anticipating such curiosity, Paul told the Corinthians:

> Someone will say, "How are the dead raised? And with what kind of body do they come?" You fool! That which you sow does not come to life unless it dies; and that which you sow, you do not sow the body which is to be, but a bare grain, perhaps of wheat or of something else. But God gives it a body just as He wished, and to each of the seeds a body of its own. All flesh is not the same flesh, but there is one flesh of men, and another flesh of beasts, and another flesh of birds, and another of fish. There are also heavenly bodies and earthly bodies, but the glory of the heavenly is one, and the glory of the earthly is another. There is one glory of the sun, and another glory of the moon, and another glory of the stars; for star differs from star in glory. (1 Cor. 15:35-41)

Paul's point in the first analogy is that a seed bears no resemblance to the plant or tree into which it will grow. As far as size is concerned, some relatively large seeds produce small plants, whereas some smaller seeds produce large trees. Many different kinds of seed look much alike, and the total variety of seeds has yet to be calculated. If given a handful of seeds that were all different and came from various parts of the world, not even an experienced farmer, much less the average person, could identify all of them. Not until it is sown and the resulting plant begins to mature can the kind of seed be accurately identified. The same principle applies in relation to our natural and spiritual bodies. We cannot possibly determine what our future spiritual bodies will be like by looking at our present physical bodies. We will have to wait to see.

Paul also points out the obvious fact that animate creatures vary widely in their appearance and nature, and that, without exception, like produces like. The genetic code of every living species is distinct and unique. No amount of attempted interbreeding or change of diet can turn a fish into a bird, or a horse into a dog or cat.

There is also variety in the heavenly bodies, an immeasurably greater variety than people in Paul's day were aware of. The apostle's point in mentioning the animals and heavenly bodies seems to be that of calling attention to the vast magnitude and variation of God's creation and to the inability of man even to come close to comprehending it.

The Bible discloses very little about the nature of a believer's resurrected body. Paul goes on to tell the Corinthians, "So also is the resurrection of the dead. It is sown a perishable body, it is raised an imperishable body; it is sown in dishonor, it is raised in glory; it is sown in weakness, it is raised in power; it is sown a natural body, it is raised a spiritual body. If there is a natural body, there is also a spiritual body" (1 Cor. 15:42-44).

Because we will ultimately be like Christ, we know that our resurrected bodies will be like His. As noted above, Paul assures us that, "if we have become united with Him in the likeness of His death, certainly we shall be also in the likeness of His resurrection" (Rom. 6:5). In his epistle to Philippi he explains further that our Lord "will transform the body of our humble state into conformity with the body of His glory, by the exertion of the power that He has even to subject all things to Himself" (Phil. 3:21).

During the period between His resurrection and ascension, Jesus' body still bore the physical marks of His crucifixion (John 20:20) and He was able to eat (Luke 24:30). He still looked like Himself, yet even His closest disciples could not recognize Him unless He allowed them to (Luke 24:13-16, 30-31; John 20:14-16). He could be touched and felt (John 20:17, 27), yet He could appear and disappear in an instant and could pass through closed doors (John 20:19, 26).

Although our redeemed bodies will in some way be like Christ's, we will not know exactly what they will be like until we meet our Savior face to face (1 John 3:2). Paul's primary purpose in 1 Corinthians 15 and Romans 8 is to emphasize that our resurrected bodies, regardless of their form, appearance, or capabilities, will be sinless, righteous, and immortal.

He continues to explain that **in hope we have been saved. Hope** is inseparable from salvation. Our salvation was planned by God in ages past, bestowed in the present, and is now characterized by **hope** for its future completion.

The believer's **hope** is not based on wishful thinking or probability, but on the integrity of the clear promises of the Lord. As already cited above, "All that the Father gives Me shall come to Me," Jesus declared, "and the one who comes to Me I will certainly not cast out" (John 6:37). Our **hope** is not that we might not lose our salvation but that, by our Lord's own guarantee, we *cannot* and *will not* lose it.

The writer of Hebrews assures us that "God, desiring even more to show to the heirs of the promise the unchangeableness of His purpose, interposed with an oath, in order that by two unchangeable things, in which it is impossible for God to lie, we may have strong encouragement, we who have fled for refuge in laying hold of the hope set before us. This hope we have as an anchor of the soul, a hope both sure and steadfast and one which enters within the veil" (Heb. 6:17-19). Paul refers to our hope of salvation as a helmet, symbolizing our divine protection from the blows of doubt that Satan sends to crush our hope (1 Thess. 5:8).

As Jesus made clear in the parable of the wheat and tares (Matt. 13) and in the story of the fruitless branches (John 15), there will always be some who bear the name of Christ who do not genuinely belong to Him. And, by the same token, there are true believers whose lives sometimes give little evidence of salvation. But as we shall continue to see to the end of this chapter, the Word of God is unequivocal in declaring that everyone who is saved by Jesus Christ will forever belong to Him. Although it is quite possible for a sinful Christian to struggle with the assurance of salvation and with the joy and comfort which that assurance brings, it is not possible for him to lose salvation itself.

It is true, on the other hand, that the completion of our salvation is presently a **hope** and not yet a reality. Explaining the obvious, Paul states the axiomatic truth that **hope that is seen is not hope; for why does one also hope for what he sees?** In other words, in this life we cannot expect to experience the reality of our glorification but only the **hope** of it. But since the believer's **hope** is based on God's promise, the completion of his salvation is more certain by far than anything **he sees** with his eyes. As we shall see later, the believer's salvation is so secure that his glorification is spoken of in the past tense (see Rom. 8:30).

Therefore, Paul continues, **if we hope for what we do not see, with perseverance we wait eagerly for it.** "For I am confident of this very thing," Paul assured the Thessalonian believers, "that He who began a good work in you will perfect it until the day of Christ Jesus" (Phil. 1:6). Because salvation is completely God's work and because He cannot lie, it is absolutely impossible for us to lose what He has given us and promises never to take away. It is in light of that absolute certainty that Peter admonishes: "Gird your minds for action, keep sober in spirit, fix your hope completely on the grace to be brought to you at the revelation of Jesus Christ" (1 Pet. 1:13). It is for their faithfully holding to that hope that Paul commends the Thessalonians, assuring them that he, Silvanus, and Timothy were "constantly bearing in mind [their] work of faith and labor of love and steadfastness of hope in our Lord Jesus Christ in the presence of our God and Father, knowing, brethren beloved by God, His choice of you" (1 Thess. 1:3-4). In other words, our certainty of salvation does not rest in our choosing God but in His choosing us, even "before the foundation of the world" (Eph. 1:4).

THE GROANING OF THE HOLY SPIRIT

And in the same way the Spirit also helps our weakness; for we

do not know how to pray as we should, but the Spirit Himself intercedes for us with groanings too deep for words; and He who searches the hearts knows what the mind of the Spirit is, because He intercedes for the saints according to the will of God. (8:26-27)

In the same way refers back to the groans of the creation and of believers for redemption from the corruption and defilement of sin. Here Paul reveals the immeasurably comforting truth that the Holy Spirit comes alongside us and all creation in groaning for God's ultimate day of restoration and His eternal reign of righteousness.

Because of our remaining humanness and susceptibility to sin and doubt, the Holy **Spirit also helps** us in **our weakness.** In this context, **weakness** doubtless refers to our human condition in general, not to specific weaknesses. The point is that, even after salvation, we are characterized by spiritual **weakness.** Acting morally, speaking the truth, witnessing for the Lord, or doing any other good thing happens only by the power of **the Spirit** working in and through us despite our human limitations.

Several times in his letter to the Philippians Paul beautifully pictures that divine-human relationship. Speaking of his own needs, he said, "I know that this shall turn out for my deliverance through your prayers and the provision of the Spirit of Jesus Christ" (Phil. 1:19). **The Spirit** supplies us with all we need to be faithful, effective, and protected children of God. In the following chapter he admonishes, "So then, my beloved, just as you have always obeyed, not as in my presence only, but now much more in my absence, work out your salvation with fear and trembling; for it is God who is at work in you, both to will and to work for His good pleasure" (Phil. 2:12-13). The Spirit of God works unrelentingly in us to do what we could never do alone—bring about the perfect will of God.

To make clear how the Spirit works, Paul turns to the subject of prayer. Although we are redeemed and absolutely secure in our adoption as God's children, nevertheless **we do not know how to pray as we should.** Paul does not elaborate on our inability to pray as we ought, but his statement is all-encompassing. Because of our imperfect perspectives, finite minds, human frailties, and spiritual limitations, we are not able to pray in absolute consistency with God's will. Many times we are not even aware that spiritual needs exist, much less know how best they should be met. Even the Christian who prays sincerely, faithfully, and regularly cannot possibly know God's purposes concerning all of his own needs or the needs of others for whom he prays.

Jesus told Peter, "Behold, Satan has demanded permission to sift you like wheat; but I have prayed for you, that your faith may not fail; and you, when once you have turned again, strengthen your brothers"

(Luke 22:31-32). Fortunately for Peter, Jesus kept His word despite the apostle's foolish bravado. Not only was Peter no match for Satan but he soon proved that his devotion to Christ could not even withstand the taunts of a few strangers (vv. 54-60). How glorious that our spiritual security rests in the Lord's faithfulness rather than in our vacillating commitment.

Even the apostle Paul, who lived so near to God and so faithfully and sacrificially proclaimed His gospel, did not always know how best to pray. He knew, for example, that God had allowed Satan to inflict him with an unspecified "thorn in the flesh." That affliction guarded Paul against pride over being "caught up into Paradise." But after a while Paul became weary of the infirmity, which doubtless was severe, and he prayed earnestly that it might be removed. After three entreaties, the Lord told Paul that he should be satisfied with the abundance of divine grace by which he was already sustained in the trial (see 2 Cor. 12:3-9). Paul's request did not correspond to the Lord's will for him at that time. Even when we do not know what God wants, the indwelling **Spirit Himself intercedes for us,** bringing our needs before God even when we do not know what they are or when we pray about them unwisely.

Paul emphasizes that our help is from **the Spirit Himself.** His divine help not only is personal but direct. **The Spirit** does not simply provide our security but is **Himself** our security. The Spirit intercedes on our behalf in a way, Paul says, that is totally beyond human comprehension, **with groanings too deep for words.** The Holy Spirit unites with us in our desire to be freed from our corrupted earthly bodies and to be with God forever in our glorified heavenly bodies.

Contrary to the interpretation of most charismatics, the **groanings** of the Spirit are not utterances in unknown tongues, much less ecstatic gibberish that has no rational content. As Paul says explicitly, the groans are not even audible and are inexpressible in **words.** Yet those groans carry profound content, namely divine appeals for the spiritual welfare of each believer. In a way infinitely beyond our understanding, these **groanings** represent what might be called intertrinitarian communication, divine articulations by the Holy Spirit to the Father. Paul affirmed this truth to the Corinthians when he declared, "For who among men knows the thoughts of a man except the spirit of the man, which is in him? Even so the thoughts of God no one knows except the Spirit of God" (1 Cor. 2:11).

We remain justified and righteous before God the Father only because the Son and the Holy Spirit, as our constant advocates and intercessors, represent us before Him. It is only because of that joint and unceasing divine work on our behalf that we will enter heaven. Christ "is able to save forever those who draw near to God through Him, since He always lives to make intercession for them" (Heb. 7:25). Jesus' divine work of redemption in a believer's heart begins at the time of conversion, but it does not end until that saint is in heaven, glorified and made as righteous as God is righteous, because he possesses the full righteousness of Christ. That is guaranteed by the heavenly high priestly work of our Lord and by the earthly indwelling Holy **Spirit,** which also make secure the divine adoption and heavenly destiny of every believer.

If it were not for the sustaining power of the Spirit within us and Christ's continual mediation for us as High Priest (Heb. 7:25-26), our remaining humanness would have immediately engulfed us again in sin the moment after we were justified. If for an instant Christ and the Holy Spirit were to stop their sustaining intercession for us, we would, in that instant, fall back into our sinful, damnable state of separation from God.

If such a falling away could happen, faith in Christ would give us only temporary spiritual life, subject at any moment to loss. But Jesus offers no life but eternal life, which, by definition, cannot be lost. To those who believe, Jesus said, "I give eternal life, . . . and they shall never perish; and no one shall snatch them out of My hand" (John 10:28; cf. 17:2-3; Acts 13:48). To have faith in Jesus Christ and to have eternal life are scripturally synonymous.

Were it not for the sustaining and intercessory work of the Son and the Spirit on behalf of believers, Satan and his false teachers could easily deceive God's elect (see Matt. 24:24) and could undermine the completion of their salvation. But if such a thing were possible, God's election would be meaningless. Satan knows that believers would be helpless apart from the sustaining work of the Son and the Spirit, and in his arrogant pride he vainly wars against those two divine persons of the Godhead. He knows that if somehow he could interrupt that divine protection, once-saved souls would fall from grace and again belong to him. But the never-ending work of Christ and the Holy Spirit make that impossible.

And He who searches the hearts knows what the mind of the Spirit is, Paul continues. **He** refers to God the Father, **who searches the hearts** of men.

In the process of selecting a successor to King Saul, the Lord told Samuel, "God sees not as man sees, for man looks at the outward appearance, but the Lord looks at the heart" (1 Sam. 16:7). At the dedication of the Temple, Solomon prayed, "Hear Thou in heaven Thy dwelling place, and forgive and act and render to each according to all his ways, whose heart Thou knowest, for Thou alone dost know the hearts of all the sons of men" (1 Kings 8:39; cf. 1 Chron. 28:9; Ps. 139:1-2; Prov. 15:11). When they were choosing between Joseph Barsabbas and Matthias as a successor for Judas, the eleven apostles prayed, "Thou, Lord, who knowest the hearts of all men, show which one of these two Thou hast chosen" (Acts 1:24; cf. 1 Cor. 4:5; Heb. 4:13).

If the Father knows the hearts of men, how much more does He know **the mind of the Spirit.** The Father understands exactly what the **Spirit** is thinking **because He intercedes for the saints according to the will of God.** Because the Spirit's will and the Father's will are identical, and because God is one, Paul's statement seems unnecessary. But he is pointing up the truth in order to give encouragement to believers. Because the three persons of the Godhead have always been one in essence and will, the very idea of communication among them seems superfluous to us. It is a great mystery to our finite minds, but it is a divine reality that God expects His children to acknowledge by faith.

In this passage Paul emphasizes the divine intercession that is necessary for the preservation of believers to their eternal hope. We can no more fathom that marvelous truth than we can fathom any other aspect of God's plan of redemption. But we know that, were not Christ and the Holy Spirit continually on guard in our behalf, our inheritance in heaven would be reserved for us in vain.

The Ultimate Security—part 1 The Infallible Guarantee of Glory

34

And we know that God causes all things to work together for good to those who love God, to those who are called according to His purpose. (8:28)

For Christians, this verse contains perhaps the most glorious promise in Scripture. It is breathtaking in its magnitude, encompassing absolutely *everything* that pertains to a believer's life. This magnificent promise consists of four elements that continue Paul's teaching about the believer's security in the Holy Spirit: its certainty, its extent, its recipients, and its source.

THE CERTAINTY OF SECURITY

And we know (8:28*a*)

In the context of the truths that follow in Romans 8, these three simple words express the Christian's absolute certainty of eternal security in the Holy Spirit. Paul is not expressing his personal intuitions or opinions but is setting forth the inerrant truth of God's Word. It is not

471

Paul the man, but Paul the apostle and channel of God's revelation who continues to declare the truth he has received from the Holy Spirit. He therefore asserts with God's own authority that, as believers in Jesus Christ, **we know** beyond all doubt that every aspect of our lives is in God's hands and will be divinely used by the Lord not only to manifest His own glory but also to work out our own ultimate blessing.

The phrase **we know** here carries the meaning of *can* know. Tragically, many Christians throughout the history of the church, including many in our own day, refuse to believe that God guarantees the believer's eternal security. Such denial is tied to the belief that salvation is a cooperative effort between men and God, and although God will not fail on His side, man might—thus the sense of insecurity. Belief in salvation by a sovereign God alone, however, leads to the confidence that salvation is secure, because God, who alone is responsible, cannot fail. Beyond that theological consideration Paul is saying that the truth of eternal security is clearly revealed by God to us, so that all believers *are able* with certainty to **know** the comfort and hope of that reality if they simply take God at His word. God's child need never fear being cast out of his heavenly Father's house or fear losing his citizenship in His eternal kingdom of righteousness.

THE EXTENT OF SECURITY

that God causes all things to work together for good (8:*b*)

The extent of the believer's security is as limitless as its certainty is absolute. As with every other element of the believer's security, **God** is the Guarantor. It is He who **causes** everything in the believer's life to eventuate in blessing.

Paul emphasizes that **God** Himself brings about the good that comes to His people. This magnificent promise does not operate through impersonal statements, but requires divine action to fulfill. God's decree of security is actually carried out by the direct, personal, and gracious work of His divine Son and His Holy Spirit. "Hence, also, [Christ] is able to save forever those who draw near to God through Him, since He always lives to make intercession for them" (Heb. 7:25). And as Paul has just proclaimed, "The Spirit Himself intercedes for us with groanings too deep for words; and He who searches the hearts knows what the mind of the Spirit is, because He intercedes for the saints according to the will of God" (Rom. 8:26-27).

All things is utterly comprehensive, having no qualifications or limits. Neither this verse nor its context allows for restrictions or conditions. **All things** is inclusive in the fullest possible sense. Nothing existing or occurring in heaven or on earth "shall be able to separate us from the love of God, which is in Christ Jesus" (8:39).

Paul is not saying that God prevents His children from experiencing **things** that can harm them. He is rather attesting that the Lord takes all that He allows to happen to His beloved children, even the worst things, and turns those things ultimately into blessings.

Paul teaches the same basic truth in several of his other letters. "So then let no one boast in men," he admonishes the Corinthian believers. "For all things belong to you, whether Paul or Apollos or Cephas or the world or life or death or things present or things to come; all things belong to you" (1 Cor. 3:21-22). Perhaps a year later he assured them in another letter: "For all things are for your sakes, that the grace which is spreading to more and more people may cause the giving of thanks to abound to the glory of God" (2 Cor. 4:15). Later in Romans 8 Paul asks rhetorically, "He who did not spare His own Son, but delivered Him up for us all, how will He not also with Him freely give us all things?" (v. 32).

No matter what our situation, our suffering, our persecution, our sinful failure, our pain, our lack of faith—in those things, as well as in **all** other **things**, our heavenly Father will work to produce our ultimate victory and blessing. The corollary of that truth is that nothing can ultimately work against us. Any temporary harm we suffer will be used by God for our benefit (see 2 Cor. 12:7-10). As will be discussed below, **all things** includes circumstances and events that are good and beneficial in themselves as well as those that are in themselves evil and harmful.

To work together translates *sunergeō*, from which is derived the English term *synergism,* the working together of various elements to produce an effect greater than, and often completely different from, the sum of each element acting separately. In the physical world the right combination of otherwise harmful chemicals can produce substances that are extremely beneficial. For example, ordinary table salt is composed of two poisons, sodium and chlorine.

Contrary to what the King James rendering seems to suggest, it is not that things in themselves work together to produce good. As Paul has made clear earlier in the verse, it is God's providential power and will, not a natural synergism of circumstances and events in our lives, that causes them **to work together for good.** David testified to that marvelous truth when he exulted, "All the paths of the Lord are lovingkindness and truth to those who keep His covenant and His testimonies" (Ps. 25:10). No matter what road we are on or path we take, the Lord will turn it into a way of lovingkindness and truth.

Paul likely has in mind our **good** during this present life as well as ultimately in the life to come. No matter what happens in our lives as His children, the providence of God uses it for our temporal as well as our eternal benefit, sometimes by saving us from tragedies and sometimes by sending us through them in order to draw us closer to Him.

After delivering the Israelites from Egyptian bondage, God continually provided for their well-being as they faced the harsh obstacles of the Sinai desert. As Moses proclaimed the law to Israel, he reminded the people: "[God] led you through the great and terrible wilderness, with its fiery serpents and scorpions and thirsty ground where there was no water; He brought water for you out of the rock of flint. In the wilderness He fed you manna which your fathers did not know, that He might humble you and that He might test you, to do good for you in the end" (Deut. 8:15-16). The Lord did not lead His people through forty years of difficulty and hardship to bring them evil but to bring them **good,** the good that sometimes must come by way of divine discipline and refining.

It is clear from that illustration, as well as from countless others in Scripture, that God often delays the temporal as well as the ultimate **good** that He promises. Jeremiah declared, "Thus says the Lord God of Israel, 'Like these good figs, so I will regard as good the captives of Judah, whom I have sent out of this place into the land of the Chaldeans. For I will set My eyes on them for good, and I will bring them again to this land; and I will build them up and not overthrow them, and I will plant them and not pluck them up. And I will give them a heart to know Me, for I am the Lord; and they will be My people, and I will be their God, for they will return to Me with their whole heart'" (Jer. 24:5-7). In His sovereign graciousness, the Lord used the painful and frustrating captivities of Israel and Judah to refine His people, and by human reckoning, the process was slow and arduous.

"Therefore we do not lose heart," Paul counseled the Corinthian believers, "but though our outer man is decaying, yet our inner man is being renewed day by day. For momentary, light affliction is producing for us an eternal weight of glory far beyond all comparison" (2 Cor. 4:16-17). Even when our outward circumstances are dire—perhaps *especially* when they are dire and seemingly hopeless from our perspective—God is purifying and renewing our redeemed inner beings in preparation for glorification, the ultimate **good.**

First of all, God causes righteous things to work for our **good.** By far the most significant and best of good things are God's own attributes. God's *power* supports us in our troubles and strengthens our spiritual life. In his final blessing of the children of Israel, Moses testified, "The eternal God is a dwelling place, and underneath are the everlasting arms" (Deut. 33:27). In His parting words to the apostles, Jesus promised, "You shall receive power when the Holy Spirit has come upon you; and you shall be My witnesses both in Jerusalem, and in all Judea and Samaria, and even to the remotest part of the earth" (Acts 1:8).

In order to demonstrate our utter dependence upon God, His power working through us is actually "perfected in weakness. Most gladly, therefore," Paul testified, "I will rather boast about my weaknesses, that the power of Christ may dwell in me" (2 Cor. 12:9).

God's *wisdom* provides for our **good**. The most direct way is by sharing His wisdom with us. Paul prayed that the Lord would give the Ephesian believers "a spirit of wisdom and of revelation in the knowledge of Him" (Eph. 1:17). He made similar requests on behalf of the Colossians: "We have not ceased to pray for you and to ask that you may be filled with the knowledge of His will in all spiritual wisdom and understanding" (Col. 1:9), and later, "Let the word of Christ richly dwell within you, with all wisdom teaching and admonishing one another with psalms and hymns and spiritual songs, singing with thankfulness in your hearts to God" (3:16).

Almost by definition, God's *goodness* works to the **good** of His children. "Do you think lightly of the riches of His kindness and forbearance and patience," Paul reminds us, "not knowing that the kindness of God leads you to repentance?" (Rom. 2:4).

God's *faithfulness* works for our **good**. Even when His children are unfaithful to Him, their heavenly Father remains faithful to them. "I will heal their apostasy, I will love them freely, for My anger has turned away from them" (Hos. 14:4). Micah rejoiced in the Lord, exulting, "Who is a God like Thee, who pardons iniquity and passes over the rebellious act of the remnant of His possession? He does not retain His anger forever, because He delights in unchanging love" (Mic. 7:18). When a child of God is in need, the Lord promises, "He will call upon Me, and I will answer him; I will be with him in trouble; I will rescue him, and honor him" (Ps. 91:15). "My God shall supply all your needs," Paul assures us, "according to His riches in glory in Christ Jesus" (Phil. 4:19).

God's *Word* is for our **good**. "And now I commend you to God and to the word of His grace, which is able to build you up and to give you the inheritance among all those who are sanctified" (Acts 20:32). Every good thing we receive from God's hand "is sanctified by means of the word of God and prayer" (1 Tim. 4:5). The more we see sin through the eyes of Scripture, which is to see it through God's own eyes, the more we abhor it.

In addition to His attributes, God's *holy angels* work for the **good** of those who belong to Him. "Are they not all ministering spirits," the writer of Hebrews asks rhetorically about the angels, "sent out to render service for the sake of those who will inherit salvation?" (Heb. 1:14).

God's *children* themselves are ministers of His **good** to each other. In the opening of his letter to Rome, Paul humbly assured his readers that he longed to visit them not only to minister *to* them but to be ministered to *by* them, "that is, that I may be encouraged together with you while among you, each of us by the other's faith, both yours and mine" (Rom. 1:12). To the Corinthian believers the apostle described himself and Timothy as "workers with you for your joy" (2 Cor. 1:24; cf. v. 1). It is both the obligation and the joy of Christians "to stimulate one another to love and good deeds" (Heb. 10:24).

Although the truth is often difficult to recognize and accept, the Lord causes even *evil* things to work for our **good.** It is these less obvious and less pleasant channels of God's blessing that Paul here seems to be emphasizing—those things among the "all things" that are in themselves anything but good. Many of the things that we do and that happen to us are either outright evil or, at best, are worthless. Yet in His infinite wisdom and omnipotence, our heavenly Father will turn even the worst of such things to our ultimate **good.**

As mentioned above, God used His people's slavery in Egypt and their trials in the wilderness not only to demonstrate His power against their enemies in their behalf but to refine and purify His people before they took possession of the Promised Land. Although the afflictions and hardships in the Sinai desert hardened the hearts of most of the people and made them rebellious, God intended those trials to be for their blessing.

When Daniel was threatened with death for refusing to obey King Darius's ban on worshiping any god but the king, the monarch reluctantly had the prophet thrown into the den of lions. When it became evident that the lions would not harm him, Daniel testified to Darius, "'O king, live forever! My God sent His angel and shut the lions' mouths, and they have not harmed me, inasmuch as I was found innocent before Him; and also toward you, O king, I have committed no crime.' Then the king was very pleased and gave orders for Daniel to be taken up out of the den. So Daniel was taken up out of the den, and no injury whatever was found on him, because he had trusted in his God" (Dan. 6:21-23). The suffering and martyrdom of many of His saints, however, is clear evidence that God does not always choose to bless faithfulness by deliverance from harm.

The evil things that God uses for the **good** of His people may be divided into three categories: suffering, temptation, and sin.

God uses the evil of suffering as a means of bringing **good** *to His people.* Sometimes the suffering comes as the price of faithfulness to God. At other times it is simply the common pain, hardship, disease, and conflicts that are the lot of all mankind because of sin's corruption of the world. At still other times the suffering comes by God's permission, and not always as punishment or discipline. The godly Naomi lamented, "Call me Mara, for the Almighty has dealt very bitterly with me" (Ruth 1:20). After the bewildering afflictions with which God allowed him to be tormented by Satan, Job responded in simple trust: "The Lord gave and the Lord has taken away. Blessed be the name of the Lord" (Job 1:21).

Often, of course, suffering *does* come as divine chastisement for sin. God promised Judah that, despite the rebellion and idolatry that caused her captivity, "I will regard as good the captives of Judah, whom I have sent out of this place into the land of the Chaldeans" (Jer. 24:5). God chastened certain members of the Corinthian church because of their flagrant and unrepentant sins, causing some to become sick and others to die (1 Cor. 11:29-30). We are not told what good God brought to those sinful believers themselves. Perhaps it was simply His means of preventing them from falling into worse sin. It is likely that He worked good for the rest of the Corinthian church as He had done in the instance of Ananias and Sapphira, whose severe discipline was a purifying force, causing "great fear [to come] upon the whole church, and upon all who heard of these things" (Acts 5:11).

Regardless of what our adversities might be or how they might come, James admonishes us to "consider it all joy, my brethren, when you encounter various trials, knowing that the testing of your faith produces endurance" (James 1:2-3). Trials that come directly because of our relationship to Christ should be especially welcomed, Peter says, "that the proof of your faith, being more precious than gold which is perishable, even though tested by fire, may be found to result in praise and glory and honor at the revelation of Jesus Christ" (1 Pet. 1:7).

Joseph is a classic Old Testament example of God's using unjust suffering to bring great **good,** not only to the sufferer himself but to all of his family, who constituted God's chosen people. If he had never been sold into slavery and cast into prison, he would not have had the opportunity to interpret Pharaoh's dream and rise to a position of great prominence, from which he could be used to save Egypt and his own people from starvation. Understanding that marvelous truth, Joseph told his fearful brothers, "And as for you, you meant evil against me, but God meant it for good in order to bring about this present result, to preserve many people alive" (Gen. 50:20).

King Manasseh of Judah brought foreign conquest and great suffering upon himself and his nation because of his sinfulness. But "when he was in distress, he entreated the Lord his God and humbled himself greatly before the God of his fathers. When he prayed to Him, He was moved by his entreaty and heard his supplication, and brought him again to Jerusalem to his kingdom. Then Manasseh knew that the Lord was God" (2 Chron. 33:12-13).

Although Job never lost faith in God, his incessant afflictions eventually caused him to question the Lord's ways. After a severe rebuke by God, however, Job confessed, "I have heard of Thee by the hearing of the ear; but now my eye sees Thee; therefore I retract, and I repent in dust and ashes" (Job 42:5-6).

An enemy aggressively afflicted pain on the apostle Paul. Very likely he was the leader of Corinthian hostility toward Paul. Paul knew that, although this person belonged to Satan's domain, his activity against the apostle was permitted by God to keep him (Paul) from exalting himself because of his visions and revelations (2 Cor. 12:6-7). Nevertheless, Paul pleaded earnestly three times that he might be delivered from the man's attacks. The Lord responded by telling His faithful servant, "My grace is sufficient for you, for power is perfected in weakness." That explanation was sufficient for Paul, who said submissively, "Most gladly, therefore, I will rather boast about my weaknesses, that the power of Christ may dwell in me. Therefore I am well content with weaknesses, with insults, with distresses, with persecutions, with difficulties, for Christ's sake; for when I am weak, then I am strong" (2 Cor. 12:9-10). Instead of turning down the trouble, God turned up the sufficient grace, so that Paul could endure the situation gladly and be humbled by it at the same time.

Through suffering of all kinds and for all reasons, we can learn kindness, sympathy, humility, compassion, patience, and gentleness. Most importantly, God can use suffering as He can use few other things to bring us closer to Himself. "And after you have suffered for a little while," Peter reassures us, "the God of all grace, who called you to His eternal glory in Christ, will Himself perfect, confirm, strengthen and establish you" (1 Pet. 5:10). The Puritan Thomas Watson observed, "A sick-bed often teaches more than a sermon" (*A Divine Cordial* [Grand Rapids: Baker, 1981], p. 20).

Suffering can also teach us to hate sin. We already hate sin to some degree, because it is the direct or indirect cause of all suffering. But personally suffering at the hands of evil men will teach us more about the wickedness of sin. Martin Luther said that he could never understand the imprecatory psalms until he himself was persecuted viciously. He could not understand why the godly David could call down God's vengeance on his enemies until he himself [Luther] had been tormented by enemies of the gospel.

We also come to hate sin when we see its destruction of others, especially its harm to those we love. Jesus groaned in agony at Lazarus's tomb, but not because He despaired for His deceased friend, because He would momentarily remedy that. He was angry and saddened because of the grief that sin and its greatest consequence, death, brought to the loved ones of Lazarus (see John 11:33). He also realized that such agony is multiplied a million times over every day throughout the world.

Suffering helps us see and hate our own sin. Sometimes it is only when we are mistreated, unfairly accused, or are debilitated by illness, financial disaster, or some other form of hardship that we come face-to-face with our temper, our self-satisfaction, or our indifference to other people and even to God. By helping us see and hate our sin, suffering is also used by God to drive it out and purify us. "When He has tried me," Job said, "I shall come forth as gold" (Job 23:10). In the last days, " 'It will come about in all the land,' declares the Lord, 'that two parts in it will be cut off and perish; but the third will be left in it. And I will bring the third part through the fire, refine them as silver is refined, and test them as gold is tested. They will call on My name, and I will answer them; I will say, "They are My people," and they will say, "The Lord is my God" ' " (Zech. 13:8-9). Through that final and unparalleled period of suffering, the Lord will refine and restore to Himself a remnant of His ancient people Israel.

Suffering divine discipline confirms that we are indeed God's children. The writer of Hebrews reminds us that "those whom the Lord loves He disciplines, and He scourges every son whom He receives. It is for discipline that you endure; God deals with you as with sons; for what son is there whom his father does not discipline? But if you are without discipline, of which all have become partakers, then you are illegitimate children and not sons" (Heb. 12:6-8; cf. Job 5:17).

As the writer of Hebrews notes, wise human parents discipline their children for the children's own welfare. Even secular psychologists and counselors have come to recognize that a child who is overindulged in what he wants, but given no bounds and held to no standards by his parents, realizes innately that he is not loved.

Three times the writer of Psalm 119 acknowledged that the Lord used suffering to strengthen his spiritual life: "Before I was afflicted I went astray, but now I keep Thy word" (v. 67); "It is good for me that I was afflicted, that I may learn Thy statutes" (v. 71); and, "I know, O Lord, that Thy judgments are righteous, and that in faithfulness Thou hast afflicted me" (v. 75).

Suffering is designed by God to help us identify to a limited extent with Christ's suffering on our behalf and to conform us to Him. It is for that reason that Paul prayed to "know Him, and the power of His resurrection and the fellowship of His sufferings, being conformed to His death" (Phil. 3:10), and that he boasted, "I bear on my body the brand-marks of Jesus" (Gal. 6:17). When we willingly submit it to our heavenly Father, suffering can be used by Him to mold us more perfectly into the divine likeness of our Lord and Savior.

God uses the evil of temptation as a means of bringing **good** *to His people.* Just as suffering is not good in itself, neither, of course, is temptation. But, as is the case with suffering, the Lord is able to use temptation for our benefit.

Temptation should drive us to our knees in prayer and cause us to ask God for strength to resist. When an animal sees a predator, he runs or flies as fast as he can to a place of safety. That should be the Christian's response whenever he is confronted by temptation. Temptation causes the godly believer to flee to the Lord for protection.

Whether Satan approaches us as a roaring lion or as an angel of light, if we are well taught in God's Word we can recognize his evil enticements for what they are. That is why the psalmist proclaimed, "Thy word I have treasured in my heart, that I may not sin against Thee" (Ps. 119:11).

God can also cause temptation to work for our good by using it to devastate spiritual pride. When we struggle with temptation, we know that, in ourselves, we are still subject to the allurements and defilements of sin. And when we try to resist it in our own power, we quickly discover how powerless against it we are in ourselves.

In His incarnation, even Jesus did not resist Satan's temptation in His humanness but in every instance confronted the tempter with the Word of God (Matt. 4:1-10; Luke 4:1-12). Our response to Satan's enticements should be the same as our Lord's while He was on earth. Christ's experience with temptation not only provides us with a divine example but provided Christ with human experience—in light of which the writer of Hebrews could declare, "For we do not have a high priest who cannot sympathize with our weaknesses, but one who has been tempted in all things as we are, yet without sin" (Heb. 4:15).

Finally, temptation should strengthen the believer's desire for heaven, where he will be forever beyond sin's allurement, power, and presence. When in frustration we cry out with Paul, "Who will set me free from the body of this death?" we can also proclaim with him, "Thanks be to God through Jesus Christ our Lord! So then, on the one hand I myself with my mind am serving the law of God, but on the other, with my flesh the law of sin" (Rom. 7:24-25). We can also confess with the apostle that, although we are willing to remain on earth to fulfill the Lord's ministry through us, our great longing is to be with Him (Phil. 1:21-24).

God uses the evil of sin as a means of bringing **good** *to His children.* That would have to be true if Paul's statement about "all things" is taken at face value. Even more than suffering and temptation, sin is not good in itself, because it is the antithesis of good. Yet, in God's infinite wisdom and power, it is most remarkable of all that He turns sin to our good.

It is of great importance, of course, to recognize that God does not use sin for good in the sense of its being an instrument of His righteousness. That would be the most obvious of self-contradictions. The Lord uses sin to bring good to His children by overruling it, canceling its normal evil consequences and miraculously substituting His benefits.

Because it is often easier for us to recognize the reality and the wickedness of sin in others than in ourselves, God can cause the sins of other people to work for our good. If we are seeking to live a godly life in Christ, seeing a sin in others will make us hate and avoid it more. A spirit of judgmental self-righteousness, of course, will have the opposite effect, leading us into the snare about which Paul has already warned: "In that you judge another, you condemn yourself; for you who judge practice the same things. And we know that the judgment of God rightly falls upon those who practice such things. And do you suppose this, O man, when you pass judgment upon those who practice such things and do the same yourself, that you will escape the judgment of God?" (Rom. 2:1-3; cf. Matt. 7:1-2).

God can even cause our own sins to work for our good. A believer's sins are just as evil as those of unbelievers. But the ultimate consequence of a believer's sin is vastly different, because the penalty for *all* his sins—past, present, and future—has been paid in full by his Savior. Although the foundational truth of Romans 8 is that, by God's unspeakable grace, a Christian is forever preserved from sin's *ultimate* consequence, which is eternal condemnation (v. 1), a Christian is still subject to the immediate, temporal consequences of sins he commits, as well as to many continuing consequences of sins committed before salvation. As noted several times above, the sinning believer is not spared God's chastisement but is assured of it as a remedial tool for producing holiness (Heb. 12:10). That is the supreme good for which God causes our sin to work.

God also causes our own sin to work for our good by leading us to despise the sin and to desire His holiness. When we fall into sin, our spiritual weakness becomes evident and we are driven humbly to seek God's forgiveness and restoration. Evil as it is, sin can bring us good by stripping us of our pride and self-assurance.

The supreme illustration of God's turning "all things," even the most evil of things, to the good of His children is seen in the sacrificial death of His own Son. In the crucifixion of Jesus Christ, God took the most absolute evil that Satan could devise and turned it into the greatest conceivable blessing He could offer to fallen mankind—eternal salvation from sin.

THE RECIPIENTS OF SECURITY

to those who love God, to those who are called (8:28c)

The only qualification in the marvelous promise of this verse has to do with the recipients. It is solely for His children that God promises to work everything for good. **Those who love God** and **those who are called** are two of the many titles or descriptions the New Testament uses of Christians. From the human perspective we are **those who love God**, whereas from God's perspective we are **those who are called**.

THE RECIPIENTS OF SECURITY LOVE GOD

to those who love God,

First, Paul describes the recipients of eternal security as **those who love God.** Nothing more characterizes the true believer than genuine **love** for **God.** Redeemed people **love** the gracious **God** who has saved them. Because of their depraved and sinful natures, the unredeemed hate God, regardless of any arguments they may have to the contrary. When God made His covenant with Israel through Moses, He made the distinction clear between those who love Him and those who hate Him. In the Ten Commandments the Lord told His people, "You shall not worship [idols] or serve them; for I, the Lord your God, am a jealous God, visiting the iniquity of the fathers on the children, on the third and the fourth generations of those who hate Me, but showing lovingkindness to thousands, to those who love Me and keep My commandments" (Ex. 20:5-6; cf. Deut. 7:9-10; Neh. 1:4-5; Pss. 69:36; 97:10). In God's sight, there are only two categories of human beings, those who hate Him and those who love Him. Jesus was referring to that truth when He said, "He who is not with Me is against Me" (Matt. 12:30).

Even during the time of the Mosaic covenant, when God was dealing with His chosen people Israel in a unique way, any person, even a Gentile, who trusted in Him was accepted by Him and was characterized by love for the Lord. God's redeemed included "also the foreigners who join themselves to the Lord, to minister to Him, and to love the name of the Lord, to be His servants, every one who keeps from profaning the sabbath, and holds fast My covenant" (Isa. 56:6).

The New Testament is equally clear that those who belong to God love Him. "Just as it is written," Paul reminded the Corinthians, "'Things which eye has not seen and ear has not heard, and which have not entered the heart of man, all that God has prepared for those who love Him'" (1 Cor. 2:9; cf. Isa. 64:4). Later in that letter he declared, "If anyone loves God, he is known by Him" (1 Cor. 8:3).

James says that those who love God, that is, believers, are promised the Lord's eternal crown of life (James 1:12). Paul refers to Christians as "those who love our Lord Jesus Christ with a love incorruptible" (Eph. 6:24).

Saving faith involves much more than simply acknowledging God. Even the demons fearfully believe that God is one and is all-powerful (James 2:19). True faith involves the surrendering of one's sinful self to God for forgiveness and receiving Jesus Christ as Lord and Savior. And the first mark of saving faith is love for God. True salvation produces lovers of God, because "the love of God has been poured out within our hearts through the Holy Spirit who was given to us" (Rom. 5:5). It is not by accident that Paul lists love as the first fruit of the Spirit (Gal. 5:22).

Love for God is closely related to forgiveness, because the redeemed believer cannot help being grateful for God's gracious forgiveness. When the sinful woman, doubtlessly a prostitute, washed and anointed Jesus' feet in the Pharisee's house, the Lord explained to His resentful host that she expressed great love because she had been forgiven great sins (Luke 7:47).

Love for God is also related to obedience. "And why do you call Me, 'Lord, Lord,'" Jesus said, "and do not do what I say?" (Luke 6:46). The persistently disobedient heart is an unbelieving and unloving heart. Because "the love of Christ controls us" (2 Cor. 5:14), His Word will also control us. "You are My friends," Jesus said, "if you do what I commanded you" (John 15:14). In context, it is clear that Jesus uses the term *friend* as a synonym for a true disciple (see vv. 8-17).

Obviously we do not love Christ as fully as we ought because we are still imperfect and are contaminated by the sinful remnants of the old self. It is for that reason that Paul told the Philippians, "And this I pray, that your love may abound still more and more in real knowledge and all discernment" (Phil. 1:9). Their love for Christ was genuine, but it was not yet perfect.

Genuine love for God has many facets and manifestations. First, godly love longs for personal communion with the Lord. It was that desire which led the psalmists to proclaim, "As the deer pants for the water brooks, so my soul pants for Thee, O God. My soul thirsts for God, for the living God; when shall I come and appear before God?" (Ps. 42:1-2), and "Whom have I in heaven but Thee? And besides Thee, I desire nothing on earth" (Ps. 73:25).

David prayed, "O God, Thou art my God; I shall seek Thee earnestly; my soul thirsts for Thee, my flesh yearns for Thee, in a dry and weary land where there is no water. Thus I have beheld Thee in the sanctuary, to see Thy power and Thy glory. Because Thy lovingkindness is better than life, my lips will praise Thee" (Ps. 63:1-3). Speaking for all faithful believers, the sons of Korah exulted, "My soul longed and even yearned for the courts of the Lord; my heart and my flesh sing for joy to the living God. The bird also has found a house, and the swallow a nest for herself, where she may lay her young, even Thine altars, O Lord of hosts, my King and my God. How blessed are those who dwell in Thy house! They are ever praising Thee" (Ps. 84:2-4).

Second, genuine love for God trusts in His power to protect His own. David admonished fellow believers: "O love the Lord, all you His godly ones! The Lord preserves the faithful" (Ps. 31:23).

Third, genuine love for God is characterized by peace that only He can impart. "Those who love Thy law have great peace, and nothing causes them to stumble" (Ps. 119:165). As believers, we have a divine and secure peace that the world cannot give, possess, understand, or take away (John 14:27; 16:33; Phil. 4:7).

Fourth, genuine love for God is sensitive to His will and His honor. When God is blasphemed, repudiated, or in any way dishonored, His faithful children suffer pain on His behalf. David so identified himself with the Lord that he could say, "Zeal for Thy house has consumed me, and the reproaches of those who reproach Thee have fallen on me" (Ps. 69:9).

Fifth, genuine love for God loves the things that God loves, and we know what He loves through the revelation of His Word. Throughout Psalm 119 the writer expresses love for God's law, God's ways, God's standards, and all else that is God's. "The law of Thy mouth is better to me Than thousands of gold and silver pieces" (v. 72); "O how I love Thy law! It is my meditation all the day" (v. 97); and "How sweet are Thy words to my taste! Yes, sweeter than honey to my mouth!" (v. 103). David testified: "I will bow down toward Thy holy temple, and give thanks to Thy name for Thy lovingkindness and Thy truth; for Thou hast magnified Thy word according to all Thy name" (Ps. 138:2).

Sixth, genuine love for God loves the people God loves. John repeatedly and unequivocally asserts that a person who does not love God's children does not love God and does not belong to God. "We know that we have passed out of death into life," the apostle says, "because we love the brethren. He who does not love abides in death" (1 John 3:14). "Beloved, let us love one another, for love is from God; and everyone who loves is born of God and knows God. The one who does not love does not know God, for God is love" (4:7-8). In the strongest possible language, John declares that "if someone says, 'I love God,' and hates his brother, he is a liar; for the one who does not love his brother whom he has seen, cannot love God whom he has not seen. And this commandment we have from Him, that the one who loves God should love his brother also" (4:20-21). In the next chapter he declares just as firmly that "whoever loves the Father loves the child born of Him. By this we know that we love the children of God, when we love God and observe His commandments" (1 John 5:1-2).

Seventh, genuine love for God hates what God hates. Godly love cannot tolerate evil. The loving Christian grieves over sin, first of all for sin in his own life but also for sin in the lives of others, especially in the lives of fellow believers. When the cock's crow reminded Peter of His Lord's prediction, he wept bitterly over his denial of Christ, which he had just made for the third time (Matt. 26:75).

On the other hand, to love the world and the things of the world is to love what God hates, and John therefore solemnly warns, "If anyone loves the world, the love of the Father is not in him" (1 John 2:15).

Eighth, genuine love for God longs for Christ's return. Paul rejoiced in the knowledge that "in the future there is laid up for me the crown of righteousness, which the Lord, the righteous Judge, will award to me on that day; and not only to me, but also to all who have loved His appearing" (2 Tim. 4:8).

Ninth and finally, the overarching mark of genuine love for God is obedience. "He who has My commandments and keeps them," Jesus said, "he it is who loves Me; and he who loves Me shall be loved by My Father, and I will love him, and will disclose Myself to him" (John 14:21). As noted above in the citation of 1 John 5:1-2, obedience to God is inextricably tied both to love for God and love for fellow believers.

Although we are commanded to love God and fellow believers, that love does not and cannot originate with us. Godly love is God-given. "Love is from God," John explains, and therefore it is "not that we loved God, but that He loved us and sent His Son to be the propitiation for our sins" (1 John 4:7, 10). We are able to love only because God has first loved us (v. 19).

THE RECIPIENTS OF SECURITY ARE CALLED

to those who are called

Second, Paul describes the recipients of eternal security as **those who are called.** Just as our love originates with God, so does our calling into His heavenly family. In every way, the initiative and provision for salvation are God's. In their fallen, sinful state, men are able only to hate God, because, regardless of what they may think, they are His enemies (Rom. 5:10) and children of His wrath (Eph. 2:3).

When Jesus said that "many are called, but few are chosen" (Matt. 22:14), He was referring to the gospel's *external* call to *all* men to believe in Him. In the history of the church nothing is more obvious than the fact that many, perhaps most, people who receive this call do not accept it.

But in the epistles, the terms *called* and *calling* are used in a different sense, referring to the sovereign, regenerating work of God in a believer's heart that brings him to new life in Christ. Paul explains the meaning of **those who are called** in the following two verses (29-30), where he speaks of what theologians often refer to as God's effectual call. In this sense, *all* **those who are called** are chosen and redeemed by God and are ultimately glorified. They are securely predestined by God to be His children and to be conformed to the image of His Son.

Believers have never been **called** on the basis of their works or for their own purposes. As Hebrews 11 makes clear, faith in God has always been the only way of redemption. Believers are not saved on the basis of who they are or what they have done but solely on the basis of who God is and what He has done. We are redeemed "according to His own purpose and grace which was granted us in Christ Jesus from all eternity" (2 Tim. 1:9). Because it operates completely according to God's will and by His power, the gospel never fails to accomplish and secure its work of salvation in those who believe (1 Thess. 2:13).

Later in Romans Paul uses Jacob and Esau to illustrate God's effectual call, which is also a sovereign call. "For though the twins were not yet born," he says, "and had not done anything good or bad, in order that God's purpose according to His choice might stand, not because of works, but because of Him who calls, it was said to her, 'The older will serve the younger.' Just as it is written, 'Jacob I loved, but Esau I hated'" (Rom. 9:11-13).

Although human faith is imperative for salvation, God's gracious initiation of salvation is even more imperative. Jesus declared categorically, "No one can come to Me, unless it has been granted him from the Father" (John 6:65). God's choice not only precedes man's choice but makes man's choice possible and effective.

Paul not only was called by Christ to salvation (see Acts 9) but was also "called as an apostle of Jesus Christ by the will of God" (1 Cor. 1:1). He describes himself as being "laid hold of by Christ Jesus" (Phil. 3:12). Paul addressed believers at Corinth as "those who have been sanctified in Christ Jesus, saints by calling" (1 Cor. 1:2), and later refers to all Christians as "those who are the called, both Jews and Greeks" (v. 24). All believers, without exception, are called by God, "having been predestined according to His purpose who works all things after the counsel of His will" (Eph. 1:11).

In its primary sense, God's call is once and for all, but in a secondary sense it continues until the believer is finally glorified. Although he acknowledged his permanent call both as a believer and as an apostle, Paul could yet say, "I press on toward the goal for the prize of the upward call of God in Christ Jesus" (Phil. 3:14).

As already noted, although salvation is by God's initiative and power, it is never accomplished apart from faith. It is therefore impossible, as some teach, that a person can be saved and never know it. No person is saved apart from conscious and willful acceptance of Christ. "If you confess with your mouth Jesus as Lord, and believe in your heart that God raised Him from the dead," Paul says, "you shall be saved; for with the heart man believes, resulting in righteousness, and with the mouth he confesses, resulting in salvation" (Rom. 10:9-10). It is possible, of course, for a weak, unlearned, or sinful Christian to have later doubts about his salvation. But a person cannot come to Christ without knowing it.

As Paul explains a few verses later, God also uses human agents in making effective His call to salvation. "How then shall they call upon Him in whom they have not believed? And how shall they believe in Him whom they have not heard? And how shall they hear without a preacher?" (Rom. 10:14).

It is through the content of His Word, specifically the truth of the gospel message, and through the power of His Holy Spirit that God brings men to Himself. Peter succinctly states the first of those two principles: "You have been born again not of seed which is perishable but imperishable, that is, through the living and abiding word of God" (1 Pet. 1:23). Paul states the second principle in these words: "For by one Spirit we were all baptized into one body, whether Jews or Greeks, whether slaves or free, and we were all made to drink of one Spirit" (1 Cor. 12:13; cf. John 16:8).

THE SOURCE OF SECURITY

according to His purpose. (8:28d)

At the end of verse 28, Paul states the source of the believer's security in Christ. God causes all things to work together for the good of His children because that is **according to His** divine **purpose**. Although the Greek text does not contain the term for **His**, that meaning is clearly implied in the context and is reflected in most translations.

Paul expands on and clarifies the meaning of God's **purpose** in verses 29-30, which will be discussed in the next chapter of this volume. Briefly explained, God's broader **purpose** is to offer salvation to all mankind. As our Lord declared at the beginning of His earthly ministry, "God so loved the world, that He gave His only begotten Son, that whoever believes in Him should not perish, but have eternal life. For God did not send the Son into the world to judge the world, but that the world should be saved through Him" (John 3:16-17). In his second letter, Peter states that the Lord does not desire the condemnation of any person but wants "all to come to repentance" (2 Pet. 3:9).

In Romans 8:28, however, Paul is speaking of the narrower, restricted meaning of God's **purpose**, namely, His divine plan to save those whom He has called and "predestined to become conformed to the image of His Son" (v. 29). The focus is on God's sovereign plan of redemption, which He ordained before the foundation of the earth.

While Israel was still wandering in the desert of Sinai, Moses told them, "The Lord did not set His love on you nor choose you because you were more in number than any of the peoples, for you were the fewest of all peoples, but because the Lord loved you and kept the oath which He swore to your forefathers, the Lord brought you out by a mighty hand,

and redeemed you from the house of slavery, from the hand of Pharaoh king of Egypt" (Deut. 7:7-8). The Jews were not chosen because of who they were but because of who God is. The same is true of God's choosing believers. He chooses solely on the basis of His divine will and **purpose.**

Isaiah wrote, "For I am God, and there is no other; I am God, and there is no one like Me, declaring the end from the beginning and from ancient times things which have not been done, saying, 'My purpose will be established, and I will accomplish all My good pleasure'; calling a bird of prey from the east, the man of My purpose from a far country. Truly I have spoken; truly I will bring it to pass. I have planned it, surely I will do it" (Isa.46:9b-11).

John wrote of Jesus, "But as many as received Him, to them He gave the right to become children of God, even to those who believe in His name, who were born not of blood, nor of the will of the flesh, nor of the will of man, but of God" (John 1:12-13).

The Ultimate Security—part 2 The Purpose and Progress of Salvation

35

For whom He foreknew, He also predestined to become conformed to the image of His Son, that He might be the first-born among many brethren; and whom He predestined, these He also called; and whom He called, these He also justified; and whom He justified, these He also glorified. (8:29-30)

From the time of the early church, Christians have debated the possibility of a believer's losing his salvation. Many bitter controversies have centered on that single issue.

As already expressed numerous times in this volume, it is my strong contention that, despite the claims of many sincere believers to the contrary, Scripture is unambiguous in teaching that every person who is genuinely saved is eternally saved. We can never be in danger of losing the spiritual life given to us by God through Jesus Christ. Romans 8:29-30 is perhaps the clearest and most explicit presentation of that truth in all of God's Word. In these two verses Paul reveals the unbroken pattern of God's sovereign redemption, from His eternal foreknowledge of a believer's salvation to its ultimate completion in glorification.

For the sake of easier understanding, the first heading in this chapter will be taken out of textual order. Because the second half of verse 29 states the purpose of the five aspects of salvation that Paul mentions in these two verses, that phrase will be considered first.

THE PURPOSE OF SALVATION

to become conformed to the image of His Son, that He might be the first-born among many brethren; (8:29c-d)

Paul introduced the truths of the believer's security and of God's purpose of salvation in the previous verse, stating "God causes all things to work together for good to those who love God, to those who are called according to His purpose" (v. 28). God's calling precedes and makes possible a person's hearing and responding in faith to that divine call. The resulting salvation is made secure by the Lord's causing everything in a believer's life to work for his ultimate good. Conversely, it is impossible for any evil to cause a believer any ultimate harm.

In the middle of verse 29, Paul states the twofold purpose of God's bringing sinners to eternal salvation. The secondary purpose is stated first: to make believers into the likeness of His Son.

TO CONFORM BELIEVERS TO CHRIST

to become conformed to the image of His Son, (8:29c)

From before time began, God chose to save believers from their sins in order that they might **become conformed to the image of His Son,** Jesus Christ. Consequently, every true believer moves inexorably toward perfection in righteousness, as God makes for Himself a people recreated into the likeness of **His** own divine **Son** who will dwell and reign with Him in heaven throughout all eternity. God is redeeming for Himself an eternally holy and Christlike race, to be citizens in His divine kingdom and children in His divine family. For a believer to lose his salvation would be for God to fail in His divine purpose and to condemn to hell those whom He had sovereignly elected to redemption. It would be for God (who cannot lie) to break His covenant with Himself, made before the foundation of the earth. It would mean that the divine seal of the Holy Spirit, imprinted by the King of kings and Lord of lords upon each of His elect children, would be subject to violation and abrogation (see 2 Cor. 1:22; Eph. 1:13; 4:30).

Leading up to the climactic truth that, without exception, God will complete the salvation of every sinner who is converted to Christ, Paul has already established that "there is therefore now no condemnation for those who are in Christ Jesus" (8:1), that God's Holy Spirit indwells every believer (v. 9), that every believer is already, in this life, an adopted child of God (vv. 14-16), that those children are therefore "heirs of God and fellow heirs with Christ" (v. 17), and that "the Spirit also helps our weakness" and "intercedes for the saints according to the will of God" (Rom. 8:26-27).

Building on the categorical declaration that no believer will again face God's condemnation, the apostle progressively establishes that "no condemnation" inevitably eventuates in glorification. There is no failure or partial fulfillment in the sovereign operation of God's salvation plan. Every believer who is saved will one day be glorified. There is absolutely no allowance for the possibility of a believer's sinning himself out of God's grace. He can no more work himself out of salvation than he could have worked himself into it. Nor is there any allowance for an intermediate state of limbo or purgatory, in which some Christians fall short of being fully **conformed to the image of** God's **Son** and must, after death, somehow complete their salvation by their own works or have it completed by others on their behalf.

Although the full truth of it is far too vast and magnificent even for a redeemed human mind to grasp, the New Testament gives us glimpses of what being **conformed to the image** of Christ will be like.

First of all, we will be like Christ *bodily.* One day the Lord will "transform the body of our humble state into conformity with the body of His glory, by the exertion of the power that He has even to subject all things to Himself" (Phil. 3:21). As the term itself denotes, glorification (our ultimate conformity to Christ) will be God's gracious adornment of His children with the very glory of **His** divine **Son.**

The writer of Hebrews tells us that "in these last days [God] has spoken to us in His Son, whom He appointed heir of all things, through whom also He made the world. And He is the radiance of His glory and the exact representation of His nature, and upholds all things by the word of His power. When He had made purification of sins, He sat down at the right hand of the Majesty on high" (Heb. 1:2-3). John assures us: "Beloved, now we are children of God, and it has not appeared as yet what we shall be. We know that, when He appears, we shall be like Him, because we shall see Him just as He is" (1 John 3:2). In the meanwhile, as long as we remain on earth, "we all, with unveiled face beholding as in a mirror the glory of the Lord, are being transformed into the same image from glory to glory, just as from the Lord, the Spirit" (2 Cor. 3:18). "For if we have become united with Him in the likeness of His death," Paul has explained earlier in Romans, "certainly we shall be also in the likeness of His resurrection" (6:5). "Just as we have borne the image of the earthy, we shall also bear the image of the heavenly" (1 Cor. 15:49).

All human beings share a common kind of physical body, but each person has his own distinctive looks and personality. In the same way, the redeemed in heaven will share a common kind of spiritual body but will be individually distinguished from one another. The Bible nowhere teaches the idea that individuality is destroyed at death and that the soul of the deceased becomes absorbed unidentifiably into some cosmic wholeness, or, worse yet, cosmic nothingness. Scripture is clear that, in eternity, both the saved and the damned will retain their individuality. The final resurrection will be of all human beings of all times, a resurrection of life for the righteous and a resurrection of death for the wicked (John 5:29; Acts 24:15).

Second, and more importantly, although not becoming deity, we will be like Christ *spiritually*. Our incorruptible bodies will be infused with the very holiness of Christ, and we will be both outwardly and inwardly perfect, just as our Lord. The writer of Hebrews gives insight into God's gracious plan of redeeming those who believe in His Son and of conforming them to His image when he writes:

> We do see Him who has been made for a little while lower than the angels, namely, Jesus, because of the suffering of death crowned with glory and honor, that by the grace of God He might taste death for everyone. For it was fitting for Him, for whom are all things, and through whom are all things, in bringing many sons to glory, to perfect the author of their salvation through sufferings. For both He who sanctifies and those who are sanctified are all from one Father; for which reason He is not ashamed to call them brethren. (Heb. 2:9-11)

TO MAKE CHRIST PREEMINENT

that He might be the first-born among many brethren; (8:29d)

God's supreme purpose for bringing sinners to salvation is to glorify His Son, Jesus Christ, by making Him preeminent in the divine plan of redemption. In the words of this text, it is God's intent for Christ to **be the first-born among many brethren.**

In Jewish culture the term **first-born** always referred to a son, unless a daughter was specifically stated. Because the **first-born** male child in a Jewish family had a privileged status, the term was often used figuratively to represent preeminence. In the present context that is clearly the meaning.

As it is in almost every instance in the New Testament, the term **brethren** is a synonym for believers. God's primary purpose in His plan of redemption was to make His beloved Son **the first-born among many brethren** in the sense of Christ's being uniquely preeminent among the children of God. Those who trust in Him become God's adopted children, and Jesus, the true Son of God, graciously deigns to call them His brothers and sisters in God's divine family (Matt. 12:50; cf. John 15:15). God's purpose is to make us like Christ in order to create a great redeemed and glorified humanity over which He will reign and be forever preeminent.

In his letter to Philippi, Paul beautifully portrays God's purpose of glorifying Christ: "God highly exalted Him, and bestowed on Him the name which is above every name, that at the name of Jesus every knee should bow, of those who are in heaven, and on earth, and under the earth" (Phil. 2:9-10). Our ultimate purpose as the redeemed children of God will be to spend eternity worshiping and giving praise to God's beloved **first-born**, our preeminent Lord and Savior, Jesus Christ. To the Colossians, Paul further explains that Christ not only is presently the "head of the body, the church," but is also "the beginning, the first-born from the dead; so that He Himself might come to have first place in everything" (Col. 1:18).

God's original purpose in creation was to make a people in His divine image who would give Him honor and glory by serving and obeying Him in all things. But when Adam and Eve rebelled, alienating themselves from God and bringing damnation upon themselves and all subsequent humanity, God had to provide a way of bringing fallen mankind back to Himself.

Through Christ, He provided that way by placing the sins of all mankind upon His sinless Son, causing "the iniquity of us all to fall on Him" (Isa. 53:6). Those who trust in that gracious sacrifice on their behalf are saved from their sins and given God's own glory.

As the redeemed of God, conformed to the image of His Son, we will forever glorify Him with the glory He has given us. Like the twenty-four elders who fell down before Christ on His throne, we will cast our crowns of righteousness (2 Tim. 4:8), of life (James 1:12; Rev. 2:10), and of glory (1 Pet. 5:4) at our Savior's feet, exclaiming, "Worthy art Thou, our Lord and our God, to receive glory and honor and power; for Thou didst create all things, and because of Thy will they existed, and were created" (Rev. 4:10-11).

We thank the Lord for giving us salvation and the eternal life, peace, and joy that salvation brings. But our greatest thanks should be for the unspeakable privilege we have been given of glorifying Christ throughout all eternity.

The Progress of Salvation

For whom He foreknew, He also predestined . . . and whom He predestined, these He also called; and whom He called, these He also justified; and whom He justified, these He also glorified. (8:29a-b, 30)

In delineating the progress of God's plan of salvation, Paul here briefly states what may be called its five major elements: foreknowledge, predestination, calling, justification, and glorification.

It is essential to realize that these five links in the chain of God's saving work are unbreakable. With the repetition of the connecting phrase **He also,** Paul accentuates that unity by linking each element to the previous one. No one whom God foreknows will fail to be predestined, called, justified, and glorified by Him. It is also significant to note the tense in which the apostle states each element of God's saving work. Paul is speaking here of the Lord's redemptive work from eternity past to eternity future. What he says is true of all believers of all times. Security in Christ is so absolute and unalterable that even the salvation of believers not yet born can be expressed in the past tense, as if it had already occurred. Because God is not bound by time as we are, there is a sense in which the elements not only are sequential but simultaneous. Thus, from His view they are distinct and in another sense are indistinguishable. God has made each of them an indispensable part of the unity of our salvation.

FOREKNOWLEDGE

For whom He foreknew, (8:29a)

Redemption began with God's foreknowledge. A believer is first of all someone **whom He** [God] **foreknew.** Salvation is not initiated by a person's decision to receive Jesus Christ as Lord and Savior. Scripture is clear that repentant faith is essential to salvation and is the first step that *we* take in response to God, but repentant faith does not initiate salvation. Because Paul is here depicting the plan of salvation from God's perspective, faith is not even mentioned in these two verses.

In His omniscience God is certainly able to look to the end of history and beyond and to know in advance the minutest detail of the most insignificant occurrences. But it is both unbiblical and illogical to argue from that truth that the Lord simply looked ahead to see who would believe and then chose those particular individuals for salvation.

If that were true, salvation not only would begin with man's faith but would make God obligated to grant it. In such a scheme, God's initiative would be eliminated and His grace would be vitiated.

That idea also prompts such questions as, "Why then does God create unbelievers if He knows in advance they are going to reject Him?" and "Why doesn't He create only believers?" Another unanswerable question would be, "If God based salvation on His advance knowledge of those who would believe, where did their saving faith come from?" It could not arise from their fallen natures, because the natural, sinful person is at enmity with God (Rom. 5:10; 8:7; Eph. 2:3; Col. 1:21). There is absolutely nothing in man's carnal nature to prompt him to trust in the God against whom he is rebelling. The unsaved person is blind and dead to the things of God. He has absolutely no source of saving faith within himself. "A natural man does not accept the things of the Spirit of God," Paul declares; "for they are foolishness to him, and he cannot understand them, because they are spiritually appraised" (1 Cor. 2:14). "The god of this world has blinded the minds of the unbelieving, that they might not see the light of the gospel of the glory of Christ, who is the image of God" (2 Cor. 4:4).

The full truth about God's omniscience cannot be comprehended even by believers. No matter how much we may love God and study His Word, we cannot fathom such mysteries. We can only believe what the Bible clearly says—that God does indeed foresee the faith of every person who is saved. We also believe God's revelation that, although men cannot be saved apart from the faithful action of their wills, saving faith, just as every other part of salvation, originates with and is empowered by God alone.

While He was preaching in Galilee early in His ministry, Jesus said, "All that the Father gives Me shall come to Me, and the one who comes to Me I will certainly not cast out" (John 6:37). But lest that statement be interpreted as leaving open the possibility of coming to Him apart from the Father's sending, Jesus later declared categorically that "No one can come to Me, unless the Father who sent Me draws him" (v. 44). New life through the blood of Christ does not come from "the will of the flesh, nor of the will of man, but of God" (John 1:13).

Paul also explains that even faith does not originate with the believer but with God. "For by grace you have been saved through faith; and that not of yourselves, it is the gift of God; not as a result of works, that no one should boast" (Eph. 2:8-9).

God's foreknowledge is not a reference to His omniscient foresight but to His foreordination. He not only sees faith in advance but ordains it in advance. Peter had the same reality in mind when he wrote of Christians as those "who are chosen according to the foreknowledge of

God the Father" (1 Pet. 1:1-2). Peter used the same word "foreknowledge" when he wrote that Christ "was foreknown before the foundation of the world" (1 Pet. 1:20). The term means the same thing in both places. Believers were foreknown in the same way Christ was foreknown. That cannot mean foreseen, but must refer to a predetermined choice by God. It is the knowing of predetermined intimate relationship, as when God said to Jeremiah, "Before I formed you in the womb I knew you" (Jer. 1:5). Jesus spoke of the same kind of knowing when He said, "I am the good shepherd; and I know My own" (John 10:14).

Because saving faith is foreordained by God, it would have to be that the way of salvation was foreordained, as indeed it was. During his sermon at Pentecost, Peter declared of Christ: "This Man, delivered up by the predetermined plan and foreknowledge of God, you nailed to a cross by the hands of godless men and put Him to death" (Acts 2:23). "Predetermined" is from *horizō,* from which we get the English *horizon,* which designates the outer limits of the earth that we can see from a given vantage point. The basic idea of the Greek term refers to the setting of any boundaries or limits. "Plan" is from *boulē,* a term used in classical Greek to designate an officially convened, decision-making counsel. Both words include the idea of willful intention. "Foreknowledge" is from the noun form of the verb translated **foreknew** in our text. According to what Greek scholars refer to as Granville Sharp's rule, if two nouns of the same case (in this instance, "plan" and "foreknowledge") are connected by *kai* ("and") and have the definite article (the) before the first noun but not before the second, the nouns refer to the same thing (H. E. Dana and Julius R. Mantey, *A Manual Grammar of the Greek New Testament* [New York: Macmillan, 1927], p. 147). In other words, Peter equates God's predetermined plan, or foreordination, and His foreknowledge.

In addition to the idea of foreordination, the term *foreknowledge* also connotes forelove. God has a predetermined divine love for those He plans to save.

Foreknew is from *proginōskō,* a compound word with meaning beyond that of simply knowing beforehand. In Scripture, "to know" often carries the idea of special intimacy and is frequently used of a love relationship. In the statement "Cain had relations with his wife and she conceived" (Gen. 4:17), the word behind "had relations with" is the normal Hebrew verb for knowing. It is the same word translated "chosen" in Amos 3:2, where the Lord says to Israel, "You only have I chosen among all the families of the earth." God "knew" Israel in the unique sense of having predetermined that she would be His chosen people. In Matthew's account of Jesus' birth, "kept her a virgin" (NASB) translates a Greek phrase meaning literally, "did not know her" (Matt. 1:25). Jesus used the same word when He warned, "Then I will declare to them, 'I never knew you; depart from Me, you who practice lawlessness'" (Matt.

7:23). He was not saying that He had never heard of those unbelievers but that He had no intimate relationship with them as their Savior and Lord. But of believers, Paul says, "The Lord knows those who are His" (2 Tim. 2:19).

PREDESTINATION

He also predestined (8:29b)

From foreknowledge, which looks at the beginning of God's purpose in His act of choosing, God's plan of redemption moves to His predestination, which looks at the end of God's purpose in His act of choosing. *Proorizō* (**predestined**) means literally to mark out, appoint, or determine beforehand. The Lord has predetermined the destiny of every person who will believe in Him. Just as Jesus was crucified "by the predetermined plan and foreknowledge of God" (Acts 2:23), so God **also** has **predestined** every believer to salvation through the means of that atoning sacrifice.

In their prayer of gratitude for the deliverance of Peter and John, a group of believers in Jerusalem praised God for His sovereign power, declaring, "For truly in this city there were gathered together against Thy holy servant Jesus, whom Thou didst anoint, both Herod and Pontius Pilate, along with the Gentiles and the peoples of Israel, to do whatever Thy hand and Thy purpose predestined to occur" (Acts 4:27-28). In other words, the evil and powerful men who nailed Jesus to the cross could not have so much as laid a finger on Him were that not according to God's predetermined plan.

In the opening of his letter to the Ephesian believers, Paul encouraged them with the glorious truth that God "chose us in Him before the foundation of the world, that we should be holy and blameless before Him. In love He predestined us to adoption as sons through Jesus Christ to Himself, according to the kind intention of His will" (Eph. 1:4-5).

Much contemporary evangelism gives the impression that salvation is predicated on a person's decision for Christ. But we are not Christians first of all because of what we decided about Christ but because of what God decided about us before the foundation of the world. We were able to choose Him only because He had first chosen us, "according to the kind intention of His will." Paul expresses the same truth a few verses later when he says, "In Him we have redemption through His blood, the forgiveness of our trespasses, according to the riches of His grace, which He lavished upon us. In all wisdom and insight He made known to us the mystery of His will, *according to His kind intention which He purposed in Him*" (Eph. 1:7-9, emphasis added). He then says that "we have obtained an inheritance, having been predestined according to His purpose who works all things after the counsel of His will" (v. 11).

CALLING

and whom He predestined, these He also called; (8:30*a*)

In God's divine plan of redemption, predestination leads to calling. Although God's calling is also completely by His initiative, it is here that His eternal plan directly intersects our lives in time. Those who are **called** are those in whose hearts the Holy Spirit works to lead them to saving faith in Christ.

As noted under the discussion of verse 28, Paul is speaking in this passage about God's inward call, not the outward call that comes from the proclamation of the gospel. The outward call is essential, because "How shall they believe in Him whom they have not heard?" (Rom. 10:14), but that outward call cannot be responded to in faith apart from God's already having inwardly **called** the person through His Spirit.

The Lord's sovereign calling of believers gives still further confirmation that we are eternally secure in Christ. We were saved because God "called us with a holy calling, not according to our works, but according to His own purpose and grace which was granted us in Christ Jesus from all eternity" (2 Tim. 1:9). Emphasizing the same truths of the Lord's sovereign purpose in His calling of believers, Paul assured the Thessalonians that "God has chosen you from the beginning for salvation through sanctification by the Spirit and faith in the truth. And it was for this He called you through our gospel, that you may gain the glory of our Lord Jesus Christ" (2 Thess. 2:13-14). From beginning to end, our salvation is God's work, not our own. Consequently, we cannot humanly undo what He has divinely done. That is the basis of our security.

It should be strongly emphasized, however, that Scripture nowhere teaches that God chooses unbelievers for condemnation. To our finite minds, that what would seem to be the corollary of God's calling believers to salvation. But in the divine scheme of things, which far surpasses our understanding, God predestines believers to eternal life, but Scripture *does not* say that He predestines unbelievers to eternal damnation. Although those two truths seem paradoxical to us, we can be sure that they are in perfect divine harmony.

Scripture teaches many truths that seem paradoxical and contradictory. It teaches plainly that God is one, but just as plainly that there are three persons—the Father, the Son, and the Holy Spirit—in the single Godhead. With equal unambiguity the Bible teaches that Jesus Christ is both fully God and fully man. Our finite minds cannot reconcile such seemingly irreconcilable truths, yet they are foundational truths of God's Word.

If a person goes to hell, it is because He rejects God and His way of salvation. "He who believes in Him [Christ] is not judged; he who does not believe has been judged already, because he has not believed in the name of the only begotten Son of God" (John 3:18). As John has declared earlier in his gospel, believers are saved and made children of God "not of blood, nor of the will of the flesh, nor of the will of man, but of God" (John 1:13). But he makes no corresponding statement in regard to unbelievers, nor does any other part of Scripture. Unbelievers are condemned by their own unbelief, not by God's predestination.

Peter makes plain that God does not desire "for any to perish but for all to come to repentance" (2 Pet. 3:9). Paul declares with equal clarity: "God our Savior . . . desires all men to be saved and to come to the knowledge of the truth" (1 Tim. 2:3-4). Every believer is indebted solely to God's grace for his eternal salvation, but every unbeliever is himself solely responsible for his eternal damnation.

God does not choose believers for salvation on the basis of who they are or of what they have done but on the basis of His sovereign grace. For His own reasons alone, God chose Jacob above Esau (Rom. 9:13). For His own reasons alone, He chose Israel to be His covenant people (Deut. 7:7-8).

We cannot understand God's choosing us for salvation but can only thank and glorify Him for "His grace, which He freely bestowed on us in the Beloved" (Eph. 1:6). We can only believe and be forever grateful that we were called "by the grace of Christ" (Gal. 1:6) and that "the gifts and the calling of God are irrevocable" (Rom. 11:29).

JUSTIFICATION

and whom He called, these He also justified; (8:30b)

The next element of God's saving work is justification of those who believe. After they are **called** by God, they are **also justified** by Him. And just as foreknowledge, predestination, and calling are the exclusive work of God, so is justification.

Because justification is discussed in considerable detail in chapters 17-18 of this volume, it is necessary here simply to point out that **justified** refers to a believer's being made right *with* God *by* God. Because "all have sinned and fall short of the glory of God," men can only be "justified as a gift by [God's] grace through the redemption which is in Christ Jesus" (Rom. 3:24).

GLORIFICATION

and whom He justified, these He also glorified. (8:30c)

As with foreknowledge, predestination, calling, and justification, glorification is inseparable from the other elements and is exclusively a work of God.

In saying that those **whom He justified, these He also glorified,** Paul again emphasizes the believer's eternal security. As noted above, no one whom God foreknows will fail to be predestined, called, justified, and ultimately **glorified.** As believers, we know with absolute certainty that awaiting us is "an eternal weight of glory far beyond all comparison" (2 Cor. 4:17).

Ultimate glory has been a recurring theme throughout Paul's epistle to the Romans. In 5:2 he wrote, "We exult in hope of the glory of God." In 8:18 he said, "I consider that the sufferings of this present time are not worthy to be compared with the glory that is to be revealed to us." He anticipated that marvelous day when "creation itself also will be set free from its slavery to corruption into the freedom of the glory of the children of God" (8:21).

To the Thessalonians Paul wrote that our ultimate glorification is the very purpose for which we are redeemed: "It was for this He called you through our gospel, that you may gain the glory of our Lord Jesus Christ" (2 Thess. 2:14).

This promise of final glory was no uncertain hope as far as Paul was concerned. By putting the phrase **these He also glorified** in the past tense, the apostle demonstrated his own conviction that everyone **whom He justifed** is eternally secure. Those who "obtain the salvation which is in Christ Jesus [receive] with it eternal glory" (2 Tim. 2:10). That is God's own guarantee.

The Hymn of Security

What then shall we say to these things? If God is for us, who is against us? He who did not spare His own Son, but delivered Him up for us all, how will He not also with Him freely give us all things? Who will bring a charge against God's elect? God is the one who justifies; who is the one who condemns? Christ Jesus is He who died, yes, rather who was raised, who is at the right hand of God, who also intercedes for us. Who shall separate us from the love of Christ? Shall tribulation, or distress, or persecution, or famine, or nakedness, or peril, or sword? Just as it is written, "For Thy sake we are being put to death all day long; we were considered as sheep to be slaughtered." But in all these things we overwhelmingly conquer through Him who loved us. For I am convinced that neither death, nor life, nor angels, nor principalities, nor things present, nor things to come, nor powers, nor height, nor depth, nor any other created thing, shall be able to separate us from the love of God, which is in Christ Jesus our Lord. (8:31-39)

Paul closes this magnificent chapter with what might be called a hymn of security. With all the apostle has said previously in this chapter about security, especially after his climactic declarations in verses 28-30, it would seem there was nothing left to add. But this closing passage is a crescendo of questions and answers regarding issues some objectors might still raise. Although verses 31-39 continue his argument in defense of security, they also amount to an almost poetic declaration of thanksgiving for God's grace, in which His children will live and rejoice throughout all eternity.

THE INTRODUCTION

What then shall we say to these things? (8:31a)

Judging from what Paul says in the rest of the passage, **these things** doubtless refer to the issues he has already dealt with in the chapter. Much of what he says in verses 31-39 relates to the doctrine of Christ's substitutionary atonement, but the specific focus is still on the security that His atonement brings to those who believe in Him.

Paul realizes that many fearful believers will still have doubts about their security and that false teachers would be ready to exploit those doubts. To give such believers the assurance they need, the apostle reveals God's answer to two closely related questions: Can any person or can any circumstance cause a believer to lose his salvation?

PERSONS WHO MIGHT SEEM TO THREATEN OUR SECURITY

If God is for us, who is against us? He who did not spare His own Son, but delivered Him up for us all, how will He not also with Him freely give us all things? Who will bring a charge against God's elect? God is the one who justifies; who is the one who condemns? Christ Jesus is He who died, yes, rather who was raised, who is at the right hand of God, who also intercedes for us. (8:31b-34)

Paul begins with an all-encompassing rhetorical question, **If God is for us, who is against us?** The word **if** translates the Greek conditional particle *ei*, signifying a fulfilled condition, not a mere possibility. The meaning of the first clause is therefore "*Because* **God is for us.**"

The obvious implication is that if anyone were able to rob us of salvation they would have to be greater than God Himself, because He is both the giver and the sustainer of salvation. To Christians Paul is asking, in effect, "Who could conceivably take away our no-condemnation status?" (see 8:1). Is there anyone stronger than God, the Creator of everything and everyone who exists?

David declared with unreserved confidence, "The Lord is my light and my salvation; whom shall I fear? The Lord is the defense of my life; whom shall I dread?" (Ps. 27:1). In another psalm we read, "God is our refuge and strength, a very present help in trouble. Therefore we will not fear, though the earth should change, and though the mountains slip into the heart of the sea; though its waters roar and foam, though the mountains quake at its swelling pride. . . . The Lord of hosts is with us; the God of Jacob is our stronghold" (Ps. 46:1-3, 11).

Proclaiming the immeasurable greatness of God, Isaiah wrote,

> It is He who sits above the vault of the earth, and its inhabitants are like grasshoppers, who stretches out the heavens like a curtain and spreads them out like a tent to dwell in. . . . Lift up your eyes on high and see who has created these stars, the One who leads forth their host by number, He calls them all by name; because of the greatness of His might and the strength of His power not one of them is missing. . . . Do you not know? Have you not heard? The Everlasting God, the Lord, the Creator of the ends of the earth does not become weary or tired. His understanding is inscrutable. (Isa. 40:22, 26, 28)

In Romans 8:31 Paul does not specify any particular persons who might be successful against us, but it would be helpful to consider some of the possibilities.

First of all, we might wonder, "Can other people rob us of salvation?" Many of Paul's initial readers of this epistle were Jewish and would be familiar with the Judaizing heresy promulgated by highly legalistic Jews who claimed to be Christians. They insisted that no person, Jew or Gentile, could be saved or maintain his salvation without strict observance of the Mosaic law, and especially circumcision.

The Jerusalem Council was called to discuss that very issue, and its binding decision was that no Christian is under the ritual law of the Mosaic covenant (see Acts 15:1-29). The major thrust of Paul's letter to the churches in Galatia was against the Judaizing heresy and is summarized in the following passage:

> If you receive circumcision, Christ will be of no benefit to you. And I testify again to every man who receives circumcision, that he is under obligation to keep the whole Law. You have been severed from Christ, you who are seeking to be justified by law; you have fallen from grace. For we through the Spirit, by faith, are waiting for the hope of righteousness. For in Christ

Jesus neither circumcision nor uncircumcision means anything, but faith working through love. (Gal. 5:2-6; cf. 2:11-16; 3:1-15)

The Roman Catholic church teaches that salvation can be lost by committing so-called mortal sins and also claims power for itself both to grant and to revoke grace. But such ideas have no foundation in Scripture and are thoroughly heretical. No person or group of persons, regardless of their ecclesiastical status, can bestow or withdraw the smallest part of God's grace.

When Paul was bidding farewell to the Ephesian elders who had come to meet him at Miletus, he warned, "Be on guard for yourselves and for all the flock, among which the Holy Spirit has made you overseers, to shepherd the church of God which He purchased with His own blood. I know that after my departure savage wolves will come in among you, not sparing the flock; and from among your own selves men will arise, speaking perverse things, to draw away the disciples after them" (Acts 20:28-30). Paul was not suggesting that true believers can be robbed of salvation but was warning that they can be seriously misled, confused, and weakened in their faith and that the cause of the gospel can be greatly hindered. Although false teaching cannot prevent the completion of a believer's salvation, it can easily confuse an unbeliever regarding salvation.

Second, we might wonder if Christians can put themselves out of God's grace by committing some unusually heinous sin that nullifies the divine work of redemption that binds them to the Lord. Tragically, some evangelical churches teach that loss of salvation is possible. But if we were not able by our own power or effort to save ourselves—to free ourselves from sin, to bring ourselves to God, and to make ourselves His children—how could it be that by our own efforts we could nullify the work of grace that God Himself has accomplished in us?

Third, we might wonder if God the Father would take away our salvation. It was, after all, the Father who "so loved the world, that He gave His only begotten Son, that whoever believes in Him should not perish, but have eternal life" (John 3:16). If anyone could take away salvation, it would have to be the One who gave it. We might argue theoretically that, because God is sovereign and omnipotent, He *could* take away salvation if He wanted to. But the idea that He *would* do that flies in the face of Scripture, including the present text.

In answer to such a suggestion, Paul asks, **He who did not spare His own Son, but delivered Him up for us all, how will He not also with Him freely give us all things?** How could it possibly be that God would sacrifice His own Son for the sake of those who believe in Him and then cast some of those blood-bought believers out of His family and His kingdom? Would God do less for believers after they are saved than He did for them prior to salvation? Would He do less for His children than He did for His enemies? If God loved us so much while we were wretched sinners that He delivered up **His own Son . . . for us,** would He turn His back on us after we have been cleansed from sin and made righteous in His sight?

Isaac was an Old Testament picture of Christ. When God commanded Abraham to sacrifice Isaac, the only son of promise, both Abraham and Isaac willingly obeyed. Abraham's willingness to sacrifice Isaac is a beautiful foreshadow of God the Father's willingness to offer up His only begotten Son as a sacrifice for the sins of the world. Isaac's willingness to be sacrificed foreshadows Christ's willingness to go to the cross. God intervened to spare Isaac and provided a ram in his place (Gen. 22:1-13). At that point, however, the analogy changes from comparison to contrast, because God **did not spare His own Son, but delivered Him up for us all.**

Isaiah extoled the wondrous love of both God the Father and God the Son when he wrote,

> Surely our griefs He Himself [Christ, the Son] bore, and our sorrows He carried; yet we ourselves esteemed Him stricken, smitten of God [the Father], and afflicted. But He was pierced through for our transgressions, He was crushed for our iniquities; the chastening for our well being fell upon Him, and by His scourging we are healed. All of us like sheep have gone astray, each of us has turned to his own way; but the Lord has caused the iniquity of us all to fall on Him. . . . But the Lord [the Father] was pleased to crush Him [the Son], putting Him to grief; if He would render Himself as a guilt offering. (Isa. 53:4-6, 10)

Jesus' sacrifice on the cross not only is the foundation of our salvation but also of our security. Because the Father loved us so much while we were still under condemnation, "He made Him who knew no sin to be sin on our behalf, that we might become the righteousness of God in Him" (2 Cor. 5:21). Because the Son loved us so much while we were still under condemnation, He "gave Himself for our sins, that He might deliver us out of this present evil age, according to the will of our God and Father" (Gal. 1:4; cf. 3:13).

Jesus promises all those who belong to Him: "In My Father's house are many dwelling places; if it were not so, I would have told you; for I go to prepare a place for you. And if I go and prepare a place for you, I will come again, and receive you to Myself; that where I am, there you may be also" (John 14:2-3). The Lord makes no allowance for any of His people to be lost again, but promises each one of them an eternal home in His eternal presence. Jesus also assures us that the Holy Spirit will be with us forever (John 14:16), again making no allowance for exceptions. What power in heaven or earth could rob the Godhead of those who have been divinely saved for eternity?

Beginning in verse 8 of chapter 12, Paul speaks almost entirely in the first and second persons, referring to himself and to fellow believers. It is the same spiritual brethren (**us**) he speaks of twice in verse 32. If the Father delivered up His Son **for us all**, he argues, **how will He not also with Him freely give us all things?** In his letter to Ephesus the apostle is also speaking of fellow believers when he says, "Blessed be the God and Father of our Lord Jesus Christ, who has blessed us with every spiritual blessing in the heavenly places in Christ" (Eph. 1:3). If God blesses **all of us**, His children, with "every spiritual blessing in the heavenly places in Christ," loss of salvation is clearly impossible. *All* believers receive that eternal inheritance.

Freely give translates *charizomai,* which means to bestow graciously or out of grace. In some of Paul's other letters the same word carries the idea of forgiveness (see 2 Cor. 2:7, 10; 12:13; Col. 2:13; 3:13). It therefore seems reasonable to interpret Paul's use of *charizomai* in Romans 8:32 as including the idea of God's gracious forgiveness as well as His gracious giving. If so, the apostle is also saying that God **freely** *forgives* **us all things** (cf. 1 John 1:9). God's unlimited forgiveness makes it impossible for a believer to sin himself out of God's grace.

In order to assure His people of their security in Him, "in the same way God, desiring even more to show to the heirs of the promise the unchangeableness of His purpose, interposed with an oath, in order that by two unchangeable things, in which it is impossible for God to lie, we may have strong encouragement, we who have fled for refuge in laying hold of the hope set before us" (Heb. 6:17-18). The two unchangeable features of God's unchangeable purpose are His promise and His oath to honor that promise. What greater proof of security could we have than the unchangeable purpose of God to save and keep His elect, the heirs of promise?

Fourth, we might wonder if Satan can take away our salvation. Because he is our most powerful supernatural enemy, if anyone other than God could rob us of salvation, it would surely be the devil. He is called "the accuser of [the] brethren" (Rev. 12:10), and the book of Job depicts him clearly in that role:

> And the Lord said to Satan, "Have you considered My servant Job? For there is no one like him on the earth, a blameless and upright man, fearing God and turning away from evil." Then Satan answered the Lord, "Does Job fear God for nothing? Hast Thou not made a hedge about him and his house and all that he has, on every side? Thou hast blessed the work of his hands,

and his possessions have increased in the land. But put forth Thy hand
now and touch all that he has; he will surely curse Thee to Thy face
(Job 1:8-11)

Satan accused Job of worshiping God out of selfishness rather
than out of reverence and love. Although Job at one point questioned
God's wisdom and was divinely rebuked (chaps. 38-41), he repented and
was forgiven. From the beginning to the end of Job's testing, the Lord
affectionately called him "My servant" (see 1:8; 42:7-8). Although Job's
faith was not perfect, it was genuine. The Lord therefore permitted Satan
to test Job, but He knew Satan could never destroy Job's persevering faith
or rob His servant of salvation.

In one of his visions, the prophet Zechariah reports: "Then he [an
angel] showed me Joshua the high priest standing before the angel of
the Lord, and Satan standing at his right hand to accuse him. And the
Lord said to Satan, 'The Lord rebuke you, Satan! Indeed, the Lord who has
chosen Jerusalem rebuke you! Is this not a brand plucked from the fire?'"
(Zech. 3:1-2). Although "Joshua was clothes with filthy garments" (v. 3),
that is, was still living with the sinful flesh, he was one of the Lord's
redeemed and was beyond Satan's power to destroy or discredit.

Satan also tried to undermine Peter's faith, and Jesus warned him
of that danger, saying, "Simon, Simon, behold, Satan has demanded permission to sift you like wheat." He then assured the apostle, "but I have
prayed for you, that your faith may not fail" (Luke 22:31-32).

Because every believer has that divine protection, Paul asks, **Who
will bring a charge against God's elect? God is the one who justifies; who is the one who condemns?** The world and Satan are continually bringing charges **against God's elect,** but those charges amount
to nothing before the Lord, because He **is the one who justifies,** the
one who decides who is righteous before Him. They have been declared
eternally guiltless and are no longer under the condemnation of God
(8:1), the only **one who condemns.** God conceived the law, revealed
the law, interprets the law, and applies the law. And through the sacrifice
of His Son, all the demands of the law have been met for those who trust
in Him.

That great truth inspired Count Zinzendorf to write the following
lines in the glorious hymn "Jesus, Thy Blood and Righteousness," translated by John Wesley:

> Bold shall I stand in Thy great day,
> For who aught to my charge shall lay?
> Fully absolved through these I am
> From sin and fear, from guilt and shame.

It is not that the accusations made against believers by Satan and the unbelieving world are always false. The fact that we are not yet sinless is obvious. But even when a charge against us is true, it is never sufficient grounds for our damnation, because all our sins—past, present, and future—have been covered by the blood of Christ and we are now clothed in His righteousness.

Fifth, we might wonder if our Savior Himself would take back our salvation. Anticipating that question, Paul declares, **Christ Jesus is He who died, yes, rather who was raised, who is at the right hand of God, who also intercedes for us.** It is because Jesus makes continuous intercession for *all* believers, **God's elect,** that "they shall never perish" and that "no one shall snatch them out of [His] hand" (John 10:28). For **Christ** to take away our salvation would be for Him to work against Himself and to nullify His own promise. Christ offers no temporary spiritual life but only that which is eternal. He could not grant eternal life and then take it away, because that would demonstrate that the life He had granted was *not* eternal.

In verse 34 Paul reveals four realities that protect our salvation in Jesus Christ. First, he says that **Christ Jesus . . . died.** In His death He took upon Himself the full penalty for our sins. In His death He bore the condemnation that we deserved but from which we are forever freed (8:1). The death of the Lord Jesus Christ on our behalf is the only condemnation we will ever know.

Second, Christ **was raised** from the dead, proving His victory over sin and over its supreme penalty of death. The grave could not hold Jesus, because He had conquered death; and His conquest over death bequeaths eternal life to every person who trusts in Him. As Paul has declared earlier in this letter, Christ "was delivered up because of our transgressions, and was raised because of our justification" (Rom. 4:25). His death paid the price for our sins and His resurrection gave absolute proof that the price was paid. When God raised Jesus from the dead, He demonstrated that His Son had offered the full satisfaction for sin that the law demands.

Third, Christ **is at the right hand of God,** the place of divine exaltation and honor. Because "He humbled Himself by becoming obedient to the point of death, even death on a cross, . . . God highly exalted Him, and bestowed on Him the name which is above every name" (Phil. 2:8-9). David foretold that glorious event when he wrote, "The Lord says to my Lord: 'Sit at My right hand, until I make Thine enemies a footstool for Thy feet'" (Ps. 110:1).

There were no seats in the Temple, because the sacrifices made there by the priests were never finished. They were but pictures of the one and only true sacrifice that the Son of God one day would make. The writer of Hebrews explains that "every priest stands daily ministering and offering time after time the same sacrifices, which can never take away sins; but He [Christ], having offered one sacrifice for sins for all time, sat down at the right hand of God" (Heb. 10:11-12; cf. 1:3).

Fourth, Christ **also intercedes for us.** Although His work of atonement was finished, His continuing ministry of intercession for those saved through His sacrifice will continue without interruption until every redeemed soul is safe in heaven. Just as Isaiah had prophesied, "He poured out Himself to death, and was numbered with the transgressors; yet He Himself bore the sin of many, and interceded for the transgressors" (Isa. 53:12). Jesus Christ "is able to save forever those who draw near to God through Him, since He always lives to make intercession for them" (Heb. 7:25).

If we understand what Christ did on the cross to save us from sin, we understand what it means to be secure in His salvation. If we believe that God loved us so much when we were wretched and ungodly that He sent His Son to die on the cross to bring us to Himself, how could we believe that, after we are saved, His love is not strong enough to keep us saved? If Christ had power to redeem us out of bondage to sin, how could He lack power to keep us redeemed?

Christ, the perfect Priest, offered a perfect sacrifice to make us perfect. To deny the security of the believer is therefore to deny the sufficiency of the work of Christ. To deny the security of the believer is to misunderstand the heart of God, to misunderstand the gift of Christ, to misunderstand the meaning of the cross, to misunderstand the biblical meaning of salvation.

Even when we sin after we are saved, "if we confess our sins, He is faithful and righteous to forgive us our sins and to cleanse us from all unrighteousness," because in Him "we have an Advocate with the Father, Jesus Christ the righteous" (1 John 1:9; 2:1). When we sin, our Lord intercedes on our behalf and comes to our defense against Satan and any others who might bring charges against us (see Rom. 8:33). "God is able to make all grace abound to you," Paul assured the believers at Corinth (2 Cor. 9:8). Through our remaining days on earth and throughout all eternity, our gracious Lord will hold us safe in His everlasting love by His everlasting power.

CIRCUMSTANCES THAT MIGHT SEEM TO THREATEN OUR SECURITY

Who shall separate us from the love of Christ? Shall tribulation, or distress, or persecution, or famine, or nakedness, or peril, or sword? Just as it is written, "For Thy sake we are being put to

**death all day long; we were considered as sheep to be slaughtered."
But in all these things we overwhelmingly conquer through Him
who loved us.** (8:35-37)

After establishing that it is impossible for any person to take away
our salvation, Paul anticipates a similar question that some will ask: "Is it
possible for circumstances to rob a believer of his salvation?" The apostle
now proceeds to show that that, too, is impossible.

The interrogative pronoun *tis* (**who**) is the same word that begins
the previous two verses. But the Greek term also can mean "what," and
the fact that Paul speaks only of things and not people in verses 35-37,
makes clear that he is now referring to impersonal things.

Unpleasant and dangerous circumstances obviously can have
a detrimental influence on the faith and endurance of believers. The
question here, however, is whether they can cause a believer to sin himself
out of salvation. In essence, this question is an extension of the one
discussed above regarding the possibility of a believer's dislodging himself
from God's grace.

Paul anticipates and refutes the notion that any circumstance, no
matter how threatening and potentially destructive, can cause a genuine
believer to forfeit his salvation. In verse 35 Paul lists a representative few
of the countless ominous circumstances that faithful believers may
encounter while they still live in the world.

First of all, it should be noted that **the love of Christ** does not
refer to the believer's love for Him but rather to His love for the believer
(see vv. 37, 39). No person can love Christ who has not experienced the
redeeming work of Christ's love for him: "We love, because He first loved
us" (1 John 4:19).

In this context, **the love of Christ** represents salvation. Paul is
therefore asking rhetorically if any circumstance is powerful enough to
cause a true believer to turn against **Christ** in a way that would cause
Christ to turn His back on the believer. At issue, then, are the power
and permanence of **the love of Christ** for those He has bought with His
own blood and brought into the family and the kingdom of His Father.

John reports that "Before the Feast of the Passover, Jesus knowing
that His hour had come that He should depart out of this world to the
Father, having loved His own who were in the world, He loved them to
the end" (John 13:1). As John makes clear in his first epistle, "the end"
does not refer simply to the end of Jesus' earthly life but to the end of
every believer's earthly life. "By this the love of God was manifested in
us, that God has sent His only begotten Son into the world so that we
might live through Him. In this is love, not that we loved God, but that
He loved us and sent His Son to be the propitiation for our sins. . . . By
this, love is perfected with us, that we may have confidence in the day of

judgment; because as He is, so also are we in this world" (1 John 4:9-10, 17). We have confidence as we face the day of judgment, because we know that the divine and indestructible **love of Christ** binds us eternally to Him.

In a majestic benediction at the end of the second chapter of his second letter to Thessalonica, Paul says, "Now may our Lord Jesus Christ Himself and God our Father, who has loved us and given us eternal comfort and good hope by grace, comfort and strengthen your hearts in every good work and word" (2 Thess. 2:16-17). Eternal comfort and good hope are the permanent gifts of God's grace, because, by definition, that which is eternal cannot end.

The first threatening circumstance Paul mentions is **tribulation,** from *thlipsis,* which carries the idea of being squeezed or placed under pressure. In Scripture the word is perhaps most often used of outward difficulties, but it is also used of emotional stress. The idea here is probably that of severe adversity in general, the kind that is common to all men.

The second threatening circumstance is **distress,** which translates the compound Greek word *stenochōria,* which is composed of the terms for narrow and space. The idea is similar to that of tribulation and carries the primary idea of strict confinement, of being helplessly hemmed in. In such circumstances a believer can only trust in the Lord and pray for the power to endure. Sometimes we are caught in situations where we are continually confronted with temptations we cannot avoid. Paul counsels believers who are under such **distress** to remember that "no temptation has overtaken you but such as is common to man; and God is faithful, who will not allow you to be tempted beyond what you are able, but with the temptation will provide the way of escape also, that you may be able to endure it" (1 Cor. 10:13). Until He provides a way of escape, the Lord provides the power to resist.

The third threatening circumstance is **persecution,** which refers to affliction suffered for the sake of Christ. Persecution is never pleasant, but in the Beatitudes Jesus gives a double promise of God's blessing us when we suffer for His sake. He then bids us to "rejoice, and be glad, for your reward in heaven is great, for so they persecuted the prophets who were before you" (Matt. 5:10-12).

Famine often results from persecution, when Christians are discriminated against in employment and cannot afford to buy enough food to eat. Many believers have been imprisoned for their faith and have gradually starved to death because of inadequate food.

Nakedness does not refer to complete nudity but to destitution in which a person cannot adequately clothe himself. It also suggests the idea of being vulnerable and unprotected.

To be in **peril** is simply to be exposed to danger in general, including danger from treachery and mistreatment.

The **sword** to which Paul refers was more like a large dagger and was frequently used by assassins, because it was easily concealed. It was a symbol of death and suggests being murdered rather than dying in military battle.

Paul was not speaking of these afflictions in theory or second hand. He himself had faced those hardships and many more, as he reports so vividly in 2 Corinthians 11. Referring to certain Jewish leaders in the church who were boasting of their suffering for Christ, Paul writes,

> Are they servants of Christ? (I speak as if insane) I more so; in far more labors, in far more imprisonments, beaten times without number, often in danger of death. Five times I received from the Jews thirty-nine lashes. Three times I was beaten with rods, once I was stoned, three times I was shipwrecked, a night and a day I have spent in the deep. I have been on frequent journeys, in dangers from rivers, dangers from robbers, dangers from my countrymen, dangers from the Gentiles, dangers in the city, dangers in the wilderness, dangers on the sea, dangers among false brethren; I have been in labor and hardship, through many sleepless nights, in hunger and thirst, often without food, in cold and exposure. (vv. 23-27)

Quoting from the Septuagint (Greek Old Testament) version of Psalm 44:22, Paul continues, **Just as it is written, "For Thy sake we are being put to death all day long; we were considered as sheep to be slaughtered."** In other words, Christians should not be surprised when they have to endure suffering for the sake of Christ.

Before Paul wrote this epistle, God's faithful people had suffered for centuries, not only at the hands of Gentiles but also at the hands of fellow Jews. They "experienced mockings and scourgings, yes, also chains and imprisonment. They were stoned, they were sawn in two, they were tempted, they were put to death with the sword; they went about in sheepskins, in goatskins, being destitute, afflicted, ill-treated (men of whom the world was not worthy), wandering in deserts and mountains and caves and holes in the ground" (Heb. 11:36-38).

The cost of faithfulness to God has always been high. Jesus declared, "He who loves father or mother more than Me is not worthy of Me; and he who loves son or daughter more than Me is not worthy of Me. And he who does not take his cross and follow after Me is not worthy of Me. He who has found his life shall lose it, and he who has lost his life for My sake shall find it" (Matt. 10:37-39). Paul assured his beloved Timothy that "indeed, all who desire to live godly in Christ Jesus will be persecuted" (2 Tim. 3:12).

If a professing Christian turns his back on the things of God or lives persistently in sin, he proves that he never belonged to Christ at all. Such people have not lost their salvation but have never received it. About such nominal Christians, John said, "They went out from us, but they were not really of us; for if they had been of us, they would have remained with us; but they went out, in order that it might be shown that they all are not of us" (1 John 2:19).

If the things of the world continually keep a person from the things of God, that person proves he is not a child of God. During Jesus' earthly ministry, many thousands of people walked great distances to hear Him preach and to receive physical healing for themselves and their loved ones. At His triumphal entry into Jerusalem, the crowd acclaimed Him as their Messiah and wanted to make Him king. But after He was convicted and crucified, and the cost of true discipleship became evident, most of those who had once hailed Christ were nowhere to be found.

Luke gives an account of three men, doubtless representative of many others, who professed allegiance to Jesus but who would not submit to His lordship and thereby proved their lack of saving faith. The first man, whom Matthew identifies as a scribe (8:19), promised to follow Jesus wherever He went. But knowing the man's heart, "Jesus said to him, 'The foxes have holes, and the birds of the air have nests, but the Son of Man has nowhere to lay His head'" (9:57-58). When the Lord called a second man, he asked permission to first bury his father. He did not mean that his father had just died but rather that he wanted to postpone commitment to Christ until after his father eventually died, at which time the son would receive his family inheritance. Jesus "said to him, 'Allow the dead to bury their own dead; but as for you, go and proclaim everywhere the kingdom of God'" (vv. 59-60). In other words, let those who are spiritually dead take care of their own carnal interests. The third man wanted to follow Jesus after he said "goodbye to those at home." To Him the Lord replied, "No one, after putting his hand to the plow and looking back, is fit for the kingdom of God" (vv. 61-62).

We are not told what any of the three men eventually did in regard to following Christ, but the implication is that, like the rich young man (Matt. 19:22), the cost of true discipleship, which is always the mark of true salvation, was too high for them.

Only the true believer perseveres, not because he is strong in himself but because he has the power of God's indwelling Spirit. His perseverance does not keep his salvation safe but proves that his salvation is safe. Those who fail to persevere not only demonstrate their lack of courage but, much more importantly, their lack of genuine faith. God will keep and protect even the most fearful person who truly belongs to Him. On the other hand, even the bravest of those who are merely professing Christians will invariably fall away when the cost of being identified with Christ becomes too great.

Only true Christians are overcomers because only true Christians have the divine help of Christ's own Spirit. "For we have become partakers of Christ," explains the writer of Hebrews, "if we hold fast the beginning of our assurance firm until the end" (Heb. 3:14). To some Jews who believed Him, Jesus said, "If you abide in My word, then you are truly disciples of Mine; and you shall know the truth, and the truth shall make you free" (John 8:31-32). Holding fast and abiding in God's Word neither merit nor preserve salvation. But the presence of those virtues confirms the reality of salvation, and the absence of them confirms the condition of lostness.

Just as we can only love God because He first loved us, we can only hold on to God because He holds on to us. We can survive any threatening circumstance and overcome any spiritual obstacle that the world or Satan puts in our way because **in all these things we overwhelmingly conquer through Him who loved us.**

Overwhelmingly conquer is from *hupernikaō,* a compound verb that literally means to hyper-conquer, to over-conquer, to conquer, as it were, with success to spare. Those who **overwhelmingly conquer** are supremely victorious in overcoming everyone and everything that threatens their relationship to Jesus Christ. But they do so entirely **through** His power, the power of **Him who loved us** so much that He gave His life for us that we might have life in Him.

Because our Lord both saves and keeps us, we do much more than simply endure and survive the ominous circumstances Paul mentions in verse 35. First of all, we **overwhelmingly conquer** by coming out of troubles stronger than when they first threatened us. Paul has just declared that, by His divine grace and power, God causes everything, including the very worst things, to work for the good of His children (8:28). Even when we suffer because of our own sinfulness or unfaithfulness, our gracious Lord will bring us through with a deeper understanding of our own unrighteousness and of His perfect righteousness, of our own faithlessness and of His steadfast faithfulness, of our own weakness and of His great power.

Second, we **overwhelmingly conquer** because our ultimate reward will far surpass whatever earthly and temporal loss we may suffer. With Paul, we should view even the most terrible circumstance as but "momentary, light affliction" that produces "for us an eternal weight of glory far beyond all comparison" (2 Cor. 4:17).

From the human perspective, of course, the over-conquest God promises often seems a long time in coming. But when, as true believers, we go through times of testing, whatever their nature or cause, we come out spiritually refined by our Lord. Instead of those things separating us from Christ, they will bring us closer to Him. His grace and glory will rest on us and we will grow in our understanding of His will and of the sufficiency of His grace. While we wait for Him to bring us through the trials, we know that He says to us what He said to Paul, "My grace is sufficient for you, for power is perfected in weakness." And we should respond with Paul, "Most gladly, therefore, I will rather boast about my weaknesses, that the power of Christ may dwell in me" (2 Cor. 12:9).

Paul probably wrote his letter to Rome during a winter in Corinth, and it is not likely that either Paul or the Roman believers realized how short the time would be before they would stand in need of the apostle's comforting words in this passage. It would not be many years before they would face fierce persecution from a pagan government and people that now tolerated them with indifference. It would not be long before the blood of those to whom this epistle is addressed would soak the sands of Roman amphitheaters. Some would be mauled by wild beasts, some would be slain by ruthless gladiators, and others would be used as human torches to light Nero's garden parties.

Consequently, the true and false believers soon would be easily distinguished. Many congregations would be saying of former members, "They went out from us, but they were not really of us; for if they had been of us, they would have remained with us, but they went out, in order that it might be shown that they all are not of us" (1 John 2:19). But those whom the world looks upon as the overwhelmed and conquered are in reality overwhelming conquerors. In God's scheme of things, the victors are the vanquished and the vanquished are the victors.

THE CONCLUSION

For I am convinced that neither death, nor life, nor angels, nor principalities, nor things present, nor things to come, nor powers, nor height, nor depth, nor any other created thing, shall be able to separate us from the love of God, which is in Christ Jesus our Lord. (8:38-39)

This chapter closes with a beautiful summary of what has just been said. The apostle assures his readers that he was not teaching them anything about which he himself was not fully **convinced**. He was convinced first of all because of the nature of salvation, which God had revealed to him and which he presents so clearly in these first eight chapters. His counsel is also a personal testimony. He was convinced because he had experienced most of the things mentioned and they did not separate him from Christ. Both revelation and experience convinced him. Paul was saying to believers in Rome the same thing he would say some years later to Timothy: "For this reason I also suffer these things, but I am not ashamed; for I know whom I have believed and I am convinced that He is able to guard what I have entrusted to Him until that day" (2 Tim. 1:12).

Paul begins his list with **death**, which, in our earthly life, we experience last. Even that supreme enemy cannot separate us from our Lord, because He has changed death's sting from defeat to victory. We can therefore rejoice in the psalmist's affirmation that "precious in the sight of the Lord is the death of His godly ones" (Ps. 116:15), and we can testify with David that "even though I walk through the valley of the shadow of death, I fear no evil; for Thou art with me; Thy rod and Thy staff, they comfort me" (Ps. 23:4). With Paul, we should "prefer rather to be absent from the body" because that will mean we are finally "at home with the Lord" (2 Cor. 5:8).

Donald Grey Barnhouse told a personal story that beautifully illustrates death's powerlessness over Christians. When his wife died, his children were still quite young, and Dr. Barnhouse wondered how he could explain their mother's death in a way their childish minds could understand. As they drove home from the funeral, a large truck passed them and briefly cast a dark shadow over the car. Immediately the father had the illustration he was looking for, and he asked the children, "Would you rather be run over by a truck or by the shadow of a truck?" "That's easy, Daddy," they replied. "We would rather get run over by the shadow, because that wouldn't hurt." Their father then said, "Well, children, your mother just went through the valley of the shadow of death, and there's no pain there, either."

The second supposed hindrance does not seem like a hindrance at all. We think of **life** as something positive. But it is in our present earthly **life** that spiritual dangers lie. Not only does death itself hold no harm for believers, but it will bring the end of all harm. It is while we still have *this* **life** that we face tribulation, distress, persecution, famine, nakedness, peril, sword (8:35) and the many other trials that Paul could have mentioned. But because we have eternal life in Christ, the threats during our present **life** are empty.

The third supposed threat is **angels**. Because the next danger on the list (**principalities**) doubtless refers to fallen angels, it seems likely that the ones mentioned here are holy **angels**. Paul's reference here to angels presupposes a purely hypothetical and impossible situation, just as did one of his warnings to the Galatians. He told the Galatian believers to stand firm in their salvation through Christ's shed blood on the cross and to refuse to accept any contrary gospel, even if preached, if that were possible, by an apostle or "an angel from heaven" (Gal. 1:8).

The fourth supposed threat is not in the least hypothetical. As already noted, **principalities** seems to refer to evil beings, specifically demons. Like the Greek term (*archē*) behind it, **principalities** indicates neither good nor evil. But the obvious negative use of *archē* in such passages as Ephesians 6:12 ("rulers"), Colossians 2:15 ("rulers"), and Jude 6 ("own domain")—as well as its apparent contrast with the term that precedes it here (angels)—seems to indicate fallen angels, the demons. If so, Paul is saying that no supernatural created being, good or evil, can sever our relationship to Christ.

Things present and **things to come** represent everything we are experiencing and will yet experience.

Powers translates *dunamis,* the ordinary Greek word for power. But in its plural form, as here, it often refers to miracles or mighty deeds. It was also used figuratively of persons in positions of authority and power. Regardless of the specific meaning Paul had in mind here, **powers** represents another obstacle that Christians need not fear.

Paul may have used **height** and **depth** as astrological terms that were familiar in his day, *hupsōma* (**height**) referring to the high point, or zenith, of a star's path, and *bathos* (**depth**) to its lowest point. If so, the idea is that Christ's love secures a believer from the beginning to the end of life's path. Or perhaps he used the terms to signify the infinity of space, which is endless in every direction. In either case, the basic meaning is that of totality.

To leave no doubt that security is all-encompassing, Paul adds **nor any other created thing**. Since only God Himself is uncreated, everyone else and everything else is excluded.

There is nothing anywhere at any time that **shall be able to separate us from the love of God, which is Christ Jesus our Lord.** Our salvation was secured by God's decree from eternity past and will be held secure by Christ's love through all future time and throughout all eternity.

Earlier in this epistle Paul declared that, "as it is written, 'There is none righteous, not even one; there is none who understands, there is none who seeks for God; all have turned aside, together they have become useless; there is none who does good.'" To make sure that no person could make an exception for himself, the apostle added, "there is not even one" (Rom. 3:10-12). In a similar way, Paul allows absolutely no exceptions in regard to the believer's security in Christ.

In this marvelous closing section of chapter 8, verses 31-34 focus on the love of God the Father, and verses 35-39 focus on the love of God the Son. One is reminded of Jesus' high priestly prayer, in which He prays on behalf of believers, "that they may all be one; even as Thou, Father, art in Me, and I in Thee, that they also may be in Us; . . . And the glory which Thou hast given Me I have given to them; that they may be one, just as We are one; I in them, and Thou in Me, that they may be perfected in unity, that the world may know that Thou didst send Me, and didst love them, even as Thou didst love Me. Father, I desire that they also, whom Thou hast given Me, be with Me where I am" (John 17:21-24).

George Matheson was born in Glasgow, Scotland, in 1842. As a child he had only partial vision, and his sight became progressively worse,

517

until it resulted in blindness by the time he was eighteen. Despite his handicap, he was a brilliant student and graduated from the University of Glasgow and later from seminary. He became pastor of several churches in Scotland, including a large church in Edinburgh, where he was greatly respected and loved. After he had been engaged to a young woman for a short while, she broke the engagement, having decided she could not be content married to a blind man. Some believe that this painful disappointment in romantic love led Matheson to write the beautiful hymn which begins with the following stanza:

> O love that will not let me go,
> I rest my weary soul in Thee;
> I give Thee back the life I owe,
> That in Thine ocean depths its flow
> May richer, fuller be.

Because our God is infinite in power and love, "we confidently say, 'The Lord is my helper, I will not be afraid. What shall man do to me?'" (Heb. 13:6). Because our God is infinite in power and love, we can say with David, "When I am afraid, I will put my trust in Thee" (Ps. 56:3) and, "In peace I will both lie down and sleep, for Thou alone, O Lord, dost make me to dwell in safety" (Ps. 4:8). Because our God is infinite in power and love, we can say with Moses, "The eternal God is a dwelling place, and underneath are the everlasting arms" (Deut. 33:27). Because our God is infinite in power and love, we can say with the writer of Hebrews, "This hope we have as an anchor of the soul, a hope both sure and steadfast" (Heb. 6:19).

Bibliography

Alleine, Joseph. *The Alarm to Unconverted Sinners*. Grand Rapids: Baker, 1980 reprint.

Barnhouse, Donald Grey. *Expositions of Bible Doctrines*, vol. 2. *God's Wrath*. Grand Rapids: Eerdmans, 1953, p. 18.

——————. *God's Remedy: Romans 3:21—4:25*. Grand Rapids: Eerdmans, 1954.

——————. *God's River: Romans 5:1-11*. Grand Rapids: Eerdmans, 1959.

——————. *God's Wrath: Romans 2—3:1-20*. Grand Rapids: Eerdmans, 1953.

——————. *Romans: God's Freedom*. Grand Rapids: Eerdmans, 1961.

Baxter, Richard. *The Reformed Pastor*. Carlisle, Pa.: Banner of Truth, 1974.

Bonhoeffer, Dietrich. *The Cost of Discipleship*. New York: Macmillan, 1959.

Bruce, F. F. *The Letter of Paul to the Romans*. Grand Rapids: Eerdmans, 1985.

Calvin, John. *Commentary on the Epistle of Paul the Apostle to the Romans*. Grand Rapids: Baker, 1979.

——————. *The Epistles of Paul the Apostle to the Romans and to the Thessalonians*. Grand Rapids: Eerdmans, 1960.

Cranfield, C. E. B. *A Critical and Exegetical Commentary on the Epistle to the Romans*. Edinburgh: T & T Clark, 1975.

Dana, H. E., and Mantey, Julius R. *A Manual Grammar of the Greek New Testament.* New York: Macmillan, 1927.

Edwards, Jonathan. *The Life of David Brainerd.* Grand Rapids: Baker, 1980 reprint.

——————. *The Works of Jonathan Edwards,* vol. 2. Carlisle, Pa.: Banner of Truth, 1986 reprint.

Haldane, Robert. *An Exposition of the Epistle to the Romans.* MacDill AFB, Fla.: MacDonald, 1958.

Henry, Matthew. *Matthew Henry's Commentary on the Whole Bible.* vol 6. Old Tappan, N.J.: Revell, n.d.

Hodge, Charles. *Commentary on the Epistle to the Romans.* Grand Rapids: Eerdmans, 1983 reprint.

Johnson, Alan. F. *The Freedom Letter.* Chicago: Moody, 1974.

Lewis, C. S. *The Problem of Pain.* N.Y.: Macmillan, 1962.

Lloyd-Jones, D. Martyn. *Romans: An Exposition of Chapter Six.* Grand Rapids: Zondervan, 1972.

Moule, Handley. *The Epistle to the Romans.* London: Pickering & Inglis, n.d.

Murray, John. *The Epistle to the Romans.* Grand Rapids: Eerdmans, 1965.

——————. *Principles of Conduct.* Grand Rapids: Eerdmans, 1957.

——————. *Redemption Accomplished and Applied.* Grand Rapids: Eerdmans, 1955.

Newton, John. *Out of the Depths: An Autobiography.* Chicago, Moody, n.d.

Needham, David C. *Birthright: Christian Do You Know Who You Are?* Portland: Multnomah, 1979.

Owen, John. *Sin and Temptation.* Portland, Ore.: Multnomah, 1983.

Pink, Arthur. *The Doctrines of Election and Justification.* Grand Rapids: Baker, 1974.

Stott, John R. W. *Our Guilty Silence.* Grand Rapids: Eerdmans, 1969.

Tozer, A. W. *The Root of the Righteous.* Harrisburg, Pa.: Christian Publications , 1955.

Watson Thomas. *A Body of Divinity.* Carlisle, Pa.: Banner of Truth, 1983 reprint.

——————. *A Divine Cordial.* Grand Rapids: Baker, 1981.

Wilson, Geoffrey B. *Romans: A Digest of Reformed Comment.* London: Banner of Truth, 1969.

Wuest, Kenneth S. *Romans in the Greek New Testament.* Grand Rapids: Eerdmans, 1955.

——————. *Wuest's Word Studies from the Greek New Testament,* vol. 1. Grand Rapids: Eerdmans, 1973.

Indexes

Index of Greek Words

Index of Hebrew Words

Index of Scripture

Index of Subjects

Abraham
faith of, 260, 263, 267
obedience of, 236, 237
spiritual descent from, 255
Abused children, 191
Abused wives, 191
Accountability, 137, 158, 293
Adam
Christ and, antithetical analogy of, 291
deception by Satan, 303
Eve and, historicity of, 294
no excuse for sin, 296
representative of human race, 293
Adoption, Roman, 436
Afflictions, of Christian, 511
AIDS, 107
Alcoholics Anonymous, 369
Allah, 336
Ambition, selfish, 133
Anarthrous construction, Greek, 255, 359
Angels, fallen, 99, 298
Anger, holy, 63
Anti-Semitism, 164
Antichrist, 92
Antinomianism, 173, 315
Apis, bull-god, 94
Apocalypse of Baruch, 452
Apocrypha, 90
Apostolic authority, Paul's, 6
Apostasy, 120, 138
Apostle
general meaning of, 22
qualifications of, 7
Aorist tense, Greek, 296
Artemis, goddess, 94
Assurance of salvation, 223, 429, 438

Astrology, 95
Atonement, Day of, 209, 402
Atonement, substitutionary, 118, 209, 274, 291, 399
Attitude, believer's, 36, 42
Attributes, divine, 70
Augustine, Aurelius, ix

Baal-zebub (see also Beelzebul), 95
Babylonian exile, 91, 157
Baptism, infant, 150, 251, 253
Baptism, water, 21, 253, 320
Baptismal regeneration, 250
Barnabas, Letter of, 250
Barnhouse, Donald Grey, xi, 23, 116, 179, 260, 273, 318, 335, 516
Baruch, Apocalypse of, 452
Baxter, Richard, 420
Beelzebul (see also Baal-zebub), 95
Behavior, Spirit-controlled, 428
Belief, true, 237
Believer
battle with sin and Satan, 332
called to divine service, 22
glorification of, 279
hatred of sin, 381, 388
holy disposition of, 326
imperfection of, 278
judgment of, 128
lifestyle of, 343
marks of a spiritual, 380
riches of, 20
superficial, 36
unredeemed humanness of, 326
work of Holy Spirit in, 415
Belshazzar, 93
Biblical Christianity, 199